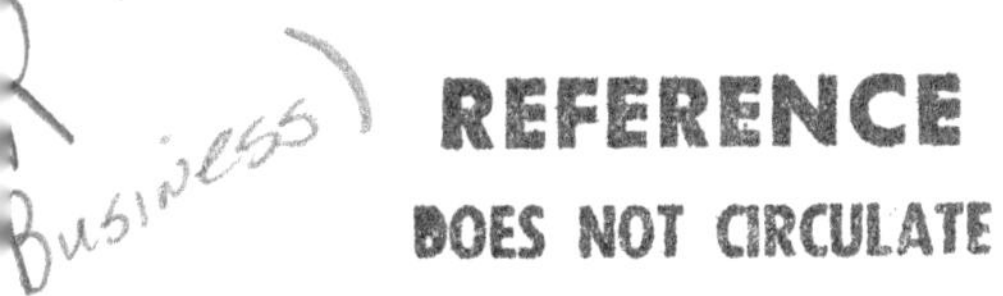

R 338.0922 Interna v.1

International directory of
business biographies

International Directory of

BUSINESS BIOGRAPHIES

International Directory of
BUSINESS BIOGRAPHIES

VOLUME 1
A-E

Edited by Neil Schlager
Produced by Schlager Group Inc.

ST. JAMES PRESS
An imprint of Thomson Gale, a part of The Thomson Corporation

EVANSTON PUBLIC LIBRARY
1703 ORRINGTON AVENUE
EVANSTON, ILLINOIS 60201

Detroit • New York • San Francisco • San Diego • New Haven, Conn. • Waterville, Maine • London • Munich

International Directory of Business Biographies
Schlager Group Inc. Staff
Neil Schlager, president
Marcia Merryman Means, managing editor

Project Editor
Margaret Mazurkiewicz

Editorial
Erin Bealmear, Joann Cerrito, Jim Craddock, Stephen Cusack, Miranda Ferrara, Peter M. Gareffa, Kristin Hart, Melissa Hill, Carol Schwartz, Bridget Travers, Michael J. Tyrkus

Editorial Support Services
Luann Brennan

Rights Acquisitions Management
Mari Masalin-Cooper, Shalice Shah-Caldwell

Imaging and Multimedia
Dean Dauphinais, Lezlie Light, Dan Newell, Christine O'Bryan

Composition
Evi Seoud

Product Design
Jennifer Wahi

Manufacturing
Rhonda Williams

© 2005 Thomson Gale, a part of The Thomson Corporation.

Thomson and Star Logo are trademarks and Gale and St. James Press are registered trademarks used herein under license.

For more information, contact
Thomson Gale
27500 Drake Rd.
Farmington Hills, MI 48331-3535
Or you can visit our Internet site at
http://www.gale.com

ALL RIGHTS RESERVED
No part of this work covered by the copyright hereon may be reproduced or used in any form or by any means—graphic, electronic, or mechanical, including photocopying, recording, taping, Web distribution, or information storage retrieval systems—without the written permission of the publisher.

For permission to use material from this product, submit your request via Web at http://www.gale-edit.com/permissions, or you may download our Permissions Request form and submit your request by fax or mail to:

Permissions
Thomson Gale
27500 Drake Rd.
Farmington Hills, MI 48331-3535
Permissions Hotline:
248-699-8006 or 800-877-4253, ext. 8006
Fax: 248-699-8074 or 800-762-4058

Cover photographs reproduced by permission of AP/Wide World Photos: (from left to right) Richard D. Parsons, chairman and chief executive officer of Time Warner; Carly Fiorina, chairwoman, chief executive officer, and president of Hewlett-Packard Company; William Clay Ford Jr., president and chief executive officer of Ford Motor Company; and Nobuyuki Idei, chief executive officer of Sony Corp.

While every effort has been made to ensure the reliability of the information presented in this publication, Thomson Gale does not guarantee the accuracy of the data contained herein. Thomson Gale accepts no payment for listing; and inclusion in the publication of any organization, agency, institution, publication, service, or individual does not imply endorsement of the editors or publisher. Errors brought to the attention of the publisher and verified to the satisfaction of the publisher will be corrected in future editions.

LIBRARY OF CONGRESS CATALOGING-IN-PUBLICATION DATA

International directory of business biographies / Neil Schlager, editor ; Vanessa Torrado-Caputo, assistant editor; project editor, Margaret Mazurkiewicz ; produced by Schlager Group.
p. cm.
Includes bibliographical references and indexes.
ISBN 1-55862-554-2 (set hardcover : alk. paper) —
ISBN 1-55862-555-0 (volume 1) —
ISBN 1-55862-556-9 (volume 2) —
ISBN 1-55862-557-7 (volume 3) —
ISBN 1-55862-558-5 (volume 4)
1. Businesspeople—Biography. 2. Directors of corporations—Biography. 3. Executives—Biography. 4. Industrialists—Biography. 5. Businesspeople—Directories. 6. Directors of corporations—Directories. 7. Executives—Directories. 8. Industrialists—Directories. I. Schlager, Neil, 1966- II. Torrado-Caputo, Vanessa. III. Mazurkiewicz, Margaret. IV. Schlager Group.

HC29.I57 2005
338.092'2—dc22 2004011756

British Library Cataloguing in Publication Data.
A Catalogue record of this book is available from the British Library.

Printed in the United States of America
10 9 8 7 6 5 4 3 2 1

Contents

Preface

■■■

Welcome to the *International Directory of Business Biographies (IDBB).* This four-volume set covers more than 600 prominent business people from around the world and is intended for reference use by management students, librarians, educators, historians, and others who seek information about the people leading the world's biggest and most influential companies. The articles, all of which include bylines, were written by a team of journalists, academics, librarians, and independent scholars. (See **Notes on Contributors**.) Approximately 60 percent of the entrants are American, while 40 percent are from other countries. Articles were compiled from material supplied by companies for whom the entrants work, general and academic periodicals, books, and annual reports. With its up-to-date profiles of important figures from the world of international business, *IDBB* complements the popular St. James Press series *International Directory of Company Histories (IDCH),* which provides entries on the world's largest and most influential companies. Leaders of many of the companies covered in *IDCH* are profiled in *IDBB.*

INCLUSION CRITERIA

The list of entrants in *IDBB* was developed by the editors in consultation with the academics and librarians serving on *IDBB*'s advisory board. (See **List of Advisers**.) The majority of people profiled here are current or recent chief executives of large, publicly traded companies such as those found on the Fortune 500 and Global 500 lists of companies compiled by *Fortune* magazine. Among this group are familiar names such as H. Lee Scott Jr. of Wal-Mart, Carly Fiorina of Hewlett-Packard, John Browne of BP, and Nobuyuki Idei of Sony. Retired or former executives like GE's Jack Welch and Vivendi Universal's Jean-Marie Messier also make the list, as do a few deceased individuals who were active in the past few years, including Jim Cantalupo of McDonald's and Chung Ju-yung of Hyundai.

In addition, we have included other high-profile individuals whose companies are privately held or are not large enough to make the *Fortune* lists but whose influence makes them valuable candidates for study, such as Kase L. Lawal of CAMAC Holdings, Oprah Winfrey of Harpo Productions, and Terence Conran of Conran Holdings. We also mix in up-and-coming executives who may not currently be chief executives but who are rapidly gaining prominence in the business world; among this group are Indra K. Nooyi of PepsiCo and Lachlan and James Murdoch of News Corporation. For these latter categories, we have attempted to highlight female and minority executives who, even in the early twenty-first century, continue to be underrepresented in the upper echelons of the corporate world.

Readers should note that our aim was to produce balanced, objective profiles of influential executives, and individuals were not disqualified if they or their companies were enmeshed in scandal. Thus, the set includes articles about executives such as Ken Lay of Enron, Dennis Kozlowski of Tyco International, and Martha Stewart of Martha Stewart Living Omnimedia, all of whom were indicted on criminal charges in the early 2000s.

ARRANGEMENT OF SET AND ENTRY FORMAT

The four-volume set is arranged alphabetically by surname. An alphabetical list of subjects is included in the frontmatter. Within each entry, readers will find the following sections:

Fact Box: This section provides details about the subject's birth and death dates, birth and death locations, family information, educational background, work history, major awards, and publications. For entrants affiliated with a specific company at the time of publication, the Fact Box also includes the company address and URL address, except in cases where the subject is no longer affiliated with a company.

Main Text: This section provides a narrative overview of the subject's life, career trajectory, and influence. The text includes subheadings to assist the reader in navigating the key periods in the subject's life.

Sources for Further Information: This section lists books, articles, and Web sites containing more information about the subject. Also included here are sources from which quotations are drawn in the main text.

See also: At the end of most articles is a cross-reference to applicable company profiles in the *International Directory of Company Histories.*

INDEXES

IDBB includes four indexes. The **Nationality Index** lists entrants according to their country of birth, country of citizenship (if different from country of birth), and country of long-term residence. The **Geographic Index** lists entrants according to the country of the headquarters of operation or the country where the subject works (if different from country of the headquarters); the index lists entrants according to their employer at the time of publication as well as significant previous companies where they were employed. The **Company and Industry Index** lists entrants according to their current and former companies of employment as well the industries in which those companies operate; in this latter index, industries are listed in small caps, while companies are listed in roman font with upper- and lowercase letters. The **Name Index** lists all entrants as well as other significant individuals discussed in the text.

ACKNOWLEDGMENTS

Numerous individuals deserve gratitude for their assistance with this project. I am indebted to everyone at St. James Press and Thomson Gale who assisted with the production, particularly Margaret Mazurkiewicz, who provided crucial help at all stages of production; I also thank Chris Nasso, Peter Gareffa, and Bridget Travers for their support. At Schlager Group, Marcia Merryman Means elucidated style matters and coordinated the copyediting and fact-checking process, while Jayne Weisblatt and Vanessa Torrado-Caputo provided valuable editorial assistance.

Neil Schlager

SUGGESTIONS WELCOME

Comments and suggestions from users of *IDBB* on any aspect of the product are cordially invited. Suggestions for additional business people to include in future new editions or supplements are also welcomed. Please write:

The Editor
International Directory of Business Biographies
Thomson Gale
27500 Drake Rd.
Farmington Hills, MI 48331-3535

Advisers

■■■

Vincenzo Baglieri, PhD
Director, Technology Management Department
Bocconi School of Management
Bocconi University
Milan, Italy

Lyda Bigelow, PhD
Assistant Professor of Organization and Strategy
Olin School of Business
Washington University in St. Louis
St. Louis, Missouri

Diane Davenport, MLS
Reference Manager
Berkeley Public Library
Berkeley, California

Karl Moore, PhD
Associate Professor
Faculty of Management
McGill University
Montreal, Canada

Mohammad K. Najdawi, PhD
Senior Associate Dean and Professor
Department of Decision and Information Technologies
College of Commerce and Finance
Villanova University
Villanova, Pennsylvania

Judith M. Nixon, MLS
Management and Economics Librarian
Purdue University
West Lafayette, Indiana

Contributors

Elisa Addlesperger
Barry Alfonso
Margaret Alic
Don Amerman
William Arthur Atkins
Kirk H. Beetz
Patricia C. Behnke
Mark Best
Alan Bjerga
Jeanette Bogren
Thomas Borjas
Carol Brennan
Jack J. Cardoso
C. A. Chien
Peter Collins
Stephen Collins
Matthew Cordon
Peggy Daniels
Amanda de la Garza
Ed Dinger
Catherine Donaldson
Jim Fike
Virginia Finsterwald
Tiffeni Fontno
Katrina Ford
Erik Donald France
Lisa Frick
Margaret E. Gillio
Larry Gilman
Meg Greene
Paul Greenland
Barbara Gunvaldsen
Timothy L. Halpern
Lauri Harding
Lucy Heckman
Ashyia N. Henderson
Eve M. B. Hermann
John Herrick
Jeremy W. Hubbell
Dawn Jacob Laney
Michelle Johnson
Jean Kieling
Barbara Koch
Deborah Kondek
Alison Lake
Sandra Larkin
Josh Lauer
Anne Lesser
David Lewis
Jennifer Long
DeAnne Luck
Susan Ludwig
David Marc
William F. Martin
Beth Maser
Doris Morris Maxfield
Ann McCarthy
Patricia McKenna
Lee McQueen
Jill Meister
Carole Sayegh Moussalli
Miriam C. Nagel
Catherine Naghdi
Caryn E. Neumann
John M. Owen
Carol Pech
David Petechuk
Anastasis Petrou
A. Petruso
Luca Prono
Trudy Ring
Nelson Rhodes
Celia Ross
Joseph C. Santora
Lorraine Savage
M. W. Scott
Cathy Seckman
Kenneth R. Shepherd
Stephanie Dionne Sherk
Hartley Spatt
Janet P. Stamatel
Kris Swank
François Therin
Marie L. Thompson
Mary Tradii
Scott Trudell
David Tulloch
Michael Vandyke
Maike van Wijk
Stephanie Watson
Valerie Webster
S. E. Weigant
Kelly Wittmann
Lisa Wolff
Timothy Wowk
Ronald Young
Barry Youngerman
Candy Zulkosky

List of Entrants

■■■

A

F. Duane Ackerman

Josef Ackermann

Shai Agassi

Umberto Agnelli

Ahn Cheol-soo

Naoyuki Akikusa

Raúl Alarcón Jr.

William F. Aldinger III

Vagit Y. Alekperov

César Alierta Izuel

Herbert M. Allison Jr.

John A. Allison IV

Dan Amos

Brad Anderson

Richard H. Anderson

G. Allen Andreas Jr.

Micky Arison

C. Michael Armstrong

Bernard Arnault

Gerard J. Arpey

Ramani Ayer

B

Michael J. Bailey

Sergio Balbinot

Steve Ballmer

Jill Barad

Don H. Barden

Ned Barnholt

Colleen Barrett

Craig R. Barrett

Matthew William Barrett

John M. Barth

Glen A. Barton

Richard Barton

J. T. Battenberg III

Claude Bébéar

Pierre-Olivier Beckers

Jean-Louis Beffa

Alain Belda

Charles Bell

Luciano Benetton

Robert H. Benmosche

Silvio Berlusconi

Betsy Bernard

Daniel Bernard

David W. Bernauer

Wulf H. Bernotat

Gordon M. Bethune

J. Robert Beyster

Jeff Bezos

Pierre Bilger

Alwaleed Bin Talal

Dave Bing

Carole Black

Cathleen Black

Jonathan Bloomer

Alan L. Boeckmann

Daniel Bouton

Martin Bouygues
Jack O. Bovender Jr.
Peter Brabeck-Letmathe
Richard Branson
Edward D. Breen
Thierry Breton
Ulrich Brixner
John Browne
Wayne Brunetti
John E. Bryson
Warren E. Buffett
Steven A. Burd
H. Peter Burg
Antony Burgmans
James Burke
Ursula Burns

C

Louis C. Camilleri
Lewis B. Campbell
Philippe Camus
Michael R. Cannon
Jim Cantalupo
Thomas E. Capps
Daniel A. Carp
Peter Cartwright
Steve Case
Cássio Casseb Lima
Robert B. Catell
William Cavanaugh III
Charles M. Cawley
Clarence P. Cazalot Jr.
Nicholas D. Chabraja
John T. Chambers
J. Harold Chandler
Morris Chang
Chen Tonghai
Kenneth I. Chenault
Fujio Cho
Chung Ju-yung
Carla Cico
Philippe Citerne
Jim Clark
Vance D. Coffman
Douglas R. Conant
Phil Condit
Terence Conran
John W. Conway
John R. Coomber
Roger Corbett
Alston D. Correll
Alfonso Cortina de Alcocer
David M. Cote
Robert Crandall
Mac Crawford
Carlos Criado-Perez
James R. Crosby
Adam Crozier
Alexander M. Cutler
Márcio A. Cypriano

D

David F. D'Alessandro
Eric Daniels
George David
Richard K. Davidson
Julian C. Day
Henri de Castries
Michael S. Dell
Guerrino De Luca
Hebert Demel
Roger Deromedi

E

F

G

K

L

M

Ma Fucai

John J. Mack

Terunobu Maeda

Joseph Magliochetti

Marjorie Magner

Richard Mahoney

Steven J. Malcolm

Richard A. Manoogian

Mohamed Hassan Marican

Reuben Mark

Michael E. Marks

J. Willard Marriott Jr.

R. Brad Martin

Strive Masiyiwa

David Maxwell

L. Lowry Mays

Michael B. McCallister

W. Alan McCollough

Mike McGavick

Eugene R. McGrath

Judy McGrath

William W. McGuire

Tom McKillop

Henry A. McKinnell Jr.

C. Steven McMillan

Scott G. McNealy

W. James McNerney Jr.

Dee Mellor

Jean-Marie Messier

Gérard Mestrallet

Edouard Michelin

Charles Milhaud

Alexei Miller

Stuart A. Miller

Akio Mimura

Vittorio Mincato

Rafael Miranda Robredo

Fujio Mitarai

William E. Mitchell

Hayao Miyazaki

Anders C. Moberg

Larry Montgomery

James P. Mooney

Ann Moore

Patrick J. Moore

Giuseppe Morchio

Tomijiro Morita

Angelo R. Mozilo

Anne M. Mulcahy

Leo F. Mullin

James J. Mulva

Raúl Muñoz Leos

James Murdoch

Lachlan Murdoch

Rupert Murdoch

N. R. Murthy

A. Maurice Myers

N

Kunio Nakamura

Robert L. Nardelli

Jacques Nasser

M. Bruce Nelson

Yoshifumi Nishikawa

Hidetoshi Nishimura

Uichiro Niwa

Gordon M. Nixon

Jeffrey Noddle

Tamotsu Nomakuchi

Indra K. Nooyi

Blake W. Nordstrom

S

T

Z

Antoine Zacharias

Edward Zander

John D. Zeglis

Deiter Zetsche

Zhang Enzhao

Zhang Ligui

Zhou Deqiang

Aerin Lauder Zinterhofer

Edward J. Zore

Klaus Zumwinkel

■ ■ ■

F. Duane Ackerman

1942–

Chairman and chief executive officer, BellSouth Corporation

Nationality: American.

Born: 1942, in Plant City, Florida.

Education: Rollins College, BS, 1964; MS, 1970; Massachusetts Institute of Technology, MBA, 1978.

Family: Married Kappy (maiden name unknown); children: four.

Career: Southern Bell Telephone and Telegraph Company, 1964–1971, various customer service and other positions; 1971–1974, division plant manager; 1974–1975, general personnel supervisor; 1975, assistant vice president, plant department; 1978–1979, general commercial and marketing manager; 1979–1983, vice president; BellSouth Corporation, 1983–1985, vice president, corporate planning and development; BellSouth Services, Incorporated, 1985–1989, executive vice president for marketing, network, and planning; BellSouth Corporation, 1989–1991, vice chairman, finance and administration; 1991–1995, vice chairman and group president; BellSouth Telecommunications, 1991–1992, president and chief operating officer; 1992–1995, president and chief executive officer; BellSouth Corporation, 1995–1997, vice chairman of the board and chief operating officer; 1997–1998, president and chief executive officer; 1998–, chairman and chief executive officer.

Awards: Honorary doctorate, Rollins College, 2000; Hall of Fame, J. Mack Robinson College of Business, Georgia State University, 2001.

Address: BellSouth Corporation, 1155 Peachtree Street NE, Atlanta, Georgia 30309; http://www.bellsouth.com.

F. Duane Ackerman. *AP/Wide World Photos.*

F. Duane Ackerman helped to steer BellSouth Corporation through both divestiture and deregulation to make the firm one of the more profitable telephone companies in the United States. He began working in customer service with Southern Bell Telephone and Telegraph in 1964, and he moved steadily upward through the company ranks. When the so-called "Baby Bell" regional telephone companies were divested from AT&T in 1984, Ackerman became a leading figure in BellSouth. He served in a variety of upper management positions before taking over as president and chief executive officer in 1997. Known for his low-key demeanor, Ackerman often made trips to the field, riding in company trucks to stay in touch with his company and its customers.

EDUCATION AND EARLY CAREER

Ackerman grew up in Plant City, Florida, a small city east of Tampa. He enrolled at Rollins College in Winter Park, Florida, where he studied physics. He joined Southern Bell Telephone and Telegraph Company, a part of the "Baby Bell" system of the American Telephone and Telegraph Company (AT&T) in 1964. Ackerman's first job with Southern Bell was in the customer service department, where he fielded customer complaints. His first five jobs with the company were related to customer service, a department that Ackerman later described as less complex in the 1960s than it had become when he took over the company more than 30 years later. On the other hand, Ackerman acknowledged that the basic premise of customer service had not changed over the intervening years, namely the importance of "treating customers with respect; listening to them and trying to understand needs and how to satisfy those needs" (*USA Today*, March 14, 2004).

Ackerman was given various assignments in Orlando and Miami between 1964 and 1971. During that time he also earned a master's degree in commercial science from Rollins in 1970. In 1971 he was promoted to division plant manager, a position that he held until 1974, when he was named general personnel supervisor at Southern Bell's headquarters in Atlanta. He was promoted to assistant vice president of the plant department in 1975.

Ackerman left Southern Bell for several years in order to do graduate work at the Massachusetts Institute of Technology, where he was named a Sloan Fellow in 1977. He earned his MBA at MIT in 1978 and returned to Southern Bell. He was named to the position of general and commercial marketing manager for the company's operations in North Carolina. Ackerman returned to Atlanta in 1979 after he was selected as vice president of the company for the Georgia network.

THE FORMATION OF BELLSOUTH

AT&T had been subject to antitrust litigation for nearly a decade during the 1970s and 1980s. By 1983 the company had agreed to divest itself of its local telephone operating companies. BellSouth Corporation was formed as a result of this divestiture. In October 1983, about two months prior to completing the breakup of AT&T, BellSouth elected 10 officers. Ackerman was chosen to serve as the company's vice president for corporate planning and development. He later admitted that the company experienced some apprehension about the impending breakup. "There was a little bit of shock and a little bit of concern," Ackerman said in 1989 (*MIS Week*, January 2, 1989).

Ackerman was elected in March 1985 to a new position as executive vice president for network planning and marketing for BellSouth Services, Incorporated. By this time, two years after the divestiture, BellSouth had already become a standout among the other regional Bell companies. It was the first of the "Baby Bells" to request permission from the divestiture court to develop and sell software and the first to begin widespread installation of optical fiber in its local networks. Ackerman demonstrated foresight regarding the use of new technologies for transmitting information. "We want businesses to use the public network to move data," he said in 1985 with regard to the improvements in the company's network (*Data Communications*, May 1, 1985).

BellSouth's strategies paid off. The company grew at a faster rate than the other regional Bell companies, adding more than 650,000 local access lines in 1987. Ackerman emphasized that BellSouth would pursue strategies for expanding its residential and small-business services, since those markets were growing along with the expanding population in BellSouth's home region. "I don't think telephone companies in the past looked at the residential markets the way we're going to look at them in the future," said Ackerman in 1988. "The demographics have changed dramatically, and I believe that will offer us opportunities" (*Telephony*, April 4, 1988).

RAPID RISE IN THE COMPANY

Ackerman's role in developing BellSouth's effective marketing strategy led to his appointment in February 1989 as vice chairman of finance and administration. The move was significant in Ackerman's career in that several other executives had more seniority than Ackerman at the time. Analysts noted that Ackerman had become a candidate to eventually become chairman of the company.

Ackerman gained broad responsibility for overseeing the company's finances, budgeting, administration, and strategic planning as well as supervising a number of department staffs. The company's chief financial officer reported directly to Ackerman in his new position. Ackerman in turn reported directly to BellSouth's chairman, John Clendenin. Under Clendenin's leadership, and with the assistance of Ackerman and fellow vice-chairman William McCoy, BellSouth in 1989 continued to outperform other local telephone companies. The company had become the most technologically advanced local telephone network in the country. In addition, it was the third largest cellular telephone company in the United States.

BellSouth Services, Southern Bell, and South Central Bell, which had previously been separate operating companies under the umbrella of BellSouth Corporation, consolidated in 1991 to form BellSouth Telecommunications. Ackerman was named vice chairman of BellSouth Corporation and president and chief operating officer of BellSouth Telecommunications. In 1992 he became president and chief executive officer of BellSouth Telecommunications.

As Ackerman rose through the ranks at BellSouth during the early 1990s, he became more involved in Atlanta civic affairs. He was appointed to the boards of the Commerce Club and Central Atlanta Progress and was highly active in the local Boy Scouts. With Ackerman's help, the Boy Scouts raised $1 million to encourage children from public housing communities to join the organization.

Ackerman adopted a low-key yet smooth management style. "Duane is so quiet, you almost can't hear him purr," said one acquaintance who served on a board with Ackerman (*Atlanta Journal and Constitution*, March 9, 1993). His management style, however, was quite effective. As vice president during the late 1980s, he demanded teamwork among subordinates. Ackerman reportedly threatened to force one employee to share a "double desk" (a desk constructed for two users, who must work side by side) with a colleague if the employee did not work more closely with the rest of his group (*Wall Street Journal*, March 1, 1989).

THE NEW CEO

Ackerman worked with BellSouth Telecommunications until 1995, when he was appointed vice chairman of the board and chief operating officer for BellSouth Corporation. Clendenin was nearing the end of his term at the helm at BellSouth, while Ackerman had emerged as the likely successor. When Clendenin announced his plans to retire as of January 1, 1997, Ackerman was named as the company's new president and chief executive officer. Clendenin expressed full confidence in Ackerman. "Duane is an extremely capable guy and just has a great grasp of the total business," Clendenin said. "We have shared ideas and points of view for many years" (*Atlanta Journal and Constitution*, April 23, 1996).

Ackerman looked forward to the challenges that came with his promotion. "I look at it with a little bit of awe," he said of his new position. "I look at it with the conviction that you've got to keep looking over your shoulder. When you wake up in the morning, you don't have to wait for the wheels to start turning. They're turning when you get up and they're turning all day long." (*Chattanooga Free Press*, November 3, 1996). Analysts said that Ackerman was taking over BellSouth during a difficult time. "He'll walk in with a plate full of challenges," said one analyst. "There's never been a more difficult and challenging time to take the reins." (*Chattanooga Free Press*, November 3, 1996).

At the time that Ackerman took control of BellSouth in 1997, the telecommunications industry was beginning to experience the effects of the Telecommunications Act of 1996, which, among other provisions, deregulated local telephone markets. BellSouth had enjoyed a virtual monopoly over its local telephone markets, but after the legislation was passed, the company had to deal with competition. Ackerman acknowledged that the company would undergo changes under his leadership, but he maintained that the transition was a result of the change in the market rather than his leadership style.

Ackerman expected BellSouth to lose as much as 20 percent of its local network revenues from competition in 1997 but vowed to build such other aspects of the business as long-distance services in order to compensate. "There's going to be a battle in our region," Ackerman said. "Our goal is to add more revenue than we're going to lose" (*Forbes*, May 19, 1997). In September 1997, the company announced that it would buy back $1 billion of its own shares in order to boost stock prices to spark the interest of investors. The company also announced in September 1997 that Ackerman would assume the duties of chairman of the board.

MAINTAINING BELLSOUTH'S INDEPENDENCE

BellSouth was the only remaining former "Baby Bell" that existed in its original form by 1999. Ackerman worked diligently to maintain the company's independence, even amid swirling rumors that the company had been targeted for acquisition by other firms. Part of Ackerman's strategy was to build the company's overseas operations. By 2000 BellSouth had built a major market share for wireless products in South America. Of the company's $25 billion in revenues, 10 percent came from its international operations.

Other companies continued to grow larger through mergers, but BellSouth remained profitable without giving up its independence. "BellSouth is the smallest of the Baby Bells, but it's still in the top 100 companies in the world," Ackerman said in 2003. "We are doing very well against our peers" (*Atlanta Journal-Constitution*, December 25, 2003).

DEDICATION TO CUSTOMER SERVICE

Ackerman was well known for spending time in the field, often riding around in company trucks. "We don't want to get too far away from what's happening with the customers and our people," Ackerman told a reporter from *BusinessWeek* on one occasion (August 2, 1999). Ackerman also remained dedicated to customer service, a commitment that went back to his first positions with the company during the 1960s. According to the University of Michigan American Customer Satisfaction Index, BellSouth led all local telephone service providers in customer service satisfaction every year between 1993 and 2003. "Those around us know we're committed [to customer service], because we live it," said Ackerman. "If you're consistent over time, it will permeate [the company]" (*USA Today*, March 14, 2004).

Ackerman also served on the boards of Wachovia Corporation and the Allstate Corporation. He was active in a number of civic organizations, including the Georgia Research Alliance, the Atlanta Chamber of Commerce, the Woodruff Arts Center, and the National Council on Competitiveness. In 2004 President George W. Bush named Ackerman as chair of the National Security Telecommunications Advisory Committee. Ackerman received an honorary doctorate from Rollins College in 2000, and was inducted into the Hall of Fame at the J. Mack Robinson College of Business at Georgia State University in 2001.

See also entries on AT&T Corp. and BellSouth Corporation in *International Directory of Company Histories.*

SOURCES FOR FURTHER INFORMATION

"BellSouth CEO Committed to Customer Service," *USA Today*, March 14, 2004.

Booker, Ellis, "BellSouth Revs into High Gear," *Telephony*, April 4, 1988, pp. 40–45.

Gannes, Stuart, and Nancy J. Perry, "BellSouth is on a Ringing Streak," *Fortune*, October 9, 1989, pp. 66–72.

Hayes, John R., "Focused," *Forbes*, May 19, 1997, pp. 124–127.

Kanell, Michael E., "Telecommunications: The Executives," *Atlanta Journal and Constitution*, July 14, 1996.

Lopez, Julie Amparano, "BellSouth's Ackerman Leapfrogs Others To Succeed White as a Vice Chairman," *Wall Street Journal*, March 1, 1989.

Rice, Marc, "Change in CEO at BellSouth 1st Since It Became 'Baby Bell,'" *Chattanooga Free Press*, November 3, 1996.

Robinson, Teri, "BellSouth Rises Again," *MIS Week*, January 2, 1989, p. 20.

Rocks, David, "Is Standing Firm Enough?," *BusinessWeek*, August 2, 1999.

Saporta, Maria, "BellSouth Officer Makes Connections To Better the City," *Atlanta Journal and Constitution*, March 9, 1993.

———, "Calm Growth Wise Policy for BellSouth," *Atlanta Journal-Constitution*, December 25, 2003.

———, "End of an Era Approaches for BellSouth CEO," *Atlanta Journal and Constitution*, April 23, 1996.

Spiegel, Peter, "The Crafty Globalizer," *Forbes*, March 20, 2000, pp. 81–83.

Wilke, John R., "BellSouth Leads the Pack with Lightwave, Data Services," *Data Communications*, May 1, 1985, pp. 68-69.

—Matthew C. Cordon

■■■
Josef Ackermann
1948–
Chairman, Deutsche Bank

Nationality: Swiss.

Born: February 7, 1948, in Mels, Switzerland.

Education: Saint Gallen University, PhD, 1977.

Family: Son of a doctor (name unknown) and Margrit (maiden name unknown); married Pirkko Anelli (a homemaker), 1977; children: one.

Career: Credit Suisse, 1977, corporate banker; 1978–1990, positions in Lausanne, London, and Zurich; 1990–1993, member of the executive board; 1993–1996, president of the executive board; Deutsche Bank, 1996–2002, member of the board of directors; 2002–, chairman of the group executive committee and spokesman of the board.

Address: Deutsche Bank, Taunusanlage 12, 60325 Frankfurt-am-Main, Germany; http://www.deutsche-bank.de.

Josef Ackermann. *AP/Wide World Photos.*

■ Josef Ackermann became renowned at Deutsche Bank for shifting the style of management from a conventional mode to one that focused on the needs of shareholders and on international expansion. Ackermann changed the distribution of power within Deutsche Bank, resulting in criticism from traditionalists and praise from those who shared his global focus, allowing him to become the most powerful man in Germany's financial industry. In his effort to turn Deutsche Bank from a bloated German lender into a lean global competitor, Ackermann eliminated 14,470 jobs, or 18 percent of the workforce, and cut costs by one-third by closing retail branches and outsourcing management of the bank's computer systems and real estate. He also sold assets totaling EUR 11 billion in worth. Described by many as a man of integrity, Ackermann charted his own course throughout his life, bearing a vision beyond what peers encouraged him to do.

A NONPROVINCIAL LIFE IN THE SWISS COUNTRY

Ackermann was born and raised in the provincial town of Mels in Switzerland. His father was the local doctor who mended the many broken bones that resulted from ski accidents over the winter holidays, and he often called on his sons to assist him. Ackermann and his two younger brothers were avid skiers themselves and maintained their fitness in the summer by playing soccer. Each learned to play an instrument; Ackermann chose the piano. As of age 12, all the Ackermann boys were encouraged to study languages abroad. The family often took trips to Munich, Germany, to watch plays.

Ackermann excelled in mathematics in high school, but rather than pursue a career in engineering he chose to study economics and social sciences with a focus on bank management at the University of Saint Gallen. His instructors there hoped that he would join the ranks of academia. In addition to his studies, Ackermann served in the army reserves, where he was quickly promoted to colonel, the highest-ranking reservist officer in his regiment. His superiors encouraged him to embark on a full-time military career, but Ackermann decided otherwise. He completed his studies in 1977 as the assistant to the Institute of National Economics, graduating with a doctorate in economics. He married the Finnish-born Pirkko Anelli, whom he had met at the university, that same year. His daughter, Catherine, was born in 1984.

COMBINING MILITARY SKILLS AND ACADEMIC KNOWLEDGE

Ackermann told *Manager Magazin* that his military experience was a better preparation for corporate competition than business school was. While business school focused on a peaceful world, the military prepared him for war and the day-to-day business crises he would come to face "every half hour" (Zehle, May 2002). More specifically, he credited the military with teaching him goal-orientation and problem-solving skills. Still, in spite of the regimental training he received, Ackermann was able to maintain an appreciation for the arts, taking singing lessons in New York and often attending the opera with his wife.

Upon graduation Ackermann joined Credit Suisse (then the Swiss Credit Institute) in New York as the assistant to the general board of directors. At age 33 he was in charge of three hundred subordinates. After stints in Lausanne, London, and Zurich, Ackermann was promoted to general director, and thus a member of the board, of Credit Suisse in 1990. In 1993 he became president of the Credit Suisse executive board, successfully merging the Swiss Volksbank into Credit Suisse that same year. CEO Rainer Gut wanted to merge the Volksbank business operations into Credit operations, but Ackermann advocated keeping the business units separate; the two also clashed over management styles and strategic plans. In what was perceived by commentators as an abrupt move, Ackermann left Credit Suisse in 1996.

ON TO DEUTSCHE BANK

That same year, after receiving at least three lucrative offers from various companies, Ackermann joined Deutsche Bank as a member of the board of directors. He spearheaded the merger of the U.S.-based Bankers Trust into Deutsche Bank in 1998 and was credited with facilitating the move by using an integrative and communicative approach. In 1999 Ackermann's leadership of the global operations and institutions department generated 60 percent of Deutsche Bank's year-end revenues. In the spring of 2000 Ackermann vetoed a merger with Dresdner Bank after insisting the deal could go ahead only if Dresdner Kleinwort Benson was sold. Maintaining this stance in spite of pressure from his peers to approve the deal solidified his reputation as a man of integrity and earned him a promotion. "If there were an enhancement to authenticity, Josef Ackermann would fit the bill," wrote A. T. Kearney's Central European Profit Center leader Michael Träm. "Those who followed his Swiss career point out his well-balanced personality, his even distribution of head vs. gut thinking, and his down-to-earth mentality. He is obviously not an actor-banker, but a banker in heart and soul" (2002).

Ackermann was then appointed to succeed CEO Rolf Breuer, who charged him with building a truly global investment bank. Ackermann served as CEO designate for almost two years before his formal appointment as spokesman of the board and chairman in May 2002. Revenue from corporate and investment banking had surged to EUR 14.3 billion in 2002, from EUR 4.8 billion in 1998, and Ackermann was intent on making an impact in this lucrative market. Even before he became head of Deutsche Bank, he made waves with his plans for restructuring. Inspired by the American leadership structure, he founded an 11-member group executive committee, disempowering the traditional German supervisory board, which he cut in half from eight to four members, all of whom were also members of the aforementioned committee.

Ackermann's vision for globalization focused on shareholders and international performance. In the long term, this created a shift in emphasis in Germany from commercial and retail banking to securities-trading/underwriting and asset-management businesses like the ones the company had acquired. The former Volkswagen CEO Carl Hahn said, "Ackermann modernized Deutsche Bank in a most impressive way" (January 26, 2004).

CHANGING DEUTSCHE BANK'S OPERATIONS

After four months at his new position, Ackermann sold retail bank branches in France and began focusing on Spain and Italy. The German retail bank market, meanwhile, was saturated with state-subsidized Sparkassen, which owned 40 percent of the market; Deutsche Bank held only 7 percent of the 8.2 million German customers in 2003. However, a European Union directive called for the phasing out of subsidies in 2005, which would create new opportunities in the retail banking environment.

Ackermann merged Deutsche Bank's previously separate divisions for retail, business, and private clients who own between EUR 250,000 and EUR 5 million in assets, into one private banking unit in order to encourage cross-selling. Between 2001 and 2004 Deutsche Bank closed 272 of 1,042 retail branches in Germany and cut the size of the retail banking workforce by 19 percent, to 13,600 employees.

In 2002 Ackermann hired Pierre de Weck to run Deutsche Bank's wealth-management business for clients with more than EUR 5 million of assets to invest. To further entice wealthy clients, in 2003 Deutsche Bank bought Rüd, Blass & Cie, the Swiss private-banking arm of Zurich Financial Services. Pretax profits from asset and wealth management rose to EUR 505 million in the first nine months of 2003—more than triple the earnings of 2002.

In 2003 Deutsche Bank reconsidered its corporate loan criteria after losing billions in the previous year. The company had granted loans based on relationships rather than on the performance of the corporations to which it loaned. Longstanding alliances with large companies were severed, including a more than 40-year relationship with Volkswagen. As a result, problematic loans were significantly reduced in number.

Ackermann also sold $5.3 billion of industrial holdings that were not earning money. The biggest disposal was a EUR 1.6 billion stake in Munich Re, the world's largest reinsurer. "People said: 'He is selling the family silver,'" Ackermann told *Fortune Europe*. However, a drop in share prices a few months later justified the decision. "If we hadn't sold it, we would not have realized this capital gain that paid for restructuring costs. But it is very difficult to explain to some people" (January 26, 2004).

While Ackermann's revisionary leadership ruffled German feathers, American colleagues described him as "smart but low-key" to *Manager Magazin*. Reporter Sybille Zehle considers Ackermann a "man without extremes: diligent, but not overworked; ambitious, but not awed by rank; casual, but not sloppy; goal-oriented, but not grim; persistent, but not stubborn" (May 2002).

REAPING THE BENEFITS

Deutsche Bank's net income rose 85 percent to EUR 929 million in the first nine months of 2003, after it had earned EUR 397 million in all of 2002. "Two years ago, Deutsche Bank was very inefficient, with a huge loan book and poor cost controls," said Rolf Zartner, a Frankfurt-based fund manager at Deka Investment. "Ackermann cleaned up the investment portfolio; he's streamlined the businesses and sold assets the bank doesn't need" (February 2004).

In 2003, 134-year-old Deutsche Bank was the world's seventh-largest bank in terms of revenue; it ranked 12th in mergers and acquisitions and 21st in terms of market capitalization. In the underwriting of international bonds, Deutsche Bank ranked second, behind Citigroup. With EUR 974 billion in assets under management, Deutsche Bank was the world's fourth-largest money manager.

In the summer of 2003 Citigroup and Deutsche Bank entered merger talks, but Deutsche Bank called the deal off. In early 2004 information about other merger discussions surfaced, with Ackermann saying that he was open to a merger as long as it would not harm the shareholders. "Domestic transactions would probably create more value for shareholders," said Ackermann. "It could happen that U.S. banks will start buying big European banks. I think we should find a European response before that happens" (February 2004).

FIGHTING FOR ANGLO-AMERICAN BUSINESS PRINCIPLES

In addition to his full-time position, Ackermann also served on other company boards, including Bayer AG, Deutsche Lufthansa AG, Linde, Mannesman, and Siemens AG. In early 2004 Ackermann was involved in a criminal trial accusing him and other Mannesman board members of *Untreue* (breach of trust) for granting payouts that were not part of the Mannesman executives' contracts. CEO Klaus Esser, supervisory board chairman Joachim Funk, and other executives of Mannesman received appreciation awards and accelerated pensions in the amount of EUR 55 million after they accepted a hostile takeover by Britain's Vodafone in 2000. The amount was considered "excessive" by German prosecutors. The prosecutors invoked a statute dating from 1871 that bans those supervising the financial assets of others from abusing their power; the original intent of the statute was to avoid fraud.

Ackermann argued that the bonuses were rewards for the executives' success in increasing Mannesmann's value by EUR 77 billion by holding out for a higher offer (EUR 192 billion) from Vodafone. "We increased Mannesmann's market value by EUR 150 billion in my five years as CFO and CEO," Klaus Esser said in an e-mail to Bloomberg. "Awarding a bonus of EUR 15 million to acknowledge an increase of EUR 150 billion is a decision most shareholders in the world will continue to agree with" (February 2004).

The court case was highly publicized, because Ackermann himself did not receive a similar bonus. Also, the case called the nature of executive pay into question in a country where CEOs were compensated significantly less than CEOs in the United States, where "golden parachutes" are customary. Some Ackermann supporters believe the trial reflected Germans' resistance to globalization. "The treatment of Josef Ackermann shows that Germany has not adopted the notion of providing strong incentives for business executives," said the president of the National Bureau of Economic Research, Martin Feldstein. "The failure to provide such incentives depresses German productivity" (February 2004).

Ackermann, who was also a member of the boards of Bayer, Deutsche Lufthansa, Siemens, and Linde, refused to plea-bargain and saw the trial as a test for Germany's business climate. "We have to fight it through," Ackermann said. "We are obliged to fight it through for the benefit of Germany and for the financial system in Europe" (February 2004). Amidst pressure to resign, Ackermann continued his work at Deutsche Bank. His goal: making Deutsche Bank one of the world's top three advisers on mergers and acquisitions and returning its status to the top ten in market value.

See also entries on Credit Suisse Group and Deutsche Bank AG in *International Directory of Company Histories.*

SOURCES FOR FURTHER INFORMATION

Baker-Said, Stephanie, and Silje Skogstad, "Deutsche Bank's Distraction," *Bloomberg Markets,* February 2004, http://www.bloomberg.com/media/markets/deutsche.pdf

Freitag, Michael, "Porträt: Josef Ackermann," *Handelsblatt,* May 15, 2002.

Guyon, Janet, "The Trials of Josef Ackermann," *Fortune Europe,* January 26, 2004, p. 53.

Träm, Michael, *Führung braucht Zeit: Der Mythos der ersten 100 Tage,* Berlin: Econ Verlag, 2002.

Zehle, Sibylle, "Porträt: Low-Key-Joe," *Manager Magazin,* May 2002, p. 76.

—Maike van Wijk

■■■

Shai Agassi

1968–

Chief technology developer, SAP

Nationality: Israeli.

Born: 1968, in Ramat-Gan, Israel.

Education: Technion, BA, 1990.

Family: Son of Reuven Agassi (retired Israeli Defense Force colonel and telecom executive); married former general manager of QuickSoft Media (name unknown); children: two.

Career: Israeli Defense Force Intelligence, 1986, computer programmer; QuickSoft, 1991, founder; TopTier Software, 1992, founder; TopManage, 1993, founder; QuickSoft Media, 1994, founder; SAP, 2002–2003, CEO of Portals, CEO of Markets, chief technology officer; SAP, 2003–, executive board member.

Awards: Most Influential Businessman in the World, *Time*, 2003.

Address: SAP America, 3410 Hillview Avenue, Palo Alto, California 94304; http://www.sap.com.

■ The entrepreneur and programming expert Shai Agassi founded a series of technology companies in Israel in the 1990s. He joined SAP in 2001 when the German company paid $400 million for his corporate portal company TopTier Software. As part of the deal Agassi joined SAP's executive board in order to guide technology strategy for the world's third-largest independent software supplier. Technology analysts described Agassi as a bold visionary with the potential to develop a service-oriented computer infrastructure that could be the industry standard for years to come.

Technology came naturally to Agassi. As a seven-year-old he began programming in a computer-science class for children at Tel Aviv University. Programming appealed to him because he could control and build things; he recalled, "While other children collect baseball cards, I collected punch cards" (*Time Canada*, December 1, 2003). After a brief term of mandatory military service as a programmer for the Israeli Defense Force, Agassi earned a bachelor's degree from Technion, the Israeli Institute of Technology, in 1990. He then began to start up technology companies, including TopTier, his most successful venture, in partnership with his father. TopTier provided the technology needed to build enterprise portals—internal corporate Web sites providing company information to employees as well as access to select public sites.

In May 2001 Agassi sold TopTier to SAP, the German firm that led the world in sales of basic applications for corporations. Typically after selling a brainchild, a computer-age entrepreneur would leave an established company in pursuit of the next exciting opportunity. Agassi, however, chose to stay with SAP, first as the chief executive officer of a subsidiary called SAP Portals, then taking responsibility for another subsidiary, SAP Markets. In 2003 he became responsible for xApps, a new set of software products designed to allow disparate applications to interact across an entire corporate network with great efficiency and little risk. He was also one of eight members of SAP's executive board, taking part in determining the future direction of the firm, which had $6.5 billion in revenues in 2002.

Agassi explained that he sold TopTier and remained with SAP because of the opportunity provided by the sale. As he described, the software giant possessed "an environment where my ideas about computing can have a real impact on the market" (*Red Herring*, March 2003)—especially since he believed that start-up companies no longer had the potential to change the software industry. Agassi was convinced that small companies with big ideas operated at an incredible disadvantage because corporate chief information officers were no longer gambling on high-risk projects. They wanted to buy products that would be around for decades; large companies offered the promise of stability.

Despite his eagerness to become part of a large company, Agassi feared the challenges that he would be undertaking. As by far the youngest member of SAP's board and an entrepreneur by nature, he was an outsider within the most conservative firm in the software industry. His introduction of the xApps idea at a high-level SAP strategy meeting led to a four-hour argument with coworkers who insisted that the company should continue with traditionally designed applications. Agassi realized that his value lay in his willingness to take risks, and he persisted. In 2003 he described himself as a "retrovirus" that could awaken the genetic material possessed by SAP (*Red Herring*, March 2003).

With xApps Agassi pushed for a new generation of applications emphasizing simplicity. While existing applications comprised collections of transactions built on top of databases, Agassi was attempting to develop applications that could build new processes without being tied to predetermined database structures. He explained, "Looking at the world from customers' eyes and then trying to understand where complexity is and then designing it out—that's been the goal of my programming" (*Network World*, December 22, 2003).

SAP came to view xApps as the linchpin of an emerging corporate strategy that would carry the firm through its next stage of growth. If SAP failed to develop the next generation of web applications, analysts believed that the company would become merely a component provider to a larger company such as Microsoft. As the self-described "quintessential outsider" (*Red Herring*, March 2003), Agassi was uncertain whether he would remain with SAP once the xApps venture was completed. He had not ruled out founding another start-up sometime in the future.

SOURCES FOR FURTHER INFORMATION

Bednarz, Ann, "SAP's Resident Entrepreneur," *Network World*, December 22, 2003, p. 42.

Hamm, Steve, "The Youngster Who's Out to Energize SAP," *BusinessWeek*, June 26, 2002.

James, Geoffrey, "Odd Man In," *Red Herring*, March 2003, pp. 40–44.

Laing, Yehezkel, "*Time* Names Israeli World's Most Influential Businessman," *Jerusalem Post*, November 27, 2003.

Taylor, Chris, "The Software Industry's New New Man," *Time Canada*, December 1, 2003, p. 51.

—Caryn E. Neumann

■■■

Umberto Agnelli

1934–2004

Former chairman, Fiat

Nationality: Italian.

Born: November 1, 1934, in Lausanne, Switzerland.

Died: May 27, 2004.

Education: University of Turin, laurea in legge, 1959.

Family: Son of Edoardo Agnelli (chairman, Fiat) and Princess Virginia Bourbon del Monte di San Faustino; married Antonella Bechi Piaggio, 1959 (divorced); married Allegra Caracciolo, 1974; children: three (first marriage, one; second marriage, two).

Career: Juventus, 1956–1961, chairman; SAI, 1959–1975, chairman; Simca Industries, 1965–1980, chairman; Fiat SpA, 1970–1976, chief executive officer; 1976–1993, vice president; 2003–2004, chairman; senator of the Italian Republic, 1976–1979; Fiat Auto, 1980–1990.

Awards: Trade Award, Ministry of International Trade and Industry, 1995; Grand Cordon of the Order of the Sacred Treasure, Japan, 1996; Grand'Ufficiale al Merito, Republic of Italy; Officier, Légion d'Honneur, France; honorary chairman, Juventus football team, 1994.

Umberto Agnelli. *AP/Wide World Photos.*

■ Throughout his life Umberto Agnelli, "the Doctor," was overshadowed by the flamboyant management and social style of his older brother Giovanni Agnelli, "the Lawyer." In the words of Cesare Romiti, the former managing director of Fiat, Agnelli "lived a nightmare of being number two. You always said 'Umberto, the brother of Giovanni'" (Hooper, "Umberto Agnelli," May 29, 2004). Yet Umberto may have been the more successful businessman of the two. In only one year as chairman of the Italian car giant Fiat, a position he had been repeatedly denied, Agnelli halved the losses and reestablished the credibility of the group for customers, creditors, and shareholders.

EARLY SUCCESSES

After a childhood marked by the deaths of both his parents, Agnelli became president of the Juventus football club at only 22 years of age, starting an enduring association with the team that would last until his death. Under Agnelli's chairmanship, the team hired important foreign players for then record sums and won four championships. The year of his graduation from law school Agnelli was thrown into the world of business and took charge of the small insurance company SAI, which at the time did business only with Fiat. During the 16 years of his presidency, Agnelli transformed the firm into one of the largest Italian insurance groups, relinquishing a centralized type of organization in favor of a segmented structure. In 1965 Agnelli was appointed chairman of the former French branch of Fiat, Simca Industries, and of Piaggio, one of the most important Italian producers of scooters. With these responsibilities, Agnelli seemed destined to become his brother's successor as leader of Fiat.

ITALIAN SENATOR AND CHAIRMAN OF THE AUTOMOBILE DIVISION OF FIAT

Despite early successes Agnelli in 1976 suddenly stepped down from all industrial positions to run for election as an independent senator on the centrist list of the Christian Democrats, Italy's ruling party at the time. Agnelli wanted to represent a constituency near his hometown of Turin, yet he was forced to accept one in Rome. Agnelli won the election but served an undistinguished three-year term. His political experience was shadowed by a scandal in which the Agnelli Foundation donated funds to the right-wing faction of the Christian Democrats, Europa 70, which had totalitarian plans.

When the parliament was prematurely dissolved in 1979, Agnelli did not seek re-election and returned to Fiat as chief executive officer and later chairman of the company's core automotive sector. In the summer of 1980 Fiat faced a severe crisis due to competition from German and Japanese companies such as Volkswagen and Toyota, which produced cars that were more reliable and durable than the vehicles produced by Fiat. Agnelli resigned his position as chief executive and was replaced by Romiti. Besieged by foreign competition, massive trade union strikes, and left-wing terrorism, Fiat was near collapse. Agnelli was convinced that Fiat could be saved only through drastic cuts in the number of employees. His plans were implemented by Romiti, who was credited for breaking the trade union front with a surprising march of 40,000 white-collar employees who supported the firm's layoff measures.

EXILED FROM FIAT

During the 1980s Agnelli devoted his energies to building the family holding firm Ifil, which, under his leadership, increased its profits from ITL 30 billion to ITL 350 billion. The purpose of the firm was to invest the family earnings in nonindustrial groups whose financial prosperity would be more stable than Fiat's and thus provide better protection of the family's wealth. Meanwhile, the crisis in the automobile sector had been countered with a policy of expansion. Fiat bought Alfa Romeo and Maserati and began to invest in developing countries. However, another economic crisis hit Fiat in 1993, and the group was forced to ask for the help of the investment bank Mediobanca, which was led by the powerful Enrico Cuccia. Cuccia's restructuring of Fiat prevented Agnelli once again from becoming the chief executive at Fiat. Mediobanca offered its help but demanded that Giovanni Agnelli and Romiti extend their terms. Thinking of his retirement, Giovanni Agnelli for the second time denied Umberto the top position, designating as his successor Umberto's elder son Giovanni Alberto Agnelli. When Romiti retired as managing director, Paolo Fresco, a manager not related to the Agnelli family, replaced him. Umberto Agnelli accepted all these decisions with his distinctive discreet style, shunning the attention of the public and the news media.

PATRIARCH AT LAST

When Giovanni Agnelli died in 2003, Umberto finally became the chairman of Fiat, Giovanni Alberto having died in 1997 of a rare form of stomach cancer. Despite a partnership with American General Motors signed in 2000, Agnelli inherited a huge debt of EUR 4.3 billion and falling stock prices. Surprising everyone, Agnelli decided not to sell the car sector but to rely on it for the group's relaunch. Replacing Fresco with Giuseppe Morchio and divesting small parts of the family's other firms, Agnelli obtained the banks' trust and was able to obtain a considerable loan, which helped to push Fiat out of the financial quagmire. Although his plans were cut short by his death of lymphatic cancer in May 2004, Agnelli managed to reduce Fiat's losses considerably and presided over the inauguration of successful new car models such as the Panda, the Idea, and the Trepiùno.

See also entry on Fiat SpA in *International Directory of Company Histories.*

SOURCES FOR FURTHER INFORMATION

Chapman, Giles, "Umberto Agnelli: Urbane Chairman of Fiat," *The Independent,* May 29, 2004, http://news.independent.co.uk/people/obituaries/story.jsp?story=525972.

Hooper, John, "Umberto Agnelli," *Guardian,* May 29, 2004.

"Obituary: Umberto Agnelli," *Financial Times,* May 29, 2004.

Tropea, Salvatore, "Al servizio di azienda e famiglia e solo un anno da patriarca," *La Repubblica,* May 29, 2004.

Volpato, Giuseppe, "Corporate Governance at Fiat SpA," http://www.insead.fr/cgep/Research/Industrystudies/CGFiat.pdf.

—Luca Prono

■ ■ ■

Ahn Cheol-soo

1962–

Chief executive officer and president, AhnLab

Nationality: South Korean.

Born: February 26, 1962, in Busan, South Korea.

Education: Seoul National University, College of Medicine, BS, 1986; Seoul National University, College of Medicine, PhD, 1991; The Penn Engineering and Wharton School, University of Pennsylvania, MS, Executive Master of Technology Management (EMTM), 1997; Strategy and Entrepreneurship in Information Technology (SEIT) program, Stanford University, 2000.

Family: Son of Youngmo Ahn (medical doctor) and Guinam Park; married Mikyung Kim (medical doctor), children: one.

Career: Seoul National University College of Medicine, 1986–1989, research assistant; Dankook University, 1989–1991, lecturer at College of Medicine and head of premedical course; Army of the Republic of Korea, 1991–1994, medical officer; AhnLab, 1995–, CEO and president; IA Security, 2000–2003, CEO and president.

Awards: 50 e-Leaders in Digital Society, *Digital Times*, 2001; 30 Asia Leaders for 21st Century, *SAPIO*, 2001; Top 3 CEOs of Korea and Top Digital CEO of Korea, *Economist Weekly*, 2002; 25 Stars of Asia, *BusinessWeek*, 2002; 18 Korean Representatives of Next-Generation Asian Leaders, *World Economy Forum*, 2002; 10 Best CEOs, *CEO Monthly*, 2002; Grand Prize for Transparency Management in the 1st Korea Ethical Management Grand Prix, Ministry of Commerce, Industry, and Energy of New Industry Management Academy, 2003.

Publications: *Virus Analysis and Vaccine Writing,* 1995; *Virus Preventing and Cure,* 1997; *Learning Korean Windows '98 with Charles Ahn,* 1998; *CEO Charles Ahn: Business with Principles,* 2001.

Address: AhnLab, Inc., 6th Floor, CCMM Building, 12 Yeouido-dong, Yeongdeungpo-gu, Seoul 150-869, South Korea; http://www.ahnlab.com.

■ Ahn Cheol-soo (Charles), born in 1962, was part of a new generation of South Korean entrepreneurs, making his fortune with intellectual capital rather than in traditional industry. He was educated in medical science and headed toward a career in medical research when his avocational interest in writing software programs to combat computer viruses took center stage in his life. By mid-2004 his company AhnLab had captured nearly two-thirds of the South Korean virus-protection market and had also expanded into Japan and China. Ahn believed that companies needed to earn profits but also contribute to society along the way. Upbeat and unpretentious, he grounded his company in core values based on self-improvement, trust in and respect for employees, and attention to customers.

EARLY LIFE

Ahn Cheol-soo was the son of a physician and destined for a promising career in medical research. He attended South Korea's leading educational institution, Seoul National University, earning both a BS and a PhD from the College of Medicine. He wrote a doctoral dissertation on cardiac electrophysiology.

Initially Ahn's interest in computers was simply a hobby; he was self-taught in computer technology. He was aware of computer viruses and the need for software security but did not develop an interest in the field until his own software became infected in 1988. He quickly understood the need to reverse-engineer computer viruses in order to neutralize them.

After his graduation Ahn began his professional career along predictable lines—as a lecturer in the College of Medicine at Seoul's Dankook University. From 1991 to 1994 he served as a medical officer in the Army of the Republic of Korea in order to complete the military service compulsory for all South Korean men.

AHNLAB, INC.—AT THE NEXUS OF SOUTH KOREA'S SOFTWARE INDUSTRY

Upon leaving military service at the beginning of 1995 Ahn founded AhnLab, Inc. with the modest seed-capital fund of $64,000, half of which was provided by Hangul & Computer Company, the country's largest software developer. The firm's mission was to provide a complete, integrated client-security solution, offering virus-protection software, online-security application service provider (ASP) service, and security consulting. His core program, the V3 Antivirus Solution, captured nearly two-thirds of the South Korean antivirus market and had the highest profit margin in the field. The program enjoyed strong customer loyalty, garnered many local awards, and was widely used for industry benchmarking studies.

Ahn's story reflected South Korea's evolution as a software-developing nation with the appropriate protections for the intellectual property of its technological innovators. The government enacted laws against copyright piracy in 1988, but enforcement was slow, and many users expected to pay only for hardware. Piracy of software was commonplace, and a legitimate local industry did not exist.

Attitudes and enforcement both evolved. By mid-2004 Ahn's virus-protection software successfully dealt with the two-hundred-odd known "native" Korean viruses. Ahn himself wrote several volumes on virus protection and software security. His corporate customers included almost all of Korea's major *chaebol*, or industry giants, and the Blue House or executive branch of the government.

SUBSTANTIAL INTELLECTUAL HORSEPOWER

Conscious of his lack of formal education in management, Ahn enrolled in an extended course of study in business. He commuted monthly to the Penn Engineering and Wharton School's Executive Master of Technology Management (EMTM) program from Seoul, staying in touch with associates and employees through the Internet and completing the program in 1997. He then went on to complete the Strategy and Entrepreneurship in Information Technology (SEIT) program at Stanford Business School in 2000, again commuting from Seoul and running his company online.

The year 2003 was prolific for Ahn. In April he was granted a patent for his system for client-computer analysis. Later in the year he filed various other patent applications, including one for a method to prevent stealth key inputs and one for a network-status display device. He had patents pending for a number of other methods, such as for detecting malicious scripts using either code insertion or static analysis, for detecting malicious behavior patterns by monitoring control flow and data flow, and for analyzing and decoding malicious encoded scripts.

PROFITS FOR A LARGER PURPOSE

Ahn believed that the meaning of existence lay in making contributions to society and indeed framed his management philosophy in spiritual terms. He believed that continuous improvement should begin with the self and expand outward, that managing the development of employees and the company's affairs should be done with respect and trust, and that the voice of the customer and the company's commitment to its customers were essential. Ahn wanted his firm to endure and defined its core values around those principles.

He was able to do this partly because, as a member of the generation of entrepreneurs coming of age in the 1990s, he benefited from the First World infrastructure built by the older generation, under the auspices of a handful of *chaebol.* During the two decades of rapid industrialization, from the 1960s through the 1980s, the very acts of building roads and bridges contributed to the common good. With a venture emerging from intellectual capital, he embedded his values in the daily work of creative development.

REPUTATION

Ahn was profiled in numerous publications and granted many awards within a relatively short period of time. In the mid-2000s, established in the domestic market, he had already expanded into overseas markets, most notably in neighboring China and Japan. Ahn himself was well regarded in the industry—a significant fact in the relationship-driven Korean business community; financial analysts cited Ahn's positive image as a factor in favorable assessments of AhnLab securities. Joel Adler, the Associate Director of the Wharton School's EMTM program, described Ahn's intellectual agility in the *Far Eastern Economic Review*, saying that he could "jump from one scientific paradigm to another" with ease (May 30, 1996).

Ahn held numerous positions of leadership in the domestic software industry: he was chairman of the Software Venture Association and the Korea Information Security Industry Association, director of the Korea Information Processing Society and the Korea Institute of Information Security & Cryptology, and counselor to the Policy Development and Research and Development Divisions of the government, the Korea IT Industry Promotion Agency, and the Electronics and Telecommunications Research Institute.

In 2000 Ahn made good on his philosophy of giving back to society by donating three-year licensed V3Pro 2000 Deluxe virus-protection software to a number of nongovernment organizations, including Green Korea United, the Korean Federation for Environment Movement, the Korean Confederation of Trade Union, and the National Farmer's Federation.

SOURCES FOR FURTHER INFORMATION

"The AhnLab Web Site," http://www.ahnlab.com/, June 2004, http://info.ahnlab.com/english/ahnlab/02_1.html.

Holloway, Nigel, "ENTREPRENEURS—Disk Doctor: Korean Medic's Business Is Curing Computer Viruses," *Far Eastern Economic Review*, vol. 159, no. 22, p. 53, http://www.feer.com/articles/archive/1996/9605_30/P058.html, May 30, 1006.

Kim Jung Min, "A Feeling of Security," *Far Eastern Economic Review*, http://www.feer.com/articles/2001/0111_08/p057money.html, November 8, 2001.

—Carole S. Moussalli

■■■

Naoyuki Akikusa

1938–

Chairman and representative director, Fujitsu Limited

Nationality: Japanese.

Born: December 12, 1938, in Tochigi, Japan.

Education: Waseda University, BA, 1961.

Family: Son of a former president of Nippon Telegraph & Telephone Corporation; married (wife's name unknown); children: two.

Career: Fujitsu Ltd., 1961–1977, general manager, public service systems engineering division; 1977–1991, group senior vice president, system engineering group; 1991–1992, senior vice president; 1992–1996, executive vice president; 1996–1997, executive vice president, group president of software and service business promotion group; 1997–1998, executive vice president, group president of China project promotion group; 1998–2000, president; 2000–2003, president and chief executive officer; 2003–, chairman and representative director.

Address: Fujitsu Limited, Shiodome City Center, 1-5-2, Higashi-Shimbashi, Minato-ku, Tokyo, 105-7123, Japan; http://www.fujitsu.com.

Naoyuki Akikusa. *AP/Wide World Photos.*

■ Naoyuki Akikusa spent his entire professional career in service to Fujitsu Limited, the company that developed Japan's first commercial computer in 1954. After expanding into mainframe computer and semiconductor production and factory automation, Fujitsu became the premiere computer manufacturer in 1979, surpassing IBM. The company entered the personal-computer marketplace in the late 1980s; by 1995 it held an 18 percent share of consumers and was expanding globally. In 1998 Fujitsu suffered from the slump in the semiconductor market and the weak Asian economy. Akikusa took over leadership of Fujitsu in this tough environment and battled to pull the company out of the slump during his five-year tenure as president. In the process he drew fire from critics for not acting according to Japanese business principles. Akikusa lost his position as president at Fujitsu because of his inability to produce short-term gains, but he continued to hold influence in the company as its chairman. Known for his innovative style, Akikusa was widely respected around the world and frequently spoke at technology conferences and seminars.

TROUBLESHOOTER AND SELF-TAUGHT TECHNICIAN

Akikusa spent the first 35 years of his career developing and proving his technical prowess. Joining Fujitsu as its first systems engineer despite his lack of an engineering background, he taught himself how to program computers and built up the company's systems integration business, where he spent most of his career. While serving as the general manager of the public service systems engineering division, he secured a mainframe contract with the Australian Bureau of Statistics that showed the global business community Fujitsu was a company to be reckoned with.

As executive vice president, Akikusa developed Fujitsu's global solutions business. His group created two products: Propose, a service product framework solution, and Solutionvision, a comprehensive solution product. Both products became key profit centers for Fujitsu.

In addition to being an innovator in systems solutions, Akikusa proved a capable leader in a crisis. On January 17, 1995, the Kobe earthquake destroyed Fujitsu's regional office in western Japan. By the end of that day, Akikusa, who was the manager of that region, drafted plans for restoring clients' computer systems and established an alternative office to take over the operations in Kobe.

SAVING FUJITSU

After assuming the role of president of Fujitsu in 1998, Akikusa had to marshal his systems expertise and troubleshooting ability to turn the company around. In 1999 Fujitsu's profits in the semiconductor business had dried up, and its other three business units were suffering. Like its competitors, Fujitsu needed restructuring because of smaller profit margins. Long a champion of global operations, Akikusa stepped up his efforts to make Fujitsu a global information technology company, attempting to grab a share of the global services and outsourcing business that IBM and EDS held. Akikusa felt that by leveraging the company's expertise in computers, communications, and systems integration, Fujitsu could become the second- or third-largest company in those segments by 2003.

In 1999 Akikusa eliminated three of Fujitsu's 12 semiconductor operations and filled the company's need for chips by outsourcing to a company in Taiwan. Recognizing that Fujitsu needed to build a global presence to compete and survive, Akikusa pushed the company into online trading, auctions, and electronic commerce services for businesses and consumers. In March 1999 Fujitsu spent $225 million to purchase Nifty Serve, the largest Internet service provider in Japan. The purchase also put Fujitsu in a good position to take advantage of the next generation of cellular phone systems and high-speed data communications.

Fujitsu reorganized again in 2001, eliminating more than 16,000 jobs and ceasing its manufacturing of hard-disk drives for personal computers. Akikusa believed that Fujitsu was facing an extremely elongated U-shaped recovery but that the IT market would grow in the long term. Experts were appalled at Fujitsu's results for the first quarter of 2001. With every major product division in the red, the company's outlook was bleak. The competition that forced the restructuring was not going away but likely to grow. By the end of 2001 Akikusa's vision for the company had not come into focus. The company had made little progress in capturing market share in Europe and the United States, despite heavy investment by Fujitsu.

Akikusa was labeled a taboo breaker because of his dramatic reorganization and extensive layoffs. A sacred principle of corporate Japan was that no matter how bad business got, employees kept their jobs. As the first of many Japanese leaders to follow a new code of conduct, Akikusa was unusual in his ability to climb the corporate ladder in Japan despite his maverick techniques. Although some critics faulted Akikusa for not establishing a focus for Fujitsu as either an Internet business firm or a hardware maker, many investors believed in Akikusa's business transformation. The company's stock was trading well when Akikusa announced Fujitsu was moving away from its core businesses and into new growth areas.

Akikusa had a down-to-earth style. At his unpretentious office he had an open-door policy, and when traveling he used his computer to keep in close touch with his managers and clients. In April 2002 Akikusa established Fujitsu University to train company executives to speak English, which Akikusa considered the language of business. Each year 6,400 employees studied English. Through the university's Global Knowledge Institute, executives with a good command of English put their skills to use in developing business models. Under the personal supervision of Akikusa, the executives had three months to devise their models and then present their research to Akikusa and other executives.

Fujitsu lost ¥380 billion in 2001 and ¥122 billion in 2002. With the goal of maximizing shareholder value, the company announced new corporate governance and business management structures in March 2002. The board was streamlined and a system of corporate executive officers introduced. In June 2003 Akikusa became chairman of the company, with Hiroaki Kurokawa succeeding him as president.

THE FUTURE

After becoming chairman, Akikusa was able to focus on long-term goals. He arranged a deal with Verizon to manufacture several hundred million dollars' worth of fiber-optic equipment for Verizon's North American operation and established a joint venture with Sun Microsystems to merge its high-end server operations with those at Fujitsu. Sun and Fujitsu would develop a Sparc processor together and then resell each other's respective product lines. In addition, he capitalized on the market to build plasma and flat screens in a joint venture with Hitachi. As a result of these deals, Fujitsu realized a ¥49.7 billion profit in fiscal year 2003. By the middle of the first decade of the 21st century, with European markets expanding and business in the United States expected to rally, Fujitsu began catching up with IBM in the global market and hoped to double its profit to more than ¥100 billion.

Akikusa also gained a reputation as a protector of the environment. According to the Silicon Valley Toxics Coalition, a diverse worldwide grassroots organization that engages in research, advocacy, and organizing around the environmental and human health problems caused by the rapid growth of the electronics industry, Fujitsu was the only firm it deemed worthy of a passing grade among its corporate peers for dealing with e-waste and promoting environmental awareness within its corporate culture. Fujitsu's grade was published in the January 4, 2003, Silicon Valley Toxics Coalition 4th Annual Report Card. Akikusa has been quoted as saying, "Environmental preservation is one of the most pressing issues we all face as members of the human race." Akikusa moved environmental issues up Fujitsu's priority list from countermeasures to strategies.

See also entry on Fujitsu Limited in *International Directory of Company Histories.*

SOURCES FOR FURTHER INFORMATION

"Fujitsu Limited Fiscal Year 2003 Year-End Report," *Company News Feed,* June 7, 2004.

"Fujitsu Selects New Head in Revamp Drive," *Nikkei Weekly,* April 28, 2003.

"Fujitsu Striving to Boost Sales, Company President Says," *AsiaBizTech,* January 5, 1999.

"Fujitsu to Invest Heavily in Hardware," *Nikkei Weekly,* March 15, 2004.

"IT Strategies in the Age of Broadband: Commoditizing IT," Second Nikkei Global Management Forum Web site, http://www.nikkei.co.jp/hensei/ngmf2000/pdf/gm_web/file/akikusa_e.html (November 6, 2000).

Kallender, Paul, "Fujitsu to Cut 16,400 in $2.5B Restructuring," *EETimes,* August 27, 2001, p. 24.

Kunii, Irene M., "A Behemoth of the Net?" *BusinessWeek,* August 30, 1999, p. 214.

———, "Fujitsu: Beyond Big Iron," *BusinessWeek,* March 29, 1999, p. 76.

———, "Japan's Tech Giants Go under the Knife," *BusinessWeek,* September 10, 2001, p. 18.

"Kurokawa to Become Fujitsu President in Late June," *Jiji Press Ticker,* April 25, 2003.

Morgan, Timothy Prickett, "Sun Throws in with Fujitsu for Future Joint Sparc Platform," *ComputerWire,* June 2, 2004.

Murakami, Mutsuko, "The Taboo Breaker," *Asiaweek,* October 26, 2001.

Rahman, Bayan, "Order Represents Turnaround for Fujitsu," *Financial Times Limited,* June 25, 2003.

Schuch, Beverly, and David Piper, "Fujitsu's Transformation," *CNNfn,* transcribed by FDCH emedia, September 17, 1999, transcription #091705cb.112.

"Silicon Valley Toxics Coalition 2002 Computer TakeBack Report Card," http://www.svtc.org/cleancc/pubs/2002report.htm#fujitsu (January 9, 2003).

—Jill Meister

■ ■ ■

Raúl Alarcón Jr.

1956–

Chairman, president, chief executive officer, Spanish Broadcasting System

Nationality: American.

Born: May 1956, in Havana, Cuba.

Education: Fordham University, BS, 1981.

Family: Son of Raul Alarcón Sr.; married Maria (maiden name unknown; divorced, 2004); children: two.

Career: Spanish Broadcasting System, 1983–1985, account executive; 1985–, president and director; 1994–, CEO and president; 1999–, chairman, CEO, and president.

Address: Spanish Broadcasting System, 2601 South Bayshore Drive, Coconut Grove, Florida 33133; http://www.spanishbroadcasting.com.

■ Controlling a Latino radio empire, Raúl Alarcón Jr. helped make the Spanish Broadcasting System (SBS) one of the largest operators of Spanish-language radio stations in the United States, with 25 stations located in eight of the largest Latino markets in the country: Los Angeles, Puerto Rico, New York, Miami, San Francisco, Chicago, San Antonio, and Dallas. Alarcón was driven by both his cultural roots and his father's dream—an American dream that mirrored, and was enabled by, the fastest-growing cultural group in the country. America's Latino population grew 61 percent—from 21.9 million to more than 35 million—between 1990 and 2001. By 2004 Alarcón's radio stations reached more than 61 percent of the U.S. Latino population.

LIKE FATHER, LIKE SON

Raúl Alarcón Jr. fled Cuba for the United States with his family in 1960. His father, Raúl Alarcón Sr., had been a radio entrepreneur when he left Cuba as a political refugee, giving up 14 radio stations and vowing to replicate the business in his adopted homeland. In New York City, Alarcón Sr. began working as an announcer at a Spanish radio station and climbed the ranks to programming director and station manager. As a teenager growing up in the Bronx section of New York, Alarcón Jr. was deeply influenced by his father's job. He worked at the station after school and listened to records with his father at night. Describing his childhood in an interview in *Billboard* (July 26, 2003), Alarcón Jr. said, "I met all his colleagues and the music people and the artists. All of that of course affected me. I grew to love it."

Despite his affinity to the business, Alarcón never planned to follow his father's career path. He was a premed student at Fordham University in New York and expected to pursue a career in medicine. However, in 1983 his father made a bold move and borrowed $3.5 million to buy an AM radio station, WSKQ (La Super 1380). Eager to help his father, Alarcón Jr. took a job in the sales department. His first advertisement contract was with an electrical repair shop on Broadway. "They would hear it on the air and it was like, wow! It was a very exciting time for me," he told *Billboard* (July 26, 2003).

TIMING IS EVERYTHING

WSKQ-AM introduced a modern Spanish-language format in New York. In 1983 father and son formed SBS and began working together to build the empire. By 1988 SBS was profitable and generated sales of about $20 million. That year the Alarcóns purchased their first FM station, regional Mexican KLAX (97.9 FM) in Los Angeles. When they bought their third station, New York's WSKQ-FM, in 1989 and reformatted it as Mega 97.9, La Mega, it seemed unlikely that a Spanish-language radio station could dominate the metropolitan New York market. Yet by 1998 WSKQ surpassed the market's longtime leader, the light-rock station WLTW-FM. Many industry analysts said a major turning point for Spanish radio happened that year when media researchers at Arbitron rated La Mega's morning show number one over that of the radio personality Howard Stern. By 2003 WSKQ was the most listened-to Spanish language radio station in the United States.

SBS was profitable in its first year, generating sales of about $20 million. The company went public in the fall of 1991, raising $435.8 million by selling 21.8 million shares at $20 per share. The success of the station, one of a dozen around the nation run by SBS in 1998, confirmed the influence of the growing Spanish-speaking audience. From 1993 to 1998 the number of Spanish stations in the United States ballooned from 365 to 454.

INSTINCT TRUMPS DUE DILIGENCE

In 2002 the company created SBS Entertainment, a concert production arm. Around the same time, it diversified by purchasing 80 percent of JuJu Media, the operator of the Spanish-English Web site LaMusica.com, which offered Latin music, entertainment, news, and culture. Later that year, at the insistence of Alarcón Jr., SBS launched KZAB-FM (La Sabrosa 93.5), targeting the Central American population in Los Angeles and offering programming distinct from anything else in the market. Alarcón attributed the bold move to a mix of research, which provided a road map, and gut instinct. In 2003 he told *Billboard*, "My opinion is that radio programming continues to be an art. It is not a science. I will not argue with the fact that research gives you a good indication, a good road map."

MAKING MONEY REQUIRES SPENDING IT

A big challenge for SBS was its heavy debt load. To avoid bankruptcy in the early 1990s, the company issued $175 million in high-yield debt and another $175 million in a privately placed issue of preferred stock that paid its holders an annual return of 14.25 percent in additional shares. The company's ratio of debt and preferred stock to operating profits in 1998 was a large 10.9, according to Bishop Cheen, a media analyst at First Union Capital Markets. With a weakened financial position, the company was vulnerable to takeover attempts. Cheen told the *New York Times* (December 14, 1998), "When they are surrounded by giants, the question is whether to consume or be consumed. What they really should have is a smart strategic partner with deep pockets."

STAYING FAITHFUL TO CORE MARKETS

Although SBS considered financial options, Alarcón remained committed to retaining the company's independence. In much of its marketing, the company proudly described itself as owned, controlled, and managed by Hispanics. In 2004, including pending transactions, SBS had a stable of 26 radio stations in the United States and Puerto Rico that offered music in a wide variety of formats, including "Cumbia," "Meringue," "Salsa," and "Tejano."

A GROWING MARKET IS SLOW TO MATURE

While Latinos were the hottest media market, Spanish-language stations ironically faced a continued stigma: advertisers still tended to favor a more mainstream audience. In 1997, when Mega 97.9 ranked third in the New York market in ratings, it was only 13th in revenue, with $21.5 million. That was well back of the top-ranked WLTW, or Lite-FM, which took in $38 million from advertisers, according to James Duncan Jr., editor of *Duncan's Radio Market Guide.*

As a savvy executive, however, Alarcón intuitively knew how to turn negatives into positives. Where others saw stigma, Alarcón sensed opportunity. While recognizing that Hispanic media revenue had increased, he acknowledged the downside of that growth. "I don't believe the Hispanic market has achieved parity in terms of being able to capture the revenue it really deserves," he told *Billboard* (July 26, 2003). "But that again is a positive. You flip it around, and that is the potential for the future. Everyone is pointing to Hispanic media as the future."

Raúl Alarcón Jr. believed that his fortunes were tied to America, as were those of the ethnic community that was his sales base. "Defeat is in acceptance, and winning is in striving," he told Laurie Flink of *AOL Latino, Latin Access.* "It certainly holds true for myself, my family, and for my company, but only as a result of the great country that we live in, the United States of America."

See also entry on Spanish Broadcasting System, Inc. in *International Directory of Company Histories.*

SOURCES FOR FURTHER INFORMATION

Cobo, Leila, "SBS: 20 Years of Success," *Billboard,* July 26, 2003, p. 25.

Fabrikant, Geraldine, "Spanish Broadcasting Builds on Growing Radio Audience," *New York Times,* December 14, 1998.

Flink, Laurie, "The Business of Spanish Radio: How One Man's Dream Is Rockin' the Country," *AOL Latino, Latin Access,* http://www.aola.com/ush/latinaccess/archives/7_raulalcan.htm.

Whithead, Mimi, "SBS's Roots in Radio Broadcasting Go Back a Generation," *Miami Herald,* January 17, 2000.

—Tim Halpern

■ ■ ■

William F. Aldinger III

1947–

Chairman and chief executive officer, Household International

Nationality: American.

Born: 1947, in Brooklyn, New York.

Education: Baruch School, City College of New York, BA, 1969; Brooklyn Law School, JD, 1975.

Family: Son of William F. Aldinger (dockworker); married Alberta (maiden name unknown); children: four.

Career: U.S. Trust Company, 1969–1975, various positions; Citibank Corporation, 1975–1986, various positions, including trust officer and vice president of private banking; Wells Fargo Bank, 1986–1994, various positions, including executive vice president of private banking group and vice chairman of private banking, consumer credit, and retail banking groups; Household International, 1994–1996, president and CEO; 1996–, chairman and CEO.

Awards: Distinguished Alumnus Award, Baruch College, 2004; Adam Smith Business Citizen Medal, 2004.

Address: Household International, 2700 Sanders Road, Prospect Heights, Illinois 60070; http://www.household.com/corp/index.jsp.

William F. Aldinger III. *AP/Wide World Photos.*

■ William F. Aldinger III was known for his leadership of Household International, the consumer-finance company acquired by the British banking firm HSBC in March 2003. Aldinger joined Household in 1994, and his accomplishments included shaping a multibusiness corporation into a lean, highly profitable firm focused on subprime lending and credit cards. Household was one of the largest consumer-finance firms in the United States in 2004. Under Aldinger, Household prospered, making acquisitions and encountering few challenges, until the early 2000s, when accusations of predatory lending by consumer activists culminated in a variety of lawsuits. A 2002 audit caused Household to restate its earnings for the previous nine years. These problems affected the stock price and made Household vulnerable to acquisition. According to former coworkers and analysts, Aldinger's priorities were to reduce costs and build shareholder value; he was an introverted leader, more likely to avoid conversation than to seek it.

A SUBPRIME START

Aldinger grew up in Brooklyn, New York, where his parents, like his future customers, were more familiar with the services offered by Household than with those of traditional banks. Unlike banks, which offered a variety of services such as loans, safe deposit boxes, and federally insured savings accounts, consumer finance companies like Household specialized in personal and mortgage loans and were often patronized by working class, low-income customers. An article in the *Guardian* reported that Aldinger "has said his father's way of life and working class ethic were captured in the Marlon Brando film, *On the Waterfront*" (May 30, 2003).

EARLY CAREER

After graduating from the Baruch School of City College of New York in 1969, Aldinger started working at the U.S. Trust Company, taking night classes at the Brooklyn Law School. He completed his law degree in 1975, the year he joined Citibank. As a vice president of sales at Citibank, he tested an incentive-compensation program designed to retain top salesmen, in part, by distributing financial awards annually instead of quarterly. An *American Banker* article quoted Aldinger as saying, "I like to keep the carrot dangling" (November 17, 1983). Aldinger left Citibank in 1986 to join the Wells Fargo Bank in San Francisco, where he held progressively important senior-leadership positions in the private-banking, consumer-credit, and retail-banking groups.

A SUCCESSFUL START AT HOUSEHOLD

Following his employment with Wells Fargo, Aldinger joined Household International in 1994 as president and CEO, leaving the banking industry for the world of consumer finance that was familiar to him from his youth. Aldinger saw banking and consumer financing as different aspects of one industry—the money business.

When Aldinger joined Household, it had multiple businesses and an art collection. He sold the art collection and eliminated unprofitable divisions, such as consumer banking and stockbrokering, leaving the credit-card and consumer-finance divisions to become the core of a streamlined organization whose lending operations served subprime borrowers. Aldinger credited Household's success to its limited focus. He further demonstrated that focus in 1997 by purchasing the consumer-finance subsidiary of Transamerica and ACC Consumer Finance, a subprime automotive-finance firm. Household shareholders benefited; stock prices increased to $100 per share, a milestone. In 1998 Household merged with rival consumer-finance firm Beneficial.

COPING WITH PROBLEMS

In the early 2000s the consumer-activist organization ACORN (Association of Community Organizations for Reform Now) started accusing Household and other subprime lenders of predatory-lending practices, which included charging high interest rates, excessively high points, failing to explain the relationship between points and interest rates, and charging financial penalties to borrowers who paid off mortgages early. To Aldinger, prepayment penalties were an acceptable method of retaining customers in the flurry of mortgage refinancing effecting the industry. He felt that without subprime lenders like Household, many of these borrowers would have no access to credit at all.

The accusations continued, however, and in 2002 Household faced multiple lawsuits. One of the most significant was filed by financial regulators and the attorneys general of 19 states and the District of Columbia; the lawsuit was settled in October, 2002 and included the establishment of a $484 million restitution fund. Aldinger agreed to the settlement primarily to avoid more negative press. There were no fines or penalties. Household did, however, reform its lending practices.

Another problem occurred in August 2002 when Household restated its financial results for the previous nine years, beginning in 1994, reducing its earnings by $386 million. KPMG, Household's new auditing firm, recommended the revision, which addressed issues with three of Household's credit-card-marketing agreements.

HOUSEHOLD PURCHASED BY HSBC

As its stock prices fell, Household became an appealing purchase for the venerable British banking firm HSBC. The purchase was announced in November 2002 and finalized in March 2003. The final Household stock price was about $30 a share, which was considered low by analysts, but the merger improved Household's ability to access funding based on HSBC's capital strength and good credit ratings. One Chicago banking official, Steve Timbers, told Janet Stewart Kidd of the *Chicago Tribune* that "At the end of the day, Bill Aldinger is a bright guy, and whatever his reasons were, I'm sure he thought it through. He's not one to do anything dumb" (November 17, 2002).

Aldinger received a three-year contract to remain as head of HSBC's Household subsidiary, with a large (especially by the standards of British shareholders) compensation package of more than $50 million. He joined the HSBC board of directors in April 2003. The "Household" name began to be phased out in 2004.

MANAGEMENT STYLE

Aldinger was an introverted leader who focused on business. He was intelligent, self-disciplined, and methodical. He served on the boards of MasterCard International, Illinois Tool Works, Children's Memorial Medical Center/Children's Memorial Hospital (a combined board), the Children's Memorial Foundation, Evanston Northwestern Healthcare, and other organizations. He was also on the board of trustees for Northwestern University and other educational institutions.

See also entry on Household International, Inc. in *International Directory of Company Histories.*

SOURCES FOR FURTHER INFORMATION

Kidd, Janet Stewart, "How Does Household's New Roof Fit Chicago?" *Chicago Tribune,* November 17, 2002.

Pratley, Nils, "Enter HSBC's 57M Dollars Man," *Guardian* (London), May 30, 2003.

Timmons, Heather, "Banker at the Helm of Household Makes Transition," *American Banker,* July 30, 1997, p. 8.

Tyson, David O., "Citibank Incentive Program Builds Current Fee Business," *American Banker,* November 17, 1983, p. 1.

—S. E. Weigant

■■■

Vagit Y. Alekperov

1950–

Founder and chief executive officer, Lukoil

Nationality: Azerbaijani-Russian.

Born: September 1, 1950, in Baku, Azerbaijan.

Education: Azerbaijan Oil and Gas Institute, PhD, 1974.

Family: Married; children: one.

Career: Kaspmorneft, 1972–1974, drill operator; West Siberian oil production, 1974–1979, team leader, deputy chief, deputy director general; Kogalymneftegaz and Basneft, 1979–1982, director general; Kogalymneftegaz Oil, 1982–1990, director general; Soviet Union, 1990–1991, deputy minister of oil and gas, acting minister of fuel and energy; Lukoil, 1991–, president.

Awards: Order of People's Friendship, Order of Honor, medal for developing the oil and gas complex in western Siberia, Order of Glory, Global Corporate Leadership Award.

Address: OAO Lukoil, 11 Sretenski Boulevard, 101000 Moscow, Russia; http://www.lukoil.com.

Vagit Y. Alekperov. *AP/Wide World Photos.*

■ Vagit Y. Alekperov created Lukoil in 1991, when he was the deputy minister of oil, as one of the first attempts by the Russian government to privatize state enterprises. Eventually acquiring a controlling stake in Lukoil, Alekperov deployed capitalist management techniques, socialist industrial practices, strong-arm tactics, and political connections to make Lukoil on of the world's leading oil companies. With 21.45 billion barrels of proven and probable reserves in oil patches across Russia as well as 25 other countries, Lukoil ranked second in the world to ExxonMobil, which had 22 billion barrels of proven reserves. Lukoil, a publicly traded company on the NYSE, remained a tightly held company in 2003; its principal shareholders were Atlantic Richfield Company (6 percent), the Russian government (8 percent), Alekperov (10 percent), and Lukoil managers (20 percent). In addition to oil reserves, Lukoil owned eight refineries and 4,700 gas stations worldwide, with 2,000 in the United States. In 2002 Alekperov ranked 327th on a list of world's richest people, with assets totaling $1.3 billion.

THE BOY FROM BAKU

Raised in Baku on the Caspian Sea, an area "seeped through with oil," Alekperov was destined to become an oilman (*Forbes*, January 22, 1996). Baku oil made several famous fortunes, including that of the Nobel brothers and the founder of Shell Oil. However, Alekperov, the youngest of five children from an Azerbaijani-Cossack family and the son of an oilman, was the first native to realize wealth from oil. His mother, who struggled as a single parent, raised him to be "a doer, not a talker" (*New York Times*, May 19, 2002). At 18, Alekperov went to work in the oil fields while pursuing an advanced degree.

Alekperov completed his studies at the Azerbaijan Oil and Gas Institute with a dissertation titled "Vertically Integrated

Oil Companies in Russia: Methodology of Forming and Realization." In that work he explored the technical complexities that a Russian oil company faced in integrating oil production—that is, controlling all aspects of exploration, extraction, refining, marketing, and distribution. From his research, Alekperov formulated a theory about integrated Russian oil production and showed that integrated companies, whether in the United States or Russia, were the most efficient means of developing oil. He posited that if Russian oil was to compete on the global market, its companies had to resemble companies like British Petroleum and Shell. While completing his doctoral degree, Alekperov established his reputation as a sound oilman with an aura of invincibility. While at work in the Caspian Sea, he survived a wellhead explosion on a drilling platform that killed two other workers.

OIL IN THE SOVIET UNION

The Soviet Union organized oil deposits into 33 associations, determined in their size and breadth by the deposits under their control. Taken as distinct private companies, 16 of these associations would have ranked among the world's 30 largest oil companies in 1991. Having proven his knowledge of oil geology and his ability to work hard, Alekperov took charge of Kogalym, an oil production town in the association of Kogalymneftegaz, in 1983. Though atop one of the world's best reserves, Kogalym had poor output figures before Alekperov arrived.

Alekperov combined two managerial techniques, blending a capitalist-style attention to production margins with a socialist-style attention to workers. One of his first acts at Kogalym was to build homes and a retail outlet for his workers; later he added a hospital and small airport. Though such materialist concerns won him a reprimand and a criminal investigation from Moscow, the boost in worker morale assisted Alekperov in restructuring work practices. His approach included a genuine solidarity with his workers. On one occasion, men nervous about repairing a pipeline were put at ease when Alekperov lay next to it and told them to get to work. In short, Alekperov had begun to create an integrated oil company, and he was not afraid to get dirty. As a result of his management, annual production at Kogalym increased from 2 million barrels to 240 million barrels of crude by 1990. Amidst the general decline of Soviet production, Alekperov's performance brought him to the attention of Mikhail Gorbechev, who was then attempting to recreate the Soviet Union.

Alekperov became deputy oil minister in 1990, charged with improving the overall efficiency of Russian oil production. Understanding that oil, whether under Communism or not, had to be developed by integrated companies using modern technology, Alekperov sought foreign investment, specifically from British Petroleum. However, Western oil executives could not imagine a post-Communist Russia and declined, fearing political risk. Alekperov, however, learned some lessons from British Petroleum: "If the company is hit by a fall in crude oil prices, it can still make money on petrochemicals" and "buying and selling goes on between competing oil companies" (*Forbes*, January 22, 1996). Alekperov added these aspects of capitalism to his already sound understanding of integration.

Although Soviet hardliners revolted against Gorbachev, their failure only accelerated the demise of the Soviet Union. Nevertheless, Gorbechev was unable to prevent Boris Yeltsin from taking the lead and establishing the Russian Republic. Meanwhile, oil's importance to the government and Alekperov's excellent managerial ability ensured his continued role as oil minister. When Yeltsin expedited privatization of state industries in 1991, Alekperov created Lukoil. The first three letters came from the largest of Russia's associations, which Alekperov had selected to anchor his company: Langepasneftegaz, Uraineftegaz, and Kogalymneftegaz. Lukoil was the first and largest of 10 Russian oil companies created at this time. By 1993 Alekperov had stepped down from his ministerial post to take control of Lukoil, becoming incredibly wealthy in the process. Alekperov's Lukoil was not released into a free market world but a world of a partially functioning capitalist bureaucracy. In addition, he had to face the Russian mafia, or *Mafiya*; the kidnapping of a Lukoil subordinate in 2002 by the *Mafiya* revealed their intransigence.

ROBBER BARON, CRONY, OLIGARCH

By the mid-1990s the Western media equated Russia's new men of wealth to the American robber barons of the late 19th century. Accordingly, *robber baron* was defined as a man who used his unique business acumen to consolidate manufacturing concerns or extract natural resources when nobody else could, all for the benefit of the economy as a whole. Using the robber-baron analogy to depict Russian businessmen obscured the deterioration resulting from the Soviet Union's demise and boosted support for global market deregulation.

However, the myth by analogy was grossly misleading. First, the historic imbalance of the late 19th century was not unique to the United States: Russia had the Swedish-born Nobel brothers to match Rockefeller in oil, and N. I. Putilov matched Andrew Carnegie in steel manufacturing. The instability of capitalist economies at the time of the historic robber barons nearly destroyed the entire system; government reform and a judicial crackdown eventually curtailed the monopolistic power acquired by the robber barons. Second, and worse, propagation of the robber baron myth allowed commentators to view Russia in the 1990s as 19-century Russia, thus ignoring the historical vestiges of a corrupt Communist bureaucracy demanding attention before a market economy would be viable. Refusing to see Russia in its post-Soviet context fostered ignorance of the true state of Russia, where incredibly high rates of alcoholism and suicide created a decline in population and a civic order verging on anarchy. Russia's new men of wealth took advantage of a power vacuum to look out for their own interests.

As Linda Randall wrote, the Russian robber baron more closely paralleled the 19th-century Russian manager, using Communist-style bureaucratic habits to operate in a global capitalist market without checks and balances. Russian administrative autocracy operated within a set of "interlocking relationships" involving managers, workers, government bureaucrats, and organized crime. Such managers had no reason to become risk-taking entrepreneurs looking out for shareholders. Rather, they worked to secure the well-being of their networks by refusing to lay off workers (who often included generations of families working at the same plant because they could not relocate), refusing to favor new policies, refusing to demand honest bureaucrats over "their" bureaucrats, and refusing to give up protection regimes. As a result, the private fiefdoms carved out of the Russian Federation's economy during Yeltsin's presidency were woefully inefficient, undervalued, and far from the standards of a market economy. As described by Randall, corporate moguls like Alekperov were a return to the past; they were 19th-century Russian managers joined with Soviet bureaucrats looking to capitalist markets to enrich their networks. Such figures looked nothing like the mythic robber barons, who ultimately had answered to market rules. A more apt comparison was the "junk bond king" of the scandal surrounding U.S. savings and loan associations in the early 1990s.

Alekperov capitalized on this misunderstanding as he constructed an image of himself for the West. The press promulgated the idea that Russia could transition to capitalism only by means laid out by the men who had violently wrested their private fiefdoms from the wreckage of the Soviet Union instead of demanding transparency and lawful market behavior. Subsequently, Western capital flowed where men like Alekperov wanted it to flow. Consolidations and operation improvement did occur during the 1990s, but in Russia a "hostile takeover" was more often accomplished with guns than with a stock purchase. Because Western investors allowed the so-called robber barons to set the terms of investment, common Russians were disillusioned. Their vouchers for stock in the new companies were made worthless in a market controlled by the powerful. Not surprisingly, Russians call privatization, *prikhvatizatsiya*, meaning "grabification." In short, the benign robber baron hid the actual theft of state resources Yeltsin had allowed to occur. Advertising himself as a safe, dependable source of oil, Alekperov never spurned a Western reporter and freely disseminated a "rags to riches" tale of his upbringing that mirrored Russia's struggle to become a rich capitalist nation.

PUTTING ON THE BAKU SQUEEZE

Alekperov delivered cheap oil to the West using the Baku Squeeze. As an oilman and, more importantly, a man of the government with friends in high places, Alekperov solved problems in Russian oil development by creating them. Alekperov used his Moscow connections to pressure local governments to bog down a foreign company in a hopeless mire of red tape. Then, just when the foreign company despaired, Alekperov promised to solve the problem if Lukoil received a share of the project. By 1996, wherever oil development had stopped in the former Soviet Union for political, technical, or financial reasons, Alekperov appeared, and oil magically flowed.

Gradually, nicknames like General and Don dropped away, and Alekperov was referred to as Alek the First (and often compared to a Turkish pasha). The nickname was an endearment but reflected the fact that Lukoil's success at moving oil occurred because Alekperov governed oil. Western oil companies admired Alekperov's ability to resolve issues and soon insisted on making deals only with Alekperov. Although control of cash flow was tantamount to control of a company in Russia, Alekperov made himself essential to the flow of a commodity in general, and Lukoil increased its holdings outside its core associations as payment for Alekperov's "help."

Alekperov also used sex and gift giving to augment his "position to demand participation in all oil and gas projects in the region," as he once told a Russian reporter (*The Economist*, July 16, 1994). Alekperov funded the development of Russian private jets to have a local source for expensive gifts. A jet worth $18 million given to the president of Kazakhstan ensured Lukoil's entry into that country's oil fields, a seat on Kazakhstan's Foreign Investments Council, and numerous marks of nobility. To polish his image, Alekperov made it company policy to hire only beautiful Russian women as Lukoil spokespersons and translators. The best-looking women were reserved for Alekperov's plane. The women became Lukoil's face, helping to smooth negotiations between Alekperov and oilmen from around the world.

MATURATION OF LUKOIL

At the end of the 1990s, Lukoil was in trouble. Vladimir Putin had become president of Russia and was determined to consolidate power. Lukoil was charged with tax fraud in fiscal year 1998–1999. To become better friends with Putin, Alekperov orchestrated the departure of one of Putin's strongest opponents, Boris Berezovsky. Using Lukoil's stake in NTV, the domestic television network that Berezovskyhad grown to a 50 percent audience share, Alekperov forced the network into bankruptcy and Berezovsky to flee to Britain.

In 2002 another Russian oil giant, Yukos, embarrassed Lukoil by surpassing it as the most valuable Russian company and the most preferred Russian stock. Lukoil shareholders and executives were furious and criticized Alekperov for the very qualities that had made Lukoil successful. One shareholder complained, "Lukoil was built on personal loyalties, not a corporate structure. You can sign a deal at the center, but you find you can't implement it" (*New York Times*, May 19, 2002). Ultimately, Alekperov defended himself in a form that had worked in the past—he cultivated reporters. He asked to be excused from blame for the immaturity of Russian capitalism. He then agreed to make Lukoil more "open" but stated, "In the Soviet school of management, nothing like that existed" (*New York Times*, May 19, 2002). Alekperov played up his image as a rustic pioneer who would ultimately succeed.

Aleperov's ability to make oil move in the former Soviet Union stuttered. By 2004 Lukoil withdrew from a number of fields it easily entered in the 1990s. Citing regional instability, cash shortages, and technical problems, Alekperov reduced work in Komi to focus on Parma. In the area of the Timan Pechora project, for which Alekperov won the admiration of Mitsui, Mitsubishi, McDermott International, Marathon, and Shell because of a Baku Squeeze, Lukoil had its exploration license revised.

LUKOIL AND RUSSIAN FOREIGN RELATIONS

A highlight in Alekperov's leadership of Lukoil came in September 2003. Two years after terrorists attacked the Pentagon and the twin towers of the World Trade Center, President Putin paid his respects in New York on his way to a meeting with President Bush. During this visit, Putin appeared at the grand opening of a Getty gas station in Manhattan, which for the occasion was renamed Lukoil. Putin appeared holding a Krispy Kreme doughnut and a cup of coffee as a visible sign of his support of Lukoil, the Russian government's investment in Lukoil, and Lukoil's claim to development rights in Iraq's West Qurna oil field. The public relations stunt by Russia's president showed Lukoil's importance to Russia's foreign policy. As Julia Nanay, a Russian oil expert, said, "The company's international expansion is focused on the Caspian and Iraq, and Putin is focused on those places" (*New York Times*, September 27, 2003).

Iraqi debt to Russia totaled $7.6 billion, an amount Russia wanted to recover. Lukoil paid Iraq $2 billion in 1997 for exploration rights to the West Qurna oil field, thought to have 7 billion to 15 billion barrels. These interests fueled Russia's disagreement with U.S. policy toward Iraq from 1996 through 2004. During that time Lukoil was unable to explore West Qurna because of UN sanctions and U.S. policy (as an NYSE company and a recipient of U.S. development aid, Lukoil had to abide by all U.S. policies on Iraqi business operations). In 2002 Saddam Hussein canceled Lukoil's contract due to inaction. In 2003 Russia refused to participate in the occupation of Iraq, in part because the United States would not guarantee Russian interests, which included Lukoil's. In 2004 Alekperov met with Iraqi ministers to lay the groundwork for Lukoil's investment in Iraq and the education of Iraqis in Russian petroleum institutes.

Oil also permeated Russia's relations with China. Officially, the Chinese economy grew by 9.7 percent early in the 21st century (analysts put the actual rate several points higher), making it desperate for oil. Consequently, China aggressively pursued supplier relations with oil-rich countries. Lukoil helped construct pipelines and developed rail transportation of Russian oil south. Investment in trade with China plus an investment in South America pushed Lukoil ahead of Yukos once again (in terms of Russian company value) and firmly in the number-two spot of global oil companies (in terms of reserves). It helped that Putin had imprisoned the head of Yukos for tax fraud in 2003.

GLOBAL OIL

A ranking of the world's largest economies listed ExxonMobil 21st, just behind Sweden but ahead of Turkey. Lukoil was not on the list. Alekperov's boast to one day buy ExxonMobil, therefore, appeared unlikely. Lukoil had better reserves but failed to approach ExxonMobil's level of capitalization. Yet Alekperov continued working toward his goal, steadily improving the chronically undervalued company by modernizing its facilities, increasing its cash flow, and fostering integration by purchasing gas stations and petrochemical concerns.

Alekperov's plan depended largely on the oil reserves of Eastern Siberia, which were at an unknown level, and Lukoil's ability to diversify its reserves. Alekperov's deputy, Leonid Fedun, put the matter succinctly: "To become an international oil major, our overseas output should account for 25 percent of total production, with 30 percent of total reserves located outside Russia" (*FSU Energy*, April 23, 2004). Though shareholders and analysts grumbled loudly about Alekperov's inability to realize Lukoil's potential as a global oil supplier because of his management style, that style defended Lukoil's Iraq investments and secured Lukoil a role in China's energy markets.

Growing up in an "oil-stained environment," Alekperov became a consummate oilman regarding the development and delivery of oil as a legitimate means of world security (December 2000). Alekperov showed no concern for the environmental impact of oil or the repercussions of oil politics in terms of war or human disease. Much of Lukoil's ability to sell oil cheaply depended on keeping labor costs low but keeping workers happy through superficial housing improvements. He used political connections and the media's gullibility to make Lukoil the world's second-largest oil company. However, his inability to operate according to the rules of transparency expected in a true market economy nearly exposed Lukoil to expensive litigation several times as the company pursued global status and greater responsibility for oil security.

See also entry on OAO LUKOIL in *International Directory of Company Histories.*

SOURCES FOR FURTHER INFORMATION

Alekperov, Vagit, "The Oil Business: A Responsible Approach," *Second Russian Energy Summit,* December 2000, http://www.mmnk.org/journal/alekperov.htm.

"Alekperov Talks Big," *FSU Energy,* April 23, 2004.

Energy Intelligence Group, "Lukoil Halves Timan-Pechora Investments," *NEFTE Compass* 11, no. 15 (April 11, 2002), p. 4.

Gabel, Medard, and Henry Bruner, *Global Inc.: An Atlas of the Multinational Corporation,* New York: New Press, 2003.

"Iraq Pact: Lukoil Signs Pact with Iraq, West Qurna Waits," *NEFTE Compass* 13, no. 12 (March 16, 2004).

Klebnikov, Paul, "Russia's Robber Barons," *Forbes,* November 21, 1994, pp. 75-82.

———, "The Seven Sisters Have a Baby Brother," *Forbes,* January 22, 1996, pp. 70-78.

"Lukoil," *Petroleum Economist,* August 2000, p. 42.

"Lukoil: Vagit Rockefeller," *The Economist,* July 16, 1994, p. 57.

Neela Banerjee, "Russia Sends Message to U.S. About Iraqi Oil Contracts," *New York Times,* September 27, 2003.

Randall, Linda M., *Reluctant Capitalists: Russia's Journal Through Market Transition,* New York: Routledge, 2001.

Rubinfien, Elisabeth, "Russian Oil Man and Firm He Formed, Lukoil, Are Making Mark on Industry," *Wall Street Journal,* April 25, 1994.

"Russia: Iraqi Leaders Meet Lukoil's President," *IPR Strategic Business Information Database,* December 24, 2003.

"Russia-Lukoil-Alekperov-Shares," *Energy News,* July 26, 2002.

Tavernise, Sabrina, "Harsh Lessons for Russian Oilman," *New York Times,* May 19, 2002.

———, "Oil Prize, Past and Present, Ties Russia to Iraq," *New York Times,* October 17, 2002.

Upperton, Jane, "Lukoil's Showpiece in Russia's Tundra," *Platt's Oilgram News* 1, no. 2 (December 14, 1994).

—Jeremy W. Hubbell

■ ■ ■

César Alierta Izuel

1945–

Chairman and chief executive officer, Telefónica

Nationality: Spanish.

Born: May 5, 1945, in Zaragoza, Spain.

Education: University of Zaragoza, JD; Columbia University, MBA, 1970.

Family: Married Ana Cristina Placer.

Career: Banco Urquijo, 1970–1985, financial analyst; Beta Capital, 1985–1996, founder and president; Tabacalera, 1996–1999, CEO; Altadis, 1999–2000, co-chairman; Telefónica, 2000–, chairman and CEO.

Awards: Aragonese Person of the Year in the Information Sector, Spanish Association of Telecommunications Engineers, 2002.

Address: Telefónica, Gran Vía 28, 28013 Madrid, Spain; http://www.telefonica.com.

César Alierta Izuel. *AP/Wide World Photos.*

■ César Alierta Izuel served as chief executive officer of two of Spain's largest corporations. In 1996 the Spanish government appointed him as CEO of Tabacalera, the country's main tobacco company; under Alierta's guidance Tabacalera became the world's largest producer and distributor of tobacco, thanks in large part to the merger he engineered with the French tobacco company Seita, which resulted in the creation of Altadis. In 2000 Alierta became the CEO of the Spanish telecommunications company Telefónica, where he guided the company through significant Latin American expansion. Alierta was described as a detail-oriented leader who focused on day-to-day business operations while shying away from the public spotlight. He was said to be an admirer of the renowned billionaire investor Warren Buffet.

EARLY CAREER

Alierta was born and raised in Zaragoza, Spain. After graduating from high school, he considered forging a career as a philosophy professor but instead obtained a law degree from the University of Zaragoza. Having developed an interest in economics, he traveled to the United States to attend Columbia University in New York, graduating with an MBA in 1970. Upon completing his U.S. studies, Alierta returned to Spain to embark on a long and varied career.

Alierta found his first job in 1970 as a financial analyst for Banco Urquijo, where he later began working as the general manager of the capital-markets division. He served in various other capacities for the bank during the next 15 years. In 1985 Alierta left Banco Urquijo in order to start a stock brokerage known as Beta Capital, where he was the largest shareholder and president. He ran Beta Capital until 1996, when he sold out to the Dutch merchant bank Mees Pierson. Alierta served as the president of the Spanish Stock Market Association (AEMV) from 1991 to 1996.

PRESIDENT OF TABACALERA

In 1996 the conservative government that had come to power in Spain appointed Alierta as the head of Tabacalera, the state-run Spanish tobacco company. Although Tabacalera had begun trading shares in 1945, no foreign investors had been allowed access to the company until 1987. At the time of Alierta's appointment there was still little foreign investment in the company; Alierta indicated that he wished to keep foreign involvement to a minimum.

Under Alierta's leadership Tabacalera became the world's leading producer and distributor of tobacco, attaining this position through expansion in the United States and Central America, especially in the cigar market. While the company had long dominated the Spanish market, Alierta wanted Tabacalera to become an important multinational corporation. This goal stemmed in part from a desire to raise the company's stock price before the 1998 privatization of the Spanish government's remaining 52 percent of Tabacalera's shares.

Even before Alierta became CEO, Tabacalera had tried to expand into the U.S. market: an attempted 1995 purchase of General Cigar Holdings, one of the largest cigar makers in the United States, had failed to materialize. Indeed, operating in the U.S. market would not be easy for the Spanish tobacco concern. While the Spanish government had essentially controlled the international tobacco trade since the 1600s and Tabacalera enjoyed a near monopoly, the U.S. tobacco market was extremely competitive. After taking over at Tabacalera, Alierta revived the possibility of expansion into the U.S. market, telling the *New York Times*, "It's impossible to be an important world player without being in the United States" (November 28, 1997).

To this end Alierta engineered the purchases of Max Rohr Importers as well as Havatampa in Tampa, Florida, the second-leading cigar maker in the United States and the owner of strong brand-name products. Alierta also bought two Central American companies that made hand-rolled cigars and would help supply Tabacalera with tobacco leaf. Along with expansion into the U.S. market, Alierta raised tobacco prices in Spain to bring them more in line with the European average; these two steps led to shares in Tabacalera stock doubling in price.

In 1999 Alierta merged Tabacalera with the French tobacco company Seita through a share exchange; the enlarged tobacco group became known as Altadis. The newly created firm benefited from strong positions in both the French and Spnaish markets and possessed an extensive tobacco-product distribution network across Europe and throughout the world. The company operated in 20 countries and employed more than 20,000 workers. Upon the creation of Altadis, Alierta became co-chair of the new company along with the Seita CEO Jean-Dominique Comolli. Comolli oversaw the company's cigarette activity, while Alierta was in charge of cigars and logistics. At the time of the merger Alierta stated, "Two companies with a centennial tradition in tobacco and logistics today face the global market challenge with their integration. Altadis is a key European player in cigarettes and logistics, and the world leader in cigars: our past will be proud of our future" (October 6, 1999, http://www.altadis.com/en/noticias/en-notisueltas/19991006.html).

HEAD OF TELEFÓNICA

In July 2000 Alierta became the CEO of the Spanish telephone company Telefónica, having served as a member of the company's board of directors since 1997. Telefóncia's board met on July 26, 2000, in order to identify a suitable replacement for the CEO Juan Villalonga, who was being investigated for controversial stock-options contracts. The meeting lasted less than an hour; Alierta was chosen. After Alierta's appointment Telefónica shares immediately increased in value.

The board believed Alierta would be able to balance the interests of the company's core shareholders with those of international investors. Upon taking over, Alierta expressed confidence in existing management and indicated that he had no plans to institute major changes. He emphasized that he wished to pay close attention to the company's day-to-day management, something his predecessor had not done. Furthermore, the new CEO favored a "back-to-basics" approach that would focus on Telefónica's mobile and fixed-line phone operations while de-emphasizing other media such as satellite television.

In being chosen as Telefónica's new CEO, Alierta was seen as somewhat of a compromise and had both supporters and detractors. In the *Financial Times* his supporters pointed to the fact that he possessed important qualities that Villalonga had lacked. One Madrid investment banker said, "He believes in teamwork and he knows how to delegate" (July 27, 2000). Others also felt that he would know how to increase the value of the company's stock. One of his supporters remarked, "There is very little about creating shareholder value that César doesn't know about" (July 27, 2000). On the other hand, Alierta's detractors felt that he lacked the ability to spot opportunities and make quick decisions, for which Villalonga had been reputed. Alierta was known to painstakingly pore over details before making decisions.

FACES MANY DIFFICULTIES

Alierta faced a series of problems after taking over at Telefónica, most notably charges of insider trading at Tabacalera, which he categorically denied. In 2002 a nine-month investigation, which also focused on Alierta's wife and nephew, indeed found evidence of such trading while Alierta had been leading Tabacalera. The charges were especially important because no senior executive in Spain had ever been put on trial. In addition to the official government investigation a Spanish consumer group representing 15,000 bank customers and stock-market investors filed a lawsuit against Alierta.

The charges stemmed from 1997, when Alierta and his wife had formed an investment company that they later sold to their nephew. The investment company purchased a large number of Tabacalera shares immediately preceding the purchase of Havatampa and the subsequent rise in tobacco prices, both of which led to an increase in the value of Tabacalera shares. In early 1998 the investment company sold these shares at a great profit.

Along with the CEOs of most large Spanish companies that invested abroad, Alierta also had to cope with the negative effects of economic problems in Latin America. At times as much as 50 percent of Telefónica's revenue came from Latin America; ties to the region led to a decline in the value of the company's shares in 2001, especially as a result of Argentina's financial crisis. A 2001 scandal in the Argentine government led to protests against president Fernando de la Rua, who soon resigned; the political crisis developed into a severe economic one in 2002. The Argentine government devalued the peso and defaulted on foreign debt, and the country suffered through record unemployment and poverty.

Despite its instability, Latin America continued to offer growth potential for Telefónica. Alierta was quick to point out that while the problems in Argentina were severe, his company had also invested in less troubled markets such as that of Brazil. He told the *Financial Times*, "The crisis in Argentina is not a Latin American crisis. We are confident that Brazil has decoupled from Argentina's problems" (December 19, 2001).

Alierta also hedged against the Argentine problems by investing heavily in Mexico. In 2000 he negotiated an all-stock transaction worth $2.6 billion to buy Motorola's operations in Mexico and other Latin American countries. In 2002 Alierta paid nearly $6 billion in cash and assumed debt for Bell South's Latin American operations. In spite of the sporadic economic issues and the concerns of some investors, Alierta would not shy away from the Latin American market.

Another problem that grabbed headlines during Alierta's term at Telefónica was a reported falling out in 2003 with Fernando Abril-Martorell, the company's chief operating officer. Abril-Martorell had resigned his position in 2000 as a result of a dispute with the former CEO Juan Villalonga; when Alierta took over at Telefónica, he asked Abril-Martorell to return to the company due to his reputation as an excellent manager and his respected position among investors. However, Alierta and Abril-Martorell apparently had their own differences with respect to corporate strategy; the latter eventually resigned. This episode left some investors worried, and Telefónica shares fell noticeably in value after news of the resignation was announced. Abril-Martorell's departure, however, gave Alierta even more power to run Telefónica in what he believed to be the most suitable manner.

See also entry on Telefónica S.A. in *International Directory of Company Histories.*

SOURCES FOR FURTHER INFORMATION

Burns, Tom, "New Face with an Eye for Detail," *Financial Times*, July 27, 2000.

Crawford, Leslie, "Telefónica Hedges against Spread of Argentine Crisis," *Financial Times*, December 19, 2001.

Goodman, Al, "Spanish Cigar Company Makes Inroads into U.S.," *New York Times*, November 28, 1997.

"Seita and Tabacalera Merge, Creating Altadis, a Leader in the European Tobacco Industry," October 6, 1999, http://www.altadis.com/en/noticias/en-notisueltas/19991006.html.

—Ronald Young

■■■

Herbert M. Allison Jr.

1943–

President, chief executive officer, and chairman, TIAA-CREF

Nationality: American.

Born: August 24, 1943, in Pittsburgh, Pennsylvania.

Education: Yale University, BA, 1965; Stanford University, MBA, 1971.

Family: Son of Herbert M. Allison Sr. (FBI agent) and Mary B. Boardman Ellison; married Simin Nazemi, 1974; children: two.

Career: Merrill Lynch & Company, 1971–1978, investment banker; 1978–1980, assistant to the president; 1980–1983, manager, market planning; 1983–1986, treasurer; 1986-1993, senior vice president, director of human resources; 1993–1997, chief financial officer; 1997–1999, president and chief operating officer; AllLearn.org, 2000–2002, president and chief executive officer; TIAA-CREF, 2002–, president, chief executive officer, chairman.

Address: TIAA-CREF, 730 Third Avenue, New York, New York 10017; http://www.tiaa-cref.org.

■ Herbert M. Allison Jr. brought equilibrium and creative, problem-solving abilities to his executive responsibilities at Merrill Lynch & Company and TIAA-CREF. Allison contributed solutions that helped the freewheeling, competitive culture at Merrill to generate better, more reliable financial results. Conversely, at the nonprofit TIAA-CREF, a pension fund and insurance company, Allison added a profit orientation in an effort to improve and expand customer service and to increase that company's share of its core market—employees of colleges, universities, and nonprofit organizations. While Allison attended well the financial aspects of business, coworkers and employees considered him less adept in employee relations, finding him unlikely to give praise or build employee confidence.

Herbert M. Allison Jr. *Evan Agostini/Getty Images.*

MERRILL LYNCH

After serving in the Navy during the Vietnam War and obtaining a master of business administration degree at Stanford University, Allison began a 28-year career with Merrill Lynch & Company in 1971. He worked as an investment banker in New York City, Paris, London, and Tehran, Iran, until 1978, then he returned to New York City to become assistant to the president. Although he never worked as a stockbroker, Allison rose to positions of greater responsibility as Merrill diversified during the 1980s from primarily a stock brokerage to a full-service investment bank. Allison was promoted to manager of market planning in 1980 then to other positions that broadened his experience and increased his responsibilities.

Allison brought a methodical but creative approach to problem solving and was instrumental in bringing balance to

Merrill's individualistic, permissive culture during difficult times. As director of human resources from 1986 to 1993, Allison changed the cash bonus structure for the company's stockbrokers after the stock market crash of 1987. Much to the dismay of the brokers, Allison eliminated the excesses of bonuses based on individual performance and replaced them with bonuses based on team performance. These options, referred to as "Herbies," were tied to return on equity of the company as a whole on the basis of a 12.5 percent benchmark as well as to return on equity for the business unit under which an employee worked. Although unhappy with the program initially, by 1990 the brokers received more bonus pay under the program than under the previous bonus structure.

In another situation Allison introduced a strategy to eliminate the extreme high and lows in Merrill's earnings, a consequence of the company's culture. With leveling of the extremes the company's stock valuation improved, particularly compared with those of competitors. During an organizational restructuring in 1993 Allison, already the treasurer, became the chief financial officer in the then-new office of the chief executive. Allison also worked as head of the investment banking, debt, and equity divisions worldwide from 1993 until 1997. In April 1997 the CEO David Komansky promoted Allison to president and chief operating officer, placing him in line for possible succession to CEO.

Despite a record of success a few obstacles prevented Allison from becoming chief executive. Foremost was that he had never worked as a broker but had risen through the company on the merits of his accounting abilities. Second, Allison pared the staff of the fixed income division to a bare minimum, which had seriously negative effects for Merrill. Observers speculated about conflicts over Internet business, a strong interest of Allison's. Another possible problem involved a risk management initiative that involved ending payment of an annual $100,000 consulting fee to a popular former executive.

In July 1999, after Komansky bypassed Allison for chief executive, Allison resigned from Merrill Lynch, ending a 28-year career with the company. Allison became a financial manager for the presidential campaign of John McCain then became chief executive of the nonprofit online education company called AllLearn.org, which had been formed through a joint venture of Yale, Oxford, and Stanford universities. Allison's interest in Internet business led to his election to the board of directors of Financial Engines, a provider of online investment advice. Allison was elected to the board of the New York Stock Exchange in June 2002. After that board was largely discredited owing to excess CEO pay, Allison was reelected in November 2003.

TIAA-CREF

Allison's experience at a full-service investment house, his nonprofit experience at AllLearn.org, and his credential of integrity in the investment business led to his being hired as CEO at TIAA-CREF, Teachers Insurance and Annuity Association College Retirement Equities Fund. A nonprofit investment house, TIAA-CREF was the largest provider of pension plans for universities and nonprofit organizations. On the surface it seemed that Allison's career at competitive, profit-oriented Merrill Lynch would conflict with the atmosphere of tradition and stability at TIAA-CREF; however, Allison's career at Merrill paralleled that company's diversification into a broad range of investment services, a strategy TIAA-CREF considered when the board hired Allison in October 2002.

Before taking action in his new position Allison initiated a study of TIAA-CREF's organization, practices, and market potential, called Decisions 2003. With McKinsey & Company consulting, six task forces analyzed the company's market positions and rising expenses and conducted customer surveys. The central issue that arose involved a lack of responsiveness to TIAA-CREF's customers in terms of bureaucratic processes and demand for services. Customers turned to other financial-planning companies for investment advice, because TIAA-CREF did not provide it. Allison found that the company's share of its core market—employees of colleges and universities, private schools for kindergarten through twelfth grade, and nonprofit hospitals—had declined from 70 percent to 50 percent.

To address these issues Allison made changes directed at returning the company to its core market, focusing on markets and services within that core. To create closer contact with customers Allison shifted the company's emphasis from back office functions to front office sales and service, a move that resulted in 500 layoffs in September 2003. Allison reorganized TIAA-CREF into several business units with decentralized accountability, a structure that allowed each segment to grow simultaneously.

Allison instituted a practice common to investment firms—dividing customer groups on the basis of assets. The "rich lecturers" owned more than $1 million in assets, the "affluent class" owned assets from $250,000 to $1 million, and an unnamed category owned less than $250,000 in assets. Within these groups Allison sought to provide better service to small investors, in the $2,000 to $100,000 asset range. New services under consideration included hedge funds, financing services to institutions, and endowment management for mid-sized universities.

See also entry on Merrill Lynch & Co., Inc. and Teachers Insurance and Annuity Association-College Retirement Equities Fund in *International Directory of Company Histories.*

SOURCES FOR FURTHER INFORMATION

McGee, Suzanne, "Stranger in a Strange Land: The Unexpected New Leader at TIAA-CREF," *Financial Planning*, October 1, 2003.

Targett, Simon, "Face to Face: Working to Make Trust a Matter of Principle," *Financial Times*, November 24, 2004.

Thornton, Emily, "More Service, Fewer Silos at TIAA-CREF," *BusinessWeek Online*, October 3, 2003.

—Mary Tradii

■ ■ ■

John A. Allison IV

1948–

Chairman and chief executive officer, BB&T Corporation/Branch Bank

Nationality: American.

Born: September 14, 1948, in Charlotte, North Carolina.

Education: University of North Carolina at Chapel Hill, BS, 1971; Duke University, MBA, 1974.

Family: Married Elizabeth McDonald; children: three.

Career: BB&T Corporation, 1971–1972, manager, financial analysis department; 1972–1973, manager, loan officer development program; 1973–1980, regional loan administrator; 1980–1981, manager, business loan administration; 1982–1987, positions unknown; 1987, president; 1989–, chairman and chief executive officer.

Awards: Honorary Doctor of Letters, East Carolina University, 1995; Consolidator of the Year, *American Banker* Best in Banking issue, 2001.

Address: BB&T Corporation, 200 West Second Street, Winston-Salem, North Carolina 27101; http://www.bbandt.com.

■ John A. Allison IV intended his job with BB&T Corporation to be a stopgap between earning his bachelor's degree and attending law school. His plan was thwarted, however, when he was bitten by the entrepreneurial bug. Allison subsequently spent his entire career with BB&T and grew the bank from less than $5 billion in assets to $97 billion as of June 2004, making it the ninth-largest bank in the nation. Mergers and acquisitions were a major component of that growth, as was Allison's all-pervasive philosophy. The company's core values were clearly stated on its Web site: honesty, integrity, justice, reason, independent thinking, reality, productivity, teamwork, self-esteem, and pride. "Everything we do is guided by our core values," Allison wrote. "These values not only guide our everyday relationships with our clients, employees, shareholders and the communities we serve, but also provide the foundation for our approach to sound corporate governance."

TINY BANK BECOMES SERIAL ACQUIRER

BB&T was established in 1872 by Alpheus Branch, the son of a wealthy planter. Branch moved to North Carolina to attend military school and began a small trade business. In North Carolina, Branch met Thomas Jefferson Hadley, who was attempting to establish an educational infrastructure. Appalled by the swindlers who were scamming citizens' money, the pair decided to set up a reliable bank, which they named Branch and Hadley. Branch bought out Hadley in 1887 and was so successful that even when dozens of North Carolina banks failed after the 1929 stock market crash, BB&T doubled its number of branches and trebled its assets in the ensuing five years.

BB&T's reputation as a serial acquirer began in the 1960s. By early 1970 the bank had spread to 35 cities. In 1995 BB&T's merger with North Carolina's fifth-largest bank, Southern National, expanded its territory to 220 cities in the Carolinas and Virginia. From the time of Allison's election as chairman and CEO in 1989 to the end of 2003 BB&T made 60 acquisitions. The company expanded into 11 states and Washington, D.C., and managed 1,350 branch offices, its business including insurance and other financial services. According to Allison, all mergers were made within the context of BB&T's 10 core values. In a March 2004 address at the Kenan-Flagler Business School of the University of North Carolina, Allison said, "We figure out why an acquisition would be good for us but also why it would be good for the other company. If it's not going to be good for them, too, we don't want to do it. Every time we've completed an acquisition, we've always kept our agreements" (April 2004).

TO BE ENTREPRENEURIAL AND AUTONOMOUS

Allison's overall goal for BB&T was that it be an entrepreneurial and highly autonomous organization. His management philosophy allowed and encouraged a high degree of independence among branches and offices. This atmosphere made for a highly decentralized and entrepreneurial structure in which independent thinkers were respected and rewarded. With independence came a high degree of accountability. In an interview with Christine Van Dusen of the *Atlanta Journal*, Allison outlined some of the strategic processes he had implemented to attain his goal. Although Allison preferred in-market acquisitions, there were times when the company had to "push out," and at those times Allison preferred to make multiple acquisitions. He preferred to focus on businesses with between $250 million and $10 billion in assets. "Our real sweet spot is about $500 million to $3 or $4 billion," he told Van Dusen, explaining the reasons were twofold. First, he said, it was less risky. "If something goes wrong, then we're much more able to fix it, and it's certainly not going to kill our whole company. Second, we can add more value" (October 7, 2001).

In January 2002 BB&T reported net earnings for final-quarter 2001 had increased 14.5 percent for a net profit of 19.6 percent. Annual net income was $973.6 million, an increase of 39.4 percent from 2000, and 2001 became the 20th consecutive year of record recurring earnings for the bank. "We accomplished our earnings goals and other key strategic objectives during a very difficult economic environment," Allison was quoted at *Oakridger.com.* "It is especially gratifying" (January 11, 2002).

SLOWDOWN AFTER BIG BITE

Early in 2003 BB&T announced that in July it would close its largest deal ever—the acquisition for $3.4 billion of First Virginia Bank, of Falls Church, Virginia, which had $11 billion in assets. Analysts sharply criticized the acquisition, and investors seemed to lose confidence. BB&T's shares plunged more than 13 percent before beginning a recovery in May. In December 2003 BB&T announced a deal to purchase for $436 million Republic Bancshares, of St. Petersburg, Florida, which had $2.8 billion in assets.

In February 2004 BB&T notified stakeholders that earnings for the year would be down, primarily owing to a higher-than-expected $85 million restructuring expense after the First Virginia Bank purchase. Allison defended his latest acquisitions, saying he believed they were good investments for the future. He told stakeholders, however, they would see fewer acquisitions in the near term. "If we don't do any acquisitions in 2004 and 2005 it'll be OK with me," he was quoted in an article by David Boraks. "We plan to get back in the game in 2006, but we're really focusing internally for the next couple of years—milking the cow we've already bought, so to speak" (February 20, 2004). Allison did not entirely rule out the possibility of doing a deal if it were "cheap enough to make sense for a company whose earnings and share price have been harmed by the years of deals," wrote Boraks, who noted that the CEO still planned to pursue appropriate deals to bolster the bank's insurance and wealth-management services. According to Richard Craver of *Knight-Ridder Tribune Business News,* Arnold Danielson, chairman of Danielson and Associates, believed that because BB&T was firmly entrenched in the banking industry's second tier, the company would ride out the slump. "They've come so far so fast . . . and taking an acquisition breather could enable them to spring forward in 2005 or 2006 in a significant way" (February 20, 2004).

Allison admitted, however, that if BB&T could not demonstrate it could keep growing, it would face pressure to sell. He reiterated the commitment to autonomy the company had made to employees and stakeholders alike. Boraks quoted Allison as saying, "We've said we have an obligation to earn the right to be independent through superior performance. We plan to get our performance up and we plan to remain independent" (February 20, 2004). Boraks also quoted the analyst Christopher Marinac of FIG Partners as taking a wait-and-see attitude when evaluating the bank's continued success. "They have struggled to meet their plan over the past few years," he said. "There's no doubt there is a huge opportunity to move the dial in some of the new markets, but that opportunity was there in 2003, 2002, and 2001."

SHORTFALL SPARKS TAKEOVER SPECULATION

In April 2004 BB&T announced that first-quarter earnings fell short of analyst predictions. The company projected diluted earnings of $2.85 to $2.95 a share, and a survey by Zacks Investment Research revealed a consensus from analysts of $2.87 a share. A reporter for *Triangle Business Journal* called the shortfall "a rare misfire" for the company and quoted Allison as calling the performance "disappointing in comparison to past trends" (April 13, 2004). However, Allison had already outlined internal growth initiatives that included the possibility of going offshore with certain back-office operations (not to include customer-service functions), improving performance in underperforming markets, and expanding in high-growth areas already within its network. Allison was confident the strategy would enhance the bank's prospects for 2005 and said he was already seeing progress in several important areas.

By June 2004 speculation of a takeover bid for BB&T had surfaced. Rumors were that San Francisco's Wells Fargo & Company, the nation's fifth-largest bank, was sizing up prospects for expansion into the Southeast. Although many analysts saw BB&T as a serious prospect, others, such as Robert R. Maneri of Victory Capital Management in Cleveland, Ohio, who managed shares of BB&T, said he never viewed the bank as a takeover target. Craver quoted Maneri as referring to BB&T's history: "Banks typically are bought, not sold, and any deal would require both John Allison's agreement and shareholder agreement that the offer was too good to pass up" (June 4, 2004). D. Anthony Plath, associate professor of finance at the University of North Carolina at Charlotte, believed the more time BB&T was given to benefit from the improving southeastern economy, the higher was the price Allison could command, thus discouraging takeover bids. Craver quoted Plath as saying, "It really comes down to how restive or how patient are BB&T's shareholders with the internal growth plan that BB&T is focused on this year" (June 4, 2004).

LEADERSHIP PHILOSOPHY INTEGRAL TO CORE VALUES

Throughout his career Allison emphasized his leadership philosophy and translated it into the bank's core values, which he firmly believed enabled BB&T to achieve its mission and purpose. In an address to students at Appalachian State University, Allison defined those philosophies. One was that good leaders allow people to make mistakes. "Good leaders . . . create a context around the mistakes, a context in which the mistakes must have a purpose consistent with the mission of the organization. The person making the mistake must learn from the mistake and must share what he or she has learned with others. In that context, mistake making is good because it permits us to learn to get better," he said (October 24, 1991). Among the dozen or more other attributes Allison believed were necessary for good leadership, one was vision. He said that vision could be big or small but must always be about being better.

Allison warned that the basic need of individuals to survive could get in the way of improving the world in which they live. While a person may be intrinsically motivated to make the world a better place, the need to survive often causes fear, and fear can cause actions that counter improving the world. "One of the great challenges, personally, for organizations and for leaders of teams, is to find a harmony between our need to make the world a better place to live and our need to survive" (October 24, 1991). He also warned against using fear as a motivator. After noting that people can be and are motivated by fear, Allison declared that fear is incredibly destructive. "When people are afraid," he said, "they literally can't think and can't be depended on to do the right thing. Good leaders do all they can to drive out fear."

Truth also was high on Allison's list of values. He noted that in his years with BB&T he saw large organizations fail, and in almost all cases it was because their leaders refused to tell themselves the truth. "They misled themselves, and therefore, a small mistake got to be bigger and became fatal. Telling yourself the truth is the first step. You can always be confident that you will get the good news out; it is more important to get the bad news out," he said (October 24, 1991).

In an address to an ethics class at his alma mater, the University of North Carolina, as in the many other presentations he gave at educational institutions, Allison emphasized honesty in all instances and defined honesty as simply being consistent with reality. He emphasized the importance of right values, high integrity, and moral principles in all walks of life, including running a multibillion-dollar business. Allison said that while having the right values does not always guarantee success in the day-to-day challenges individuals and companies face, it does increase the possibility. An article in the *Daily Objectivist* quoted Allison as saying, "Regardless of the short-term benefits, acting inconsistently with our principles is to our long-term detriment."

SOURCES FOR FURTHER INFORMATION

Allison, John A., IV, "Leadership," October 24, 1991, http://business.appstate.edu/ceo/past/allison.asp.

"BB&T Corp. CEO and Chairman of the Board Speaks on Leadership and Values," *UNC Kenan-Flagler News*, April 2004, http://www.kenan-flagler.unc.edu/newsletter/alumni/2004/Apr/alumniDept.cfm.

"BB&T Misses 1Q Profit Target," *Triangle Business Journal*, April 13, 2004, http://www.bizjournals.com/triangle/stories/2004/04/12/daily9.html.

"BB&T Reports Net Earnings Up 14.5 Percent in Quarter," *Oakridger.com*, January 11, 2002, http://theoakridger.com/stories/011102/bus_0111020098.html.

Boraks, David, "Why an Active Buyer Will Sit This Round Out," *American Banker*, February 20, 2004, p. 1.

"Corporate Governance: Message from John A. Allison, Chairman and Chief Executive Officer, BB&T Corporation," http://www.bbandt.com/investor/corpgovernance/default.asp.

Craver, Richard, "Winston-Salem, N.C.-Based BB&T Bank May Not Pursue Acquisitions in 2004-05," *Knight-Ridder Tribune Business News*, February 20, 2004, p. 1.

———, "Winston-Salem, N.C., Leaders Nervous about BB&T Takeover Rumors," *Knight-Ridder Tribune Business News*, June 4, 2004, p. 1.

"Hero of the Day, John A. Allison," *Daily Objectivist*, http://www.dailyobjectivist.com/Heroes/johnallison.asp.

Van Dusen, Christine, "Q & A: Acquisitions Keep BB&T in the Game," *Atlanta Journal, Atlanta Constitution*, October 7, 2001.

—Marie L. Thompson

■ ■ ■

Dan Amos

1951–

Chairman of the board, chief executive officer, and president, American Family Life Assurance Company (AFLAC)

Nationality: American.

Born: August 13, 1951, in Pensacola, Florida.

Education: University of Georgia Business School, BBA, 1973.

Family: Son of Paul Amos (cofounder and former chairman of the board of AFLAC) and Mary Jean Roberts; married Mary Shannon Landing (a philanthropist); children: two.

Career: AFLAC, 1973–1982, sales representative; 1983–, president; 1987–1990, COO; 1990–, CEO; 2001–, chairman of the board.

Awards: Distinguished Alumnus Award, University of Georgia Business School, 1990; Silver Award, *Financial World* CEO of the Year competition, 1994; Executive of the Year, Georgia Securities Association, 1995.

Address: AFLAC, 1932 Wynnton Road, Columbus, Georgia 31999; http://www.aflac.com.

■ Dan Amos's father, Paul, said that he raised his son to become the leader of American Family Life Assurance Company (AFLAC), but Dan Amos proved to be more than a scion taking over a family business. He was a charismatic leader who attracted bright, hardworking people and who guided his company through dramatically changing business environments. His innovations kept AFLAC at the forefront of the supplemental insurance industry, and in the first four years of his tenure as CEO, AFLAC's income grew from $2.7 billion to $9.6 billion. According to the AFLAC Web site, he remarked: "Give your employees everything they need to succeed and they will give everything they can to help the business succeed." AFLAC prospered under his leadership, and it did so while being consistently rated as one of the best businesses for which to work.

RAISED TO LEAD

Amos was only four years old when AFLAC was established by his father, Paul, and his uncles, John and Bill, in 1955. The company focused exclusively on supplemental cancer coverage. By the time Dan Amos entered the University of Georgia Business School in 1969, he seemed to have formed most of the core values that directed his management style, especially his Christian views. When he graduated in 1973 with a bachelor's degree, with a focus on insurance management and risk management, he immediately became a salesman for AFLAC. For ten years he worked in various aspects of sales, assuming leadership roles by directing the work of other salespeople, and he became one of AFLAC's top earners. In 1983, when the flamboyant company president John Amos died, Dan Amos became the new president. It may have been tough succeeding his charismatic and much-loved Uncle John, but Dan Amos proved to be charismatic himself. Unlike his uncle, who wore white linen suits, Dan dressed conservatively and fit the image of a buttoned-down business executive.

SERVING JAPANESE SUBSCRIBERS

In 1974 AFLAC had won permission from Japan's government to be one of only two foreign insurance companies in the country. Cancer was the leading cause of death in Japan, and AFLAC quickly attracted Japanese subscribers, who made payments through payroll deductions as Americans did. As president of AFLAC, Amos took it upon himself to build strong relations with Japanese salespeople, who tended to be retirees selling to their old employers, as well as with AFLAC subscribers. He improved working conditions and made sure that some AFLAC profits were reinvested in Japan. For instance, when AFLAC built new corporate buildings in Japan, at Amos's direction AFLAC used Japanese construction companies rather than American ones, which might have charged much less. This decision made AFLAC resemble a native Japanese business, respected even more than Japanese insurance companies. Amos's son, Paul Amos II, even learned Japanese in preparation for joining the business.

In 1990 Dan Amos became CEO and had to chart AFLAC's direction during a period in which Japan's economy almost ceased to grow and new subscriptions in the United States began to stagnate. Amos decided that diversification was the answer, and he devised new ways in which AFLAC could serve its customers. For instance, in Japan, AFLAC offered a plan that would provide treatment for senile dementia and a policy called Super Cancer, which made sure that an AFLAC policy would cover all shortcomings in government assistance for cancer sufferers. These moves were big hits in Japan. By 1996 AFLAC drew 75 percent of its income from Japan, where 23 percent of Japan's people were covered by AFLAC policies and 96 percent of publicly held companies offered them as payroll deductions. In the United States, expanding services to coverage of disability attracted new subscribers. Yet AFLAC's core product, cancer insurance, remained Amos's passion.

TREASURING EMPLOYEES, AN AMOS MANAGEMENT STYLE

Amos invested heavily in cancer research and developed Georgia's AFLAC Cancer Center at Atlanta's Egleston Children's Hospital, which in 1999 merged with the Scottish Rite Children's Hospital and took the name Children's Healthcare of Atlanta. Amos and his wife, Mary, devoted much of their time to this hospital, which treated cancer-afflicted children, and they and AFLAC contributed millions of dollars to cancer research.

In an effort to attract high-quality employees in the 1990s, AFLAC offered to pay for the college educations of business students who would then come to work for AFLAC. This program was a disappointment and was discontinued before the end of the 1990s. More successful was the creation of an attractive, friendly working environment that included child care and flexible work hours, particularly suitable for working mothers. In 2001 women held 29 percent of top-management positions and represented 42 percent of the top earners for AFLAC.

In 2000 AFLAC began a television-advertising campaign featuring the AFLAC duck. Amos fretted when he saw the first commercial, worrying that the company's board of directors would not like it, but thanks to the duck, by 2004 polls indicated that AFLAC was recognized by 96 percent of all Americans. On May 7, 2001, Amos's father, Paul, retired as chairman of the board for AFLAC and was replaced by Dan Amos, making Amos president, CEO, and chairman all at once.

ANTICIPATING CUSTOMER NEEDS

From 1997 to 2004 AFLAC's annual profits grew to more than $1 billion, roughly tripling. In 2002 AFLAC opened an enormous customer service center in Omaha, Nebraska, a key aspect of Amos's hope of expediting payments of claims, and by 2004 AFLAC had created a computer center that could be accessed through the Internet, allowing clients to file claims online.

See also entry on AFLAC Incorporated in *International Directory of Business Biographies.*

SOURCES FOR FURTHER INFORMATION

Bremner, Brian, "How AFLAC Laid a Golden Egg in Japan: Can the Insurer Keep Racking Up Huge Profits?," *BusinessWeek*, November 11, 2002, p. 56.

"Company Philosophy," https://www.aflac.com/about_us/corp_overview_philosophy.asp

Hardman, Adrienne, "American Sumo: Heft May Come from Japan, but Its Agility Is Georgia Bred," *Financial World*, August 3, 1993, pp. 42–43.

McLean, Bethany, "Duck and Coverage: Insurance Seller AFLAC Has Had an Extraordinary Ride to the Top—Some of It on the Back of a Mascot," *Fortune*, August 13, 2001, p. 142.

Williams, Chuck, "Two Columbus, Ga., Companies Honored by Magazine," *Working Mother* Magazine, *Columbus Ledger-Enquirer*, October 10, 2001.

—Kirk H. Beetz

■ ■ ■

Brad Anderson

1949–

Chief executive officer and vice chairman, Best Buy Company

Nationality: American.

Born: 1949, in Sheridan, Wyoming.

Education: Waldorf College, AA, 1969; University of Denver, BA, 1971.

Family: Married Janet (maiden name unknown); children: two.

Career: Sound of Music (became Best Buy Company in 1983), 1973–1981, audio-components salesperson, then store manager; 1981–1986, vice president; 1986–1991, executive vice president; 1991–2001, president; 2001–2002, president and COO; 2002–, CEO and vice chairman.

Awards: Retail Executive of the Year, *Retail Merchandiser*, 2002; Alumni Distinguished Service Award, Waldorf College, 1997.

Address: Best Buy Co., Inc., 7601 Penn Avenue South, Richfield, Minnesota 55423; http://www.bestbuy.com.

■ Brad Anderson rose from salesperson to CEO at Best Buy Company by focusing on the customer. In 2004 Best Buy was the largest consumer electronics retailer in the United States and had over 750 locations in all of North America. The chain was named Company of the Year in the January 12, 2004, issue of *Forbes* magazine.

POOR STUDENT WHO FINDS STRENGTHS

A below-average high school student, Anderson was advised by his guidance counselor to forgo higher education; yet he found a love for learning at Waldorf College, then a junior college. He later studied sociology at the University of Denver. As quoted in the *Fort Wayne News-Sentinel*, Anderson reflected on his struggle to find his strengths in a keynote speech at the Indiana University–Purdue University Fort Wayne Business Management Seminar: "I'm not the only guy out there who could deliver more than I and other people thought was possible" (April 1, 2004).

Brad Anderson. *AP/Wide World Photos.*

STARTS IN SALES

Anderson joined Sound of Music, which later became Best Buy, as a sales associate in a Minneapolis store in 1973. He was described in *Training* magazine as "knowing what it's like to be the new person on the sales floor, simultaneously struggling to understand the products, customers, cash register, and the company. It's where he started" (November 2002).

Anderson next became a store manager, then joined the corporate office as vice president in 1981 when the Best Buy chain comprised only seven stores. The company opened its first supercenter in 1984 and quickly entered a period of rapid growth. Anderson's career advanced steadily as he was named executive vice president and a company director in 1986 and then president in 1991.

WEATHERS DIFFICULTIES

Despite rapid growth, Best Buy had become barely profitable in 1997 when the stock price bottomed out. Anderson sought out consultants to address the company's merchandise/inventory and marketing systems. Management implemented changes throughout the retail stores that returned the chain to a position as a market leader. Anderson would continue to emphasize the importance of hiring outside advisors when necessary. Best Buy later ran into difficulties stemming from the 2001 acquisition of the Musicland chain. Through the Musicland acquisition, Best Buy was attempting to reach new customers and to increase sales of consumer electronics at Musicland stores. However, there were overall declines in mall traffic and in CD sales, partially due to music piracy, and Musicland customers did not purchase more electronics. Anderson developed a new company strategy focusing on existing Best Buy customers and sold the money-losing Musicland group in 2003.

"CUSTOMER CENTRICITY" INITIATIVE

Anderson led an initiative that he termed "customer centricity" at Best Buy, the idea behind which was to create new stores that reflected the shopping patterns of local communities. Customer centricity was described in *Forbes* as involving "a massive effort to identify and serve the company's most profitable shoppers by rebuilding stores, adding to staff, and upgrading wares"; Best Buy management reviewed products "to see what sold and what didn't in order to adjust merchandise according to the income level and buying habits of shoppers at every location." Further, in naming Best Buy the company of the year, *Forbes* described Best Buy as boldly "reinventing itself while at the top of its game" (January 12, 2004).

MANAGEMENT STYLE

Anderson believed successful management required a commitment to developing and facilitating the expression of employee capabilities. He found leaders at Best Buy who could develop the strengths of those under their charge. *Training* found Anderson to be "a passionate reader of biographies and the leadership lessons they conveyed" (November 2002).

Anderson was named Retail Executive of the Year by *Retail Merchandiser* magazine because he was "an executive of a $17 billion company who had never forgotten his roots as a humble sales associate" (February 2002). Anderson was considered by his industry colleagues to be "the nicest man in the business" and "a humble, caring person whose word was his bond"; Anderson was quoted as saying, "We all work together. It's a family type of thing. We are all committed to giving the customer the best experience we can" (February 2002).

SERVICE TO THE COMMUNITY

An extension of Anderson's leadership was his service to the community; he was a director of the Best Buy Children's Foundation and the national Junior Achievement organization, a trustee of the American Film Institute and Minnesota Public Radio, and a member of the board of regents at Waldorf College. In the retail industry he served as a leader of the International Mass Retail Association.

See also entry on Best Buy Company in *International Directory of Company Histories.*

SOURCES FOR FURTHER INFORMATION

"CEOs Who Get It: *Training* Celebrates 11 CEOs Whose Commitment to Workforce Development Remains in Stellar and Lackluster Economic Times," *Training*, November 2002, pp. 24–35.

Frazier, Lynne McKenna, "Looking Differently at Jobs," *Fort Wayne News-Sentinel*, April 1, 2004.

———, "Unlocking the Potential," *Fort Wayne News-Sentinel*, April 2, 2004.

Gibson, Elizabeth, and Andrew Billings, *Big Change at Best Buy*, Palo Alto, Calif.: Davies-Black Publishing, 2003.

Hisey, Pete, "Conquering the Digital Divide at Best Buy: *RM*'s Retail Executive of the Year, Brad Anderson, Says Best Buy Will Be a $100 Billion International Retailer by 2010," *Retail Merchandiser*, February 2002, pp. 19–21.

Pieper, Mary, "Waldorf Gift: $5.5 Million," *Mason City (IA) Globe-Gazette*, November 18, 2003.

Tatge, Mark, "Fun & Games," *Forbes*, January 12, 2004, pp. 138–144.

—Jean Kieling

■■■

Richard H. Anderson

1956–

Chief executive officer, Northwest Airlines

Nationality: American.

Born: 1956, in Galveston, Texas.

Education: University of Houston, BS, 1979; South Texas College of Law, JD, 1982.

Family: Son of Richard Anderson.

Career: Harris County Criminal Court, Texas, 1978–1987, chief counsel, then assistant district attorney; Continental Airlines, 1987–1990, staff vice president and deputy general counsel; Northwest Airlines, 1990–1994, vice president and deputy general counsel; 1994–1996, senior vice president of labor relations; 1997–1998, senior vice president of technical operations and airport affairs; 1998, executive vice president of technical operations, flight operations, and airport affairs; 1998–2001, executive vice president and COO of facilities, airport affairs, and regulatory compliance; 2001–, CEO.

Address: Northwest Airlines, 2700 Lone Oak Parkway, Eagan, Minnesota 55121; http://www.nwa.com.

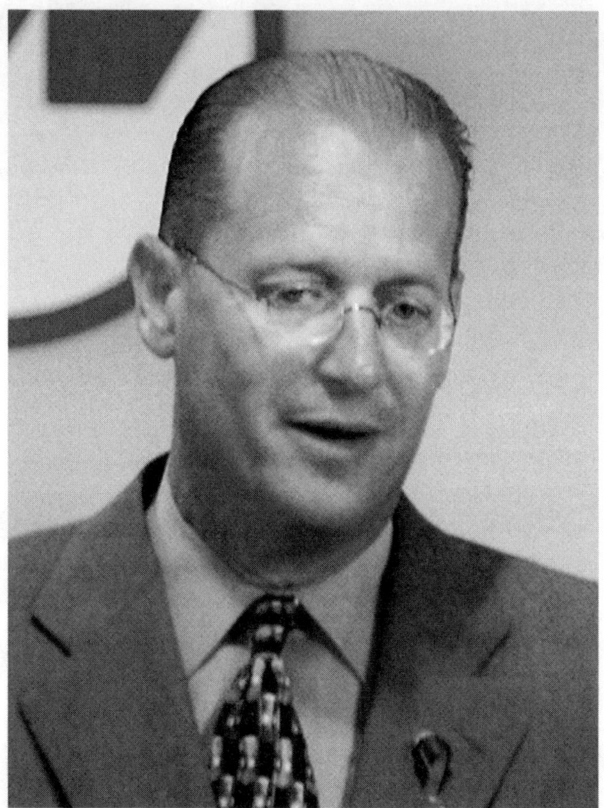

Richard H. Anderson. *AP/Wide World Photos.*

■ In February 2001 Richard Anderson was appointed chief executive officer of the holding company NWA and its principal subsidiary Northwest Airlines. The promotion recognized Anderson's earlier achievements in making Northwest the country's most on-time airline in the 1990s and also his role in expanding the airline's key facilities in Detroit. The early focus at Northwest during Anderson's tenure as CEO was on managing the effects of the September 11, 2001, terrorist attacks against the United States. By aggressively cutting costs while also attending to Northwest's problematic labor relations, Anderson averted the need to file for bankruptcy protection, as other major carrier networks were forced to do in 2002.

EARLY YEARS AS LEGAL COUNSEL

Anderson was born and raised in Galveston, Texas. After his parents died when he was 19, Anderson put himself through college and law school by working as a laborer in the building and construction industries. Between 1978 and 1987 Anderson worked as the chief counsel and then as the assistant district attorney in the Harris County Criminal Court in Texas. He moved to the air-transportation industry in 1987, working as staff vice president and general counsel for Continental.

EXECUTIVE VICE PRESIDENT AND COO OF NORTHWEST AIRLINES

In 1990 Anderson began working for Northwest Airlines as vice president and general counsel. Over the next seven years he gained a breadth of experience at Northwest in the areas of operations, staff relations, and legal problem solving.

In early 1997 Anderson was appointed executive vice president in charge of technical operations, flight operations, and airport affairs. A year later he was appointed chief operating officer, with responsibility for facilities, airport affairs, and regulatory compliance. In these roles he considerably improved fleet maintenance, working especially closely with Steve Gorman, the manager of engine maintenance. Together with Gorman, Anderson significantly reduced the airline's backlog of repairs and increased the number of Northwest planes in service, resulting in improved performance and a reduction in flight cancellations. Northwest was deemed the most on-time airline of the seven major American network carriers during the 1990s based on statistics compiled by the Department of Transportation.

APPOINTED CEO AND DIRECTOR OF NORTHWEST

Anderson was appointed CEO of Northwest Airlines in February 2001. Simultaneously, Douglas Steenland was appointed president, and the two would effectively maintain a collaborative style of leadership. In October 2001 Anderson was appointed to the airline's board of directors.

As the newly appointed CEO, Anderson promised to continue his predecessor John Dasburg's focus upon product integrity and customer service. In February 2002 Anderson opened the new $1.2 billion midfield terminal at Detroit's Metro Airport, a project he had been instrumental in initiating in 1994. The new terminal offered enhanced capacity and faster connection times, enabling Northwest Airlines to expand its already extensive service to Asia and to increase its competitiveness among business travelers. With a state-of-the-art architectural design, the new facility offered a change in image from the previous terminal and was intended to generate improved customer experiences.

At a company known for low employee morale, Anderson was committed to improving labor relations. In an interview broadcast on Minnesota Public Radio, Anderson extended an olive branch to Northwest labor unions, saying, "We have to go down the road today of building relationships, and you have to build those relationships while you're not in negotiations" (June 18, 2001). He thereafter undertook a nationwide tour of Northwest sites to establish rapport with employees and hear their concerns. In April 2001 he successfully negotiated a new contract with the Aircraft Mechanics Fraternal Association, which represented 9,795 Northwest mechanics, cleaners, and custodians. This resolution ended a dispute that had begun in 1996.

After the September 11, 2001, terrorist hijacking of four jetliners, Anderson strove to balance his commitment to labor relations with the pressing need to reduce operating costs. In an interview with the *New York Times*, Anderson said of Northwest's stance, "In the last two and a half years, we've been the most aggressive in the industry in terms of getting out in front of the problems that we faced. It's necessitated some very hard decisions" (August 7, 2003). Anderson failed to get union support for wage and benefit concessions to the tune of $950 million by July 2003, which the company had claimed would be necessary to stave off bankruptcy proceedings. Despite this threat Northwest did not subsequently file for Chapter 11 bankruptcy protection, as United and U.S. Airways had done in 2002. By restructuring in order to reduce operating costs, Anderson and Steenland eliminated 17,000 jobs from the payroll and cut $1.6 billion in annual expenses between 2001 and 2003.

Anderson emerged as an industry leader in talks with the federal government regarding financial assistance for the air-transportation industry in the wake of the 9/11 attacks. He helped develop tighter security mandates with the Federal Aviation Administration and was part of the Bush administration's Airport Safety Committee, which was formed in the days following the attacks. In these talks Anderson sought federal government assistance in the form of payment of increased security costs, reductions in the taxes and fees imposed on airlines, and increased flexibility for mergers and alliances in order to promote sales. His role as industry spokesperson was expanded when he was appointed chairman of the executive committee of the Air Transport Association in December 2002.

Anderson's dual attendance to operating performance and labor relations improved Northwest's public image and commercial performance. In July 2002 Standard & Poor's deemed Northwest to be one of the two most stable megacarriers in the industry; Anderson's leadership in the wake of the 9/11 attacks was an important factor in this judgment. Joel Denney, the analyst with the Minneapolis-based U.S. Bancorp, Piper Jaffray, praised the performances of both Anderson and the Continental Airlines CEO Gordon Bethune in turning around the fortunes of their respective companies. Speaking to the *Minneapolis–St. Paul Business Journal* in 2002, Denney said of the pair, "It's not that they knew the future, but they prepared for the unknown" (July 26, 2002).

As CEO of Northwest, Anderson was committed to involvement in the Minnesota and Michigan communities, serving on the boards of Hamline University of St. Paul, Minnesota, and Medtronic, among numerous other local and business organizations. In 2000 he was appointed first chairman of the Minnesota Business Leadership Network.

MANAGERIAL STYLE

Anderson was known for his open and personable managerial style. As CEO he fostered good staff relations by encouraging direct, informal communication among all Northwest staff. His work e-mail address was simply "Richard." His accessible approach helped him to initiate and maintain the dialogue necessary between unions and management to resolve the company's labor disputes.

Calmness under pressure was another characteristic of Anderson's executive leadership. After the opening of the Detroit midfield terminal in 2002, the *Knight Ridder-Tribune Business News* journalist Tom Walsh commented on Anderson's visible pride and excitement with respect to the new facility. Such a response was unusual for the business leader better known, as described by Walsh, for being "even keeled, unflappable, and easygoing" (February 25, 2002).

See also entry on Northwest Airlines Inc. in *International Directory of Company Histories.*

SOURCES FOR FURTHER INFORMATION

Carey, Susan, "The Thrifty Get Thriftier: Northwest Airlines Has Long Had a Reputation as a Cost Cutter; Now It Needs to Cut Some More," *Wall Street Journal,* May 10, 2004.

Maynard, Micheline, "NW Chief Says Airline Will Not File for Bankruptcy," *New York Times,* August 7, 2003.

Tellijohn, Andrew, "Overpaid CEOs Underpaid: Richard Anderson; Bad Year Takes Toll on Anderson, NWA," *Minneapolis–St. Paul Business Journal,* July 26, 2002, p. 15.

Walsh, Tom, Detroit Free Press Tom Walsh Column, *Knight Ridder-Tribune Business News,* February 25, 2002.

Zdechlik, Mark, "Anderson Putting His Imprint on Northwest Airlines," Minnesota Public Radio, June 18, 2001, http://news.minnesota.publicradio.org/features/200106/18_zdechlikm_nwaanderson.

—Ann McCarthy

■ ■ ■

G. Allen Andreas Jr.

1943–

Chairman and chief executive officer, Archer Daniels Midland Company

Nationality: American.

Born: June 22, 1943, in Cedar Rapids, Iowa.

Education: Valparaiso University, BA, 1964; JD, 1969.

Family: Son of Glenn Allen Andreas Sr. (bank president) and Vera Irene Yates; married Toni Kay Hibma, 1964; children: three.

Career: U.S. Treasury Department, Denver, 1969–1973; Archer Daniels Midland Company, 1973–1986, lawyer; treasurer, 1986–1989; chief financial officer of European operations, 1989–1994; vice president and counsel to the executive committee, 1994–1996; member of the office of the chief executive, 1996–1997; president and chief executive officer, 1997–1999; chairman and chief executive officer, 1999–.

Address: Archer Daniels Midland Company, 4666 Faries Parkway, Decatur, Illinois 62526; http://www.admworld.com.

■ G. (Glenn) Allen Andreas joined Archer Daniels Midland Company (ADM) as a member of the legal team in 1973. ADM is an agribusiness specializing in the processing of oils from seeds and grains. In 1999 three top executives, including Michael Andreas, pled guilty to charges of price fixing. Michael, who had been next in line to run the company, was given a three-year prison sentence. Michael's father, Dwayne Andreas, former director and chief executive officer (CEO), resigned his post and appointed his nephew, the current CEO, G. Allen Andreas as chairman. Some board members were concerned by this move. In a letter to *BusinessWeek Online*, Timothy E. McKinney, a New Hampshire investor, reported, "I thought it was classic nepotism, but have been pleasantly surprised by the direction he has provided and the job he has done." Analysts did not see much improvement as of 2001. John M. McMillin, an analyst at Prudential Securities, told Julie Forster of *BusinessWeek*, "Whether it's his fault or not, Andreas hasn't yet moved the needle." But investors and analysts were satisfied with his eventual turnaround of the company. Under Andreas's direction, major decision-making processes were changed, a department of corporate compliance and regulatory affairs was established, and new health and nutritional products were introduced. During fiscal year 2003 ADM invested $1.25 billion on property, plants, and equipment. Profits were increasing slowly but steadily, with a five-year record increase by the third quarter of 2004.

REBUILDING THE COMPANY

For Allen Andreas, who spent most of his early years at ADM dealing with finances and legal matters, the appointment to CEO came at a difficult time. In addition to a class-action lawsuit and fines totaling over $200 million resulting from the price-fixing charges, ADM was hit by a declining agricultural economy in the mid-1990s. As the only family member available to take over at the time, though, he accepted the responsibility. He began the task of rebuilding the company image, incorporating new products, and gaining the acceptance of the board, shareholders, and employees.

Under Dwayne Andreas the board of directors was composed of people with political ties that benefited the company. The top three executives made major company decisions. In a *Chief Executive* magazine profile, Bill Leach, a food-industry analyst, recalled that Dwayne Andreas gave "one-sentence press releases where ADM wouldn't even reveal pretax earnings" (March 1, 2004). Allen Andreas wanted more open leadership and to change the way major decisions were made. He appointed a new president and reduced the board of directors, handpicking the members who were to step down. Under Allen Andreas's leadership each of the company's operations (ADM Natural Health and Nutrition, ADM Specialty Ingredients, and ADM BioProducts and Feed) were to function as separate divisions with individual leadership, leaving room for individual growth and a better chance to increase product lines and profits. Andreas personally recruited or promoted 80 percent of the people running each business unit, and he committed himself to improving communications with shareholders. In 2001 ADM won the *Investor Relations Magazine*'s Most Improved Relations Award.

On top of building sales and shareholder support, Andreas also saw the importance of building employee relationships.

His strategy was to motivate employees to think like owners. He provided stock options and investment plans for employees to create an entrepreneurial corporate culture.

NEW PRODUCT LINES

In 2000, in line with Andreas's aims to reduce reliance on sales of food and feed products and increase newer high-margin retail sales, ADM adapted a new mission statement. "To unlock the potential of nature to improve the quality of life" (press release, October 27, 2000). The new mission statement emphasized the company's focus on nutraceuticals (over-the-counter medications made from agricultural chemicals) and other dietary supplements. The new products, along with the production of ethanol (a gasoline additive made from corn) and veggie burgers (a product he ate for lunch with a salad almost every day) resulted in a 13 percent earnings increase over the fiscal year 1999. In 2001 a new logo and ad campaign were designed to accompany the new mission statement. That same year, in conjunction with the American Menopause Foundation, ADM's Nova Soy Natural Power Tool was introduced. Andreas actively promoted a nationwide tour that offered bone-density screenings to stress the importance of soy supplements in maintaining bone and heart health during menopause. In 2003 Envoa, a cooking oil designed to help reduce fat and obesity, was added to the U.S. product line. It had been a big seller in Japan since 1999 and was expected to increase U.S. sales by $150 million per year. By the third quarter of 2004, five years after becoming chairman and CEO, Allen Andreas was on the road to accomplishing his goals, with earnings increasing 94 percent in that quarter.

THE LOW-CARBOHYDRATE DIET

When low-carbohydrate diets became popular in the United States, the demand for flour declined. In response, Andreas closed some of the company's mills. The new diet also had a positive effect for ADM, as it increased consumer demand for poultry, pork, and beef products. This in turn increased the need for animal feed, another of ADM's core products.

See also entry on Archer-Daniels-Midland Co. in *International Directory of Company Histories.*

SOURCES FOR FURTHER INFORMATION

"ADM Announces New Mission," company press release, October 27, 2000, http://www.biotech-info.net/ADM_mission.html.

Burns, Greg, "Archer Daniels Midland Tells Unhappy Shareholders of Plans to Cut Costs," *Knight Ridder/Tribune Business News,* October 21, 1999.

Buss, Dale, "Heartland Transformation: ADM CEO Allen Andreas Has Led the Giant Out of Scandal and Put it on the Winning Path," *Chief Executive Magazine,* March 1, 2004.

"Cultivating His Garden," interview, *Institutional Investor,* December 2000, p. 28.

Forster, Julie, "A Different Kind of Andreas at ADM," *BusinessWeek,* July 9, 2001, p. 62.

McKinney, Timothy E., letter to editor, *BusinessWeek Online,* http://www.businessweek.com/print/magazine/content/01_33/c3745022.htm.

—Valerie J. Webster

■ ■ ■

Micky Arison

1949–

Chairman and chief executive officer, Carnival Corporation

Nationality: American.

Born: 1949.

Education: Attended University of Miami.

Family: Son of Ted Arison (cofounder of Norwegian Caribbean Cruises and founder of Carnival Cruises).

Career: Carnival Cruise Lines, 1972–1974, sales; 1974–1976, reservations manager; 1976–1979, vice president of passenger traffic; 1979, president; 1990–, chairman and chief executive officer.

Awards: Seatrade Personality Award, *Seatrade*, 2003.

Address: Carnival Corporation, 3655 NW 87th Avenue, Miami, Florida 33178-2428; http://www.carnivalcorp.com.

Micky Arison. *AP/Wide World Photos.*

■ Micky Arison built his father's Carnival Cruise Lines business into the world's largest and most successful cruise-ship company, Carnival Corporation. He served as president of the business beginning in 1979 and has been the corporation's chairman and chief executive officer since 1990. Under Arison's direction, Carnival, which was founded by his father in 1971, became the industry leader by the traditional avenue of new ship construction to expand its fleet and by entering into new market segments, such as the fast-growing European market. Described as an extremely competitive person who hated to lose, Arison was commended by industry analysts for his keen attention to marketing and the bottom line.

LEARNS BUSINESS FROM THE GROUND UP

Arison decided to follow in his father's footsteps in 1972 when he dropped out of college to join Carnival's sales department and learn the business from the ground up. Two years later he was made reservations manager and began working with his father and others to devise new marketing strategies for Carnival Cruise Lines. One of the early successful strategies that Arison helped develop was to institute a more affordable pricing plan that would include shorter trips. The packages included airfare to and from the port of departure as well as entertainment, meals, and activities on ship. As a result of these moves, Carnival's trips quickly became competitive with other vacation packages and attracted a younger demographic, along with older people who had never taken a cruise.

In 1976 Arison became vice president of passenger traffic. In 1979, a year after the company announced that it would build the largest purpose-built cruise ship in the world, Arison was named the company's president. With company profits steadily growing, he oversaw the building of three more ships in the mid-1980s. But Arison was not interested in building ships that offered the same environment as the cruise ships and luxury liners of old. Instead, his new ships were destinations in themselves and offered vacationers distinct vacation environments that included, for example, retired streetcars and buses serving as dining cafés and shops.

ESTABLISHES IPO TO SECURE EXPANSION FUNDS

Arison's successful strategy of focusing on steady growth and on attracting a new demographic of people who wanted to take cruises resulted in the company's going public in 1987. With the influx of a $400-million initial public offering (IPO), Carnival began to expand its fleet further and to diversify into land-based resort operations, such as the construction of the Crystal Palace Resort and Casino in the Bahamas for an estimated $250 million. Arison continued to enlarge the company's market segment and engineered the acquisition of Holland America, one of the world's oldest and most revered cruise lines. This acquisition allowed Carnival to move into the luxury, premium segment of the cruise industry. Looking back on the company's successful rise to the top by the late 1980s during an interview for *U.S. News & World Report*, Arison proudly noted, "We went from being bottom feeders to No. 1 in 10 years" (October 16, 1995).

In 1990 Arison's father stepped down as the company's CEO and named Arison as his replacement. Maintaining a steady course of expansion and acquisition, Arison led the company to acquire a stake in Seabourn Cruise Line and its ultra-luxury cruise ships in 1992. With his eye on Europe, Arison also engineered the acquisition of Europe's leading cruise company, Costa Cruises, in 1997 and the luxury operator Cunard Line in 1998. Arison's vision for Carnival was so successful that the cruise line was operating at 100 percent of capacity for several years by 1996, compared with an average 85 percent capacity for Carnival's competitors. Under Arison's guidance, the once-struggling company became the undisputed king of the cruise-line industry.

HITS SNAGS IN UNCHARTED WATERS

Flush with success, Arison continued to expand the company's fleet and ordered the building of 15 more ships during 1997–1999. By 2001 Carnival had a 35 percent market share and was a $16.3-billion company. Despite the success and overwhelming market share, Arison soon faced what many other CEOs had to contend with, a faltering economy and recession. Arison was forced to slash cruise prices in the fourth quarter of 2000 by approximately 3 percent. According to one leisure-industry analyst, this was the largest percentage decline for the company in nearly two decades.

By the first quarter of 2001 the company's profits had fallen 25 percent, from $172 million ($0.28 per share of stock) to $128 million ($0.22 per share). Furthermore, Arison admitted that his company had made a marketing mistake when it consolidated its high-end companies Seabourn and Cunard in 1999, thus blurring the brands. Problems were compounded that same year when faulty engines caused some ships to go adrift and several fires occurred; Arison believes that these mishaps also turned away potential customers.

Carnival and the entire cruise industry was dealt another blow after the terrorist attacks of September 11, 2001, in New York, Pennsylvania, and Washington, D.C. Although the attacks primarily affected the airline industry, people cut back in general on travel plans to go anywhere that was a potential terrorist target, including cruise ships. In addition, insurance costs for Carnival and other cruise lines soared.

REBOUNDS AND ENGINEERS VICTORIOUS ACQUISITION

In the two months following September 11, the company's advance bookings for 2002 cruises dropped dramatically because of a significant slowdown in travel. Although Carnival reported flat first-quarter earnings in 2002, the earnings were viewed as a rebound by industry analysts, because they greatly exceeded early expectations and were not the sharp decline in earnings that many had predicted.

Arison continued to keep an eye on Carnival's expansion and set out to add P&O Princess Cruises to the company's roster of brands. P&O had a long history in the maritime industry and had established markets in the United Kingdom, Australia, and the United States through its base in Los Angeles. But Arison found himself in a battle as P&O decided to merge with one of Carnival's primary competitors, Royal Caribbean. In a last-ditch effort to acquire P&O, Arison raised the bid to $5.4 billion. Arison and Carnival faced stiff competition from Royal Caribbean for P&O, and when questions about the legality of the acquisition surfaced, the U.S. Federal Trade Commission and the European Commission begun antitrust investigations. At issue was the belief that the company's combined 43 percent global market share after the acquisition would allow it to control prices.

Arison and Carnival were successful in gaining regulatory approval and finally persuaded P&O shareholders to go with his better offer, which Arison had improved by offering to create a single company that would be listed on both the U.S. and British stock markets. The offer also stipulated that 74 percent of the company would be owned by Carnival and 26 percent by P&O.

The acquisition of P&O was an enormous victory for Arison, cementing his company's status as the world's largest cruise company. When asked during an interview for *NYSE Magazine* why the acquisition of P&O was such a milestone for his company, Arison noted that intense competition among those in the industry greatly limited the opportunities for such an acquisition. He also said, "But it's also a very difficult time for the leisure travel, so taking on a huge capacity is exciting and challenging at the same time" (April 2003).

In the fourth quarter of 2003 Carnival Corporation reported a net income of $205 million, in line with the company's previous fourth-quarter earnings-per-share guidance of $0.24–0.28 per share. Arison was ranked 104 on *Forbes* magazine's list of the world's richest people, with a net worth of $3.2 billion. Arison did not rest on his laurels; he continued to expand the company's fleet, with several new Carnival ships and Cunard's *Queen Mary 2* entering service in 2004. At 150,000 tons, the *Queen Mary 2* was the world's largest ocean liner.

MANAGEMENT KEYS TO SUCCESS

Industry analysts have pointed to many reasons for Arison's success in guiding Carnival to the top of the cruise-line business. They noted that his father was a good teacher and felt confident enough in his son to effectively delegate most of the company's daily operations to him by 1979. Arison has been known for his hands-on, open-door management style. Many of his employees even call him "Micky." On the other hand, Arison, too, believes in delegating authority. "Working with various aspects of the company taught me that if you've got the right people in the right spots, let them do their thing," Arison said in an *NYSE Magazine* interview. He went on to note, "My management style is not to get in their way" (April 2003).

Another aspect of Arison's success was his keen attention to company marketing (including glitzy television ads) and growth priorities. As noted by Jill Jordan Sieder in *U.S. News & World Report*, Arison always relied primarily on one strategy: "Built it, make it splashy, and they will come" (October 16, 1995). He applied that philosophy even to the Miami Heat professional basketball team when he took over his family's interests in the team in 1994. He hired a successful and expensive coach, Pat Riley, and pushed for a new, ritzy arena to showcase the team.

Finally, industry insiders and business analysts have noted that throughout Arison's career he has imposed tight cost controls on Carnival cruise ships. These controls include standardizing the Carnival fleet from ship design and construction down to bedspreads and furniture. Julia Boorstin in *Fortune* also noted, "Arison's pack-'em-in approach helps too" (June 9, 2003). For example, the Carnival line has typically run at 100 percent or more occupancy by such tactics as providing bunk beds for children. This strategy has led to a win-win situation. Passengers pay less per person for a room, but they end up spending more money onboard, which generates profits for Carnival.

BEGINS TO SELL COMPANY STOCKS

In 2003 Arison and his family began to sell some company stocks as part of their estate planning and to diversify their investments. During the last four months of 2003 Arison sold more than $100 million of his Carnival stock, slightly reducing the Arison family's controlling stake in the company. This was the first time in nearly eight years that Arison sold any significant amount of his shares, and the sale reduced his holdings at that time from 65 percent to 60 percent. Commenting on the Arison family's sale of stocks, the industry analyst Joseph Hovorka told the *Miami Herald*, "They're doing a bit of estate planning and nothing more. They still have a significant investment in the company" (August 27, 2003).

See also entry on Carnival Corporation in *International Directory of Company Histories.*

SOURCES FOR FURTHER INFORMATION

Boorstin, Julia, "Cruising for a Bruising?," *Fortune,* June 9, 2003, p. 143.

Dupont, Dale K., "Arison Family Plans to Sell Some Shares," *Miami Herald,* August 27, 2003.

Fredericks, Alan, "Q&A with Micky Arison," *Travel Weekly,* November 4, 2002.

"Mick Arison, Chairman and CEO, Carnvial Corp. Winning Vacations," *NYSE Magazine,* April 2003, http://www.nyse.com/events/1057189596704.html.

"Micky Arison: When the Carnival Comes to Town," *International Cruise & Ferry Review* (Spring–Summer 2003), p. 15.

Sieder, Jill Jordan, "Full Steam Ahead: Carnival Cruise Line Makes Boatloads of Money by Selling Fun," *U.S. News & World Report,* October 16, 1995, p. 72.

—David Petechuk

■■■

C. Michael Armstrong

1938–

Former chairman and chief executive officer, AT&T Corporation

Nationality: American.

Born: October 18, 1938, in Detroit, Michigan.

Education: Miami University of Ohio, BS, 1961; Dartmouth Institute, Advanced Management Program, 1976.

Family: Married Anne Gossett; children: three.

Career: IBM Corporation, 1961–1978, various positions; 1978–1980, president of Data Processing Division; 1980–1983, corporate vice president and assistant group executive; 1983–1986, senior vice president and group executive for Information Systems and Communications Group; 1986–1987, director general of IBM Europe and president and a member of the board of directors of the IBM Europe/Middle East/Africa Corporation (EMEA); 1987–1988, president director general of IBM Europe and CEO of EMEA; 1988–1992, president and chairman of EMEA; General Motors Corporation, 1992–1997, chairman and CEO of Hughes Electronics; AT&T Corporation, 1997–2002, chairman and CEO; Comcast Corporation, 2002–2003, chairman; 2003–2004, nonexecutive chairman.

Awards: Honorary Degrees, Pepperdine University, 1997; Loyola Marymount University, 1998; Worcester Polytechnic Institute, 2000.

C. Michael Armstrong. *AP/Wide World Photos.*

■ The 31-year IBM employee and former AT&T chairman and CEO C. Michael Armstrong retired as nonexecutive chairman of the board of Comcast Corporation in 2004. In a bold, historic move to reestablish itself as an end-to-end carrier during the dot-com boom, Armstrong's AT&T acquired two of the four largest U.S. cable-television companies for $102 billion in 1998. With the dot-com collapse, fraud-assisted telecom depression, unyielding regulatory battles, high debt load, and the sheer complexity and size of the acquisitions, Armstrong was forced to break AT&T up in 2001. He had joined AT&T in 1997 after five and a half years as chairman and CEO of the Hughes Electronics subsidiary of General Motors Corporation. At Hughes, Armstrong expedited development of DirecTV to establish one of the first digital-broadcast systems. Armstrong had joined Hughes after 31 years with IBM Corporation, where he eventually led international operations and was a member of IBM's senior executive committee. He was described by analysts and co-workers as a strong, affable, and intensely competitive sales and marketing executive who managed to salvage many investor assets during the fraud-plagued dot-com era.

PERSONAL HISTORY

The eldest of three sons born in pre–World War II Detroit, Armstrong was president of his high school senior class, earned college-football scholarships, and went on his first date with his future wife, Anne Gossett, at the age of 14. A college fraternity brother described Armstrong to *BusinessWeek* by saying, "You could almost quote the Boy Scout motto: loyal, friendly, trustworthy" (June 20, 1988).

Armstrong's athletic and future U.S. Marine Corps careers ended due to a gridiron shoulder injury. Surgery upon the shoulder resulted in his right arm being shorter than his left. In the place of football Armstrong made time to be the president of his fraternity, Sigma Nu, and to work for the all-fraternity council, the college publications board, and the honorary business society. In the April 22, 1996, issue of *BusinessWeek* he recalled how his mother's motto—"no limits"—inspired the family while his father struggled to start a business after being laid-off; Armstrong worked odd jobs to pay for tuition, successfully attaining his degree in business and economics in 1961.

Shortly after his graduation Armstrong married Gossett and joined IBM Corporation in Indianapolis as a systems engineer. Once inside the rapidly growing computer company he soon moved over to sales and marketing, attending sales training programs with the future IBM CEO John Akers. Colleagues described Armstrong as intensely competitive; with respect to the tennis played during the training programs, one colleague told *BusinessWeek*, "He'd always be the last guy off the court" (June 20, 1988).

Following Akers up the IBM corporate ladder, Armstrong attended a Dartmouth Institute for advanced-management education, which he finished in 1976. In 1978 he was named president of a high-level IBM division, Data Processing, and in 1980 became corporate vice president. In 1983 he was named a senior vice president and group executive in the communications division, where he was responsible for the development and manufacture of minicomputers, personal computers and software, and communications-network technology—the last of which included an early joint attempt at global communications networking, dubbed Satellite Business Systems, with the future competitor MCI Corporation.

CLIMBING THE IBM SENIOR-EXECUTIVE LADDER

In 1986 Armstrong received his toughest assignment from the CEO Akers: to reenergize IBM's European operations, in which annual sales had stagnated at $19 billion; although the European market for computing products had been growing at 10 percent annually, revenues for IBM Europe had remained flat. Customers and analysts alike said that IBM's lack of success in Europe was due to the company's single-minded devotion of attention to the U.S. market—IBM failed to either focus on individual-country markets or prepare for the single-market structure that emerged in Europe in 1992. In most ways IBM's European efforts were no different from U.S. efforts to boost sales and customer satisfaction, cut bureaucracy, and contain costs—all in the shadow of the growing threat to IBM's computing architecture from the personal-computing alliance of Microsoft and Intel.

Making immediate use of his sales background, Armstrong scheduled his first meetings as IBM's European director-general with the presidents and CEOs of prominent client firms; at one point he spent 45 consecutive days on the road meeting with major customers. His down-to-earth midwestern mannerisms proved charming, and his prior experiences with major U.S. clients such as General Motors and Boeing provided him with enough knowledge of internal IBM pathways to allay the bureaucratic concerns of major European customers. Armstrong lived in Paris and took lessons in French.

After European sales rose more than 25 percent during a two-year period, in September 1988 Armstrong was brought back to the United States and named as one of five members of IBM's highest-level executive committee. Additionally he was given responsibility for IBM operations in Asia Pacific and throughout the Americas. In June 1989 he was made chairman and president of IBM World Trade Corporation, the company's international division, reporting directly to Akers. After 28 intense, energetic years in U.S. and global operations, sales, and marketing, Armstrong was considered a possible successor to Akers as chairman and CEO.

FROM MAINFRAMES TO ELECTRONICS

Armstrong surprised the business world in February 1992 when he announced that he would leave IBM after 31 years in order to become the CEO and chairman of Hughes Aircraft Company, the defense unit of General Motors Corporation's Hughes Electronics group. It was later disclosed in *BusinessWeek* that Akers had privately told Armstrong that, for reasons unspoken and unasked, he would not recommend that his protégé be appointed as IBM's CEO. Observers noted that Armstrong was only three years younger than Akers—a relatively small age difference between successive CEOs. Meanwhile the Microsoft-Intel alliance continued to negatively impact IBM, which in 1991 reported its first-ever annual loss. In April 1993 an IBM outsider, Louis V. Gerstner, the former chairman and CEO of RJR Nabisco, replaced Akers.

Armstrong was the first Hughes CEO to come from outside not only the billionaire Howard Hughes's former research facility but the entire defense industry. The announcement of Armstrong's appointment, which followed an earlier reorganization wherein focus was shifted to nondefense markets after the collapse of the Soviet Union, was a clear message that Hughes would be targeting commercial markets, including communication and satellite systems. GM officials believed that in order to reach global commercial markets a sales and marketing executive with international experience was needed, such that customer needs would be met and costs controlled.

At that time Hughes had a reputation for its highly advanced design and engineering work—at prices that made

Pentagon officials wince. During the Reagan-era defense buildup Hughes's nonthrifty strategy worked, but sales and profits were being squeezed in the post-Cold-War world. Further, Hughes had been slow to divert its attention from defense to commercial markets at a time when similar companies were already converting their defense facilities—and sometimes faltering.

By the time Armstrong arrived, in a period of economic recession Hughes' annual sales had been flat, and profits had declined for three consecutive years, alarming GM executives. With respect to the company's shift in focus from defense to commercial markets, 65 percent of 1992 revenues came from defense, compared to the peak of 85 percent. In 1992 employees numbered 65,000, compared to the peak of 82,000 in 1985; the steady decline in the size of the workforce had a negative effect on staff morale.

Before accepting the Hughes post, Armstrong spent eight days reviewing the backgrounds of the Hughes executive team in order to determine whether changes should be made immediately. The Detroit native—and former IBM executive in charge of the GM account—met with top GM executives to confirm that he would have operating autonomy.

During his first days at Hughes, Armstrong met with Pentagon officials and ordered a minimum 30 percent reduction in costs across the entire organization. Later, with defense orders continuing to decline and in order to fund new projects such as DirecTV and OnStar, Armstrong closed several factories and ordered 16,000 layoffs. To prevent morale from diminishing further, those who were laid off received above-average severance packages.

Armstrong expected every Hughes employee to be accountable for satisfying customers, controlling costs, and increasing production efficiency; bonuses became tied to profits and performance. To ensure that employees understood the message being sent, he met with small groups of employees without their managers present. Research scientists were required to take finance classes and work closely with product groups.

Armstrong's performance in orchestrating Hughes's turnaround pleased GM executives, as sales and profits steadily increased. The tracking stock for GM Hughes Electronics had been mired in the $20 range when Armstrong arrived in 1992; it was valued at almost $70 by April 1996. During that period operating profits more than doubled. Within a year Armstrong was made chairman of both Hughes Electronics and its corporate sibling AC Delco Electronics, both GM units. In June 1995 Armstrong was elected to the seven-member GM Presidents' Council.

Armstrong's greatest accomplishment at Hughes was the launch of DirecTV, one of the first successful digital broadcast systems, which drew on Hughes's strengths in communications and satellite technology. A year before Armstrong's arrival Hughes had attempted to launch DirecTV in partnership with NBC and Rupert Murdoch's News Corporation, but talks broke down over marketing and other concerns. Armstrong was able to persuade the GM board to invest $750 million in the DirecTV project's technology and marketing despite the economic recession.

DirecTV signed up one million customers in its first 13 months of existence, with interest spurred by special sports lineups and 175 channels of programming. By 1996 Armstrong decided to use DirecTV's strong U.S. base to expand internationally, forming DirecTV Global to support management operations in Latin America and Japan. The growing success of DirecTV drew a $137 million investment from a communications company seeking to expand its line of products: AT&T Corporation.

FROM SATELLITE TELEVISION TO LONG DISTANCE

Following the successful launch of DirecTV and the market turnaround at Hughes Electronics, Armstrong was tapped in October 1997 to become chairman and CEO of the iconic yet uncertain U.S. business giant AT&T. He was selected after an unusual search during which three CEO-designees were selected over a two-year period.

Armstrong became the first outsider to hold the CEO spot at AT&T. His predecessor Robert G. Allen had lost the board's confidence after a series of public gaffes that negatively affected stock-market price performance, including several unprofitable acquisitions, an attempt to merge with SBC Communications that was foiled by the Federal Communications Commission, and his personal selection of one successor who left after only eight months. The day after Armstrong's appointment was announced, AT&T stock rose 5.1 percent in heavy trading to $47.50 a share.

At that time AT&T, as the leading U.S. long-distance carrier, was profitable with little debt but facing serious market challenges, such as changing regulations, rapid technological evolution, and the rise of the Internet as a communications medium. A few computer buffs were starting to use the Internet to make free long-distance calls, and the trend was expected to grow quickly.

First achieved on the foundation of Alexander Graham Bell's patent, AT&T's dominance of local and long-distance telephone service and telecom-equipment markets eventually resulted in a long series of antimonopoly rulings. In a 1984 court decision AT&T long distance and the local rate-regulated Bell System companies were separated, with AT&T and its long-distance competitors alike paying access charges to the Bell companies in order to complete calls. Notably, the "Baby Bells" were awarded the wireless cellular licenses, which AT&T executives then believed to be of little value.

When the breakup occurred, AT&T began losing direct contact with its customer base, and long-distance market shares were being sapped away by highly competitive rivals such as MCI (later a WorldCom unit) and Sprint. In 1996 the Telecom Reform Act authorized the Baby Bells as well to enter the long-distance market once there were credible amounts of competition in their respective local markets.

When Armstrong assumed the top spot at AT&T, he said that his goals were clear: to quickly bring head-count and operating costs in line with those of competitors such as MCI; to profitably mass market local phone and Internet services; to finish implementation of a national cellular network; and to increase global network capacity. In order to achieve those goals and compete in a changing environment, Armstrong had to alter the staid, risk-adverse, monopolistic mind-set within AT&T. Analysts would later assert that that monopolostic mind-set more than anything else prevented progress at the company.

Heartened by Armstrong's take-charge attitude and heated by the Internet's skyrocketing rise, investors quickly bid up AT&T's stock price, which doubled within six months of Armstrong's appointment. The addition of more than $50 billion in common-stock value, along with the high-yield bonds used to finance cable systems, helped fuel an 18-month acquisitions binge on Armstrong's behalf totaling more than $125 billion.

Within 10 days of his arrival at AT&T, Armstrong began addressing the issue of local access by reviewing past attempts at acquiring Teleport Communications Group (TCG). Started by Merrill Lynch in order to cut local businesses' telecom-access costs by bypassing New York Telephone and directly connecting to long-distance carriers, TCG had been acquired in part by three of the four then-dominant U.S. cable companies—TCI, Comcast, and Continental—for a nationwide launch.

Given the economic importance of telecommunications for commercial uses, the $20 billion business sector had always possessed more profit potential than the residential sector. In January 1998 Armstrong announced the acquisition of TCG for $11.3 billion, an eye-popping price for a young, still-unprofitable company with just $500 million in annual sales. Still, the next trading day after the announcement of the purchase AT&T stock rose 8 percent, effectively reducing the acquisition cost by approximately 40 percent. Around this time Armstrong took several other actions in order to improve AT&T's economic standing: he ordered an immediate hiring freeze; ended a $4 billion program wherein local Bell service was resold, which consistently lost money due to regulated costs; tied compensation to results; and cut myriad costs—disposing of the AT&T executive limo service, for example.

BECOMING A CABLE GIANT

In June 1998, with the dot-com boom continuing to drive up telecom stock prices—and, as a result, the supply of acquisition capital—Armstrong stunned the communications industry by announcing a $48 billion deal to buy Tele-Communications (TCI), the largest U.S. cable company. Armstrong explained to Wall Street and the public that TCI's coaxial links to homes would provide local cable-telephony links to the AT&T network, thus allowing AT&T to bypass local companies and avoid having to pay billions in local-network access fees to the Bells. In 1993 Bell Atlantic (later Verizon) had proposed buying TCI for $26 billion, but the deal collapsed when the FCC cut cable rates, lowering TCI's earnings expectations.

Several analysts immediately questioned the AT&T-TCI deal, noting that cable telephony was then a still-unproven technology that required high-quality networks. Further, they asserted that upgrading cable networks in order to handle voice traffic and persuading enough consumers to leave the Bell companies would be expensive and time-consuming. They also noted that the formerly monopolistic AT&T had no experience in operating entrepreneur-founded cable systems and navigating through their complex, tax-sheltered structures. Several AT&T insiders reportedly raised these same questions.

Armstrong countered by noting that the multiple opportunities in cable-driven video, voice, and high-speed Internet data—popularly referred to as "convergence"—would prove to be long-term profit generators and would help reestablish AT&T as a full-service communications provider. AT&T's stock price dipped 13 percent upon news of the TCI announcement, but along with the rest of the Internet-fueled stock market later recovered and continued upward.

Armstrong's local cable-telephony strategy relied on establishing network relationships with other cable companies. Staying true to his track record as a sales superstar, Armstrong immediately began talks with Time Warner Cable, Comcast, Cablevision, and other cable systems on forming local cable-telephony partnerships. Those talks on networking, marketing, and financing—which were long, difficult, and often acrimonious—would later take a toll on confidence in Armstrong.

At first investors had cheered Armstrong on as he ambitiously cut costs. A long-promised reduction in 18,000 positions was achieved through generous early retirement and severance packages. Much-needed additions were made to data and international networks. A new cellular-service plan providing free network-roaming and free long-distance boosted profits, attracted high-end users, and upset the Bell companies because some users were starting to eliminate home phone lines.

In March 1999, after learning of an unsolicited $49 billion bid by Comcast Corporation for the fellow cable giant Media-One Group, Armstrong put forth his own offer and set off a bidding contest. AT&T was ultimately victorious with a $54 billion offer, after negotiating with Comcast to sell it certain cable systems and to work with AT&T on cable telephony. After Wall Street analysts raised concerns about what the MediaOne acquisition's effect on AT&T earnings would be, Armstrong announced that more cost cuts would be made if necessary.

Having acquired so many cable assets so quickly—and having amassed an historic debt load of more than $55 billion—Armstrong experienced increasing pressure to deliver results, and fast. In the clubby, insular world of the cable industry, concerns were raised as to whether placing so much of AT&T's future in the hands of one person—Armstrong—without a succession plan was prudent. Complicating potential succession plans, large numbers of AT&T staff were leaving for dot-com start-ups or for the lucrative early-retirement packages.

As AT&T negotiations with other cable providers over cable-telephony deals became bogged down, Armstrong publicly suggested in late 1999 that non-AT&T-affiliated cable operators would find themselves competing with AT&T via other networks, such as the fixed wireless network. A dispute later arose as to whether AT&T had been privately negotiating with America Online about network access. To the tightly bound cable community Armstrong's words bordered on treason and displayed untrustworthiness. Investors raised concerns about the degree to which Armstrong was trusted by his fellow cable CEOs and whether that level of trust would affect his ability to acquire a sufficient number of cable-telephony customers.

By May 2000, with long-distance revenues continuing to drop due to price wars with MCI WorldCom, Armstrong announced that AT&T's profits that year were projected to be 5 percent less than originally expected. As the fact that the lost revenue would have provided capital for new services was common knowledge, the stock-market reaction was swift and terrible. Over the next two days AT&T's stock price dropped 19 percent to $39.75, shaving off $28 billion in shareholder value, never to recover. Shortly afterwards a leading AT&T board member and former Bell Labs staffer, the legendary cable executive John Malone, publicly suggested making the long-distance unit a stand-alone company.

On August 11, 2000, a front-page *Wall Street Journal* article reported that more than half of AT&T's top 550 business customers had reduced spending over concerns about service levels. Analysts criticized Armstrong and other AT&T executives for focusing too much on cable and not enough on the company's core customer base. Armstrong transferred support staff to the business long-distance unit to win back customers.

In October 2000, with AT&T stock at $24—20 percent less than when he had arrived—Armstrong announced that he would break AT&T up into four separate firms: cable/broadband, cellular/wireless, business, and consumer/residential. He said that the move would allow investors to more clearly see the financial and operating results of the individual units and would also provide incentive for the employees of each unit to perform better.

Armstrong stood by his assertions that AT&T needed to venture into new products and services, especially given the rapidly declining market for stand-alone long-distance service and the fact that the Bells were essentially blocking access to their local networks. Yet many analysts described Armstrong's breakup plan as a reversal of his original cable-centric strategy. Also, as some had predicted, cable telephony had proven more technically complicated than originally envisioned, such that initial marketing expenses were 50 percent higher than projected. To make their organizational clout visible during the breakup plan review, AT&T unions, along with their pension funds and political supporters, began publicly questioning Armstrong's strategy.

Many analysts agreed that Armstrong had put on a strong performance as AT&T's CEO during the turbulent dot-com era—calling on major customers, keeping employees focused on customer needs, meeting with bankers, and working with regulators. Nevertheless, the huge debt load that resulted from his cable acquisitions overshadowed noticeable improvements in the finances of cellular, data, and international services.

In July 2001 Comcast announced an unsolicited bid of $41 billion for AT&T's broadband unit. Armstrong averred that the offer was too low and began soliciting offers from Disney, Microsoft, and others. In December 2001, following the September 11 attacks and with recession looming, Comcast announced its acquisition of AT&T Broadband for $50.5 billion. As part of the deal Armstrong was given the mostly honorific title of chairman of the board; actual control lay in the hands of the founding Roberts family, who were well known for their thrifty, hands-on management. One year later Armstrong was named nonexecutive chairman; he then retired in May 2004.

RETIRED—BUT STILL COMPETING

On the eve of his retirement, having spent 40 years in corporate life, Armstrong made several public comments that were reported on in the *Wall Street Journal*. He challenged assertions that his AT&T strategy had failed due to defective assumptions and poor personnel selection. Also, he charged that due to the record-setting accounting fraud perpetrated by WorldCom and its MCI Corporation long-distance unit, U.S. long-distance prices were driven to unsustainable levels, sending the telecom industry into a downward spiral. Still, analysts maintained that Armstrong had overreached in buying too many cable systems and assuming that cable telephony would work as planned.

In 2004 Armstrong watchers noted with irony the two-to-one market advantage that cable modems had over the Bells' digital subscriber lines (DSL) and the fact that cable operators were beginning to embrace cable telephony. Detailed, conclusive analyses of Armstrong's moves would be years away; regardless of the answers reached, given all of the issues faced by AT&T in the late 1990s and early 2000s, the lasting question might be whether any corporate leader would have been capable of returning AT&T to its formerly dominant market position.

See also entries on AT&T Corp. and Comcast Corporation in *International Directory of Company Histories.*

SOURCES FOR FURTHER INFORMATION

ABCNews.com, "Reference/Bios," http://abcnews.go.com/references/bios/armstrong.html.

Blumenstein, Rebecca, "Hanging Up: AT&T Now Is Facing Erosion in Key Sector," *Wall Street Journal*, August 11, 2000.

———, "On the Hook: Former Chief Tries to Redeem the Calls He Made at AT&T," *Wall Street Journal*, May 26, 2004.

Lynch, David J., "The Armstrong Approach," *Orange County Register*, October 3, 1993.

Peterson, Thane, "Mike Armstrong Is Improving IBM's Game in Europe," *BusinessWeek*, June 20, 1988, pp. 96–99.

Schine, Eric, "A Guy Who Focuses on the Doable," *BusinessWeek*, April 22, 1996, pp. 147–152.

———, "Liftoff," *BusinessWeek*, April 22, 1996, pp. 136–141.

—C. A. Chien

■■■

Bernard Arnault

1949–

Chairman, chief executive officer, Moét Hennessy Louis Vuitton

Nationality: French.

Born: March 5, 1949, in France.

Education: École Polytechnique, BA, 1971.

Family: Married Helene Mercier (concert pianist), 1991; children: five.

Career: Ferret-Savinel, 1971–1983, engineer; Dior and Boussac Saint-Frères, 1984–1989, owner; Moét Hennessy Louis Vuitton, 1989–, chairman, chief executive officer.

Address: Moét Hennessy Louis Vuitton, 22 avenue Montaigne, 75008 Paris, France; http://www.lvmh.com.

■ Bernard Arnault made it his business to own the most attractive names across the spectrum of luxury goods, cosmetics, and beverages. As chairman and CEO of Moét Hennessy Louis Vuitton (LVMH), he had an intense drive and seemingly insatiable corporate appetite that earned him a reputation as a financier interested only in profits. Yet those who dismissed him as an angry caricature missed the point; his shrewd moves proved that his expertise in brand management was unmatched by the competition. In 2002 LVMH had $13 billion in sales, distributing luxury products that included Dom Perignon and Moét & Chandon champagnes; Hennessy and Hines cognacs; Louis Vuitton and Loewe luggage, leather goods and accessories; Christian Dior and Givenchy perfumes and cosmetics. LVMH also had interests in the DFS and Sephora retail groups.

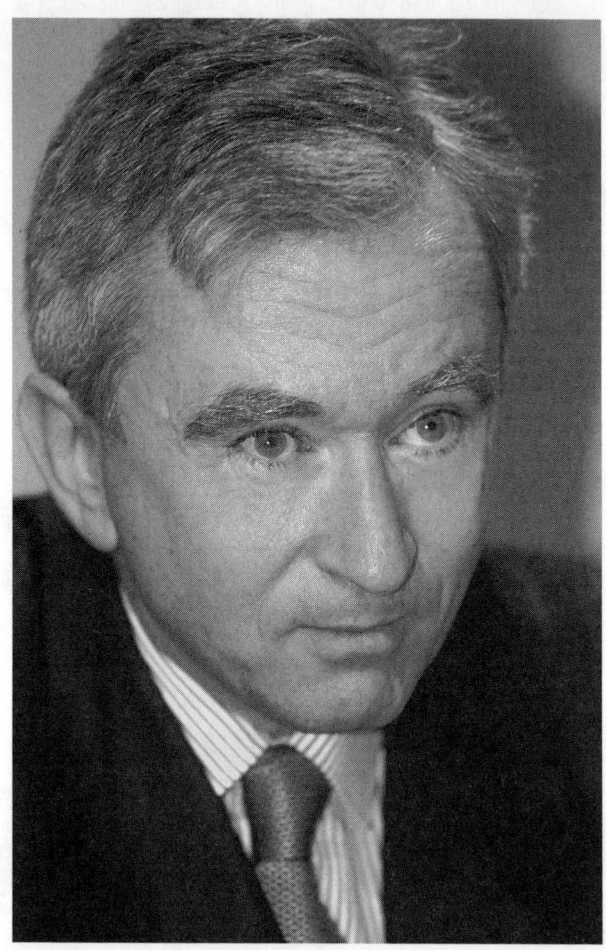

Bernard Arnault. *AP/Wide World Photos.*

LEARNING THE FAMILY BUSINESS

Arnault grew up in Roubaix, northern France. After graduating from the École Polytechnique, France's esteemed engineering school, Arnault worked as an engineer and ran his family's construction and property business firm, Ferret-Savinel. Years ahead of the competition, he spearheaded the company's move into the lucrative new niche of building timeshares on the Riviera. However, when the French Socialists rose to power in 1981, Arnault immigrated to the United States with his wife and two young children. He prospered, developing condominiums in Palm Beach, Florida, but after three years turned to developing a U.S. branch of his family's property business. His time in America left an indelible impression. Before leaving, he sold his Mediterranean-style home in suburban New York to a neighbor, the mogul John Kluge, who promptly had it removed to improve his view. The unfortunate fate of his beautiful home taught Arnault a useful lesson: "When something has to be done, do it! In France we are full of good ideas, but we rarely put them into practice" (*Forbes*, June 2, 1997).

ENTRÉE INTO THE LUXURY MARKET REQUIRES POWERFUL BACKING

The French Socialists switched to a more conservative economic course in 1983, prompting Arnault to return to his native France. His rise to control of the world's largest luxury group began with an opportunity created when a textile firm, Boussac, went bankrupt. The French government was looking for someone to take over the textile empire, which comprised several foundering businesses, including a disposable diaper company and the once-prized couture house of Christian Dior.

Arnault soon gained a powerful friend in Antoine Bernheim, managing partner of the investment firm of Lazard Fréres. Bernheim arranged the financing for Arnault's acquisition of Boussac. The Arnault family put up just $15 million of their own money, with Lazard supplying the rest of the reported $80 million purchase price. The main reason Arnault bought Boussac was to get Dior, which he viewed as the potential cornerstone of a "luxury-goods supermarket," where a rising global bourgeoisie would shop. Arnault quickly expanded Dior to include new brands: the fashion house of Christian Lacroix and Celine, a leather-goods house known for its loafers.

A BRUTAL RISE TO POWER

Next Arnault unloaded Boussac's disposable-diaper business and much of its textiles operations, gaining a $400 million windfall in the process. This sale enabled him to buy his way into LVMH in 1989, purchasing $1.8 billion in LVMH shares and forging a deal that gave him control of 24 percent of the group. A bitter power struggle ensued between Arnault and Henry Racamier, the former chairman of LVMH's Louis Vuitton subsidiary and a member by marriage of one of the firm's founding families. After more than a year, Arnault won a series of court battles, Racamier was ousted, and Arnault purged LVMH's top Vuitton executives. His takeover of LVMH was one of the roughest in France's business history and earned Arnault a reputation for viciousness that was solidified by the numerous layoffs that followed his rise to power. According to a former officer of Louis Vuitton who was fired in the purge, "He's an asset shuffler, a raider, a French Donald Trump" (*BusinessWeek*, July 30, 1990). But many people respected Arnault's business strategy and penchant for risk taking. Among his admirers was Gilles Cahen-Salvador, who at the time ran the financial firm LBO France. "People like him are setting good examples for the French economy," said Cahen-Salvador (*BusinessWeek*, July 30, 1990).

BALANCING COMMERCE AND ARTISTRY

With the LVMH victory Arnault began assembling the pieces of his "luxury-goods supermarket," following a business model that balanced sound practices and creativity. He believed that to raise creative energy, a company must have managers with a certain love for and understanding of artists. In an interview with Suzy Wetlaufer for *Harvard Business Review* (October 2001), Arnault said, "If you deeply appreciate and love what creative people do and how they think, which is usually in unpredictable and irrational ways, then you can start to understand them. And finally, you can see inside their minds and DNA." Putting his model into action, at Dior, Arnault hired John Galliano, an up-and-coming designer with a flair for melodrama and unusual creations, including dresses fashioned out of newspapers. The move represented a new direction for the haute couture company. Said *Vogue*'s editor-in-chief, Anna Wintour, "What I think is so brilliant about Bernard is that he realized that to revitalize this boring, dusty, fuddy-duddy old house, he had to go with the shock of the new. Most businessmen wouldn't understand. They wouldn't have that sensibility and that flair" (*Washington Post*, April 28, 2002). This aspect of Arnault's competitive edge came partly from his background as an amateur artist. Although he concluded early in life that he did not have the mettle for a career as a concert pianist, Arnault was classically trained and made time to practice Chopin, Liszt, and Schumann. Both his wife and mother were pianists as well.

Unique among the world's leading CEOs, Arnault had the ability to relate to both the creative and financial aspects of running a business. Although he did not believe in limiting his artists' innovation, he insisted on financial discipline when producing, marketing, and selling his company's products. He understood that, in a successful corporate culture, the counterbalance to creativity must be commerce. He never hesitated to reign in, or outright terminate, creative executives who did not produce. In 1995 Arnault fired the heads of Dior perfumes and a top manager at Givenchy, replacing them with executives from U.S. consumer brands from outside the fashion industry. The new executives, with Arnault's blessings, made unpopular but profitable changes, including eliminating the cellophane inside the Givenchy perfume box, arguing that the cost outweighed any added cachet. The results were some "star brands" that were both modern and timeless. "Our strategy is to have some stars—and there are not many stars in the luxury business. What is a star? It's a name that is the very best. It's a name that is very profitable. But the number of true stars is less than I can count on both of my hands" (*New York Times*, March 25, 2001).

A BOURGEOISIE SHOPPING SPREE

Throughout the 1990s Arnault amassed an empire of indulgence, purchasing dozens of luxury-goods makers;

strengthening his presence in Europe, North America, and Asia; and expanding into South America and Australia. To his company's roster he added wine and spirits as well as Louis Vuitton luggage and Givenchy clothes and perfume. He bought up watches (TAG Heuer), a cosmetics line (Sephora), and even a magazine (*Art and Auction*). Initially, many of his competitors told him his company was getting too big, that he should focus on one brand. Soon, however, LVMH had its imitators. In Italy, Gucci expressed a similar appetite for the luxury-goods market, as did the owner of Cartier in Switzerland. Of his competition, Arnault said in the *Washington Post* (April 28, 2002), "They saw it was working. And then they said, 'Okay, now we are going to do the same thing.' I think, really, they underestimate the difficulty. They underestimate the time required to make it successful. And my guess is that they will have a very tough time."

A COMPANY IN NEED OF CASH

In the short term, however, many of Arnault's acquisitions failed to generate the kind of cash that would justify the amount of money spent on them. In 1999 LVMH and Prada together purchased a 51 percent stake in Fendi, only to see the brand's sales flatten. LVMH ultimately acquired Prada's share of the business. In 2001 operating margins for the LVMH watch and jewelry brands were about 7 percent, less than the 10 percent of competitors. In addition, the companies under its selective retailing division, including an auction house and the duty-free shops ubiquitous in airports, were barely profitable.

Although LVMH's operating profit rose 26.6 percent to a record $1.74 billion in 2000, the results failed to match expectations. Arnault's shopping sprees appeared to have decreased operating margins to about 17 percent in 2000, down from 25 percent in 1995. In January 2001 several analysts cut their recommendation for LVMH from "buy" to "neutral." Andrew Gowen, a securities analyst who followed LVMH at Lehman Brothers in London, said in the *New York Times* (March 25, 2001), "What started to bug me was a misallocation of capital. A lot of acquisitions pushed them into several low-margin, low-return businesses." Arnault ultimately put the brakes on his acquisition strategy in favor of generating some much-needed cash. LVMH sold its interest in the Phillips auction house, and stockholders urged that similar decisions be made about other struggling divisions.

THE FUTURE OF FASHION AND LUXURY

Arnault faced a host of challenges in early 2004. The luxury market struggled from declines in tourist travel, crucial to the sale of designer goods, and several LVMH brands suffered from their own financial troubles. Japan's economy was another factor; in 2001 the country accounted for 40 percent of sales at LVMH, but Japan's economy had been in a recession since 2003. It even seemed questionable that mass-market brands could continue to command top dollar. Nonetheless, Arnault was optimistic that he could continue to generate a steady flow of profit from his brands while ensuring the highest level of quality and creativity. As he told the *Washington Post* (April 28, 2002), "The possibility of creating very appealing products with architects, with designers and making it commercially very successful is what I am good at, I think, and what I like to do."

See also entry on LVMH Moët Hennessy Louis Vuitton SA in *International Directory of Company Histories.*

SOURCES FOR FURTHER INFORMATION

Givhan, Robin, "The French Connection: Bernard Arnault Built a Fashion Empire, but Don't Expect Any Air Kisses," *Washington Post*, April 28, 2002.

Levine, Joshua, "Liberté, Fraternité—but to Hell with Egalité!" *Forbes*, June 2, 1997, p. 80.

Tagliabue, John, and Cathy Horyn, "Suddenly, at LVMH, Money Is an Object," *New York Times*, March 25, 2001.

Toy, Stewart, and Andrea Rothman, "Meet Monsier Luxury," *BusinessWeek*, July 30, 1990, p. 48.

Tully, Shawn, "King of Chic—and Artful Deals," *Fortune*, January 2, 1989, p. 40.

Wetlaufer, Suzy, "The Perfect Paradox of Star Brands: An Interview with Bernard Arnault of LVMH," *Harvard Business Review*, October 2001, p. 116.

—Tim Halpern

Gerard J. Arpey

1958–

President and chief executive officer, AMR Corporation and American Airlines

Nationality: American.

Born: July 26, 1958, in New York City, New York.

Education: University of Texas, BBA, 1980; MBA, 1982.

Family: Married Lisa (maiden name unknown); children: three.

Career: AMR Corporation and American Airlines, 1982–1983, financial analyst; 1983–1985, senior financial analyst; 1985–1987, manager of financial analysis department; 1987–1988, director of airline profitability analysis; 1988–1989, managing director of financial analysis and planning; 1989–1992, vice president of financial planning and analysis; 1992–1995, senior vice president of financial planning; 1995–1999, senior vice president of finance and planning and chief financial officer; 2000–2002, executive vice president of operations; 2002–2003, president and chief operating officer; 2003–, president and chief executive officer.

Address: P.O. Box 619616, Dallas–Fort Worth International Airport, Dallas, Texas 75161-9616; http://www.amrcorp.com.

Gerard J. Arpey. *AP/Wide World Photos.*

Gerard Arpey was president and chief operating officer of American Airlines and its parent company AMR in the early 2000s when the U.S. economy suffered a major downturn, partly as a result of the 9/11 hijackings of four passenger jets, two of which belonged to American Airlines. The entire airline industry fell into financial disarray, and American was facing Chapter 11 bankruptcy. Arpey took over as chief executive officer early in 2003, when the presiding chief executive was fired following a scandal involving huge executive bonuses and pension-plan benefits at a time when lesser employees were taking enormous cuts in salaries. Functioning in an internally hostile environment and an externally ailing economy, within nine months Arpey pulled American away from the brink of bankruptcy and developed considerable employee and shareholder confidence in his leadership abilities and in the corporation as a whole.

A ONE-COMPANY AVIATOR

Arpey was a one-company employee, and his relationship with aviation was both personal and professional. He hailed from an airline-industry family—his father was a career airline employee and an executive with Texas Air (now part of Continental Airlines)—and started with American loading luggage into airplanes. After college he became an analyst in the finance department, which, according to Micheline Maynard of the *New York Times,* was a "stellar training ground for airline executives" (April 25, 2003). Under the tough leadership style of the then CEO Robert Crandall, who gained a reputation as American's "iron hammer," Arpey developed an ethic for hard work. Aviation even became his hobby; an avid pilot, he earned his Federal Aviation Administration multiengine instrument pilot rating and flew private multiengine planes. In the *Washington Post,* Sara Kehaulani Goo quoted George

Hamlin, the aviation analyst with Global Aviation, as saying, "He's got some kind of kerosene in his blood" (April 25, 2003).

American Airlines, the largest airline in the world, serviced more than 250 cities in 41 countries and territories in 2003 and owned 1,100 aircraft that made a combined total of 4,400 flights a day. While working his way up the corporate ladder, Arpey was responsible for profitability analyses, fleet planning and scheduling, financial planning, strategic planning, and partnership activities. As chief financial officer, he oversaw the company's entire financial operations. As executive vice president of operations, he managed flight operations worldwide, which included engineering and maintenance, purchasing, corporate real estate, operations planning, the flight department, and AA Cargo and American Eagle.

BECOMES CEO AMID HOSTILITY AND SKEPTICISM

Following 9/11 and the major economic downturn of the early 2000s, American, along with other major carriers, suffered a financial freefall. Donald J. Carty, the chief executive officer at the time, appealed to American's employees and negotiated with union leaders for huge employee concessions and cutbacks. Indeed, employees voted in favor of slashing their own salaries to help the company survive. Meanwhile, Carty hid the fact that he and top executives, including Arpey, had agreed to accept huge retention bonuses and lucrative pension deals. When the cover-up was revealed to the public, enraged employees and union officials stirred up a furor; Carty was fired. Arpey was thrust into the position of CEO, albeit amid serious concerns from union leaders, financial analysts, and employees about his involvement in the executive compensation debacle. Maynard quoted Kevin Mitchell, president of the Business Travel Coalition, who expressed the reservations of many when he said, "My concern with him is that he was right there. What was his advice and counsel on what should have been done?" (April 25, 2003).

Regardless of the overarching skepticism, American's shares jumped 96 percent following the announcement that Arpey would replace Carty. Highly regarded for his analytical skills, determination, company loyalty, and strong belief in its employees, Arpey took over the helm of American when the company was carrying $11 billion in long-term debt and employee morale was at its lowest—and he was obligated to ask employees to sacrifice even more. In *Business Week*, Wendy Zellner quoted Arpey as saying, "People are being asked to work harder for less pay. That obviously does not create an environment for happiness" (March 22, 2003).

Arpey set about the Herculean task of keeping the company airborne, realizing that little could be done successfully until teamwork and trust were reestablished. Pilot Thomas W. Hoban, whose $157,000 annual salary became $95,000 while his hours on the job increased, had high regard for Arpey's ability. "I think he understands the employee relationship problem we have here and the impact it has on the bottom line," he told Zellner (March 22, 2003). A spokesman for the Allied Pilots Association commented that the union had "quite favorable dealings" with Arpey over the years, and, according to Goo, association president John Darrah expressed confidence in Arpey. "I can honestly tell you there's not a person I have more respect for or trust in, not only at this company, but on the planet," he said (April 25, 2003).

BUILDS EMPLOYEE CONFIDENCE

While some industry analysts, union executives, and employees still held reservations about Arpey's credibility, there was a consensus that he was making a concerted effort to communicate with employees in rehabilitating the company with his "pull together and win" attitude. John Ward, president of the flight attendants union, was instrumental in negotiating a new cost-cutting program with Arpey. Ward said that although his union would not fly by faith alone, he was encouraged by Arpey's willingness to negotiate openly, a phenomenon that was virtually nonexistent during Carty's tenure. Arpey firmly believed in open communication and even more firmly in cooperative involvement. He maintained that inviting employees to participate in the decision-making process was essential to their understanding of the conclusions eventually reached at the top.

Operating under his belief that actions speak louder than words, Arpey selected high-level managers who not only had the necessary technical skills to help turn the corporation around but also were people oriented. Furthermore, he agreed to have senior executives meet on a regular basis with union leaders. Goo quoted him as saying, "There is definite need to rebuild trust within our company, and that starts at the top" (April 25, 2003). In an action that spoke volumes to employees, Arpey did more than reject a pay increase when he was promoted: he took a 14 percent pay cut and refused stock awards for the upcoming year. In a novel approach that allowed managers and board members to engage in dialogue openly, he invited senior executives to make slide presentations at a board meeting to explain their new business strategies and present their own thoughts and ideas. Board member David L. Boren was quoted by Edward Wong of the *New York Times* as calling the approach "refreshing—what I see as a board member is more strategic thinking about the future going on from the leadership than we've seen in recent years" (October 10, 2003).

One industry analyst felt that while Arpey had a decent rapport with employees, who saw him as being gentle yet firm, he was still part of the leadership team that had created the aura of mistrust and disillusion in the first place. On the other hand, another analyst thought that Arpey was highly appropriate for the position because of his extensive experience with the corporation. The latter analyst expressed hope that Arpey would learn from the mistakes of his predecessors.

BANKRUPTCY AVOIDED, BUT A LONG ROAD AHEAD

By the end of 2003 Arpey—one of the youngest CEOs in the corporation's history—had adopted several major plans that proved to be milestones in the company's recuperation. He implemented his Turnaround Plan, which aimed at making American more competitive, and created employee stock-option and profit-sharing plans that would kick in when pretax profits exceeded $500 million. He sold the company's 26 percent interest in a computer-reservation company for $180 million in cash and negotiated a savings of $175 million with suppliers, all in all more than doubling American's unrestricted cash balance. Less tangibly, he changed the stuffy and arrogant image American had earned over the years to a more open and relaxed one. As evidence of this, corporate executives became exempt from having to wear neckties.

Veteran captain Tim Whitby expressed his elation at Arpey's election as CEO in an interview with Lisa DiCarlo of *Forbes* (April 30, 2003). Whitby recalled how he had sent a scathing letter to corporate management while Carty was still CEO, documenting how "screwed up and shabby the company was in terms of service and attitude." When Arpey took over, he called Whitby to his office. Whitby had felt he was going to be fired but was instead invited to lunch at a restaurant in a strip mall that was, according to Whitby, "a complete dump." "The funny part is," he said of Arpey, "the staff all knew his name." Over tacos and enchiladas, Arpey listened attentively to Whitby's opinions and agreed that changes needed to be made. Whitby said it was amazing to him that Arpey wanted to hear employees' "gripes" and was willing to take them into account in order to help turn the company's image around.

In December 2003 Captain Sam Mayer, chairman of American's crew base at La Guardia, New York, expressed confidence in Arpey's skills but skepticism about his ability to overcome twenty years of company inertia. According to Margaret Allen of the *Dallas Business Journal*, Mayer said, "It's like trying to turn a battleship, which takes miles and miles. I just don't know if he's going to have the horsepower to do it" (December 26, 2003). In point of fact, as employee confidence in Arpey gradually increased, financial losses steadily decreased. His financial strategy raised revenues by 4 percent over the eight-month period following his appointment as CEO and cut costs by almost 12 percent. Although the corporation still lost money, net losses were reduced from $3.51 billion in 2002 to $1.23 billion in 2003. The amount lost per share dropped from $22.57 in 2002 to $7.76 in 2003. Fourth-quarter losses per share equaled $0.70 in 2003 compared with $3.39 in 2002, which defied industry analysts' predictions of losses of at least $1 per share.

Arpey refused to take credit for the turnaround, instead deferring to the company's employees. And while encouraging employees and management to pull together to ensure that the worst was behind them and the best yet to come, Arpey acknowledged that the company was far from being out of the woods. Allen quoted him as saying: "The first six months in this job was absolutely a sprint. Now we're not talking or worrying about bankruptcy. We're back to running the company again. We're still sprinting—but we recognize it's a marathon" (December 26, 2003).

See also entries on AMR Corporation and American Airlines in *International Directory of Company Histories.*

SOURCES FOR FURTHER INFORMATION

Allen, Margaret, "AMR Corp.'s CEO Off to a Flying Start," *Dallas Business Journal*, December 26, 2003.

DiCarlo, Lisa, "Arpey Could Give American a Fresh Start," *Forbes.com*, April 30, 2003. http://www.forbes.com/2003/04/30/cx_ld_0429arpey.html.

Goo, Sara Kehaulani, "Key Union Accepts Cuts at American," *Washington Post*, April 26, 2003.

Maynard, Micheline, "History of Loyalty Helps Successor Reach Top, but May Not Calm Unions," *New York Times*, April 25, 2003, http://www.mccombs.utexas.edu/news/mentions/arts/2003/04.25.nyt_arpey.asp.

Wong, Edward, "A Market Revival, and Less Turmoil, at American Air," *New York Times*, October 10, 2003.

Zellner, Wendy, "A First Officer: 'For Many Years to Come,'" *BusinessWeek Online*, March 22, 2003.

—Marie L. Thompson

■■■

Ramani Ayer

1947–

Chairman, president, and chief executive officer, Hartford Financial Services Group

Nationality: American.

Born: May 27, 1947, in Kerala, India.

Education: India Institute of Technology, BS, 1969; Drexel University, MS, 1971; PhD, 1973.

Family: Immigrated to the United States, 1969; naturalized American citizen; married Louise (maiden name unknown); children: two.

Career: Hartford Financial Services Group (The Hartford), 1973–1978, operations researcher; 1978–1979, property casualty actuarial researcher; 1979–1981, assistant secretary and staff assistant to chairman; 1981–1983, secretary and director, corporate reinsurance (HartRe); 1983–1984, vice president, HartRe; Hartford Specialty Company, 1984–1986, executive vice president; 1986–1989, president; The Hartford, 1987, vice president; 1989–1990, senior vice president; 1990–1991, executive vice president; 1991–1997, president and chief operating officer, property-casualty operations; The Hartford Financial Services Group, 1997–, chairman, president, and chief executive officer.

Awards: Polaris Award, Leadership Greater Hartford, 1993; Distinguished Alumnus Award, India Institute of Technology, 1998; *Forbes*, one of the Most Powerful People of 2002; honorary doctor of laws, University of Hartford, 2003.

Address: Hartford Financial Services Group, Hartford Plaza, 690 Asylum Avenue, Hartford, Connecticut 06105; http://www.thehartford.com.

■ Ramani Ayer served as president, chairman, and chief executive officer of the Hartford Financial Services Group (The Hartford), one of the largest investment and insurance companies in the United States. Ayer joined The Hartford in 1973 and worked his way up from a position in the operations research department to becoming chairman, president, and chief executive officer in 1997. During Ayer's tenure at The Hartford, his hard work, intelligence, and problem-solving skills kept The Hartford technologically current and competitive as the technology and business of the insurance and financial industry changed. Employees and colleagues described Ayer as a modest yet articulate and innovative leader who challenged his employees constantly to explore new opportunities and ideas.

DEVELOPING PROBLEM-SOLVING SKILLS

In India, Ayer began honing his innovative problem-solving abilities out of necessity. His father was a low-paid government servant in the accountant general's office in Bombay. In college Ayer could barely afford the materials needed for his classes. To decrease expenses Ayer developed a plan with his friend Parag Rele to share Rele's books. For five years Ayer arranged his schedule so that he could study late at night. After a night of studying Ayer would slip the books under Rele's door so that they would be ready for Rele. The book time-share plan enabled Ayer's graduation in 1969 from the India Institute of Technology with a bachelor of science degree in mathematics and his acceptance as an engineering student at Drexel University, in Philadelphia, Pennsylvania.

After obtaining his master's degree and doctorate in chemical engineering from Drexel in 1971 and 1973, Ayer made the unusual decision to join the strategic planning team at The Hartford instead of accepting the more traditional engineering research job he was offered at Air Products and Chemicals. In 1978, after five years of hard work, Ayer did not believe he was being used to his full potential at The Hartford and brought his concerns to executives. Recognizing Ayer's potential, the executives persuaded him to stay, and DeRoy "Pete" Thomas, the chairman, offered him a staff assistant position. Ayer accepted the position and turned the role into the career boost he needed to meet his potential. Over the next 20 years Ayer honed his leadership skills and set his analytic mind to broadening his knowledge about the insurance and financial industry. Over this time Ayer became an invaluable member of the management team at The Hartford.

INDUSTRY INNOVATIONS

In Ayer's various executive roles, his scientific approach to exploration and implementation of new ideas brought a fresh and innovative perspective to The Hartford. While in the positions of senior vice president of The Hartford and president of Hartford Specialty Company, Ayer found that corporations had begun shifting the primary responsibility of buying insurance to their financial officers. Ayer noted that treasurers and chief financial officers would review the insurance policies and shop around for better prices with more frequency than they had in the past. Instead of trying to persuade companies to return to the old way of buying insurance or lowering insurance prices, Ayer recognized that corporate insurance marketing strategies and education should change with the customer's change in policy. Ayer developed targeted information projects to educate the newly responsible individuals on corporate insurance and policies. In this way he increased revenues and developed a loyal base of educated customers.

As an executive at The Hartford, Ayer developed a set of goals for keeping The Hartford ahead of its competitors. He focused on improving the ease with which The Hartford's clients could contact and work with the company, increased the efficiency of internal procedures at the company, and used technology to improve The Hartford's business decisions and practices. By concentrating on these priorities, Ayer kept ahead of The Hartford's rivals in the investment and insurance sectors. For example, in 2003 and 2004 Ayer implemented innovations that included an electronic claim submission method for agents and cooperative development of a buyer protection plan service on eBay. On the basis of Ayer's changes, The Hartford created a strong record of deploying advanced technology for improved agency interaction.

A crucial component of Ayer's success at The Hartford was his ability to complement his problem-solving with an atmosphere of interactive discussion and free exchange of ideas. In an article by Julie Gallagher in *Insurance and Technology*, the chief information officer of The Hartford characterized Ayer as "a real thinker . . . [who] loves to question, probe, and drill down, exploring options and possibilities" (June 1, 2002). By surrounding himself with other individuals focused on the development of new and innovative ideas, Ayer created a forward-looking team with the ability to adapt to the needs of the changing insurance and financial services marketplace. For example, the increasing volatility in the 2003 equity markets could have reduced the number of individuals investing in retirement funds. To encourage investors to remain in the market, Ayer and his team created a fund to help investors concerned about market volatility. The fund allowed investors to withdraw over a period of years the money they originally invested, even if the original investment funds had been lost owing to downward financial trends.

EXPANDED LEADERSHIP ROLE

After the terrorist's attacks on September 11, 2001, Ayer expanded his leadership role beyond his responsibilities at The Hartford by joining a team of insurance chief executives invited by President George W. Bush to discuss the insurance industry and its stability after the terrorism and associated insurance claims. Although they reported to Bush that the industry could bear the financial burden of the terrorist attacks, the executives determined that legislation should be developed to protect the insurance industry if another attack were to occur. Ayer served as a strong advocate for the development of new national insurance legislation and policy development. In part as the result of Ayer's work, the Terrorism Risk Insurance Act of 2002, which provided a federal backstop for terrorism insurance, was signed into legislation on November 26, 2002. Ayer continued his larger leadership role in the business community as a director of the American Insurance Alliance, the chairman of the Insurance Information Institute, a director of the Metro Hartford Regional Economic Alliance, a chairman of the American Institute of Property and Liability Underwriters, and a trustee of the Business Roundtable.

CORPORATE COMMUNITY

Perhaps remembering the challenges he faced obtaining an education, Ayer took his innovative problem-solving skills to a leadership role in public education. After becoming chairman, president, and chief executive officer of The Hartford in 1997, Ayer focused the company's philanthropic activities on improving educational opportunities for students in the Hartford area and helping them further their academic careers. The goal Ayer developed for The Hartford was to help ensure that by 2010 every student being graduated from Hartford high schools was academically prepared for college. To meet that goal Ayer focused The Hartford's attention on developing, staffing, and funding several new public education initiatives. In 2003 The Hartford donated nearly $3 million, and its employees volunteered 20,000 hours to Hartford city schools. The Hartford also supported two programs, the STAG and the Alliance, which provided college scholarships, employment at The Hartford, and mentoring for city high-school graduates attending specific colleges. In a speech on November 12, 2003, Ayer conveyed his commitment to education by saying, "Nothing is more important to the future of American enterprise, or indeed to the strength of our country, than providing the best possible education for all our nation's youth" (November 12, 2003). Following Ayer's lead, several other Hartford corporations began funding local education initiatives and developing partnerships with area schools. In November 2002 the Urban League of Greater Hartford presented its highest honor, The Founder's Award, to Ayer and The Hartford for philanthropic efforts to improve educational opportunities for the city's young people and for the company's commitment to making the city of Hartford a better place in which to live and work.

SOURCES FOR FURTHER INFORMATION

Gallagher, Julie, "Tech-Focused Way of Life: At The Hartford, CEO Ramani Ayer's Scrutiny of Ideas Leads to Enterprise-Wide Innovation," *Insurance and Technology*, June 1, 2002, p. 34.

"The Hartford's CEO Ramani Ayer to Be Honored for Support of Public Education," November 12, 2003, http://www.thehartford.com/press/corpnews/2003/1068641422890.html.

Reich-Hale, David, "'Good Cop' Ayer Still Waits for Terror Insurance Fix," *American Banker*, June 27, 2002, pp. 1–4.

—Dawn Jacob Laney

■■■

Michael J. Bailey

1948–

Chief executive officer, Compass Group

Nationality: British.

Born: October 14, 1948, in United Kingdom.

Education: Westminster College.

Family: Son of Sidney William Bailey and Joyce Mary (maiden name unknown); married (wife's name unknown; separated); children: two.

Career: Gardner Merchant, 1964–1985, food service manager, then later executive director; 1985–1991, president of U.S. subsidiary; 1991–1992, managing director of contract feeding business; Nutrition Management Food Services Company, 1992, executive vice president; Compass Group, 1993–1994, group development director; 1994–1999, CEO of North America Division; 1999–, CEO.

Address: Compass Group, Compass House, Guildford Street, Chertsey, Surrey KT16 9BQ, United Kingdom; http://www.compass-group.com.

Michael J. Bailey. © *Bryn Colton/Assignments Photographers/Corbis.*

■ Michael J. Bailey had a long career in the food service industry: from his first job as a canteen chef he rose through the ranks to become the group chief executive of Compass Group, one of the world's largest catering and franchise food-brand companies. Bailey helped turn the small UK-based catering company into an international market leader; Compass Group became an FTSE 100 company with over 375,000 employees in 90 countries and annual revenues of more than £10 billion.

EARLY CAREER

Bailey originally left school at the age of 15 because he was fed up with classes; he quickly found a job as a canteen chef at a Ford Motor Company facility in the United Kingdom. He also served as a chef for British troops stationed in Afghanistan. Bailey eventually returned to school, graduating from Westminster College in London and attending a number of additional classes and lectures on business topics.

In 1964 Bailey moved to the large catering company Gardner Merchant and slowly worked his way up the corporate ladder. He started out as a food service manager; in 1985 he became the president of the company's U.S. subsidiary, helping it increase in value from $40 million to $225 million. In 1991 Bailey became the managing director of Gardner Merchant's contract feeding business. In 1992 he left to become an executive vice president of Nutrition Management Food Services Company in the United States.

COMPASS GROUP

Bailey then joined Compass Group in 1993 as group development director. Compass Group evolved out of the company Factory Canteens, which was established in 1941 in the United Kingdom to provide the compulsory hot meal that was guaranteed to wartime munitions workers. Acquired by Grand

Metropolitan (later Diageo) in 1960, the firm became Grand-Met Catering before being relaunched in 1984 as Compass Services. Compass Group was then formed from Grand Metropolitan in 1987 as a management buyout, listing on the London Stock Exchange in 1988.

In the early 1990s Compass Group was almost wholly a UK-based concern, with 99 percent of its business being done in the United Kingdom; the remaining 1 percent consisted of catering for a remote Alaskan site. The UK market was entering a period of recession so the company decided on a program of overseas expansion. Compass Group acquired both Scandinavian Service Partner and Letheby & Christopher, the UK-based sports and events food-service provider, in 1993.

Bailey was a key player in Compass Group's new strategy. As group development director he brought into existence the branded food-service subsidiary New Famous Foods, which sold both the company's own brands—such as Ritazza, Upper Crust, and StopGap—and franchised brands such as Burger King. The use of branded products proved to be a great success for Compass: familiar brands offered the consumer security and a set of expectations that would be consistently fulfilled; if quality was maintained, satisfaction with the brand would grow.

Compass developed Ritazza, its international café brand, to branch out into the growing market for espresso and gourmet coffee. In 1998 only a single outlet sold Ritazza coffee; by 2004 the brand was being sold in 20 countries at over 1,600 locations, including airports, universities, hospitals, and shopping malls. The StopGap brand provided European customers with American-style convenience-store products, including snacks, confectionaries, books, magazines, and even gifts and greeting cards. Sales of StopGap products spread quickly across 13 countries; the brand was sold in the education, health-care, travel, business, and industry sectors.

Bailey was instrumental in the 1994 buyout of Canteen Corporation from the U.S. company Flagstar. At the time Canteen was the largest vending company in the world, and its acquisition opened up new opportunities for the marketing and distribution of Compass brand products. Compass Group acquired other companies as well, such as Eurest International in 1995, which specialized in the delivery of meals for business and industry as well as in offshore and remote-site service, such as for the armed forces.

Bailey became chief executive of Compass Group's North America Division from 1994 to 1999, during which time the division nearly tripled its sales and profits. Bailey moved back to the United Kingdom in July 1999 when he was appointed group chief executive. As CEO he was to oversee the complicated merger and subsequent demerger of Compass with Granada, which forged the world's largest food-service company.

GRANADA COMPASS—BRIEFLY

The hospitality and media company Granada wished to shed the hospitality side of its business, and Compass was interested in the food-service portion of that division. The merger brought about by Bailey was rather complex and at first caused some shareholder confusion, especially due to uncertainty regarding the share price. A straight sale would have come with a large tax bill, however, so a plan to merge the two companies was put into motion, creating Granada Compass. The companies then demerged, with Compass retaining the hospitality portions of Granada; the arrangement saved Compass over £1 billion in taxation.

As Bailey told *FoodChain Magazine*, "What we were left with were the existing Compass businesses plus Granada's very successful Sutcliffe Catering business and motorway and roadside food-service outlets—and a hotel portfolio valued by the market at approximately £3 billion" (May/June 2001). Yet many shareholders were unhappy with the merger, seeing Compass's entry into the hotel industry as a potential liability; in response those assets were later sold for over £1.4 billion.

MANAGEMENT STYLE

Bailey saw growth and globalization as the keys to the contract food business. In an interview with the *Wall Street Transcript* Bailey noted that clients were looking for a single point of contact—a company that could provide all of their food-service needs in all of their locations without any hassle and could deal with any problems or issues that might arise. Through continued expansion and increased diversity within the framework of contract food, Bailey deemed Compass able to deliver such service.

Greater size gave Compass the ability to leverage purchasing and the flexibility clients demanded—as well as savings in terms of economies of scale. Bailey noted that the contract food market was vast, with plenty of room for further growth. As new manufacturing concerns were born in developing countries, the demand for employee meals grew. Bailey felt Compass to be ideally positioned as an established, reliable, global outsourcing food caterer that could provide all of the services required by new customers.

Bailey offset international expansion with reductions in overhead costs. Under his leadership Compass sold off many of their physical assets in order to focus on the core business of food service. While Compass needed to retain depots, vehicles, and vending machines—as well as restaurants in airports, museums, and stadiums—the largest portion of the company's business remained outsourced contract catering, where the equipment and premises of others were used, which reduced overhead costs. Bailey told *Food Chain* magazine, "Essentially our business is about providing a better-quality service cheaper than a self operator" (May/June 2001).

Bailey saw employee happiness and motivation as key in Compass Group's service-oriented industry. A share-investment incentive was launched in 2001 to help employees "share in the success" of the company; the scheme included a share savings plan for all permanent employees. Compass introduced a "great ideas" competition to reward innovative employees, with a prize of one hundred shares. Such promotions created additional challenges, however, when share prices fell upon the announcement of the merger with GrandMet. A dropping stock value had the potential to demotivate employees, so Bailey introduced a biannual video in which he personally explained the business results of such occurrences to staff.

MOTO

An example of the innovative branding and marketing undertaken by Compass during Bailey's tenure was the Moto brand. One of the assets gained by Compass after the merger/demerger with Granada was a chain of 47 motorway service stations. These had reputations as poor-quality, overpriced rest stops that relied on the captive nature of the motorway-bound consumer. While some considered these stations to be a liability, Bailey saw them as a goldmine. The stations were given total makeovers in terms of image, product lines, and service, and renamed Moto; Compass found these stations to be the perfect sites at which to sell more of its branded products. Familiar goods at standard—not gouging—prices counteracted the negative assumptions customers had previously held with regard to motorway outlets.

The most popular feature instituted at Moto was the continual maintenance of clean restrooms. The company found that the majority of their customers headed straight for the restrooms. Dirty facilities could easily turn customers away from food; when restrooms were clean and hygienic, motorists were more likely to stay and eat. The changes to the motorway service stations were modeled after the successful Italian autostrada rest areas, and the name Moto was chosen to evoke an association with those popular stops.

Commentators remarked that Bailey had statistics at his fingertips and could always offer facts and examples from his long history in the food-service business to support his case in an argument. Throughout his career Bailey remained passionate about food. He loved to cook—and eat—and knew he was not alone. He told the *Mail on Sunday*, "People will always want to eat. All that stuff about us living off pills is nonsense. It will never happen in my lifetime" (January 6, 2002). In Bailey's opinion the demand for food would be a constant if not increasing need, and he helped Compass to satisfy an ever-growing portion of that demand.

See also entry on Compass Group PLC in *International Directory of Company Histories.*

SOURCES FOR FURTHER INFORMATION

Bailey, Michael, "Compass Group PLC, CEO Interview," *Wall Street Transcript*, August 27, 2001, http://www.twst.com/ceos/cpg_l.html.

Carlino, Bill, "Flik International Corp.: Walking the Fine Line between a Family Operation and a Growing Corporation—Compass Group USA," *Nation's Restaurant News*, March 2, 1998, http://articles.findarticles.com/p/articles/mi_m3190/is_n9_v32/ai_20354009.

"From office chef to global sandwich maker," The City Interview, *Mail on Sunday*, January 6, 2002, also available at http://www.thisismoney.com/20020106/nm42477.html.

O'Hanlon, John, "Broad Compass—Part One," *Food Chain Magazine Online*, May/June 2001, http://www.foodchain-magazine.com/0106/01-compass.html.

———, "Broad Compass—Part Two," *Food Chain Magazine Online*, July/August 2001, http://www.foodchain-magazine.com/0108/ad_compass.html.

—David Tulloch

■■■

Sergio Balbinot

1958–

Co–chief executive officer, Assicurazioni Generali

Nationality: Italian.

Born: 1958, in Italy.

Career: Assicurazioni Generali, 1983–1989, insurance-operations department; 1989–1992, head of Swiss branch; 1992–1995, head of International Activity of Europe Assistance; 1995–1996, area manager for German-speaking countries and France; 1996–1998, assistant general manager and head of group-insurance operations; 1998–2002, deputy general manager; 2002–, co–chief executive officer.

Address: Assicurazioni Generali, Piazza Duca degli Abruzzi, 2, 34132 Trieste, Italy; http://www.generali.com.

■ Sergio Balbinot became the co-CEO of the Italian insurance company Assicurazioni Generali in 2002 after nearly two decades with the firm. After acquiring a degree in business management, Balbinot went to work for Generali in 1983. He held positions throughout the company's European offices, working in Munich, Trieste, Zurich, and Paris. It was this expertise in international operations, along with his quiet and diplomatic management style, that earned him the appointment as co-CEO.

LONG CAREER WITH GENERALI

Balbinot joined Assicurazioni Generali, one of Europe's largest insurance companies, in 1983, taking a position with the firm's Munich office. In 1986 he moved to Generali's main offices in Trieste, where he joined the insurance-operations department. In 1989 Balbinot took over at the Swiss branch of Generali in Zurich. In 1992 he relocated to Paris to take responsibility for International Activity of Europe Assistance. Balbinot returned to Trieste in 1995, becoming the area manager for the German-speaking countries and France. In 1996 the company appointed him to the positions of assistant general manager and head of group-insurance operations. In 1998 Balbinot moved up to the post of deputy general manager.

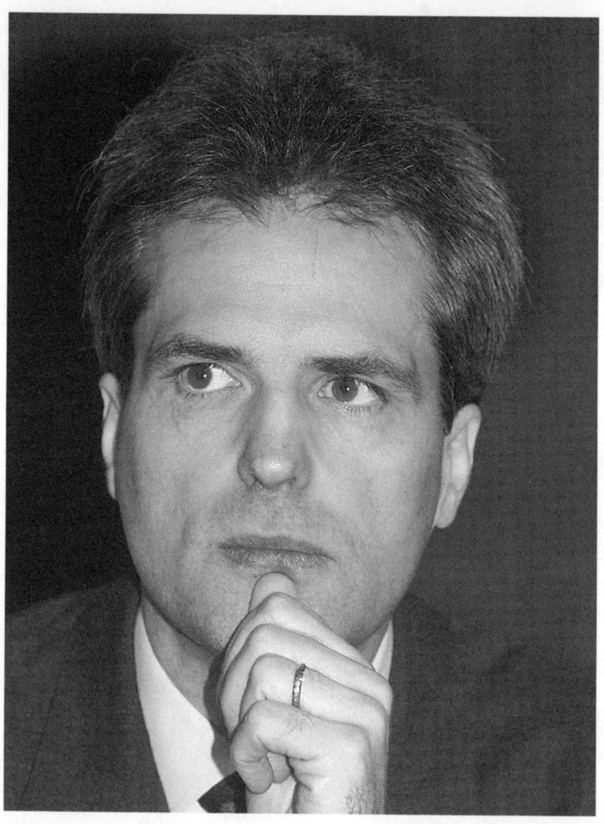

Sergio Balbinot. *AP/Wide World Photos.*

BALBINOT BECOMES CO-CEO OF GENERALI

In 2002 Balbinot joined Giovanni Perissinotto as co-CEO after a shake-up of the company's board of directors. The changes were a result of a feud between Vincenzo Maranghi of Mediobanca, Generali's biggest shareholder, and Antonio Fazio, head of Italy's central bank. Mediobanca, Italy's most-influential investment bank, increasingly had sought to dictate decision making at Generali, especially in regard to choosing top-level management. Fazio sought to limit the growing power of Mediobanca, and Generali was caught in the middle.

As a result of the shake-up, Generali reduced the number of CEOs from three to two. The appointment of Balbinot to join Perissinotto was designed to make the top management at the insurance company younger and more dynamic. The Balbinot appointment also seemed to be an indicator that the firm sought to expand outside of Italy, since he had previously headed Generali's non-Italian operations.

Along with Perissinotto, Balbinot did a good job of explaining Generali's strengths and strategies to investors. Known as a quiet diplomat, the new co-CEO promised change at the company by cutting costs, and promoting younger managers. Balbinot needed to restore the reputation of a company that had not performed as well as its rivals in the late 1990s and early 2000s. For example, Generali's market capitalization in 2002 was half of what it had been in 2001. "We still have a lot to do," Balbinot reported to the *Financial Times* (November 25, 2002).

The co-CEOs created a new sense of openness, transparency, and coherence at the company. Before the shake-up, the company's top executives rarely spoke openly, and they avoided meetings with investors. Balbinot and Perissinotto presented a three-year strategic plan for Generali, the first time the insurer had ever done so. The new plan set targets and sales goals, along with a new compensation system to encourage productivity.

Balbinot's main role as co-CEO was to oversee Generali's international operations. He immediately went to work on cutting costs by streamlining dozens of international companies under Generali's control, and he expanded Generali's presence beyond Europe. He helped to create Generali China Life Insurance, a joint venture with China National Petroleum Company. Generali opened offices in Canton in 2002 and in Beijing in 2004. Balbinot considered China fundamental to the company's future and envisioned it as one of Generali's biggest markets within 10 years of entering the country. He told *Insurance Day* that "our group is among the first to enter the important Beijing area and thus gain a significant competitive advantage over other qualified international operators" (February 9, 2004).

In April 2004 Generali's shareholders gave three-year mandates to its co-CEOs as well as the chairman, Antoine Bernheim. They hoped to create a degree of stability in the company's management after several years of turmoil and rapid change. Past managers had failed to stand up to the principal shareholder, Mediobanca, and many investors assumed that the investment bank called the shots at Generali. Among Balbinot's main early goals was to persuade shareholders to take a more active role in order to free the insurer from Mediobanca's meddling.

See also entry on Assicurazioni Generali SpA in *International Directory of Company Histories.*

SOURCES FOR FURTHER INFORMATION

Caswell, Nim, "Generali Reshapes Board in Shake-Up," *Financial Times*, April 29, 2002.

"Fiasco," *Economist*, March, 8, 2003, p. 69–70.

"Generali Steps Out," *Economist*, November, 23, 2002, p. 71.

"Generali Venture Gets Key to Chinese Capital," *Insurance Day*, February 9, 2004.

Kapner, Fred, "Generali Chiefs Get 3-Year Mandates," *Financial Times*, April 26, 2004.

———, "Generali MDs to Put Emphasis on Clarity," *Financial Times*, November 25, 2002.

—Ronald Young

■ ■ ■

Steve Ballmer

1956–

Chief executive officer, Microsoft Corporation

Nationality: American.

Born: March 24, 1956, in Detroit, Michigan.

Education: Harvard University, BS, 1977.

Family: Son of Frederic Henry Ballmer (manager, Ford Motor Company) and Beatrice Dworkin; married Connie Snyder (public relations executive), 1990; children: three.

Career: Proctor & Gamble, 1977–1979, brand assistant; Microsoft Corporation, 1980–1983, business manager; 1983–1984, vice president of marketing; 1984–1989, vice president of systems software; 1989–1992, senior vice president of systems software; 1992–1998, senior vice president of sales and support; 1998–2001, president; 2000–, chief executive officer.

Address: Microsoft Corporation, 1 Microsoft Way, Redmond, Washington 98052-6399; http://www.microsoft.com.

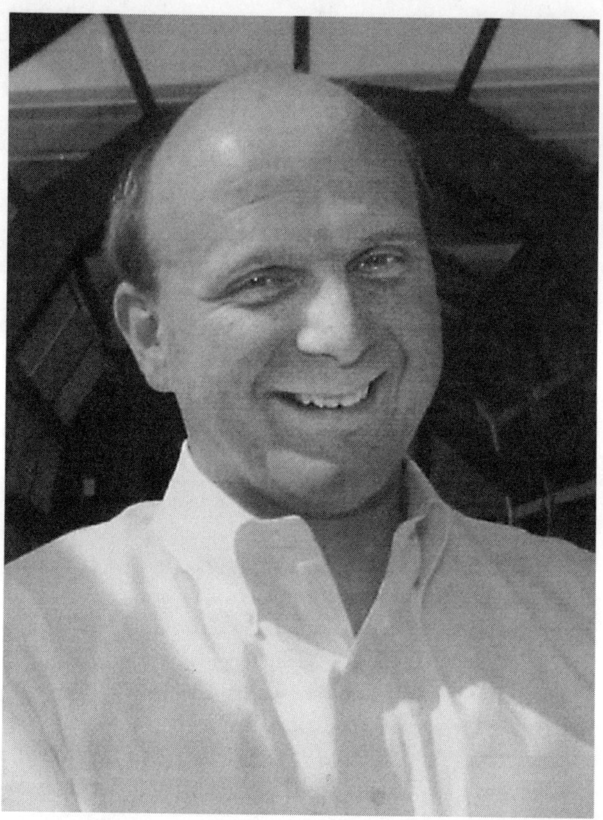

Steve Ballmer. *A/P Wide World Photos.*

■ Steven A. Ballmer joined a tiny startup called Microsoft in 1980 at the invitation of his college friend, founder Bill Gates. In a variety of roles that placed him second only to Gates, Ballmer played a crucial role in Microsoft's growth into the most powerful force in the computer industry. He became Microsoft's chief executive officer in 2001. Ballmer's exuberant, aggressive, and highly competitive personality helped shape the company's strategy and was critical to its success. Many consider him the author of Microsoft's more aggressive and questionable tactics, aimed not simply at strengthening Microsoft but at weakening the competition. Unquestionably, those tactics achieved results—including both dominance of the software market and numerous legal challenges over the years. The most prominent legal challenge was the 1998 antitrust case brought by U.S. Justice Department, which accused Microsoft of abusing its power as an illegal monopoly. Additionally, as of 2004 it faced antitrust charges in the European Union.

COMPETITIVE FROM THE START

Ballmer and his sister, Shelly, grew up in a wealthy suburb of Detroit, where their father, a Swiss immigrant, had a midlevel management job at Ford Motor Company. At Detroit Country Day School, which he attended on a scholarship, Ballmer was perceived as an overachiever. A highly intelligent and enthusiastic student with a talent for math, he earned a 4.0 grade point average, played on the football and track teams, managed the basketball team, and participated in various school clubs. He repeated this experience at Harvard University, where he studied applied mathematics, managed the football team, and worked on the *Harvard Crimson* newspaper and the university literary magazine. He also played poker with a classmate, Bill Gates, who dropped out in their junior year to start a software company.

After earning a BS degree at Harvard, Ballmer spent a year and a half at Procter & Gamble, marketing brownie and muffin mixes. He entered Stanford University's Graduate School of Business in 1979, and after his first year, visited his college friend Gates in Seattle, hoping for a summer job at Gates's company, Microsoft. Instead, Gates persuaded him to take a full-time job managing the company's operations. Ballmer's earliest role was as head recruiter for the fast-growing firm; although he was not a programmer himself, Ballmer could recognize technical talent. Not long after Ballmer was hired, Microsoft signed a contract to create an operating system for IBM's new line of what eventually would be called personal computers. Under a tight deadline, Microsoft licensed a program called QDOS from a small Seattle company, rewrote it, and renamed it MS-DOS.

The roles of the major players were set: Bill Gates and his partner and cofounder, Paul Allen, oversaw the technical side, while Ballmer handled the business end. In 1981 Ballmer reorganized the partnership into a corporate structure in which Gates held 53 percent of the equity, Allen 35 percent, and Ballmer 8 percent. He also implemented a stock option plan for Microsoft employees, which kept programmers from leaving until their options vested and would ultimately result in the creation of numerous "Microsoft Millionaires." Faced with health problems, Allen left the company in 1983, leaving the team of Gates and Ballmer in charge.

MAKING MICROSOFT

During the 1980s Ballmer headed the development of operating systems, the core of the company's business. He was quick to realize that the graphical user interface (GUI) introduced by Apple's MacIntosh in 1984 was a major step toward making personal computers easier to use and more popular. In addition, it was a potential threat to Microsoft's goal of making MS-DOS the industry standard. To stave off the competition and ensure that developers would continue creating applications for the MS-DOS platform, Microsoft announced Windows, a GUI for MS-DOS, in late 1983. Windows was heavily promoted during the two years between its announcement and the product's actual release in October 1985, gaining a reputation as *vaporware* (an industry term for products announced far in advance of any release, which may or may not actually take place). The Windows interface used the visual metaphor of a desktop and file folders, which was originally created at Xerox's Palo Alto Research Center in the early 1970s and first brought to market by Apple. Although some aspects of the desktop interface were licensed to Microsoft for use in Windows 1.0, Apple sued Microsoft in 1988, claiming that the "look and feel" of Windows 2.0 infringed its copyright. Apple lost this suit in 1992.

Microsoft became a publicly held company in 1986, making Ballmer a multimillionaire before he turned 30. But Gates and Ballmer were not solely motivated by wealth; their ambition was for Microsoft to control every aspect of the software market. They were particularly successful with the Microsoft Office suite of applications, comprising word-processing, spreadsheet, and presentation software (Word, Excel, and PowerPoint, respectively). By 2004 Microsoft Office had achieved a 90 percent market share. Windows 3.0, released in 1990, had finally resolved many of the technical problems of earlier versions. In 1993 the company introduced Windows NT, an operating system for mainframes and large networks, to compete with UNIX. Ballmer was ahead of Gates in recognizing the importance of the Internet in the early 1990s, and in 1995 the company launched the Microsoft Network and its own Web browser, Internet Explorer, to compete with Netscape, one of the earliest browser programs. The launch of Windows 95, another long-delayed upgrade to the operating system, became a media event.

LEGAL TROUBLES

But increasing criticism mirrored the company's growth. Many industry observers expressed the view that Microsoft dominated the market because of its success at crowding out smaller competitors by any means available, not because of the quality of its products. Microsoft's aggressive business practices resulted in a number of legal challenges in the 1990s. One lawsuit came from Sun Microsystems, which had created the platform-independent Java Web programming language. Microsoft had licensed Java from Sun in 1995, and in 1997 Sun sued, claiming that Microsoft had created a version of Java that was incompatible with non-Windows platforms. The suit was settled in 2001.

The most serious charges came in 1998, when the U.S. Justice Department and 18 states joined to prosecute Microsoft on antitrust charges. The case focused largely on the "bundling" of Internet Explorer with the Windows operating system, making it difficult to use competing Web browsers such as Netscape, and on other illegal anticompetitive actions. The government accused Microsoft of being a monopoly and of using that monopoly power to illegally expand and protect its Windows operating system. In 1999 a district court judge ruled that Microsoft was a monopoly and in 2000 found the company had violated the Sherman Antitrust Act. In June 2000 the judge ordered that Microsoft be split into two companies. Microsoft, of course, appealed, and while the appeals court upheld the monopoly and antitrust rulings, it threw out the order to split up Microsoft. A tentative settlement that would keep Microsoft intact but restrict its activities was issued in November 2001. In May 2003 Microsoft settled with AOL Time Warner, owner of the competing browser Netscape, in a deal that included a $750 million payment to AOL Time Warner and plans for the two companies to work together. However, litigation continued: in 2004 the European Union rejected a settlement offer in its long-running antitrust case against Microsoft that focused on the bundling of Media Player, its audio and video software, into Windows. Ballmer, always a passionate, outspoken advocate for the company and its products, vigorously defended Microsoft in the media, declaring that the company's only goal was to provide the best possible products to its customers.

A KEY PLAYER PLANS FOR THE FUTURE

From 1980 to 1998 Ballmer headed several Microsoft divisions, including operations, operating systems development, and sales and support. In July 1998 he was promoted to president, and in January 2000 he was named chief executive officer, a position Gates had held since the company began. The concerns he faced as the new CEO included Microsoft's tarnished reputation as a fair and ethical competitor; escalating attacks by hackers pinpointing vulnerabilities in Explorer, Windows, and other products; and the growing popularity of open-source operating systems like Linux. Ballmer also found a need for internal changes at Microsoft. Under Gates, who was more of a technical visionary than a business manager, the company had been highly centralized. As CEO, Ballmer divided the company into seven operating divisions, worked to create systematic procedures for everything from product development to strategic planning to employee and management evaluation, and revamped the compensation plan by eliminating stock options in favor of outright grants of restricted stock.

By the early 2000s Microsoft's strategy had shifted away from the PC-centered approach to focus on Microsoft.net, an architecture based on XML technology, which would enable the integration of data and applications. Ballmer viewed this focus on interoperability as a major shift in the information technology industry, comparable to the introduction of the graphical user interface in the 1980s. As ever, he energetically promoted Microsoft's role as the dominant player, setting the standards and selling the software behind the next big thing in computing.

Since 1980 Microsoft's growth has been driven by Ballmer's fierce loyalty and managerial talent. Although he was described as affable and easygoing, he was best known for a loud, boisterous style, and a high-energy personality that dominated most interactions. Such exuberance had its price: in 1991 he damaged his vocal cords at a meeting in Japan by screaming "Windows!" But the defining characteristic of Steve Ballmer was his passionate belief in Microsoft Corporation.

See also entry on Microsoft Corporation in *International Directory of Company Histories.*

SOURCES FOR FURTHER INFORMATION

Maxwell, Frederic Alan, *Bad Boy Ballmer, the Man Who Rules Microsoft,* New York: HarperCollins, 2002.

Schlender, Brent, "Ballmer Unbound: How Do You Impose Order on a Giant, Runaway Mensa Meeting? Just Watch Microsoft's CEO," *Fortune,* January 26, 2004, p. 116.

Shepard, Stephen B., "Steve Ballmer on Microsoft's Future," *BusinessWeek,* December 1, 2003.

—Sandra M. Larkin

■ ■ ■

Jill Barad

1951–

Former chairman, president, and chief executive officer, Mattel, Incorporated

Nationality: American.

Born: May 23, 1951, in New York, New York.

Education: Queens College, BA, 1973.

Family: Daughter of Lawrence Elikann (television director) and Corinne Schuman; married Thomas Kenneth Barad (film producer), 1979; children: two.

Career: Coty Cosmetics, 1976–1977, assistant product manager, marketing; 1977–1978, product manager, marketing; Wells Rich Greene, 1978–1979, account executive; Mattel Toys, Incorporated, 1981–1982, product manager, marketing; 1982–1983, director, marketing; 1983–1985, vice president, marketing; 1985–1986, senior vice president, marketing; 1986–1988, senior vice president, marketing development; 1988–1989, executive vice president, product design and development, and executive vice president, marketing and worldwide product development; 1989–1990, president, girls' and activity toys division; Mattel USA, 1990–1992, president; 1992–1997, president and chief operating officer; Mattel, Incorporated, 1997–2000, chairman, president, and chief executive officer.

Awards: Frontrunner Award, Sara Lee Foundation, 1994; Exemplary Leadership in Management Award, Anderson School of Management at UCLA, 1995; award, Girls Incorporated, 1998; named one of Women of the Year, Los Angeles County Commission for Women, 1998.

Jill Barad. *AP/Wide World Photos.*

■ Jill Elikann Barad used her marketing ability and eye for consumer trends to reestablish the Barbie doll as an American icon. She rapidly climbed the corporate ladder to become president, chairman, and chief executive officer of Mattel, Incorporated, one of the world's largest toy companies. As one of four women at the helm of a Fortune 500 company in the late 1990s, Barad broke through the corporate "glass ceiling" and inspired other businesswomen from her position as chief executive officer to overcome obstacles to success in a male-dominated corporate climate. Barad helped usher in a period of growth and prosperity for Mattel in the 1990s through mergers, acquisitions, and the use of high-level marketing skills. After three years as Mattel's CEO, however, Barad made the unwise decision to acquire the Learning Company. This acquisition led to financial losses for Mattel and forced Barad to resign her position. Prior to her resignation, she was described by her coworkers and employees as an ambitious and competitive perfectionist with keen insights into product development and marketing.

DEVELOPING MARKETING SKILLS

Barad learned about marketing, sales, and customers in the mid-1970s when she went to work for Coty Cosmetics as a traveling cosmetician and trainer. Although Barad had begun her cosmetics career during a year-long hiatus from college during which she sold make-up for Love Cosmetics, she became more interested in the marketing aspect of products after graduating from college in 1974. During this time she began to pay attention to store displays of cosmetics and think about ways to make her company's products stand out from the competition. Using her powers of intuition and keen observation, Barad designed a wall display to improve the presentation of Coty products and sent it to the company's headquarters. Barad's unique department store wall display brought the Coty products to the front of the cosmetics section and increased the number of impulse buys of Coty products by customers. Recognizing the exceptional visual impact and the competitive advantage provided by the wall display, Coty's managers used Barad's design for the next 20 years.

Following Barad's job with Coty, she moved to Los Angeles in 1978 and accepted a position with an advertising agency representing Max Factor & Company. She left the job after she married Thomas Barad in 1979 to become a stay-at-home wife and mother. Soon after Barad's first son was born, she realized that she was spending her days critiquing displays in local clothing stores. She decided that she needed to make use of her marketing ability to retain a sense of challenge and purpose in her life. Her husband recalled coming home from work in 1981 ". . . and all this unspent energy would hit me. I told her to go back to work" (*BusinessWeek*, May 25, 1998).

TAKING MATTEL BY STORM

Taking her husband's advice, Barad joined Mattel in 1981 as an employee in the novelty section of the well-known toy company. One of her first noteworthy marketing efforts was a presentation for a product called "A Bad Case of Worms." The toy consisted of rubber worms that were supposed to slither down after being thrown at a wall. The night before a commercial for the toy was to be sent to Toys 'R' Us, however, Barad found that the worms simply fell off the wall rather than slithering down as advertised. In order to salvage the project, she spent the night creating a new commercial that did not focus on the worms' supposed ability to slither. The commercial was a success and helped to sell a good many worms before the product was discontinued.

Although the worms commercial was not enough by itself to salvage an inferior product, it did bring Barad's marketing skills, innovative ideas, and demands for a more challenging position to the attention of Mattel's management. A former Mattel CEO, Tom Kalinske, remembered being impressed by Barad's ability to create an effective marketing campaign around mediocre products as well as by her ambition and feisty nature as she stormed into his office and asked what she needed to do to obtain a better assignment. Barad remembers saying, "There must be something better than worms" (*BusinessWeek*, May 25, 1998). She was confident that she could accomplish more for the company in a higher position and therefore set out to earn and demand promotions. Barad's hard work and successful marketing campaigns for Barbie and other best-selling dolls helped to bring Mattel back from a brush with bankruptcy in the early 1980s when the company's Intellivision game console failed to make money. Barad's successes won her an important place on the Mattel team. She was promoted to director of marketing by 1983, only two years after she began working at Mattel.

By 1989 Barad had become an executive vice president but still felt she was not moving up quickly enough. She used her understanding of Mattel's competitive corporate culture to engineer her next promotion. As a bargaining chip, Barad threatened to leave the company to join Reebok International unless she was promoted even higher. Mattel's CEO at the time, John Amerman, recognized Barad's importance to the business and made her co-president of Mattel USA.

In 1992 Barad returned to Amerman to demand an assurance that she would succeed him upon retirement. This demand was unusual because Amerman was not close to retirement. He granted Barad's request, however, made her chief operating officer and president, doubled her compensation, and put into place a contract that would pay her five years' compensation if she were not made chief executive officer when he eventually retired.

EARLY SUCCESSES

Once Barad became Mattel's chief operating officer, her first success was raising sales of the Barbie doll, perhaps Mattel's best-known product. When Barad had joined Mattel in 1981, the doll's sales were stagnant, partly because Barbie had become a symbol of sexist standards of beauty and demeaning attitudes toward women. By 1993 the doll's annual sales had reached a plateau of about $320 million. In 1995, however, Barad began to market Barbie as a professional role model with the tagline "We Girls Can Do Anything," accompanied by the message that Barbie could be a doctor, dentist, teacher, or executive. The new aggressive marketing campaign meant that Barbie became a symbol of achievement rather than an image of high-fashion attractiveness. That year the new Barbie dolls accounted for $1.4 billion in sales or 35 percent of Mattel's gross revenue. In 1997 Barad became living proof of Barbie's "We Girls Can Do Anything" slogan by moving into the position of Mattel's chief executive officer when John Amerman retired.

As CEO, Barad brought about several successful mergers that boosted Mattel's profits. In 1997 she brokered a merger with Tyco Toys, the maker of Matchbox cars and holder of the primary toy license for the popular television show "Sesame Street." In 1998 Barad led Mattel into a merger with the Pleasant Company, the maker of the American Girl brand of dolls and clothes, as well as collaboration with Intel, the world's largest manufacturer of computer chips, to design and develop new generations of interactive "smart toys." Barad's marketing skills and executive experience resulted in her election to the corporate boards of Microsoft, Reebok International, and BankAmerica.

DIFFICULTIES IN MANAGEMENT

Barad was known for her powerful marketing strategies, keen insights into product development, fierce competitive streak, and driving ambition. During her climb to CEO, however, other Mattel executives came to regard her as too demanding and outspoken. She was often described as refusing to be a team player. On the other hand, one of Barad's former supervisors, Judy Schakelford, noted that Mattel's corporate culture was intensely competitive and that Barad's personality was well suited to scaling the company's corporate ladder. Other observers remarked that criticisms of Barad's perfectionism and hard-driving style would not have been as loud or as frequent if she had been a male executive.

As Mattel's chief executive officer, Barad instituted such innovations as flexible hours and half-day Fridays; however, the same personality traits that facilitated her rise to power led to problems in managing others. Barad held all Mattel employees to high standards without acknowledging their contributions or giving them adequate financial compensation. She was also accused of being controlling and temperamental. These traits led to the resignation of many top-level Mattel executives during the three years of Barad's tenure as CEO. The resignations were attributed to Barad's penchant for micromanagement, as she continued to be a hands-on marketing executive while carrying out her duties as CEO. For example, Barad had all the options for a new Barbie doll presented to her on one occasion and then unilaterally selected the styles of Barbie's clothing and hair for production. Mattel's marketing team thought that her examination of each design concept might speed up the marketing of one particular product but was also intrusive and meddling.

Although Barad's management style was seen as too hard-edged and hands-on by some of her colleagues, she was effective at first in expanding Mattel's reach into new global markets through innovative marketing as well as the centralization of the company's European warehouses and shipping. She added to Mattel's list of toy licenses related to child-focused television shows and films from Walt Disney and Nickelodeon. One profitable agreement between Mattel and Disney included the manufacturing and marketing of toys for such successful films as *Toy Story 2, A Bug's Life, The Lion King,* and *Snow White.* These deals brought in 10 percent of Mattel's operating profits in 1998.

OVEREXPANSION

Although Barad had increased Mattel's visibility and profits in the early 1990s through clever marketing and lucrative mergers, the company's share price declined by 56 percent between 1996 and 1999 while Barbie doll sales dropped 32 percent. Barad's skills led her to recognize good merger targets from a marketing perspective but did not include the ability to manage a company and sustain profits. Sydney Finkelstein attributed Barad's downfall to her habit of ruthlessly eliminating upper-level subordinates ". . . if she thought they harbored serious reservations about the way she was running things" or weren't completely behind her vision for the company (*Ivey Business Journal,* January/February, 2004).

Barad's major error in judgment came in 1999, when she led Mattel's acquisition of the Learning Company, a software maker, for $3.5 billion in stock. She expected the purchase to help Mattel cross into the high-tech toy market. Instead of increasing the company's profits, however, the ill-considered acquisition resulted in a loss of at least $50 million. Barad resigned as CEO in 2000 after pressure from shareholders and investors over the company's dismal financial performance and her poor strategic planning. Barad received a $1.2 million annual pension as part of a compensation package of $50 million. Her large severance package became a highly publicized example of corporate inequality in executive payment compared to company profit, in that her payout was equal to the amount of money Mattel lost from acquiring the Learning Company. Despite Barad's resignation, many of the changes she instituted continued to increase Mattel's profits after her departure. In fact, Mattel's sales in 2000 rose 2 percent to $4.7 billion, with sales of Barbie dolls 10 percent higher thanks to Barad's redesign and marketing strategy.

After leaving Mattel, Barad focused her attention on such nonprofit organizations as the Children Affected by AIDS Foundation, Children's Medical Network, Town Hall of California, and the International Women's Fellowship.

See also entries on Coty, Inc. and Mattel, Inc., in *International Directory of Company Histories.*

SOURCES FOR FURTHER INFORMATION

Finkelstein, Sydney, "The Seven Habits of Spectacularly Unsuccessful Executives," *Ivey Business Journal,* January–February, 2004, pp. 1–6.

Morris, Kathleen, "The Rise of Jill Barad," *BusinessWeek,* May 25, 1998, pp. 112–118.

—Dawn Jacob Laney

■■■

Don H. Barden

1943–

Chief executive officer, Barden Companies

Nationality: American.

Born: December 20, 1943, in Detroit, Michigan.

Education: Attended Central State University, 1963–1964.

Family: Son of Milton Barden (mechanic and auto laborer) and Hortense (maiden name unknown); married Bella Marshall (Barden Companies' president and COO); children: one.

Career: Record store, 1960s, owner; newspaper owner, 1967–1972; *Lorain County Times*, 1974, partner; Lorain City Council, 1972–1975, council member; Don H. Barden Inc., 1976–1981, president; WKYC-TV, 1977–1980, talk-show host; Barden Cablevision, 1982–1994, CEO; Barden Companies, 1994–, CEO.

Awards: Trumpet Award, Turner Companies, 2004; Seven Living Legends, Mayor Kwame Kilpatrick and the Detroit City Council, 2004.

Address: Barden Companies, 163 Madison Avenue, Suite 2000, Detroit, Michigan 48226.

■ Don H. Barden started up his first business with only $500 and a dogged determination to control his destiny; in the 1960s, using an instinctive entrepreneurial acumen, he opened a record store. From this humble beginning Barden made inroads into the cable industry, eventually achieving success as the first African American cable-company owner. He then moved on to the casino industry; he first acquired a riverboat casino in Gary, Indiana, then used his experiential expertise and an uncanny knack for being in the right place at the right time to purchase three more casinos—including one in Las Vegas, making him the first African American to own a casino there.

STARTED VARIOUS COMPANIES

Don Barden was born on December 20, 1943, in Detroit, Michigan. His parents, Milton and Hortense, taught all of their 13 children the value of hard work and determination. During high school Barden excelled at sports as a member of his school's basketball and football teams. He went on to Central State University, in Wilberforce, Ohio, but money for college was scarce; he left after his freshman year. Barden moved to Lorain, Ohio, and worked various odd jobs while saving money. He soon amassed $500 and opened a record store, where he began promoting shows and booking bands. Before long he had started a small record label as well as a public-relations firm.

Though Barden gained experience through his various businesses, he was not reaping the level of profit he desired. That changed when he moved into the field of real estate and helped the U.S. government find a location for a new military-recruiting station. After Barden identified a building, he secured a commitment from the government for the military to lease the facility. Bearing the letter of commitment, he procured a bank loan with which to make the purchase; he sold the building two years later for $50,000, doubling his investment.

Barden soon switched gears once more: he started a newspaper with a partner, creating the successful *Lorain County Times.* He later enjoyed a short political career with his election to the Lorain City Council, serving two terms between 1972 and 1975.

HIGH VISIBILITY LED TO CABLE OPPORTUNITIES

After leaving the public-service arena, Barden became a talk-show host on WKYC-TV in Lorain. He soon learned of openings in the cable industry; he helped put together a deal wherein 4 percent of the cable-television franchises in Lorain and another community were set aside for investment by African Americans. Barden himself purchased a share of each franchise for $2,000 apiece, shares which he later sold for $200,000.

Perceiving cable to be the future of television, Barden began locating primarily black communities to wire. The City of Inkster, Michigan, awarded Barden his first home-wiring contract. He completed the work on time and under budget, earning himself a reputation as a reliable and respectable contractor; he soon won contracts in other communities.

STARTED BARDEN CABLEVISION

In 1982 the mayor and city council of Detroit, Michigan, began seeking bids to wire the city. Barden invested $500,000 to write a proposal, and his efforts paid off when he was awarded the contract. However, in spite of his business know-how and good reputation, Barden still lacked the capital to fund the project, which involved laying wire both above and below ground.

The Canadian company Maclean Hunter of Toronto agreed to purchase 25 percent of Barden Cablevision for $230,000. Maclean would eventually own 60 percent of the cable company, with Barden owning 40 percent and maintaining 51 percent of the voting rights. In addition, Maclean loaned the company $15 million; Barden also received an $80 million loan from a Canadian bank.

Barden began wiring Detroit in 1986 and used an unorthodox approach in order to lure customers and expand his business. While most cable operators sought affluent customers as subscribers, Barden targeted the less well-off. He began the practice of "churning," or signing new customers while canceling delinquent accounts. Barden Cablevision soon grew to include 120,000 subscribers.

SOLD COMPANY TO OPEN CASINO

In 1993 the State of Indiana approved the operation of riverboat casinos. Barden first teamed up with President Riverboat Casinos in an effort to make a purchase; unfortunately for Barden, President Riverboat was unable to produce its pledged half of the money. Following Maclean Hunter's lead, Barden sold his share of Barden Cablevision to Comcast Cable for $300 million. He then placed a successful bid with Gary, Indiana, to secure a contract for his riverboat casino, the Majestic Star, to open for gaming in 1996.

In Detroit, meanwhile, voters approved a proposal to bring casinos to their city. Barden, wanting to help in the rebuilding process, placed a bid. He was unsuccessful but undeterred. He argued for and won a chance to place a referendum before the voters, partnering with superstar Michael Jackson in an attempt to create the Majestic Kingdom—a complex that would comprise a casino, hotel, restaurants, and a theme park. Voters, however, turned down the referendum. Still unfazed, Barden tried—once again unsuccessfully—to purchase Greektown Casino in Detroit. In 2002 he and the Lac Vieux Desert Band of Lake Superior Chippewa Indians claimed that the 1997 Detroit Casino bidding process was unconstitutional. It seemed Barden would finally realize his goal of opening a casino in Detroit, but in 2004 a judge put another stop to this dream becoming a reality.

Barden eventually shifted his focus to acquiring three Fitzgeralds casinos that had filed for bankruptcy. To garner funds to make the purchases, Barden visited 40 institutions in a dozen cities. As selling points he cited the facts that the Majestic Star had a proven track record; the Fitzgeralds casinos were still generating profits and had excellent growth potential; and the casinos were being bought at a significant discount. He was able to secure $135 million and also put up $14 million of his own cash.

BECAME FIRST AFRICAN AMERICAN CASINO OWNER IN LAS VEGAS

In 2002 Barden took possession of the Fitzgeralds casinos. One was based in Tunica, Mississippi, another in Black Hawk, Colorado, and the third in downtown Las Vegas. With the Las Vegas casino Barden became the city's first African American casino owner.

Barden Companies, with over four thousand employees, earned $347 million in 2002, 90 percent of which came from Barden's four casinos, his Tunica-based casino being the most profitable. Not one to rest on his laurels, Barden tried to acquire the rival Trump Casinos' riverboat casino in Gary, Indiana, and planned to open a hotel-casino on the Turks and Caicos Islands in the West Indies—all while trying to purchase another bankrupt casino in Black Hawk, Colorado.

EXPANDING INTO VARIOUS TECHNOLOGIES

Barden was involved in implementing innovations. His Barden Technologies company developed computerized voting machines; another company, Barden Entertainment, developed digital video jukeboxes that played music videos. Barden expected the voting machines to be certified and ready for use in 2006 and the jukeboxes to bring in $100 million by the same year.

Barden was described in a profile in *Black Enterprise* magazine, which gave its Company of the Year award to Barden Cablevision in 1992 and to Barden Companies in 2003, as a "soft-spoken man" (June 1992). He showed that he had great negotiating skills, whether for real estate or for licenses for new technology, and was a risk taker. With each new acquisition he gained more experience, and he continually used his new skills to move his companies forward. As quoted in *Black Enterprise*, U.S. Representative Richard Gephardt, a Democrat from Missouri, stated, "Don's success is a direct result of his sharp intellect and his dedicated work ethic" (June 2003).

In addition to being a member of the Executive Committee of the Democratic Party, Barden was the chairman of the board of directors for the Booker T. Washington Business Association. He was married to Bella Marshall, who was also Barden Companies' president and chief operating officer. The couple resided in Detroit with their son, Keenan.

SOURCES FOR FURTHER INFORMATION

Bray, Hiawatha, "Wired for Success," *Black Enterprise,* June 1992, pp. 134–137.

Dietderich, Andrew, "Barden Buys Three Casinos," *Crain's Detroit Business,* February 25, 2002, p. 18.

Huey, Erik C., "Fitzgeralds Owner Upbeat on Downtown," *Las Vegas Review-Journal,* February 20, 2004.

Hughes, Alan, "The House Always Wins," *Black Enterprise,* June 2003, pp. 126–133.

Lam, Tina, "CEO of Casino Operator Continues Fight to Build Property in Detroit," *Knight Ridder/Tribune Business News,* February 23, 2004.

—Ashyia N. Henderson

■ ■ ■

Ned Barnholt

1943–

President, chief executive officer, and chairman of the board, Agilent Technologies

Nationality: American.

Born: 1943, in New York City, New York.

Education: Stanford University, BS, 1965?, MS, 1966.

Family: Married (wife's name, Jimi); children: three.

Career: Hewlett-Packard, 1966–1973, research and development engineer; 1973–1980, marketing manager; 1980–1984, general manager, Microwave and Communications Group; 1984–1988, general manager, Electronic Instruments Group; 1988–1993, vice president; 1990–1999, general manager, Test and Measurement Organization; 1993–1996, senior vice president; 1996–1999, executive vice president; Agilent Technologies, 1999–, president and chief executive officer; 2002–, chairman of the board.

Awards: AeA Medal of Achievement, 2002; Excellence in Leadership Communication Award, International Association of Business Communicators, 2003; Spirit of Silicon Valley Lifetime Achievement Award, Silicon Valley Manufacturing Group, 2003; National Day Award, Singapore, 2004.

Address: Agilent Technologies, 3000 Hanover Street, Palo Alto, California 94304-1112; http://www.Agilent.com.

■ Edward W. "Ned" Barnholt received his MS in electrical engineering at Stanford University and went from there to Hewlett-Packard's Palo Alto headquarters, where he became a true believer in "the Hewlett-Packard Way," a style of management that involved a great deal of interaction among management staff and employees. His experience in marketing as well as his leadership of a new division in Seattle made him a candidate for running the Agilent spin-off from Hewlett-Packard in 1999. He took over leadership of Agilent just as the market for Agilent's high-tech products went into a steep and prolonged decline. His response to the crisis that followed put his skills to a severe test.

THE HEWLETT-PACKARD WAY

When Barnholt joined Hewlett-Packard in 1966, both Bill Hewlett and Dave Packard were still running the company. Packard made it a habit to mingle with workers and to visit his company's various work sites. The corporate culture focused on innovation, trust of employees, respect for employees, and management integrity. These would be the ideals Barnholt espoused when he ran Agilent. In 1973 Barnholt had tired of his work on production and secured a transfer to marketing, where he proved to be an able salesman. This experience would become very important when he tried to direct Agilent out of a nearly catastrophic decline in sales in 2000–2002. From 1973 to 1976 he worked in the Stanford Park division, moving in 1976 to the Santa Clara (California) division, where he served until he was sent to Spokane, Washington, in 1980 to open and manage a new division for Hewlett-Packard's Microwave and Communications Group.

Originally, measurement and testing equipment had been the heart of Hewlett-Packard's manufacturing, but during the 1980s there was a marked shift in the company's focus, with computer and printer products replacing measurement and testing devices as the company's big moneymakers. By 1998 computer and printer products accounted for about 80 percent of Hewlett-Packard's profits. The president and chief executive officer (CEO) of Hewlett-Packard, Lewis E. Platt, decided to have the company focus on computers and printers, having the other aspects of the business spun off into a new corporation; he tabbed Barnholt to lead the change.

Barnholt had his doubts about the potential for a spin-off to succeed, but he also saw a chance to preserve the corporate values that he thought Hewlett-Packard was losing. He wanted to maintain what he called Hewlett-Packard's "foundation values," and since the new company would include the Measurement Organization, which had once been Hewlett-Packard's only focus, he saw an opportunity to do so. Many of the workers who were to join the new company thought that they should retain the name "Hewlett-Packard," because their organization had been Hewlett and Packard's first corporate endeavor, but their new company was given the name "Agilent," derived from the word "agile," which is what Barnholt hoped the company would be when responding to developments in the high-tech marketplace.

In March 1999 Agilent brought with it not only the Test and Measurement Group but also the Life Sciences and

Chemical Analysis Group and the Semiconductor Products Group. One-third of Hewlett-Packard's researchers joined Agilent. At its inception Agilent had $8.3 billion in funding and manufactured 20,000 measurement devices. Agilent's initial public offering was valued at $2.1 billion, although Hewlett-Packard retained an 84 percent interest in the spin-off. The new company started well, with its stock going up in value, but then the worldwide recession hit, with a dramatic reduction in purchases by Agilent's customers. Perhaps as much as 50 percent of orders for Agilent's products were cancelled in 2000.

Barnholt's response to the crisis included diversifying the company by acquiring smaller companies that produced high-tech components that complemented Agilent's own products; he also instituted a $135-million advertising campaign in 2001 that featured the slogan "Dreams Made Real." In 2001, 55 percent of Agilent's sales were in electronics and telecommunications, and the decline in orders was sharpest in those very areas.

HANDLING MASSIVE LAYOFFS

From 2000 to 2001 Agilent's business dropped 50 percent. Barnholt initiated a company-wide effort to economize, and employees strove to cut costs by recycling equipment parts, cutting back on toll calls, and doing without unessential supplies. These economies helped, but Agilent was still losing hundreds of millions of dollars. When Agilent began, it had 42,000 employees; by November 2000 it had 47,000 employees. Barnholt was loath to lay off any workers, believing that the Hewlett-Packard way was to cut employees only as a last resort. Thus, in early 2001 he sold Agilent's health-care services division to Holland's Philips Electronics NV; this move sent five thousand employees and their jobs out of Agilent. In March 2001 he released five thousand temporary employees.

Barnholt blamed "excess capacity" for the problems in high-tech industries; when demand slumped, companies such as Agilent had more manufacturing capacity than there were orders, which meant that there was a huge overhead in maintenance of facilities and in underemployed workers that had to be compensated for elsewhere in the company. If Agilent's divisions had still been part of Hewlett-Packard, the computer and printer divisions would have picked up the slack, but Agilent itself had no such moneymakers to help out.

To keep Agilent afloat, Barnholt cut employee's salaries and wages by 10 percent in 2001. He carefully explained what was happening to his employees and even took a pay cut himself (to $950,000 annually). Employees by and large responded by working longer hours, regarding the pay cuts as part of Barnholt's efforts to save their jobs. Still, Agilent continued to hemorrhage money. In the third quarter of 2002 alone Agilent lost $228 million. For the entire year losses were $1 billion, with sales of $6 billion. Despite such losses, Barnholt was made chairman of the board that year. He remarked, "How you communicate bad news is an important challenge, because how you treat people who leave has a great impact on the attitude of those people who stay" (Agilent press release, June 11, 2003). Barnholt told every employee in all Agilent's offices about the massive layoffs by broadcasting the announcement. More than eight thousand people were laid off in 2002.

The response of employees to the layoffs was remarkable. The general impression of the employees was that Barnholt had done all he could to save their jobs, and those who were laid off stuck with their jobs, working hard, until the end of their last day with Agilent. The Hewlett-Packard way had paid off in employees who were not angry with the company and thus would be willing to be rehired by Agilent should the company manage to end its steep decline. An internal survey by Agilent's management revealed that nearly 90 percent of employees thought that those who had been laid off had been treated well; this resulted in a high level of motivation among the employees who remained. By 2004 Agilent had only 28,000 employees, but the company seemed to be stabilizing.

NAVIGATING ROUGH SEAS

Quoting an African adage, Barnholt asserted that "calm seas do not make skillful sailors" in a 2002 speech to a *BusinessWeek* CEO summit (Agilent press release, September 30, 2002). Not everything was gloomy during Barnholt's first years running Agilent. In 2001 life sciences sales, primarily in chemical analysis, grew by 25 percent. Sales of measurement devices, the heart of the original Hewlett-Packard company, brought in about $600 million. Agilent established public relations offices in fourteen countries around the world, and by 2004, 55 percent of the company's income came from outside the United States.

Barnholt took a forward-looking approach to his direction of Agilent. He made alliances with small companies to help with manufacturing components for Agilent's products, outsourcing much of what the released temporary workers had done; this move cut down on the overhead for storage of parts. In February 2001 he founded Agilent Ventures, even though Agilent was entering very rough seas. Agilent Ventures was a research division devoted to finding promising high-tech start–ups, especially in telecommunications, and funding the research of those startups with an eye to having the startups create new technologies that Agilent could use.

Perhaps Barnholt's hardest decision was to end work on photonic, or optical, switches; these had the potential to revolutionize semiconductors, because the switches operated at the speed of light and many more of them could be put on a chip than could electrical switches. But there was no market for chips using photonic technology. Many potential customers were deciding that the processing chips they had were good enough for what they wanted to do, and sales for processing chips of all kinds declined in 1999–2002.

On the other hand, Agilent took a lead in the manufacture of fiber-optics products, and its host of measurement products made it the place to shop for customers who had many different measurement needs, such as manufacturers of hospital monitors. Agilent brought forth "system on a chip" technology that allowed it to put several processes on one chip, rather than on several different chips. Interest in this technology was slow to grow, but in 2003 demand began to rise, because the system-on-chip design saved space, expense in maintenance (only one chip to look after), and the cost of buying several different chips to do what one system on a chip could do. In 2003 Agilent seemed to have turned around, earning $6.056 billion in profits for the year.

AGILENT LABORATORIES

One of Agilent's strategies countered the latest thinking about corporate research, which was that it should be decentralized, with research laboratories focused on only one project and making the project succeed. Instead, Barnholt wanted a central research facility that was charged with conducting all of Agilent's research. He wanted communication among Agilent's researchers, and putting them together seemed like a good way to make sure they all knew what others were doing and could help when necessary. Thus was founded Agilent Laboratories.

The laboratories were to focus, in Barnholt's vision, on research that would have identifiable practical applications rather than on pure research. One of the laboratory's first triumphs was the development in 2000 of the DNA chip. This involved laying DNA on semiconductors that would detect and arrange in proper order strands of DNA, occasionally rebuilding damaged genes. By 2002 Agilent was spending $1 billion on Agilent Laboratories, but hard times forced cutbacks, with research funding cut by 18 percent for 2003. The halting of the development of the photonic switching platform had to have been a blow to research staff personnel, but Barnholt insisted that the photonic switch would be taken up again by Agilent when the world was ready for it.

See also entries on Hewlett-Packard Company and Agilent Technologies Inc. in *International Directory of Company Histories.*

SOURCES FOR FURTHER INFORMATION

"Agilent Chairman, President and CEO Ned Barnholt Receives IABC EXCEL Award," Agilent press release, http://www.agilent.com/about/newsroom/features/2003jun11_IABC.html, June 11, 2003.

Meade, Peter, "The '$8B Start-up' Starts Out," *Communications News*, July 2000.

"Ned Barnholt, Agilent President and CEO, Discusses 'Culture, People and Processes' at the 2002 *BusinessWeek* CEO Summit," Agilent press release, http://www.agilent.com/about/newsroom/features/2002sep30_bizweek.html, September 30, 2002.

Roth, Daniel, "How to Cut Pay, Lay Off 8,000 People, and Still Have Workers Who Love You: It's Easy, Just Follow the Agilent Way," *Fortune*, February 4, 2002, pp. 62–65.

Sperling, Ed, and Jeff Chappell, "Biggest Test," *Electronic News*, November 25, 2002, pp. 22–23.

—Kirk H. Beetz

■■■

Colleen Barrett

1944–

President and chief operating officer, Southwest Airlines Company

Nationality: American.

Born: 1944, in Bellows Falls, Vermont.

Education: Becker Junior College, 1964.

Family: Married, 1970 (divorced).

Career: Mathews & Branscomb law firm, 1968–1970, secretary; Southwest Airlines Company, 1978–2001, began as corporate secretary and became vice president of administration and then executive vice president of customers; 2001–, president and chief operating officer.

Awards: Compass Award, Woman's Leadership Exchange, 2002; Kupfer Distinguished Executive Award, 2002.

Address: Southwest Airlines, 2702 Love Field Drive, P.O. Box 36611, Dallas, Texas 75235-1611; http://www.southwest.com.

Colleen Barrett. *AP/Wide World Photos.*

■ Colleen Barrett joined Southwest Airlines Company in 1978 as a corporate secretary and rose through the ranks to become the company's president and chief operating officer. Barrett's development of Southwest's innovative customer-focused culture made her a driving force in the airline's growth into one of the largest and most profitable major airlines. Barrett is highly regarded by industry analysts for her ability to meet the needs of employees, customers, and shareholders.

TAKING ADVANTAGE OF OPPORTUNITIES

As a girl, Barrett was fascinated with the law and worked as a legal secretary for an uncle. She could not afford to attend law school, however, so she went to a junior college in her home state of Vermont. In 1968 the 23-year-old college graduate was hired by the law firm of Mathews & Branscomb in San Antonio, Texas. She ended up working with Herb Kelleher, marking the beginning of a long-term business relationship that was to change her life. Looking back on those early days, Barrett recalled that Kelleher took her everywhere, from court rooms to the state's legislative halls in Austin, Texas. She thought that all legal secretaries engaged in this sort of work. In an interview with Margaret Allen of the *Houston Business Journal*, Barrett recalled, "I wasn't smart enough to know I was being given some golden opportunities that most people don't get in a lifetime" (August 24, 2001).

Barrett soon became indispensable to the eccentric Kelleher. When he and the San Antonio businessman Rollin King decided to create Southwest Airlines, Barrett became an integral part of Kelleher's efforts to gain legal approval for the fledgling airline. The two ended up spending many sixteen-hour days together in the effort to get the airline off the ground. Barrett maintained ties with Kelleher but did not officially join the airline staff until 1978, when she became corporate secretary. Barrett's intuitive business sense helped her move up the corporate ladder to become vice president of administration and then vice president of customers. Nevertheless, she remained Kelleher's personal spokesperson and confidante and continued to oversee his scheduling. In fact, the two became so inseparable at Southwest that they were known simply as "Herb and Colleen."

ARCHITECT OF CORPORATE CULTURE

Although sometimes described as shy and introverted, Barrett is credited with the Southwest corporate culture that stresses customer satisfaction and employee participation. In an interview with Sharon Shinn for *BizEd*, Barrett noted, "We tell job applicants we're in the customer service business. We just happen to provide airline transportation" (March/April 2003). Barrett's success in guiding the company along this path was evident when she worked as vice president in the customer relations department. Under her guidance, Southwest typically beat all the other airlines year in and year out in the airline industry's "Triple Crown" of performance ratings. The airline routinely scored highest in on-time record, lowest in lost luggage, and lowest in customer complaints.

As a longtime leader of the company's hiring program, Barrett focused on hiring employees who wanted more than just a job. She told Erika Rasmusson in an interview for *Sales & Marketing Management*, "We start from day one, trying to make people understand that we are looking for people who want to join a cause, not get a paycheck" (December 2001). To achieve her goals with employees, Barrett strengthened the company's efforts at mentoring and coaching to include imparting knowledge about the airline's history and an understanding of what type of company the employees had joined. Southwest's reputation as a good company to work for became so well known that in 2000 Southwest received 216,000 résumés for a little more than five thousand positions. Southwest consistently has had one of the lowest employee turnover rates in the industry.

BECOMES COMPANY DIRECTOR

Barrett was rewarded for her continuing commitment to Southwest with her appointment to the post of president and COO in 2001, after Kelleher retired. Her promotion took place only three months before the terrorist attacks of September 11, 2001. The attacks, which used commercial airlines, had a tremendous negative impact on most airlines and resulted in a big decline in ticket sales. Although Southwest experienced passenger loads well below normal, Barrett and the company slowly built up passenger confidence, partly through an advertising campaign that began on September 19—just eight days after the attacks. The ads focused on Southwest employees' uniting to get Americans to fly again. Less than a week later Barrett and Southwest launched an airfare sale that offered travelers another incentive to resume flying. Barrett also gave refunds to passengers who wanted to cancel their flights and took a pay cut to help the airline through the crisis.

Barrett noted in *Sales & Marketing Management*, "We have tried to be a constant in what has otherwise been an uncertain environment" (December 2001). Part of that constancy was that Southwest maintained all of its 2,700 daily flights and retained its 32,000 employees. Barrett's efforts produced results, and the airline went on to have profitable years in both 2001 and 2002. In fact, through 2003 Southwest was the only major carrier to remain consistently profitable since the 2001 terrorist attacks. Its fourth-quarter profit in 2003 was $66 million, or eight cents per share, which marked an increase from the $42 million, or five cents per share, of a year earlier.

APPROACH TO MANAGEMENT

If anything typified Barrett's approach to management and business, it was hard work—she usually worked 16-hour days. Nevertheless, industry analysts described her as having a laid-back management style. Although she stressed customer satisfaction, her fundamental philosophy put employees first and customers second. Barrett always believed that making employees happy resulted in better service for the customers, who would then want to fly Southwest. Barrett also emphasized honesty and direct communication with employees. She has garnered complete loyalty from Southwest employees by fostering ownership of the company as a family. For example, in addition to traditional approaches, such as sending out cards on employees' birthdays or anniversary dates of hire, the company sends notes of sympathy and condolence to employees when their family members are sick or die.

Barrett is also known for her ability to respond to difficulties and crisis, as in the aftermath of the terrorist attacks, a trait she credits to her mentor, Kelleher. Noting that opportunities usually come only once, she told Shinn in *BizEd*, "If you don't take them, someone else will" (March/April 2003).

RECOGNIZED FOR LEADERSHIP

Barrett's success made her the top-ranked woman executive in the airline industry. In January 2004 J. C. Penney Company's board of directors elected her a director of the company. Throughout her career, Barrett was known for her honesty and dedication. During a ceremony at Texas A&M, when Barrett received the 2002 Kupfer Distinguished Executive Award, Kelleher was quoted on *Mays Business Online* as saying, "She is the antidote to the questions about integrity in American business" (May 2002).

See also entry on Southwest Airlines Co. in *International Directory of Company Histories.*

SOURCES FOR FURTHER INFORMATION

Allen, Margaret, "Southwest Airlines Head Takes Flight with Ground Control," *Houston Business Journal*, August 24, 2001, p. 2.

Clark, Kim, "Nothing But the Plane Truth," *U.S. News & World Report*, December 31, 2001, p. 58.

Engeler, Amy, "A Busy Boss Can Never Fly Solo," *Business Month*, August 1990, p. 22.

Rasmusson, Erika, "Flying High: How Southwest Airlines Is Inspiring Loyalty in Trying Times," *Sales & Marketing Management*, December 2001, p. 55.

Shinn, Sharon, "LUV Colleen," *BizEd*, March/April 2003, pp. 18–23.

White, Judith Macintosh, "Colleen Barret: Redefining the Rules," *Mays Business Online*, http://maysbusiness.tamu.edu/2002/may/features/barrett.htm.

—David Petechuk

■ ■ ■

Craig R. Barrett

1939–

Chief executive officer, Intel

Nationality: American.

Born: August 29, 1939, in San Francisco, California.

Education: Stanford University, PhD, 1964.

Family: Married Barbara (lawyer and politician who ran for governor of Arizona in 1994); children: two.

Career: Stanford University, 1965–1974, faculty member; Intel, 1974, focused on quality assurance; 1984, vice president; 1992, elected to board of directors; 1993, COO; 1997, president and COO; 1998, CEO.

Awards: NATO Fellowship to conduct research at National Physical Laboratory in England, 1965; Hardy Gold Medal of American Institute of Mining and Metallurgical Engineers, 1969; Fullbright Fellowship to Technical University of Denmark, Copenhagen, 1972.

Publications: *The Principles of Engineering Materials* (with William D. Nix and Alan S. Tetelman), 1973.

Address: 2200 Mission College Boulevard, Santa Clara, California 95052–8119; http://www.intel.com.

Craig R. Barrett. *AP/World Wide Photos.*

■ In his first ten years working for Intel, Craig R. Barrett earned a reputation for his creative solutions to nettlesome production problems. In the early 1980s Intel was on the verge of being swamped by Japanese manufacturers of computer chips, and Barrett was tapped to find ways to make Intel more competitive against these manufacturers. Through intense study and then determined leadership over reluctant departmental managers, Barrett brought greater efficiency to Intel's manufacturing of chips and higher quality to the chips that were produced. This success helped Intel survive a mid-1980s decline in revenues and made Barrett one of Intel's stars. When he became CEO, Barrett responded to the 1999–2001 decline in the computer chip market by diversifying and expanding Intel's manufacturing capacity. His diversifying program and the expansion of Intel's manufacturing capability enabled Intel to respond to a boom in demand for high-technology products that began in 2002, which helped the company retain its dominant position in the manufacturing of microprocessors.

UNIVERSITY FACULTY MEMBER

As a college student, Barrett was very much interested in how pure science could become applied science. At the age of 26, he earned a doctorate at Stanford University in materials science, a field that allowed him to combine his interests in physics and in engineering. As a faculty member at Stanford (1965–1974), he made a name for himself by publishing 40 scientific papers along with *The Principles of Engineering Materials*, which quickly became a standard textbook and, after periodic revision, remained in use in classrooms even in the 2000s.

Barrett wanted to see his theoretical research turn into practical, useful products, so he was happy to take a sabbatical from Stanford during 1973 and join Intel as a consultant. Although it was still a young company, Intel was grossing $66 million per year in sales of its DRAM (dynamic random-access memory) and related chips. The company had developed ceramic casings for its chips, allowing them to survive wide variations in temperatures. This meant that computers using these chips did not require the same isolation in cold rooms that computers had previously required. This development laid the foundation for modern personal computing, because computers could be put in almost any room, even in a home.

Still, there was a problem. Only about 20 percent of the chips Intel manufactured were functional; others would work for a while and then fail. It turned out that when they were in use, the chips generated enough heat to vaporize water in the ceramic casings, and the water corroded the metal circuits in the chips. Barrett's assignment was to solve the water vapor problem. His solution was to drill small holes in the casings and then bake the chips. While this method did remove the water vapor, the baking usually destroyed the chips. When Barrett returned to teaching at Stanford, his work at Intel seemed to have failed.

BARRETT HAD WHAT WAS WANTED

George Moore, Robert Noyce, and Andy Grove, Intel's leaders, were able to build a successful high-tech manufacturing company partly because of their astute recognition of talent. Barrett had qualities and qualifications these people especially admired—a PhD, a creative mind, leadership in academe, and expertise in both physics and engineering. His passion for his work was evident. Grove admired Barrett's persistence in trying to solve problems. Barrett had been glad to leave Intel in 1973 and return to teaching, but in 1974 he found himself dissatisfied with being a university teacher. At Intel he had worked on a real problem that had effects on people's lives, and he missed that kind of work. In 1974, when Intel offered him a chance to return on a full-time basis, he did so. His academic background, as well as his insistence on orderly, carefully reasoned research, quickly earned him the nickname "the Professor." Given that his mandate from Moore, Noyce, and Grove was to find ways to make production more efficient, he focused on manufacturing.

MAKING INTEL COMPETITIVE

In the 1970s Intel had two major lines of products: DRAMs and microprocessors, with DRAMs being the core of its business. Noyce had been the one who turned the DRAM into the major alternative to the magnetic memory cores that previously had been required by computers. A small DRAM chip from 1970 could hold four times (1,024 bits) more memory than the magnetic memory cores could hold. When Intel began manufacturing DRAMs in quantity, 70 percent of them were functional at the end of the manufacturing process, which in those days was a very good success rate; it meant that Intel could sell enough of them to be profitable. In 1970 Intel's introduction of the DRAM to mass production began the revolution that would make computers small enough to fit on desks.

The chips were made in factories called "fabs," short for "fabrication." Chips were circuited in big blocks that eventually were sliced into wafers, the working parts of the chips. The wafers would be encased in ceramic and then tested to see whether they worked. Those that failed the test would be broken up and their materials recycled. The rest would be sold to computer manufacturers, manufacturers of calculators, manufacturers of medical monitoring equipment, and others.

However, there were problems with Intel's fabs, which became evident as the marketplace for computer components became more competitive. The fabs were big, awkwardly laid out, and clumsy, which resulted from the experimental nature of Intel's enterprise: Intel scientists and engineers devised the production process as they went along, adding and subtracting equipment as they sought to improve the products. Much of the equipment for manufacturing chips was invented by Intel's workers in this way. Barrett focused on pulling together into coherent production plans the work that his colleagues were doing. He achieved straightforward outlines for the layout of the fabs as a way to meet Intel's production goals.

Barrett was helped by Intel's hiring practices for assembly workers. These workers had starting wages of $30,000 per year, a princely sum in the 1970s, which attracted intelligent, well-educated people to do the dull jobs required in the fabs. Even so, the incessant demands that they work long hours and meet ever-higher production goals created problems with morale. Barrett became a buffer for the workers, absorbing the demands of management and then finding ways for them to be met. When he transmitted the demands to the fab workers, he would also provide the solutions for meeting those demands. His efforts resulted in more efficient workplaces and contributed to his becoming a vice president in 1984.

THE CHALLENGE FROM JAPAN

Barrett's rise to power was affected by one of Intel's production problems in the early 1980s: only 50 percent of its DRAM chips were functional when they came out of the fabs. During the 1970s this rate had not been a problem. Through aggressive marketing and advances in the amount of memory in its DRAMS and the power of microprocessors, Intel sold its products in such high volume that it realized big profits even when quality declined. It was becoming a billion-dollar company when Japanese manufacturers knocked the legs out from under Intel's most important products, the DRAMs.

Japanese high-tech corporations were tough competitors, employing industrial spies, manufacturing illegal copies of

Intel's 8086 microprocessor, and refusing to pay royalties when they had licensing agreements with Intel to use Intel technology. The Japanese corporations Fujitsu, Hitachi, NEC, and Toshiba invested heavily in research, and in 1979, Fujitsu had a 64k (64,000 bits of memory) DRAM chip ready for the mass market, beating Intel to the 64k level by two years. This advantage meant that Fujitsu had a huge market advantage over Intel—one that Intel was not able to overcome. Further, the Japanese corporations had much greater financial reserves than Intel, and they started a price war for the U.S. market. Hitachi told its salespeople to undersell all producers of DRAMs by 10 percent, no matter how low the price went. (This practice is known as "dumping," the selling of products below the cost to manufacture them in order to drive competitors out of business.) By 1985 Intel was the tenth-largest manufacturer of semiconductors in the world, and it was losing money at a prodigious rate.

Will Kaufman, vice president in charge of quality assurance, identified some of the aspects of manufacturing that the Japanese manufacturers did better than Intel, but his views were not accepted by his superiors. Kaufman learned that Japanese manufacturers were achieving a 75 percent success rate in manufacturing DRAMs (meaning that only 25 percent of new chips failed testing) and 98 percent success with microprocessors, in contrast to Intel's 50 percent and 80 percent rates of manufacturing viable DRAM and microprocessing chips, respectively. Barrett seemed to have paid attention, because he launched an extensive study of manufacturing practices at Intel's fabs in Arizona, California, Oregon, Israel, and Malaysia. He found that the Oregon and Malaysian fabs outproduced the other operations. Especially interesting was the Malaysian fab, where workers were paid much less than their counterparts at Intel, yet achieved quality and productivity comparable to those of the Japanese manufacturers.

With Intel's DRAMs losing money by the millions of dollars per year, Moore and Grove eventually decided to give up manufacturing DRAMs and focus on microprocessors. The company had already been heading in that direction. The managers of fabs were subject to rigorous evaluations of their performances, including how much revenue their fabs generated for Intel. With Intel's DRAMs losing money and the microprocessors generating 70 percent margins, fab managers were already taking manufacturing time away from DRAMs and adding it to microprocessors.

MANAGEMENT STYLE

Barrett was devoted to exercise. He was known to do two hundred sit-ups every day when bad weather prevented him from pursuing his more demanding outdoor exercise regimen. At six foot, two inches in height, with the muscular build of a professional athlete, he was an intimidating figure. He had a short temper, but he was not prone to the loud tirades that typified Grove's and other executives' responses to poor employee performance. Instead, Barrett spoke in a low voice, almost a monotone, while he patiently described what he wanted from employees.

Although he did not receive the official title of COO until 1993, Barrett had assumed that role by 1985. With a mandate to focus Intel's production on microprocessors, he began what Intel employees called "death marches." The death marches consisted of Barrett's traveling to every Intel facility in the world repeatedly. He wanted each Intel facility to run like every other Intel facility, and he wanted fabs to look exactly alike. Thus, any solution to a problem in one plant could apply to all the others and be duplicated with precision in each. One goal was to make Intel's production predictable. This aim became important as U.S. corporations adopted a "just-in-time" process that reduced inventory expenses with the purchase of parts, such as microprocessors, for delivery just before they were needed. By creating a production process in which Intel's production of chips could be predicted, the company was able to deliver chips where they were wanted, when they were needed.

Moreover, Barrett was interested in how the Malaysian fab in Penang succeeded in outproducing the other fabs in quality. One result was the creation of an uncluttered, straightforward arrangement of fab equipment. The fab in Penang had burned down and had been rebuilt using some of what Intel's engineers had learned from experimenting with the fab process during the 1970s. Barrett encouraged employees to learn how other fabs worked and to cooperate instead of compete with one another to meet production goals.

The tangible results of Barrett's efforts were $1.9 billion in gross revenues for Intel in 1987 and $2.9 billion in gross revenues for 1988, a remarkable 60 percent increase in one year. By the end of the 1980s the 8086 microprocessor had evolved into the 80386, the most advanced chip for the mass market in the world; it was appearing in computers large and small in part because Intel's new predictable productivity and improved quality made it ideal for the manufacturers of computers. By then "the Professor" had a new nickname at Intel: "Mr. Quality."

HEIR APPARENT

By 1993, when Barrett was named COO, his work on making the fabs efficient and reliable had had a valuable side effect. Back in the 1960s Gordon Moore, who was to become Intel's longtime CEO, had coined "Moore's law," which first stated that the power of computer chips would double every year but was soon revised to project doubling every eighteen months. With the 80386, Intel learned that advances in its chips' architectures had predictable limits, allowing Intel to know when a new chip, such as the 80486 or the Pentium, would be needed to replace the previous chip architecture. Combined with predictable manufacturing, Intel was able to tell customers when its next big chip would be available and what processing power could be expected.

Despite vigorous competition from Advanced Micro Devices (AMD) and Cyrix, both U.S. manufacturers of microprocessors, Intel dominated the microprocessor market both for mass consumer computers and for high-end corporate computers. By the time Barrett became president in 1997, more than 80 percent of the world's computers had Intel chips in them. By then, Barrett was widely thought to be the person who would replace Andy Grove as CEO. Although he was only a few years younger than Grove, Barrett still seemed like a youthful up-and-comer who could replace the venerable master when the time came.

Barrett continued his long-distance trips, always flying on commercial airliners and eschewing private corporate aircraft—he was conscious of economizing and saving the company money. He lived in Arizona and used the local Intel fab as his headquarters. His shares in Intel had made him a millionaire. With his wealth he purchased 10,000 acres of wild land in Montana, where he enjoyed hiking and hunting. When Grove was named Intel's chairman of the board in 1998, Barrett replaced him as CEO. The transition was hailed in the press as a model of consistency.

DECLINE AND TRIUMPH

Then the world crashed in on Barrett and Intel. A worldwide recession dampened demand for computers. Corporate leaders began to believe that buying every new, faster microprocessor was not necessarily a benefit to their companies' bottom lines. AMD's new Athlon microprocessors were gaining more and more admiration, stealing clients from Intel. From 1998 to 2000 AMD's market share grew from 11 percent to 20 percent, at Intel's expense. For about nine months in 2000, AMD actually was marketing the world's fastest computer chip, displacing Intel, which had held the top spot for 10 years. That its latest version of its Pentium 4 microprocessor eventually reclaimed the top spot did not prevent Intel from losing millions of dollars to AMD. Such publications as *Fortune* and *Business Weekly* said that Barrett was at fault for Intel's problems and derided Barrett's efforts to repair the damage done to it as weakening the company. Intel shares worth $250,000 in June 2000 fell to a value of only $65,000 in six months. In 2001 Intel laid off five thousand employees. Profits declined from $10.5 billion in 2000 to $700 million in 2001.

Barrett's response to declining revenues was to diversify his company's products and to make multibillion-dollar capital improvements to Intel's manufacturing capacity, flying in the face of a declining demand for Intel's products. Barrett drove himself hard. Intel had 30 different business locations around the world, and he continued to visit each one every year. Moreover, he worked Mondays and Fridays at corporate headquarters in Santa Clara and Tuesdays through Thursdays in Arizona. He was constantly in motion.

It was his opinion that computers were undergoing a transformation in which electronic commerce (dubbed "e-commerce"), the Internet, and telecommunications would dominate the marketplace. In 2001 Barrett directed the investment of $11.5 billion (45 percent of revenues) into research and manufacturing. Intel actually accelerated production of its Pentium chips in a weak market; $7.5 billion went to upgrading fabs. Billions more were spent on acquiring existing manufacturers of parts for cell phones, Internet servers, and Website hosting. For instance, $2 billion was spent to purchase Giga, a manufacturer of chips used with fiber-optic switches. Another $2 billion went to purchase Level One Communications, a chip manufacturer for broadband communications. By and large, journalists thought Barrett was trying to spend himself out of a desperate situation that he had created by not responding sooner to the changing marketplace.

In 2002 Intel's fortunes turned around. The world began recovering from the recession, and the market for chips to be used for telephones to high-end computers boomed; out of all the world's chip manufacturers, Intel was best situated to take advantage of the economic recovery. By then Intel had invested $28 billion in new technology. Barrett told his subordinate managers that they were to take on responsibility for making decisions about production without having to clear those decisions with him first. This new freedom resulted in greater flexibility and speed in responding to market changes. Furthermore, Intel was able to offer complete chip sets for products, whereas competitors could offer only one or two of the chip sets needed for a given product; this convenience made Intel a one-stop place in which to shop for many corporate consumers.

In 2003 the acquired companies grossed over $5 billion dollars for Intel, and Intel's net earnings were $5.4 billion, up 60 percent. Research enabled Intel to manufacture chips thinner than human hair, improving the company's productivity relative to raw materials. Its Pentium 4 continued its predictable course of development, peaking at 4.5 gigahertz (4.5 billion clock cycles per second) with the last version of the chip arriving in February 2004, released several months ahead of its deadline. The company forged ahead with its development of the Titanium chip, which would be 10 gigahertz and serve the needs of high-end users, such as manufacturers of automobiles and space-exploration technology. Barrett had the reputation of being a risk taker, but he took on the image of a prophet after Intel's exploitation of a burgeoning market.

See also entry on Intel Corporation in *International Directory of Company Histories*.

SOURCES FOR FURTHER INFORMATION

Edwards, Cliff, and Ira Sager, "INTEL," *BusinessWeek*, October 15, 2001, p. 80.

Jackson, Tim, *Inside INTEL: Andy Grove and the Rise of the World's Most Powerful Chip Company*, New York: Dutton, 1997.

Popovich, Ken, "Barrett Inside: Intel Diversifies—CEO Steers Company into Net, Communications," *eWEEK*, November 6, 2000, p. 1.

Roth, Daniel, "Craig Barrett Inside: Can This Nature-Loving Onetime Professor Lead Intel out of the Woods?" *Fortune*, December 18, 2000, p. 246.

Schlender, Brent, "Intel Unleashes Its Inner Attila: Why in the World Are Craig Barrett and Andy Grove Smiling?" *Fortune*, October 15, 2001, p. 168.

—Kirk H. Beetz

■ ■ ■

Matthew William Barrett

1944–

Chief executive officer, Barclays Bank

Nationality: Irish.

Born: September 20, 1944, in County Kerry, Ireland.

Education: Attended Harvard Business School.

Family: Married Irene Korsak, c. 1967 (divorced, 1995); married Anne-Marie Sten, 1997 (separated); children (first marriage): four.

Career: Bank of Montreal, 1962–1967, clerk; 1967, management trainee; 1967–1987, held various management positions; 1987–1989, chief operating officer; 1989, CEO; 1990–1998, chairman and CEO; Barclays Bank, 1999–, CEO.

Awards: Canadian Catalyst prize; Officer of the Order of Canada, 1994; Canada's Outstanding CEO of the Year, 1995; Communicator of the Year Award, British Association of Communicators in Business, 2001.

Address: Barclays Bank, 54 Lombard Street, London, EC3P 3AH, England; http://www.barclays.com.

Matthew William Barrett. © *AFP/Corbis.*

■ Matthew William Barrett worked for the Bank of Montreal for more than 30 years, serving as CEO for the final 10 years. He retired in 1998 but was persuaded to join the troubled Barclays Bank in London as CEO in 1999. Within three years he improved the bank's performance to the point that Barclays shares outperformed the FTSE All-Share Index (which includes approximately eight hundred companies) by more than 39 percent. Industry analysts say that Barrett believed strongly in value-based management analysis and was able to get the most out of his staff thanks in part to his charm and wit.

A DEFINING CHANGE

Barrett was born and raised in County Kerry, Ireland, where his father struggled to make a living as a musician playing in local dance halls in the 1950s. Since the family was relatively poor, Barrett was encouraged by his father to enter the banking business; in 1962, at the age of 18, he became a clerk at the London headquarters of the Bank of Montreal. Shortly afterward Barrett's father died of a heart attack, and Barrett was left as the sole supporter of his mother and sister. In an interview with Ruki Sayid for the *Mirror*, Barrett recalled, "It aged me overnight. I was the man of the family; it changed me from being a young man having a good time into a serious career banker" (October 18, 2003).

With his newfound focus, Barrett impressed his employers enough to win a promotion to management trainee at the Bank of Montreal's main office in Canada in 1967. As part of his training he attended Harvard Business School, eventually becoming an expert in retail banking. Barrett steadily rose through the ranks at the Bank of Montreal and was appointed president in 1987. In 1989 Barrett took over as chief executive officer.

Barrett paid close attention to the bank's diversification strategy, in terms of both line of business and geography. He oversaw nine years of record profits, and by the time he left the bank, more than half its earnings came from outside Canada. He was also credited with guiding the company into the realm of Internet banking. Overall, during Barrett's 10-year tenure as chief executive, the Bank of Montreal's market cap quadrupled.

MERGER FAILURE LEADS TO NEW JOB

Although he had been extremely successful in turning around the weak Bank of Montreal, Barrett's plans for continued expansion finally met a roadblock. He planned for the bank to merge with the Royal Bank of Canada; his goal was to form a North American behemoth that could compete head to head with any bank in the world and would reinvigorate Canada's role in global financial services. The Canadian government eventually ruled against the merger, and shortly afterward Barrett decided to retire, a decision many analysts credited to the failed merger.

Barrett's retirement did not last long. In October 1999, at the age of 55, he decided to accept an offer to become the CEO of Barclays Bank in England. Many saw Barrett's appointment as a new start for what banking insiders described as a stuffy 300-year-old British institution. Succeeding the previous "blue-blood" bosses, Barrett was a rare non-British leader of the bank.

EXPANDS BUSINESS AND REDUCES OVERHEAD

Barrett took over the reins of Barclays during a period of upheaval. The company had been Britain's largest bank in 1982, with assets that ranked fifth in the world. In 1988 it had 4,200 branches in 83 countries and $190 billion in assets. However, the British banking industry faced turbulent times in the late 1980s and 1990s, and many competitors from both within and without Britain were successful in luring customers away from Barclays. Many blamed the bank's demise on its "inbred culture," and according to John H. Christy, writing in *Forbes*, "Barrett was a blast of fresh air" (July 23, 2001).

One of the first areas Barrett focused on as CEO was that of the Internet. He used his Web savvy to establish a number of online banking services, including free Internet access for life for new Barclays customers and online share dealing. In 2000 he oversaw the launch of the company's business-to-business Web site.

Barrett proceeded to attack what many analysts saw as Barclays' swollen overhead. Setting a target of $1.4 billion in cut costs by 2003, Barrett ordered the shutting down of 171 Barclays branches, mostly in rural areas, and the laying off of numerous staff. At the same time, he focused on widening the bank's product range, as he had done at the Bank of Montreal. In August 2000 he negotiated Barclays' $7.6 billion purchase of Woolwich, Great Britain's leading mortgage banker. The move also added Woolwich's Internet operation, making Barclays the biggest Internet bank in Great Britain, with 1.4 million online customers.

Barrett further bolstered Barclays' business by forming a distribution alliance with Legal & General, one of Great Britain's leading suppliers of pension plans and life and health insurance, a move which gave Barclays customers a wider range of savings options. Banking analysts saw the Woolwich takeover and the relationship with Legal & General as overcoming two of Barclays' biggest challenges, namely, its weaknesses in Great Britain's mortgage business and in long-term savings.

THE PR WARS

While Barrett was making headway in quickly turning Barclays around, he committed a few missteps, especially in terms of public relations. His closure of many Barclays branches in rural areas resulted in a massive public outcry. Many complained that the closings left rural communities with no banking options. Customers demonstrated, and Barrett and Barclays apologized for the way the closings had been handled; the bank then forged a deal with post offices so customers could cash and pay in checks.

Barrett took additional criticism when it was learned that he received £1.3 million for just three months' work at a time when the bank was drastically cutting costs that directly affected customers. Barrett further raised the ire of many in the public when he commanded the closure of one hundred Woolwich branches by the end of 2000, a move which resulted in the losses of one thousand jobs.

In spite of bad publicity, many analysts saw Barrett's tenure at Barclays as successful. By the end of 2002 Barclays had experienced a steady rise in profits. The bank's 2003 pretax profit increased 15 percent over the previous year, surpassing analysts' estimates. The bank's private-client, corporate, and investment banking units all grew stronger in 2003, while credit quality improved.

VALUE-BASED MANAGEMENT

According to industry analysts, Barrett based much of his business strategy on value-based management. The approach focuses on creating value for all stakeholders in an organization, including customers, shareholders, employees, and vendors. Essentially, value is created as long as the return on a business or an investment is higher than the cost of capital invested in the business. Barrett's adherence to this approach was evident when he led Barclays out of the car-leasing business because the cost of capital was not keeping up with economic earnings. He then invested the realized capital from the sale elsewhere. Writing in *Forbes*, the analyst John H. Christy noted, "By tying many of Barclay's incentive schemes to economic—not reported—profit, Barrett sets higher hurdles for his managers to clear" (July 23, 2001).

Barrett, who preferred to be called "Matt" over the more formal "Matthew," was long seen as an employer who stressed communication with his employees and the importance of ethics in the banking industry. Within his first two years at Barclays, he spoke with more than 14,000 employees at events in the United Kingdom, Paris, New York, Madrid, and Lisbon. In accepting the Communicator of the Year Award, Barrett was quoted in the *CiB enews* as saying, "It's through communications that strong leaders have an ability to add value to colleagues. There needs to be a conscious value take-out by the recipient—knowledge should be shared, not hoarded" (November 2001). Barrett's belief in the sharing of knowledge was evident at the Bank of Montreal as well. In 1994 he created the bank's Institute of Learning in order to create an atmosphere of continued intellectual engagement, so that the bank and its employees could maintain a competitive advantage in the rapidly and constantly changing environment of the banking world.

Barrett was known for his efforts to ensure employee diversification, including through the hiring of women and minorities. He received the Canadian Catalyst prize for fostering the advancement of women in the banking industry. In his 10 years as chairman of the Bank of Montreal he constantly updated the bank's mode of operation, actively encouraging the employment of women and members of minority groups in senior positions and bringing in social scientists to advise senior executives. He continued to use this approach at Barclays.

Another aspect of Barrett's management approach was his willingness to lead banking into new areas of operation. He initiated computerization at the Bank of Montreal long before any of his competitors did so; he similarly strengthened the Internet-banking component at Barclays. A proponent of a leader's ability to think laterally, Barrett commented in the *CiB enews* that company leaders "need to catch the waves of change early, and be prepared to take ideas and input from a variety of different sources" (November 2001).

MOVING ON

In late 2003 Barclays announced that Barrett would be leaving his post as CEO of Barclays to become chairman of the board by the end of 2004. The appointment came under criticism by some industry insiders, who noted that Barrett did little to assuage the public's perception of him as a "fat cat." He committed another public-relations gaff when he stated that he would not use bank credit cards because the interest rates were too high. However, the communications management consultant George Pitcher wrote in *Marketing Week* that Barrett's comment was to be commended, calling it "a simple point. But not one you would expect MPs, with their tax-free allowances, their wives as secretaries and credit from any number of organizations in the form of freebies, readily to understand" (October 23, 2003).

See also entries on Bank of Montreal and Barclays PLC in *International Directory of Company Histories.*

SOURCES FOR FURTHER INFORMATION

"Canada Dry at Barclays," *Observer*, February 17, 2002, http://observer.guardian.co.uk/business/story/0,6903,651338,00.html.

Christy, John H., "Phoenix Rising," *Forbes.com*, July 23, 2001, http://www.forbes.com/global/2001/0723/032.html.

Jones, Neil, "Making the Light Bulbs Go On," *CiB enews*, November 2001, http://www.abraca.net/cib_enews/cib_archives/barrett_profile.html.

Pitcher, George, "Barclays Boss Should Be Credited for Card Claims," *Marketing Week*, October 23, 2003, p. 29.

Sayid, Ruki, "Secret Life of Barclays Plank Barrett," *Mirror*, October 18, 2003, http://www.mirror.co.uk/news/allnews.

—David Petechuk

■ ■ ■

John M. Barth

1946–

Chairman and chief executive officer, Johnson Controls

Nationality: American.

Born: 1946.

Education: Gannon College, BS, 1977.

Career: Johnson Controls, 1969–?, industrial engineer; ?–1990, head of plastics group; 1990–1992, head of automotive business; 1992–1998, executive vice president; 1998–2002, president and COO; 2002–2004, CEO; 2004–, chairman and CEO.

Address: Johnson Controls, 5757 North Green Bay Avenue, Milwaukee, Wisconsin 53209-4408; http://www.jci.com.

■ John M. Barth embodied the success story of the loyal, longterm employee who worked his way to the top of a company. In its 117 years Johnson Controls had only six chief executives; Barth was hand groomed for the job by the well-liked chief who preceded him, James Keyes, who stayed on as chairman for another three years after stepping down as CEO. Barth's challenge would not be to turn his company around; in fact, Johnson Controls was an unequivocal leader in its industry. Rather, Barth needed to find a way to sustain the momentum and success that had already been instilled at the company by his predecessors. Adding a warm, personal approach to the executive role, he both met that challenge and created his own legacy to match those of previous CEOs. By 2004 Johnson Controls had enjoyed its 29th consecutive year of earnings growth while also advancing its visibility as an involved and responsible corporate citizen.

As of 2004 Johnson Controls, Wisconsin's largest company, employed over 118,000 persons worldwide. Founded in 1885, the firm began as a producer of electric room thermostats, later expanding its inventory to include other energy and security products and services for buildings. Later entering the automotive-supplier market, Johnson manufactured and marketed batteries and seats, eventually becoming a leading producer of interiors and electronics for new vehicles.

A LOYAL EMPLOYEE

Born in 1946, Barth joined Johnson Controls just a few years after his completion of schooling at Carnegie Tech. His first position with the company was as an industrial engineer in 1969. He later returned to school, earning his bachelor's degree from Gannon College in 1977. Loyal and committed to the success of the company, he served in a variety of operating-management positions over the next 15 years, heading Johnson's plastics group and, starting in 1990, its automotive business in Michigan.

Barth's technical skills and management abilities assured him of continued success; also of key importance was his close relationship with the former CEO James Keyes, who had joined the company two years before Barth. The two worked together for many years, predating Keyes's own promotion to CEO in 1988. They shared corporate philosophies and objectives and jointly trained several other managers for higher positions.

During Keyes's tenure as chief executive officer Barth was elected executive vice president in 1992, then became president and chief operating officer in 1998. He held those positions through 2002, at which time he took over for Keyes as CEO. When Keyes finally retired from his duties as chairman in 2004, Barth was named to head the company's board.

AN OUTSTANDING CORPORATE CITIZEN

When Johnson's board of directors announced Barth's election in July 2002, Keyes stated in a company press release, "John Barth and I have worked together for 17 years, and I am confident that he will strengthen Johnson Controls' commitment to our customers and our shareholders, as well as our employees, our suppliers, and our communities" (July 24, 2002, http://www.prnewswire.com/cgi-bin/stories.pl?ACCT=105&STORY=/www/story/07-24-2002/0001770789). True to his commitment, Barth continued Johnson's legacy of success while also keeping the company visible in social and civic communities.

During Barth's term of leadership, Johnson Controls became the only company to twice win the Management Excellence Award—in 2002 and 2003—bestowed by Robert W. Baird & Company and the Executive MBA Alumni Association at the University of Wisconsin–Milwaukee. The company was honored as Corporation of the Year in 2003 by the National Minority Supplier Development Council. The award represented the highest recognition a corporation could receive for conducting business with minority- and women-owned firms. In 2004 Barth was named chairman of that council.

With Barth at the helm, Johnson Controls became the only automotive-parts supplier to make *BusinessWeek*'s Top 50 Performers list in 2004. Barth told the magazine that he considered customer relations to be the job of every employee. He also stated that in order for a company to improve its bottom line, the company had to focus on helping its customers improve their bottom lines. Also in 2004 the World Environment Center selected Johnson Controls for its Gold Medal for International Corporate Achievement in Sustainable Development. Elsewhere Barth committed a hefty company contribution toward the creation of the National Underground Railroad Freedom Center and museum in Cincinnati, Ohio.

Barth had endeared himself to the community before: In 2003, five days after the 77th annual Milwaukee Holiday Parade was canceled due to a lack of financial support, Barth heard the news on the radio while getting out of the shower. He and his wife had just relocated to downtown Milwaukee from the Detroit area; realizing what a tradition the parade had become for the community, Barth hurriedly gathered a number of corporate managers. Later, from the company's downtown lobby—with a choir of boys and girls singing Christmas carols behind him—Barth announced that Johnson Controls would rescue the parade, which would go on as planned. Yes, Virginia, Santa was alive and well—and living in Milwaukee.

See also entry on Johnson Controls, Inc. in *International Directory of Company Histories.*

SOURCES FOR FURTHER INFORMATION

Content, Thomas, "Executive to Become CEO at Glendale, Wis.–Based Auto-Interior Supplier," *Milwaukee Journal-Sentinel*, July 25, 2002.

———, "Milwaukee-Based Automotive Systems Maker Selects New Chairman," *Milwaukee Journal-Sentinel*, July 24, 2003.

Heinen, Tom, "Johnson Controls Official Rescues Milwaukee Holiday Parade," *Milwaukee Journal-Sentinel*, October 13, 2003.

"John Barth Selected to Chair National Minority Supplier Development Council," May 17, 2004, http://biz.yahoo.com/prnews/040517/cgm051_1.html.

"Johnson Controls Elects John Barth CEO; Additional Appointments and Dividend Announced," company press release, July 24, 2002, http://www.prnewswire.com/cgi-bin/stories.pl?ACCT=105&STORY=/www/story/07-24-2002/0001770789

—Lauri R. Harding

■ ■ ■

Glen A. Barton

1939–

Former chairman and CEO, Caterpillar

Nationality: American.

Born: August 1939, in Alton, Missouri.

Education: University of Missouri–Columbia, BS, 1961.

Family: Married Polly (maiden name unknown).

Career: Caterpillar, 1961–1964, trainee; 1964–1968, 1972–1975, sales associate for Caterpillar Overseas; 1975–1977, manager for South American Sales; 1977–1983, manager of Merchandising Division, General Offices; 1983–1984, sales and product support manager in Industrial Lift Truck Division; 1984–1986, manager in Products Control; 1987–1989, vice president of Caterpillar, president of Solar Turbines; 1989–1990, executive vice president; 1990–1998, group president; 1999–2004, chairman and CEO.

Awards: Faculty-Alumni Award and member of Civil Engineering Academy of Distinguished Alumni, University of Missouri–Columbia, 1999; Distinguished Service Award, University of Missouri–Columbia Alumni Association, 2002; Volunteer of the Year, American Red Cross.

Address: Caterpillar, 100 Northeast Adams Street, Peoria, Illinois 61629; http://www.cat.com.

■ Glen A. Barton completed a career of nearly 43 years with Caterpillar in February 2004. Headquartered in Peoria, Illinois, Caterpillar—with its trademark yellow-colored machines—is the world's largest manufacturer of mining and construction equipment, earth-moving machinery, industrial gas turbines, and natural gas and diesel engines. From 1999 to 2004 Barton led the Fortune 500 company, informally known as CAT, in producing machines to build the world's infrastructure on all seven continents, in the areas of construction, electric-power generation, electronics, energy, financing, forestry, logistics, mining, and transportation. Caterpillar products and components are manufactured in 50 U.S. facilities and in 65 other locations around the world.

IMPRESSED BY CATERPILLAR MACHINERY

The young Barton, growing up in Alton, Missouri, enjoyed taking things apart. He liked playing with Tinkertoys, dismantling his bike and the washing machine, and using a gas motor to power carts and wagons. Barton first started driving a tractor at the age of five, as a way to help his grandfather pick blackberries. He was in his junior year in the College of Engineering's cooperative program at the University of Missouri–Columbia when he helped supervise roadwork for the Missouri Highway Department. The Caterpillar equipment used by the crew impressed Barton so much that when he graduated in 1961 with a bachelor's degree in civil engineering, he applied for a job with Caterpillar.

FROM TRAINEE TO MANAGEMENT

Barton began his career when he joined Caterpillar as a trainee in 1961. In the years that followed, he held numerous management and marketing positions in North America, South America, Europe, and Japan. He worked in marketing during his two terms with Caterpillar Overseas in Geneva, Switzerland, from 1964 to 1968 and from 1972 to 1975 and, in 1975, became the manager for South American Sales. During this time, he learned comprehensive global business knowledge—which he would need later in his career—through living and working in various locations around the world. In 1977 Barton completed the Stanford University Executive Program, furthering his managerial expertise.

Upon completion of the Stanford program, Barton became manager of the Merchandising Division General Offices. In 1983 he moved to Mentor, Ohio, where he became the sales and product support manager for the Industrial Lift Truck Division. From 1984 through 1986 Barton worked as the manager of Products Control. His duties included product development and strategic planning. In 1987 Barton was elected a vice president of Caterpillar and president of Solar Turbines, a Caterpillar subsidiary in San Diego, California.

In 1989 Barton assumed the position of executive vice president, with responsibility for worldwide marketing. On July 1, 1990, Barton became group president with oversight of the design, development, and production of most of Caterpillar's comprehensive product line of construction, forest, and mining equipment. His tasks also included sales and marketing operations in North America, South America, Latin America, and Japan. During this time, Barton played a critical role in reorganizing the company into business units and streamlining the company's product-management strategy and product-introduction process.

LEADING CATERPILLAR

On February 1, 1999, Barton was nominated chairman and chief executive officer of Caterpillar, succeeding Donald V. Fites, who had served as chairman and CEO since 1990. When Barton was selected to replace him, Fites said of his successor, "Glen's global experience, his broad knowledge of our customers and our industry, as well as his breadth of understanding of our product line and manufacturing capabilities, give him a powerful perspective from which to lead Caterpillar into the 21st century" (January 12, 1999).

Barton began his direction of Caterpillar at a time when there was weakened demand for its products in many markets around the world. By quickly redirecting its efforts into areas that showed more demand (such as smaller machines and truck engines), the company substantially outperformed its stiff competition. In 1999 Caterpillar was able to return a respectable profit to its stockholders, even though many industries served by Caterpillar were in the middle of or emerging from recession. That year was additionally stressful for the new CEO because Caterpillar had only recently completed one of its most volatile periods of labor negotiations with the United Automobile Workers of America. Barton proceeded to lead the company to an improved relationship with the union, giving much of the credit for the company's financial success during his reign to the excellent support provided by all of its employees.

SUCCESSFUL LONG-TERM STRATEGY

Barton's long-term strategy emphasized continued diversification of products and services, including a new line of compact construction machines; strengthened interactions with major acquisitions; new dealer-rental stores; dramatically increased e-business; cost reductions; and internal process improvements. This combination of focuses placed the company on a solid path toward the goal Barton had set of reaching $30 billion in sales and revenues by the middle part of the first decade in the twenty-first century. With projected incremental growth of approximately $10 billion, $5 billion was to come from the engines business unit, $4 billion from machines, and $1 billion from financial products.

As CEO, Barton emphasized Caterpillar's reputation for quality and integrity as the global leader in its industry. He focused the company's employees on delivering greater value with its products and services and providing increasingly better financial and technical expertise. When the Environmental Protection Agency (EPA) set stringent environmental standards for diesel engines, Caterpillar's competition chose to fall back on known technology that met the new standards but sacrificed reliability and fuel efficiency. Barton, on the other hand, opted to develop technology that not only met the EPA standards but also maintained performance and fuel efficiency. Barton noted that Caterpillar did not choose the easy or the safe route, but a more expensive route that would allow the company to continue to meet EPA standards without neglecting quality.

LEADERSHIP STYLE

When asked to define his leadership style, Barton stated that his goal as a leader was to encourage innovation among his employees and to foster the natural creativity of everyone so as to achieve solutions in the best way possible. Barton noted that the best performances produced by Caterpillar employees are achieved when sufficient time is allowed to ask questions before important decisions are made, to learn from customers' opinions and suggestions, and to incorporate valuable past experiences into new projects. He added that performance should be judged not only by the results but also by the means used to achieve the end. Charlie Rentschler, an analyst with Langenberg & Company, said of Barton's leadership style, "He's got people pulling in the right direction. The company is a lot stronger than it was a decade ago. I don't think there's any question they've put some distance between themselves and their competition" (Dennis).

EMBRACING SIX SIGMA

Under Barton's leadership, Caterpillar implemented "six sigma," an integrated, disciplined strategy geared toward efficiently improving measurable facets of an organization based on historical information and data. "Sigma" is a term used to stand for "standard deviation," that is, how far from the average (mean) is some measurable quantity. The concept of six sigma was developed for practical use, to measure quantities in millions of possibilities (such as the number of defects in millions of products). Using the six-sigma structure beginning in 2001, Caterpillar uniformly achieved continuous improvement in the working culture by maximizing customer value, minimizing corporate expenses, stimulating efficiency gains in employees, and improving overall shareholder value. Barton attributed much of the company's successful financial returns to the six-sigma concept, with specific improvements occurring in the areas of costs, manufacturing, product quality, and volume.

LOOKING BACK ON A CAREER

During Barton's five-year term of leadership, the company was able to remain profitable even during harsh economic times. Upon his retirement, Barton deemed his guidance of Caterpillar through those troubling years to be his most important accomplishment and believed that the company's success was due to its ability to demonstrate, especially to the investment community, its diversity of products and services, such as its expanded line of smaller equipment. Barton took aggressive steps to ensure Caterpillar's competitive leadership in the global marketplace, including building a superior dealer network worth $7.1 billion and investing in research at a rate of $4 million per day. Caterpillar's 2003 corporate sales and revenues totaled $22.76 billion, with profits of $1.1 billion, or $3.13 per share. More than half of all sales went to customers outside the United States.

LEAVING CAT STRONG AND LEAN

Barton retired from Caterpillar at age 64 on January 31, 2004, due to the company's mandatory retirement rule. He felt that Caterpillar's future success would depend on its ability to take care of its customers, maintain a high level of integrity, recognize shareholder value, and acknowledge that its employees were vital to operations. Upon notification of Barton's retirement, the board of directors at Caterpillar named James W. Owens as CEO, to whom Barton passed on a strong and lean company ready to meet the challenges of the future. Owens joined Caterpillar in 1972 and had been group president of the Component Products and Control Systems Division and an executive office member of Caterpillar.

SERVING COMPANY AND COMMUNITY

During his professional career, Barton served on the Dean's Engineering Advisory Council at the University of Missouri–Columbia as well as on the boards of directors of Inco and Newmont Mining Corporation, North America's largest gold producer. Barton also served as a trustee of the Malcolm Baldridge National Quality Award Foundation; a member of the Illinois Business Roundtable and the President's Export Council; and chairman of the board of trustees of Bradley University.

After retiring, Barton continued to involve himself with the communities surrounding Caterpillar. He planned to stay active with Peoria NEXT, a community organization dedicated to high-technology business growth, and with Civic Federation, a private group comprising the area's top 40 business leaders. He was committed to helping improve area school systems and finding ways to deal with the issues of local health-care costs.

See also entry on Caterpillar Inc. in *International Directory of Company Histories.*

SOURCES FOR FURTHER INFORMATION

"Barton to Succeed Fites as Caterpillar Chairman and CEO Feb. 1," PR Newswire, January 12, 1999, http://www.findarticles.com/cf_0/m4PRN/1999_Jan_12/53554053/p1/article.jhtml.

Dennis, Jan, "CEO Ends 43-year Ride with Caterpillar," *Beacon News Online.*

—William Arthur Atkins

■ ■ ■

Richard Barton

1967–

Founder, Expedia, Inc., and director, IAC/InterActiveCorp

Nationality: American.

Born: June 2, 1967.

Education: Stanford University, B.S. (industrial engineering), 1989.

Family: Son of Jim Barton (a retired executive at Union Carbide) and Betsy (a homemaker; maiden name unknown); married Sara (an obstetrician and gynecologist; maiden name unknown); children: three.

Career: Alliance Consulting Group, 1989–1991, strategy consultant; Microsoft Corporation, 1991–1994, product manager, then general manager of Expedia unit, 1994–1999; Expedia, Inc., 1999–2003, president, chief executive officer, and director; IAC/InterActiveCorp, 2003–, director.

Awards: Named "One of the Best Managers of 2002" by *BusinessWeek* magazine.

Address: IAC/InterActiveCorp, 152 West Fifty-seventh Street, 42nd Floor, New York, New York 10019; http://www.usainteractive.com/index.html.

■ Richard Barton founded Expedia, Inc., a popular operator of online travel planning services, in 1994 and acted as its president, chief executive officer, and director from November 1999 to March 2003. The company was founded within the offices of the Microsoft Corporation and spun off into a separate unit in 1999. During his tenure at Expedia, Barton successfully established one of the few Internet companies of the late-1990s boom to actually make money for its investors.

DEVELOPING ENTREPRENEURIAL SKILLS

Born in the Midwest, Barton honed his entrepreneurial talents while growing up in New Canaan, Connecticut. After learning how to drive, Barton started a summer business by driving an ice-cream truck in New Canaan. He taught himself to price the merchandise, determine the daily route, and carry a large amount of inventory in ice cream and Popsicles for his customers. Later, for two years, Barton hired out as a golf caddy at the local country club.

Although his parents funded his college education, Barton supported himself for his other expenses. He hesitated at the large profit percentage that a painting company wanted from him, so he started his own company. During summer vacations away from college, Barton painted houses using his own multiple-person crew. Reflecting upon the experience in an interview in the *New York Times,* Barton said of himself, "It taught me how to run a business, hire people, manage clients, do quality work. I fell in love with running my own thing. And painting made me feel really good, especially when I was finished" (August 5, 2001).

JOINS MICROSOFT AND FOUNDS EXPEDIA

Before founding Expedia, Barton was employed by Microsoft from 1991 to 1994 in various product management capacities. He was involved in the research and development of such products as the MS-DOS 5, MS-DOS 6, Windows 3.1, and Windows 95 operating systems. He pushed (and eventually succeeded) in selling MS-DOS with a "DOS for Dummies" book even though it was published by a Microsoft rival. Barton felt novice computer users would be more apt to buy DOS if it came with an easy-to-read user's guide.

Later, while traveling on a CD-ROM work project to create travel guides—interestingly enough called Expedia—Barton came up with the idea of "e-travel," or using electronic resources to assist travelers. He informed Bill Gates, his boss at Microsoft, that he thought the CD travel guide project would fail but that his e-travel concept would succeed. Gates liked the idea, and Expedia, in its new form, was created. Barton began working on the concept in 1994.

Barton persuaded Microsoft to invest $100 million in order to make a group of personal computers do what in the past only a mainframe airline-reservation system could do—retrieve flight information and purchase a ticket. With this investment Barton and his team created software that allowed users the ability to build customized trips rather than to buy prepackaged ones, a key development that helped Expedia to rapidly grow its business.

Barton's success with Expedia was made possible by the company's approach to the hotel business. Instead of selling rooms on commission, Expedia bought them at a discount, using its growing size to negotiate low prices. It then resold the rooms to customers at a higher price, often packaged with airfares. Barton was very adept at using technology to constantly reduce the costs of the travel process.

Expedia first appeared on the Internet in 1996. At that time Barton imagined that Expedia would become the online destination for individuals who booked travel reservations—such as for hotels, airplane trips, and rental cars—from their personal computers. In addition, Barton developed other travel-related features for the Expedia Web site, including chat rooms, frequent flyer tracking tools, and maps. During this time Expedia bought two of its competitors, Travelscape.com and VacationSpot.com. These acquisitions were instrumental in helping Expedia to expand its customer service operations.

FROM EXPEDIA IPO TO SALE TO USA INTERACTIVE

In the fourth quarter of 1999 Microsoft spun off Expedia (while still maintaining a controlling interest) with an initial public offering (IPO) of $14 per share. The stock jumped 280 percent on the first day of trading, producing a market cap of $2 billion and making Barton a rich man. Shortly thereafter Barton told a reporter at *BusinessWeek,* "We've been driving this Ferrari in the suburbs. Now we're taking it out on the highway and seeing what it can do" (January 31, 2000).

In early 2000 Barton began to invest considerably in building a comprehensive merchant inventory and improving the company's computer system. According to Barton, Expedia's new searching and pricing system and related package business led to a dramatic increase in customers. As a result, revenue from merchant business nearly doubled from a year earlier, to about $67 million, while agency revenue grew about 88 percent to $34 million. This milestone, as Barton declared, was the direct result of travel-savey consumers seeking out Expedia's technology.

In July 2001 Microsoft agreed to sell control of Expedia for an estimated $1.3 billion to 's USA Interactive, the cable television company. (USA Interactive later operated under the name IAC/InterActiveCorp.) With the help of Expedia's new parent company, Barton expanded Expedia to what he called a "travel superstore on the Internet," one that sold everything from discount air fares, vacation packages, and island hideaway rentals to tickets to professional sporting events. Under Barton's guidance, Expedia expanded from 50 original employees to more than 1,300 worldwide in 2003, while going from several offices at Microsoft headquarters to its own building in Bellevue, Washington, along with worldwide sites in Las Vegas, Canada, Britain, Germany, France, Italy, and the Netherlands.

MANAGEMENT STYLE

Expedia's success was in large measure due to Barton's imagination and leadership. Some industry analysts, such as those with Bear Stearns, praised Barton's vision and his ability to steer Expedia to profitability in an era of Internet company failures. At the same time, colleagues remarked on his good interpersonal skills and ability to motivate his employees. Barton's former boss at Microsoft, Brad Chase, who until April 2001 was a senior vice president with Microsoft, compared Barton to the lion, tin man, and scarecrow in *The Wizard of Oz.* Chase told Monica Soto of the *Seattle Times,* "He's sort of got the courage of his convictions and he's smart—he's got a brain. At the same time, he's got a heart. He cares about the people around him" (May 27, 2002).

Friends and coworkers described Barton as highly competitive and very passionate, sometimes forgetting to put on his shoes before walking down the hallway. Passion sometimes landed Barton in trouble. Just after Expedia was spun off from Microsoft, Barton told a *BusinessWeek* reporter that Expedia would sell $1 billion in travel products by the year 2000. The statement was seen as an outlandish boost from the boss at the small ex-division within Microsoft. Expedia did meet that goal, but at the time Barton was politely asked to "tone" himself down when speaking to the press.

RESIGNS FROM EXPEDIA, MOVES TO PARENT COMPANY

Barton resigned as president and CEO of Expedia effective March 31, 2003. Barton left the company at the height of its financial earnings history, with the company having booked $5.3 billion in gross revenue for the 2002 calendar year. He listed personal reasons for his departure, specifically the desire to live in Europe for a year. In February 2003 he assumed a position on the board of directors at Expedia's parent company, IAC/InterActiveCorp. The InterActiveCorp position allowed Barton to continue his involvement with Expedia. Barton also served on the board of directors of Ticketmaster, Netflix, and AtomShockwave.

See also entry on Expedia, Inc. in *International Directory of Company Histories.*

SOURCES FOR FURTHER INFORMATION

"The Best Managers," *BusinessWeek,* 13 January 2003, pp. 60–69.

Levere, Jane L. "New Journey of a Travel Pioneer," *New York Times,* 5 August 2001.

Mullaney, Timothy J. "Expedia: Changing Pilots in Mid-Climb," *BusinessWeek,* 24 February 2003, pp. 120–123.

"Multiple Microsofts May Be Better than One," *BusinessWeek,* 31 January 2000, p. 43.

Soto, Monica, "High-energy CEO Puts Expedia at Front of Pack," *Seattle Times,* 27 May 2002.

—William Arthur Atkins

■ ■ ■

J. T. Battenberg III

1944–

Chairman, CEO, and president, Delphi Corporation

Nationality: American.

Born: 1944.

Education: Kettering University, BS, 1966; Columbia University, MBA, 1969.

Career: General Motors, 1961–1986, assembly line, plant superintendent, comptroller, production manager, plant manager, managing director of the General Motors Continental Division in Belgium, general manager of overseas truck operations in England; 1986–1992, vice president of Buick-Oldsmobile-Cadillac Group's luxury car division; 1992–1995, vice president of Automotive Components Group Worldwide; 1995–1998, executive vice president; Delphi Corporation, 1995–1998, president; 1998–, chairman, CEO, and president.

Address: Delphi Corporation, 5725 Delphi Drive, Troy, Michigan 48098; http://www.delphi.com.

■ J. T. Battenberg III rose through the ranks of General Motors to become president of Delphi, a world-leading diversified automotive supply company, when it was first organized as a separate division of GM in 1995. Battenberg gained the additional title of chairman of the board when Delphi reorganized as an independent corporation in May 1999. Under Battenberg's leadership, Delphi gained recognition when it ranked 57th in the Fortune 500 in 2000, continuing the aggressive global expansion that started when the company was still a division of GM.

J. T. Battenberg III. *AP/Wide World Photos.*

AN INSIDER RISES TO CEO

Battenberg is a classic example of an insider who rose through the ranks to reach the top of a company. He started working on the assembly line at General Motors in 1961. He received a bachelor's degree in 1966 from the General Motors Institute, now known as Kettering University; three years later he earned an MBA from Columbia University and then underwent management training at Harvard University. Later, Battenberg was given the opportunity to progress through the ranks of GM in both the United States and Europe. In *Good to Great: Why Some Companies Make the Leap and Others Don't,* Jim Collins, author of several well-known studies of corporate management, notes that 10 of 11 CEOs coming from inside companies are "good to great"; Battenberg fell into this category.

In a keynote presentation to the Automotive News World Congress in January 2003, Battenberg reflected on the auto industry over the period of his working experience. He noted that one of the passions that guided his management style was his interest in data, including demographics. He attributed this interest to his years spent looking for new customers as well as focusing on the character of the workforce. He further commented that his job had been made easier by an "oversupply of educated, skilled, internet-savvy and highly motivated people" to fill jobs. However, he said, there had been a serious decline in the United States in the number of 35- to 50-year-old workers, the group Battenberg described as having the highest productivity.

LEAN, MULTIFUNCTIONAL MATRIX MANAGEMENT

As chairman, CEO, and president, Battenberg was the ultimate authority at Delphi and used a lean, multifunctional matrix approach to management. The board comprised Battenberg and 20 senior executives representing the three product sectors and the company's world and regional headquarters staff. Each product sector was managed by its own strategy board, which was responsible for the profitability of that sector's various products and businesses. The differences in the nature of the products within a sector made it necessary to manage the three sectors separately.

Matrix management is one strategy used by top industry leaders in response to developments such as globalization, the intensification of competition, and the complexities of relationships with customers, employees, and governments that these changes have created. Matrix management provides a parallel reporting structure as a mechanism to handle diverse and sometimes conflicting needs of functional-product and geographic-management groups. It is a multidimensional organization scheme that can, under the right leadership, respond well to external complexity. Battenberg was able to make this scheme work at Delphi.

The company reported organizational refinements that included the consolidation of product lines and realignments made to sharpen focus. For cost savings, support staffs were joined across headquarters, divisions, and regions. While additionally consolidating product lines in single divisions, Delphi announced in November 2003 that it had acquired a German company so as to expand its product line primarily for the European automotive original-equipment market. Battenberg also strengthened the company's competitive position in China through continued globalization.

GLOBAL OPPORTUNITIES

When Battenberg started working on the assembly line in 1961, the government was filing antitrust lawsuits within the auto industry. However, antitrust is no longer an issue in the auto industry, owing to the proliferation of foreign competition. Working under the CEO Jack Smith Jr. in the 1990s, Battenberg adopted a doctrine of global focus for broader markets and, as with most manufacturing industries under profit pressure, outsourcing for cheaper labor.

While the automotive systems division was led by Battenberg under GM, operations were set up in China. After investing more than $400 million in China over a decade, Delphi realized $700 million in sales in 2002. Delphi was the largest auto parts manufacturer in China by the end of 2003. Most of the production manufactured in China stayed there, because demand was so great within the country. Delphi also outsourced manufacturing to Eastern Europe to lower manufacturing costs on products for Western European markets.

See also entry on Delphi Corporation in *International Directory of Company Histories.*

SOURCES FOR FURTHER INFORMATION

Bartlett, C. A., and Sumantra Ghoshal, "Matrix Management: Not a Structure, a Frame of Mind," *Harvard Business Review,* July–August 1990.

Battenberg III, J. T., "Keynote Dinner Remarks," Automotive News World Congress, January 13, 2003, http://www.autonews.com/files/jtbattenberg113.doc.

Collins, Jim, *Good to Great: Why Some Companies Make the Leap and Others Don't,* New York: HarperCollins, 2001.

Muller, Joann, et al., "Autos: A New Industry," *BusinessWeek Online,* July 15, 2002, www.businessweek.com/magazine/content/02_28/b3791001.htm.

Tichy, Noel M., *The Leadership Engine: How Winning Companies Build Leaders at Every Level,* New York: HarperBusiness, 1997.

—M. C. Nagel

■ ■ ■

Claude Bébéar

1935–

Former chairman and chief executive officer, AXA Group

Nationality: French.

Born: July 29, 1935, in Issac, France.

Education: École Polytechnique, 1958.

Family: Married (wife's name unknown); children: five.

Career: Anciennes Mutuelles, 1958–1964; 1964–1966, founder of life-insurance branch of Provinces Unies; 1975–1978, chairman; Mutuelles Unis, 1978–1985, chairman; AXA Group, 1985–2000, chairman and CEO.

Awards: Commander of the Legion of Honor; Officer of the National Order of Merit; Manager of the Year, *Nouvel Économiste*, 1988.

Publications: *Le courage de réforme,* 2002; *Ils vont tuer le capitalisme* (with Philippe Manière), 2003.

Address: AXA Group, 25 avenue Matignon, Paris 75008 France; http://www.axa.com.

Claude Bébéar. *AP/Wide World Photos.*

■ Claude Bébéar, who was called the "godfather of French capitalism," built the global insurance giant AXA Group by taking over obscure or struggling financial companies and making them hugely profitable. The company and the man were almost synonymous because Bébéar spent his whole career at the firm, and under his leadership it grew enormously in size and influence. At the end of 2003 AXA Group was the number-one insurer in the world, with 50 million clients in 50 countries and $979 billion in client assets under management.

AN ASPIRING ENTREPRENEUR

Bébéar grew up in southwestern France in the Dordogne region. His parents were teachers and placed a high value on academic success. After attending local schools and preparing at the Lycée Saint-Louis in Paris, Bébéar began his college education at the elite École Polytechnique, one of France's *grandes écoles,* which groom future business leaders and politicians.

André Sahut d'Izarn, the father of Bébéar's college roommate, headed Anciennes Mutuelles, a small, undistinguished insurance company in Rouen, Normandy. When d'Izarn failed to interest his own son in a position at the firm, he approached Bébéar with a similar offer. Although Bébéar believed his education had prepared him for a more glamorous future—perhaps in the French civil service—the opportunity to grow with a company and become a successful entrepreneur intrigued him; he began his career at Anciennes Mutuelles in 1958.

Bébéar worked his way up through the company's hierarchy, gaining both skills and responsibilities as he progressed. From 1964 to 1966 he worked in Canada, where he created the life-insurance division of Provinces Unies, a subsidiary of Anciennes Mutuelles. He gained firsthand experience working in the aggressive, freewheeling business environment he found there, a culture that contrasted sharply with his native France.

"CROCODILE CLAUDE"

Bébéar's successful resolution of a workers' strike in 1974 impressed the board, and he became chairman of Anciennes Mutuelles after d'Izarn's death in 1975. In 1978 the firm, renamed Mutuelles Unies, acquired the practically bankrupt Mutuelle Parisienne de Garantie. Then in 1982, when the leftist government wanted to nationalize the insurance sector, Bébéar took on the Drouot Group, at the time the leading private insurance company in France, which became the first of his many conquests. As described in *Fortune* magazine, Bébéar's skill at taking over smaller rivals, or "his appetite in gobbling up companies," earned him the nickname of "Crocodile Claude" (December 20, 1999).

Under Bébéar's leadership the firm's name was changed to AXA Group in 1985; the choice was astute because, although the letters did not stand for anything, they would come at the beginning of alphabetical lists, and people worldwide could pronounce the name. Bébéar's skill at operating outside his country's borders was becoming apparent.

According to an article in *Fortune*, Bébéar "benefited from a charming, easygoing exterior that masked a steely determination" (December 20, 1999). His interest in hunting wild game generated many comparisons to his supposed stalking and capturing of weaker companies. Rugby, his favorite sport, was also used as a metaphor for his no-holds-barred approach. Bébéar became one of the first of a new breed of European CEOs who understood how essential it was for France to enter global markets.

By 1988 AXA was the second-largest French insurance company, just behind UAP. In what was described as a turning point in his career, Bébéar made a $1 billion investment in Equitable, the fifth-largest U.S. life insurer in 1991, and turned it into a unit of AXA. The move gave him international credibility and secured a place for AXA on the New York Stock Exchange the following year.

Bébéar eventually negotiated a merger with UAP, a company that represented the old way of doing business in France. UAP's falling stock prices had made it vulnerable to the American firm AIG, and Bébéar prevailed on sentiments of national pride to keep the business in France. AXA doubled in size and became a formidable presence in all of Europe.

Still further acquisitions meant entry into the world markets in Asia, Australia, and elsewhere. Bébéar traveled extensively and became known for his adventurous meetings with his executive teams, engaging in such activities as camping near the Great Wall of China and exploring the Nigerian desert.

NEW CHALLENGES IN THE INSURANCE INDUSTRY

In a speech in Berlin at the 35th Annual Seminar of the International Insurance Society in 1999, Bébéar said insurers needed to make changes in order to remain competitive. He cited research by Andersen Consulting that found that insurance agents were in touch with their clients on average only every eight years, in contrast to banks, which had contact with clients every three weeks. As people were buying insurance via telephone-based services, supermarkets, and even mail order, Bébéar emphasized effective branding and the importance of keeping agents close to their customers. He added that consumers of certain types of insurance and other financial products would continue to require personal contact with professional, highly trained advisers.

BÉBÉAR REMAINS INFLUENTIAL

Although he officially retired as AXA's director when he turned 65 in 2000, Bébéar remained active as the chairman of AXA's supervisory board. In its August 11, 2003, issue, *Fortune* included Bébéar on its list of the 12 most powerful business leaders outside the United States.

In 2001 Bébéar headed the committee to locate the 2008 Olympics in Paris. He also helped found the Institut Montaigne, a think tank that analyzed French economic challenges. Bébéar resisted overtures to become involved in his country's volatile political scene, twice turning down offers to become finance minister, although he did not rule out future involvement.

His book *Ils vont tuer le capitalisme* (They Are Going to Kill Capitalism), published in 2003 and coauthored with the French economist Philippe Manière, discussed globalization and its effects on the French economy. Bébéar deplored the corporate scandals that sapped the confidence of both investors and employees, without whose participation capitalism would be impossible. He explained that the need for highly paid specialists in international law and finance hamstrung business leaders and complicated their decision making. Bébéar called for a return to more vigorous audits and closer scrutiny of company finances.

See also entry on AXA Colonia Konzern AG in *International Directory of Company Histories.*

SOURCES FOR FURTHER INFORMATION

de Hasay, Anthony, "Capitalism and Virtue: Politicians Do Not Understand the Economy, but Do Managers?" *The Library of Economics and Liberty*, June 2, 2003, http://www.econlib.org/library/Columns/y2003/JasayVirtue.html.

Howard, Lisa S., "AXA Cites Threats from New Insurance Players," *National Underwriter Property & Casualty-Risk & Benefits Management*, August 2, 1999, p. 15.

Rossant, John, and Carol Matlack, "A Talk with the Godfather: Claude Bébéar on What French Business Needs Now," *BusinessWeek*, July 29, 2002, p. 58.

Tagliabue, John, "French Business Champion, or a Corporate Puppeteer?" *International Herald Tribune*, November 15, 2003.

Tully, Shawn, "Watch Out! Here Comes Crocodile Claude: AXA's Claude Bébéar Became the World's Largest Insurer by Hunting Down Dogs like Equitable and Making Them Winners," *Fortune*, December 20, 1999, p. 206.

—Anne Lesser

■■■

Pierre-Olivier Beckers

1960–

President, chief executive officer, and director, Delhaize Group; chairman and chief executive officer, Delhaize America

Nationality: Belgian.

Born: 1960.

Education: I.A.G, Univerite catholique de Louvain, bachelor's degree; Harvard Business School, MBA.

Career: Delhaize Group, 1983–1996, began as U.S. operations group store manager, became director of purchasing and executive committee member; 1996–, executive vice president of executive committee in charge of international activities; 1999–, president and chief executive officer; Delhaize America, 1999–2002, chairman; 2002–, chairman and chief executive officer; CIES–The Food Business Forum, 2002–2004, chairman; Food Marketing Institute, director.

Awards: Manager of the Year, *Trends/Tendances* magazine, 2000.

Address: Delhaize Group, rue Osseghemstraat 53, Molenbeek-St.-Jean, B-1080 Brussells, Belgium; http://www.delhaizegroup.com/en.

Pierre-Olivier Beckers. © *Reuters NewMedia Inc./Corbis.*

■ A Belgian native who earned his master's degree in the United States, Pierre-Olivier Beckers simultaneously held the top executive positions with the Delhaize Group, the Belgian-based, international owner and operator of food retail stores, and the group's U.S. subsidiary, Delhaize America. In 2002 he was elected to a two-year term as chairman of the Paris-based CIES–The Food Business Forum, an international network interfacing with more than four hundred food retailers and suppliers from 50 countries.

STORE MANAGER BECOMES SUPERMARKET STAR

Beckers began his lifelong food-industry career in Belgium in 1982 as a store manager for a bakery chain. He joined Delhaize Group in 1983 and spent the next three years in the United States running the company's U.S. operations. After his return to Belgium, Beckers gained considerable experience as a buyer before becoming director of nonperishables purchasing. By 1999 his hands-on experience in several of the corporation's operational areas had earned him the position of chief executive officer of the entire Delhaize Group. Beckers thus held jurisdiction over seven hundred retail stores in Belgium and more than 2,500 stores functioning under more than 20 separate identities in nine countries throughout Europe and Asia and in the United States. He was elected chairman of the board at Delhaize America in 1999 and was then elected CEO in 2002.

In Belgium, Delhaize—"Le Lion"—operated stores under banners such as AD Delhaize, Delhaize Di (health and beauty products), Tom & Company (pet products), and Proxy (convenience stores). In the United States, Delhaize America operated approximately 1,485 supermarkets under the banners Food Lion (1,225 stores in 11 Southeast and Mid-Atlantic states), Hannaford (114 stores in New England), and Kash n' Karry (138 stores in Florida).

EXPANDING IN THE UNITED STATES

In April 1999 U.S. native Bill McCanless, the then CEO of Delhaize America, was named president and CEO of Food Lion, Delhaize's chain of budget food stores. At the same time, Beckers was named Food Lion's chairman. Rose Post of the *Salisbury Post* quoted Laura Kendall, Food Lion's chief financial officer, as commenting, "Delhaize views Food Lion as its growth opportunity in the United States, and with Pierre in the chairman's slot they will be able to work with Bill in focusing on strategies such as acquisitions of stores and driving sales momentum" (April 8, 1999).

As chairman of Delhaize America, Beckers was strategically positioned to help navigate Food Lion into a greater market share of the U.S. food retail-store industry. Beckers told shareholders that Food Lion was a vitally important component of Delhaize's global growth strategy and that Delhaize intended to create new areas of development for the Food Lion chain, implying that the company would look into acquisitions if appropriate targets became available.

A year after Beckers's appointment, Food Lion's acquisition of Hannaford, an upmarket food chain in New England, was imminent. Not all Food Lion shareholders were happy about the prospect, however. In a special report to the *Salisbury Post,* Ralph Ketner, the 1957 cofounder of Food Lion, expressed his dissatisfaction with the direction in which Delhaize's senior executives were taking his company. The annual stockholders meeting, held in Salisbury, North Carolina, ever since the late 1950s, had been moved to Tampa, Florida, and the Delhaize board chose not to allow cumulative shareholder voting, thus denying 44 percent of class B stockholders input into business decisions. Ketner called Food Lion's planned merger with Hannaford a disaster because Delhaize offered roughly $1 billion too much for the company. (Hannaford's shares were trading at $63, and Delhaize offered $79.) He also cited other huge outlays, such as $2.5 billion in goodwill, and the fact that Food Lion would need to borrow $3 billion at 7.8 percent to complete the deal, which meant $234 million annually in interest alone. "Can Food Lion afford or justify this?" he wrote. "From my detailed studies of their projections, absolutely not! And obviously, Wall Street investors also think 'not,' as the stock has plunged from $12 to $6 just sincc Delhaize's announcement" (April 17, 2000).

Ketner was also distressed at what he considered Delhaize's freedom with Food Lion stocks and Beckers's lack of responsiveness to shareholders. He noted that McCanless received 200,000 shares in Food Lion, pointing out that such stock options were usually given as a hiring incentive or for outstanding performance, neither of which, he said, was applicable in that instance. McCanless had been on board for twelve months, and stock values had plummeted. Ketner wrote, "Almost daily, I am asked by stockholders and employees, 'What is happening to our company?!' I have repeatedly written to Pierre Beckers, but have received no satisfactory answer. It seems to many of us that Delhaize is interested only in mergers and acquisitions and not in 'minding the store'" (April 17, 2000).

Regardless, with Beckers as Food Lion's chairman, merger plans went ahead, and Hannaford was acquired in 2000. Beckers's reasoning behind the acquisition grew out of Delhaize's unsuccessful attempt in the early 1980s to take Food Lion into noncontiguous states when they opened a store in Texas that ultimately failed. Beckers was quoted by David Orgel in *Supermarket News* as commenting, "We came out with the realization that it was not going to be easy to take Food Lion into every state across the U.S." (December 8, 2003). Learning from the failure, Beckers saw acquisition as the most favorable way to open up growth opportunities for Food Lion in new geographic regions.

Beckers believed that a common vision needed to be maintained for acquisitions to succeed. Toward that end, he kept Hannaford's management team intact. "Success begins with human resources," he told David Ghitelman in an interview with *Supermarket News.* "If you keep that in mind, the rest falls into place. When acquisitions fail, it's usually due to a lack of communication. We're past that. We've known each other a very long time" (April 30, 2001).

TACKLING AN UNFAVORABLE ECONOMIC ENVIRONMENT

While the acquisition of Hannaford succeeded, Food Lion's revenues slumped. By 2002 the chain's sales lagged amid a general industry downturn. McCanless was removed from his role as CEO of Delhaize America to become vice chairman, and Beckers stepped into the role of chief executive because of his extensive operations experience. "For me, with 75 percent of our operations in the U.S., it is very important that I focus much of my energy and time on this part of the operations," Beckers told Mark Hamstra in an interview with *Supermarket News.* "It was really the next logical step for Delhaize in terms of streamlining the organization" (November 11, 2002). Although the executive restructuring occurred during a low ebb in Food Lion's performance, Becker insisted the transition had been planned two years earlier and was not due to short-term pressure.

In his attempt to increase Food Lion's visibility and market share, Beckers readily entertained new ideas. Drawing on his company's experience in Belgium and Europe, he took a multi–pronged approach to reviving Food Lion's performance.

While retaining their low-price reputation, revitalization plans included redesigning stores, increasing convenience and levels of customer service, and bolstering Food Lion's fresh-food image, as heightened consumer awareness of health and nutrition had shifted demand toward more variety and better quality.

Analysts saw Beckers's focus on convenience and customer service as perhaps the most significant aspect of Food Lion's growth strategy. Beckers noted to Hamstra that the chain had more than 1,200 stores in the states in which they operated, and thus there was a "Food Lion near your home in just about every area" (November 11, 2002). Developing the convenience model even further, the company experimented with building smaller stores with the same array of products in several underserved communities. Beckers also felt that in-store convenience needed to be improved. One tactic used to address this issue was to place self-serve items, such as deli products, in the front of the store for easy customer access. Beckers believed that increased customer service and convenience made Food Lion a major competitor of the mammoth American retailer Wal-Mart: "I know there's this feeling out there that Wal-Mart is the 800-pound gorilla that takes market share away for all retailers. But we experience every time we open a new store next to Wal-Mart that we are taking sales away from that competition," he told Hamstra (November 11, 2002).

STREAMLINING TO STAY ON TRACK

Unlike the often sudden and daring business moves made by many U.S. enterprises, Delhaize maintained a slow and steady approach, a philosophy that Beckers believed was the most favorable method of integrating acquisitions in the United States. While realizing that U.S. investors often sought the more exciting approach, Beckers believed that exciting consumers was far more important, and building relationships between employees and consumers was a major part of the process.

In March 2003, however, still struggling amid the general economic downturn, 41 Food Lion stores were closed; meanwhile Hannaford, the more upmarket chain, continued to fair well. Early in 2004, primarily due to the weakness of the dollar against the euro, the Delhaize Group closed 34 Florida-based Kash n' Karry stores and was nearing the end of a restructuring phase that closed several stores and initiated the sale of certain other interests internationally. The restructure included the sale of Delhaize's 49 percent stake in the Singapore retailer Shop N Save. Beckers pointed out that in contrast to the image Delhaize portrayed as a result of these bail-out transactions, the company met its 2003 indebtedness and cash-flow targets. "We had announced the creation of one billion dollars of free cash flow and of an indebtedness ration of 100 percent to equity capital in 2003, and we are in line with these objectives," he told a reporter for the Belgian daily newspaper *L'Echo* (January 31, 2004).

RECOGNIZED FOR ACHIEVEMENTS

In 2000 Beckers received a prestigious distinction when Belgium's leading business magazine named him Manager of the Year. In 2002 he was elected chairman of CIES–The Food Business Forum, the independent, Paris-based, global association established in the mid-1900s as a liaison between food marketing industries and grocery manufacturers in more than 50 countries. When Beckers became chairman, company membership in the association included two-thirds of the world's largest food retailers and their suppliers as well as smaller companies from developing nations. At the age of 42, Beckers was the youngest person ever to be named CIES chairman.

See also entries on Delhaize "Le Lion" S.A. and Food Lion, Inc. in *International Directory of Company Histories.*

SOURCES FOR FURTHER INFORMATION

CIES–The Food Business Forum, "Pierre-Olivier Beckers, CEO of Delhaize Group: New Chairman of CIES–The Food Business Forum," press release, June 20, 2002, www.ciesnet.com/pdf/presse/p-o_beckers_new_cies_chairman.pdf.

"Delhaize Nearing End of Restructuring Phase," *Forbes.com,* January 31, 2004, http://forbes.com/reuters/newswire/2004/01/31/rtr1237040.html.

Ghitelman, David, "All Together Now," *Supermarket News,* April 30, 2001, p. 1.

Hamstra, Mark, "Making Food Lion Roar," *Supermarket News,* November 11, 2002, p. 10.

Ketner, Ralph, "What Is the Future of Food Lion? Board Representation, Merger Are among Cofounder's Concerns," *Salisbury Post,* April 17, 2000, http://www.salisburypost.com/2000april/041700g.htm.

Orgel, David, "Four Key Lessons Delhaize Group Learned in America," *Supermarket News,* December 8, 2003, p. 8.

Post, Rose, "McCanless President, CEO; Beckers Chairman of Board," *Salisbury Post,* April 8, 1999. http://www.salisburypost.com/newscopy/040899lion_1.htm.

—Marie L. Thompson

■■■

Jean-Louis Beffa

1941–

Chairman and chief executive officer, Groupe Saint-Gobain

Nationality: French.

Born: August 11, 1941, in Nice, France.

Education: École Polytechnique, 1960.

Family: Son of an engineer and a teacher; married; children: three.

Career: Corps des Mines, 1967–1974, various positions including ingénieur des mines and ingénieur en chef des mines; Saint-Gobain, 1975–1977, chief operating officer; Pont-à-Mousson, 1977–1979, deputy manager and managing director; 1979–1982, chairman and managing director; Saint-Gobain, 1982–1986, chief operating officer; 1986–, chairman and chief executive officer.

Awards: Elected manager of the year, Nouvel économiste, 1989.

Address: Les Miroirs, 18 avenue d'Alsace, 92096 La Défense Cedex, France; http://www.saint-gobain.com.

Jean-Louis Beffa. © *Pasquini C/Corbis SYGMA.*

■ Jean-Louis Beffa, CEO of the glass and building-materials giant Groupe Saint-Gobain, oversaw the company's privatization in 1986. In subsequent years he restructured the company, eliminating some 60,000 jobs while presiding over the group's diversification and expansion into international markets. Saint-Gobain grew under his direction into a group of some 1,200 different companies, and in the early 21st century it was one of the 100 largest industrial companies in the world and the world leader in building materials.

Established in 1665 as part of France's King Louis XIV's royal glassworks, Saint-Gobain manufactured the glass used in Versaille's Galerie des glaces (the Hall of Mirrors) and in 2004 was the only surviving company that had been created by Colbert, the finance minister under Louis XIV. In the early 2000s it manufactured an extensive line of building products ranging from pipes to flat glass, insulation, and glass containers. Its products were of both cultural and commercial interest. Saint-Gobain provided the glazing for the architect I. M. Pei's pyramid at the entrance to the Louvre and produced some 30 billion glass containers a year.

Beffa's appointment as CEO of Saint-Gobain at the age of 45 made him one of the youngest people ever to attain such a high position in that country, and hence he was one of the longest-serving CEOs in France. He assumed virtually complete control over the group's activities during his tenure. Known for being meticulous and for emphasizing rational and conservative business practices, he still demonstrated complete confidence in his carefully chosen executives. As his appointed successor, Christian Streiff, said in *Le Figaro*, "He has a lot of authority, but he is not authoritarian" (April 7, 2003). Beffa's larger mission, as he saw it, was to protect and promote a French and European model of capitalism.

ÉCOLE POLYTECHNIQUE: A DECISIVE AND FORMATIVE INFLUENCE

Beffa was educated at the prestigious École Polytechnique, which is administered by the Ministry of Defense and produces many of France's top CEOs. He found the military aspects of its educational system appealing, in particular the physical training provided by the staff, the ceremonial uniform the students wore, and the geographically and socially unbiased atmosphere. Both the military and scientific aspects of his training at the school strongly influenced his personal style as a CEO.

As a child, Beffa had a keen interest in history, but his growing interest in mathematics steered him toward the École Polytechnique, largely for the unique opportunities it provided to students who wished to pursue a career in business. He graduated in 1960 and continued his engineering studies at the highly prestigious Corps des Mines. There he rose to the rank of chief engineer and held a position in the Ministère de l'Industrie. Upon recommendation from the Corps des Mines, Beffa joined Saint-Gobain in 1974 at the age of 33.

SAINT-GOBAIN: CLIMBING THE CHAIN OF COMMAND

Beffa's joining Saint-Gobain was an obvious and logical move. His temperament was perfectly suited to the prevailing culture at Saint-Gobain, given his love of the solid, the concrete, and the mathematically precise. He was appointed chief operating officer, which matched his fundamental skills to the task at hand: tightening budgets, making meticulous one-year assessments, and drawing up detailed three-year operational plans.

In 1977 Beffa was promoted to director and then to chairman of Pont-à-Mousson, a pipe manufacturer and a mainstay of Groupe Saint-Gobain. Acquired in 1970, the company was facing difficulties when Beffa arrived. He imposed an austerity plan, which involved cutbacks, elimination of jobs, and restructuring. His success there gave him confidence in his future as a potential director of the Saint-Gobain group.

Roger Fauroux chose him as his successor in 1982 over Alain Gomez, Jean-Marie Descarpentries, and Francis Mer. Fauroux based his decision on Beffa's reserved and prudent temperament, which seemed apt to steer the group through a difficult period of nationalization. Another quality that recommended Beffa during these trying times was his political neutrality. Beffa had a reputation for disliking conflict and refusing to engage in lengthy disputes. This made him appealing to a variety of French administrations. In 1986, as the group was being privatized, he was named CEO by the administration of Laurent Fabius and confirmed in that position later by the administration of French President Jacques Chirac.

AT THE HELM: A WORLDWIDE STRATEGY BASED AT HOME

Beffa's strategy for Saint-Gobain was completely in accordance with his character. A Catholic who regularly attended Jesuit meetings, he was something of a traditionalist who was distrustful of new industries like information technology and proud of the group's main, albeit unglamorous, businesses in the building-materials sector. In the 1980s the group made a hapless foray into computers and electronics with the acquisition of key stakes in Bull and Olivetti. Beffa, unlike his predecessor, did not regret that the government forced Saint-Gobain to backtrack and shed its assets in these areas.

Nevertheless, Beffa vigorously pursued Fauroux's diversification program while recentering the group's activities on more closely related industries. In 1996, for example, Saint-Gobain acquired Poliet, a leading building-materials distributor in France. Beffa dismissed initial criticism that he was blurring the group's focus on manufacturing while transforming it into a conglomerate. In the *Financial Times* he defended the decision to acquire Poliet as a point of strategy: "When you are in the specialized distribution of building materials, you know the consumer's needs. You are able to take account of these needs to prepare the new products of the future" (June 11, 1996). Acquisition of Poliet pushed Saint-Gobain to within the FRF 100 billion mark in total sales.

A salient feature of Beffa's long-term strategy was to reduce the business's cyclical nature by expanding into international markets and by promoting the Groupe Saint-Gobain as a blue-chip stock to shareholders. In the early 1990s Saint-Gobain bought the North American abrasives and ceramics manufacturer Norton for FRF 11 billion; by 2004 it provided 20 percent of American households with insulation. Having consolidated a strong home and regional base in France and Europe, the group next set its sights on the emerging markets of South America, China, India, Indonesia, and Thailand.

This strategy, however, created a dilemma, which Beffa in part resolved through the acquisition of Poliet. Before this move, France accounted for only 29 percent of the group's turnover and had more employees in North America than in its home market. These figures conflicted with Beffa's vision of a French and European model of capitalism, which emphasizes less dependence on the stock markets in favor of greater fiscal autonomy and a greater accountability to society as a whole rather than exclusively to the shareholders. "If capitalism is to be acceptable, then so must its behavior," Beffa asserted in *L'Express* (October 10, 2002).

Beffa, however, was not without troubles of his own. In 1994 he was placed under investigation during the Trager affair. The scandal involved allegations that Pont-à-Mousson had paid an improper commission to the French Republican

Party in connection with a public contract for a water supply system. Ironically, the incident resulted in Beffa's being unceremoniously passed over in favor of Jean-Marie Messier as head of the state-owned Compagnie Générale des Eaux, later Vivendi-Universal.

The Trager affair was soon forgotten, and Beffa worked to secure his vision of French capitalism as he neared retirement in 2007. This vision was reflected by his choice of successor, the ferociously competitive and highly principled Christian Streiff. Streiff had spent most of his career in Germany and was 100 percent Saint-Gobain, making him the ideal representative of the European model of capitalism that Beffa devoted his career to promulgating and defending.

SOURCES FOR FURTHER INFORMATION

Beffa, Jean-Louis, "Comment réformer le capitalisme, conservons notre identité européenne," *L'Express*, October 10, 2002.

Owen, David, "Companies and Finance: Europe. How to Diversify without Becoming a Conglomerate: Saint-Gobain's Takeover of Poliet Has Not Blurred Its Focus, Chairman Jean-Louis Beffa Tells David Owen," *Financial Times*, June 11, 1996.

Rovan, Ann, "Jean-Louis Beffa: 'J'imagine toujours le pire,'" *Le Figaro*, April 7, 2003.

—John Herrick

■■■

Alain Belda

1943–

Chairman, chief executive officer, and president, Alcoa

Nationality: Brazilian.

Born: June 23, 1943, in Meknes, Morocco.

Education: Universidade MacKenzie, BA, 1965.

Family: Married Haydee (maiden name unknown; a philanthropist); children: at least two.

Career: BASF, 1965–1969, accountant; Alcoa Aluminio (Brazilian subsidiary of Alcoa Inc.), 1969–1982, financial planner; 1979–1994, president; Alcoa Inc., 1982, vice president; 1991–1994, president of Latin American operations; 1994, executive vice president; 1995, vice chairman; 1997–1999, president and COO; 1999–2001, CEO and president; 2001–, chairman, CEO, and president.

Awards: Person of the Year, America, Brazilian American Chamber of Commerce, 1999.

Address: Alcoa, 201 Isabella Street, Pittsburgh, Pennsylvania 15212-5858; http://www.alcoa.com.

■ Alain Belda had seemed a safe choice when he was tapped to become Alcoa's president and chief operating officer in 1997: he was a company man through and through, having spent 30 years climbing Alcoa's corporate ladder. Rather than maintaining the status quo, however, he proved to be an advocate of change, reshaping Alcoa from a traditional economic model into one that more closely resembled modern high-tech companies than the commodities company Alcoa had long been. He spoke five languages—English, French, Italian, Portuguese, and Spanish—and had a firm understanding of the global marketplace. Evolving out of his international experience was his vision of Alcoa as a global entity at home in many different cultures.

MERITOCRACY

Belda was born to a Spanish father and a Portuguese mother in what was then called French Morocco. His father was skilled at turning failing companies around and traveled the world doing so. When Belda was three years old, his family moved to São Paolo, Brazil; when he was 13, his father's work took the family to Canada; when he was 17, his father was killed in an auto accident. Belda and his family returned to Brazil, where he eventually became a naturalized citizen in 1982. When he accepted the post of executive vice president at Alcoa in 1994, which required him to work in the United States, his wife and children remained in Brazil, although two of his children attended Brown University in Rhode Island. Belda often said that the United States was the only place where he could rise so high in a corporation, declaring American business to be a "meritocracy."

It was by chance that Belda had his first opportunity with Alcoa in Brazil. In 1969 he had a lunch appointment with his younger brother, Ricardo, who sent word that his work at Alcoa Aluminio, Alcoa's Brazilian subsidiary, would keep him late. Belda met his brother at the Alcoa Aluminio office and, while there, applied for a job in the financial department. Alcoa Aluminio offered to double the salary Belda was receiving from the German chemical company BASF, and he accepted the offer.

Belda worked in both finance and planning for Alcoa Aluminio for 10 years before being elevated to president, becoming the first person from outside the United States to hold that post. His language skills were put to good use when he was placed in charge of Alcoa's Latin American operations in 1991. He resisted assignment to posts in the United States, preferring to remain in his beloved Brazil, but in 1994 he took the next big step in his career and accepted the post of executive vice president at Alcoa, which required him to move to Pittsburgh, Pennsylvania.

PHILOSOPHY AND VISION

When he was later appointed by Alcoa's board of directors to the offices of president and COO, Belda immediately began introducing new business practices to the world's largest producer of aluminum. A far-reaching change was the introduction of the Alcoa Business System (ABS), which was derived from the Toyota Production System (TPS), with modifications by Belda and his staff. The most significant aspect borrowed from the TPS was the focusing of production on specific items demanded by customers. Until then, Alcoa had followed a typical commodities-company model in which it produced as much of its primary product as possible, sold what it could in the industrialized world for a profit, and then dumped what was left on the rest of the world's markets. This often led to Alcoa merely breaking even rather than turning a profit. In the ABS introduced by Belda, Alcoa's salespeople learned what their customers wanted, and Alcoa produced exactly that and nothing more.

Belda also expanded on the TPS model by emphasizing respect for all employees and for their opinions. If Alcoa were to succeed at production on demand, it would need to be nimble in its manufacturing, deftly shifting emphasis from one product to another. When management listened to its workers, it could develop better ways of shifting gears. As part of this strategy, in 1997 Belda introduced a three-year plan aimed at cutting production costs by $1 billion; by 2000, through worldwide cooperation from employees, Alcoa had cut costs by $1.1 billion. At that point Belda introduced a second three-year plan with emphasis on the ABS, achieving another $1 billion in savings over the course of the year. For his part, Belda took a 40 percent reduction in total compensation from 2000 to 2001 and another 20 percent reduction from 2001 to 2002.

The American and international marketplaces for Alcoa's products were chaotic during the 1990s and into the 2000s. From Belda's point of view, the ABS, though successful, was not enough to keep Alcoa economically sound. Competitors such as Alcan were expanding their shares of the marketplace; meanwhile, the dumping of Russian aluminum that had piled up unused during the cold war drove down prices. Where Alcoa would typically step up production and dump aluminum on the marketplace in order to prevent customers from straying, Belda instead took a page from the high-tech industrial giants such as Intel and heavily invested capital in acquisitions and manufacturing.

The purchase of Cordant Technologies for $2.9 billion offered Alcoa new avenues for increasing revenue, and Cordant's sales force brought along an extensive list of clients who became new customers for all of Alcoa's products. In August 1999 Belda declared that Alcoa would pursue a hostile takeover of Reynolds Metals Company, which succeeded on May 3, 2000, when Alcoa bought Reynolds for $4.8 billion in cash and stock; Reynolds remained a separate corporate entity within the Alcoa family. Reynolds's emphasis was on consumer products such as aluminum foil, giving Alcoa closer contact with end users. The acquisition also ensured that Alcoa would remain the world's foremost producer of aluminum products, harboring 15 percent of world revenues.

In 1999 Alcoa's net revenue surpassed $1 billion for the first time, but integrating acquisitions into the ABS soaked up a portion of these funds. In the early 2000s Alcoa had over 127,000 employees, with business locations expanding to 40 countries. Belda addressed labor unrest by establishing Alcoa's Ethics and Compliance Program, with toll-free phone numbers set up for use by any employee. Further, Belda established long-term goals for effecting environmental changes by the 2010s that stimulated 40 percent reductions in airborne pollutants from Alcoa plants worldwide as of 2004.

See also entry on Alcoa Inc. in *International Directory of Company Histories.*

SOURCES FOR FURTHER INFORMATION

"Alcoa's Business Ethics and Compliance Program: A Global Investment," *Ethnic News,* Fall 2003.

Arndt, Michael, "Alcoa Wants One of These, and One of Those," *BusinessWeek,* September 11, 2000, pp. 63–68.

Belda, Alain, interview by Michael Arndt, "Thinking Young at Alcoa: An Old Economy 'Classic,'" *BusinessWeek,* June 28, 2000.

—Kirk H. Beetz

■■■

Charles Bell

1960–

Chief executive officer and president, McDonald's Corporation

Nationality: Australian.

Born: November 7, 1960, in Kingsford, Australia.

Family: Son of a travel agent (name unknown) and Margaret (maiden name unknown); married; children: one.

Career: McDonald's Corporation, 1975–1979, crew member; 1979–1983, store manager; 1983–1985, manager, McDonald's Europe development company; 1985–1990, operations director and regional manager, McDonald's Europe development company; 1990–1993, vice president of marketing; 1993–1999, managing director of McDonald's Australia; 1999–2001, president of Asia Pacific, Middle East, and Africa group; 2001–2002, president of McDonald's Europe; 2003, president and COO; 2004–, CEO and president.

Address: McDonald's Corporation, 1 Kroc Drive, Oak Brook, Illinois 60523-2275; http://www.mcdonalds.com.

■ Charles Bell began working for McDonald's in Australia in 1975 as a teenager. A hard worker who was highly ambitious, he rose quickly through the ranks, becoming the youngest McDonald's manager ever in 1979. By 1993 Bell was running the Australian operation, which became a model for the company's global operations. In 2002 he came to the United States to become the corporation's chief operating officer. An affable and shrewd manager, Bell was a major player under the CEO James Cantalupo in reversing McDonald's decline in the early 2000s. In 2004, at 43 years of age, Bell became one of the youngest CEOs in the world when he replaced Cantalupo as president and CEO of McDonald's. He was also the company's first foreign CEO.

"LIFE IS NOT A REHEARSAL": RISE OF A McAUSSIE

Charles Bell was born in Kingsford, Australia, on November 7, 1960. His father was a travel agent; his mother, Margaret Bell, lived in the same Sydney suburb through the early 2000s. In 1975 Bell was a student at Marcellin College of Randwick, a select Catholic boy's school, where he learned religious instruction, teamwork, and discipline as well as some technical training. Not far from Marcellin was one of the first McDonald's outlets opened in Australia, of which Bell learned from a friend while riding home on the bus. He applied for a position serving hamburgers and was hired. Although his first night was so difficult that he told his parents he felt like quitting, he did not. Bell stuck with his job, dressing hamburgers, unloading trucks, and cleaning restrooms.

Having opened its first outlet in Sydney at the end of 1971, McDonald's Australia was a fledgling operation which failed to turn a profit through most of the 1970s. Visiting the Kingsford outlet, the Australian manager Peter Ritchie met the young Bell and quickly sized him up as a future company leader. Bell readily agreed with Ritchie with regard to his own prospects; as Ritchie told the *Sydney Morning Herald*, "He was ready to tell us how the place should have been run from 15 onwards" (April 21, 2004). Bell was often arrogant and upfront about his ambition, but in a charming, irreverent Australian way. Ritchie saw not a ranting fool but a potential leader.

The aspiring young manager gained a few lessons in cross-cultural operations during the 1970s. Helping to lead an American company in Australia, where businessmen were not seen as the heroes they were in the United States, proved to be a challenge. Unions were much stronger and taxes higher. The Shop Assistants' Union sought to organize Bell's workers; the union took McDonald's to court and struck the company's food suppliers, denouncing McDonald's for maintaining unfair labor practices, serving rotten plastic food, and even for subverting Australian culture. Ritchie sued the union for defamation and won through his presentation of McDonald's Australia as an Australian company run by Australians. Bell learned from Ritchie how to counter the anti-Americanism that had stung McDonald's: by marketing the company as a local one. Enough Australians were convinced for McDonald's Australia to finally begin earning a profit in the early 1980s.

Such experiences would help Bell when he was posted to Europe in 1983 as operations director and regional manager of McDonald's European development in Frankfurt. The first European McDonald's opened in Amsterdam in 1971; Britain and Germany would eventually become the company's leading markets, followed by France. In 1993, at age 32, Bell became managing director of McDonald's Australia, which he turned into a model subsidiary, with productivity higher than any other subsidiary and sales above the company's global average. Cantalupo, who through the 1990s headed McDonald's International, was enormously proud of Bell's accomplishments and told the *Business Review Weekly* that "Australia is one of our top countries around the world" (June 5, 2003)—and that Bell deserved much of the credit. Cantalupo went on to praise the example Bell and his friend and successor Guy Russo set, making McDonald's Australia the training ground even for American executives: "We've paraded a lot of people to Australia, even from the United States, to recalibrate our standards, to see what McDonald's looks like in the ideal environment" (June 5, 2003).

"IF YOU WANT TO BE THE POPE, YOU HAVE TO COME TO ROME"

Even before Cantalupo became CEO, as early as 1996, he knew of Bell's abilities and wanted him to go to Illinois—to McDonald's headquarters. Bell, however, a conservative Australian with strong family ties as well as strong political ties to his friend Prime Minister John Howard, did not want to emigrate. Cantalupo sought to persuade Bell that only by coming to America could he make the impact that he had the potential to make; even the Asian operation would not be moved to Sydney. But Bell, a "dinkum Aussie" through and through, did not want to relocate. "If Bell wanted to be Pope, he would have to live in Rome," said Cantalupo in an article in *Business Review Weekly* (June 5, 2003). Bell went to Illinois in 1999.

From Oak Brook, Illinois, Bell oversaw McDonald's Asia Pacific, Middle East, and Africa group and was then put in charge of McDonald's Europe in 2001. Bell's operations in China, where McDonald's outlets marketed spicy chicken burgers and wings, proved particularly profitable. No sooner had Bell taken over the European operation than he had to confront the ramifications of "mad cow disease" in Britain. By 2002 McDonald's was encountering further trouble. In spite of McDonald's International's healthy growth, the parent company's markets in the United States were reaching a saturation point. By 2002 worldwide sales and profits were both dropping, as was the value of McDonald's stock. Customers complained of cold food, slow service, and a lack of cleanliness. The board called James Cantalupo out of retirement and elected him CEO, effective January 2003.

"I'M LOVIN' IT": BELL'S TURNAROUND STYLE

Cantalupo turned to Bell, appointing him chief operating officer that same month. As COO Bell became not only Cantalupo's right-hand man but also his heir apparent. Bell was placed at the heart of Cantalupo's 2003–2004 turnaround marketing strategy. If McDonald's was to save its brand, it was believed, the company would have to change its controversial and tarnished image. In April 2003 Bell launched the company's worldwide "I'm Lovin' It" media campaign. Pop singer Justin Timberlake was enlisted to help persuade millions of disillusioned consumers that McDonald's was a new company. The goal was to win back customers and revitalize the McDonald's brand.

Bell's management style was quite similar to Cantalupo's in that he was affable but very direct. "I can be as subtle as a brick through a window when I need to be," he told the *Australian*'s Rodney Dalton; "I think Australians can be very blunt and I sort of use that to my advantage where necessary" (May 26, 2003). He and Cantalupo would show up at McDonald's outlets and hand the managers cards evaluating their performances. Bell showed zero tolerance for dirty bathrooms, cold food, and slow, rude service. Having started at the bottom, Bell easily perceived that many managers and public-relations workers had lost touch with their customers. He voiced this perception in a candid comment in *Business Review Weekly*: "A lot of marketing people can get too theoretical in their meeting rooms so I take them to the real world and say, 'This is what it's all about'" (June 5, 2003). In the same article Bell related how he would take his out-of-touch managers to the growing city of Blacktown, 30 miles from the heart of Sydney. In Blacktown he would tell the managers that the practical, upwardly mobile homeowners of Blacktown were their real customers, and not the monied elites of Sydney, whom Bell called the well-dressed people "who wear black lycra at lunch down at the Crow's Nest Hotel."

Bell waged more than a public-relations campaign. He and Cantalupo cut back on expansion in favor of improved service. They attempted to respond to the charge that McDonald's served unhealthy food by introducing menus featuring salads and other leaner cuisine. Several hundred outlets, mostly overseas, were closed. By the middle of 2003 the price of McDonald's stock was on the rise. Bell shared in the praise given to Cantalupo, and many believed that within three or four years he would become his successor. The coronation proved to be much more sudden.

McPRESIDENT OF THE WORLD

On April 19, 2004, Jim Cantalupo died from a heart attack at the age of 60. Some feared that his death would be a serious setback for the company. How could McDonald's profess to market healthy food when its own CEO had died possibly as a result of bearing too much fat? The board quickly named Bell chief executive officer of McDonald's Corporation, and the company seen as the very symbol of American globalization was now led by an Australian. Overnight Bell rocketed from relative obscurity to a position as one of the most influential Australians in the world, in a class with Rupert Murdoch and Mel Gibson. There seemed little doubt that he would continue to follow in the footsteps of his mentor, Cantalupo.

Concern about the company's future was reinforced when Bell underwent surgery and subsequent chemotherapy for colorectal cancer in May 2004, only two weeks after becoming CEO. Questions also remained, however, as to whether Bell would succeed in maintaining Cantalupo's turnaround strategy. Critics and pessimists felt that the company's revival was a mere illusion resulting from global economics and changes set in place by Cantalupo's predecessor, Jeff Greenberg. They pointed out that the youthful Bell, 43, had virtually no American experience and no career experience outside McDonald's, aside from his having headed a task force on small business for Prime Minister Howard. Optimists, however, believed Bell, who knew every facet of the company and its worldwide operations, to be the perfect man for the job. Who better to reinvent the McDonald's brand, which would depend more than ever on global markets, than an international executive?

See also entry on McDonald's Corporation in *International Directory of Company Histories.*

SOURCES FOR FURTHER INFORMATION

Arndorfer, James B., "Greenberg Resigns: McD's Shuffle Signals Bell as Heir Apparent; Europe Prez in Line to Succeed Cantalupo," *Advertising Age*, December 9, 2002.

Buckley, Neil, "McDonald's Earnings Looking 12 Percent Healthier," *Financial Times* (London), October 23, 2003.

Cock, Anna, "Australian Given Key to Golden Arches," *Melbourne Herald-Sun*, April 21, 2004.

Dalton, Rodney, "Bell to Ring In New Era for Macca's," *Australian*, May 26, 2003.

Day, Sherri, "McDonald's Chief Stresses Food Safety," *New York Times*, May 23, 2003.

Elliott, Stuart, "McDonald's Campaign Embraces a Loving Theme," *New York Times*, June 12, 2003.

Friedman, Thomas L., *The Lexus and the Olive Tree: Understanding Globalization*, New York, N.Y.: Farrar, Strauss & Giroux, 2000.

Gibbs, Stephen, and Caroline Overton, "McDonald's Tragedy Turns Kingsford Boy into New Burger King," *Sydney Morning Herald*, April 21, 2004.

Gibson, Richard, "McDonald's Is Recuperating, but Full Recovery a Way's Off?" *Wall Street Journal*, December 9, 2003.

Guy, Sandra, "Running McD an Inside Job," *Chicago Sun-Times*, December 8, 2002.

Herman, Eric, "Australian Bell Appointed New CEO of McDonald's," *Chicago Sun-Times*, April 20, 2004.

Horovitz, Bruce, "It's Back to Basics for McDonald's," *USA Today*, May 21, 2003.

———, "McDonald's CEO Could Be One to Copy—or Console," *USA Today*, December 23, 2003.

Love, John F., *McDonald's: Behind the Arches*, New York, N.Y.: Bantam Books, 1995.

Lusetich, Robert, Vanessa Walker, and Blair Speedy, "Aussie the Biggest Mac," *Australian*, April 21, 2004.

Patrick, Aaron, "Burger Meister," *Business Review Weekly* (Australia), June 5, 2003.

———, "McChief: Charlie Bell's Rise to the Top," *Business Review Weekly* (Australia), June 5, 2002.

Serwer, Andrew E., "McDonald's Conquers the World," *Fortune*, October 17, 1994, pp. 103–104, 106, 108, 112, 114, 116.

"Wannabe Boss Now McDonald's Head Honcho," *Sydney Morning Herald*, April 20, 2004.

—David Charles Lewis

■■■

Luciano Benetton

1935–

Chairman, Benetton

Nationality: Italian.

Born: May 13, 1935, in Treviso, Italy.

Family: Son of Leone (owner of a car and bike rental business) and Rosa Carniato; married Teresa (maiden name unknown), 1961; children: five.

Career: Benetton Group, 1965–, chairman; Italian Republic, 1992–1994, senator.

Awards: Master in Business Administration Honoris Causa, Instituto de Empresa, Madrid, 1992; honorary degree in law, Boston University, 1994; Laurea in Economia Aziendale Honoris Causa, Università ca' Foscari di Venezia, 1995.

Publications: *Io e i miei fratelli,* 1995.

Address: Villa Minelli 1, Ponzano, Treviso, Italy; http://www.benetton.com.

Luciano Benetton. *AP/Wide World Photos.*

■ With an aggressive marketing style and a precise target social group—teenagers and youngsters who were not particularly wealthy—Luciano Benetton transformed the small wool sweater firm that he founded with his sister Giuliana in 1965 into a global phenomenon studied by international business scholars. Throughout the years the group's core business remained clothing, and Benetton expanded in the sector to include not only the United Colors of Benetton but also a children's line sized 0–12, the more fashionable and trendy Sisley, and the sportswear brands Playlife and Killer Loop. Through the family's company, Edizione Holding, Benetton also controlled highway and urban catering services, infrastructures and services for mobility and communications, real estate, and agriculture. Though a global phenomenon, Benetton's management style was firmly rooted in the economic and business heritage of northeastern Italy, which combined a strong artisan tradition with an abundance of labor due to shrinking agricultural production.

THE LEGEND OF THE ORIGINS

As with all phenomena that attain a near-mythical status, the Benetton Group has a legend about its founder. According to the story Luciano, after the sudden death of his father, left school at age 14 and worked in a clothing store to support his family. He sold his bicycle in order to buy the company's first knitting machine. In 1965 Luciano, together with his sister and his two brothers, set up a small company producing pullover sweaters. From the start the tasks were diversified: Luciano acted as the marketing representative, while Giuliana designed the products and was in charge of production.

More important for the development of the group than Luciano's bike, however, was the founder's trip to Scotland. Here he became acquainted with a wool-softening process, which allowed manufacturers to knit in off-white yarn. The wool was dyed only at the last stage of production, an innovation that allowed the firm to keep up with ever-changing fashion trends. The bright colors that resulted from this process became the distinctive trademark of Benetton.

DEVELOPING THE GLOBAL BUSINESS

Luciano was the mind behind the so-called "industrial fashion," fashionable clothes that were sold through a cost-effective system of production and distribution. Success arrived almost immediately, and Benetton shops began to open throughout Europe, even in the challenging Parisian market. Luciano did not opt for centralized production and wide distribution, and his intuition regarding this crucial business decision paid off. He created his own clothing empire through subcontracts and franchising. Benetton licensed out most manufacturing to smaller textile producers and specialized in design, dying, and cutting. Through franchise agreements he contracted with independent retailers so that they would stock only Benetton clothing. Thanks to this marketing strategy and to profitable exchange rates in the 1980s and the early 1990s, the group was able to make surprising gains given the context of recession in which it operated.

During the 1980s Luciano also started to diversify the group's industrial activities with the purchase of Toleman's Formula One team, the sponsorship of Treviso's volleyball team, and the commercialization of Benetton watches, make-up, and perfumes. Benetton understood that the home market was saturated and started to open stores in the new American and Japanese markets.

FASHIONABLY SHOCKING

From the 1980s until 2000, Benetton collaborated with the advertising photographer Oliviero Toscani to create promotional campaigns that became as distinctive to the firm as its clothing. At first the advertisements focused on multiracial and multicultural themes. Toscaniand Benetton rejected the idea of creating standard fashion photographs simply featuring sexy models and stunning clothes: "With Benetton, we started out with the notion of color. By definition, Benetton means colors. So, to convey this idea of colors, we showed a group, made up of people with different colored skin. It was fantastic, so exhilarating to show the products in such a new and simple way" ("The Company's History," benetton.com). Yet, as the group began to face its first serious crisis with lawsuits from enraged franchisers who claimed not to have been adequately supported, advertising campaigns increasingly featured shocking images. They included an AIDS victim on his deathbed, an African guerrilla holding a Kalashnikov rifle and a human leg bone, a boat overcrowded with Albanians, a car in flames after a Mafia bombing, and even a series of male and female genitals.

These scandalous images produced heated debates. Benetton claimed to be drawing attention to social issues that were being shunned by the establishment: "We are forging a new form of communication. . . . We spread no lies. We say, in this world there is sickness, war and death" ("The Company's History," benetton.com). His detractors claimed that such advertising, far from rendering consumers socially conscious, subordinated social conscience to shopping.

GLOBAL MEETS LOCAL

In spite of the controversies about his advertisements, Benetton managed to retain a clear image for his group. He was not involved in the numerous judicial inquiries that caught many Italian politicians and businessmen during the 1990s. He also served as an Italian senator for the center-left Republican Party from 1992 to 1994, although he was largely disappointed and frustrated by that experience. As he remarked, "Running for office was a form of protest, I had hoped that everybody would roll up their sleeves and get to work but it wasn't like that" ("Interview with Foreign Press," www.made-in-italy.com).

By the middle of the 1990s Benetton had changed his distribution strategy. Rather than relying on the capillary network of small shops with which Benetton began, the commercial organization switched to a program of investment in megastores, some of them controlled directly by the group. Given their large dimensions and their prestigious locations either in historic buildings or in commercial centers, they formed distinctive urban landmarks. Benetton expanded into more than 120 countries with 5,000 stores. Despite the global expansion, however, in the early 21st century both the group and its founder remained inextricably linked to northeastern Italy. Older employees maintained that the Benettons still talked to them in the local dialect rather than in formal Italian. In addition, the group's close relations with its local origins were embodied by the cultural activities of the Fondazione Benetton Studi e Ricerche and through sports programs in a vision that went beyond athletic excellence to focus on the community-building aspects of athletic teams.

See also entry on Benetton Group S.p.A. in *International Directory of Company Histories.*

SOURCES FOR FURTHER INFORMATION

"The Company's History," *Benetton.com,* http://www.museedelapub.org/pubgb/virt/mp/benetton/pub_benetton.html.

"Interview with Foreign Press," *made-in-italy.com*, http://www.made-in-italy.com/fashion/fashion_houses/benetton/interview.htm.

Levine, Joshua, "Even When You Fail, You Learn a Lot," *Forbes*, March 11, 1996, p. 58.

Mirodan, Seamus, "The A-List Celebs Move In," *New Statesman*, May 1, 2004, p. 10.

Rossant, John, "The Faded Colors of Benetton," *BusinessWeek*, April 10, 1995, pp. 87, 90.

Sullivan, Ruth, "Dropping the Shock for the New," *Marketing*, April 20, 1995, p. 23.

—Luca Prono

■■■

Robert H. Benmosche

1944–

Chairman, chief executive officer, and president, Metropolitan Life Insurance Company

Nationality: American.

Born: May 29, 1944, in New York City, New York.

Education: Alfred University, BS, 1966.

Family: Married Denise V. (maiden name unknown); children: two.

Career: Arthur D. Little and Information Science, 1966–1975, computer consultant; Chase Manhattan Bank, 1975–1979, systems group; 1979–1982, vice president of technology; PaineWebber, 1984, vice president of marketing; 1984–1986, senior vice president of marketing group; 1986–1987, CFO in retail business; 1989–1995, executive vice president and director of securities operations; Metropolitan Life Insurance Company, 1995–1997, executive vice president of Individual Business Department; 1997–2004, president; 1997–, director; 1998–, chairman and CEO.

Address: Metropolitan Life Insurance Company, One Madison Avenue, New York, New York 10010-3603; http://www.metlife.com.

■ Robert H. Benmosche, a complete outsider who lacked any insurance-industry experience, would be remembered as the chief executive who attempted to remake Metropolitan Life Insurance Company. He demutualized the company in 2000, converting it from a policyholder-owned to a stockholder-owned firm. The new structure opened the doors for MetLife to win a larger piece of the financial-services pie, supplying it with the wealth to make acquisitions that would have previously been out of its league. By 2004 the level of success incurred through Benmosche's grand plan had yet to be determined.

With over $12 billion in premiums written and $220 billion in assets in 2003, MetLife was publicly traded and the largest life-insurance company in the nation with respect to total life insurance in effect and total admitted assets. Subsidiaries included GenAmerica, the independent-agency distribution network; Metropolitan Property and Casualty, for auto, home, and related coverages; and State Street Research, providing asset-management products and services to institutions and individuals. The company also had a retail-banking business unit, MetLife Bank.

MetLife's Institutional segment offered group benefits, through insurance, retirement products, and prepaid legal plans; its Individual segment offered many of the same types of products to individual consumers; and its International segment offered the same primarily to groups and individuals in Latin America and Asia Pacific. The company provided property and casualty protection through its Auto & Home operations as well as retail and institutional investment-management services—such as retirement plans, mutual funds, and more—through its Asset Management segment. A sixth segment focused on reinsurance.

THE DEATH OF A FATHER SHAPES A SON

Benmosche spent his childhood in the bucolic Catskills town of Monticello, New York. His formative years were shaped more than anything by a single event: the death of his father at age 50. The elder Benmosche left Robert, his three siblings, and their mother struggling with a mountain of debt. They continued to run the family hotel and restaurant, the Patio Motel, where the young Benmosche took on some of the housekeeping responsibilities and helped out with the switchboard. During high school and college he funded most of his tuition through a truck-driving job, delivering Coca-Cola. His uncle Julius Cohen, who worked with the family at the hotel, told *American Banker*, "He always had ambition. Whatever he had to do, he did to reach what he wanted" (January 8, 2001).

THE ARMY PRODUCES A TECHIE

After earning his bachelor's degree in mathematics from Alfred University in 1966, Benmosche served for two years as an army lieutenant. After a tour of duty in Vietnam, he spent about a year in Korea in the U.S. Signal Corps, where he set up field communications and acquired a love for technology. Benmosche then began his career with Arthur D. Little and

Information Science as a consultant. In the mid-1970s he moved to Chase Manhattan Bank, where he became a vice president of technology. In *BusinessWeek* James C. Curvey, the Chase colleague who became chief operating officer of Fidelity Investments, was quoted as saying, "He was one of the smartest, hardest-working, most intense executives there. He's very results oriented" (December 14, 1998).

A SALES AND MARKETING STAR

Benmosche joined PaineWebber in 1982, helping develop the Central Asset Brokerage Account, which propelled the company to second place in total account sales and first place in average customer balance among firms exceeding $200,000 in assets under management per customer within the financial services industry. In 1984 he became senior vice president in PaineWebber's marketing group, responsible for marketing IRAs, insurance, financial planning, retirement plans, and money-market funds through the firm's 4,500 retail brokers. Benmosche later became director of brokerage operations and launched a reengineering plan that relied heavily on technology. As a result PaineWebber was able to handle a fourfold increase in volume with 40 percent less staff.

A MERGER SPECIALIST

Benmosche's last major assignment at PaineWebber was to lead the firm's Southern division, where he concentrated on reducing the high broker turnover at 80 branch offices employing more than 1,500 retail brokers. He also oversaw the complex merger of Kidder Peabody's operations and systems with those of PaineWebber. In 1995 MetLife hired Benmosche to the position of executive vice president, which entailed leading its forthcoming merger with New England Financial.

REBUILDING AFTER A SCANDAL

The toughest challenge of Benmosche's career came when he was named MetLife's president and COO, responsible for both the Individual and Institutional businesses as well as the company's international insurance operations. At the time the sales force had been hampered by a scandal; an investigation had revealed that agents in the company's Tampa office had sold life insurance to nurses under the guise of a retirement plan. The publicly aired scandal sent agents running from the company, and sales plummeted. But under Benmosche's watch the sales force rebounded. Focusing on agent retention instead of recruitment—at the time an internally divisive strategy—he visited many of the company's 428 sales offices, meeting with agents one on one and in group meetings. Agents ceased to abandon the firm, and productivity per agent increased from $19,000 to $23,000.

REINVENTING METLIFE

In July 1998 Benmosche was named chairman and CEO and took on the challenge of reinventing the 132-year-old MetLife—known by its employees as Mother Met. Benmosche, who lacked experience in the insurance industry, later commented that he had been attracted to the firm's history; it was founded in New York three years after the Civil War from the remnants of the National Union Life and Limb Insurance Company. Yet, in spite of his appreciation for the company's past, Benmosche had revolutionary plans for its future. At the time of his appointment insurance companies were beginning to recognize that customers were demanding a wider range of financial services from a single provider.

THE JOB OF A LIFETIME

All of Benmosche's prior roles had prepared him for the ultimate test; his 14 years of experience in the securities industry would serve him well as MetLife pushed into the financial-services industry. One of his primary goals would be to strengthen the sales force to which he had become so connected as president and COO—and which he called in *National Underwriter* the company's "strongest individual franchise" (April 6, 1998). When Benmosche took over in 1998, MetLife employed 10,500 U.S. agents; he said that he planned to increase that number by four hundred annually over the coming five to 10 years.

A TOUGH MANAGER AT EASE WITH HIS TROOPS

At both PaineWebber and MetLife, Benmosche developed a reputation as a tough manager who regarded productivity as more important than people, sometimes bruising egos in order to achieve the desired results. His military training certainly played a part in his leadership style; rather than let his troops create their own battle plans, Benmosche played the role of a hands-on sergeant who delineated exactly what to do and how to get it done. Martin A. Stein, the vice chairman at BankAmerica Corporation who worked with Benmosche for more than 25 years, said in *BusinessWeek*, "You love him, or you don't like him at all, because of his sometimes confrontational style" (December 14, 1998).

Indeed, Benmosche may have been most at ease when he was in the trenches with his troops. He once spent four hours convincing about 40 brand managers to start taking accountability for their problems instead of blaming the company for poor results. As described by *BusinessWeek*, he gave out his direct phone number and offered to meet "anyone anytime anywhere" to offer assistance with problems (December 14, 1998).

TAKING METLIFE PUBLIC

Benmosche's largest contribution to MetLife was his push to take the company public. Insurance companies had historically been mutual companies owned by the insurance policyholders—the insured. In essence Benmosche wanted to convert MetLife from a policyholder-owned company into a stockholder-owned company. MetLife would distribute all of its shares to policyholders, who could then sell them once additional shares were issued to the public. Around the same time as MetLife's planned conversion, Prudential Insurance Company of America and John Hancock Mutual Life Insurance Company announced plans to convert.

Benmosche's primary justification for the dramatic move was that in his opinion MetLife's age-old business structure was stymieing its competitive potential. Washington had opened the gates for insurers, banks, and brokers to aggressively compete in one another's businesses, but without the capital that would be raised by a stock offering, MetLife's ability to expand through acquisitions was greatly limited. Benmosche told *BusinessWeek*, "This sleeping giant is no longer asleep. We're going to wake up the world" (December 14, 1998).

A FORMIDABLE CHALLENGE

In retrospect Benmosche perhaps should have tempered his enthusiasm. MetLife did not start out of the gate from a position of strength: the company's average return on assets in 1998 was 0.38 percent, one of the lowest of any large mutual company, according to Standard & Poor's. Additionally, competition was formidable. Around the time that Benmosche announced his plans, American International Group bought SunAmerica, a growing annuity firm. SunAmerica's return on assets was 2.25 percent—six times MetLife's. Robert Barker said in a *BusinessWeek Online* editorial, "What's plain from its financials is that, despite a flair for friendly marketing, MetLife is a lot like the blimps that keep its name—and Snoopy—aloft: all puffed up and pretty slow" (February 21, 2000).

SNOOPY TAKES A BOW

As the company prepared to go public, MetLife sent a strong message to its customers indicating that it was no longer their grandfather's insurance company. For nearly 15 years MetLife's advertising campaigns had featured the adventures of Snoopy and other characters from the celebrated "Peanuts" comic strip. In early 1999 the company relegated Snoopy to a supporting role, announcing a campaign that would supplant the dog with stories about MetLife's history, told by actors and actresses playing a multicultural group of agents. Snoopy made only cameo appearances at the end of the commercials and in marketing brochures. In the *New York Times* Benmosche said of the former campaign, "I felt it was too much Snoopy. When you talk about MetLife, you say, 'That's Snoopy's company,' and that's important. But we also want the ads to begin to remind people why to do business with MetLife" (March 12, 1999).

A SLOW START FOR THE REINVENTED METLIFE

Benmosche took MetLife public in April 2000, adding about $2.5 billion in capital to the former mutual insurer. Benmosche promised 15 percent growth in per-share earnings, but analysts warned that beneath the lofty numbers and promises, the company was struggling, and pressure was building on its CEO. By January 2001 MetLife had made no large acquisitions and earnings were still sagging.

Colin Devine, the insurance analyst with Solomon Smith Barney who was one of six analysts to downgrade their ratings on MetLife's stock, noted in *American Banker*, "They're still on mutual time—to make this work as a stock they need to turn this into a growth company. They need more new blood there. You've got people thinking they're doing a great job, but the problem is they're not" (January 8, 2001).

METLIFE GOES TO THE BANK

Benmosche had his work cut out for him; one of his main priorities in restructuring the company would be to expand outside of insurance. About four months after MetLife's initial public offering he purchased a small bank based in Kingston, New Jersey, for $80 million. Customers had access to the bank's products and services through MetLife's agents and through the company's Web site. Caitlin Long, the insurance analyst at Credit Suisse First Boston, remarked in *American Banker*, "Met's strategy is to use the bank to try to hold onto some of the $20 billion-plus per year that it pays out in the form of benefits and claims payments to its customers. It fits into the vision that Benmosche has of increasing the penetration into the customer base" (January 8, 2001).

MAPPING A STRATEGY

To turn his vision into reality, Benmosche was prepared to enforce accountability. New standards placed considerable pressure on the sales force, and the lowest-rated agents risked losing their jobs. He planned to push distributors like Merrill Lynch to ratchet up sales of MetLife annuities. Priority was placed on the development of new products, such as a more competitive variable life-insurance policy and long-term-care insurance that could be sold to existing customers. With regard to the company's Institutional business, Benmosche planned to increase sales to small and midsize companies while expanding product offerings to large businesses by selling accidental-death and dismemberment benefits in addition to basic life and short-term-disability coverage.

Expenses would be reduced through advances in technology and cutbacks in noncore businesses. As he told *American Banker*, Benmosche felt confident that the new MetLife would succeed: "A big product of the whole demutualization was an enormous self-confidence in our company. We want to transform our culture, so people feel empowered and have the freedom to act" (January 8, 2001).

A COMPANY RESPONDS TO A NATIONAL TRAGEDY

The impact of September 11, 2001, on the New York–based MetLife was extraordinary. In addition to losing employees in the tragedy, the company paid the largest amount in life-insurance claims resulting from the attacks of any insurer. Within two weeks of the attacks more than $53 million had been approved for payment to beneficiaries; the first payment had been finalized just three days after September 11. In hearings a few weeks later MetLife estimated its losses at $250 million to $300 million. During the crisis the company took steps to allow family members of victims to easily access benefits. The company waived the traditional death-certificate requirement, relying instead on communication with employers. MetLife also established a toll-free call-in number so that anyone affected by the tragedy could quickly obtain needed information.

While Benmosche focused mainly on paying claims to the beneficiaries of victims, he also responded to government leaders' pleas to take the necessary steps to strengthen the nation's economy. As part of a program to increase MetLife's investment in public equity markets, Benmosche announced that MetLife would invest $1 billion in a broad array of publicly traded stocks. As recorded in Federal Document Clearing House Political Transcripts, Benmosche said, "We have made this move because we have enormous confidence in the resilience of the country and its economy, and it's time to put our money where our beliefs are" (September 26, 2001).

SIGNS OF GROWTH

In the first quarter of 2004 MetLife came one step closer to bearing the profile of a true growth company. It boasted $362.9 billion in assets under management—an 18 percent increase over the prior year period and the fourth consecutive quarter of double-digit growth. The company notched record annuity deposits of $3.4 billion and earned total premiums and fees of $6 billion, for increases of 32 percent and 12 percent, respectively, over the prior year period. All told, in the first quarter of 2004 the company posted a 44 percent increase in net income over the first quarter of 2003.

With respect to the auspicious quarter, Benmosche declared to Business Wire, "During the quarter, we continued to demonstrate our ability to grow premiums and fees as well as annuity deposits through our leading market positions, innovative products, diversified distribution channels and improved sales-force productivity. At the same time, we are operating in a dramatically improved credit and equity market environment compared to the prior year period" (May 3, 2004).

See also entry on Metropolitan Life Insurance Company in *International Directory of Company Histories.*

SOURCES FOR FURTHER INFORMATION

Barker, Robert, "MetLife: I Wouldn't Take This Puppy Home," *BusinessWeek Online*, February 21, 2000, http://www.businessweek.com/2000/00_08/b3669143.htm.

Elliott, Stuart, "Snoopy and the 'Peanuts' Gang Will No Longer Be Metropolitan Life's Main Representatives," *New York Times*, March 12, 1999.

Gjertsen, Lee Ann, "Does Bob Benmosche's New MetLife Have What It Takes to Break Out?" *American Banker*, January 8, 2001, p. 1.

"MetLife Announces First Quarter 2004 Results: Reports Net Income of $0.69 per Share, a 47 Percent Increase," Business Wire, May 3, 2004.

Murray, M. Christian, "Met Names Benmosche CEO," *National Underwriter—Life & Health*, April 6, 1998, p. 3.

Spiro, Leah Nathans, "Fighter Pilot," *BusinessWeek*, December 14, 1998, p. 124.

"U.S. Representative Michael Oxley (R-OH) Holds Hearing on Impact of Terrorist Attacks on Securities and Insurance Industries," Federal Document Clearing House Political Transcripts, September 26, 2001.

—Tim Halpern

■■■

Silvio Berlusconi

1936–

Founder and former chairman of Fininvest and prime minister of Italy

Nationality: Italian.

Born: September 29, 1936, in Milan, Italy.

Education: University of Milan, JD, 1961.

Family: Son of Luigi (bank clerk) and Rosella (secretary) Berlusconi; married Carla Dall'Ogglio (divorced); married Veronica Lario (actress), 1990; children: five (first marriage, two; second marriage, three).

Career: Cantieri Riuniti Milanesi, 1962, founder; Edilnord, 1963, founder; Telemilano, 1974, founder; Fininvest, 1978–1994, founder, chairman; Canale 5, 1980, founder; Italian government, 1994, 2001–, prime minister.

Awards: Cavalliere del Lavoro, 1977; honorary degree in managerial engineering from Calabria University, 1991; named Man of the Year by the International Film and Programme Market of Television, Cable, and Satellite, 1991.

Address: Presidenza del Consiglio dei ministri, Palazzo Chigi, Piazza Colonna 370, 00186 Rome, Italy; http://www.governo.it/index.asp.

■ Silvio Berlusconi was noted for his entrepreneurial spirit and flamboyance in his rise to the heights of Italian business and politics. His investments in real estate, media, and sports made him Italy's richest man, and he served two separate terms as the country's prime minister. He was also controversial. Lasting just seven months, his first stint as prime minister ended with his resignation amid charges that his business interests conflicted with his duties as head of state. In 2004, three years into his second term, he was tried on charges of having, in the 1980s, bribed judges who were hearing a case involving one of his competitors. Nicknamed "The Cavalier," he was known for living lavishly while catering to populist tastes in entertainment, for emphasizing his status as a self-made man and promoting himself unabashedly, and for making outrageous statements, including negative comments about Muslims and positive ones about former Italian dictator Benito Mussolini. Nonetheless, his influence remained far-reaching. Touching on almost every aspect of Italian life, his holdings included three television networks, Italy's largest publishing house, department stores, and a soccer team. In 2004 *Forbes* magazine ranked Berlusconi the richest person in Italy and the 30th wealthiest worldwide, with a net worth of $10 billion.

A YOUNG ENTREPRENEUR

Berlusconi grew up in a lower-middle-class Milanese family, but even as a youth he showed entrepreneurial zeal and determination to improve his status. He put himself through college with a variety of jobs: selling vacuum cleaners, writing papers for his classmates (for a fee), and singing on cruise ships. After he received a law degree, with honors, from the University of Milan in 1961, he borrowed money from the bank where his father worked and went into real estate development, setting up the companies Cantieri Riuniti Milanesi in 1962 and Edilnord in 1963. With Italy's prosperity in the 1960s had come a huge demand for housing, and Berlusconi was there to take advantage of it. His projects included Milano 2, a suburban development of 4,000 housing units on the outskirts of Milan, completed in 1969. He followed this with another residential development, Milano 3, in 1976.

NEW OPPORTUNITIES IN TELEVISION

Berlusconi went into television by establishing the cable TV company Telemilano in 1974 and bringing this service to the housing complexes he had built. A 1976 court decision paved the way for more television ventures. Italy's Constitutional Court ruled that while the public-sector network, Radio Televisione Italiana, could have a monopoly on national broadcast television, local markets were open to all.

Setting up a holding company, Fininvest, in 1978 as an umbrella for his various projects, Berlusconi delved into numerous aspects of the television industry. He rented films to local TV stations; in turn, the stations had to carry advertising they bought through Fininvest's advertising agency, Publitalia. In 1980 he set up the Canale 5 television network. To avoid running afoul of regulators, Canale 5 operated legally as a group of local stations. However, all the stations carried the same programs simultaneously by means of videotape, making it a national network in practice. Renato Brunetta, one of Berlusconi's political advisers, told the London *Observer*, "What Berlusconi did was what he always does. He cut to the core"—and the core was that the purpose of television was to sell advertising nationally (January 18, 2004). According to Brunetta, Berlusconi then put all "his energy and imagination" into creating a virtual national network that could compete with the public TV network for advertising, a concept the political adviser called "pure genius."

In 1981 Italy's Constitutional Court decided to allow privately owned networks to broadcast nationally. Berlusconi responded by buying Canale 5's primary competitors, Italia 1 in 1983 and Rete 4 in 1984, giving him about 45 percent of the national broadcast market, equivalent to Radio Televisione Italiana's share. His networks broadcast soap operas and game shows, which proved popular in contrast to the highbrow programming on the public network. The Constitutional Court, however, also favored strong antitrust regulations on private broadcasters and urged the Italian parliament to pass such legislation. Despite this, and despite widespread criticism of Berlusconi's large market share, the parliament in 1990 enacted a very weak antitrust law.

INTO POLITICS

Berlusconi kept expanding his holdings, adding broadcast operations outside Italy and such diverse acquisitions as the AC Milan soccer club in 1986, La Standa department stores in 1988, and the Arnoldo Mondadori Editore publishing house in 1990. The Fininvest empire grew to about 150 companies. His critics continued to object to the degree of control he exercised over national television, but in the 1990s, demonstrating his trademark determination and tenacity, he fought back by going into politics. In 1993 he formed the political party Forza Italia, which means "Go Italy," a cheer used by fans of his soccer team. Berlusconi forged a coalition with two right-wing parties, the National Alliance and the Northern League. His personal popularity, enhanced by his status as a political outsider at a time when many insiders had been accused of enriching themselves at public expense in a widespread scandal known as Tangentopoli (Bribesville), helped him win the office of prime minister in 1994. Berlusconi had climbed to the top in national politics by "using the same methods and many of the same people as he had used to become a billionaire" (*Independent*, June 21, 2003).

Berlusconi stepped down as Fininvest's chairman in 1994, but the company remained under his ownership. Many Italians called for the new prime minister to sell some of his businesses, which he declined to do. Public outcry increased when he proposed that one of Fininvest's advisers, the merchant bank Mediobanca, assist in the privatization of state-run companies. Moreover, some of his appointees in the new government had been involved in the Tangentopoli scandal, and conflicts arose with the leaders of the National Alliance and the Northern League. Berlusconi was forced to resign as prime minister in December 1994, after only seven months in office.

Berlusconi then made some conciliatory moves, such as selling stakes in some of his businesses to outside investors. In 1995 he sold 28 percent of Mediaset, a company he had formed to unite his television, advertising, film, and recording ventures, to outside investors, and in 1996 he announced a public stock offering to further reduce his share. That year, he was elected to parliament, despite having been accused over the years of crimes that included tax evasion, bribery, and antitrust violations. Although convicted of some corruption-related charges, he appealed and stayed out of jail. In 2004 he was taken to court again, this time on charges of bribing judges. He maintained his innocence of all the charges brought against him, which he contended were politically motivated.

Many Italians continued to support Berlusconi, electing him prime minister again in 2001 to a term ending in 2006. In 2003 he became president of the European Union, a post that rotates among European heads of state every six months. He remained "one of Europe's most unusual and flamboyant leaders, a media magnate and political titan who has amassed, or at least sought, an astonishing degree of power, yet always seems to be dancing one small step ahead of disaster" (*New York Times*, February 16, 2003). Despite some of the charges and criticisms he faced, Berlusconi was to many Italians "the ordinary Joe next door who by dint of incredible hard work and determination has landed on top of the heap . . . Italy's master of the universe, their proudest son" (*Independent*, June 21, 2003).

SOURCES FOR FURTHER INFORMATION

Bruni, Frank, "Italy's Leader Balances Ambitions and Trials," *New York Times*, February 16, 2003.

Carlin, John, "All Hail Berlusconi," *Observer*, January 18, 2004.

Popham, Peter, "Silvio Berlusconi: The Two Faces of Italy's Billionaire Premier," *Independent*, June 21, 2003.

—Trudy Ring

■■■

Betsy Bernard

1955–

Former president and chief executive officer of consumer long-distance unit, AT&T

Nationality: American.

Born: May 16, 1955, in Holyoke, Massachusetts.

Education: Saint Lawrence University, BA, 1977; Fairleigh Dickinson University, MBA, 1981; Stanford University, MS, 1989.

Career: American Telephone and Telegraph (AT&T), 1976, summer intern; 1977–1995, various positions including account executive, sales manager, operations manager, and product manager; Pacific Bell Communications, 1995–1997, president and CEO; Pacific Telesis, 1996–1997, head of Business Market Group; Avirnex Communications, 1997–1998, president and CEO; U.S. West, 1998, president and CEO of Long Distance; 1998–2000, executive vice president of retail markets; Qwest Communications, 2000–2001, executive vice president of national mass markets; AT&T, 2001–2002, president and CEO of consumer long-distance unit; 2002–2003, president.

Awards: Sloan Fellowship, Stanford University, 1988; Honorary Doctorate of Laws, Pepperdine University, 2003; Emerging Leader of the Year Award, Women's Vision Foundation, 2003.

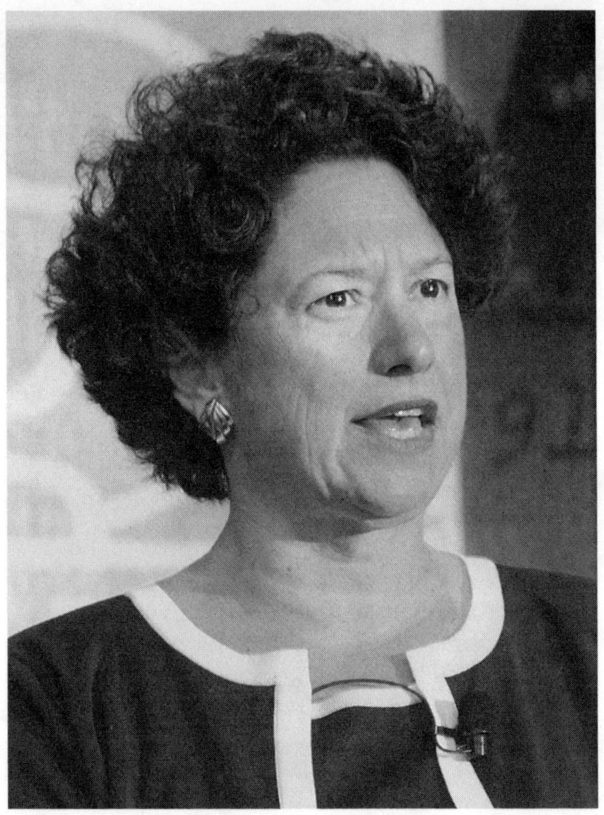

Betsy Bernard. © *Naljah Feanny/Corbis.*

■ Betsy Bernard spent much of the 1990s on *Fortune* magazine's list of the 50 most powerful women in business, eventually rising to 12th in 2003 before her resignation from AT&T. She was respected for her toughness when making difficult decisions. During her years as a top executive, she adhered to a set of ideals that had begun forming while she was in college and were shaped and refined when she became a feminist in her 30s.

EXPERIENCE

Bernard was born and raised in Massachusetts, where she was inspired by her mother, a radio personality, television talk-show host, and writer. She credited her experiences while attending Saint Lawrence University, especially a semester spent in Kenya, with helping her learn to cope with work outside her comfort zone, which helped her tackle ever-more-challenging tasks during her career. Her employment at AT&T began during her junior year in college when she received a call from a recruiter; in 1976 she interned at AT&T Long Lines in Albany, New York, where she first developed a passion for the telecommunications business. By 1979 she was running an office of 50 people in New Jersey. During her first 18 years at AT&T she worked in finance, marketing, strategy, and customer service.

In 1995 Bernard left AT&T to become president and CEO of Pacific Bell Communications. From there, she became the head of the Business Market Group of Pacific Telesis but wanted to return to being a CEO; thus, she took charge of the high-tech startup Avirnex Communications. She then moved to U.S. West, helping the company earn $9 billion in annual revenues before it became part of Qwest Communications, where she helped develop the company's markets.

In 2001 Bernard was lured back to AT&T with the promise that she would eventually become the CEO of a new spin-off company. At the time, she took charge of long distance, network services, AT&T Labs, and AT&T's business division. Altogether, she oversaw more than 55,000 employees; the business division alone was a $27 billion concern, with four million customers. On October 1, 2002, Bernard became AT&T's first woman president; but all was not well. In 2003 AT&T Business laid off 3,500 workers in an attempt to stabilize its bottom line. Further, AT&T was no longer planning on spinning off the company that Bernard had been expected to lead. Thus, in April 2003 she and Dave Dorman, AT&T's CEO, began arranging for her departure from the company. She left on December 1 of that year in the hope of finding employment as a CEO elsewhere.

APPLIED THEORY

Bernard noticed the rarity of women and ethnic minorities in executive positions in her industry, and she tried to enhance the chances of advancement for people she believed had been subject to discrimination. She cited Abraham Lincoln as her inspiration, saying her goals were "to lift artificial weights from all shoulders,/To clear the paths of pursuit for all,/And to afford an unfettered start and a fair chance in the race of life" (Bernard, August–September 2003). To this end, in 2000 she established the Emerging Leaders Program at AT&T, 60 percent of its members were women. The intent of the program was to provide mentoring for management employees.

Among the ideas she taught were that performance and communication with employees were essential for success. With respect to the former, one should lead by example by actually putting in the hours necessary to achieve one's goals. With respect to the latter, clear communication of instructions and of goals to be attained was considered crucial.

SEVEN GOLDEN RULES

In addition to being a powerful business leader, Bernard may be remembered for her "seven golden rules of leadership," which she enumerated at the Women & Diversity Leadership Summit on October 24, 2002 (Bernard, December 15, 2002). The first of these rules was that "everyone's time is valuable." Wasting employees' time costs businesses money and perhaps hundreds of millions of dollars in lost productivity in America every year. Further, a leader's wasting the time of his employees, for instance by making them wait before commencing meetings, is demoralizing and tends to suggest that wasting time is acceptable.

Her second rule also employed the use of basic courtesy: "No temper tantrums." Bernard thought displays of ill temper were infantile. She observed that such behavior created a corporate climate in which managers, their subordinates, and their subordinates' subordinates all communicated violently, thus degenerating interaction to the point of nonsensicalness. Bernard herself was noted for her calm demeanor. Effective communication was also the basis of her third rule: "Get to the bloody point!" A leader should know what he or she wants to say before speaking and should be concise. A wandering discourse leaves subordinates guessing as to what their boss wants.

The fourth rule, "Be candid," was a further refinement of the communication essential to leadership. Talking entirely about success was mere "bragging" in Bernard's view; employees needed to know exactly what the problems were so that they could try to fix them in their everyday work. Her fifth rule, "Just say thank you. And mean it," noted that a successful manager is one who shares credit and recognizes that no business organization succeeds without the cooperation of many.

Bernard was particularly mindful of her sixth rule, "Integrity is everything," after the Exxon and Enron scandals of the early 2000s. For her, integrity was reflected in daily behavior and in the way in which managers treated the work of their employees. She knew of and reviled business gatherings where company money was lavishly spent on luxuries such as $600 bottles of wine. Employees had worked hard to earn that $600, and wasting company money in such a fashion communicated to them that their work was not valued.

Her final rule: "If you don't know, who does?" A leader should have "vision" and should know what is needed and how to get it. In her mind, a brilliant person with every asset but "vision" would be a poor leader. People need to know what they are supposed to achieve in order to work together toward a common goal.

Bernard is a member of the board of directors of BearingPoint, Principal Financial Group, United Technologies Corporation, and URS Group.

See also entry on AT&T Corp. in *International Directory of Company Histories.*

SOURCES FOR FURTHER INFORMATION

Bernard, Betsy J., "Leadership and Diversity," *Executive Speeches*, August–September 2003, pp. 16–19.

———, "Seven Golden Rules of Leadership," *Vital Speeches of the Day*, December 15, 2002, pp. 152–156.

Black, Jane, "AT&T's Betsy Bernard Goes the Distance," *BusinessWeek Online*, May 29, 2003, http://www.businessweek.com/technology/content/may2003/tc20030529_5598_tc111.htm.

—Kirk H. Beetz

Daniel Bernard

1946–

Chief executive officer and chairman, Carrefour

Nationality: French.

Born: 1946, in France.

Education: École des Hautes Études Commerciales.

Career: Director of hypermarket chains Mammouth and Delta; Metro, 1975–1981, various positions; 1981–1992, managing director of Metro France; Carrefour, 1992–1998, CEO; 1998–, chairman and CEO.

Awards: Most Influential People in Trade, *World Trade Magazine*, 2000; Global Corporate Achievement Award, Economist Intelligence Unit, 2002.

Address: Carrefour, 6, avenue Raymond Poincaré, Paris 75771 France; http://www.carrefour.com.

Daniel Bernard. © *Corbis SYGMA.*

Daniel Bernard was the dynamic leader of Carrefour, the French general-merchandise chain and grocery retailer that was the second largest such company in the world, behind Wal-Mart. The group operated hypermarkets (sprawling stores with broad varieties of products and services), supermarkets, "hard discounters" (small specialty stores), convenience stores, cash-and-carry wholesale operations, and food services. The first three of the aforementioned outlets were Carrefour's primary focus and were prevalent in Asia, Latin America, and Europe. Carrefour invented the superstore in the 1970s and had become a rival to Wal-Mart in many regions of the world by the beginning of the 21st century.

A GROCER WITH A GLOBAL REACH

Daniel Bernard quickly climbed the retail and merchandise industry ladder to run the world's number-two discount chain and France's number-one grocery and retail chain. Bernard joined Carrefour in 1992 as chief executive officer and by 2004 had amassed 27 years of retail experience. Before arriving at Carrefour, Bernard had headed the German food retailer Metro, a large French retailer with a presence in six other countries, for 10 years. In his posts at both companies, Bernard's drive to expand into foreign markets was relentless and ongoing and central to his profit strategy.

Bernard cultivated Carrefour's corporate image into that of a leading merchandiser, particularly in fresh food, and Carrefour developed into an omnipresent standard across Europe. The company advanced to that point under the strong leadership of Daniel Bernard. Called "bright, effusive, confident, sophisticated, and well spoken" by a commentator for *MMR* (March 10, 2003), Bernard transformed Carrefour from "a French retailer with stores in other countries to the French-based retail company that happens to be the premier global retailer. His vision, more than any other ingredient, is responsible for Carrefour's astonishing metamorphosis, in one decade, into a world-class retailing power" (March 10, 2003).

BusinessWeek called Bernard "a low-key" CEO (June 11, 2001). He listened carefully to his audiences, both within and outside the company. He was determined to expand the company's retail storefront presence around the world and, as a result, its market share. His attention to pleasing customers manifested itself in his ongoing market studies and catchy promotions. Under Bernard, Carrefour garnered a reputation for making the most of clever advertising, displays, and promotions.

Bernard constantly tried to modernize the hypermarket and tailor it to consumer needs and convenience. His zeal for improvement was evident in the company's top-secret, two-year test market in a Paris warehouse. This full-size mock store, stocked with plastic foods, tested different product arrangements and store designs on consumers.

CARREFOUR HAD THE IDEA FIRST

The first retail giant in Europe, Carrefour was by 2004 France's largest and the world's second-largest such company, at a quarter of the size of Wal-Mart. Carrefour was known as the inventor of the superstore and the hypermarket. Its stores were especially visible to the general consumer; they were situated outside town centers and known as "crossroads" of products, from groceries to garden supplies. Additional services included eyeglass repair, travel and rental-car agencies, and mobile-phone service.

Carrefour was active in all types of retail distribution but specialized in food sales. Its stores offered competitive prices and variety in products and brands. The company, a marketing pioneer in the "consumer staples" industry, opened the world's first hypermarket in 1963. The company was known worldwide for its discount Ed markets and Picard frozen foods.

STRATEGY: TAKING ON THE WORLD

Carrefour operated in Latin America beginning in 1975 and opened new purchasing centers and supermarkets in China through the early 2000s. Bernard was instrumental in expanding the company outside its traditional base in France and Spain. Referring to Carrefour's expansion into regions avoided by Wal-Mart, Bernard told *BusinessWeek*, "We are pioneers" (June 12, 2000). At the end of the 1990s Carrefour had expanded through a major merger at a time when Europe's common currency created the trends of increased competition and industry consolidation.

Part of Bernard's strategy was to target areas of the world where Wal-Mart lagged. Carrefour had particular strengths in merchandising and international sales and marketing. Bernard sustained business growth through mergers and joint acquisitions; he built and converted existing stores and shaped them according to his standards of the hypermarket concept. Discounts and promotions lured customers to new stores.

Bernard was skilled at successfully assessing and moving into international markets. He devoted at least a year to the study of a target market before moving forward with development plans. His attention to local needs ensured smooth transitions and quick customer interest in new stores. Part of his strategy was to tailor Carrefour's retailing to local markets and choose the most appropriate formats, be they supermarkets, hypermarkets, or discount stores. He undertook an aggressive expansion into emerging markets such as China, Poland, and Brazil.

TURNING POINT: THE PROMODÈS ACQUISITION

Bernard's $17 billion friendly acquisition of the French Promodès Group in 1999 solidified Carrefour's national position as the largest retailer and made the company a formidable opponent to Wal-Mart in Latin America and Asia. The acquisition added an effective inventory and distribution system as well as an additional string of stores with a concentration in Spain. Bernard initiated the acquisition to preempt Wal-Mart's doing the same, particularly in light of its already aggressive moves into Europe. The acquisition created a behemoth with a combined $50 billion in annual sales, nine thousand stores, and 240,000 employees in 26 countries and was called by *Time* magazine a "marriage of convenience" to ward off Wal-Mart (September 13, 1999).

Despite the sound reasoning behind the acquisition, the consequent transition had its rough moments. In 1999 the company began losing out to competitors as its expansion and absorption of hundreds of small stores worldwide became unwieldy. After the merger Carrefour slashed prices on toys, clothing, and food to increase sales. The end of 2000 and beginning of 2001 was another tough period for the company, due to the general economic downturn in Europe. Critics blamed Bernard in part for Carrefour's problems; in spite of his reputation for putting customers first, *BusinessWeek* accused him of forgetting "retailing's Rule No. 1: Know your customer" (June 11, 2001). The publication noted that Bernard turned off many longtime Promodès customers through his remodeling of the stores and product lines. Carrefour's market share decreased from 18.1 to 17.4 percent, with the stock price dropping 30 percent from its 1999 high. Carrefour was forced to continue to rely on Europe for the majority of its sales—85 percent in 1999.

REINVENTION THROUGH EXPANSION

Bernard eventually put the company back on track, slashing prices in the domestic market and driving into more foreign markets because the market in Western Europe had reached the saturation point. He redirected the retailer after confronting economic problems in Brazil and Argentina in 1999 and the costly logistics of reinventing its added Promodès stores worldwide.

Carrefour's operations profits reached $270 million in 2000, by which time *BusinessWeek* placed the company in "Wal-Mart's rear-view mirror" (June 12, 2000). Sales totaled $70 billion in 2001; by that time, however, the merged group's retail sales had begun to decline in France, quickening Bernard's enthusiasm for global expansion.

Under Bernard's leadership Carrefour overtook Wal-Mart as the largest retailer in Brazil and competed successfully against Wal-Mart in Argentina. Carrefour had an especially strong presence in the latter country, where the brand name was both common and popular. Bernard proved apt in studying local Argentine customs and tastes and with its localized products managed to appeal to customers far more than did Wal-Mart. Carrefour's success there and in Brazil, Korea, and Mexico made the company a strong rival on the global scene. Bernard also expanded rapidly in Central Europe in 1999, where the market was not yet saturated, as it was in Western Europe.

Elsewhere Bernard invested $800 million in South Korean operations. Bernard told South Korea's commerce minister Yoon Jin Sik that he would commit $200 million a year to operations in the Asian nation from 2004 to 2007. Carrefour had first entered the South Korean market in 1996 with the opening of two dozen retail stores—the company's largest investment in any Asian country.

After several years of careful study of Japan's economic downturn, Bernard made a "concerted push" into the Japanese market in 1999, according to the *Wall Street Journal* (June 10, 1999). Bernard had concluded that the country's slump would provide an opportunity to move in with hypermarkets at a time when consumer attitudes were changing. He told the *Journal* that "greater openness to foreign brands and products made a place for hypermarkets that offer good value" (June 10, 1999). This move evidenced Bernard's confidence in targeting local markets and analyzing consumer attitudes in foreign countries as well as in his own.

COMMITMENT TO A TIME-TESTED FORMAT

Bernard's commitment to the hypermarket format and global corporate reach connected local retailers to larger economic trends and businesses. His experience in Argentina, where the French company became the commonplace Argentine grocery store, was an example. At the CIES World Food Business Summit in Barcelona, Bernard emphasized that globalization brought more products to more people, presenting consumers with choices they had never had before. Bernard typically closed acquired stores and then simply reopened them under the Carrefour name, emphasizing the use of local resources. Carrefour purchased many of its products locally—rather than exclusively introducing unknown foreign brands—trained local managers rather than importing its own, and used local channels of distribution.

Bernard invested $2.7 billion in 2002 to open new stores, refurbish others, and expand in Europe and Asia. He was optimistic about the expansion, believing that consumer demand would continue to justify the growth. He planned over four hundred store openings a year, including 40 hypermarkets, one hundred supermarkets, and three hundred discount stores. Rather than struggle with already saturated markets in North America and Europe, Bernard looked to countries and regions where supermarket retailers were few, in places that needed variety and high-quality products at affordable prices.

The *Wall Street Journal* complimented Carrefour's "international track record—the envy of other retailers now struggling belatedly to go global" (June 10, 1999). When asked if he had any plans to merge with Wal-Mart, he replied, "We have a lot of respect for the people at Wal-Mart. But we have different identities" (June 10, 1999).

By 2004 Carrefour's hypermarkets had begun to lose ground to smaller discount stores. In response Bernard was not afraid to challenge the traditional French manner of grocery shopping; Bernard commanded the acquisition of Comptoirs Modernes, a chain of 550 supermarkets in France and Spain.

Bernard strove to stick with a global branding strategy, stepping outside of his native France to create a brand recognizable not only throughout Europe but across the world, from Latin American to Asia. While under this strategy Carrefour faced temporary setbacks, as some customers were lost in the interim, the company was able to later cut prices to win them back.

The company's profits rose 17.9 percent from the second half of 2002 to reach $514 million in 2003. In that year one-fourth of Carrefour's hypermarket openings worldwide were in China, raising the number of stores in that country to around 50—including a $16 million venture in Shanghai. China, as an emerging market expected to someday be the largest in the world, was the ideal place for Bernard to focus his attention.

Bernard's efforts through the difficult periods paid off. The company was ranked 33rd on *BusinessWeek*'s list of the 50 best companies in Europe in 2003. By 2004 Carrefour operated 9,600 stores worldwide under a couple dozen names in 30 countries in Europe, Latin America, and Asia. More than half of its retail sales were reaped in France. The company was Europe's number-one retailer through 2004 and continued to present Wal-Mart with strong competition.

Daniel Bernard's success as the CEO of the world's second-largest retailer was based on his broad range of skills. He cultivated a studied understanding of local tastes; his sharp sense of timing enabled him to move into markets at the right moments—particularly before the American giant Wal-Mart attained a foothold. Bernard knew that well before a store opened, customer needs and tastes had to be investigated and tested. Then, Bernard knew that when the store was up and running, Carrefour would have to constantly woo and amaze consumers. Finally, Bernard knew he would have to always reinvent the wheel and try different approaches. He consistently incorporated all of the above factors into his sales efforts and kept his finger on the economic pulse in every store and in every region of the world in which Carrefour operated.

See also entry on Carrefour SA in *International Directory of Company Histories.*

SOURCES FOR FURTHER INFORMATION

Bernard, Ariane, "Profit for Retailer," *New York Times,* August 29, 2003.

"Carrefour Has Many Managers; It Has Only One Leader," *MMR,* March 10, 2003, p. 20.

"Carrefour Profit Rises," *New York Times,* August 29, 2002.

Cowell, Alan, "French Chains Plan to Merge into a Giant," *New York Times,* August 31, 1999.

"Daniel Bernard," *BusinessWeek,* June 12, 2001, p. 82.

Kapner, Suzanne, "Two Big European Retailers Contrast in Strategy and Profit," *New York Times,* August 31, 2001.

Krauss, Clifford, "Selling in Argentina (as translated from the French)," *New York Times,* December 5, 1999.

Labi, Aisha, "A Gallic Grocery Giant," *Time,* September 13, 1999, http://www.time.com/time/magazine/article/subscriber/0,10987,1107990913-30978,00.html.

"A Look at the Leaders," *BusinessWeek Online,* July 28, 2003, http://www.businessweek.com/@@HbAVSIUQHGzZsRYA/magazine/content/03_30/b3843711.htm.

Matlack, Carole, and Adeline Bonnet, "What's Shackling France's Big Chains," *BusinessWeek Online,* May 17, 2004, http://www.businessweek.com/@@HbAVSIUQHGzZsRYA/magazine/content/04_20/b3883073_mz054.htm.

Orr, Deborah, "Shoplifters!" *Forbes,* March 5, 2001, http://www.forbes.com/forbes/2001/0305/097.html.

Reed, Stanley, "Commentary: A Year They'd Like to Forget," *BusinessWeek,* June 11, 2001.

"Retailer Plans Expansion," *New York Times,* December 1, 2001.

"Talks in France May Bear No. 2 World Retailer," *New York Times,* August 30, 1999.

Tschang Chi-Chu, "Carrefour Readies for Growth in China," *International Herald Tribune,* April 8, 2003, http://www.iht.com/search/ihtsearch.php?id=92371&owner=(Bloomberg percent20News)&date=20001121010000.

Woodruff, David, "Carrefour Adds Japan to Its Expansion, but Retailer Faces Challenges in Europe," *Wall Street Journal,* June 10, 1999.

—Alison Lake

■ ■ ■

David W. Bernauer

1944–

Chairman and CEO, Walgreen Company

Nationality: American.

Born: 1944.

Education: North Dakota State University, BS, 1967.

Family: Married Mary (maiden name unknown); children: three.

Career: Walgreen Company, 1967–1979, pharmacist and then also store manager; 1979–1987, district manager; 1987–1990, regional vice president; 1990–1992, vice president and treasurer; 1992–1994, vice president of purchasing and merchandising; 1994–1997, vice president and chief information officer; 1997–1999, senior vice president and CIO; 1999–2002, president and COO; 2002–2003, CEO; 2003–, chairman and CEO.

Awards: Distinguished Alumni Award, North Dakota State University, 1999; Honorary Doctorate of Pharmacy, North Dakota State University, 2000.

Address: Walgreen Company, 200 Wilmot Road, Deerfield, Illinois 60015; http://www.walgreens.com.

■ David W. Bernauer spent his entire career at Walgreen Company, advancing over the span of 36 years from his first position as a pharmacist in a Walgreens drugstore to chairman and CEO. Before becoming CEO, Bernauer played a primary role in many of the chain's activities in store expansion, merchandising, finance, and technology. Colleagues and industry analysts described Bernauer as a low-key, soft-spoken leader with a consistent and determined approach to management.

DECIDES ON PHARMACY RETAILING CAREER

Growing up in Wadena, Minnesota, Bernauer worked in a J. C. Penney retail store managed by his father. He found that he liked retailing and noticed that some of the most successful retailers in town owned pharmacies. Bernauer decided he wanted to own his own pharmacy one day and thought that the best way to achieve his goal would be to study the subject.

Bernauer began his career at Walgreens as a pharmacy intern in 1966, the year before he graduated from North Dakota State University. The following year he joined the company as a pharmacist with the plan of learning as much as he could about the retail business before starting out on his own. In a quote from an article for his alma mater's pharmacy newsletter, Bernauer recalled, "After a few years it was pretty clear that I could have more fun and just as much freedom running a store for Walgreen as I could owning my own store" (2000).

GROOMED FOR MANAGEMENT

Over the next decade Bernauer held several store-manager positions before being appointed a district manager in Phoenix in 1979 and then in San Francisco in 1984. Walgreen's upper management identified Bernauer as someone with significant potential and followed the company's long tradition of grooming management successors from within the company. In 1987 Bernauer was named regional vice manager of Walgreen's western operations.

Over the next few years Bernauer was appointed to a series of positions that included regional vice president, vice president, and treasurer and then vice president of purchasing and merchandising. In 1995 Bernauer let it be known that he was interested in becoming the company's chief information officer when the then CIO announced his impending retirement. But the company's president and COO, L. Daniel Jorndt, thought Bernauer needed more experience in merchandising and was looking at several outside candidates. In the end he appointed Bernauer. In an interview for *Drug Store News*, Jorndt noted, "I realized that none of them were in Dave's league. This guy is so talented" (October 16, 2000).

Bernauer continued his slow but steady rise in the company as he succeeded in a variety of areas, including store operations, purchasing, and finances. In 1999 he was named president and COO. Jorndt, who had become CEO, noted that he could not think of anyone more qualified within the company to assume the position of president and COO and extend the company's remarkable growth.

One of Bernauer's most noted accomplishments before he became president and COO was his overseeing of the development of Walgreen's Intercom Plus, an advanced pharmacy computer and workflow system based on Internet technology.

The system was seen as a way to streamline operations so that Walgreens pharmacists could have more time to spend with customers. In order to handle store-to-store prescription transfers and automatic drug reorders from Walgreen's more than three thousand satellite-connected stores, the system implemented an integrated infrastructure that could process several million transactions a day.

Although Bernauer was convinced that computer technology and the Internet could improve Walgreen's business, he did not see the company becoming an Internet retailer. Rather, he thought that the Internet would be a medium through which to give better service to Walgreens customers and thus develop a stronger relationship with them. As he noted in *Drug Store News*, the Internet would help business "because it enables us to provide customers with information, with better service, and to expand what a pharmacy means to them" (October 16, 2000).

PROMOTES EXPANSION AND NEW TECHNOLOGY

In 2000 one of Bernauer's goals for Walgreen was to use his broad experience in operations to build the company to six thousand stores by 2010. He said that building Walgreens stores on roads that people traveled during their daily commutes would help families with two working parents deal with the time crunches they faced.

Bernauer also touted a new technological process called Basic Department Management, which gave Walgreen the ability to customize merchandise quantities according to data accrued through its computer system. According to Bernauer, instead of relying on individual store managers to decide on what to stock and how to control promotional space, the BDM system would itself customize each store at the stock-keeping level. With BDM, Walgreen could identify the items that sold well in each store location and then offer more of those items. In addition, the company could eliminate items that sold poorly in particular regions, as those items served only as distractions on the shelves. Bernauer believed the implementation of this process would have a positive impact on both sales and inventory control.

In 2002 Bernauer was named CEO of Walgreen, replacing the retiring Jorndt. Industry commentators observed that Bernauer had been thoroughly groomed for the job. The stock analyst Tom Goetzinger noted in *Supermarket News*, "He knows the business inside and out, and that's an important trait for a CEO, especially in retailing" (July 21, 2003).

MANAGEMENT STYLE: LOW-KEY

Industry analysts noted that Bernauer's appointment as CEO did not represent a change in the management philosophy at Walgreen, such as one that occurs when an outsider is brought in to take over the reins. However, Bernauer was seen as a much "mellower" and more soft-spoken manager than his predecessor. Bernauer's colleagues noted that he had an encyclopedic knowledge of the company, was extremely enthusiastic, and paid close attention to details.

Industry analysts also said that Bernauer accomplished what many people in retail management could not—that is, a smooth and seamless advancement through the ranks to become a company's leader. As noted by the retail consultant Neil Stern in *Supermarket News*, Bernauer stayed firmly within the corporate culture at Walgreen and distinguished himself by, in essence, not distinguishing himself. Stern noted, "You're not going to see Bernauer write a book about management principles or go on the podium speaking at industry events; that's not his style" (July 21, 2003).

BECOMES CHAIRMAN

In 2003 Bernauer was named Walgreen's chairman of the board in addition to his post as CEO. Over the previous four years he had helped oversee Walgreen's market share increase from 15.4 to 21.2 percent. Nevertheless, Walgreen did face questions, especially when its third-quarter operating performances in 2003 were not as high as expected. Bernauer maintained that the company's long-term strategy of expansion would not be sacrificed to meet quarterly expectations. The following quarter, Bernauer and Walgreen announced record sales and earnings, primarily because of an increase in prescription drug sales. Overall, sales for the quarter ending August 31, 2003, rose 14 percent to $8.2 billion, and sales for the year rose 13.3 percent to $32.5 billion. Bernauer noted that the company was budgeting more than $1 billion in capital investments for the 2004 fiscal year to include expenditures for new stores and a new distribution facility in Southern California. He also said that the company was going to focus on reaching seven thousand stores by 2010, upping the previous goal by one thousand. In addition to his duties at Walgreen, Bernauer is on the board of directors of the National Association of Chain Drug Stores, the board of trustees of Chicago's Field Museum, and the board of directors of Students in Free Enterprise.

See also entry on Walgreen Co. in *International Directory of Company Histories.*

SOURCES FOR FURTHER INFORMATION

Baeb, Eddie, "Headaches Awaiting Walgreen's New CEO," *Crain's Chicago Business*, July 23, 2001, p. 3.

Frederick, James, "Still Leading, Walgreens Stays on Course with New President," *Drug Store News*, April 26, 1999, p. 83.

Frederick, James, "Walgreens Caps Strong '03 with Plans to Invest in '04," *DSN Retailing Today*, January 26, 2004, p. 7.

"Putting Customers First by Meeting Changing Needs," *Drug Store News*, October 16, 2000, p. 79.

"SN's Power 50 (Part Six)," *Supermarket News*, July 21, 2003, p. 54.

—David Petechuk

■■■

Wulf H. Bernotat

1948–

Chairman and chief executive officer, E.ON

Nationality: German.

Born: September 14, 1948, in Göttingen, Germany.

Education: University of Göttingen, JD, 1976.

Family: Married Dorte (maiden name unknown); children: two.

Career: Shell, 1976–1981, legal-department counsel; 1981–1984, Business Development Manager for Eastern Europe; 1984–1986, head of Lubricant and Fuel Trading Business for Germany; 1986–1987, strategic planning; 1987–1988, Erdgas marketing; 1988–1989, head of distribution for Aviation and Public Authorities; 1989–1992, general manager for Portugal; 1992–1995, area coordinator for Africa and coordinator of Southern Hemisphere Coal Business; 1995, board of management member; VEBA, 1996–1998, board of management member; 1998–2000, head of downstream marketing and distribution; Stinnes, 2000–2002, chairman; E.ON, 2003–, chairman and CEO.

Address: E.ON, E.ON-Platz 1, 40479 Düsseldorf, Germany; http://www.eon.com.

■ Wulf H. Bernotat spent his entire career working in the energy industry. In 2003 he became the CEO of E.ON, Europe's second-largest utility.

LEGAL BACKGROUND

Bernotat received a doctorate in law—with a specialization in cartel law—in 1976, and his first employment position was in the legal department at Shell in Hamburg, Germany. Although he later transferred to the business side of the energy industry, he did not seem to lose his interest in law; as late as 1997 newspaper and magazine interviews indicated his knowledge of and comfort with the legal complexities of European business.

Wulf H. Bernotat. *AP/Wide World Photos.*

ENERGY MANAGEMENT

In 1981 Bernotat went to England to become Shell London's business development manager for Eastern Europe. He never returned to legal practice, advancing thenceforth exclusively in the field of corporate management. He remained with Shell until 1996, working in various European offices with increasing amounts of administrative responsibility: in London he became Shell's coordinator of business interests in Africa as well as of coal-business interests in the entire Southern Hemisphere; in Lisbon he was general manager for Shell in Portugal; and in France he became a member of Shell Paris's board of management.

In Germany in 1996 Bernotat joined VEBA, one of two holding companies for state-owned mining and electricity businesses. VEBA had been founded in Berlin in 1929 and was privatized in 1987. Bernotat was named to the board of management with partial responsibility for downstream marketing and distribution; in 1998 he was given overall responsibility in that area.

Later in 1998 Bernotat joined Stinnes, an international provider of transportation and freight services, as chairman of the board of management. During his two years with Stinnes, Bernotat was instrumental in separating the company from peripheral business in order to concentrate on the core activity of transportation. In 1999 he guided the company through an initial public offering.

Bernotat remained on the management board of VEBA until 2000. In that year VEBA merged with another former state-owned industrial enterprise, VIAG, in a $14 billion deal; the resulting company was named E.ON. Two years later Bernotat was appointed chairman of the board of management and chief executive officer of E.ON, a position he assumed on May 1, 2003.

E.ON

E.ON began its existence as a German conglomerate but by 2003 had become an international multiutility. E.ON owned Powergen, a British energy provider; LG&E, an American utility; and Rurhgas, Germany's number-one supplier of natural gas. As CEO of E.ON Bernotat adhered to his driving corporate philosophy: to concentrate on core business. Under his direction the company divested itself of or was preparing to divest itself of Ruhrgas; Viterra, a real-estate operation; Degussa, a chemical company in which E.ON had a significant stake; and Bouyges Telecom. At the same time E.ON planned on increasing its presence in specific European power markets as well as on establishing significant investments in its electric network.

Bernotat took part in several meetings with other German energy companies and with the government in order to discuss the future of German energy policy in light of global warming and protests against nuclear power.

Bernotat was a practical, methodical administrator. His education and early experience prepared him to be a lawyer; he was insistent on working within the framework of established dictates. His career path took him higher and higher up in the European energy industry, and he exhibited an appreciation for the importance of networking continental resources in order to assure absolute efficiency.

See also entry on E.On AG in *International Directory of Company Histories.*

SOURCES FOR FURTHER INFORMATION

"E.ON Plans to Sell Rurhgas Industries,"*AFX News Limited*, April 28, 2004.

"Germany Puts at Risk Future Power Investment,"*Reuters, Electricity Forum News*, November 3, 2003, http://www.electricityforum.com/news/nov03/germany.html.

—Barbara Gunvaldsen

■■■

Gordon M. Bethune

1941–

Chairman and chief executive officer, Continental Airlines

Nationality: American.

Born: 1941, in Austin, Texas.

Education: Abilene Christian University, BS; Harvard Business School, Advanced Management Program, 1992.

Family: Married; children: three.

Career: U.S. Navy, 1958–1978, aircraft maintenance officer; Braniff Airlines, 1979–1980, maintenance manager; 1980–1982, vice president, maintenance; Western Airlines, 1982–1984, vice president, engineering and maintenance; Piedmont Airlines, 1984–1988, senior vice president, operations; Boeing Commercial Airplane Group, 1988–1994, vice president and general manager, Renton Division; Continental Airlines, 1994, president and chief operating officer; 1994–1996, president and chief executive officer; 1996–, chairman and CEO.

Awards: Top 25 Global Managers, *BusinessWeek*, 1996; Laureate in Aviation Trophy, National Air and Space Museum, 1997; 25 Most Influential Executives, *Business Travel News*, 1998, 2000; 50 Best CEOs in America, *Worth*, 2001, 2002, 2003; Airline Person of the Year, *Travel Agent*, 2001.

Publications: *From Worst to First: Behind the Scenes of Continental's Remarkable Comeback* (with Scott Huler), 1999.

Address: Continental Airlines, Incorporated, 1600 Smith Street, Dept. HQSEO, Houston, Texas 77002; http://www.continental.com.

■ In more than a decade as the chairman of Continental Airlines, Gordon M. Bethune piloted the company from the brink of a third bankruptcy into the ranks of America's best airlines. He also managed to steer the carrier through the disastrous aviation industry slump that followed the terrorist attacks of September 11, 2001. In early 2004 Bethune announced plans to retire at the end of the year—a prospect that saddened both the airline's regular fliers and its stockholders.

EARLY CAREER

Born in Austin, Texas, in 1941, Bethune grew up in Austin and San Antonio. At age 17 he dropped out of high school to join the navy, where he found his niche as an aircraft mechanic and aviation electronics specialist. While in the navy he completed his high school education and went on to earn a bachelor's degree from Abilene Christian University. He was eventually promoted to the rank of chief petty officer. After completing a 20-year hitch in the navy, Bethune hired on as a maintenance manager for Texas-based Braniff Airlines and rose through the ranks to become the carrier's vice president for maintenance. In 1982 Bethune moved to Western Airlines as vice president for engineering and maintenance after Braniff went out of business. Two years later he was hired by Piedmont Airlines as its senior vice president for operations.

In 1988 Bethune left Piedmont after it was purchased by U.S. Airways and took a job with the Boeing Commercial Airplane Group as vice president and general manager of its division in Renton, Virginia. When he received an offer to join Continental Airlines as president and chief operating officer in early 1994, he jumped at the chance—only to discover later that the airline was in far worse shape than he had believed. In *From Worst to First*, the book he co-wrote with Scott Huler in 1999, Bethune described the Continental he took over in 1994 in these words: "We weren't just the worst big airline. *We lapped the field.*" By November 1994 Bethune was named Continental's CEO, to which was added the position of chairman in September 1996.

CONTINENTAL TURNS AROUND

What happened next confounded almost everyone in the airline industry. Continental, which had lost an average of $960 million a year from 1990 through 1993, trimmed its loss in 1994 to $619 million. By 1995 it was back into the black, posting a profit of $215 million. The airline's net income climbed further to $319 million in 1996, $383 million in 1997, and $385 million in 1998. In 1999 the airline posted a record profit of $455 million—a figure inflated, however, by a one-time $182 million gain from the sale of its interest in Amadeus Global Travel Distribution. Continental's net income in 2000 was $342 million. According to a report by Bill Hensel Jr. in the *Houston Chronicle*, Bethune built passenger confidence in the airline and sharply increased its traffic by refocusing its strategy on three basic concepts—"clean, safe, reliable" (December 28, 2003).

And then came 2001. The terrorist attacks on September 11, 2001, resulted in a dramatic drop in passenger flights for the remainder of that year. The impact of 9/11, which triggered a worldwide economic slump, continued to be felt over the next few years. The financial bloodletting would have been much worse if Bethune had not acted quickly to cut back sharply on operations and spending. Nevertheless, the airline posted losses of $95 million in 2001 and $413 million in 2002. By 2003, however, Bethune had once again guided Continental back to profitability.

One measure of the degree to which Bethune succeeded in remaking Continental into an airline respected for its reliability and quality of service were the many awards the airline won in the years after he took over as CEO. In 1996 and again in 2001, *Air Transport World* named Continental its airline of the year. In December 1999 *Fortune* referred to it as the "best airline in the U.S." *SmartMoney* rated Continental the best U.S. airline for business travel in 2000, while *Investor's Business Daily* named it the number two U.S. airline in 2001. In March 2002 *Fortune* rated Continental second in its separate rankings of the most admired U.S. and global airlines.

MANAGEMENT STYLE AND STRATEGY

Bethune offered some valuable insights in an interview with *Texas Monthly* into the strategy he used to turn Continental around. He observed that an important way to achieve success is to motivate others to aid success. Cooperation at all levels of an organization, Bethune contended, is essential to smooth operation and effective management. "And the only way you're going to get that [help] is to openly acknowledge and appreciate the contribution of others to the success of whatever it is you're doing." That means, he said, that a manager receiving an award must make clear that the accomplishment for which he's being honored was mostly the result of the hard work of others. "And they [the employees] sit up straight and feel real good, and the next day they work harder to help you be successful" (July 2000).

Of the five largest U.S. airlines, only Continental and Northwest managed to post a profit in 2003. Under Bethune's leadership, Continental reported a net income in 2003 of $87 million on revenue of nearly $8.9 billion. Although Northwest also showed a profit in 2003, AMR, which operates American Airlines; UAL (United); and Delta Airlines, the country's three largest carriers, all posted their third net loss in as many years.

In the first quarter of 2004, Continental reported a jump of 11.1 percent in its revenue to a total of just over $2 billion; however, record high fuel prices pushed the carrier into the red. It reported a net loss for the quarter of $124 million. Losses were also posted by the other four airlines in the top five. Only UAL, which was emerging from reorganization under Chapter 11 of the Bankruptcy Code, reported a larger rise in revenue than Continental—17.2 percent— during the first quarter. AMR's revenue rose only 2.8 percent, while Northwest and Delta posted revenue increases of 8.1 and 3.1 percent, respectively.

See also entries on Boeing Company and Continental Airlines, Inc. in *International Directory of Company Histories.*

SOURCES FOR FURTHER INFORMATION

Akron Roundtable, "Gordon M. Bethune, Chairman and Chief Executive Officer, Continental Airlines, Inc.," June 8, 2004, http://www.akronroundtable.org/speakers/individuals/bethune.html.

"Bethune: My Last Year Running Continental," *Pacific Business News* (Honolulu), January 16, 2004.

Continental Airlines, Incorporated. "Gordon Bethune," June 13, 2004, http://www.continental.com/company/investor/bios.asp?SID=2187E471BC55425BBB4C03DFCC0A4B7A#01.

"Continental's Bethune to Step Down at Yearend," *Air Transport World*, February 1, 2004.

"Gordon M. Bethune, Chairman of the Board, Chief Executive Officer at Continental Airlines, Inc.," *Forbes.com*, June 8, 2004, http://www.forbes.com/finance/mktguideapps/personinfo/FromMktGuideIdPersonTearsheet.jhtml?passedMktGuideId=461726.

Hensel, Bill, Jr., "Continental CEO Won't Rest on His Laurels," *Houston Chronicle*, December 28, 2003.

Huey, John, "Outlaw Flyboy CEOs," *Fortune*, November 13, 2000, p. 237.

McConnico, Patricia Busa, "Gordon Bethune," *Texas Monthly*, July 2000, p. 54.

O'Reilly, Brian, "The Mechanic Who Fixed Continental," *Fortune*, December 20, 1999, p. 176.

Schmit, Julie, "New CEO Changes Airline's Approach," *USA Today*, November 7, 1994.

—Don Amerman

■■■

J. Robert Beyster

1925–

Former chairman and chief executive officer, Science Applications International Corporation

Nationality: American.

Born: 1925.

Education: University of Michigan, BSE, MS, PhD (dates unknown).

Family: Married Betty (maiden name unknown); children: three.

Career: Westinghouse, early 1950s, senior scientist; Los Alamos National Scientific Laboratory, mid-1950s, research scientist; General Atomic Company, 1957–1969, chairman of the Accelerator Physics Department; Science Applications International Corporation, 1969–2004, chairman and CEO.

Awards: Lifetime Achievement Award, CONNECT Program in Technology and Entrepreneurship of the University of California, 1994; Engineering Manager of the Year, American Society of Engineering Management, 2000; Next Millennium Award for Excellence in Education (23rd Annual Leavey Awards for Excellence in Private Enterprise Education), 2000; Lifetime Achievement Award, Defense Special Weapons Agency, 2000; Spirit of San Diego Award, San Diego Regional Chamber of Commerce, 2001; Lifetime Achievement Award, Ernst & Young, 2003.

Publications: *Slow Neutron Scattering and Thermalization* (with D. E. Parks, M. S. Nelkin, and N. F. Wikner), 1970.

■ J. Robert Beyster founded Science Applications International Corporation (SAIC) with a small group of scientists in 1969 and guided the engineering company for 35 years as its chairman and CEO. During that time, he built SAIC into one of the largest and fastest-growing employee-owned companies in the world. SAIC sustained revenue and earnings growth throughout its history by fostering diversity and building a corporate culture exemplary in its integration of teamwork and independence. Industry analysts acknowledge that Beyster was the company's driving force by virtue of his visionary outlook toward employee ownership and the business of science.

FROM SCIENCE TO BUSINESS

Beyster, who was a lieutenant commander in the navy during World War II, attended the University of Michigan, where he ultimately earned his doctorate in engineering and physics. He began his career in the early 1950s as a senior scientist at Westinghouse and then worked at the Los Alamos National Scientific Laboratory in New Mexico, where he conducted nuclear energy research. In 1957 he joined General Atomic as chairman of the Accelerator Physics Department and established and managed the company's 100-million-volt traveling-wave linear accelerator facility, which was a government-supported research laboratory. He conducted extensive research on neutron thermalization, which is an important aspect of operating nuclear reactors.

In 1969 Beyster decided to establish his own scientific consulting firm, focusing on the knowledge that he had gained working in nuclear energy. He mortgaged his house and, with a small group of colleagues, set up Science Applications International Corporation in a tiny office neighboring a ballet studio in La Jolla, California. In the beginning, the fledgling company struggled to land federal contracts in nuclear power and nuclear weapons.

Beyster and business analysts have both acknowledged that a turning point came when Beyster was struck by the inspiration to give away stock to the researchers who worked for the company and brought in much of the business. Before long SAIC had attracted a wide foundation of experts in many emerging areas of engineering and technology. In little more than a decade Beyster established SAIC as a respected provider of information-technology software and systems and as one of the leading research and engineering companies in the country. He also led the company to become an early leader in the development of renewable energy sources and energy-efficient technologies.

TIME TO REORGANIZE

SAIC experienced steady growth, and by 1985 Beyster realized that the company's continued expansion required him to rethink its mode of operation. In addition, SAIC was facing new competition in areas where the company had once been nearly the sole provider of services. Beyster began to reconsider the company's disconnected internal structure, in which all of the various divisions were virtually autonomous. In a 1985 interview with Tim O'Reiley for the *San Diego Business Journal*, Beyster noted, "We have seen a great number of changes for SAIC. And we can expect to see more changes. We are driven by the business climate and tend to respond rapidly" (June 24, 1985).

In spite of the necessity for SAIC to evolve, Beyster remained reluctant to tamper excessively with the company's approach to business. At the end of the fiscal year on January 31, 1985, the company's sales had risen 19 percent from the previous year to $420.3 million, and profits had risen 11 percent to $14.7 million. As 28 percent of the company's assets were in cash or cash equivalents, Beyster was able to fund an aggressive capital improvement program without borrowing from the outside while carrying a high load of accounts receivable. Beyster was determined to remain committed to employee ownership and to the company's focus on extremely high-technology design contracts, such as those it possessed in the areas of submarine warfare, artificial intelligence, and the federal Strategic Defense Initiative, popularly known as "Star Wars."

Nevertheless, the growing magnitude of SAIC projects led Beyster to broaden the company's thin corporate staff, who oversaw divisions that were used to a degree of freedom so high as to verge on entrepreneurship. The level of management Beyster then assembled included a new chief financial officer and treasurer. Beyster told O'Reiley, "The importance of skilled project managers is becoming extremely obvious to the company" (June 24, 1985).

At this time Beyster began to place a greater emphasis on risk aversion within the company because the standard cost-plus-profit margin contracts it typically garnered in the field of research and development had grown fewer. In their place, fixed-price contracts were gaining favor, especially within the government. As a result, Beyster knew that SAIC needed to pay closer attention to accurate bidding.

Over the span of its life up to that point, SAIC had worked in relative anonymity, known primarily to the select few in the government and private sectors who needed its services. For many years, SAIC had attained nearly three-quarters of its work from sole-source contract (contracts negotiated with one source only and not put out for general bidding), because no company had been able to compete with its unique capabilities. As a response to the new competition, Beyster spearheaded a new marketing effort while trying to maintain his aversion to publicity, which was so great that the company's name did not even appear on its main office buildings.

CONTINUED EXPANSION OF EXPERTISE

Long known for its experience in space and missile systems and its support for national security policy, SAIC branched into advanced systems for military command, control, and communications. Beyster recognized the rapidly advancing computer-technology sector of private business and the dawning of a global economy; consequently, SAIC developed Internet-based solutions for companies such as the SAIC subsidiary, Network Solutions (a global registrar for high-level Internet domains). This greater focus on commercial customers ultimately led to setting up offices in more than 150 cities worldwide.

In 1997 Beyster anticipated the growing need for advanced communications networks to be integrated with sophisticated information-technology systems. Thus, he oversaw the acquisition of Bellcore, which became Telcordia Technologies, to focus on the technological aspects of wireless communications and telecommunications software. By the end of the 20th century, SAIC had grown far beyond its roots. In 1994, 90 percent of the company's revenues came from U.S. government programs. By 1999, half of its revenues came from commercial clients. SAIC had become a major provider of plant management and automation software and services for a variety of clients, including oil, utility, and health-care companies. The move into the commercial market meant greater returns for stock-owning employees. Throughout SAIC's history, the quantity of employee-owned stock grew an average of 15 to 20 percent yearly; from 1994 to 1999 employees saw annual returns of more than 27 percent.

THE RIGHT TIMING

Like most companies in the United States and throughout the world, SAIC experienced some hardships once the booming economy of the late 1990s went into recession. The company's annual sales in the commercial and international arenas dropped to 15 percent of total annual sales. Nevertheless, SAIC continued to perform well largely because of its diversity. In an interview with Diane Lindquist for *Chief Executive*, Beyster observed, "What's helped us during downturns is that there is usually some business area that we're in that's doing pretty well" (March 2002). As an example, Beyster pointed to the huge slump that the dot-com business underwent beginning in 2001, when SAIC lost clients just as many other companies did. On the other hand, SAIC's defense business with the government expanded considerably following the terrorist attacks of September 11, 2001.

Part of the reason SAIC fared especially well after September 11 was that Beyster had established the company's technical expertise in terrorist investigations and homeland security in 1993, following the first bombing of New York's World Trade Center. Realizing that terrorism would most likely be a dominant national security issue for decades, Beyster and SAIC formed the Center for Counterterrorism Technology and Analysis in 1997 and named the former United Nations weapons inspector David Kay the center's director. SAIC was prepared to help both the government and commercial customers prepare for possible terrorist attacks through such efforts as assessing the vulnerability of facilities, providing contingency planning, and recommending strategies for lessening the threat of biological or nuclear attacks. SAIC also sent employees to Afghanistan and Iraq to work alongside American troops in the war against terrorism, responding to the need for new technologies such as unmanned vehicles and advanced information solutions.

CUTS STILL NEEDED TO BE MADE

Despite SAIC's diversity, Beyster recognized that the company had to respond to reduced business in a variety of ways, such as by minimizing expenditures and focusing on both shorter-term and smaller research projects. As a last resort, Beyster reluctantly realized that the company would be forced to cut staff.

SAIC's telecommunications activities, in particular, had suffered a large decline in business. As a result, Beyster and SAIC ordered a reduction of two thousand to three thousand Telcordia staff members, and Beyster also approved the trimming of one thousand positions within SAIC itself. He managed to soften the blow to company morale by cutting the staff primarily through attrition, that is, by not hiring new employees after others quit or retired.

MANAGEMENT STYLE: THERE IS NO "I" IN TEAM

According to Diane Lindquist, Beyster was "considered the premier advocate of spread-the-wealth management" (March 2002). Throughout SAIC's history Beyster owned barely more than 1 percent of company stock, with the remainder being owned by SAIC's employees, who numbered more than 42,000 worldwide in 2004. Beyster established a form of employee ownership different from that which is predominant among other companies with employee stock-ownership policies, where most of the stock is withheld in the retirement plan. This more common approach can lead to problems such as those that followed the bankruptcy of Enron in 2002, when many employees experienced huge personal losses in retirement savings. Alternatively, Beyster established a flexible program in which the employees owned the stock on a primarily individual basis, with performance being the foundation for ownership. In an interview for *Washington Technology*, Beyster noted that SAIC's generous stock offerings initially attracted employees. Then, he added, "to keep people we build up their holdings where if they leave, they would lose a lot of money" (September 11, 2000).

Beyster's insistence on keeping SAIC an employee-owned company led to success, with the company amassing $5.9 billion in annual revenue by the summer of 2003. Despite the company's tremendous growth, Beyster was able to adhere to his philosophy of minimizing the layers of bureaucracy and management by maintaining a flexible and decentralized organizational structure. He stressed technical excellence, high standards of ethical conduct, and a firm belief in customer service. According to industry analysts, Beyster created a business based on numerous small organizations with hundreds of leaders, each involved in the entrepreneurial culture that Beyster had fostered.

Beyster was known for his extraordinary relational skill, both in making employees feel as if they were working for him personally and in making clients feel that they were unique and important. Industry analysts commended Beyster for his intelligence and for his ability to apply that intelligence to both science and business environments. He was well regarded for his facility in tracking the details on the hundreds and sometimes thousands of projects that SAIC typically handled at one time. With respect to his personality, Beyster noted on the SAIC Web site, "I was not the brilliant, flash-of-inspiration type of entrepreneur. I was more of a persistent, builder type."

LEAVES SUCCESSFUL LEGACY

In 2004 the 78-year-old Beyster retired as the company's CEO and later left his post as chairman. Assessing Beyster's importance to SAIC over the years, David Overskei, a former SAIC employee who became the president of a defense software company, asked Brad Graves in the *San Diego Business Journal*, "How many other companies under the leadership of one individual have gone this far and done so well?" (April 14, 2003). In addition to his achievements at SAIC, Beyster established the Foundation for Enterprise Development and the Beyster Institute for Entrepreneurial Employee Ownership. These nonprofit organizations are dedicated to advancing the use of entrepreneurial employee ownership nationally and internationally and in both the public and private sectors.

See also entry on Science Applications International Corporation in *International Directory of Company Histories.*

SOURCES FOR FURTHER INFORMATION

"About SAIC: Founder's Profile," http://www.saic.com/about/profile.html.

Graves, Brad, "SAIC Looks to Replace Its 'Heart and Soul,'" *San Diego Business Journal*, April 14, 2003, p. 9.

Lindquist, Diane, "There's No 'I' in This Team," *Chief Executive*, March 2002, p. 57.

O'Reiley, Tim, "Beyster Pushes Changes at Science Applications," *San Diego Business Journal*, June 24, 1985, p. 1.

Wakeman, Nick, "SAIC's Beyster Takes Road Less Traveled," *Washington Technology*, http://www.washingtontechnology.com/news/15_12/cover/1752-1.html.

"Where Owners and Workers See Eye to Eye," *BusinessWeek*, June 21, 1999, p. 160.

—David Petechuk

■■■

Jeff Bezos

1964–

Chairman, chief executive officer, and president, Amazon.com

Nationality: American.

Born: January 12, 1964, in Albuquerque, New Mexico.

Education: Princeton University, BS, 1986.

Family: Son of Miguel Bezos (Exxon engineer) and Jackie Gise Jorgensen; married McKenzie Tuttle (former D. E. Shaw & Company researcher); children: one.

Career: Fitel, 1986–1988; Bankers Trust Company, 1988–1990, software developer; 1990, vice president; D.E. Shaw & Company, 1990–1992; 1992–1994, senior vice president; Amazon.com, 1995–, chairman, CEO, and president.

Awards: Person of the Year, *Time*, 1999.

Address: Amazon.com, 1200 12th Avenue South, Seattle, Washington 98144; http://www.amazon.com.

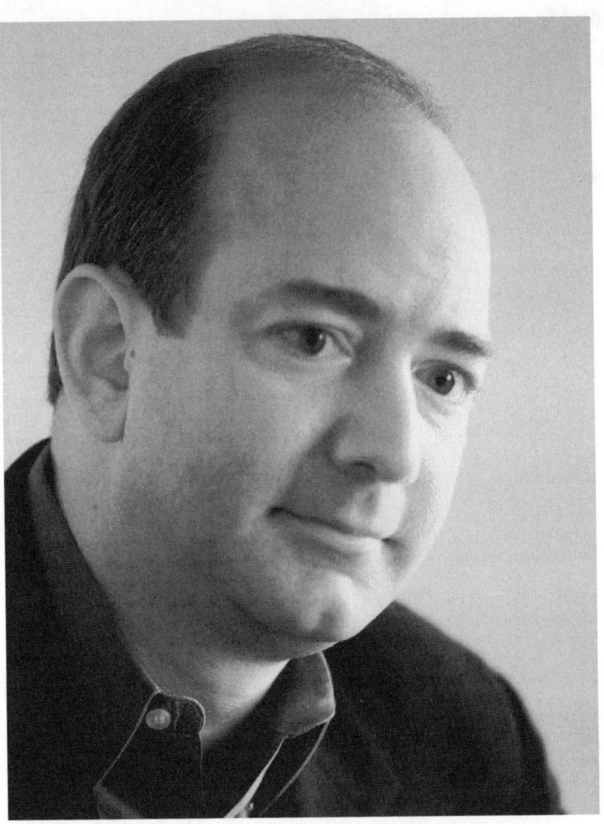

Jeff Bezos. *AP/Wide World Photos.*

■ Jeff Bezos founded Amazon.com in 1995 as an online bookstore. Due to customer demand the company later expanded and added other products to its inventories, including videos, DVDs, electronics, toys, apparel, software, household items, and gourmet food. In an interview published in *Dealerscope* magazine, Bezos indicated that books were chosen as Amazon.com's first product category "because they offered so much selection"; in the same interview, Bezos stated, "I think the main thing that has differentiated Amazon.com from conventional retailers is its obsessive/compulsive focus on the end-to-end customer experience. That includes having the right products, the right selection, and low prices" (January 2003).

Started up in Seattle, Washington, Amazon.com had its first base of operation in the Bezos's garage, which was converted into a workspace initially housing three Sun workstations. Amazon grew to be an international enterprise and eventually expanded to include sites in Canada, the United Kingdom, France, and Japan. Coworkers and chroniclers of the Amazon story characterized Bezos as a visionary and as a man who on the surface was easygoing but kept his employees on demanding schedules. Bezos demanded quick turnaround time for project completion. He scheduled weekly management meetings which often ran as long as four hours, with managers reporting on new products and pricing and taking on questions from the CEO. Bezos promoted innovative efforts among his employees through the Just Do It program, which rewarded those who came up with and executed ideas that helped the company—without first obtaining permission from their bosses. Bezos was committed to hiring the best employees, always looking for intelligent and innovative individuals.

DEVELOPING ENTREPRENEURIAL SKILLS

Jeff Bezos was a gifted child; at the age of three, tired of sleeping in a crib, he found a screwdriver and took the crib apart. He subsequently tinkered with models and with a Radio Shack electronics kit. Every summer Bezos stayed at his grandfather's ranch, where he would repair windmills and the tractor and brand cattle, among other tasks. An avid young inventor, he created a solar microwave and a door buzzer that alerted him when his siblings were entering his room. When asked who his heroes were in a *Time* magazine interview, Bezos cited Thomas Edison and Walt Disney. He visited Disney World six times and was impressed with Disney's powerful vision: "He knew exactly what he wanted to build and teamed up with a bunch of really smart people and built it" (December 27, 2003).

Bezos was a model student who was profiled (under an assumed name) in the 1977 book entitled *Turning on Bright Minds: A Parent Looks at Gifted Education*, by Julie Ray. Bezos was named class valedictorian when he graduated from high school in 1982 and won the Silver Knight Award from the *Miami Herald.* He graduated summa cum laude from Princeton in 1986, earning Phi Beta Kappa membership.

Bezos's entrepreneurial spirit became evident when he obtained his first post-graduation position at Fitel, a start-up that focused on creating a network for international financial trade. After two years, when Fitel failed to get off the ground, Bezos moved on to Bankers Trust, where he was responsible for developing software applications for pension-fund clients. He eventually became a vice president at Bankers Trust. He then moved on to D. E. Shaw & Company, a financial-trading company on the cutting edge of computer technology. David Shaw, the company's founder, was an inspiration to Bezos. Shaw was likewise impressed with Bezos and rapidly promoted him to senior vice president. In an interview with *Time*, Shaw characterized Bezos as "sort of an entrepreneurial odd-jobs kind of a person" (December 27, 2003). In 1994 Bezos left D. E. Shaw, having decided to build and operate his own company.

AMAZON.COM: THE EARLY YEARS

Bezos had paid close attention to the rapid rise of the World Wide Web, noting in 1994 that it was growing at an annual rate of 2,300 percent, and therein looked for a purer entrepreneurial outlet. He began his research by making a list of the top 20 mail-order companies, observing that there were no book mail-order companies because a comprehensive catalog would have needed to be thousands of pages long and thus expensive to mail. Bezos decided that an Internet-based company would have the capability to offer a substantrially wider selection of printed matter to consumers. Thus, he made a thorough study of the book business, beginning by attending the American Booksellers' Association's annual convention.

When Bezos told Shaw that he was leaving to launch an online book business, Shaw advised him to take some time to reconsider. Bezos eventually came to his decision in a characteristically creative way. He told *Time* that he pictured himself at 80 years of age and was certain that he would regret neither missing out on a six-figure Christmas bonus nor having tried to build an online business and failing. He stated, "In fact, I'd have been proud of myself for having taken that risk and tried to participate in that thing called the Internet that I thought was going to be such a big deal. And I knew if I didn't try this, I would reget it. And that would be inescapable" (December 27, 1999).

Bezos's parents supported his decision, investing the $300,000 they had saved for retirement in their son's venture (which was later amply rewarded; they became billionaires). Bezos initially planned to name his company Abracadabra; that name was later scrapped in favor of Amazon, inspired by the river. Bezos and his wife, McKenzie, moved to Seattle to start the company and persuaded the highly successful programmer Shel Kaphan to be among the first employees hired. Bezos officially founded Amazon.com in 1994. In June 1995 the first Web site was tested. On July 16, 1995, Amazon.com was made available to consumers in every state and 45 other countries. Sales were immediate. Bezos told *Time*, "Within the first few days, I knew it was going to be huge" (December 27, 1999). The media noticed and reported on Amazon, and as a result of the publicity the company's consumer base rapidly increased. Bezos owned and operated his own warehouses for the book inventory; as of 2003 Amazon had six.

After the Web site was launched, it was fine-tuned by Bezos and his employees to include features such as one-click shopping and customer reviews. Investors were able to buy stock in Amazon.com beginning in 1997 when the company went public. Over the next few years Bezos expanded the company by launching Web sites in Canada, the United Kingdom, Germany, France, and Japan.

Bezos constantly tapped into exactly what his customers wanted. He told *Dealerscope*, "We were doing such a good job with books, and we started getting these e-mails, initially for other media categories, like music, DVDs, or VHS" (January 2003). Bezos then actively asked customers what they wanted Amazon to sell, which led to further expansion into products such as electronics, toys, kitchenware, and gourmet foods. In early 2003 Bezos reported that electronic products were the second-largest category of items sold, after books.

MANAGEMENT STYLE

On the surface Bezos was easygoing with a sense of humor. On the other hand, employees and chroniclers found that he was adamant in his expectations of quick turnaround time on project completion and high productivity, as well as of innovativeness and intelligence. At managers' meetings Bezos personally asked his team questions about new Amazon initiatives.

He was a hands-on leader and reviewed everything from press releases that quoted him to average customer contacts per order to breakdowns of e-mail contracts and other details of the business. In a 2003 *Fortune* magazine article, Fred Vogelstein reported that 20 of Amazon's 50 top executives left between 2001 and 2003. Consequently, Bezos was characterized as a relentless recruiter of talented, innovative individuals. Bezos and personnel managers were known to thoroughly examine prospective employees' college transcripts and SAT scores. According to Bezos, "People here like to invent, and as a result other people who like to invent are attracted here. And people who don't like to invent are uncomfortable here. So it's self-reinforcing" (May 26, 2003).

To encourage new ideas, Bezos instituted the Just Do It program, wherein the winners were those who proceeded with projects that they felt would help the company without first asking their bosses' permission. Bezos believed in the benefits of communication with customers and listened to and used their ideas for expansion. Via the Web site Amazon customers were encouraged to recommend their favorite books and products through reviews, and many compiled lists of their favorite items.

Bezos looked to growth and expansion of Amazon.com through partnerships with other companies. In 1999 Amazon partnered with Sotheby's to provide online auctions of items ranging from fine art to collectibles. Additionally, Amazon acquired the International Movie Database and bought the companies Back to Basics and Tool Crib of the North. Amazon.com partnered with Toys "R" Us in 2000 to establish a cobranded toy and video-game store.

In 2000 Bezos and his company were put to the ultimate test. At a time when many dot-com companies were going out of business, Amazon's stock price fell from $106 in December 1999 to $41.50 in September 2000. To deal with this crisis, Bezos was forced to lay off 1,300 employees in February 2001. He also cut back on products, eliminating those that had yet to prove profitable for the company.

In 2001 Amazon formed an agreement with Borders to provide inventory, order fulfillment, and customer service for Borders.com. Funds also came into Amazon via cooperation with America Online and the purchase of assets from Egghead.com. Through the efforts of Bezos and his team Amazon turned a profit in the last quarter of 2001. Continuing expansion efforts in 2002, Amazon started selling clothing from established names such as The Gap, Land's End, and Nordstrom. In January 2004 Amazon.co.uk, the company's United Kingdom site, formed an agreement with the British Library to make rare and out-of-print books available for sale online.

Amazon not only survived the crisis of 2000 but flourished. For the fourth quarter of 2003 the company posted a net income of $73.2 million. The *Wall Street Journal* reported that in 2003 Amazon reported an annual net profit for the first time. Between January 2003 and 2004 company stock prices tripled.

See also entry on Amazon.com, Inc. in *International Directory of Company Histories.*

SOURCES FOR FURTHER INFORMATION

De Jonge, Peter, "Riding the Wild, Perilous Waters of Amazon.com," *New York Times*, March 12, 1999.

Keefe, Collin, "Jeff Bezos: Founder and CEO, Amazon.com," *Dealerscope*, January 2003, p. 76.

Quittner, Joshua, "An Eye on the Future," *Time*, December 27, 1999, pp. 55–56.

Saunders, Rebecca, *Business the Amazon.com Way: Secrets of the World's Most Astonishing Web Business*, Milford, Conn.: Capstone USA, 1999.

Vogelstein, Fred, "Mighty Amazon," *Fortune*, May 26, 2003, p. 60.

Weill, David, and Denise M. Bonilla, *Leaders of the Information Age*, New York, N.Y.: H. W. Wilson, 2003.

Wingfield, Nick, "Amazon Reports Annual Net Profit for the First Time," *Wall Street Journal*, January 28, 1994.

—Lucy Heckman

■■■

Pierre Bilger

1941–

Former chairman and chief executive officer, ALSTOM

Nationality: French.

Born: 1941, in France.

Family: Married (wife's name unknown); children: five.

Career: Compagnie Générale d'Électricité, 1982–1991; GEC Alsthom, 1991–1998, chairman; ALSTOM SA, 1998–2003, chairman and CEO.

Awards: Honorary Commander of Order of the British Empire, 2002.

■ Formerly one of France's top business leaders, Pierre Bilger stepped down earlier than planned from his post as chairman of the international, French-based ALSTOM engineering conglomerate. Under his stewardship, the once-giant company eventually found itself on the brink of bankruptcy. Although credited with having served ALSTOM and its predecessors well during his 20-plus-year career, Bilger received harsh criticism for his actions during the final years of his tenure. He gained more positive renown when he became the first corporate executive in France's history to hand back a huge severance package. Bilger received an honorary CBE in 2002, just prior to ALSTOM's failure.

Pierre Bilger. © *James Leynse/Corbis.*

BIG AMBITIONS BUILD AUTONOMY

Bilger began his career with France's Ministry of the Economy and joined Compagnie Générale d'Électricité in 1982. By 1989 the French-based corporation was a giant in the telecommunications world and had changed its name to Alcatel Alsthom. That same year, Alcatel Alsthom embarked on a joint venture with the multinational, U.K.-based, electrical-engineering giant General Electric Company (now known as Marconi). The two conglomerations combined their capabilities in power-generation and distribution in a 50-50 partnership deal. The new venture was named GEC Alsthom; Bilger joined the new company and in 1991 became chairman.

In June 1998 GEC Alsthom was spun off by its parent companies and renamed ALSTOM SA in order to present, according to Joseph Fitchett in the *International Herald Tribune,* "an international image that signals it is making something new of something old" (June 2, 1998). Bilger was elected CEO. Before it floated, the new company was valued at between 40 and 50 billion French francs ($6.66–8.33 billion) and paid its parent companies EUR 1.2 billion in a special dividend. The payment left the company virtually penniless. However, in its initial public offering (IPO), just over half of ALSTOM's shares went on the market in what became the largest public stock offering in Europe that year. Shares sold at around 205 French francs (slightly more than EUR 31) on stock exchanges in Paris, London, and New York. Stock market value was estimated at $4.3 billion, and a jubilant Bilger noted that the global IPO was more than three times oversubscribed. A BBC news article quoted him as saying, "We begin life as a publicly-quoted company with a quality shareholder base and a sound platform on which to realise our ambitions" (June 22, 1998).

Bilger's ambitions were grand. According to Fitchett, Bilger said of the new company, "We will be managing our destiny for ourselves and no longer as part of a much larger ensemble" (June 2, 1998). However, while GEC Alsthom was given day-to-day autonomy, it remained under the control of—and funneled its profits into—its parent companies and had to incorporate the objectives and opinions of two separate groups of shareholders. Bilger's goal was to take the new company to world-class levels in several areas, particularly in the sectors of power generation and distribution and rail transit. Another major goal was to take the company's core business—building turbines—into the global marketplace. Fitchett wrote, "In meeting their own targets of performance and clear governance, ALSTOM has the advantage of a proven team in Mr. Bilger and Mr. Cronin [managing director and deputy CEO], both of whom were present at the creation of GEC Alsthom a decade ago" (June 2, 1998).

At the time of its inception, ALSTOM was renowned for its profitability and somewhat unique position as a joint French-British operation. In the transportation industry, ALSTOM's banner product was its French-engineered, high-speed TGV trains. It also manufactured Eurostar trains and was contracted to supply tilting trains for the West Coast line between Glasgow and London. On the shipping side, it built ships for major cruise lines, including the Queen Mary 2—the largest cruise ship ever built—for Carnival. It also built naval vessels and natural-gas tankers.

In the field of power generation and distribution, ALSTOM was still behind the giant U.S. company General Electric and two other world leaders—Siemens, the German-based electrical-engineering and electronics conglomerate, and the Swiss engineering group Asea Brown Boveri (ABB). In March 1999, in pursuit of his goal to make ALSTOM a world leader in the power industry, Bilger announced that ALSTOM and ABB would embark on a 50-50 joint merger of their power generation businesses, which they named ABB ALSTOM Power. To account for the differences in the sizes of the two companies, ALSTOM paid ABB a cash compensation of EUR 1.4 billion. In a press release on the ABB Web site, Bilger stated, "This move will be a strong accelerator for the performance of both parent companies." A year later ALSTOM gained further autonomy when it bought ABB's share of ABB ALSTOM for EUR 1.25 billion. The new company became known simply as ALSTOM Power.

TOO BIG TOO FAST?

Four months later in July 2000 ALSTOM began to experience financial difficulties. There were serious and costly problems associated with the heavy-duty gas-turbine technology purchased from ABB. Although Bigler announced to shareholders that the difficulties would not affect profit margins, shares fell 15 percent on the day of the announcement. Next, following the September 11, 2001, terrorist attacks in the United States, several major cruise-liner orders failed. One of ALSTOM's clients, Florida-based Renaissance, filed bankruptcy. On September 24, Jean-Christophe Mounicq, writing for *Tech Central Station*, accused Bilger of bad management. Mounicq referred specifically to the Renaissance failure, noting that ALSTOM had taken on the contract without demanding collateral. Once again, an announcement from ALSTOM's corporate offices reassured shareholders that the company was covered against such incidents, but it also confirmed that the company's exposure could be as high as EUR 684 million. Once again, shares dropped—this time by almost 40 percent over two days.

In March 2002 Bilger announced his Restore Value plan, which was ultimately unsuccessful. In March 2003, nine months ahead of schedule and as the former showcase of French technology was bound for bankruptcy, Bilger proposed he step down as chairman and that Patrick Kron, recently elected CEO, take his place. Kron praised Bilger for developing the company into a world leader in transport and energy with a strong reputation for innovation. According to a report produced by the InterNet Bankruptcy Library, Kron said: "Together with the Board members and all the staff of the Company, I pay tribute to Pierre and his strong personal commitment" (March 14, 2003). Kron then announced a restructuring plan, but the next day ALSTOM stocks fell 50 percent to less than EUR 1. In the 2003 fiscal year ALSTOM suffered a net loss of EUR 1.38 billion. The company was forced to sell off its most profitable arm and Bilger's baby—its power transmission capabilities.

Shortly thereafter, in an incident unrelated to the company's crash, Bilger and two other former ALSTOM executives were taken into custody as part of a judicial investigation into allegations of illegal commissions paid out during the 1994 construction of new ALSTOM transport headquarters in Paris. Judicial sources said the secret commissions were worth several million euros.

More bad news was yet to break: in June 2003, ALSTOM executives revealed that the U.S. Federal Bureau of Investigation and the Securities and Exchange Commission were conducting investigations into "significantly understated" losses experienced by ALSTOM's U.S. transport unit. Outside auditors discovered $58 million in unreported losses, and the company was charged that amount for accounting irregularities, further adding to its fiscal-year loss of $1.56 billion on sales of $24 billion. Between 2001 and 2003, under Bilger as chairman and chief executive, the company's debt soared to more than $5 billion and its share prices plummeted by 90 percent. London-based Deutsche Bank analyst Andrew Carter was quoted in *BusinessWeek* as saying, "ALSTOM's future is in the hands of the banks. Its shares are worthless" (July 21, 2003). Mounicq stated, "Alstom was the showcase of French technology. It is now the showcase of French bankruptcy" (October 24, 2003). ALSTOM staved off bankruptcy, however, after a highly controversial EUR 3.4 billion bailout by the French government in return for a 31.5 percent stake in the company. Analysts still wondered whether the bailout would be sufficient to revive the company, which did 90 percent of its business outside of France.

In a *Business Week* article, Carol Matlack noted that Kron indirectly defended Bilger's leadership of ALSTOM, believing the company was a victim of circumstances beyond anyone's control. He said that the company could not have been scuttled by one factor alone, but the combined circumstances had disastrous consequences. Matlack wrote, "Fair enough. But Alstom's previous management made things worse by repeatedly assuring investors that the company's problems were under control, only to acknowledge later that the woes were far worse than previously disclosed" (July 21, 2003). Regardless of such criticism, ALSTOM's board awarded Bilger a EUR 4.1 million severance payout that many called a "reward for failure." The payout enraged French investors, most of who blamed the company's collapse on Bilger's ambition and reckless leadership. John Tagliabue noted in the *New York Times* that Bilger was "bitterly criticized" during the company's July 2003 shareholder meeting for accepting the payout (August 19, 2003).

AN UNPRECEDENTED ACTION—PAYING BACK THE PAYOUT

On August 14, 2003, in an entirely unprecedented move, Bilger sent a letter to his successor stating that he would return the payout—the first time an executive had returned a payout to a French corporation. According to Noah Barkin, writing for *Forbes.com*, Bilger stated that he made the decision so as not to be an "object of scandal for the roughly 100,000 ALSTOM employees that it was my honour to direct for 12 years, nor among shareholders who trusted me from 1998." He also said he wanted to be able to look himself in the mirror when he thought about the people with whom he had worked. Some analysts, however, suggested Bilger's move was due to pressure from the French government. Colette Neuville, president of the shareholder group that so heavily criticized Bilger, was quoted by Tagliabue as saying, "We welcome it, even if it was not entirely spontaneous" (August 19, 2003). Tagliabue also said Bilger may have been trying to head off investigations that could have led to more and deeper problems.

Others gave Bilger considerable credit for his actions, contrasting him with Jean-Marie Messier, the former head of the troubled Vivendi, who, according to David Gow of the *Guardian*, received a EUR 20.5 million payoff "on the say-so of just one director without board approval and who faces French court proceedings to prevent him receiving the money" (August 19, 2003). Messier refused to relinquish the payoff of his own volition. Bilger did declare that his payout was his contractual due and was approved by the full board, and he was adamant that it was no golden parachute but was appropriately calculated in recognition of his more than 20 years of service since joining Compagnie Générale d'Électricité. He also stated that returning the money was unfair to his family, who had been profoundly affected by his complete dedication to the company over those twenty years. Alex Duval Smith and Katherine Griffiths of the *New Zealand Herald* quoted Bilger as remarking, "Whatever anyone may say, I have always been very careful to respect the principles of corporate governance" (August 23, 2003).

See also entries on Compagnie Générale d'Électricité and ALSTHOM in *International Directory of Company Histories.*

SOURCES FOR FURTHER INFORMATION

"ABB and ALSTOM Create World Leader in Power Generation," ABB, Press Releases, http://www.abb.com/global.

"ALSTOM SA: Patrick Kron Succeeds Pierre Bilger as Chairman," InterNet Bankruptcy Library, March 14, 2003. http://bankrupt.com/TCREUR_Public/030314.mbx.

"Alstom Steams Ahead," BBC News, June 22, 1998, http://news.bbc.co.uk/1/hi/business/the_company_file/117556.stm.

Barkin, Noah, "Ex-Alstom Chief to Waive Severance Package," *Forbes.com*, August 18, 2003, http://www.forbes.com/newswire/2003/08/18/rtr1059813.html.

Fitchett, Joseph, "GEC Alstom Flotation to Unleash Major Player in Power and Rail," *International Herald Tribune*, June 2, 1998, http://www.iht.com/IHT/DIPLO/98/jf060298.html.

Gow, David, "Former Alstom Chief to Return His £2.7m Payoff," *The Guardian*, August 19, 2003, http://www.guardian.co.uk/executivepay/story/0,1204,1021483,00.html.

Matlack, Carol, "Can Alstom Get Back on Track? It's a Financial Wreck, and the Rescue Plan May Not Work," *BusinessWeek Online*, July 21, 2003, http://www.businessweek.com/magazine/content/03_29/b3842135_mz034.htm.

Mounicq, Jean-Christophe, "Liberté, Égalité, Bankruptcy!" Tech Central Station, October 24, 2003, http://www.techcentralstation.com/102403E.html.

Smith, Alex Duval, and Katherine Griffiths, "Conscience Sparks Return of $7.8m," *New Zealand Herald*, August 23, 2003. http://www.nzherald.co.nz/employment.

Tagliabue, John, "Alstom's Ex-Chief Rejects Severance Pay Package," *New York Times*, August 19, 2003, http://www.timesizing.com/1gmktrin.htm.

—Marie L. Thompson

■ ■ ■

Alwaleed Bin Talal

1957(?)–

Entrepreneur, investor

Nationality: Saudi Arabian.

Born: July 9, 1957(?), in Riyadh, Saudi Arabia.

Education: Menlo College, BA, 1979; Syracuse University, MA.

Family: Son of Prince Talal; married Princess Kholood; divorced twice; children: two (previous marriage).

Career: Kingdom Establishment for Trading and Contracting, 1979–, owner; Kingdom Holding Company and Kingdom Hotel Investment Group, owner.

Address: Kingdom Holding Company, Takhassussi Road, PO Box 2, Riyadh, Saudi Arabia 11321.

■ Prince Alwaleed bin Talal bin Abdulaziz al-Saud was an internationally renowned businessman and investor who became a self-made billionaire at the age of 31. He was ranked the fourth-wealthiest person in the world by *Forbes* magazine in 2004. Although he started investing in businesses in Saudi Arabia, Bin Talal amassed his large fortune by investing in companies around the world in a variety of industries, including construction, banking, media, hotels, and technology.

Alwaleed Bin Talal. *AP/Wide World Photos.*

ROYAL BEGINNINGS

Bin Talal was born in Saudi Arabia. His paternal grandfather, Abdulaziz ibn Saud, united the Arabian peninsula and formed the kingdom of Saudi Arabia, while his maternal grandfather, Riad al-Solh, was the first prime minister of the Republic of Lebanon. His father, Prince Talal, was the brother of the king of Saudi Arabia. Despite his influential and wealthy family tree, Bin Talal was proud of the fact that he earned his fortune through his own hard work.

Bin Talal's parents divorced when he was a young child, and he spent part of his childhood in Beirut. In order to instill more discipline in the young Bin Talal, his father made him return to Riyadh to attend the King Abdul Aziz Military Academy. Like many other members of the royal family, he pursued his college education in the United States. He earned a business administration degree from Menlo College in California and later finished a master's degree in political science from Syracuse University.

To start his business career, Bin Talal's father gave him $15,000 cash and a house. Bin Talal invested this money in construction. The initial cash investment was quickly spent, but his father refused to lend him any more money. Bin Talal mortgaged his house to support his fledgling business. Just one year later he got his first big break when he joined two other small companies to win a contract for a $16 million military academy. By 1981 Kingdom Establishment had over $1.5 billion in revenues. Bin Talal expanded his construction business to maintaining and operating existing buildings in Saudi Arabia.

INTERNATIONAL SUCCESSES

Bin Talal made his mark on the international scene in 1990 when he bought almost 5 percent of Citicorp's shares. At that time the company was on the verge of bankruptcy, but in only a couple of years it turned around, and Bin Talal profited billions. In subsequent years Bin Talal bought minority stakes in numerous foreign companies, including some of America's largest firms. In 2003 he owned small percentages of stock in Amazon.com, eBay, AOL Time Warner, Ford Motor Company, Hewlett-Packard, Motorola, Pepsi, and the Walt Disney Company, among others.

Although this investment strategy was successful for Bin Talal, he had very diverse business interests. He partnered with other investors to purchase large shares of hotel stocks, such as the Four Seasons and the Fairmont Hotels. He also invested heavily in Saudi Arabia and other Arab countries, particularly in media and technology. For example, Bin Talal owned part of Arab Radio and Television, Lebanese Broadcasting Centre, and the Palestine Development and Investment Company. Aside from Kingdom Holding Company, which was largely responsible for his international business activities, Bin Talal also owned several other companies in Saudi Arabia, including Kingdom Hotel Investment Group, Kingdom Centre, Kingdom City, Kingdom Hospital, and Kingdom Schools.

Not all of Bin Talal's investments were successful. For example, EuroDisney, Planet Hollywood, and Motorola continued to struggle even after Bin Talal's stock purchases. While he was praised for knowing when to make wise acquisitions, he was also criticized for not recognizing when to sell bad stocks.

LEADERSHIP AND BUSINESS STRATEGIES

Bin Talal owed his success as an investor to his practices of diversifying successfully and refusing to be limited by national borders. He invested primarily for long-term gains and had a good track record for selecting undervalued companies. He was also cautious and searched continually for bargains. Bin Talal had a sharp mind and was an excellent deal maker, conducting negotiations in Arabic, English, and French.

Reputed to be an extremely hard worker, Bin Talal surrounded himself with a staff that shared this value. He was a direct communicator and a demanding leader. Addicted to news, he traveled with a technology crew who kept him in touch with global developments no matter where he happened to be. Bin Talal also moved easily between the traditional Arab world and Western cultures. He lived primarily in Saudi Arabia, wore traditional Arab garb while he was there, and observed cultural and religious practices according to the laws and customs of the kingdom. At the same time, he traveled extensively across the globe, spoke American slang, and dressed in stylish business suits while working in the West.

CHANGING PERCEPTIONS OF SAUDI ARABIA

Not only did Bin Talal become a successful businessman, but he also helped to change international perceptions of the kingdom of Saudi Arabia. While the business world in the early 21st century tended to think of Saudi Arabia as traditional and private, Bin Talal was an example of a very modern businessman who was open to the media and the public. "I want my voice to be heard," Bin Talal told *Forbes* magazine (August 8, 1988). "I would love to be a corporate leader."

Bin Talal was also a very generous businessman. In a country that did not have income taxes, he donated considerable amounts of money to charitable causes. "It is my responsibility to take advantage of my position to make the world a better place," Bin Talal told the *Middle East Economic Digest* (May 3, 2003). In 2001 he donated $10 million to New York City to help with the recovery after the September 11 terrorist attacks. However, Mayor Rudolph Giuliani refused to accept the donation because Bin Talal also made some controversial political remarks about America's policies in the Middle East.

By 2004 Bin Talal had established himself as a successful international investor and one of the wealthiest businessmen in the world. He continued to look for new bargain investments both in Saudi Arabia and around the world. In 2004 he was also entertaining the idea of publicly trading the $21 billion Kingdom Holding Company.

SOURCES FOR FURTHER INFORMATION

Barrett, William P., "'I'm Not Finished Yet.' (Saudi Arabia's Prince Bin Talal Bin Abdulaziz Al Saud Self-Made Billionaire at 33)," *Forbes*, August 8, 1988, pp. 86–87.

MacLeod, Scott, "The Prince and the Portfolio," *Time*, December 1, 1997, pp. 62–68.

"The Mystery of the World's Second-Richest Businessman," *The Economist*, February 27, 1999, p. 67.

"A Prince with Divided Loyalties," *BusinessWeek*, October 15, 2001, p. 64.

Rossant, John, and Stephen Baker, "The Prince and the Public," *BusinessWeek*, April 26, 2004, p. 13.

Serwer, Andrew, "The Prince: His Royal Highness Prince Bin Talal Bin Abdulaziz al-Saud," *Money*, October 1988, pp. 108–110.

"The View from the Top," *Middle East Economic Digest*, May 2, 2003, pp. 4–6.

—Janet P. Stamatel

■ ■ ■

Dave Bing

1943–

Owner and president, Bing Group

Nationality: American.

Born: November 29, 1943, in Washington, D.C.

Education: Syracuse University, BA, 1966.

Family: Son of a contractor; mother's occupation unknown. Twice married (divorced); children: three.

Career: Detroit Pistons, 1966–1975, basketball player; Bank of Detroit, 1967–1975, management trainee; Washington Bullets, 1975–1977, basketball player; Boston Celtics, 1977–1978, basketball player; National Paragon Steel, 1978–1980, management trainee; Bing Steel, 1980–, owner and president.

Awards: National Basketball Association Rookie of the Year, 1967; National Minority Small Businessperson of the Year, 1984; Basketball Hall of Fame, 1990; Black Enterprise Company of the Year, 1998.

Address: Bing Group, 11500 Oakland Avenue, Detroit, Michigan 48211; http://www.binggroup.com.

■ Dave Bing was one of the most successful black business owners in the United States. After completing a career as a superstar in the National Basketball Association, Bing started a steel service company in 1980. The Bing Group is one of the largest African American–owned businesses in the United States. Bing is dedicated to improving the city of Detroit and to providing job opportunities for its citizens.

As a youth growing up in Washington, D.C., Bing developed an interest in business. His father, a building contractor, often took his son to construction sites. Bing decided early that he wanted one day to own his own company. An outstanding high school basketball player, he was recruited by Syracuse University. He was named All-American at Syracuse before graduating in 1966 with a degree in economics and marketing. Business was to be his second career.

Bing was drafted by the Detroit Pistons in 1966 and played professional basketball for twelve years, at a time when salaries were modest. To earn extra money during the off-season and prepare for his business career, he worked as a bank management trainee for seven years and participated in an auto dealer–training program for two years. After retiring from basketball in 1978, Bing was offered a public relations job at Paragon Steel in Detroit, but he declined the job when he realized the company wanted to hire him simply because of his fame. Instead, he entered a management-training program at Paragon. After two years he started his own steel service company, Bing Steel, which cut steel to size for the auto industry.

BATTLED RECESSION AND PREJUDICE

Bing started his company in the middle of one of the worst recessions in the steel industry. He battled not only the economy but also prejudice from people who did not believe that a black athlete could succeed in business. He told *Black Enterprise* magazine, "As a black with the stigma of being an ex-jock, the toughest thing for me was getting people to realize I had the intellect to get things done and that I was serious about making the leap from athletics to business" (June 1998).

Bing Steel lost $90,000 in its first six months, but after landing a contract with General Motors, the business turned around. It became profitable within two years, and by 1990 sales had reached $61 million. In order to insulate his company from the ups and downs of the steel industry, Bing diversified by starting four other automotive supply companies. Collectively, the five companies are known as the Bing Group. Four of the five companies are headquartered on a 30-acre campus in Detroit's empowerment zone, where property was inexpensive. In the early years Bing did a lot of the building renovation himself, to help contain costs.

LESSONS FROM THE BASKETBALL COURT

The soft-spoken Bing credited basketball for teaching him the discipline and competitiveness that helped him succeed in business. Teamwork was another aspect of Bing's management style that carried over from athletics. He had a reputation for taking good care of his employees. As he once put it, "It doesn't matter if you're the executive vice-president of Bing Steel or one of my hourly workers, you're going to get respect from me. Team effort is important here. We all work together to get the job done" (*Black Enterprise*, January 1985).

Lear's CEO, Kenneth Way, who entered into a joint venture with the Bing Group to produce auto seating, praised Bing's character. Bing has "always been an individual of very high integrity and character," he said. "You can trust him and trust that he has the business experience and track record to make an operation work" (*Black Enterprise*, June 1998).

Bing also earned the respect of General Motors, which named the Bing Group Supplier of the Year in 1997, 2002, and 2003. When the auto supplier's quality declined during the late 1990s, GM suggested improvements. The Bing Group rose to the challenge, and defects per million parts dropped from 1,200 to 17 in just two years.

DEDICATED TO DETROIT

Giving back was an important principle of Dave Bing's. He served on the boards of several civic and charitable organizations and was a benefactor of Detroit schools. He felt strongly about improving the city of Detroit and creating employment opportunities for African Americans. Frustrated at not being able to find qualified employees, Bing could have moved his company out of Detroit. Instead, he partnered with Ford (his biggest customer) to build a $4 million training facility for minority workers in Detroit in 1999. Eighty percent of the Bing Group's workforce was African American in the early 2000s.

The center taught workers the technology they needed to work in a manufacturing facility and the importance of good work habits. During their first three months, workers who missed work without calling in or who were late four times were fired. Those who met Bing's high standards were rewarded. Bing always paid his workers above the minimum wage, and managers received equity in as little as three years. Bing told *Forbes*, "It's a very strong feeling walking around the plant and seeing the faces of people everybody else quit on" (September 18, 2000).

In 2002 the Bing Group's sales totaled $344 million, and the company had a staff of 1,120. It was ranked seventh on *Black Enterprise*'s list of the top black-owned businesses. In 2003 Bing announced a plan to buy additional companies as a way to triple sales to $1 billion by 2008. A key to that growth, Bing told the *Detroit News*, is to change automaker's attitudes toward minority suppliers. "There was a small slice of the pie designated for minority businesses and that's not what we want. We want to compete for the whole pie," he said (August 26, 2003).

See also entry on The Bing Group in *International Directory of Company Histories.*

SOURCES FOR FURTHER INFORMATION

Garsten, Ed, "Bing Ties Success with Teamwork: Once-Struggling Firm Named Top GM Supplier for Second Year in a Row," *Detroit News*, August 26, 2003.

Gite, Lloyd, "Scoring with Steel," *Black Enterprise*, January 1985, pp. 63–66.

Kellner, Tomas, "Rebound Man," *Forbes*, September 18, 2000, pp. 198–200.

Smith, Eric L., "Motor City's Man of Steel," *Black Enterprise*, June 1998, pp. 124–130.

Telander, Rick, "Life Lessons from a Man of Steel: Dave Bing Has Made the Leap from NBA Star to Successful Businessman," *Sports Illustrated*, August 19, 1991, pp. 48–51.

—Barbara Koch

■ ■ ■

Carole Black

1945–

President and chief executive officer, Lifetime Entertainment Services

Nationality: American.

Born: 1945.

Education: Ohio State University, BA, 1965.

Family: Children: one.

Career: Proctor & Gamble, 1970–1983, marketing executive; DDB Needham, 1983–1986, senior vice president; Walt Disney Company, 1986–1993, held positions of vice president of worldwide marketing and senior vice president of marketing and television; NBC 4, 1994–1999, general manager; Lifetime Entertainment Services, 1999–, president and chief executive officer.

Awards: Named one of the Fifty Most Powerful Women in Business, 2001 and 2002, *Fortune*; named one of the Top 25 Managers of the Year 2002, *BusinessWeek*; named one of New York's Most Influential Women in Business, 1999, *Crain's New York Business*; named one of America's One Hundred Most Important Women of the Twentieth Century, *Ladies Home Journal*.

Address: Lifetime Entertainment Services, 309 West 49th Street, New York, New York 10019; http://www.lifetimetv.com.

HELPING LIFETIME RISE IN THE WOMEN'S MARKET

■ Under Carole Black's leadership, Lifetime Television established itself as one of the highest-rated cable television networks in the United States and the leader in women's television in programming. In 2001 Nielsen Media Research cited Lifetime Television as the number one basic-cable network in prime time. By doubling the corporation's marketing budget and making women's issues the focus of programming, Black successfully positioned the network for continued growth in the cable market, especially in that important demographic.

EARLY WORK EXPERIENCE

Carole Black displayed her strong leadership skills early in life. Indeed, as the president of her high school student body she was already a pioneer of sorts—that Cincinnati high school had never elected a female president until Black came along. After graduating from Ohio State University in 1965, Black began her career in her home town of Cincinnati as a marketing executive with Proctor & Gamble. She married and gave birth to a son. After divorcing her husband, she left Proctor & Gamble in 1983 for the advertising firm DDB Needham, where she developed a passion for working on marketing specifically targeted to women. Black worked on the Sears account, and one of her duties was to make Sears stores more engaging and appealing to women customers. In this she succeeded.

WITH DISNEY

Accepting a position with the Walt Disney Company in 1986 meant leaving the cozy confines of her home and life in the Midwest, but the move to the West Coast proved to be a great success. In her seven years with Disney, Black was credited with drawing more working women, especially busy working mothers, to the home-video market. This was considered quite revolutionary at the time. Videos had not been widely promoted for their convenience, something that as a mother Black recognized and was able to emphasize. As vice president of marketing and television she was directly responsible for increased video sales to working mothers.

Black decided to move on, and perhaps it seemed odd at first that she would leave Disney to head the NBC affiliate in Los Angeles. Since she had very little television know-how, it was an opportunity for Black and something of a gamble for NBC. The station wanted to extend its share of female viewers, and it took particular note of Black's track record and abilities in that regard. Black succeeded in increasing the station's exposure among women viewers, and she was credited with making NBC 4 the number one news station in the area.

LIFETIME'S LIFELINE

In 1999 Black became the first woman to head the Lifetime Television cable network. The network felt that her business acumen could easily provide a boost to Lifetime's viewership, but it is not clear that at the time they fully appreciated her potential for the network. Carole Black was not timid about implementing immediate and significant changes in the company. She swiftly replaced four people in top management positions. She realized that Lifetime could save money by producing much of its daytime programming in house, and she provided ways for that to happen quickly and efficiently. She ensured that all programming was for and about women, and in response large numbers of women began to take notice. Lifetime became number one in that important demographic and remained there through Black's tenure.

Black expanded the distribution of Lifetime's Movie Network and launched Lifetime Real Women, the company's third cable network. Moreover, Lifetimetv.com consistently rated high and became the fastest-growing women's Web site on the Internet. Also under Black's tutelage, *Lifetime* magazine, which was developed jointly with Hearst, was launched in April 2003 with a commitment to "real life, real women," Lifetime's slogan. The magazine had a target circulation of 500,000 and was intended for women in their thirties. By 2004 Lifetime served over 85 million households nationwide and was available on more than 11,000 cable and alternative delivery systems.

See also entries on Walt Disney Company and Lifetime Entertainment Services in *International Directory of Company Histories.*

SOURCES FOR FURTHER INFORMATION

Hundley, Heather, "The Evolution of Gendercasting: The Lifetime Television Network—Television for Women," *Journal of Popular Film and Television,* Winter 2002.

Larson, Megan, "Job of a Lifetime," *Brandweek,* May 8, 2000.

"The Top 25 Managers of the Year," *BusinessWeek,* January 14, 2002.

—Susan French Ludwig

■■■

Cathleen Black

1944–

President, Hearst Magazines

Nationality: American.

Born: April 26, 1944, in Chicago, Illinois.

Education: Trinity College, BA, 1966.

Family: Daughter of James Hamilton Black (food-company executive) and Margaret Harrington; married Thomas Harvey (attorney); children: two.

Career: Curtis Publishing, 1996, telephone ad salesperson; *Holiday*, 1966–1970, ad salesperson; *New York*, 1970–1972, ad salesperson; *Ms.*, 1972–1975, advertising director; 1975–1977, associate publisher; *New York*, 1977–1979, associate publisher; 1979–1983, publisher; *USA Today*, 1983, president; 1984–1991, publisher; Newspaper Association of America, 1991–1995, spokesperson and lobbyist; Hearst Magazines, 1995–, president.

Awards: Woman of the Year, *Adweek*, 1985; 30 Most Powerful Women in American Business, *Fortune*, 1998–2000; Publishing Executive of the Year, *Folio*, 2000; 100 Most Influential Business Leaders, *Crain's New York Business*, 2002.

Address: Hearst Magazines, 959 8th Avenue, New York, New York 10019-3795; http://www.hearstcorp.com/magazines.

■ Cathleen Black became president of Hearst Magazines in 1995. Her success in expanding the company's titles' advertising sales, circulation, and presence on both national and international levels made her a notable figure in publishing history. She was described as a person who met challenges head on, a great presenter, a charming colleague, and a hands-off supervisor who trusted her editors to do their work without her intervention. She described herself as performance- and results-driven and was noted for breaking through gender barriers throughout her career.

ENTERING THE PUBLISHING WORLD

Black grew up surrounded by arts and culture in her home town of Chicago. From an early age she perused the newspapers and chatted about current events with her parents. She earned a degree in English from Trinity College in Washington then headed to New York City with the hope of working in the publicity industry. She started her career by selling advertising for magazines.

Black was called on to help launch *Ms.* magazine as advertising manager in 1972—at a time when staunch feminism was not widely accepted. She managed to convince clients that women who were entering the workplace would represent an economically sound subset of the population that would respond to their ads. Her success in sales led to her promotion to associate publisher in 1975.

MAKING PUBLISHING HISTORY

Her success with *Ms.* did not go unnoticed. The media mogul Rupert Murdoch soon asked her to return to the East Coast to work at *New York* magazine as an associate publisher. She agreed—with the stipulation that if she met her goals and turned the magazine around, she would be named publisher. In 1979, after working there for two years, Black was indeed named publisher of *New York*, making her the first woman to hold that title for a weekly consumer magazine.

Black then moved to *USA Today* in 1984, where she would be credited with boosting the daily publication's circulation and making it profitable. She then headed the American Newspapers Publishers Association, where she worked mainly as a spokesperson and lobbyist. She expanded the lobbying program by increasing its budget sevenfold and merging six separate trade groups into one under the new name of the Newspaper Association of America. Noting her success with the job for which he had recruited her, the Hearst president and CEO Frank Bennack Jr. then asked Black to join Hearst as president of its magazine division.

FROM NAA TO HEARST MAGAZINES

In 1995 Black was hired to run Hearst Magazines, which at the time produced 16 publications, including *Cosmopolitan*, *Marie Claire*, and *Good Housekeeping*. The move made Black the first woman president of the privately held family company that had been well known for its "old boy network." Within a year she made remarkable progress in improving ad sales and the visibility and image of the company. She stressed the importance of branding each magazine and encouraged editors to think of themselves as marketers as well. Throughout her tenure she expanded on these ideas, working to apply the Hearst titles to more than 3,500 products on the world market and promoting growth in licensing, Internet presence, and international distribution. Black brought Hearst publications to more than 41 countries through 101 international editions. Her success with Hearst and throughout her career led her to be nicknamed "The First Lady of American Magazines."

See also entry on The Hearst Corporation in *International Directory of Company Histories.*

SOURCES FOR FURTHER INFORMATION

"Cathleen Black," *Folio,* April 30, 1999.

"Cathleen Black, President, Hearst Magazines," Hearst Corporation, Corporate Biographies, http://www.hearstcorp.com/biographies/corp_bio_black.html.

"Magazine Chief Shakes Things Up at Hearst," *New York Times,* June 2, 1997.

"Meet Cathleen Black, Trinity Alumn," *Trinity Times,* September 25, 2003.

—Jeanette Bogren

Jonathan Bloomer

1954–

Group Chief Executive, Prudential Public Limited Company

Nationality: British.

Born: March 23, 1954.

Education: Imperial College, London, FCA.

Family: Married; children: three.

Career: Arthur Andersen, joined company in 1974; 1991–1995, senior partner of European Insurance Practice; Prudential Public Limited Company, 1995–1999, group finance director; Prudential Public Limited Company, 1999–2000, deputy group chief executive; Prudential Public Limited Company, 2000–, group chief executive.

Address: Prudential Public Limited Company, Laurence Pountney Hill, London, EC4R OHH, United Kingdom; http://www.prudential.co.uk.

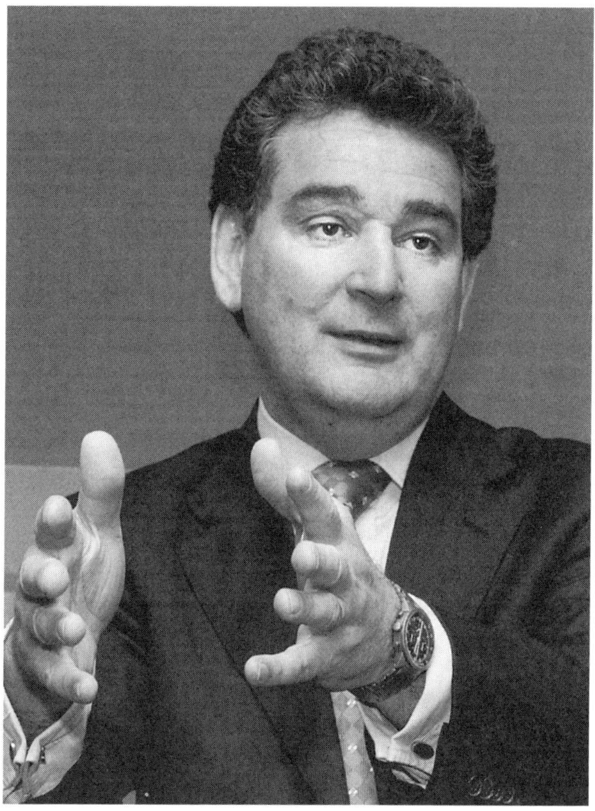

Jonathan Bloomer. *John Li/Getty Images.*

Jonathan Bloomer took over as group chief executive of Prudential Public Limited Company (no relation to Prudential Insurance Company of America), the worldwide life insurance and saving-products company, just as the international economic downturn began in 2000. As a result, Bloomer, like many other insurance company executives, struggled to reverse a steady decline in profits and stock prices. While Bloomer successfully guided the company to the beginnings of a recovery in sales, he faced ongoing difficulties in turning around the company's profit margins. Industry analysts have noted that Bloomer's background in accounting made him well suited to lead the insurance company because of his ability to understand the numerous and complex financial and actuarial concepts involved in the insurance business.

APPOINTED HEAD OF PRUDENTIAL

After graduating from Imperial College in London, Bloomer went to work for the accounting firm of Arthur Andersen, where he first began to learn about the insurance business. He worked on behalf of insurers in both the United Kingdom and Europe in the areas of acquisition reviews, strategic planning and structuring, and operations reviews and investigations. He also served as senior partner of Arthur Andersen's European Insurance Practice.

In 1995 Bloomer left Arthur Andersen and joined Prudential as group finance director. In May 1999 he was appointed deputy group chief executive and then assumed the post of group chief executive, or chief executive officer, on March 1, 2000.

FACES SETBACKS

After taking over as CEO, Bloomer immediately began to address Prudential's falling profits by attempting to take over the U.S. insurance company American General, thus adding to Prudential's U.S. subsidiaries, Jackson National Life and PPM America. Bloomer announced that he believed the companies would work well together because of their complementary business operations and similar strategies in broadening their product ranges and distribution channels.

Bloomer's efforts to purchase American General, however, fell through when the global insurance giant American International Group outbid Prudential for control of the Houston-based insurance company. Part of the reason Bloomer's acquisition plans failed was that he had offered $26.5 billion in Prudential stock to acquire the company. However, Prudential's stock price dropped after the announcement because investors thought the offer was too high. This devaluation in stock price led to a decline in the deal's value by about $20 billion.

Bloomer's failure to acquire American General was somewhat tempered by a reported $600 million break fee paid by American International Group to Prudential to cover Prudential's expenses in attempting to make the deal. However, Bloomer once again angered shareholders when it was announced that he was in a position to make up to £4.6 million if the company met performance targets. At the very least he was scheduled to earn a bonus of £900,000 on top of his £600,000 salary. The stockholder outcry led Prudential's board to reassess the deal.

A CONTINUING STRUGGLE

Bloomer continued to struggle with Prudential's declining profits, especially in the first half of 2002 when the company announced a nearly 50 percent decline in profits compared with the same time the previous year. Bloomer laid the blame for part of the decline on a $230 million loss on investments in U.S. corporate bonds. The company also suffered a steep decline in share prices.

Despite the setbacks, Bloomer announced that he was confident that Prudential would weather the global stock market downturn. He pointed out that the company's strategic expansion in Asian markets, including China, had resulted in a 27 percent increase in new business in these markets. The *BBC News* reported Bloomer as saying, "Our financial strength will enable us to continue to deliver growth in [the] future" (July 24, 2002).

Part of Bloomer's growth strategy was to continue to broaden the company's international markets and refine distribution approaches. The strategy appeared to be working in January 2003, when the company reported that insurance sales rose 12 percent and total sales for Prudential UK rose 6 percent. The improved performance was driven by sales of bulk and individual annuities, with individual annuity sales rising 39 percent. But Bloomer noted that the company expected to continue to encounter difficult market conditions.

By mid-2003 Bloomer once again angered shareholders when he cut the company's dividend by 40 percent. In a video interview on the Prudential Web site, Bloomer noted that he thought the dividend cut was a fair balance between future business investment and a shareholder dividend. He noted that the purpose of the dividend cut was "to ensure that we've got that balance and that we can invest for the future and we can grab those opportunities as they arise, as markets improve going forwards" (July 29, 2003).

MANAGEMENT STYLE: KEEPING A LOW PROFILE

Although Bloomer has been described by market analysts and colleagues as having a healthy ego, they add that his style is to keep a low profile and not to rub people the wrong way. This approach, analysts have noted, helps keep him and the company out of the sights of British Parliament members and regulators who have been examining many insurance companies. Bloomer is also known for his attention to detail.

Bloomer's management approach to foreign markets has been to stress the importance of establishing partners in countries where the company is not well known. He has emphasized recruiting local management who know the foreign markets best. Bloomer is also a strong proponent of investing in the insurance company's thousands of employees through training courses, especially online learning.

LOOKING TO THE FUTURE

By January 2004 Prudential was showing a revival with a strong rebound in policy sales during the last three months of 2003. Although the full-year sales for 2003 slid 19 percent to £148 million, the October-to-December sales rose 10 percent compared with sales in the previous quarter. As many British financial services companies were coming under regulatory review, Bloomer noted in the *Times Online* that he expected Prudential to benefit "from savers choosing those companies with clear financial strength" (January 22, 2004). Nevertheless, the following month Prudential reported a 30 percent slide in full-year profits. Bloomer was also having difficulty trying to sell Prudential's unprofitable online banking effort called Egg, which analysts noted would provide a £1.3 billion cash injection into the company. In addition to his role at Prudential, Bloomer has served as a member of Great Britain's Urgent Issues Task Force, nonexecutive director of Railtrack Public Limited Company, and deputy chairman of the Financial Services Authority's practitioner panel.

See also entries on Arthur Andersen & Company and Prudential plc in *International Directory of Company Histories*.

SOURCES FOR FURTHER INFORMATION

Ackman, Dan, "Top of the News: Transatlantic Insurer Merger," *Forbes.com* http://www.forbes.com.

"Profits at UK Insurer Prudential Take 30 Percent Beating," *Knight Ridder/Tribune Business News*, February 24, 2004.

"Prudential Interim Results," July 29, 2003, http://www.prudential.co.uk/prudentialplc/investor_home/presentations/?view=Standard&archive=yes.

"Red Tape May Trip Up Prudential Revival," *Times Online*, January 22, 2004. http://business.timesonline.co.uk/article/0,,8903-972959,00.html.

"Shareholders Revolt Costs Man from the Pru Pounds 4.6m," *Times* (London), May 9, 2002.

"Stock Market Woes Hit Pru Profits," *BBC News*, July 24, 2002.

—David Petechuk

■■■

Alan L. Boeckmann

1948–

Chairman of the board and chief executive officer, Fluor Corporation

Nationality: American.

Born: 1948.

Education: University of Arizona, BS, 1973.

Career: Fluor Corporation, 1974–1992, engineer; 1992–1996, various management positions including assignments in California, Texas, South Carolina, South Africa, and Venezuela; 1992–1996, president of Chemicals, Plastics and Fibers; 1996–1999, group president of Chemicals and Industrial Processes; Fluor Daniel, 1999–2001, president and chief operating officer; Fluor Corporation, 2001–2002, president and chief operating officer; 2002–, chairman of the board and chief executive officer.

Awards: Technology and Management Distinguished Service Award, University of Arizona, 2001.

Address: Fluor Corporation, One Enterprise Drive, Aliso Viejo, California 92656; http://www.fluor.com.

■ Alan L. Boeckmann, who was the chairman and chief executive officer of Fluor Corporation in the early 2000s, was actively involved in the fight against corruption in the international engineering and construction industry. Boeckmann had been a Fluor executive at various levels since 1992 and held the company's top job after February 2002. As of 2004 Fluor Corporation was a Fortune 500 firm, one of the world's largest publicly owned engineering, procurement, construction, and maintenance service companies. With revenues close to $9 billion in 2003, Fluor did business around the world. The global scope of its operations meant that it had to deal with the manifold challenges of bribery, corruption, and international terrorism.

Alan Boeckmann's long experience in engineering management at all levels in various locations around the world made him a natural choice to succeed Phillip J. Carroll, Jr. as Chairman and CEO of the Fluor Corporation in February 2002. Carroll had been the company's CEO since 1998. After completing a bachelor's degree in electrical engineering from the University of Arizona, Boeckmann joined Fluor in 1974 as an engineer.

KNOWING THE BUSINESS

After a variety of management-level assignments that took Boeckmann to locations in California, Texas, South Carolina, South Africa, and Venezuela, he was made the president of the chemicals, plastics, and fibers group of Fluor Daniel, which was the corporation's engineering and construction division. Boeckmann assumed his new position in 1992. Four years later he became the president of Fluor Daniel's chemical processes and industrial business group. In 1999 Boeckmann became Fluor Daniel's president and chief operating officer. Once installed as president, Boeckmann monitored the changes in his industry related to the growth of the Internet, e-commerce, and the globalization of the workforce. To remain competitive, Boeckmann directed Fluor's investments toward advanced technology and the employee training needed to use that technology effectively.

Boeckmann was promoted to president and chief operating officer of Fluor Daniel's parent corporation in January 2001. He became Fluor's chairman and chief executive officer in February 2002. Shortly before Boeckmann became Fluor's CEO, however, he was confronted by the highly publicized crises that affected several well-known public corporations across the United States. Media headlines highlighted what appeared to be systemic problems in the way top managers conducted business. A roll call of corporate mismanagement began to unfold just as Boeckmann started his new job, shaping his resolve to strengthen Fluor's efforts to promote fairness, transparency, accountability, and responsibility in its business dealings. He intended to keep Fluor Corporation among the majority of companies that did not make the news.

CORPORATE GOVERNANCE ISSUES

The high-profile corporate scandals of 2002 resulted in the passage of the Sarbanes-Oxley Act, also known as the Public Company Accounting Reform and Investor Protection Act. Sarbanes-Oxley, named for the two members of Congress who had sponsored it, was the latest in a series of laws governing the American stock market that began with the Securities Act of 1933. In 1934 the Securities Exchange Act established the Securities and Exchange Commission (SEC) and gave it broad authority over all aspects of the securities industry, including the power to prohibit the types of misconduct that had led to the corporate scandals of 2002. The Sarbanes-Oxley Act in essence strengthened the powers of the SEC.

Fluor already had in place some of the procedures recommended by the SEC, such as naming outsiders to its board of directors and having committees in place to monitor the external auditors who checked the company's financial records. In addition, all Fluor employees had already been required to subscribe in writing to the company's code of business conduct. Since these policies alone were not foolproof, as the 2002 scandals indicated, Fluor made several additional changes in its governance that were consistent with the new law.

TAKING A STAND AGAINST CORRUPTION

The issue of corruption in business, although it made headlines across the United States in 2002, is neither new nor confined to North America. Business corruption at the global level was addressed at a series of special sessions at the World Economic Forum's annual meetings. As chairman of the Engineering and Construction Governors of the World Economic Forum, Boeckmann played a major role in the multinational task force charged with establishing the benchmark business principles that were presented at the forum's annual meeting in January 2004. According to a PR Newswire press release, Boeckmann said, "This is an issue that I'm absolutely passionate about. Corruption has a corrosive impact on market opportunities and the general business climate" (July 30, 2003).

Fluor's status as a company incorporated in the United States meant that it was subject to the provisions of the Foreign Corrupt Practices Act of 1977. This act made it unlawful for any American company to pay bribes to foreign officials to secure business deals. Ethical companies, however, paid a price in lost income for refusing to engage in bribery. Boeckmann reported in 2003 that according to the U.S. Commerce Department, "... during the period 1994–2002 as many as 474 large offshore contracts worth $237 billion involved bribery of foreign officials" (*World Energy Magazine* 6, no. 4, 2003).

Until 1998 U.S. companies had to face unfair competition alone. In that year, however, they got help when more than 30 countries implemented the strong anti-bribery measures mandated by the Organization for Economic Co-operation and Development (OECD) Convention on Combating Bribery of Foreign Public Officials in International Business Transactions. As of early 2004, Fluor continued to do business on six continents.

See also entry on the Fluor Corporation in *International Directory of Company Histories.*

SOURCES FOR FURTHER INFORMATION

Boeckmann, Alan L., "Taking a Corporate Stand against Corruption," *World Energy Magazine* 6, no. 4 (2003), pp. 2–5.

"Engineering and Construction Industry Tackles Global Corruption," PR Newswire, July 30, 2003.

"Managing New Risks," World Economic Forum, Annual Meeting 2004, www.weforum.org.

"No Longer Business as Usual—Fighting Bribery and Corruption," OECD, October 1, 2000, www.oecd.org.

—M. C. Nagel

■■■

Daniel Bouton

1950–

Chairman and chief executive officer, Société Générale

Nationality: French.

Born: April 10, 1950, in Paris, France.

Education: Earned degrees from National Institute of Political Studies and National School of Administration.

Family: Married; children: two.

Career: French Ministry of Finance, 1973–1976, inspector of finance; 1977–1986, budget department; 1986–1988, chief of staff of deputy minister in charge of budget; 1988–1991, head of budget department; 1990–1991, inspector general of finance; Société Générale, 1991–1993, executive vice president; 1993–1997, chief executive officer; 1997–, chairman.

Awards: Knight of the Ordre Nationale de la Légion d'Honneur; Knight of the Ordre Nationale de la Légion du Mérite.

Address: Société Générale, 17, cours Valmy, Paris la Defense, F-92972 Cedex, France; http://www.socgen.com.

Daniel Bouton. *AP/Wide World Photos.*

■ Daniel Bouton spent nearly two decades as a civil servant in the French government before joining the French bank Société Générale in 1991. As chief executive officer and later chairman, Bouton fostered an aggressive but careful acquisition program involving banks and firms within France and overseas. By 2002 Bouton had made Société Générale into the most profitable European corporate and investment bank. Industry analysts have noted that Bouton established a good balance in Société Générale's activities among retail banking, investment banking, and asset management.

FROM GOVERNMENT SERVICE TO PRIVATE ENTERPRISE

After receiving a degree in political science from the National Institute of Political Studies, Bouton continued his studies and graduated from the elite National School of Administration. He then began his career as part of the French financial controllers' civil service corps and went on to hold a number of positions in France's Ministry of Finance. From 1986 to 1988 he served as chief of staff to Alain Juppé, who was France's deputy minister in charge of the budget. In 1988 Bouton was appointed head of the budget department.

Bouton left government service in 1991 and joined Société Générale, which had been a state-run institute that was privatized in 1987. As an executive vice president, Bouton's duties included the crucial responsibility of helping to establish a management team to institute protective measures designed to enable the bank to deal with the risks inherently associated with being a private market enterprise.

TAKES OVER THE REINS

In 1993 Bouton was named the bank's chief executive officer. As CEO, Bouton played a seminal role in acquiring a 63 percent stake in the French bank Crédit du Nord and in establishing Société Générale's strong domestic retail presence, which accounted for 50 percent of the bank's profits. He also built up a potentially powerful franchise in international capital markets and asset management.

Bouton was named chairman of Société Générale in 1997, taking over the position at what analysts considered to be the most crucial period in the institution's 130-year history. Many of Europe's banks were undergoing upheavals as they found themselves competing against global rivals. The new competition was a result of Europe's ongoing and profound economic and political transformation as barriers to cross-border trade and competition were falling. By the late 1990s, 12 Eurozone markets had been integrated and 10 new countries were expected to join. Old taboos were being broken, and European banks were stretching out more into wider domestic and global markets, with many looking toward a goal of eventually establishing a single financial market for member states of the Eurozone.

As chairman, Bouton responded to these changes by focusing on three core business lines: retail banking, corporate and investment banking, and asset management and private banking. He bolstered the bank's investment banking activities by acquiring Great Britain's Hambros banking services, which gave Société Générale an entry into private banking and corporate finance. Bouton also oversaw the purchase of the U.S. firm Cowen and Company, a Wall Street securities firm.

Bouton soon set his sights on a merger with the French investment bank Paribas, which was part of the Compagnie Financier de Paribas Group. Paribas was the fourth-ranked French bank in assets, right behind Société Générale at number three. Bouton saw Paribas's strong standing in the bond market and leadership in European currency unit issues as a complement to Société Générale's own investment banking activities in such areas as derivatives and structured finance. Although the deal was nearly finalized, the agreement was thwarted when Banque Nationale de Paris (BNP) outbid Société Générale and purchased Paribas.

At the same time that BNP secured a 65 percent share in Paribas, it was seeking to secure a controlling share of Société Générale as part of its efforts to compete in the newly unified financial markets of Europe. Bouton, however, vehemently opposed the BNP takeover and eventually succeeded in keeping BNP's share of Société Générale down to 31.8 percent.

SETS A NEW COURSE

After the failed takeover of Paribas, Bouton announced that Société Générale would seek to grow on its own, primarily through acquisitions and partnerships outside its home market in France. Although many of Europe's top banks were focusing on cross-border mergers as a way to consolidate their earnings, Bouton said he believed that alliances or partnerships had a lower execution risk than mergers, which were overly complicated. Nevertheless, Bouton knew that the fundamental style of banking in Europe was changing. He told Thomas Kamm for an article in the *Wall Street Journal*, as quoted in the *Indian Express*, "We are at the start of an accelerated evolution of the European banking landscape. In the second half of the next decade, banks will break out of their boundaries" (October 6, 1999).

By the end of 1999 Bouton noted that the bank would attempt to reduce its exposure in investment banking and emerging markets over the following two years. Instead, he wanted to focus on areas that provided for recurring profits as he tried to increase the bank's return on equity to 18.4 percent. As a part of that effort, he carried out an audacious coup by taking a 3.8 percent stake in Crédit Lyonnais SA. At the time, the troubled former French state bank was being eyed for a takeover by France's largest bank, Crédit Agricole. Bouton's acquisition effectively gave Crédit Lyonnais SA enough power to fight off the takeover. Bouton also continued to oversee acquisitions of other banks in various countries, usually rebuilding the bank in Société Générale's own image. A prime example was the Czech Republic's Komercni Bank. Acquiring a 60 percent stake in the bank in 2000, Bouton established a broader range of consumer loans and life insurance at Komercni, as well as Internet banking.

In addition to acquisitions, industry analysts also noted that Bouton had been consistently gathering together a protective group of core shareholders to help prevent Société Générale from being taken over. One of the additions to this core was Spain's largest banking group, Banco Santander Central Hispano, which raised its stake in Société Générale to 7 percent in early 2000.

FACES LEGAL CRISIS

In January 2002 Bouton and two other Société Générale executives were taken into custody for questioning by the French police as part of a money-laundering inquiry. The initial investigation centered on the issue of check controls as opposed to deliberate criminal activity. Société Générale and several other banks were part of a wide-ranging investigation involving stolen French checks that were being sent to Israel, where they were signed over to new beneficiaries. These beneficiaries then cashed the checks at various moneychangers and presented them to Israeli banks for payments. The Israeli banks then sent the checks to be cleared by the correspondent banks in France, including Société Générale.

Upon Bouton's arrest, Société Générale issued a statement denying that any of its employees knowingly participated in money-laundering transactions. Bouton, who was the most senior banking executive to be questioned, received a vote of confidence from the French Finance Minister Laurent Fabious, who was quoted in the *Business Recorder* as saying, "I know Daniel Bouton. We studied together. And I know he is honest" (January 16, 2002).

The bank officially protested that its only involvement was a failure to carefully scrutinize its check-cashing procedures and that it could not possibly monitor the huge number of checks cleared through the bank each day. More than a year and a half later, in October 2003, a French judge ordered Société Générale and seven other banks to stand trial on money-laundering charges. In all, 32 bank executives and directors were ordered to stand trial, including Bouton.

The investigation and trial sparked a controversy over revising the French judicial system. Industry analysts noted that Bouton had been known and publicly endorsed as a respectable banker. They also pointed out that he was being held responsible not for trying to make himself rich, but for failing to enforce the money-laundering regulations. His arrest further stirred up France's already exasperated business community, and the banking federation renewed calls for clarifications of France's 1996 money-laundering laws.

CAUTIOUS BUT OPTIMISTIC

Although Société Générale had a good performance in 2002 with a 16.3 percent return on equity excluding restructuring costs, Bouton remained concerned about the uncertainty of the economic situations in the countries where the bank had expanded its holdings. He was especially looking for a recovery in the U.S. economy, which had developed into Société Générale's second-biggest market.

Nevertheless, Bouton continued his strategy of acquisitions in the United States in 2003 when the bank acquired Constellation Financial Management and formed a new unit called SG Constellation. According to industry analysts, this purchase added structured products, such as hedge funds, that the bank could sell to institutional investors.

Bouton has been described by industry analysts as a firm but cautious decision maker. He has remained reluctant to form a merger with another bank and stuck to his philosophy that Société Générale would best move forward through strategic tie-ups rather than headline-grabbing cross-border mergers. Although he said that the bank might look favorably on either a domestic or cross-border consolidation, Bouton pointed out that even without them, Société Générale was one of the best performers among European banks. Fiscal year 2003, for example, saw Société Générale's net banking income rise 7 percent and its operating income rise 4 percent. As a result, Bouton maintained that Société Générale did not need to merge because of the company's continued growth, profitability, and its division's leadership positions in the Eurozone. Nevertheless, Bouton did not completely rule out a merger. As he told the *Euromoney* contributor Jennifer Morris, "We will marry when we find the right girl and it's proven that marriage is better for our shareholders, customers and employees than being a bachelor" (April 2003). In addition to his duties at Société Générale, Bouton held directorships at Schneider Electric, TotalfinaElf, and Veolia.

See also entry on Société Générale in *International Directory of Company Histories.*

SOURCES FOR FURTHER INFORMATION

Cameron, Doug, "Will SocGen Become Too Big for Its Boots?," *European*, February 23, 1998, p. 53.

"French Police Question Société Générale Officials," *Wall Street Journal Europe*, January 15, 2002.

Kamm, Thomas, "Societe Generale to Seek Growth on Its Own through Acquisition," *Wall Street Journal in the Indian Express*, October 6, 1999, http://www.indianexpress.com/fe/daily/19991007/fec07001.html

Morris, Jennifer, "France's Banking Model," *Euromoney*, April 2003, p. 42.

"Societe Generale Denies Wrongdoing in Money Launder Probe," *Business Recorder*, January 16, 2002, http://www.paksearch.com/br2002/Jan/16/Societe%20Generale.htm.

—David Petechuk

■ ■ ■

Martin Bouygues

1952–

Chairman and chief executive officer, Bouygues

Nationality: French.

Born: April 1952.

Education: Attended University of Paris, Dauphine.

Family: Son of Francis Bouygues; married (wife's name unknown); children: none.

Career: Bouygues Group, 1974–1978, site supervisor, manager; Maison Bouygues, 1978–1986, manager; Saur, 1986–1989, chairman and chief executive officer; Bouygues, 1987–1989, vice chairman; 1989–, chairman and chief executive officer.

Address: Bouygues SA, 1, avenue Eugène Freyssinet, 78061 Saint-Quentin-en-Yvelines Cedex, France; http://www.bouygues.fr.

Martin Bouygues. *AP/Wide World Photos.*

■ After he took over from his father, Martin Bouygues (pronounced "bweeg") developed the Bouygues Group into a giant corporation gathered into two primary arms—construction and services—that controlled more than 40 subsidiaries and affiliates in 80 countries. More than 22 percent of the huge corporation was controlled by the brothers Martin (the younger) and Olivier through the holding company SCDM. Martin, who shunned the public eye and was named among the richest people in the world beginning in 2000, earned his way to the top, beginning as a construction-site supervisor in 1974 after dropping out of the University of Paris.

The Bouygues company was founded by Francis Bouygues, the son of an engineer in Paris, the year Martin was born. Francis borrowed $1,700 and started an industrial works and construction business he named Entreprise Francis Bouygues. The company expanded into property development in 1956, entered the civil engineering and public works fields, and expanded from the Paris region throughout France. The company was listed on the Paris stock exchange in 1970. In 1974 Francis Bouygues created Bouygues Offshore and began building oil platforms. Martin Bouygues joined the business and supervised construction of the vast Parisian Les Halles shopping complex. He entered the business's commercial arm in 1978 and established Maison Bouygues, which specialized in catalog sales of single-family homes. That same year the Bouygues Group won a contract to build Roissy Terminal at Charles de Gaulle Airport, Paris, and in 1981 embarked on a monumental four-year project to build the University of Riyadh in Saudi Arabia, at the time the world's largest building project. In 1984 Bouygues acquired ETDE, a power transmission and supply firm, and Saur, the third-largest water treatment and supply company in France. Martin Bouygues played a significant role in the latter deal and was appointed chairman and chief executive officer two years later.

In 1986 the Bouygues Group acquired the Screg Group. Colas, France's largest highway contractor, was part of that group. Also in 1986 Jacques Chirac, the prime minister of

France, announced he would privatize Société Télévision Française 1 (TF1), the state-owned television network, and set a minimum price of FRF 4.5 billion ($750 million). Francis Bouygues saw this event as a major diversification opportunity and quickly organized a consortium, which won the bid the following year. Patrick Le Lay, a long-time construction engineer with Bouygues, became the chief executive of TF1 and immediately fired all but one of the network's 30 top executives. In their stead he placed Bouygues Group managers who had been trained at the construction company and who, like Le Lay, knew nothing about television. Under the watchful eye of Martin Bouygues, who became chairman and chief executive officer of the Bouygues Group in 1989, Le Lay grew the network into a highly diversified and successful media group. In an interview with John H. Christy of *Forbes*, it was apparent that the younger Bouygues had learned well from his father's example. He said, "It's much better to go into a new business with men who are extremely smart but don't know a damn thing about it. There are no prejudices that way. We start with a clean slate and build everything from the foundation. We're not pulling the deadweight of the past with us" (June 12, 2000).

In 1988 the Bouygues construction arm, by then one of the world's largest building and engineering companies, began building the Channel Tunnel between France and England, a project that lasted until 1994. In 1989 in failing health, Francis Bouygues, known as the "Emperor of Concrete," abdicated to Martin but remained on the board until his death in 1993. "Now the issue is," wrote a columnist for the *The Economist*, "whether the younger, and still unproven, Mr. Bouygues can hold together the empire built by his famously tough father" (September 9, 1989). The columnist went on to comment, however, that Bouygues already had built a competent team around him and that the company appeared to be bid-proof, the Bouygues family holding 17 percent of the stock and friendly institutions holding another 25–27 percent.

No one need have worried about the company's survival, and few could have predicted its exponential growth in the ensuing decades. From a builder of buildings, the University of Paris dropout became a builder of businesses, and he wasted no time. Only one month after succeeding his father in 1989 Martin Bouygues acquired a majority interest in the largest flour mill in France, Grands Moulins de Paris (sold in 1998). This deal took the company into three entirely new areas: flour milling, frozen foods, and property development. The following year Bouygues purchased the Swiss construction group Losinger.

In 1993 Bouygues made the leap into the telecommunications industry. Skeptics wondered what cement and telecommunications had to do with each other. However, Bouygues Telecom was awarded France's third mobile license in 1994. In 1996 Bouygues began mobile telephone operations and formed a partnership with Telecom Italia. Coverage throughout France was achieved in record-breaking time. The company had more than 1 million customers by 1998 and continued on to unrivaled success across Europe. In 2001 Bouygues caused a huge controversy throughout Europe when he refused to bid for a universal mobile telecommunications system (UMTS)—also known as third-generation (3G) wireless—license because of the exorbitant minimum price the French government had placed on the license. This lack of a bid meant Bouygues Telecom was the only mobile services provider in all Europe without a major investment in 3G technology. Regardless, Bouygues Telecom's revenues had by that time reached EUR 2.7 billion, operating profits were EUR 52 million, and the company had 6.1 million active customers.

Bouygues had other businesses to run, and 1996 was a busy year. Bouygues Offshore listed 40 percent of its shares on the Paris and New York stock exchanges; Bouygues Construction was created when Bouygues spun off the company's construction arm; and Bouygues oversaw a partnership that launched the digital Télévision par Satellite package at TF1, which by 2003, had 1.2 million subscribers and was Europe's most-watched general-interest channel. In 1999 Bouygues acquired the Norwegian engineering firm Kvaerner, and by 2003 the Bouygues construction arm had won huge and prestigious contracts around the globe. Contracts outside France contributed to more than half of the group's sales. The Bouygues Group by then employed 124,000 persons, sales were EUR 21.8 billion (EUR 6.1 billion outside France), and market capitalization was EUR 9 billion.

CARTELS AND CONTROVERSIES

In 1995, pursuant to France's 1993 anticorruption clampdown, French police raided the Bouygues Group headquarters and held Bouygues for investigation on huge frauds involving illegal deposits allegedly made to a Swiss bank account that investigators believed may have been used to fund the reelection campaign of the former mayor of Lyon, Michael Noir. In 1996 Bouygues, along with two other prominent French business executives, was again investigated on allegations that ranged from accounting fraud to bribery. A year later Bouygues, Le Lay, and Philippe Chalendon, the commercial director of an arm of Bouygues Offshore, were placed under investigation in a case of alleged false billing and misuse of corporate assets involving approximately 40 companies in and around Paris. David Owen of the *Financial Times* wrote, "Bouygues would last night make no comment . . . except to emphasise that the men would continue 'fully' to exercise their corporate functions" (February 28, 1997). Owen noted that Bouygues was among several companies fined the year before by the French competition council for "price-fixing and other anti-competitive behavior in public sectors. The council accused 36 French companies of creating cartels for contracts ranging from the TGV high-speed railway to the Normandy suspension bridge over the Seine. The company is appealing the decision."

In 1998 the Bouygues Group and two of France's other largest construction companies were subjected to a major investigation for an alleged agreed system for misappropriating public funds. An extensive article on the Public Services International Research Unit Web site read, "The companies participated in a corrupt cartel over building work for schools in the Ile-de-France region between 1989 and 1996. Contracts worth FF 28 billion (approximately $500 million) were shared out by the three groups, in meetings that took place in a hotel near the Champs-Elysees in Paris" (February 9, 1999).

Another major controversy erupted in 2000 when Bouygues refused to bid for a 3G technology license. The government was demanding a flat-rate fee of $4.5 billion. Bouygues balked, and Europe was stunned. "Martin Bouygues has taken a harsh line over recent months in denouncing the asking price for French UMTS licences," wrote a reporter for *Tech Europe* (February 2, 2001). Bouygues maintained that the exorbitant price demanded for the license, coupled with the expenses required to get up and running, would virtually bankrupt the entire European telecom industry, and he lodged a complaint with the European Commission. Although the company was under intense pressure, spending such a huge sum on unproven technology was, to Bouygues, sheer madness. On May 6, 2000, Bouygues wrote one of several highly critical letters warning the entire continent of the dangers of doing so. The letter appeared on the front page of *Le Monde.* In it Bouygues said that many telecom providers faced a no-win situation: Either they quit the business, as a result of not bidding for a license, or they buy the license and drown in a sea of debt. An article in *BusinessWeek* quoted from that letter: "What should I tell my employees? . . . That we have a choice between a sudden death and a slow one?" (June 3, 2002).

Bouygues's warnings went unheeded, but in 2002 his prediction came to fruition when 3G technology stumbled due to poor timing and a range of other issues. Investors became nervous, stocks plummeted, and financial losses hurt many of Europe's largest telecommunication companies. "Europe's phone giants—after spending half a trillion dollars on licenses, acquisitions, and networks—are treading madly to stay afloat in a sea of debt. . . . Deutsche Telekom is sitting on $60 billion in liabilities and casting about frantically for assets to sell," wrote the author of the *BusinessWeek* article (June 3, 2002). All Bouygues had to do was wait. "To entice him to even bid for a license, the French government had to slash the fees from $4.4 billion to $557 million," noted the *BusinessWeek* reporter. In 2002 Bouygues pocketed a cut-price license and announced his intention to launch I-mode with technology licensed from the experienced and successful Japanese NTT DoCoMo. Bouygues promised the company not to disclose the cost. "Bouygues now plans to roll out his new network—slowly," commented the *BusinessWeek* reporter. According to an article on the *ANANOVA* Web Site, when questioned about his lengthy stonewalling, Bouygues merely said, "I regret nothing." He commented that without his standoff, the government would not have cut prices. By May 2004 the I-mode service had become hugely successful, amassing more than 666,000 customers. "The company remains true to its philosophy of offering high-quality services that are easy to use, practical and affordable," Bouygues wrote in his corporate profile on the Bouygues Web site.

MANAGEMENT STYLE

Bouygues arrived at the company's gigantic and palatial headquarters outside Versailles by dawn each day. True to his philosophy of beginning a new company with "people who are extremely smart but don't know a damn thing about it," when Bouygues made the leap from construction into the unknown realm of the telecom industry in 1994, he wrote down the names of 30 Bouygues managers he thought would do the best job. All were appointed by that evening. "Bouygues approached the telecom services rollout like any other construction project," commented Christy in *Forbes,* "paying close attention to costs and deadlines" (June 12, 2000). Bouygues believed the construction business was an excellent foundation on which to build both managers and businesses. As did Bouygues himself (he and his brother never received one share from their father), almost all managers at the Bouygues company started as entry-level employees on construction sites. "Construction is an extremely difficult business," Bouygues told Christy. "Competition is fierce, and margins are thin. It's a wonderful management training school. It breeds managers that love challenges and are very quick on their feet."

Bouygues kept his employees quick on their feet by continually rotating them through the company. "I judge my top managers on their ability to turn over their best people to other parts of the company. If you do that, you'll be seen as someone who helps people advance, and people will want to work for you" (June 12, 2000). Bouygues rewarded his employees well, however, awarding them stock options and including them in profit sharing—a rare form of compensation in France.

See also entry on Bouygues S.A. in *International Directory of Company Histories.*

SOURCES FOR FURTHER INFORMATION

"Bouygues Chairman Says Worst Still to Come for Overpaying UMTS Entrants." *ANANOVA,* http://www.ananova.com/business/story/sm_569062.html?menu=.

Christy, John H., "Clean Slate," *Forbes,* June 12, 2000, p. 184.

Owen, David, "News, Europe: French Businessmen in Probe—Chairman of Bouygues and TF1 Chief Alleged to Have Misused Corporate Assets," *Financial Times*, February 28, 1997.

"Royal Retirement," *Economist*, September 9, 1989, p. 78.

"SAUR and Bouygues," Public Services International Research Unit, February 9, 1999, http://www.labournet.org/1999/Feb/saur.html#_Toc443286717.

"Tale of a Bubble: How the 3G Fiasco Came Close to Wrecking Europe," *BusinessWeek*, June 3, 2002, p. 46.

"UMTS/France: Only Two Candidates for Four Licences, (Government Activity)," *Tech Europe*, February 2, 2001, p. 208.

—Marie L. Thompson

■ ■ ■

Jack O. Bovender Jr.

1945–

Chief executive officer and chairman, Hospital Corporation of America

Nationality: American.

Born: August 16, 1945.

Education: Duke University, BA, 1967; MHA, 1969.

Family: Married Barbara (maiden name unknown), 1966; children: one.

Career: U.S. Navy, Naval Regional Medical Center, Portsmouth, Virginia, 1969–1975, lieutenant; Medical Center Hospital, Largo, Florida, chief executive officer; West Florida Regional Medical Center, chief executive officer; Health Corporation of America, 1975–1985, associate hospital administrator; 1985–1992, senior level positions; 1992–1994, executive vice president and chief operating officer; retired, 1994–1997; Health Corporation of America, 1997–2001, president and chief operating officer; 2001–, chief executive officer; 2002–, chairman.

Awards: Order of Achievement, 2001.

Address: Hospital Corporation of America, One Park Plaza, Nashville, Tennessee 37203; http://www.hcahealthcare.com.

Jack O. Bovender Jr. *AP/Wide World Photos.*

■ Jack O. Bovender Jr. joined the Hospital Corporation of America (HCA) in 1975 as an associate hospital administrator in Pensacola, Florida. Starting in 1985 Bovender held senior management positions in HCA, and in 1992 he was appointed HCA's executive vice president and chief operating officer. He retired in 1994, when HCA and Columbia merged to form Columbia-HCA. In 1997 Bovender was lured out of retirement to be HCA's president and COO. He had been in health care administration for 31 years when he was named CEO of HCA in 2001. At that time he had over 20 years' experience with HCA.

BAD TIMES AND GOOD TIMES

Thomas Frist, MD, one of HCA's three founders, was Bovender's mentor for many years. Frist took over as CEO after Richard Scott was forced out of HCA because of a federal investigation of billing fraud practices. Frist, the company's key strategist and Bovender's friend, convinced Bovender to come out of retirement to accept the positions of president and COO in August 1997. There were major legal and operational issues to address—the Columbia-HCA hospital conglomerate had been charged by the government with systematic billing abuses or fraud and was signing below-cost contracts with managed care companies in exchange for building market share.

A settlement with the government was negotiated for the fraud charges. By 1999, in a move to unload the less profitable hospitals, about one-third of HCA's approximately 350 hospitals had been sold to LifePoint Hospitals and Triad Hospitals. In 2002 HCA purchased the nonprofit, 13-hospital Health Midwest system of Kansas City, Missouri, for $1.125 billion.

HCA also invested $450 million into capital improvements for the Kansas City system. The strategy was to move away from a national, only-market-share-matters mentality to focus on larger, high-growth markets. The second major change was to drop managed care contracts if reimbursement was unfair. In late 1988 the renegotiation of contracts between HCA's 56 Florida hospitals and Humana was a significant turning point in managed care contracts.

In 2001 Bovender was named CEO of HCA and in 2002 was appointed chairman. In 2001 Bovender received $1 million as salary and $1.2 million in restricted stock; 400,000 stock options; and $203,000 in other compensation. In 2002 he received a salary raise to $1.1 million and over $2 million in restricted stock; 225,000 stock options; and $291,000 in other compensation as the U.S. Department of Justice concluded its investigation of HCA, which was accused of health-care fraud. While admitting no wrongdoing, HCA paid $1.7 billion to settle the Medicare fraud charges.

During the peak of the government investigation, HCA stock fell to below $18 per share. From 2000 through 2003 HCA has posted quarterly profits. An icon of investment, Warren Buffett bought 10 million shares of HCA in 2003. By late 2003 the stock was selling at $35 to $40 per share.

COMMUNITY AND FAMILY LIFE

Bovender served on several private and public boards and was active in the community. He served on the boards of Quorum Health Group, American Retirement Corporation, and the Nashville Electric Service during his brief retirement from 1994 to 1997. He also served on the Nashville Community Foundation, the Nashville Healthcare Council, and St. Luke's Community House. In addition, he served in several capacities at Duke University, including positions at the Fuqua School of Business, on the Divinity School Board of Visitors, and on the Divinity School Capital Campaign Committee.

Flying airplanes was Bovender's hobby, an interest often shared with his son. He reported that flying is more pragmatic than playing golf. However, it is a little riskier, unless one has a habit of routinely playing golf during thunderstorms.

MANAGEMENT STYLE

Bovender's expertise was in operations management. He had a hands-off approach to management. One of Bovender's colleagues, Chip Caldwell, stated, "He's clear at setting expectations and then leaving those who report to him with the task of execution" (*HealthLeaders Magazine*, February 1, 2002). Bovender was a devout Episcopalian, and this background was reflected in his values-based management style. He had an ability to impose strict demands on those who reported directly to him, and he got results. Caldwell noted that Bovender set aggressive goals and insisted on individual accountability. "He also set up a positive, powerful learning environment and strongly encouraged us to replicate best practices," according to Caldwell. "There was a friendly competition to be recognized as someone who could present something innovative" (*HealthLeaders Magazine*, February 1, 2002). Bovender stressed a team-oriented style and remarked, "When I read about basketball, it's not just looking at the guy who scored the most points, I always go and want to see who got the most assists." He valued experience. Bovender stated, "There's no substitute if you're the CEO of a company with 190 or so hospitals to have run a hospital or two, to know what the pressures are. I know what it's like to have two or three patients in an intensive-care unit 'go bad' at the same time. There's no substitute for having been there" (*HealthLeaders*, February 1, 2002).

See also entry on Hospital Corporation of America in *International Directory of Company Histories.*

SOURCES FOR FURTHER INFORMATION

"Bovender and Templeton Receive Order of Achievement," *Lambda Chi Alpha*, http://www.lambdachi.net/foundation/happenings.asp.

Cashill, Jack, "HCA's Investment to Energize KC Healthcare," http://www.ingramsonline.com/november_2002/hca.html.

"Columbia May Sell 108 Hospitals," *News Herald* (Panama City, Florida), November 18, 1997, http://www.newsherald.com/local/col1118.htm.

"Cover Story: The Sequel," *HealthLeaders*, February 1, 2002, http://www.healthleaders.com/magazine/print.php?contentid=31879.

Russell, Keith, "COO Steps Up to Lead HCA," *Tennessean Business*, January 9, 2001, http://www.tennessean.com/business/archives/01/01/01739924.shtml?Element_ID=1739924.

Vogt, Katherine, "HCA Revival: Hospital Company Makes a Profitable Turnaround, *AMNews*, October 20, 2003, http://www.ama-assn.org/amednews/2003/10/20/bisa1020.htm.

—Mark A. Best

■ ■ ■

Peter Brabeck-Letmathe

1944–

Chief executive officer and vice chairman of the board, Nestlé

Nationality: Austrian.

Born: November 13, 1944, in Villach, Austria.

Education: University of World Trade, degree in economics.

Family: Married; children: three.

Career: Findus, 1968–1970, ice-cream sales and delivery; Nestlé Chile, 1970–1980, sales manager and director of marketing; Nestlé Ecuador, 1981–1983, managing director; Nestlé Venezuela, 1983–1987, president and managing director; Nestlé S.A., 1987–1992, senior vice president of Culinary Products Division; 1992–1997, executive vice president of strategic business groups; 1997–, chief executive officer; 2001–, chief executive officer and vice chairman of the board of directors.

Address: Nestlé, 55 Avenue Nestlé, 1800 Vevey, Switzerland; http://www.nestle.com.

Peter Brabeck-Letmathe. *AP/Wide World Photos.*

■ Peter Brabeck-Letmathe spent his entire career working for Nestlé, rising to the position of chief executive officer (CEO) in 1997 and also assuming duties as vice chairman of the board in 2001. During his tenure as CEO of the Switzerland-based company, he turned Nestlé into the fastest-growing food-company giant in an otherwise slow-growth sector. He achieved this primarily by focusing on buying up leading food brands, getting rid of under-performing brands, and slashing costs wherever possible. According to industry analysts and co-workers, Brabeck-Letmathe, who spoke five languages, was an articulate leader whose focus on substance over style included a strong dedication to discipline and a long-term approach to growing a business.

LEARNS EARLY LESSONS

Born in Austria six months before the end of World War II, Brabeck-Letmathe and his family faced hard economic trials after the war. The surrounding Swiss Alps were his playground, and he began climbing with ropes by age 10. As a teenager his penchant for adventure grew as he took long overnight hikes in the Alps with his friend Hans Thomassen. After graduating from high school, Brabeck-Letmathe enrolled at the University of World Trade in Vienna, where he studied economics. During his summer vacation in 1967, he went on a climbing expedition to Tirich Mir, the highest peak in the Hindu Kush of Pakistan. Unfortunately, the trip ended in disaster when Thomassen and another friend were killed after falling off an ice wall during the climb. Brabeck-Letmathe was not there; he had lost a poker game to decide who would turn back, since there was only enough food for two. The event changed his life. He told Peter Gumbel for an article in *Time*, "When you lose your best friends in such an expedition it makes you more aware of the relativity of the risks but also of the relativity of the individual."

After graduating from college, Brabeck-Letmathe took a job in 1968 with a company named Findus. He sold and delivered ice cream in a freezer truck that he drove around the Swiss Alps to cafes and supermarkets. Initially, Brabeck-Letmathe did not know that the company was a Nestlé subsidiary. When he discovered who the parent company was, he realized he had an opportunity to broaden his career horizons beyond his native Austria. In an article in *BusinessWeek* he explained, "When I was growing up, career opportunities depended on your status in a political party, because 75 percent of the Austrian gross domestic product was state-owned."

In 1970 Brabeck-Letmathe was assigned to a post in Chile, where he became a sales manager and eventually director of marketing. He admitted that his initial joy at getting the assignment had more to do with the opportunity to explore some of Chile's wide-open spaces and mountains than with business. When Brabeck-Letmathe arrived in Chile he discovered that Nestlé's business concerns were facing a Socialist government under the presidency of Salvador Allende, who was threatening to nationalize the company. Nestlé Chile decided not to pull out in the face of crisis. Brabeck-Letmathe is credited with spending a good deal of his time dissuading government officials from nationalizing the production of milk. He also worked with militant labor officials to keep them from ordering workers to strike and bringing Nestlé's operations to a standstill. The Allende government was overthrown in a bloody coup in 1973.

Although he was posted back in Switzerland for a short while in 1975, Brabeck-Letmathe jumped at the chance to return to Chile within three months to take over as the marketing director, a post three other Nestlé executives had turned down because of the country's ongoing political instability. Brabeck-Letmathe continued to work in Latin America for Nestlé and was assigned to Nestlé Ecuador as managing director in 1981. He quickly turned around the ailing subsidiary by focusing on factory closures and laying off more than half of Nestlé's workers. In 1983 he became president and managing director of Nestlé Venezuela. Overall, the Latin American experience provided Brabeck-Letmathe with some solid training; he told *Business Week*, "I learned to manage through turmoil."

BECOMES VALUED EXECUTIVE AT HEAD OFFICE

By 1987 Brabeck-Letmathe was back in Switzerland, serving as senior vice president in charge of the Culinary Products Division. At about the same time, the company's CEO, Helmut Maucher, set out to redefine Nestlé's product and branding strategy, and he turned to Brabeck-Letmathe to lead the way. In 1992 Brabeck-Letmathe was appointed executive vice president of the company, with worldwide responsibility for marketing, communications, and public affairs for the strategic business groups Food, Buitoni, Chocolate and Confectionery, Ice Cream, Petcare, and Industrial Products.

Over the next few years Brabeck-Letmathe put into place Nestlé's unique branding policy, characterized by a strict hierarchy of strategic brands on the global, regional, and local levels. The six global strategic brands included Nescafe, Nestea, and Nestlé itself. For brands that did not carry the name of Nestlé, Brabeck-Letmathe oversaw the creation of a "Nestlé Seal of Guarantee" that was put on the back of products to ensure consumers of the product's quality and relationship with Nestlé. In an interview with Andrew J. Parsons for *McKinsey Quarterly*, Brabeck-Letmathe noted, "For consumers, relevance of Nestlé as a company comes first of all through contact with products that are branded Nestlé. If we want to be perceived as the world's leading food company, we have to offer consumers an increasing amount of products that they can identify as Nestlé's."

BECOMES CEO

After helping to launch the product and branding strategy, Brabeck-Letmathe decided he was ready for another adventure and asked to be reassigned away from the home office in Vevey, Switzerland. Maucher, who was nearing retirement, valued Brabeck-Letmathe and wanted to keep him in Switzerland. Reportedly, Maucher asked Brabeck-Letmathe what he needed to do to keep him at the head office in Vevey, and Brabeck-Letmathe replied that he wanted to be Maucher's successor. Several months later it was announced that Brabeck-Letmathe would become Nestlé's next CEO.

After becoming CEO in 1997, Brabeck-Letmathe began stressing internal growth. He took a more conservative approach than his predecessor to improving business. Over the next couple of years he slashed costs by increasing the efficiency of manufacturing operations, got rid of mature businesses with little potential for profit growth, and focused investment on fast-growing fields. Brabeck-Letmathe ensured higher efficiency in all of the company's manufacturing facilities worldwide. By the end of 2000 Nestlé accrued $3.2 billion in net profits and also had cash reserves of $3.8 billion. In addition, the company's market capitalization tripled by 2001 to close to $100 billion. Market analysts recognized this growth as a significant achievement because food prices had been flat or falling worldwide, causing major brands such as Coca-Cola and Kellogg to struggle.

With a significant increase in market capitalization providing a financial safety cushion, Brabeck-Letmathe purchased the Ralston Purina pet-food company in January 2001 for $10.3 billion. Six months later he guided the company into purchasing Chef America for $2.6 billion. Chef America was the leading maker of frozen snacks in the United States, and Brabeck-Letmathe saw the purchase as a way to further enhance Nestlé's sales and earnings growth. Nestlé also purchased Dreyer's Grand Ice Cream in a complex deal for approximately $2.6 billion in stock. At the same time, he continued to streamline the company by selling or spinning off less-profitable commodity businesses, such as Nestlé's European frozen-food, tomato-processing, and Italian-meats businesses. Brabeck-Letmathe managed to consistently meet Nestlé's publicly stated internal growth target of 4 percent a year.

PICTURE NOT ENTIRELY ROSY

Despite establishing Nestlé as the world leader in the food and beverage industry, some industry analysts expressed concerns over Brabeck-Letmathe's leadership and the future of the company. The overall $15.5 billion purchases of Ralston Purina, Chef America, and Dreyer's, for example, were criticized by some as an unwelcome shift in strategy on Brabeck-Letmathe's part. Some analysts saw the acquisitions as forsaking the successful focus on sales and earnings of the existing company products and as a potentially disastrous grab for higher market share. The Dreyer's deal in particular came under criticism because even though Nestlé became the leader in premium ice-cream sales in the United States, the demand for ice cream in this market had been increasing only 2 percent a year since 1966. Many market analysts saw the purchase as primarily benefiting the minority shareholders of Dreyer's while offering little benefit for Nestlé. In a 2002 article in *Institutional Investor*, a London-based analyst noted, "Before Brabeck-Letmathe came in, this was a company that had a habit of paying [too much] for acquisitions, and people are clearly worried that could happen again."

Further troubling analysts was the fact that, under Brabeck-Letmathe's leadership, Nestlé's debt had quadrupled to $13.8 billion in 2001, and the company's stock was typically trading at a discount compared with other companies in the food sector. Many believed that this lower value was due in part to the fact that the company reported profits only twice a year as opposed to four times a year like most other companies. In addition, Nestlé had a lower operating margin than many other European food companies. For example, even though the company's shares rose 77 1/2 percent under Brabeck-Letmathe by the end of 2002, a contributor to *Institutional Investor* noted that "the company's enterprise value as a multiple of earnings before interest, taxation, depreciation and amortization" was only 8.4, which lagged behind competitors such as Unilever at 9.1 and Kraft Foods at 10.9. As a result, the company's stocks traded at about 15 times estimated 2002 earnings, less than many of its major rivals, including Kraft, Kellogg, and Hershey Foods, all of which traded at price-earnings multiples of about 20.

Brabeck-Letmathe remained unfazed by the naysayers. He maintained that the company's first priority was to achieve real internal growth and that acquisitions were only an additional tool to accelerate this growth while maintaining a long-term outlook. A *Nation's Restaurant News* contributor quoted Brabeck-Letmathe as saying, "Our long-term investment in Dreyer's speaks to the tremendous upside we see in the ice-cream business in North America and our confidence that Dreyer's has the right team in place to lead the industry."

Brabeck-Letmathe also pointed out that the acquisition of Ralston Purina put Nestlé on par with the global leader in pet food (Mars). He added that future acquisitions would be small. As for the company being undervalued, Brabeck-Letmathe stressed that this was not because of Nestlé's margins but because it is a complex company with a wide range of activities and business efforts. He noted that potentially the best growth markets for the company, including China and Russia, required a decade of investment before they were significantly profitable. He told *Time* magazine, "If I had run the company based on the opinion of financial analysts, it would already have been bankrupt."

INSTITUTING GLOBE

Part of Brabeck-Letmathe's plan to streamline Nestlé and make the company more efficient was to invest in new technology. The company's most important technology project was a complex and costly data project called GLOBE (for "global business excellence"). Brabeck-Letmathe directed the company to spend over $1 billion to automate and integrate all of its operations, from procurement through production to distribution. The revamping also included Nestlé's research and development unit to facilitate better coordination among the group's different businesses.

As a part of this strategy, Brabeck-Letmathe had the company buy and install $200 million worth of software from SAP to centralize Nestlé's sourcing of supplies. The software linked the company's five major e-mail systems, which enabled it to keep a tighter rein on raw material purchases around the world. Brabeck-Letmathe felt that the centralized control created by GLOBE would allow him to unify the company's wide-ranging negotiations and contracts with suppliers and, as a result, better centralize production. The effort led Brabeck-Letmathe to close 38 factories and cut $1.6 billion in costs while improving the company's ability to obtain volume discounts.

The GLOBE project involved up to two thousand people worldwide in defining and standardizing every aspect of the company onto a common information-technology platform. The result was that the company was able to eliminate mass duplications and redundancies in its systems, such as eliminating thousands of customers listed in several databases along with vendors who were no longer in business. Brabeck-Letmathe put a strong emphasis on GLOBE, making it the foundation for his promise to cut an additional $4 billion in costs.

MANAGEMENT STYLE

Nestlé's success under Brabeck-Letmathe stemmed largely from his unique ability to guide a global company while emphasizing that there was no such thing as a global consumer in the food and beverage industry. For example, while he streamlined the company and instituted more centralized control of raw materials, he continued to emphasize the regional aspects of Nestlé's market. In an interview with Tom Mudd for *Industry Week*, he noted, "This is fundamental to our thinking. . . . That means that our products, our brands, and our communications will always stay local in order to stay relevant to the local consumer."

Brabeck-Letmathe recognized the importance of short-term performance, but stressed that it must be balanced against the long-term development of the company. He pointed to the company's experience in Chile as an example. Instead of quitting because of a change in the political situation that could potentially be harmful in the short term, the company stayed and its Chile operations eventually prospered. Brabeck-Letmathe told the *McKinsey Quarterly*, "When you are forever looking out for your short-term interests, you are not a reliable partner."

Brabeck-Letmathe stressed communication as an integral part of his leadership style. He traveled constantly, meeting with an estimated two to three thousand Nestlé employees every year. He was especially interested in young managers and made an effort to get to know them and their families. This interest was driven in part by his plan to get managers throughout the world to buy into his idea that fundamental changes in the company were necessary. He set up a working group of national managers to help figure out how to make proposed changes work. He told *Time* that this approach stemmed from his mountain-climbing experience: "You learn very early on that you're better off working in a team."

Industry analysts and coworkers noted that although Brabeck-Letmathe had an adventurous spirit, when it came to business he was circumspect. Vreni Spoerry, a Nestlé director for more than a decade, told *Time*, "He's good at anticipating what might happen and seeing where the risks lurk." Perhaps Brabeck-Letmathe summed up his management style best when he told a *BusinessWeek* correspondent, "My job is to take an athlete who can run the 100 meters in 10 seconds and improve it to 9.8 seconds."

MOVING FORWARD

Brabeck-Letmathe sought to have Nestlé's management structure pay less attention to national boundaries in its operations. For example, he centralized management of the company's water business as a global operation based in Paris. He pursued a joint venture with L'Oreal to develop nutritional supplements that enhance beauty. He remained committed to Nestlé's individual national organizations manufacturing much of what they sell locally. In addition to his duties at Nestlé, Brabeck-Letmathe served as president of the Swiss component of Nestlé's beverage, chocolate, dairy, and other food-manufacturing businesses. He served as vice chairman of the boards of directors of Credit Suisse Group, Credit Suisse, and Credit Suisse First Boston, he was a member of the boards of directors of L'Oreal and Roche Holding, and he was a member of the International Association for the Promotion and Protection of Private Foreign Investments, the European Round Table of Industrialists, and the Council of the Prince of Wales Business Leaders Forum.

See also entry on Nestlé S.A. in *International Directory of Company Histories.*

SOURCES FOR FURTHER INFORMATION

Gumbel, Peter, "Nestlé's Quick," *Time*, January 27, 2003.

Mudd, Tom, "Nestlé Plays to Global Audience," *Industry Week*, August 13, 2001.

"Nestlé S.A. Buys Large Stake of Ice-Cream Maker Dreyer's," *Nation's Restaurant News*, July 1, 2002.

Parsons, Andrew J., "Nestlé: The Visions of Local Managers," *McKinsey Quarterly* 5, no. 2 (spring 1996), p. 5.

"Peter Brabeck-Letmathe," *BusinessWeek*, June 11, 2001

"Peter Brabeck-Letmathe of Nestlé," *Institutional Investor* 20, no. 2 (November 2002), p. 20.

—David Petechuk

■■■

Richard Branson

1950–

Executive, Virgin

Nationality: British.

Born: July 18, 1950, in Shamley Green, Surrey, England.

Education: Attended Stowe School, 1964–1967.

Family: Son of Edward (barrister) and Eva Huntley-Flindt (dancer and flight attendant) Branson; married Kristen Tomassi, 1972 (divorced 1979); married Joan Templeman, 1989; children: two.

Career: *Student*, 1966–1970, editor; Virgin, 1970–, executive.

Awards: Knighthood, Queen Elizabeth II, 2000.

Publications: *Losing My Virginity* 1998.

Address: 120 Campden Hill Road, London, United Kingdom, W8 7AR; http://www.virgin.com.

Richard Branson. *AP/Wide World Photos.*

■ Richard Branson founded Virgin, a loosely knit family of more than two hundred companies, as a mail-order record business in 1970. As CEO or majority shareholder, he developed successful ventures in music, air travel, financial services, retail marketing, telecommunications, and other fields. Branson's idiosyncratic approach to business and his risk-taking personal life made him a British folk hero as well as one of his nation's wealthiest men. Under Branson's supervision the Virgin group fostered creativity among its employees and allowed the Virgin brand to evolve and diversify with the marketplace.

TEENAGE ENTREPENEUR

Branson overcame dyslexia as a child and began to show his entrepreneurial talents early. Born into a middle-class English family, he displayed both a natural intelligence and a competitive spirit on the playing field. His first business ventures included growing Christmas trees and breeding birds. As he reported in his autobiography, "Losing My Virginity," chafing under authority Branson left boarding school at age 16. At the time his headmaster reportedly told him, "Branson, I predict that you will either go to prison or become a millionaire."

In 1966 Branson launched *Student*, a youth-oriented magazine. As the editor Branson interviewed John Lennon, Mick Jagger, Vanessa Redgrave, and other celebrities. He also started the Student Advisory Center, a nonprofit referral service for troubled youth. In 1970 local authorities charged the center with obscenity for using the words "venereal disease" in its promotional material. Branson was successful in getting the charges dropped, setting a precedent for his future battles with authority.

After selling *Student* to a larger company in 1970, Branson started a mail-order record company, Virgin Mail. The following year he opened a retail store, which by 1972 had become a chain of 14 shops around the United Kingdom. Charged with evading purchase taxes on import record sales, Branson escaped prosecution by paying an out-of-court settlement. Saddled with $90,000 in fines and debts, a sobered Branson expanded his chain of stores and purchased a small castle in Wales, turning it into a recording studio. His next project was to launch a record company of his own. With his cousin Simon Draper as the creative director and Nik Powell as the business manager, Branson inaugurated Virgin Records in 1973. Among the label's first releases was Mike Oldfield's album *Tubular Bells*, which topped the U.S. charts in 1974 and sold more than 13 million copies. Virgin had suddenly become one of the most successful independent record companies in the United Kingdom. Despite his image as a "hippie capitalist" dabbling in business, Branson proved an astute negotiator from the start, signing his artists to long contracts, acquiring worldwide rights to recordings, and owning copyrights for as long as possible.

RISKY VENTURES AND DARING EXPLOITS

After its impressive start Virgin Records entered a stagnant period in the mid-1970s. Branson failed to sign such established acts as the Rolling Stones and had to rely on Oldfield's sales to keep the label profitable. Matters did not begin to improve until Virgin signed the Sex Pistols in 1977. Undaunted by the punk band's controversial image Branson sold 100,000 copies of the single "God Save the Queen" in one week. Virgin did not pull out of the doldrums until it released Culture Club's debut album in 1982. The phenomenal popularity of the lead singer Boy George helped the band to sell 1.4 million albums in the United Kingdom the following year. Hit albums and singles from Phil Collins and the Human League also did well for Virgin. The label quadrupled its size in four years. Branson used his earnings to launch a Virgin American record label and to invest in new ventures, including Virgin Vision (a film and video distribution company), Virgin Games (a computer games publisher), Virgin Rags (a clothing line), Vanson Property (a property development company), and several London-area nightclubs.

In February 1984 Branson was approached by the American attorney Randolph Fields with an offer to invest in a new transatlantic airline. Despite the objections of his business partners, Branson was immediately intrigued by the possibility. Rather than adopt Fields's initial idea of an all-business-class airline, Branson envisioned a low-cost carrier that would compete with People Express. The decision to pursue the project caused ill feelings with Draper and other Virgin staff members and met with disfavor with Branson's bankers. It was something of a personal triumph for Branson when, on June 22, 1984, Virgin-Atlantic Airways embarked on its maiden flight between London's Gatwick Airport and Newark, New Jersey. From a single leased aircraft Virgin-Atlantic slowly grew during the 1980s, adding routes to Los Angeles and Tokyo while seeking access to London's Heathrow Airport. Branson emphasized his company's commitment to service by talking with customers during flights. He was even known to dress as a flight attendant and serve refreshments.

To help promote the airline Branson began to raise his media profile by performing promotional stunts and feats of daring. In 1985 he was rescued off the coast of Ireland when his powerboat *Virgin Atlantic Challenger* crashed during an attempt to break the transatlantic speed record. A year later Branson succeeded in breaking the record with *Virgin Atlantic Challenger II.* In 1987 Branson set out with the aeronaut Per Lindstrand on a transatlantic hot-air balloon trip, crashing into the Irish Sea after making it across the ocean. The pair completed the first successful transpacific hot-air balloon ride in 1991, although they ended the trip stranded on a frozen Canadian lake before being rescued. Such death-defying adventures won Virgin invaluable publicity and emphasized Branson's image as a fearless risk taker.

Not all of Branson's corporate moves turned out as he had hoped. In 1985 Branson took Virgin public, attracting 100,000 applications for shares. While he gained greater financial stability, Branson disliked the restraints of working with a board of directors. "Previously, I had always felt confident about any decision we made, but now that Virgin was a publicly quoted company, I began to lose faith in myself," he recalled. "I felt uneasy about making the rapid decisions I had always made and wondered whether every decision should be formally ratified and minuted at a board meeting." Branson fought with the board over paying out large dividends rather than reinvesting profits in new projects, as Virgin had previously done. The October 1987 stock market crash helped to convince Branson to buy back his company. He announced Virgin's management buyout in July 1988 and began to seek investors, including the British retailer W. H. Smith and the Japanese media company Fujisankei, for joint ventures. These relationships were especially important in establishing a chain of Virgin Megastores, which were devoted to music as well as other Virgin consumer items, across Europe, North America, and Japan. Also in 1988 Branson launched Virgin Hotels and a new music division, Virgin Classics.

UNIQUE CORPORATE STRUCTURE AND FREEWHEELING STYLE

By the late 1980s Virgin's unorthodox corporate structure was well established. Behind the Virgin logo was a constantly multiplying array of wholly owned subsidiaries and outside partnerships, Branson always maintaining a controlling interest. Each business remained independent though linked to others with similar concerns. "Outside accountants would immediately look at our 200 buildings, 200 switchboards, and all that comes with them and say, 'You're bleeding money'," Branson told Betsy Morris in an interview for *Fortune.* "But I say, 'Look at what you get!' People who have worked for small companies and then big companies will tell you that it's not as much fun. In a small company, you can create a different kind of energy. People feel cared for."

Branson oversaw his operations from his residences in London's Holland Park and on Necker Island in the Caribbean. In most cases he supervised each business's startup phase, delegated management, and stepped back in only as a troubleshooter. An exception was Virgin's airline and travel businesses, of which Branson remained CEO. Branson kept informal lines of communication open even as his roster of companies kept growing. "We don't have formal meetings," he told David Sheff of *Forbes.* "People who leave companies with formal structures don't leave because of salaries. If they come up with a good idea, they're told to wait until the next meeting. . . . With Virgin, we make decisions on the phone. If you've got a good idea and I like it, you can get on with it." Branson prided himself on treating his employees well. During one difficult financial period he was able to persuade some staff members to take sabbaticals to avoid layoffs. He was known for recognizing talent at any level within the Virgin ranks. In 1996, for instance, he promoted a Virgin-Atlantic flight attendant to run Virgin Bride, the largest bridal shop in Europe. Branson became known for dropping in on employees and writing down their comments about Virgin's problems in a small notebook he kept with him at all times. The notebook remained with Branson even as others adopted laptop computers and personal digital assistants—Branson never embraced computer technology.

Lacking conventional business school training, or even a high school diploma, Branson continued to make huge financial decisions according to his own whimsical methods. "In the same way that I tend to make up my mind about people within thirty seconds of meeting them, I also make up my mind about a business proposal within thirty seconds and whether it excites me," he wrote in *Losing My Virginity.* "I rely far more on gut instinct than researching huge amounts of statistics." This approach was criticized by members of his own staff, according to Des Dearlove's book *Business the Richard Branson Way.* Some employees referred to Branson's method of trusting his own instincts without conducting further market research as "VSO," or "Virgin's system of one."

Perhaps Branson's most radical achievement was to make his own freewheeling, antiestablishment personality synonymous with the Virgin brand. Whatever caught his eye, whether it was a punk band, an airline, or a line of cosmetics, Branson marketed with style and playfulness. The challenge of entering a new field became part of the game and only added to the Virgin mystique. Assessing Branson's goals and methods for *Forbes,* Betsy Morris wrote, "Branson likes being a disruptor—taking on industries that charge too much (music) or hold consumers hostage (cellular) or treat them badly and bore them to tears (airlines). His goal was never to be the most profitable." Branson said much the same thing in *Losing My Virginity,* noting, "First and foremost, any business proposal I like must sound fun. If market is served by only two giant corporations, it appears to me that there's room for some healthy competition. . . . I love giving big companies a run for their money—especially if they're offering expensive, poor-quality products."

VINDICATION AND EXPANSION IN THE 1990S

Virgin-Atlantic became Branson's chief personal focus during the 1990s. In July 1991 he reached his key goal of expanding service to London's Heathrow Airport. This achievement was a signal victory in Branson's bitter struggle with British Airways, which had sought to block Virgin-Atlantic's growth through political influence and underhanded tactics. Among the latter was the establishment of an espionage unit to spy on Branson and harass Virgin customers in person and by telephone. Lord King, the British Airways chairman, spread rumors that his competitor was about to go bankrupt. Virgin's chronic cash flow problems lent credence to these stories. In 1992 Branson made the painful decision to sell Virgin Music Group to Thorn-EMI for approximately $1 billion to keep Virgin-Atlantic aloft. The sale brought Branson immense personal wealth and enabled him to upgrade his airline with such luxuries as seat-back video screens, full-sized sleeper seats, in-flight massages and manicures, and free ground transportation by limousine. Virgin-Atlantic's problems with lenders and overdrafts continued, however, as did the ongoing battle with British Airways. The British press wondered whether Branson had finally taken on a battle he could not win. An editorial in the London, England, *Sunday Telegraph* wondered whether Branson was "too old to rock 'n' roll, too young to fly" (March 15, 1992). Branson fought back, casting himself as an upstart David against a greedy Goliath. He continued to accuse British Airways of unethical tactics, prompting Lord King to question Branson's truthfulness publicly. Branson sued British Airways for libel in December 1992, and British Airways offered the highest uncontested libel payment (£610,000) in British history. Branson shared the settlement with the Virgin-Atlantic staff. The court victory marked a turning point for the airline. By the end of the 1990s it had become the third-largest European carrier and the most profitable company in the Virgin group.

Branson emerged from his fight with British Airways an immensely popular figure. A May 1993 survey conducted by TSB ranked Branson the number one role model for Britain's young people. In the mid-1990s Branson branched out with joint ventures as diverse as financial services (Virgin Direct), Internet services (Virgin Net), spirits (Virgin Vodka), and soft drinks (Virgin Cola). Some companies fared better than others. Virgin Trains, Branson's British express rail franchise, gained a reputation for poor service. An attempt with the television personality David Frost to take over the independent U.K. television network ITV was halted by the British government. Despite stumbles Branson's empire kept growing, partnering with Malaysia Airlines to expand Virgin-Atlantic into

Southeast Asia and Australia and entering into an agreement with the copy shop giant Kinko's to open locations in Britain and France. Branson remained a presence in the pop music world, creating a new music label, V2 Records while remaining nonexecutive president of the EMI-owned Virgin Music Group. In November 1997 Virgin Music Group oversaw the production of the commemorative album *Diana, Princess of Wales Tribute*, which raised more than $100 million for charity.

By 1998 Branson's golden touch showed signs of fading. Except for Virgin-Atlantic most of the Virgin corporate family was floundering. Virgin Vodka was withdrawn, and Virgin Cola struggled to find a market. Publicly traded companies such as the Brussels-based airline Virgin Express and the U.K. clothing retailer Victory Corporation did poorly on the stock market. Critics wondered whether the middle-aged Branson could continue to play the role of the brash outsider to a younger generation of consumers. Branson responded by cutting his losses with some companies and launching new ones. In 1999 Virgin Cinemas sold its U.K. theaters to a French company for £215 million. Also in 1999 Branson sold 49 percent interest in Virgin-Atlantic to Singapore Airlines for $960 million, reportedly to help finance weaker Virgin companies. He also hired a new strategy chief, Gordon McCallum, to bring greater discipline and focus to marketing the Virgin brand overall.

Branson took a financial beating, according to some estimates having lost more than half of his personal fortune by 2001. (His net worth was estimated by his financial advisers to be $2.6 billion in 2003.) Branson continued, however, to dream up new ventures, including a chain of U.K. health and fitness clubs (Virgin Active) and an online music service (Virgin Digital). One project, Virginstudent.com, was a youth-oriented Web site that recalled Branson's *Student* days. In interviews Branson dismissed talk that the Virgin brand had become overextended. "That's been said for about 30 years," he told Gyles Bandreth of the *Sunday Telegraph*. "I'm not somebody who believes in money sitting on deposit in bank accounts. When I make money I reinvest it straight away in new ventures. We're Britain's largest group of private companies. Last year we turned over about £3 billion. In three years time I expect that to be £6 billion" (February 25, 2001).

During the period of retrenchment Branson remained a high-profile spokesman for the Virgin group. His stature as one of the world's most famous and influential businessmen appeared to survive his setbacks. Branson became Sir Richard when he was knighted by Queen Elizabeth II in 2000. He continued to champion causes such as his ultimately unsuccessful campaign in 2003 to save the Concorde aircraft. In March 2004 Branson signed a contract with Fox Television to star in his own reality series involving several aspiring billionaires sharing adventures with him around the world. Well into his third decade as an entrepreneur Branson continued to blur the line between business and pleasure, money making and gamesmanship. "He's not driven like other people. He's driven to do stuff," the Virgin executive Tom Alexander told Betsy Morris for *Forbes*. "The money is the byproduct. If it makes money, well, then great, because then he can go off and do more stuff. Doing nothing is not an option. If you've ever been on holiday with him, it's hard work."

See also entry on Virgin Group in *International Directory of Company Histories*.

SOURCES FOR FURTHER INFORMATION

Bandreth, Gyles, "How Does It Feel to Fail, Richard?" *Sunday Telegraph*, February 25, 2001.

Branson, Richard, *Losing My Virginity*, New York: Times Books, 1998.

Cowe, Roger, "Virgin: A Brand Too Far?" *Marketing*, September 17, 1998.

Dearlove, Des, *Business the Richard Branson Way*, New York: AMACOM, 1999.

Jackson, Tim, *Virgin King*, London: HarperCollins, 1994.

Morris, Betsy, "What a Life," *Fortune*, October 6, 2003.

Sheff, David, "Richard Branson: The Interview," *Forbes*, February 24, 1997.

—Barry Alfonso

■ ■ ■

Edward D. Breen

1956–

President and chief executive officer, Tyco International

Nationality: American.

Born: 1956, in Pennsylvania.

Education: Grove City College, BS, 1978.

Family: Married Lynn Branster; children: three.

Career: General Instruments, 1978–1988, salesman; 1988–1994, senior vice president of sales; 1994–1997, various positions as president of Broadband Networks Group, president of Eastern Operations for the Communications Division, and vice president of Terrestrial Systems; 1997–2000, chairman, president, and chief executive officer; Motorola, 2000–2001, executive vice president of Motorola, president of Broadband Communications Sector (BCS), and subsequently head of the Networks Sector (which included the Global Telecom Solutions Sector; the Commercial, Government, and Industrial Solutions Sector; and BCS); 2001, president; 2002, president and chief operating officer; Tyco International, 2002–, president and chief executive officer.

Awards: Vanguard Award, National Cable Television Association, 1998; one of 100 Most Influential People in Cable, *CableFAX* magazine, 1999.

Address: Tyco International, 90 Pitts Bay Road, 2nd Floor, Pembroke HM 08, Bermuda; Tyco International (U.S.), 9 Roszel Road, Princeton, New Jersey 08540; http://www.tyco.com.

Edward D. Breen took over as president and CEO of the troubled Tyco International in July 2002. Made notorious by scandals that included questionable accounting practices and former CEO Dennis Kozlowski's unwarranted personal use of company funds, Tyco had become known as one of America's most corrupt companies. According to industry analysts, Breen's reputation as a man of honesty and integrity, as much as his standing as a successful, world-caliber executive at both General Instruments and Motorola, landed him the position at Tyco.

Edward D. Breen. *Getty Images.*

PROVES CAPABILITIES AT GENERAL INSTRUMENTS

Breen grew up in suburban Pennsylvania and attended Grove City College, a small Christian school just north of Pittsburgh. He began his career with General Instruments (GI), where he sold cable television converter boxes. Breen was successful enough as a salesman to be appointed senior vice president of sales at GI in 1988. In this position he oversaw the worldwide sales organization for the company's terrestrial products, an organization that encompassed sales personnel and activities in the United States, Canada, Latin America, Europe, and Asia Pacific.

Breen's managerial capabilities led to a series of appointments as the head of several subdivisions at GI, including the Broadband Networks Group and Eastern Operations for the Communications Division. He was eventually appointed executive vice president of Terrestrial Systems, where he directed the sales of terrestrial products worldwide and managed the division's strategic business units, including the distribution and telephony units. In 1997 he took over the reins as chairman and CEO at GI.

During his career at GI, Breen was credited with many of the company's successes. He led GI through the digital broadband revolution and expanded the company's market share in cable set-top boxes. According to one of his former bosses at GI, Hal Krisbergh, Breen's salesmanship led the company to dominate the cable set-top box market, which expanded from $200 million to $10 billion within 10 years. One of the keys to Breen's success in this area was his ability to persuade customers to sign up for multiyear contracts, which effectively shut out rivals. In an interview with John Kador for *Electronic Business*, Krisbergh noted, "Stars shine early, and Ed Breen was no exception" (February 2002).

A SHORT STINT AT MOTOROLA

In January 2000 Motorola bought GI, primarily because the former company had been attempting to enter the broadband business without much success. After the merger Breen was named executive vice president of Motorola and president of the company's Broadband Communications Sector. He quickly set out to integrate the two companies' cable businesses.

Having established himself as a key executive within Motorola, Breen was made head of the company's Network Sector. In October 2001 he was named Motorola's president, and on January 1, 2002, he assumed the additional duties of COO. Over time, Breen acquired a reputation for instituting cost-cutting and other programs to make operations more efficient and effective. For example, when he first joined the company, he promptly disposed of overlapping modems and discontinued unprofitable models. During his time at Motorola, Breen was credited with playing an instrumental role in leading the company back to profitability.

TYCO CALLS

Although he was seen as the heir apparent to Motorola's chief executive Christopher Galvin, in late July 2002, after seven months as COO, Breen decided to accept the job of CEO at the troubled Tyco International. He had previously turned down the top jobs at Lucent Technologies and Nortel Networks Corporation. Industry insiders were surprised by Breen's decision to take over the helm of a company that not only was carrying $25 billion in debt but also was suspect for its overly acquisitive growth strategy. Some analysts speculated that Breen's decision had more to do with personal ambition than with dissatisfaction at Motorola, where the CEO was many years away from retirement age.

Breen's reputation soon caused Tyco's stock to soar 53 percent, adding $9 billion to its market value within two weeks of the announcement of his taking over the position of CEO. He quickly developed specific plans to further repair the reputation of the company. In *Lightwave*, Breen was quoted as saying that one of his top priorities was to "restore confidence in Tyco with our employees, suppliers, customers, and the financial community and enhance and strengthen the core businesses" (October 2002). One of the first steps he took toward this end was to oust most of the top personnel from the previous administration. In an interview with Len Boselovic for the *Pittsburgh Post-Gazette*, Breen noted, "I went in with two thoughts: I needed to replace the board and I needed to replace most of the senior management" (November 16, 2003).

Despite Breen's belief that some of the company's directors were worth keeping, investors persuaded him to make a clean sweep. He eventually replaced the entire corporate board and 100 of Tyco's top 110 executives. He also created the monitorial position of senior vice president of corporate governance. Breen's next move was to start clearing up Tyco's financial mess, which included $26 billion of debt and a market value that had declined by some $90 billion by the time he assumed control of the company.

Part of Breen's plan for mending Tyco was to shift the company's growth strategy away from dependence on acquisitions toward maximization of the profitability of existing businesses. He focused on reducing the company's debt load in part by selling off some of the holdings the company had obtained during its overly aggressive acquisitions binge. On November 4, 2003, Breen announced his intention to sell Tyco Global Network, a $3.5 billion undersea fiber-optic network that had been built during the height of the telecom boom. He also produced plans to sell 50 smaller businesses and lay off 7,200 of 260,000 employees, and he greatly reduced executive compensation, limiting bonus payouts for executives to $29 million in 2003, compared with the $79 million executives had received the year before. Breen's announcement of these strategies drove Tyco's stock up 7 percent on November 4, 2003, to $22.50, the highest price the stock had reached since he took over.

MANAGEMENT STYLE EMPHASIZES INTEGRITY

According to industry analysts, Breen had many attributes that make a good manager. In *Electronic Business*, his former boss Krisbergh noted, "He is quickly able to identify strategic impacts of decisions; he recruits well; and he can manage large organizations through major technical innovations" (February 2002). Breen was also well regarded for his willingness to cut losses and abandon projects that he saw as being ultimately unprofitable.

Breen had had a reputation for being able to change the dysfunctional aspects of a company's culture, which was one of the main reasons he was hired by Tyco. High-tech market analysts note that Breen had the hustle and conviction to "make a bet" on products and then program and move forward quickly. Breen also placed a strong emphasis on customers—some analysts say to the point of reverence.

Perhaps the greatest aspect of Breen's importance to Tyco was his integrity, as evidenced by traits such as his dislike of ostentatious management perks, in a place where the former CEO notoriously had spent $6,000 on a shower curtain. Although he received a high salary for his duties, he was modest by nature and told Melanie Warner in an interview in *Fortune* that when he first saw his own office, which included a kitchen the size of some New York City apartments, he thought, "This is embarrassing" (April 28, 2003). He has since moved the corporate headquarters from New York City to more spartan facilities in New Jersey. Ralph Whitworth of Relational Investors summed up Breen's qualities to Warner in *Fortune* this way: "Ed is full of energy and has impeccable integrity" (April 28, 2003).

THE BATTLE CONTINUED

Breen's effort to restore Tyco's image and profitability was an ongoing battle, as the Securities and Exchange Commission and the Internal Revenue Service continued to probe Tyco in 2003 concerning accounting improprieties. Nevertheless, Breen remained confident that he could spur Tyco to regrowth. His goal was to increase earnings by 10 to 12 percent, to approximately $3 billion in 2005. He said that once Tyco's operations had become more efficient, he would look back into the prospect of making acquisitions.

See also entries on General Instruments, Motorola, Inc., and Tyco International Ltd. in *International Directory of Company Histories.*

SOURCES FOR FURTHER INFORMATION

Boselovic, Len, "Tough Decisions Awaited Tyco's New CEO: Grove City's Breen," *Pittsburgh Post-Gazette*, November 16, 2003, http://post-gazette.com/pg/03320/240433.stm.

"Fiber-to-the-Home (FTTH) Council," *Lightwave*, October 2002, p. 96.

"Ed Breen: Biography," http://www.gcc.edu/news/biographies/breen/default.htm.

Kador, John, "Shall We Dance: Ed Breen Likes to Boogie While Chris Galvin Wants to Waltz," *Electronic Business*, February 2002, p. 56.

Symonds, William, "Tyco: The Vise Grows Ever-Tighter," *BusinessWeek*, October 7, 2002, p. 48.

Warner, Melanie, "Exorcism at Tyco," *Fortune*, April 28, 2003, p. 106.

—David Petechuk

■ ■ ■

Thierry Breton

1955–

Chairman and chief executive officer, France Télécom

Nationality: French.

Born: January 15, 1955, in Paris, France.

Education: École Supérieure d'Électricité.

Family: Married (wife's name unknown); children: three.

Career: French school Lycee Francais in New York City, 1979–1981, teacher; Forma Systèmes, 1981–1986, chairman and CEO; French Ministry of Education and Research, 1986–1990, adviser; CGI Group, 1990–1993, CEO; Bull Group, 1993–, deputy managing director; Thomson Multimedia, 1997–2002, CEO; France Télécom, 2002–, CEO.

Publications: *Softwar* (with Denis Beneich), 1986; *The Pentecost Project,* 1987.

Address: France Télécom, 6 Place d'Alleray, 75505 Paris Cedex 15, France; http://www.francetelecom.com/en.

Thierry Breton. *AP/Wide World Photos.*

■ Over the course of his career Thierry Breton became known as a turnaround king. During the 1990s he rescued both the French computer-maker Bull and the consumer-electronics maker Thomson Multimedia from the brink of extinction. He orchestrated the two turnarounds through a combination of disciplined cost cutting and bold sales goals, persistently pressuring staff to meet his demands. Breton's biggest challenge came in 2002 when he became chief executive of France Télécom, Europe's second-largest phone company. At the time France Télécom was saddled with a $76 billion debt, which Breton drove down to just $53 billion over the course of 18 months. Known as a high-energy manager, Breton achieved results because he expected them; according to the *Wall Street Journal,* one of his favorite sayings was, "Anything but results is philosophy" (September 13, 2002).

BEGAN CAREER AS TEACHER

Breton was somewhat of an anomaly in the corporate world: as a young man the curly-haired computer whiz failed his entrance exams to the French *grandes écoles,* the country's best institutions of higher education. He instead attended the École Supérieure d'Électricité for engineering in Paris, going on to teach mathematics and information technology at a French high school in New York City from 1979 to 1981.

His first foray into the business world came in 1981, when he became chairman and chief executive officer of Forma Systèmes, a systems-analysis and software-engineering concern, for which he served until 1986. That year he took a position as an adviser with the French Ministry of Education and Research. From 1986 to 1990 Breton was also busy designing an open-air science and technology theme park in Paris called Futuroscope.

In 1990 Breton became the chief executive officer of CGI Group, a service-development company. He stayed until 1993, when the French government hired the computer genius to become deputy managing director of Bull Group, the troubled French computer maker. Breton's strategic restructuring delivered the company from the brink of bankruptcy and gave the young executive his first successful corporate recovery.

TURNED AROUND TV-MAKER THOMSON

In 1997 Breton was named chairman and CEO of France's Thomson Multimedia, a government-owned consumer-electronics company that was on the verge of collapse. A year before Thomson had been in such a shambles that France's prime minister had tried to unload the company on the South Korea–based Daewoo for a single franc—yet had been unable to seal the deal.

Intent on turning things around, Breton decided to learn everything he could about the company, which sold televisions and VCRs under the Thomson, Kenwood, and RCA names. Instead of relying on managers to tell him about the operation and its products, Breton took his education upon himself: soon after his start Breton pulled on a red salesman's blazer, complete with his first name scrawled across the breast, and spent several days working under cover at Darty, a Paris-based electronics outlet. There Breton learned firsthand what customers thought of Thomson's products. He spent much of one day struggling to persuade a grandmother that her grandchildren's photographs would not tumble off the top of the slanted Thomson television set.

An aggressive CEO, Breton was not afraid to slash costs and face objections to his plans. After taking over at Thomson, Breton closed inefficient factories in Germany and the United States, moving production to Latin America and Eastern Europe, and slashed U.S. management ranks by 20 percent. He made stock offerings in order to generate cash and diversified the company's businesses, figuring that consumer-electronics products were not high-end enough to consistently earn profits over the long haul. Breton involved Thomson in interactive television, electronic publishing, and the Internet, as well as the higher-margin business of digital film-editing services. He also initiated a venture into an interactive version of *TV Guide*; Thomson began manufacturing televisions with built-in software to run the electronic reference. Breton hoped the innovation would generate both subscriber and advertiser revenue.

Thomson's new ventures instilled investors with renewed confidence in the company and allowed Breton to lure big-name companies into buying stakes. Partners came to include Microsoft, Alcatel, NEC, and the DirecTV division of Hughes Electronics. By 1999 Thomson was turning a $230 million profit on sales of $6.5 billion. By the time Breton left in 2002, revenues had increased by more than 80 percent and Thomson was outperforming Sony, Matsushita, and Philips, its major consumer-electronics competitors.

Some industry analysts believed that Breton received too much credit for the Thomson turnaround, saying the company's recovery had more to do with agreements made before Breton had come on board. For instance, when Thomson bought RCA from General Electric in 1988, the French company agreed to let General Electric keep RCA's patents for 10 years as part of the purchase agreement. Thomson began reaping patent revenues in 1999; in 2001 patents and licensing earnings generated EUR 398.8 million for the company. Breton dismissed the theory, saying the company's recovery had been under way well before patent revenues started coming in. Others criticized Breton for the problems the computer-maker Bull Group ran into during the early 2000s, suggesting that the troubles stemmed from Breton's earlier tenure.

TOOK OVER STRUGGLING FRANCE TÉLÉCOM

In 2002 the French government called upon Breton again, this time to rescue France Télécom. At the time the firm's $76 billion debt burden was so great that all of its cash was being eaten up simply to pay interest payments, with nothing left over to reduce the principals on its loans. The company was carrying one of the largest debt loads in the world.

Within weeks of Breton's takeover, investors demonstrated their faith in the new leader by driving stock prices up to double the rock-bottom low. The French finance ministry's level of trust was evident in the code name Breton was given during hiring negotiations: "Mister Cash."

The task of turning the company around was formidable, but Breton's peers—and former rivals—anticipated success. The Sony chairman Nobuyuki Idei told the *Wall Street Journal*, "Thierry Breton is a brilliant person who took a nearly bankrupt company and turned it around. We have a lot of respect for him" (July 16, 2002).

Known for his youthful energy, Breton wasted no time in formulating a strategy. He took over on October 2, 2002, and gave himself a December 2 deadline for having a plan in place. Over the last weekend in October Breton asked the company's executives to hand over documents explaining their portions of the business. He also asked them to include examinations of their successes and failures. Breton took the piles of papers and headed into seclusion at a Paris hotel in order to study them; he had done the same thing five years before after taking over Thomson. Besides his own investigation, Breton put together a team of 120 consultants and advisers to conduct internal audits. He was aided by teams from Ernst & Young, Deloitte, Sullivan & Cromwell, and McKinsey and Bain. After 45 days the team produced a 1,500-page report.

Breton was determined to have a firsthand say about who would help him run the company—rather than relying on top managers to make such decisions. Breton spent his first two months speaking to up-and-coming managers over long breakfast meetings; he relied on his instincts in picking some of those managers to be appointed to top posts.

FORMULATED AGGRESSIVE RECOVERY PLAN

Just two months after taking over, Breton delivered his rescue plan to France Télécom's board of directors. Through his and others' studies, Breton generated a three-tiered plan that called for cutting costs to increase cash flow, refinancing debt, and generating $16 billion from shareholders through a capital increase, all in efforts to save $30 billion over three years. At the time of Breton's takeover some of France Télécom's ventures, such as Orange wireless and Wanadoo Internet, were operating on their own; Breton brought them back into the fold of the parent company, saving management costs and allowing him a more direct say with regard to their operations.

Breton was eager to start implementing his plan and was serious about showing his managers that he meant business. As soon as France Télécom's board gave him approval, Breton put out a message to the company's 50 top managers asking them to immediately join a conference call—it was eleven o'clock at night in Paris, and Breton wanted to prep managers to start executing his plan the very next morning. He characteristically made his managers feel challenged rather than comfortable.

Another trademark of Breton's management was extreme demands for accountability. At both Thomson and France Télécom he set up a system to review the performances of top managers every six months instead of annually; he connected their compensation to their meeting of his performance targets.

After only 18 months on the job at France Télécom, business was looking up. In that span of time Breton increased 2003 revenues 3.4 percent over the previous year to $58 billion, chiefly on gains in wireless and broadband Internet technologies. He boosted 2003 operating income to $12 billion—a 45 percent increase—through tighter financial controls and cost cutting. The company's $76 billion debt fell to $53 billion.

BELIEVED INNOVATIVE TECHNOLOGY WOULD GENERATE STABILITY

Breton's vision for France Télécom also relied on diversification of the company's services. Breton hoped that technical innovations would bump his company ahead of the pack, which was evident in the fact that his first excursion as CEO was to France Télécom's research and development laboratories. In 2003 Breton told *BusinessWeek* that while high-speed Internet and mobile service were growing sectors of the business, France Télécom could not rely on those technologies alone: "For the future, we don't know what technologies will be the most important. That means you can't just bet on one technology" (February 11, 2003).

An avowed technology junkie, Breton also told *BusinessWeek* that he adored technology and always tried out the lab's latest developments in his own home. At the end of 2003 France Télécom rolled out "wi-fi" (wireless fidelity) kits that allowed customers to hook up wireless networks in their homes; naturally Breton personally tested the technology first.

Breton also had a vision to merge his company's traditional phone service with its wireless and Internet networks, creating one integrated service that would let people communicate without considering which medium they were using. The unification would eliminate the need for different phone numbers for wired and mobile services. Breton told *BusinessWeek*, "Customers don't care about the network. They just want services" (June 7, 2004).

GAINED PUBLICITY FOR SCIENCE-FICTION BOOKS

Besides having respect in the corporate world, Breton also earned a reputation in the science-fiction world during the 1980s when he wrote a few books. One of his most popular titles was *Softwar*, which he coauthored with Denis Beneich. Originally written in French, the book was translated into English in 1986. *Softwar* was a Cold War thriller, its plot revolving around the very real conflict between the former Soviet Union and the United States during that time period. In the story the Soviets attempt to buy a supercomputer for military use. The sale is negotiated through France, since the United States would never have been able to sell a computer directly to the Soviets.

The United States then sends a computer scientist to Paris to booby-trap the computer by saddling it with programs called "softbombs," which could be set off from the outside. These softbombs could freeze up the computer or have a variety of other effects on its operations. Parts of the book were highly technical and demonstrated Breton's vast knowledge of computer programming. He followed *Softwar* with 1987's *The Pentecost Project*, a tale about a secret global-communications network overseen by the Vatican.

See also entries on France Télécom Group and THOMSON Multimedia S.A. in *International Directory of Company Histories.*

SOURCES FOR FURTHER INFORMATION

Ascarelli, Silvia, Almar Latour, and Kevin J. Delaney, "Leading the News: French Government Backs Breton to Take Top France Télécom Post," *Wall Street Journal*, September 13, 2002.

Bryan-Low, Cassell, "With Debt Down, France Télécom Aims to Separate Itself from Rivals: One-Stop Shopping Is Seen as Critical to Firm's Success, but Can It Deliver on Price?" *Wall Street Journal*, June 10, 2004.

Delaney, Kevin J., "A Rare Success Story in a Business Rife with Woes—CEO of French Company that Makes Electronics Manages a Quick Rebirth," *Wall Street Journal*, July 16, 2002.

———, "New CEO Tackles France Télécom's Woes," *Wall Street Journal*, December 18, 2002.

Lanchner, David, "Calling Up 'Mister Cash,'" *Institutional Investor*, January 2004, p. 63.

Matlack, Carol, and Andy Reinhardt, "Vive la Telecom?" *BusinessWeek*, February 17, 2003, p. 26.

"Thierry Breton," *BusinessWeek*, June 7, 2004.

"Thierry Breton," *BusinessWeek Online*, February 11, 2003, http://www.businessweek.com/technology/content/feb2003/tc20030211_1251_tc070.htm.

—Lisa Frick

■■■

Ulrich Brixner

1941–

Chairman and chief executive officer, Deutsche Zentral-Genossenschaftsbank

Nationality: German.

Born: January 6, 1941, in Munich, Germany.

Education: PhD.

Family: Married (wife's name unknown); children: two.

Career: Sudwestdeutsche Genossenschaftliche Zentralbank, 1991–1998, member of managing board; 1998–2000, chairman; Genossenschaftliche Zentralbank, 2000–2001, chairman; Deutsche Zentral-Genossenschaftsbank, 2001–, chairman and CEO.

Address: Deutsche Zentral-Genossenschaftsbank, Platz Der Republik 1, Frankfurt Am Main 0325, Germany; http://www.dz-bank.de/internet_en.

■ Ulrich Brixner was a banker with experience in both German and international banking. He was the first chairman of the board of directors of Deutsche Zentral-Genossenschaftsbank (DZ Bank). His successful career reflected both a deep understanding of the intricacies of the banking industry and a need for solid control of operations.

RISE IN GERMAN BANKING

Brixner gained prominence in the credit and cooperative banks of Germany. By 1991 he had been helped into a position of authority by Bernd Thiemann; Brixner was heading Genossenschaftliche Zentralbank (GZ Bank), the smaller of Germany's two credit bank cooperatives—the other being Deutsche Genossenschaftsbank (DG Bank). Thiemann was then chairman of Nord/LB (a German financial institution) while Brixner headed its smaller competitor GZ Bank. In that year Brixner declined an opportunity to merge with the larger of Germany's credit banks, DG Bank, which named Thiemann to be its chairman. The two men became rivals in a relationship that would come to a head 10 years later.

Under Brixner's leadership GZ Bank came to include not only three of Germany's major credit banks (Genossenschaftliche Zentralbank in Stuttgart, Sudwestdeutsche Genossenschafts-Zentralbank in Frankfurt, and Westdeutsche Genossenschafts-Zentralbank in Düsseldorf) but also the largest of the German building societies and several mortgage banks, investment companies, leasing and manufacturing companies, and a large insurance group.

EXPANSION INTO NON-GERMAN BANKING MARKETS

As Germany took a prominent role in the economic development of the European Union, German companies expanded across the continent; the more aggressive German banks followed these firms into new markets. Brixner and GZ Bank, meanwhile, looked even farther abroad. In November 1995 GZ Bank opened an office in Singapore with plans to convert the outlet into a merchant-banking operation by 1998. This move was made because of the growing number of German companies in the Asia Pacific region.

MERGER OF GERMAN COOPERATIVE BANKS

In 1991 Brixner and GZ Bank had declined merger possibilities, but during the following years it became clear that a merger of Germany's top cooperative banks would be beneficial. The number of cooperative banks in Germany was somewhere between 1,700 and two thousand but had been declining steadily. The three top banks—DG Bank, GZ Bank, and WGZ Bank (Westdeutsche Genossenschafts-Zentral Bank)—then entered into negotiations. The last of the three soon dropped out; DG Bank and GZ Bank continued talking in a painful public process until the formal merger was completed in September 2001. DG Bank was the larger of the two, but Brixner's GZ Bank had been the better performer; in the end Brixner overcame his rival Thiemann to become chairman of the new entity, which was to be called Deutsche Zentral-Genossenschaftsbank (DZ Bank).

DZ Bank was the sixth-largest bank in Germany and was to manage a large number of the country's credit unions and rural cooperatives, mostly in Baden-Württemberg, Hessen, Rheinland-Pfalz, and Saarland. On the one hand the new bank faced increased opportunities and markets as a result of the combination; on the other hand management changes and job redundancy issues were difficult obstacles that would have to be confronted. Furthermore, Brixner found that DG Bank had brought along significant liabilities. In an interview published by the *Banker* on March 1, 2002, Brixner said that DG Bank had made loans that were economically unsupportable; GZ Bank had followed an extremely conservative loan policy and had not faced the same problem.

In the months following the completion of the merger Brixner was able to secure greater control by reducing the number of DG Bank representatives in positions of authority. In January 2002 the announcement was made that three ex-DG executives would be leaving the governing board. The board comprised only 10 members altogether, five of which, including Brixner, had come from GZ.

DZ BANK GAINS SOLID FOOTING

In a 2002 interview with the *Banker*, Brixner stated that in addition to the expected problems of merging two organizations—and of dealing with DG Bank's large number of failed debtors—another immediate problem was the poor economic situation that followed the terrorist attacks of September 11, 2001, in the United States. Redundancies approached one thousand jobs, but duplication was finally eliminated. DZ Bank also cut material costs in its general reduction of expenditures and liabilities.

Brixner moved to increase company income by applying GZ Bank's conservative loan policies and moving aggressively to recover the faulty loans. He hoped to decrease DZ Bank's cost-to-income ratio from over 70 percent to 60 percent. Brixner and DZ Bank also planned to expand into an increasing number of national and international markets, which would bring the company into direct competition with Deutsche Bank and other large banks. He stated that increased competitiveness in retail and other noncooperative bank sectors would be necessary because of the decreasing number of cooperative banks controlled by DZ.

By June 2004 DZ Bank had become both a central bank and a commercial bank and was one of the world's eight largest cooperative banks. It had branches, subsidiaries, and representative offices all over the world. Brixner remained unconvinced by skeptical criticism regarding his firm. He applied the same focused, conservative attention to DZ Bank as he had to GZ Bank, and he expected to enjoy similarly positive results. His optimism was based on logical business methodology.

SOURCES FOR FURTHER INFORMATION

"Brixner Brings DZ Bank under His Control," *Global News Wire/Europe Intelligence Wire* (abstracted from *Financial Times Deutschland*), January 31, 2002.

"Brixner Replaces Thiemann at DG Bank," *Global News Wire* (abstracted from *Frankfurter Allgemeine Zeitung*), p. 21.

"GZ Bank Appointment," *Global News Wire/Borsen-Zeitung*, February 3, 2000, p. 6.

Raj, Conrad, "German Banking Group Opens Office in Singapore," *Business Times* (Singapore), November 24, 1995, p. 3.

SEC Edgar Filings: Kreditanstalt Fuer Wiederaufbau (2004) and Landwirtschaftliche Rentenbank (2003, 2004), 18-K.

"SGZ Bank Wants to Unite Forces in the Southwest," *Global News Wire/Die Welt*, February 10, 1999, p. 20.

Wagner, Jan F., "A Merger of Equals?" *Banker*, March 1, 2002.

—Barbara Gunvaldsen

■■■

John Browne

1948–

Group chief executive officer, BP

Nationality: British.

Born: February 20, 1948, in Hamburg, Germany.

Education: Cambridge University, BS, 1969; Stanford University, MS, 1981.

Family: Son of Edmund (British army officer) and Paula Browne (homemaker); never married; children: none.

Career: British Petroleum Company, 1966–1968, apprentice; 1969–1979, petroleum engineer; 1979–1980, regional petroleum engineer; 1981–1983, manager; 1983–1984, manager of Aberdeen office; 1984–1986, group treasurer; BP Financial International, 1984–1986, chief executive officer; Standard Oil Company of Ohio, 1986–1987, executive vice president and chief financial officer; Standard Oil Production Company, 1987–1989, chief executive officer; BP America, 1987–1989, executive vice president and chief financial officer; BP Exploration and Production, 1989–1995, chief executive officer; British Petroleum Company, 1995–1998, group chief executive officer; BP Amoco, 1998–2000, group chief executive officer; BP, 2000–, group chief executive officer.

Awards: Knighthood, Queen Elizabeth II, 1998; Partners Award, American Oceans Campaign, 1999; Prince Philip Medal, Royal Academy of Engineering, 1999; United Nations Environment Programme, Earth Day Award, United Nations, 1999; Britain's Most Admired CEO, *Management Today*, 2000, 2001, and 2002; Award for Responsible Capitalism, *FIRST*, 2000; Ernest C. Arbuckle Award, Stanford Business School Alumni Association, 2001; dubbed Lord Browne of Madingley, Queen Elizabeth, 2001; Public Service Award, Society of Petroleum Engineers, 2002.

Address: BP, 1 Saint James Square, London, SW1Y 4PD, United Kingdom; http://www.bp.com/home.do.

John Browne. *AP/Wide World Photos.*

■ Edmund John Phillip Browne, known as John, was always reluctant to talk about himself and his personal life. When Browne spoke, it was so softly that people strained to understand him, yet as Andrew S. Grove of Intel remembered, everyone in a meeting would become quiet and listen intently. Browne was tough and cerebral and a workaholic who frightened subordinates with his calm, penetrating assessments of their work. He was even tempered, however; practically the only way to make him angry was to pry into his mother's past. Browne was short and slim, dapperly dressed, and given to orderliness that made his offices so clean and tidy that they looked as though no one worked in them, even though he worked tirelessly. Pedantic in his speech, given to wry humor, shy and studious, Browne also was coldly ruthless in managing BP's affairs. His quiet charm overlay a daring personality that would in one moment dispassionately cut costs and jobs and in another moment bet hundreds of millions of dollars on a gamble based on his understanding of the science that underlay his oil business. Browne consistently had his thoughts turned to the future. He believed that a manager's responsibility was to build a company with a long-term future without sacrificing long-term gains for short-term profits.

DIFFICULT BEGINNINGS

Browne's mother, Paula, survived the Holocaust, having been slated for extermination in the Nazi death camp at Auschwitz. Her family perished in Nazi death camps. She was a refugee from Transylvania, Romania, when she met Browne's father. Paula Browne was private and had a horror of discussing or even hearing mentioned her experiences during World War II. Her son was very protective of her, steering the curious away from her as best he could.

Browne's father, Edmund, was a tough, determined officer in the Black Rats tank regiment. Like his wife and as his son came to be, Edmund Browne was a private personality. The most obvious legacy to his son was Edmund's love of smoking cigars. It was also through his father that Browne was drawn to work for British Petroleum, the company that would become his passion. From his mother Browne seemed to have acquired his taste for fine art. He became a collector of 18th-century English furniture, modern paintings, pre-Columbian art, and Robert Mapplethorpe photographs of flowers.

Browne's family moved often, exposing Browne to a variety of cultures. It was probably during a posting in the Middle East that Browne's father became acquainted with the Anglo-Iranian Oil Company, later renamed British Petroleum Company, and in 1958 he took a job with the company. That year Browne was sent to a boarding school, King's School, Ely, United Kingdom. He was a brilliant student, and in 1966 he won a scholarship to attend Cambridge University. He majored in physics while working holidays for British Petroleum. When he was graduated in 1969, Browne seemed destined to pursue graduate studies and a career as a college don. At his father's urging, however, Browne joined British Petroleum for a year and asked for a posting to the United States, hoping to go to New York. Instead he was sent to Prudhoe Bay in Alaska to work as an engineer on a pipeline for British Petroleum's new 14-million-barrel oil field. Browne was enthralled by the work, learning not only about oil engineering but also about business and politics.

Instead of returning to school Browne spent 10 years traveling America, moving from one British Petroleum office to another, all the while absorbing the business and loving the United States. The failure of a love affair in America appeared to permanently taint Browne's personal life. While posted in San Francisco, Browne spent his spare time studying at Stanford University, earning a master of science degree in business. He loved Stanford and would often return there. In 1980 Browne's father died of diabetes. Browne took his mother with him when he was posted to London in 1981, and they lived in an apartment in Chelsea, near the River Thames.

BEGINNING TO REMAKE BRITISH PETROLEUM

In 1982 Browne made his presence felt in British Petroleum when he devised a strategy for selling 0.25 percent interests in British Petroleum's Forties field in the North Sea to other British oil companies. This arrangement allowed the companies to count their drilling expenses against North Sea oil production and lower their British taxes. British Petroleum made $300 million from selling the interests. Browne's cleverness attracted the attention of executives in the company, notably Robert Horton, who in 1986 was sent to Cleveland, Ohio, to straighten up Standard Oil Company of Ohio (Sohio), in which British Petroleum held a 55 percent interest. Horton took Browne with him, in April 1986 making Browne chief financial officer and executive vice president of the company. Browne astounded Horton with the amount of work he did, working all day, every day. Jack E. Golden, a staff geologist, believed huge oil deposits were beyond the continental shelf in deep water in the Gulf of Mexico. Browne acted by spending all of Sohio's exploration budget of $50 million on exploring the deep water of the gulf. It was one of Browne's legendary gambles, and it paid off. British Petroleum not only discovered oil but also bought the rights to much of the new area before other oil companies got there. By 1989 British Petroleum was the largest petroleum producer in the United States. By 1995 the deepwater wells in the Gulf of Mexico were among British Petroleum's most productive and cost-effective. Although drilling costs were as high as 50 times those of drilling on dry land, pumping costs proved so small that British Petroleum's expenses were only $6 per barrel of oil. In the 1990s the value of a barrel had varied from $16 to $32. Golden became chief of deepwater exploration under CEO Browne.

In 1987 Browne oversaw British Petroleum's buyout of the remaining 45 percent of Sohio for $7.9 billion. That year Browne became executive vice president and chief financial officer of BP America. He analyzed the business units of BP America and concluded that most ventures were not profitable. In his typically unemotional manner, Browne sold BP America's production holdings except for those in Alaska and the Gulf of Mexico. That year British Petroleum's worldwide workforce peaked at 129,000 employees. In September 1989 Browne, having that year been appointed CEO of BP Exploration and Production, engineered the sale of some British Petroleum assets to Oryx Energy Company—a November 1988 spinoff of Sun Company. In the process Browne cut more than 1,700 jobs (two hundred in the United States) and $150 million in overhead. Oryx received some of British Petroleum's North Sea assets as well as British Petroleum's Dubai, Gabon, and Italian assets. Overall in 1989 Browne sold assets for $1.3 billion. Meanwhile he advocated aggressive exploration of new areas for petroleum and natural gas.

In September 1991 Browne was elected to the board of directors of British Petroleum. By then Horton was the company's CEO and was leading the company in aggressive expansion into markets such as pet foods and trying to stabilize company earnings in an effort to shield the stock value from the inevitable ups and downs of oil prices in the world marketplace. The expansion did not work as hoped. Oil prices plunged in the early 1990s, and in 1992 British Petroleum lost $624 million. In June 1992 David Simon, the chief operating officer, replaced Horton as CEO. By then British Petroleum's debt was $16 billion.

A NEW WAY OF DOING BUSINESS

On June 10, 1995, Browne was made CEO of British Petroleum, and David Simon became chairman of the board. Simon had done much to stabilize the company and with Browne's help had sold off much that was extraneous to the company's core businesses: petroleum and natural gas. At the time, competitors derisively called British Petroleum a "two-pipe company," meaning it had large reserves only in Alaska and the North Sea, both of which seemed past their peak periods of production. The decline of these reserves would mean British Petroleum's decline. Then British Petroleum's Neptune well in the Gulf of Mexico hit a rich reserve of petroleum, giving British Petroleum a third "pipe."

Browne established three new rules for employees and the company: First, do not spend money you do not have; second, no surprises; and third, ask for help. Browne reorganized the exploration department into small units, each unit being responsible for its own finances. Then he instituted a teamwork strategy that had geologists, petroleum engineers, and drillers meeting together to analyze potential drilling sites. Browne wanted the team members to talk together as a unified group until they had worked out a drilling strategy that met the requirements of the geologic characteristics of the site and the abilities of drilling technology. The previous method had been for geologists to map sites, petroleum engineers to select where to drill, and then drillers to set up platforms and try to drill. The geologists, engineers, and drillers rarely talked to one another, and it could take weeks to ask questions and receive answers. The result was that drilling equipment required many adjustments before achieving success. In 1995 it took one hundred days to drill a deepwater well. By 1997 Browne's team strategy of putting all interested parties together to plan their drilling reduced actual drilling time to 42 days. Furthermore, in 1995 Browne began his intimidating monthly reviews of each business group within British Petroleum. He amazed and even awed scientists and business managers alike with his ability to absorb immense amounts of information and make sense of it. The monthly meetings were sessions during which Browne grilled managers on every aspect of their work. Those who produced positive results were rewarded with challenging projects and promotions; those who did not were let go. A reluctant socializer, Browne found his new job required that he hobnob with business and government leaders. He took to bringing his mother with him to social events, and she proved to be ideal for such occasions, being careful in her speech.

In 1996 Browne began opening British Petroleum gasoline stations in Russia. In Europe he formed a partnership with Mobil, combining British Petroleum's and Mobil's operations and elevating them from being secondary competitors with dim futures in Europe's lubricants market to being a unified major competitor. By the end of the year Browne was looking for companies to acquire. His first step was to sound out Mobil, which was not interested in a full worldwide merger.

On May 19, 1997, in a speech at Stanford University, Browne declared that evidence suggested that global warming could be real. He argued that evidence that burning of fossil fuels was contributing to global warming was sufficient for the matter to be taken seriously by oil companies. This speech was received with horror by other oil companies and with suspicion by environmentalist organizations. Yet Browne made the term "green" a fundamental part of his company's operations. Because carbon dioxide was thought to be a major contributor to the warming of the earth's climate, Browne established a goal of reducing British Petroleum's carbon dioxide output 10 percent by 2010, a reduction of 30 million tons per year. British Petroleum met this goal of 10 percent reduction in 2002. Browne committed British Petroleum to producing cleaner fuels and cleaning up its production waste. The company improved the efficiency of its turbines and cut down on the flaring of gas at its drilling sites. Browne said that British Petroleum should monitor its carbon dioxide emissions, expand solar energy activities, and support research into causes of global warming. British Petroleum spent $160 million building solar panel plants in California and Spain and $40 million on research into solar power. Browne began having British Petroleum plant new forests, because trees absorb carbon dioxide, with two projects in 1997. An internal survey showed that employees at British Petroleum were concerned about the environment. This finding reassured Browne that his green efforts would have wide support in his company. In a disagreement over environmental issues British Petroleum left the American oil industry group Global Climate Coalition, which argued that there was no connection between burning fossil fuels and a warming climate.

Meanwhile Browne had cut his workforce to 53,000 employees, mostly by selling assets unrelated to the business of producing power. British Petroleum's debt had been reduced to $9 billion. There was controversy over British Petroleum's conduct in Colombia, where the company was accused of buying arms and training paramilitary forces to protect the company's oil pipeline from its oil field to the sea. In Russia, British Petroleum purchased 10 percent of Sidanco for $484 million. This deal was Browne's opening effort in British Petroleum's involvement in the development of Russian petroleum fields.

ONE OF THE THREE SISTERS

There were two companies known as "supermajors" in the oil business—Exxon and Shell. By the end of 1998 there would be a third supermajor, and the trio would be dubbed the "three sisters." In May 1998 Browne called H. Laurance Fuller, the chairman of the board of Amoco, about acquiring Amoco. In August 1998 British Petroleum purchased Amoco for $57 billion, and British Petroleum renamed itself BP Amoco. On December 31, 1998, Browne's title became group CEO. Stephen F. Gates, the general counsel for Amoco, became Browne's chief of staff. BP Amoco gained oil and natural gas fields in Azerbaijan, the Gulf of Mexico, the North Sea, Trinidad, the United States, and Venezuela. The purchase of Amoco made BP Amoco's workforce 99,000 employees. In 1999 this number was cut to 89,000. This and other cuts in expenses eventually saved the company $2 billion annually. Not all went Browne's way in 1998. In Russia, Sidanco went bankrupt, and the Russian company Tyumen Oil, which was run by the young tycoon Mikhail Fridman, manipulated Russian courts to gain control of an oil field that Browne had coveted. In a bright spot in Browne's personal life in 1998, Queen Elizabeth II made him a knight, upholding a British tradition whereby the monarch bestowed honors each year on her birthday.

In January 1999 Browne had a pleasant surprise when Mike R. Bowlin, the head of the Atlantic Richfield Company (ARCO), offered to sell ARCO to BP Amoco. In April 1999 BP Amoco purchased ARCO for $27 billion in BP Amoco stock. ARCO owned 22 percent of Prudhoe Bay, and BP Amoco owned 51 percent, but U.S. government regulators wanted BP Amoco to give up its ARCO Alaskan holdings. BP Amoco sold these holding to Phillips Petroleum for $7 billion, leaving BP Amoco with control of 45 percent of Alaska's oil. More important to Browne were ARCO's natural gas holdings. BP Amoco owned 13 percent of Prudhoe Bay's natural gas, but ARCO owned 43 percent, and the ARCO Tangguh facility in eastern Indonesia had 14 trillion cubic feet of natural gas. Browne later explained that he foresaw petroleum decreasing in importance while he believed the reserves of cleaner-burning natural gas to be in essence infinite and therefore the future in supplying the world with inexpensive power. Browne also hoped to retain talented executives by keeping them challenged with buying financially troubled ARCO, which required much work to be made successful. During the negotiations with ARCO, Browne's six-cigar-per-day habit caused him breathing problems when he exercised.

In keeping with Browne's belief that demand for alternatives to oil would grow faster than demand for oil would, on April 6, 1999, BP Amoco bought Solarex, making BP Amoco the world's largest solar power company. Also in that month BP Amoco began equipping two hundred British gasoline stations with solar panels. Meanwhile BP Amoco discovered the Crazy Horse Tract in deep water in the Gulf of Mexico. The tract contained 1.5 billion barrels of petroleum. By then BP had 3.7 percent of the world's oil supply. Trouble came from human rights activists when BP Amoco paid hundreds of millions of dollars to the government of Angola for rights to deep-water drilling off the nation's coast. The money was used to finance the government's war against rebels.

In March 2000 BP Amoco purchased Burma Castrol, a maker of lubricants, for $4.7 billion. In late 2000 BP Amoco began removing the word "Amoco" from all nine thousand American stations. The worldwide cost of renaming all BP stations over 4 years was $4.5 billion. BP regained its Sidanco assets and bought a 25 percent stake in the company from Tyumen Oil, which had been renamed TNK. Although BP was the world's largest producer of solar cells, Browne said he believed hydrocarbons would be the most important source of energy at least into the 2010s. He believed solar power would not become truly important until as late as 2050. Browne viewed wind power as too unsightly and too noisy to be acceptable to consumers. Meanwhile he and the leaders of Ford Motor Company began talks about cooperating to produce cleaner automobile emissions. In Atlanta, BP introduced clean fuels and experienced a jump in its sales in the city. It was in 2000 that Browne's mother died.

In 2001 BP changed its logo to lowercase "bp" and a green sun to symbolize that BP was an environmentally friendly company. The company's motto became "Beyond Petroleum." At TNK Fridman wanted help building his oil business, so he and Browne began talks about merging. Since 1995 BP had established a process of exploring, building, and pumping that dramatically reduced costs. BP had 20 "hives," $500,000 rooms for three-dimensional images of drilling sites where drillers, engineers, and geologists gathered to plan drilling in a site. Use of this system shortened planning time from weeks to hours. In 2001 Browne was made Lord Browne of Madingley.

In 2002 Browne said he believed mandatory government standards were necessary to make oil companies control their emissions. On August 29, 2003, Browne concluded an $8.1 billion agreement with Russia's TNK. BP had a 50 percent share of TNK-BP (composed of Tyumen Oil and Sidanco), which produced 1.2 million barrels per day of crude petroleum in Siberia and the Ural Mountains. The deal increased BP's petroleum reserves 30 percent. BP assigned 110 of its managers to the new company, including TNK's chief financial officer and its CEO.

See also entry on BP p.l.c. in *International Directory of Company Histories.*

SOURCES FOR FURTHER INFORMATION

Fisher, Daniel, "Going Deep: How Sir John Browne Turned BP Amoco into the Hottest Prospect in the Oil Patch," *Forbes.com,* April 2, 2001, http://www.forbes.com/global/2001/0402/044.html.

Ghazi, Polly, and Ian Hargreaves, "BP's Chief Executive Is Making the Running on Green Strategy: But How Does That Square with Controversy in Colombia and the Atlantic Ocean?" *New Statesman,* July 4, 1997, pp. 34–37.

Guyon, Janet, "A Big-Oil Man Gets Religion," *Fortune.com,* March 6, 2000, http://www.fortune.com/fortune/investing/articles/0,15114,371800,00.html.

———, "When John Browne Talks, Big Oil Listens," *Fortune.com,* July 5, 1999, http://www.fortune.com/fortune/articles/0,15114,378121,00.html.

"Odd Man Out among the Oil Barons," *Sunday Times,* January 21, 2001, http://www.bpamoco.org.uk/company/01-01-21stim.htm.

—Kirk H. Beetz

■ ■ ■

Wayne Brunetti

1942–

Chairman and chief executive officer, Xcel Energy

Nationality: American.

Born: October 13, 1942, in Cleveland, Ohio.

Education: University of Florida, BS, 1964; Harvard University, Program for Management Development, 1974.

Family: Son of Henry Joseph and Lillian Lupo; married Mary Kelly, 1963; children: two.

Career: Florida Power & Light Company, 1964–1968, accountant; 1968–1969, systems analyst; 1969–1972, project coordinator; 1972–1973, manager of property accounting; 1973–1977, manager of corporate accounting and assistant comptroller; 1977–1980, assistant to the vice president of public affairs; 1980, director of energy management; 1980–1983, vice president of energy management; 1983–1984, vice president; 1984–1987, group vice president; 1987–1991, executive vice president; Management Systems International, 1991–1994, CEO and president; Public Service Company of Colorado, 1994–1996, president and COO; 1996–1997, CEO and president; New Century Energies, 1997–2000, president and COO; 2000, CEO and president; Xcel Energy, 2001–2003, chairman, CEO, and president; 2003–, chairman and CEO.

Awards: Distinguished Leadership Award, Rocky Mountain Electrical League, 2000.

Publications: *Achieving Total Quality: Integrating Business Strategy and Customer Needs,* 1993.

Address: Xcel Energy, 414 Nicollet Mall, Minneapolis, Minnesota 55401-1993; http://www.xcelenergy.com.

■ Wayne Brunetti brought nearly 40 years of quality improvement and management experience to his role as chairman and chief executive officer of Xcel Energy, the electricity and natural-gas provider for consumers in 11 states. Xcel was formed in August 2000 by the merger of New Century Energies of Denver, of which Brunetti had been chairman and CEO, and Northern States Power of Minneapolis. Colleagues described Brunetti as a knowledgeable and methodical leader who was deeply committed to the energy industry and had a strong vision for his company.

Wayne Brunetti. *AP/Wide World Photos.*

EARLY CAREER

After graduating from the University of Florida in 1964 with a degree in business administration, Brunetti was hired by Florida Power & Light as an accountant. Over 28 years with the company he moved steadily up the corporate ladder into various management positions, including project coordinator, assistant to the vice president of public affairs, vice president of energy management, group vice president, and finally executive vice president. Brunetti left the company in 1991 to strike out on his own, relying on his expertise in quality improvement to start a consulting company called Management Systems International.

With the goal of helping the senior management of companies improve the quality of their organizations, much of Brunetti's work took him to Europe. He told the *Denver Business Journal*, "This was very personally rewarding because as much as I taught them, they taught me. And I learned a lot about different businesses, different approaches to running a business, and the different management philosophies of running a business" (November 21, 1997). He compiled the knowledge he gained into a book, *Achieving Total Quality: Integrated Business Strategy and Customer Needs*, which was published by Quality Resources in 1993.

XCEL ENERGY AND ITS PREDECESSORS

In 1994 Brunetti was recruited by Public Service Company of Colorado to fill the role of president and chief operating officer. While he was initially wary of the offer, he accepted; he informed the *Denver Business Journal*, "I felt it was at a time when many things were going to happen in the industry that had not happened in the last 50 years, and I really wanted to be a part of that. I always had ideas about how to run a utility differently. I always was a little bit of a maverick" (November 21, 1997). He became CEO of Public Service in 1996.

In 1997 Public Service merged with the Texas-based Southwestern Public Service Company to form New Century Energies, and Brunetti was appointed vice chairman, president, and chief operating officer; he became president and chief executive officer in 2000. During his tenure with the two companies Brunetti focused on improving service quality; to refer to his main goals he used the acronym "RSVP": reliability, safety, value added, and price. Brunetti told the *Journal* that he helped Public Service make "dramatic improvements in its customer service, reliability, and cost containment" (November 21, 1997).

Yet another merger occurred in August 2000, this time with the Minneapolis-based Northern States Power Company, creating Xcel Energy. Brunetti was named chairman, president, and chief executive officer in 2001, with Richard Kelly relieving him of the position of president in 2003. In 2004 Xcel provided services to 3.3 million electricity customers and 1.7 million natural gas customers in 11 states, making it the fourth-largest electricity and natural gas company in the United States.

Brunetti's expertise and commitment to the industry led to his appointment to the National Petroleum Council, an advisory body to the U.S. Department of Energy. In 2004 Brunetti was elected chairman of the Edison Electric Institute, and he once served as the chairman of the Colorado Association of Commerce and Industry. He also served on the boards of Capital City Partnership, the Juran Center for Leadership and Quality, and the Denver Chamber of Commerce.

UPS AND DOWNS

Brunetti came under fire for several reasons during his early years with Xcel. In 2002 the company lost a struggle to save its flagging NRG Energy unit from bankruptcy. After stock values dropped 60 percent and the per-share dividend was cut from $1.50 to $0.75, Xcel was sued by investors who claimed that senior management had held back crucial information. Xcel's board of directors received a letter from Minnesota's attorney general asking for Brunetti's resignation because of the possible financial effects on the state's electricity users. In 2003 the company rebounded, however, defying analysts' expectations and posting a share price that was 54 percent higher than it had been in 2002.

In 2004 Brunetti and other Xcel executives faced further criticism from shareholders regarding the company's executive compensation and pension program, which Brunetti and Kelly defended, stating in the *Rocky Mountain News* that all Xcel employees were paid "market-based rates" (May 21, 2004).

In spite of the occasional controversies Brunetti's colleagues described him as a highly committed and visionary leader. In the *Denver Business Journal* George Dibble, the former president of the Colorado Association of Commerce and Industry, noted, "He's very precise in his approach to things. He's very well attuned to what is going on in the state and what we need to do to move the business community forward." Steve Coffin, the vice president of government and regulatory affairs for Colorado Interstate Gas, said, "He is a very thoughtful, thorough, smart person. He is a strong leader with a strong vision and a strong understanding of how to get from here to there, not only in his business but in his community as well" (November 21, 1997).

See also entry on Public Service Company of Colorado in *International Directory of Company Histories*.

SOURCES FOR FURTHER INFORMATION

Aven, Paula, "Sparking a New Century," *Denver Business Journal*, November 21, 1997.

Blahnik, Mike, "For CEO Pensions, Rank Has Its Privileges," *Star Tribune* (Minneapolis-St. Paul), May 18, 2003.

Chakrabarty, Gargi, "Xcel Shareholders Fume over Bonuses," *Rocky Mountain News*, May 21, 2004.

"Wayne Brunetti Elected EEI Chairman," PR Newswire, June 14, 2004.

—Stephanie Dionne Sherk

■■■

John E. Bryson

1943–

Chairman of the board, president, and chief executive officer, Edison International; chairman of the board, Southern California Edison

Nationality: American.

Born: July 24, 1943, in New York, New York.

Education: Stanford University, 1965; Yale University, LLB, 1969.

Family: Married Louise (maiden name unknown).

Career: Natural Resources Defense Council, 1969–1979, lawyer; California Public Utilities Commission, 1979–1983, president; Morrison and Foerster, 1983–1984; partner; Edison International, 1984–1990, senior vice president for legal and financial affairs; 1990–1999, chairman of the board and chief executive officer; 2000–, chairman of the board, chief executive officer, and president; Southern California Edison, 1990–2003, chairman of the board and chief executive officer; 2003–, chairman of the board.

Address: Edison International, PO Box 800, Rosemead, California 91770; http://www.edison.com.

John E. Bryson. *AP/Wide World Photos.*

■ John E. Bryson had a background as an environmental activist before joining Edison International in 1984. After becoming chairman and CEO of the company, one of the largest investor-owned utility companies in the nation, Bryson faced the task of steering the Edison through deregulation and dealing with the California energy crisis of 2000–2001, both of which led the company to the brink of bankruptcy. Long considered by analysts as a top leader in a changing industry, Bryson garnered both praise as a cost-efficient chief executive and criticism from some who believe he turned his back on his environmental concerns.

BATTLES, THEN JOINS UTILITY

Bryson received his law degree from Yale University. In 1969 he and six other staff members of the *Yale Law Journal* founded the Natural Resources Defense Council, a group dedicated to fighting for environmental issues through the courts. In the 1970s Bryson led the legal battle that successfully blocked a proposal to dam the American River in California. In 1976 he was appointed chairman of the Water Resources Board by the governor of California, Jerry Brown, and then became president of the California Public Utilities Commission (PUC) in 1979.

According to business analysts, Bryson's leadership instincts emerged while he was serving on the Public Utilities Commission. Under Bryson the PUC became one of the first commissions in the country to lessen a utility's dependence on kilowatt-hours sold for its ability to garner maximum earnings. The move meant that California utilities were able to invest in energy-saving equipment as part of their rate base, effectively allowing them to profit from conservation. Richard Clarke, then chairman of Pacific Gas and Electric, told Peter Nulty for a *Fortune* magazine article, "Bryson stood above the zealots and visualized a balance of interests" (October 21, 1991).

Bryson left the commission in 1983 and spent a year in private practice as a lawyer. He was then recruited by Edison International and Southern California Edison (SCE), its subsidiary, in 1984. Ironically, as head of the California Public Utilities Commission, he had sued Southern California Edison for $6 million for not negotiating in good faith with nonutility power companies. Nevertheless, the chairman of SCE, Howard Allen, wanted Bryson to join the company to bring a new perspective into the business.

One of Bryson's first assignments was to oversee the creation of Mission Energy, a new unregulated subsidiary of SCE. Mission Energy went on to build small power plants throughout the United States. By 1993 it had become the third-largest independent producer of power that sold electricity under fixed-price contracts to other utilities.

COMBINES CHAIRMANSHIP WITH ENVIRONMENTALISM

Bryson became chairman and chief executive officer of Edison International and Southern California Edison in October 1990. Facing growing concerns from the government and the public about pollution created in the process of providing energy, Bryson supported a strong effort by Edison to promote demand-side management as a conservation and clean-up effort. The approach allowed utilities to factor the cost of conservation efforts into their rate base, thus providing financial support for their efforts to clean up and improve power production. These efforts included replacing inefficient electric motors with efficient ones and offering rebates to consumers who bought more expensive but also more energy-efficient fluorescent lightbulbs. For low-income families, who could not purchase the bulbs, Bryson had SCE provide more than one million bulbs free.

Bryson guided Southern California Edison to an agreement to cut carbon dioxide emissions by 20 percent by the year 2010, making SCE one of the most forward-thinking utility companies in addressing the issue of greenhouse gases. Bryson had company engineers redesign facilities to reduce the strength of electromagnetic fields produced by power lines and substations. He also promoted nontraditional technologies, including electrified trains that would reduce automobile traffic and smog in Los Angeles and efficient photovoltaic cells for solar energy use. However, Wall Street analysts debated whether these environmental policies would improve company earnings.

RESHUFFLES MANAGEMENT TO FACE CHALLENGES

By early 1992 Bryson decided that he wanted more control over Edison's interaction with state regulators and larger corporate power consumers. Edison had enjoyed a large market monopoly but was becoming less dominant because of growing state and federal regulations. In fact, in January 1992 SCE suffered its first annual profit decline in six years with $7.5 billion in revenues, and its share price fell 13 percent. Bryson's decision to take a more hands-on approach led to him realign management and take direct control over several departments that he considered crucial, including regulator affairs and customer services.

Bryson faced several challenges over the next decade, including deregulation that led to stiffer competition. In addition, PUC regulations on bidding for new power plants had further decreased Edison's ability to compete. Edison's shift from being a power supplier to being more of a power transporter meant that it was more susceptible to losing customers if it provided bad customer service.

FACES ENVIRONMENTAL CRITICISMS

Although Bryson kept the company's bottom line squarely in sight, he took a less combative, more conciliatory approach in dealing with regulators and consumer watchdogs. Michael Shames, executive director of Utility Consumers Action Network, told Todd White in the *Los Angeles Business Journal* that Bryson's approach was better for customers and noted, "The personality of John Bryson is slowly creeping its way through the Edison hierarchy" (March 2, 1992). Other environmental activists, however, did not see Bryson and Edison in the same light. They perceived most of the company's decisions as cosmetic damage control meant to bolster the utility's image rather than producing real change, allowing it to continue with antienvironmental activities.

Some environmentalists criticized Bryson and Edison for failing to move quickly to improve its Mohave Generating Station's coal-fired power plant that stood within 100 miles of the Grand Canyon. Environmentalists charged that the plant was responsible for a lot of the haze in the Grand Canyon. Bryson defended the company, saying that it was just one the plant's owners and that Edison had worked hard with the other three owners to put more controls on the plant. In an *Energy Daily* article, Bryson told Howard Buskirk, "I have a personal commitment to . . . environmental values and as a business we have worked hard to find those places where business values and environmental interests intersect" (March 12, 1999).

FACES HARD TIMES

Although Edison managed an improvement in the second quarter of 2000, with $137.2 million in earnings, up from

$128.4 million for the same period the previous year, Bryson and Edison were soon to face an energy crisis that threatened the company's solvency. As a summer heat wave hit California, the company suddenly found itself paying as much as six times more for power than a year earlier, because Edison was buying much of its power supply from other sources and transporting it. The purchase rates for power far exceeded the limits established when the state had deregulated the utility industry in 1996. Edison and other California power companies could not cover their costs and quickly began to lose billions of dollars. Bryson saw that the wholesale market was badly flawed, but he could do little because a price freeze by the California Public Utilities Commission prevented the company from raising the price it charged consumers. As a result, shares of Edison lost 5.7 percent in the third quarter of 2000.

Bryson worked hard to forge a settlement with the California Public Utilities Commission in October 2001, after Edison had threatened to file for bankruptcy and sued the PUC in court. The commission agreed to allow Edison to increase its electric rates to pay off some $3.6 billion of debt acquired during the year-and-half-long electricity crisis in California. For its part Edison agreed not to pay dividends until 2003. Nevertheless, in November the subsidiary Southern California Edison reported a loss of $134 million for the third quarter of 2001.

While Bryson was pleased with the agreement, it soon came under attack when a San Francisco–based consumer rights group sued to overturn it. In August 2003 the California Supreme Court ruled that the settlement was legal, thus effectively saving Edison from bankruptcy. The ruling sent Edison's shares to a near 52-week high of $21.25. In December 2003 Bryson announced that Edison would resume paying dividends on its common stock for the first time since the utility had been pushed to the brink of bankruptcy. Although the 20 cents a share payable on January 31, 2004, to shareholders was less than the 28 cents a share Edison had paid when it had last declared a quarterly dividend in September 2000, analysts saw it as Edison's return to financial stability and a benefit to customers because the company's borrowing costs—which were paid by consumers—would be reduced. The *Knight Ridder/Tribune Business News* quoted Bryson as saying, "This is a day of celebration for us. It's the culmination of a lot of steps."

MANAGEMENT STYLE: ALL HANDS ON DECK

Industry analysts noted that Bryson's efforts to help save Edison from bankruptcy required both his hands-on approach in dealing with company problems and his ability to work with people throughout the organization to get the most out of them. Bryson himself said that one of the keys to his management success was an even temperament and a bright outlook, which he bolstered by doing regular exercise and spending time with his family. He also admitted to being tenacious.

Although Bryson and Edison took a large role in supporting 1996 deregulation plans in California and even helped draft the legislation, Bryson believed that the regulators did not implement the plan properly, which led to problems for both the company and consumers. To counteract the failures, Bryson took a no-nonsense approach. He was quoted in *Utility Business* as saying, "But we just buckle down, do our jobs and deal with the issues" (March 1, 2001).

While he was known for his tenaciousness, Bryson's less-combative approach to dealing with problems may also have helped him and the company forge another agreement with regulators in 2004. The agreement provided for asset growth within the utility, the ability to add to the company's generation capabilities, and the ability to grow through cash redeployment. In addition to his duties at Edison and Southern California Edison, Bryson has been a director of the Boeing Company, the W. M. Keck Foundation, and the Walt Disney Company. He also served on a number of educational, environmental, and other nonprofit boards, including as chairman of the California Business Roundtable and a trustee of Stanford University.

See also entry on Edison International in *International Directory of Company Histories.*

SOURCES FOR FURTHER INFORMATION

Berry, Kate, "Court Ruling on Edison Bailout Could Restore Utility's Health," *Los Angeles Business Journal*, August 18, 2003, p. 29.

Buskirk, Howard, "Environment Is a Personal Issue for Edison International's Bryson," *Energy Daily*, March 12, 1999.

"Crisis Management," *Utility Business*, March 1, 2001, p. 40.

Nulty, Peter, "Finding a Payoff in Environmentalism," *Fortune*, October 21, 1991, p. 79.

"Parent of Southern California Edison to Again Pay Dividends," *Knight Ridder/Tribune Business News*, December 12, 2003.

White, Todd, "Bryson Takes Control of Edison Regulatory Dealings," *Los Angeles Business Journal*, March 2, 1992, p. 1.

—David Petechuk

■■■

Warren E. Buffett

1930–

Berkshire Hathaway Holdings, chairman and chief executive officer

Nationality: American.

Born: August 30, 1930, in Omaha, Nebraska.

Education: Attended University of Pennsylvania; University of Nebraska, BA, 1952; Columbia University, MA, 1953.

Family: Son of Howard Buffett (banker, investment broker, and four-term U.S. representative) and Leila Stahl (clerk, secretary, and homemaker); married Susan Thompson; children: three.

Career: Buffett Partnership, partner, 1956–1969; Berkshire Hathaway, 1969–, chairman and chief executive officer.

Address: Berkshire Hathaway, 1440 Kiewit Plaza, Omaha, Nebraska 68131; http://www.berkshirehathaway.com.

Warren E. Buffett. *AP/Wide World Photos.*

■ Warren E. Buffett was considered the second-wealthiest person in the United States in the early 2000s and the only one to have made his money through stock investing, as president and chief executive officer of Berkshire Hathaway Holdings, the most expensive and profitable listing on the New York Stock Exchange. Buffett, a deceptively shy and self-effacing man, sustained a reputation as the most astute investor in the United States for half of the twentieth century. He had become a genius at value investing and in the critical discernment of corporate talent and management. Conservative to a fault where money was concerned, he sustained a liberal, almost libertarian image in public life. Investors who followed his lead all became comfortably well off or even extraordinarily wealthy. His every investment was founded on an obligation to his investors to outperform every performance indicator.

LAYING THE FOUNDATION

Buffett created Berkshire Hathaway in 1969, after shutting down his 13-year-long partnership with a select group of seven recruited investors (from among his family and friends). This group, formed in 1956, put in a total of $105,000, of which only $100 was Buffett's. By 1962 the group's capital had grown to more than $7 million, more than $1 million of which belonged to Buffett. He charged a fee of only 25 percent of profits above 6 percent, and he would forgo his fee if his performance did not exceed the return on government bonds, which yielded the same 6 percent.

Buffett alone had authority to make investments for the partnership, and he would answer no questions regarding them. New investments were allowed only once or twice annually, and he broadened his investor base as his profits grew, bringing in 90 more limited partners from throughout the nation at $100,000 each. (Laurence Tisch of Loews and CBS put in $300,000.) Buffett incorporated the group as Buffett Partnerships Limited and opened an office in Kiewit Plaza. This location would endure as the headquarters for what was to become Berkshire Hathaway, the most successful investment company in history. Within 10 years Buffett had assets of $44 million, of which nearly $7 million was his. In 1969 he determined that further suitable investments were unavailable and began to liquidate the partnership. By then the assets had grown to $104 million; Buffett's share came to more than $25 million. He had always said that someday he would be wealthy, but for Buffett this was only the beginning.

Buffett had become a master at arbitrage investing, taking large positions in stocks of companies that his research showed to be ripe for mergers, liquidations, or takeovers. He used margin borrowing to gain leverage, which helped him establish partnership positions that put him on corporate boards, where he could exercise influence. Undervalued companies were a specialty, as they proved vulnerable to large investments that enabled him to exert pressure for control. This was his key to gaining control of Berkshire Hathaway, which was to become the keystone of his rise to financial power.

He was joined in his enterprise in 1962 by Charles Munger, who became virtually an alter ego. Munger was possessed of a brilliant mind and a rapier wit and tongue, and the two became partners for over 40 years. During the years of the Buffett Partnership, they invested in a group of stagnant knitting mills that were slowly withering in New England. This was Berkshire Hathaway, which consisted of a struggling milling entity in the town of New Bedford, Massachusetts. Buffett examined the books of the company and began to discern greater value than was evident at first glance. The long history of the fabric industry in New England and the resolute men who had shaped it intrigued Buffett. He set about quietly purchasing blocks of shares as the stock began to slide. An internal fight between relatives over the future of the company played into his hands.

He visited the main plant in New Bedford and was shown the operations by Kenneth Chace. Chace was open and candid and shared with Buffett forty years' worth of corporate statements regarding the company. Buffett continued buying the stock both directly and through brokerage houses, and he saw in Chace a man who was virtually the model of the kind of business personality that interested him. Buffett invested in companies, but he always made sure that he was investing in the right kind of people. Chace was offered the presidency of the company as soon as Buffett took controlling interest. When he liquidated his original partnership, Buffett kept 29 percent of Berkshire, which would become the foundation of his new enterprise, the holding company Berkshire Hathaway.

THE BOY BECOMES THE MAN

When he was asked how he had discerned any value in his investments, Buffett said simply that he read thousands of annual reports and corporate statements. Value Line, Moody's, and Standard and Poor's were the core of his studies, followed by corporate publications. Buffett saw the library as the true basis of anyone's education; the fact that it was cheaper than the cost of attending college warmed his conservative heart even more. Buffett did not like to spend; he was a gatherer and a holder. His childhood was replete with stories of youthful enterprise, beginning at the age of six, when he bought six-packs of cola for 25 cents and then sold individual bottles for 5 cents each. He scoured golf courses for lost balls, which he then sold individually and by the dozen. When his father went to the U.S. Congress, Buffett took over several paper routes conveniently confined to large apartment houses. He kept careful records of all his customers, and when someone did not renew a subscription, he was quick to remind them and even to sell them a competing newspaper.

Buffett was grateful when his father, who had served four terms in the U.S. Congress, lost one of his campaigns, and the family left Washington, D.C. His father was a staunch conservative and a member of the John Birch Society, which was dedicated to combating liberal, socialist, or communist tendencies in society. His father always asked whether legislation "would add or subtract from human liberty." When he returned to Omaha, he put the young Warren to work in his brokerage office, chalking prices and quotations. With his mathematical mind, he enjoyed the job immensely, and the experience was to serve him well in his future career.

Back home in Omaha, Buffett used $1,200 saved from his paper routes to buy 40 acres of land, which he leased out to a farmer. He also developed a keen interest in horse racing. The statistics involved with weights, speed ratings, pace, past performance, and breeding variables intrigued him. He formed a partnership with a friend to print the "Stable Boy's Tip Sheet," sold at Ak-Sar-Ben racetrack. He and a partner also went into the pinball machine business, which generated a nice profit. His first venture into the stock market was at the age of 11, when he bought three shares each of Cities Service stock for his sister and himself at $38 and saw it drop to $27 and then climb to $40, at which point he sold, garnering a profit after costs of $5. The same stock then began to climb, reaching $200. This was a lesson to Buffett about staying in the market.

FOUNDATIONS OF LEARNING

While Buffett admired and loved his father, he tried to stay clear of his mother, who was given to rages that traumatized her children. To keep out of her way, Buffett spent more time in his father's offices. He was fascinated by numbers and money, especially how money could grow through compound interest. The notion of compounding interest never ceased to intrigue and delight him. He could compute and project interest rates off the top of his head in mid-conversation. His lifelong guiding credos were "Number One: Never Lose Money!" and "Number Two: Never Forget Number One!"

Buffett entered the Wharton School of Business at the University of Pennsylvania in 1947 and, after two years, determined that the instructors knew less about finance than he did. He returned to Omaha and finished undergraduate work at the University of Nebraska. Buffett then applied to Harvard graduate school but was denied admission. In the meantime, he had read what was to become a classic, *The Intelligent Investor*, by Benjamin Graham. Graham taught at Columbia University, and Buffett determined to go there to study; he soon became a Graham disciple. Graham believed that profits could be generated through ownership of stocks that were undervalued on the market. His concept was that stocks of companies that were well managed, sound, and grounded in a belief in their product could and should prosper as investments. Buffett's penchant for research and analysis, joined with a dogged conservatism about money, made him a natural believer in the Graham principles. He sought a job in Graham's investment firm, Graham and Newman, but was rejected. Graham was Jewish and was dedicated to providing openings in finance to Jewish students, who had a limited presence in investment houses. So Buffett went back to Omaha to sell stocks for his father.

In 1952 he married Susan Thompson, a student and friend of Buffett's sister at Northwestern University. In the early days of their marriage, he attempted to run a gas station, which did not succeed. In 1954, however, Graham relented and hired Buffett. He stayed with the firm for two years and became immersed in the Graham formula for money management and investments. Then Graham retired and closed down his company, but by then Buffett had generated a net worth of $140,000 and a wealth of knowledge and confidence about value investing. At the age of 26, he returned to Omaha and set about forming his own company, the Buffett Partnership.

PHILOSOPHY

His experience, combined with a reputation for honesty, hard work, and an encyclopedic knowledge of securities and finance stood him in good stead. Buffett possessed an ability to fuse self-interest with a desire to have his investors do well. He did not believe in stock tips, preferring instead that investors do the work, as he did, to find a stock worthy of investment. He believed that all stewardship of funds demanded an accounting and that leaving money at rest was unconscionable when there were opportunities to put it to work.

His personal ethics and business acumen played out in private and in public. He once took umbrage when Boys Town of Omaha continued to plead poverty and exploit orphaned and homeless children to gain contributions, which Buffett found were simply hoarded by the home. He forced an exposé in the Omaha papers that compelled the home to change its practices. As a money manager, he insured that all investments made by Berkshire Hathaway returned cash to the headquarters in Omaha. He had a basic instinct about the capability of people and required only that they submit a monthly financial statement and, in the event of bad news, to report it immediately. His company moved to gain control of Borsheim Jewelry, Scott and Fetzer, Blue Chip Stamps, GEICO and General Reinsurance, Western Financial, the Omaha *Sun Herald*, See's Candies, the Omaha Furniture Mart, Executive Jet, and the *Buffalo News* as well as taking large stakes in Salomon Securities, Coca Cola, McDonald's, and International Bridge. He was always wary of getting a reputation as a liquidator or parasite bent on draining a company of its assets. Only the *Buffalo News* acquisition, through the auspices of Blue Chip Stamps, bore the heavy handprints of a take-no-prisoners capitalist assault.

Buffett and his personal newspaper agent from Omaha, Stanford Lipsey, sought to gain a monopoly on newspapers in the city of Buffalo. He made no secret that challenging the Buffalo *Courier-Express*'s right to control publication of a Sunday edition would inevitably cause that paper's demise. The Sunday edition was the lifeblood of the *Courier*, a morning paper. The *Buffalo Evening News* was constrained as an evening paper with no Sunday edition. The message Buffett gave to the unions at both papers was that their influence and numbers were to be severely curtailed and that their best interests would be served by agreeing to publication of a weekend edition by the *Evening News*. The unions understood their position, and the collapse of the *Courier* soon followed. Buffett, in his triumphant, though hardly his finest, hour, coldly told the existing unions, which had assumed they would be rewarded financially for their help, that the workforce made no worthy contribution to production of profits, given the solitary control of the market by the new *Buffalo News*.

ECONOMIC DISCIPLINE

Buffett's foremost strength was loyalty. He possessed an unyielding faith in his system, and his investors placed great faith in him in return. His admonition "Don't sell B-H stock!" was a watchword never to be taken lightly. His own children disappointed him by selling some of their stock when they could more easily have borrowed against it as collateral. He encouraged his investment partners to hold on to their stakes through good times and bad. Though he insisted on complete control over investment decisions, he also believed that business leaders had to provide an accounting to investors. He despised the practice of doling out options to executives and board members. To him, this was virtual charity. He also did not care for dividend distributions, which represented an inability of the managers to usefully devote the funds to the company's growth.

From his first investing experience in Cities Service to the creation of Berkshire Hathaway, Buffett stayed the course of his convictions. By the early 2000s, he and his wife controlled almost 39 percent of Berkshire Hathaway, some $40 billion in value. Wealth as a way to fund personal expenditures was insignificant to Buffett. It meant more to him to have the ability to buy without actually making a purchase. He continued to live in the house that he had bought for $31,500. He owned just one car, a Lincoln Continental. His only luxury was a personal jet; though he named it *Indefensible*, he justified having it by pointing out that commercial aircraft had become uncomfortable for him after he became well known.

In a speech at the Wharton School of Business (April 21, 1999), Buffett laid out four rules for investment: 1. Understand the business in which you are investing. Look for businesses within a circle of personal competence. 2. Look for sound, fundamental economics. Seek out companies that have a sustainable economic advantage, one he called "a castle with a moat around it," using Coca Cola as an example whose brand name has endured for generations and which could not be bought even for millions of dollars. 3. Find competent leadership. Honest, capable, hardworking leaders are needed to lead companies with a sustainable economic advantage. His instruction to Berkshire Hathaway managers was to "Widen the moat. That keeps the castle valuable." 4. Buy at the right price if you want an investment to pay off. He explained how he had gone through company after company in Moody's investment manuals, searching for those that had large cash values yet were selling at low percentages of that value.

SOCIAL CONCERNS

Buffett did not like to give money away, which meant that he was losing it. His tastes were simple; he ate hamburgers and drank cherry Coke, and he loved to use baseball metaphors in his talks about investing. He gave over $1 million dollars to keep minor league baseball in Omaha. He also helped Grinnell College in Iowa purchase (for $13 million) a public radio station. Two years later, to Buffett's dismay, the college sold it for $48 million dollars. His wife was prone to take up causes in poor neighborhoods and pushed him to donate to them. He did so reluctantly, and inevitably his better sense proved correct, as the money ended up being wasted, in his view. He also supported the formation of a liberal magazine in Washington that proceeded to fail. Abortion and birth control were two of his wife's special projects, as was the welfare of the homeless and street youths. The two formed a group called the Glide Foundation as a vehicle to channel money to that cause. In the early 2000s it seemed that a Buffett foundation would be the eventual beneficiary of his wealth, but Buffett preferred not to think about it.

See also entry on Berkshire Hathaway Inc. in *International Directory of Company Histories.*

SOURCES FOR FURTHER INFORMATION

Bianco, Anthony, "The Warren Buffett You Don't Know," *BusinessWeek Online* July 5, 1999, http://www.businessweek.com/1999/99_27/b3636001.htm.

Cohen, Laurie P., "Buffett Shows Tough Side to Salomon—and Gutfreund," *Wall Street Journal,* April 11, 1988.

Graham, Benjamin, *The Intelligent Investor,* New York: Random House, 1949.

Hagstrom, Robert, Jr., *The Warren Buffett Portfolio,* New York: John Wiley & Sons, 1999.

Kilpatrick, Andrew, *Of Permanent Value: The Story of Warren Buffett,* Birmingham, Ala.: APKE, 1994.

Lewis, Michael, "The Temptation of Warren," *New Republic,* February 17, 1992, pp. 22–25.

Loomis, Carol J., "The Inside Story of Warren Buffett," *Fortune,* April 11, 1988, pp. 21–36.

Lowenstein, Roger, *Buffett: The Making of an American Capitalist,* New York: Random House, 1995.

O'Laughlin, James, *The Real Warren Buffett: Managing Capital, Leading People.* London: Nicholas Brealey Publishing, 2003.

Olson, Chris, "Mrs B Uses Home to Eat and Sleep," *Omaha World-Herald,* October 28, 1984.

Pagel, Al, "Susie Sings for More than Her Supper," *Omaha World-Herald* April 17, 1977.

Pandya, Mikul, "Warren Buffett on Investing and Leadership: 'I'm Wired for This Game,'" *Leadership Digest* April 21, 1999, http://leadership.wharton.upenn.edu/digest/04-99.shtml.

Vick, Timothy, *How to Pick Stocks like Warren Buffett: Profiting from the Bargain Hunting Strategies of the World's Greatest Value Investor,* New York: McGraw-Hill, 2000.

—Jack J. Cardoso

■■■

Steven A. Burd

1949–

President, chief executive officer, and chairman of the board, Safeway

Nationality: American.

Born: 1949, in Valley City, North Dakota.

Education: Carroll College, BS, 1971; University of Wisconsin, MA, 1973.

Family: Married Chris (maiden name unknown); children: two.

Career: Southern Pacific Transportation Company, 1974–1982, marketer; Arthur D. Little, 1982–1987, management consultant; Safeway, 1986–1987, consultant; self-employed, 1987–1991, management consultant; Stop & Shop, 1988–1989, consultant; Fred Meyer, 1989–1990, consultant; Safeway, 1991, consultant; 1992–, president; 1993–, chief executive officer; 1998–, chairman of the board.

Address: Safeway, 5918 Stoneridge Mall Road, Pleasanton, California 94588-3229; http://www.safeway.com.

■ Steven A. Burd was an evangelical Christian and a tough leader, a combination that puzzled his opponents but that put him in the mainstream of a movement that resulted in the election of another evangelical Christian, George W. Bush, as president of the United States in 2000; Burd was one of Bush's most prominent supporters in California. Burd's strength, and perhaps his bane, was his remarkable skill as a micromanager; he could increase sales from a store by merely rearranging the shelving on an aisle, and he could save his company money by adjusting how plastic bags were ordered.

RAILROAD TO CONSULTING

Burd's father was a railroad-yard superintendent, and Burd was raised primarily in Minot, North Dakota. He earned a BS in economics from Carroll College in 1971, and in 1973 he earned an MA in economics from the University of Wisconsin, after which he took a job in marketing with the Southern Pacific Transportation Company.

In 1982 Burd joined the industrial management consulting firm of Arthur D. Little in New York City, where he earned a reputation for fixing broken companies. While at Arthur D. Little he attracted the attention of the management of Kohlberg Kravis Roberts & Company, a firm that specialized in leveraged buyouts of troubled companies. In 1986 Burd worked at Safeway as a management consultant after Kohlberg Kravis Roberts bought the ailing supermarket chain. In 1987 he went into the consulting business for himself while continuing to help Safeway with its organizational problems.

AILING CHAINS

In 1988 Kohlberg Kravis Roberts asked him to consult at Stop & Shop, a chain of stores that was losing its customer base. Burd helped fix the chain's problems with product selection, which had not kept up with changing consumer tastes. In 1989 he went to Oregon to help the local supermarket chain Fred Meyer. Although Burd had no official title and was technically an outsider, as the representative of the parent company, Kohlberg Kravis Roberts, he found he had real muscle behind him when he ordered changes. His most significant contribution to the chain's recovery was to set up management systems to keep track of operating expenses and how supplies related to sales.

By the end of 1990 the mismanagement of Safeway was legendary, with tales of employees driven to suicide and others killed by work-related stress appearing in newspapers and magazines. Employee morale was awful, amid chronic fears of sudden, seemingly arbitrary dismissals and store closings. Safeway's prices were higher than those of its competitors, driving away customers, and it was losing money rapidly. Fresh from his two-year turnaround success at Fred Meyer, Burd was asked to consult again at Safeway.

TURNING SAFEWAY AROUND

When he returned to Safeway, Burd found a paranoid corporate culture, outraged labor unions, customers who felt betrayed by a chain that closed profitable local stores, and an accounting system that was so neglected that management could not know what was making money and what was not.

On October 26, 1992, Kohlberg Kravis Roberts forced Safeway's management to accept Burd as its new president. It had to have been a tough situation for Burd, because the man most widely blamed for Safeway's woes, Peter Magowan, remained chief executive officer (CEO). Magowan was supposedly Burd's superior in the governance of the company, but in terms of micromanagement Burd had few peers, and he soon made his presence felt throughout the company. The chain had 1,100 stores, mostly in the far west of the United States and in Canada. It had nine regional companies, each run independently of the others.

It took Burd years to make the nine divisions partners. He began with seemingly simple matters such as the procurement of plastic bags for bagging groceries. He found that each of the nine companies had its own individual deals with plastic-bag manufacturers, seven altogether. As he would for procurement in general, Burd centralized at corporate headquarters in Oakland, California, the ordering of plastic bags by narrowing the suppliers to two, which translated into a savings of $2.5 million per year. Burd introduced streamlined systems of cost analysis, which also resulted in savings. For example, store managers reported that in-store salad bars were earning 40 percent margins, a big boost for a company that was losing money. Yet when Burd examined the losses due to spoilage and the cost of labor to maintain the salad bars, he discovered that they were actually losing money, so he had them eliminated. For 1992 Safeway grossed $15.2 billion, and its shares sold for about $5.

On April 30, 1993, Burd was appointed CEO as well as president of Safeway, with Magowan remaining as chairman of the board but no longer involved with the day-to-day operations of the company. Burd took to visiting individual stores to study layouts, products, and even the ambient music and lighting. He began adjusting each store's produce section to suit the ethnic preferences of the neighborhood; adding, for example, more mangos in predominantly Hispanic neighborhoods. He was distressed by the amount of produce and other perishables that was spoiling on shelves and pressured store managers to keep their produce fresh. He introduced organic produce to Safeway, reasoning that low prices alone would not make customers loyal and that special, high-quality products could help cement consumer loyalty.

Burd succeeded at lowering shelf prices to make Safeway competitive with other supermarkets. The savings that resulted from his management reforms were used to lower prices further, remodel stores, train employees to give better service, and to introduce the Safeway Select line of premium in-house products, which became very successful at attracting and retaining customers who wanted a brand line they could trust. Although Kohlberg Kravis Roberts had reintroduced Safeway to the stock market in 1990, it still held 67 percent of the shares, and its support helped Burd's reforms stick. By the end of 1993 Safeway had achieved a 1 percent profit margin, about the industry standard, which at the time was regarded as significant evidence of Safeway's new efficiency and improved customer service. On September 7, 1993, Burd was elected to Safeway's board of directors.

In 1995 Burd began the Safeway Category Optimization Process, which considered a store's offerings aisle by aisle rather than by product category. The idea was to put products on the aisles where customers would expect to find them. In 1996 Safeway owned 35 percent of Vons, a southern California supermarket chain. Burd forced a buyout of the remaining 65 percent of shares from a reluctant Vons management. This expanded Safeway's holdings to 1,377 stores, employing 140,000 workers. Customer service improved throughout Safeway's stores, with employees remembering frequent customers by name and escorting customers to the appropriate aisles when they asked about a specific product. Insistence that employees smile at customers may have backfired when some women employees protested that their smiles elicited unwanted interest from male customers. The price per share of Safeway stock rose to $80. Burd believed that enabling employees to invest in Safeway stock was good for the financial health of both the employee and the company, and he believed shares needed to be priced low enough that employees could easily invest in them, so in 1996 he had Safeway split its shares two for one.

By 1997 one-fourth of Safeway's employees owned 15 percent of the company's stock. Burd developed a program of sending anonymous inspectors into individual Safeway stores to check on the service provided to customers. Safeway's private-label plants were selling their products to other Kohlberg Kravis Roberts chains, increasing the profits realized at each plant. Safeway's sales increased 48 percent, and the chain tried to underprice its competitors on average shelf prices. Kohlberg Kravis Roberts lowered its holding of Safeway stock to 50 percent. Safeway netted $1.3 billion in 1997, and Burd sought to use the money to acquire new stores, believing that by increasing its size Safeway would achieve an economy of scale that would allow it to survive the looming challenges of discount chains such as Wal-Mart and Target.

EXPANSION

On May 12, 1998, Burd was elected Safeway's chairman of the board, with Magowan remaining only as a director. This was Burd's chance to fully shake loose from his predecessor. Meanwhile, Kohlberg Kravis Roberts brought its holding in Safeway down to 16 percent, meaning that Burd was largely free of their oversight, too. By October 1998 Safeway's shares were selling for $43.63 (after the split) and its financing seemed strong enough for Burd to make a daring move: In November 1998 Safeway bought Dominick's Finer Food of Illinois for $1.8 billion, consisting of cash and an assumed debt of $646 million. Dominick's had 113 stores and was a chain known for its premium products. Three years earlier the chain had been purchased for $693 million by Yucaipa Companies, owned by Los Angeles magnate Ron Burkle; the sale to Safeway was a big windfall for him, and financial analysts criticized Safeway for paying too much. Dominick's had cost Safeway about $16 million per store, compared with $11.3 million per store in the 1996 Vons deal.

Burd was sure he could turn Dominick's into a powerful asset the way he had made Safeway into one—by careful attention to details. Safeway invested $294 million into improvements at Dominick's, rearranging store layouts, widening aisles, and introducing Safeway's highly successful house brands. Dominick's employees were paid about $3 per hour more than those at local rival Jewel, owned by Albertsons, making it difficult to compete on shelf price. Burd cut staffing at Dominick's to try to lower expenses. The initial results were not good. Customers were unhappy that comfortable old layouts had been replaced by Safeway's open configuration and that Safeway brands had replaced premium name brands. For three consecutive years Dominick's income declined, and its regional market-share fell from 28 percent to 23 percent. To be fair to Burd, high-quality Safeway brands had achieved margins as high as 30 percent in the Vons chain as well as at other Safeway stores, giving reason to expect them to find appreciative buyers in Illinois.

In 1999 Safeway purchased Randall's Food Markets of Texas. To realize quick savings, Safeway reduced the chain's product selection and, as at Dominick's, introduced its house brands to customers unfamiliar with them. At both Dominick's and Randall's understaffing caused long lines at checkout registers, angering customers and lowering employee morale. Burd had long believed that high employee morale would result in better customer service, and he believed Safeway could excel in customer service, making its stores more attractive to shoppers than those of competitors, so the decline in morale was to him a serious problem.

Burd believed that a key asset was store location—placing stores where they were most convenient for shoppers. Thus, he was always looking for ideal store locations. In May 2000, for example, Safeway bought six stores in Houston from Albertsons because they seemed well placed. Burd's aggressive moves to acquire more stores created excitement among investors and journalists, and by 2001 rumors were rife about what his next moves would be. That year Safeway's stock peaked at a little over $60 per share, an increase in value of $10 billion since 1993. The chain's sales had doubled since 1993, and the profit margin was 4 percent, a big increase over 1993.

In February 2001 Safeway bought 11 stores in Arizona from Abco Foods, then purchased the Genuardi's Family Markets supermarket chain in Pennsylvania for $528 million. Genuardi's had 44 stores. Thereafter Genuardi's developed a reputation for poorly stocked shelves and poor produce. Burd viewed Safeway's advantages as location, selection, perishables, and service, but market forces were turning against him. In October 2001 United Food and Commercial Workers Union (UFCW) members struck three Safeway stores in Thunder Bay, Ontario, Canada. Burd said that Safeway had to contain its labor costs in order to compete with challenges from discount chains, and he threatened to close the stores rather than give in. In June 2002, after months of negotiations, he did just that.

In 2002 Safeway took over $1.2 billion in write downs (admitting the value of assets had gone down), a $589 million charge on Dominick's in April (taking a loss in value), and a $788 million charge on Dominick's again in November 2002. In November 2002 Safeway put Dominick's up for sale. Safeway's books valued Dominick's at only $315 million. Ron Burkle's Yucaipa Companies offered Safeway $350 million to buy back Dominick's, but Safeway turned him down; Burkle said he felt slighted by Safeway. In August 2003 Safeway sued Burkle for interfering in negotiations with Dominick's union, costing Safeway a purchaser for the chain because the purchaser could not reach an agreement with the union. Increases in costs of meat and dairy products further hurt Safeway's bottom line, because in a low-inflation economy it would have a hard time justifying increases in prices to its shoppers. Meanwhile, conditions at Genuardi's had deteriorated so badly that Safeway ran newspaper ads apologizing to customers and asking them to forgive Safeway and to try shopping at Genuardi's stores again. For 2002 Safeway grossed $35.7 billion, but it lost $828 million.

RIDING A HURRICANE

Events in 2003-2004 almost cost Burd his career and Safeway its financial strength. Wal-Mart announced that it would open 40 supercenters—stores that sold a full line of groceries as well as Wal-Mart's other offerings—in California. Discount chains in general, but Wal-Mart in particular, worried Burd and other supermarket leaders because they could significantly underprice traditional supermarkets. The biggest advantage for Wal-Mart seemed to be in the cost of labor. Wal-Mart employees were paid on average about $8 per hour less than Safeway employees and received few benefits, whereas Safeway's employees enjoyed some of the best benefits for retail workers anywhere in the country. The charge by the federal government in 2003 that Wal-Mart employed illegal immigrants who received no benefits only heightened the anxiety Wal-Mart caused its competitors.

Burd said that labor costs were a threat to the supermarket industry's survival, that high wages and benefits made it impossible for the chains to compete with Wal-Mart and Target, which were nonunion. On October 11, 2003, the UFCW went on strike against Safeway's Vons stores in southern California. Vons had 326 stores and generated 19 percent of Safeway's sales. In support of Safeway, Albertsons and Ralph's, which was owned by Kroger Company, locked out UFCW workers. Union leaders said they chose to strike only Vons because Vons would have the toughest negotiators. The three supermarket chains made Burd their spokesperson. Mindful of his belief that employee morale translated into customer service, Burd moved to mitigate some of the hardships of striking Vons workers by setting up a fund to aid workers with mortgage bills, car payments, and other expenses, hoping to alleviate the hard feelings that would result from a strike. On October 16, 2003, Burd said the three supermarket chains had made their final offer to the union, declaring that the only changes that could be made to the offer would be to make it "less good" (SignOnSanDiego.com, October 26, 2003). Burd wanted to cut Safeway's contributions to health care from $3.85 per hour worked to $1.35 per hour worked. For its part, the UFCW feared that Safeway could set a precedent that would affect contract negotiations throughout the United States.

Safeway's share price fell to $22 on October 24, 2003, which was still much higher than it had been in 1993. While Burd talked publicly about the long-term future of the industry and labor costs, he was working on revolutionary changes in how the supermarket industry dealt with vendors. For decades supermarket chains charged vendors for shelf space and shelf position; that is, in order to have its products placed in a good position on stores shelves, the vendor would pay the chain in cash. In 2003 Burd was reworking, in his typically meticulous fashion, the relationship between Safeway and vendors, demanding not cash for product placement, but price concessions. He saw Safeway's future in buying products for the lowest real-market value and then passing on the lowered prices to consumers. The prices might not beat those of discount chains, but they could be low enough that with superior products and service Safeway would attract customers away from Wal-Mart and its ilk. Further, he started having stores remodeled to be more comfortable for shoppers, installing imitation wood floors and softer lighting, for example. Market studies had indicated that shoppers found Wal-Mart stores chaotic and anxious; Burd sought to make Safeway's stores welcoming and calming. For 2003 Safeway grossed $35.6 billion but lost $170 million, failing to make a profit because it lost $696 million in the fourth quarter of the year, mostly due to lost revenue from its Vons stores.

The West Coast leader of the UFCW was Sean Harrigan, a friend whom Burkle had helped become president of the California Public Employees Retirement System (CalPERS). In March 2004 CalPERS and the pension funds of New York, Illinois, and Connecticut, each owning shares in Safeway, urged fellow shareholders to oppose Burd during the May 20, 2004, meeting of shareholders. A few financial analysts recommended that their clients vote to oust Burd. In January 2004 about 250 demonstrators tried to march to Burd's home but were stopped by the gates and guards. They prayed and called Burd evil. He was vilified in the press and on Web sites for being greedy, for costing shareholders $20 billion in stock value during a decline since 2001, and for abusing the rights of employees.

The southern California strike was settled in February 2004 in an arbitrated compromise that left workers with wages and benefits higher than in other retail businesses. Safeway's stock value was increasing, to over $28 per share. Shareholders complained that Safeway's board of directors lacked independence and profited from doing business with Safeway. Thus, the board dismissed three directors. Burd and two other longtime directors from the 1980s were targeted in the shareholders meeting, but each was reelected with over 80 percent of the vote. A proposition to separate the offices of CEO and chairman of the board received only 33.2 percent of the vote. Even so, a new position of lead independent director was created to help look after the interests of shareholders.

See also entry on Safeway Inc. in *International Directory of Company Histories.*

SOURCES FOR FURTHER INFORMATION

Barron, Kelly, "The Sam Walton of Supermarkets?" *Forbes,* October 19, 1998, pp. 64–65.

Green, Frank, "The Point Man," *SignOnSanDiego.com,* October 26, 2003, http://www.signonsandiego.com/news/business/20031026-9999_mz1b26point.html.

Weinstein, Steve, "The Resurrection of Safeway," *Progressive Grocer,* January 1997, pp. 16–22.

Whelan, David, "Unsafe at Safeway," *Forbes,* June 7, 2004, pp. 66–68.

—Kirk H. Beetz

■■■

H. Peter Burg

1946–2004

Chairman and chief executive officer, FirstEnergy Corporation

Nationality: American.

Born: April 9, 1946.

Died: January 13, 2004.

Education: University of Akron, BS, MBA.

Family: Married, Eileen (maiden name unknown); children: three.

Career: Ohio Edison, 1968–1973, financial analyst trainee, associate financial analyst, economic analyst, and director of financial studies; 1974–1985, treasurer; 1985–1989, vice president; 1989–1996, senior vice president; 1994–1995, Pennsylvania Power (Ohio Edison subsidiary), interim president; 1996–1999, Ohio Edison, president; 1997, CEO and CFO; FirstEnergy Corporation; 1999–2000, president and CEO; chairman and CEO, 2000–2004.

Awards: University of Akron Alumni Honor Award; University of Akron, Dr. Frank L. Simonetti Distinguished Business Alumni Award, 1992; University of Akron Sports Hall of Fame, 1995; American Red Cross National Volunteer Fundraiser of the Year Award, 2003.

■ Over the three-and-a-half decades of his career, H. Peter Burg rose from being a financial analyst trainee with an Ohio-based electric power company to chairman and CEO of the fifth-largest power system in the nation. While he was highly regarded among industry and community leaders alike, several difficult situations during the final two years of his career drew both governmental and public criticism. Before Burg had an opportunity to see his company through troubled times, he died at age 57 of complications from treatment for leukemia.

SMALL TOWN BOY MAKES THE BIG TIME

Burg grew up in the working-class neighborhood of Goodyear Heights in Akron, Ohio, and attended Saint Vincent High School, where he starred in football and basketball. He earned a BA and MBA from the University of Akron. In 1968, while he was still in college, he began his career with Ohio Edison electric power company in Akron. Working his way through the company's ranks, he became CEO and CFO in 1997. Under his direction, Ohio Edison merged with Cleveland-based Centerior Energy in 1997. Thus, FirstEnergy Corporation was born, and Burg was named president and CEO in 1999. When handing over the reins, Burg's predecessor, Willard Holland, said: "I leave FirstEnergy with the utmost confidence in Pete Burg and his outstanding management team" (*Business Wire*, November 16, 1999). Nine months later the position of chairman was added to Burg's responsibilities.

In August 2000, in an $11 million deal, FirstEnergy bought GPU, a New Jersey-based public utility holding company. The merger doubled FirstEnergy's size. After a brief period as vice chairman, Burg again took the helm as chairman and CEO. FirstEnergy was the fifth-largest investor-owned electric services provider in the United States and the parent company to seven electric utility companies serving 4.3 million customers in Ohio, New Jersey, and Pennsylvania. The company provided natural gas to more than 150,000 customers in the Midwest, conducted natural gas and oil exploration, and was involved in marketing and conveyance of natural gas.

ELECTED TO PRESTIGIOUS PRESIDENCY

On October 18, 2003, as evidence of the respect he had gained in his leadership role at the energy giant, Burg was elected president of the Association of Edison Illuminating Companies (AEIC) by the association's membership. AEIC, established in 1885, was the longest-running association of its kind in the world. Its membership comprised investor-owned electric power corporations in the United States and their international affiliates and included independent power producers, electric utilities, international electric corporations, and companies that generate, transmit, and distribute electric energy.

DIFFICULT TIMES

In 2002 and 2003 Burg and FirstEnergy came under heavy scrutiny. In March 2002 just after the company's stocks hit an all-time closing high, Burg had to shut down the Davis-Besse nuclear power plant near Toledo, Ohio, following the shocking discovery of a boric acid leak that ate almost entirely through a six-inch-thick reactor cap. It was to date the worst such episode at a U.S. nuclear reactor, and the plant's temporary shutdown cost FirstEnergy more than $500 million. Tom Breckenridge, a *Plain Dealer* reporter, wrote that after the incident "FirstEnergy has not been the same" (September 14, 2003). Adding to the company's financial difficulties, a deal to sell four power plants in Ohio for $1.5 billion collapsed.

August 2003 proved to be a particularly difficult month for Burg. First, investors were jolted when earnings were restated back to 2002 and the 2003 earnings forecast also was restated. Second, after having spent millions of dollars between 1984 and 1998 updating a coal-fired power plant in Jefferson County, Ohio, FirstEnergy was cited by a federal judge for failing to install the latest pollution-control equipment, thus violating the federal Clean Air Act. Third, several mishaps that apparently triggered the gigantic power blackout of August 14 were traced to FirstEnergy's Ohio facility. Spanning eight states from New York to Michigan and into Canada and affecting 50 million people, the blackout was to date the worst in North American history, at a cost of more than $7 billion. Fourth, later that month, the company experienced its biggest one-day stock drop—9.3 percent—since its formation in 1997. Then in October, FirstEnergy found itself facing a class action suit from the U.S. District Court of Akron, which charged the company and upper management with violating federal security laws. In November, 100,000 members of the Ohio Citizen Action ecology group demanded Burg's resignation.

FALLOUT FROM THE BLACKOUT

The August 14 blackout brought Burg under attack from many quarters and raised serious questions about his—and his company's—competence. Until his broadcast testimony before the U.S. House Committee on September 4, Burg refused to hold interviews or publicly address questions, giving the company's public relations department that responsibility. Breckenridge noted that Jeffrey Christian, CEO of the executive search firm Christian and Timbers in Cleveland, Ohio, believed that Burg would have done better to have appeared publicly and addressed people's concerns as soon as the lights were back on. As an example, Christian referred to the immediate public appearances of former New York mayor Rudolph Guiliani following the September 11 terrorist attacks on the World Trade Center. Christian noted that Guiliani's high public profile helped calm fears and rebuild confidence. Christian did note, however, that, unlike politicians, company executives are not trained for such events: "[Burg] has to spend more time with government and regulators than with his customers" (Breckenridge, September 14, 2003).

On September 4, 2003, following three weeks of investigation into causes of the power outage, a grim Burg appeared before the Full Committee on Energy and Commerce of the U.S. House of Representatives. In defense of his company, he said: "Clearly, and as we have said from the outset, events on our system, in and of themselves, could not account for the widespread nature of the outage. After much more evaluation, we continue to believe this is true" ("Blackout 2003"). After responding to a barrage of questions with what Breckenridge, in the *Plain Dealer*, called "cordial, cautious answers," Burg was severely berated by Ed Markey, Democratic representative from Massachusetts, who accused Burg of refusing to take responsibility. Breckenridge noted that Markey clearly blamed Burg's company for the mishap: "FirstEnergy should not have a license to drive a car, much less operate nuclear power plants and transmission systems." Before Burg had a chance to respond, the hearing ended. According to Breckenridge, University of Akron president Luis Proenza said: "It was a low blow, political grandstanding." Holland reiterated his initial confidence in Burg, saying that he believed that Burg and his management team were doing a good job.

ILLNESS INTERFERES

In December 2003 Burg temporarily stepped down from his leadership role with FirstEnergy to undergo treatment for recently diagnosed leukemia. On January 12, 2004, just one day before Burg's death of complications relating to that treatment, a *BusinessWeek* article declared Burg one of "the worst managers" in 2003, citing FirstEnergy's predicaments that year but focusing particularly on the August 14 outage. The author noted the fact that a joint report by U.S. and Canadian authorities blamed the blackout on FirstEnergy's failure to trim trees under high-tension power lines, maintain a functional computerized warning system, and adequately train its staff. The author accused Burg of failing to respond when the first signs of trouble appeared: "Not only did FirstEnergy bumble its way to a history-making outage on his watch, but Burg has seemingly written the book on how not to respond in a crisis."

Burg's untimely death meant that he had no opportunity to respond to the criticism. However, a FirstEnergy board member, George M. Smart, did so. In the February 2, 2004, issue of *BusinessWeek*, Smart said that the company's board always had complete confidence in Burg's leadership and that Burg was undeserving of the harsh press he received in the article. "Pete Burg was an excellent manager and helped build First-Energy into one of the five largest investor-owned utilities in the U.S. He provided strong leadership during the past troublesome year and was a man of the highest integrity and honesty."

INDUSTRY AND COMMUNITY PILLAR

Regardless of the difficulties Burg encountered during his final two years with FirstEnergy, he remained highly regarded among his peers, community leaders, friends, and family. In a professional capacity, he served on the boards of the Edison Electric Institute, Energy Insurance Mutual, KeyBank, Nuclear Electric Insurance Limited, the Nuclear Energy Institute, and the Institute of Nuclear Power Operators. His community involvement included serving as steering committee chairman of Team NEO, an organization that helped existing companies expand and attracted new ones to Northeast Ohio, and board member at Akron Children's Hospital, Akron Tomorrow, Catholic Diocese of Cleveland Foundation, Cleveland Tomorrow, Musical Arts Association, Ohio Business Roundtable, Ohio Foundation of Independent Colleges, United Way of Summit County, and the Summit County Chapter of the American Red Cross.

Tom Breckenridge, writing in the *Plain Dealer*, noted that colleagues described Burg as "unflappable, a leader who sees himself as part of a team rather than an autocrat . . . a quick study with numbers and with people . . . a behind-the-scenes civic powerhouse" (September 14, 2003). William Considine, president of Akron Children's Hospital, said of Burg in the Breckenridge article: "Being a leader, being a cool head in a frenzy, that's Pete." M. R. Kropko of the *Sacramento Bee* quoted Anthony J. Alexander, who stepped into Burg's position, as saying: "Pete was a great leader, a man of integrity and ethics, and an outstanding person who dedicated his life to his family, his company, and his community."

See also entry on Ohio Edison Company in *International Directory of Company Histories.*

SOURCES FOR FURTHER INFORMATION

"The Best & Worst Managers of 2003—The Worst Managers," *BusinessWeek Online*, January 12, 2004, http://www.businessweek.com/magazine/content/04_02/b3865726.htm.

"Blackout 2003: How Did It Happen and Why?" Full Committee on Energy and Commerce, September 4, 2003, http://energycommerce.house.gov/108/Hearings/09042003hearing1062/Burg1681.htm.

Breckenridge, Tom, "First Energy's CEO Generates Praise for Work under Pressure," *Plain Dealer*, September 14, 2003.

Kropko, M. R., "FirstEnergy Chairman, CEO H. Peter Burg Dies at 57," *Sacramento Bee*, January 13, 2004.

Smart, George M., "In Defense of Peter Burg's Record," *BusinessWeek Online*, February 2, 2004. http://www.businessweek.com/magazine/content/04_05/c3868022_mz004.htm.

"Willard R. Holland to Retire as Chairman of FirstEnergy Corp." *Business Wire*, November 16, 1999. http://www.findarticles.com/cf_dls/m0EIN/1999_Nov_16/57601072/p1/article.jhtml.

—Marie L. Thompson

■ ■ ■

Antony Burgmans

1947–

Chairman, Unilever N.V.; vice chairman, Unilever PLC

Nationality: Dutch.

Born: February 13, 1947, in Rotterdam, The Netherlands.

Education: University of Stockholm, Sweden, BA (date unknown); University of Lancaster, United Kingdom, MA (date unknown).

Family: Married; children: two.

Career: Lever Brothers, 1972–1982, marketing assistant and marketing and sales positions; Unilever Netherlands, 1982–1985, marketing and sales director; Unilever Germany, 1985–1988, marketing director; Unilever Indonesia, 1988–1990, chairman; Unilever, 1991, director; 1991–1994, personal products coordinator; 1994–1996, European Foods Business; 1996–1998, Business Group president, Ice Cream and Frozen Foods Europe, and chairman, Unilever Europe Committee; Unilever N.V., 1998–1999, vice chairman; 1999–, chairman; Unilever PLC, 1999–, cochairman.

Address: Unilever N.V., Weena 455, 3013AL Rotterdam, the Netherlands; http://www.unilever.com.

■ Antony Burgmans chaired Unilever N.V. and cochaired Unilever PLC, the giant Anglo-Dutch multinational company and largest manufacturer of food and personal-care products in the world. In recognition of his long and distinguished career with the company, in 2003 he was awarded an honorary doctor of laws degree by his alma mater, Lancaster University in the United Kingdom. Oliver Westall, orator at Lancaster Management School's graduation ceremony on December 3, 2003, at which Burgmans received his honorary doctorate, said that Burgmans "demonstrated flair while a student, financing his studies in part by taking cash from faculty at poker." In a more serious vein, Westall singled out three areas in which Burgmans had made outstanding contributions: as one of the top marketing executives in the world, in helping steer Unilever through a major transformation, and in advocating social and ecologic responsibility by big business.

Antony Burgmans. *AP/Wide World Photos.*

ROAD TO INTERNATIONAL ACHIEVEMENT

Burgmans was born in Rotterdam, the Netherlands, and attended Nijenrode, a business school. He studied political and social sciences at Sweden's University of Stockholm and earned a master's degree in business at Lancaster University in the United Kingdom. He began his career in 1972 with Lever Brothers, which had originated in 1884 when William Hesketh Lever, a shopkeeper's son, began selling Sunlight soap in the north of England. Unilever was created in 1930, when Lever merged with the Dutch margarine-manufacturing company Margarine Unie. Through a long succession of mergers, acquisitions, and expansions, Unilever had become, by the end of the 20th century, the largest manufacturer of packaged consumer products in the world. By early 2000 their 1,600 brands included Birds Eye, Dove, Lipton, Sunlight, Wishbone, Sunsilk, Pepsodent, and Bertolli, and they even provided out-of-season fruit and flowers grown in such countries as Kenya to markets throughout Europe.

During his early years in marketing with Unilever, Burgmans contributed substantially to the international success of the company. After spending 1988 through 1990 as chairman of Unilever Indonesia, he returned to the Netherlands, was made a board member and assumed responsibility for the company's international home- and personal-care products operations. Under his guidance the company purchased Chesebo-rough-Ponds. In 1996 Burgmans was given responsibility for ice cream and frozen foods throughout Europe and later that year was appointed chairman of the European Committee with the responsibility of coordinating the company's entire European operations.

After becoming vice chairman with Niall FitzGerald of Unilever PLC in 1999, Burgmans helped implement the company's radical "Path to Growth" strategy. The objective of the five-year plan was to focus on fewer but more profitable brands to stimulate faster economic growth. Burgmans told a reporter for the *Africa News Service* that internal analyses showed that the further the company moved from brands and into businesses, such as shipping lines and chemical manufacturers, the less profitable it became (September 4, 2003). Thus, the decision was made to concentrate on what he called "fast-moving consumer goods." Burgmans explained in an interview with *Nikkei Business* that the three-part plan for growth would reduce Unilever's 1,600 brands to 400; dispose of assets unrelated to the company's strategy while acquiring stronger brands, such as Best Foods, Knorr, Hellmann's, and Ben and Jerry's ice cream; and invest approximately EUR 6 billion to reduce annual costs by about EUR 3 billion (January 6, 2003). Over the course of the program, 100 of Unilever's 350 factories in 90 countries were slated for closure and 25,000 of the 250,000 jobs worldwide for elimination—10 percent of the company's workforce. This transition constituted one of the largest workforce reductions to date by a European company.

A *BBC News* report commented that senior Unilever staff members in the United Kingdom viewed Burgmans as the "hatchet man" (August 21, 2001). When asked during the interview with *Nikkei Business* about the proposed cutbacks, Burgmans responded: "If you plant all the seeds you have in your garden . . . they will not grow well. With ample space . . . they will grow swiftly. The same applies to business. With less brands and use of more management resources for them, the brands are certain to grow" (January 6, 2003).

As the company implemented its strategy, initial reports were positive. By the third quarter of 2003, slightly more than a year before the end of the five-year plan, operating margins had improved, and the sale of 110 less-profitable businesses meant that leading brands represented 92 percent of sales. By the end of the year, however, *Delaney Report* noted that Unilever share prices had dropped drastically and the company had twice lowered its annual growth target for that year (November 24, 2003).

MANAGEMENT STYLE—TYRANNY OR TENACITY?

The *Delaney Report* said that as profits dropped, Burgmans and FitzGerald began to micromanage, traveling to offices around the globe and focusing heavily on cost control. The report quoted a U.S. Unilever source as saying that Burgmans "has been a bully. He has come to [the U.S.] and has been beating up on everybody in North America, telling them they're responsible for [Unilever's] poor growth. He doesn't have the loveliest management style and you can imagine how he has made people feel." While some Unilever employees may have perceived Burgmans's management style as less than positive, Westall described him as tenacious, direct, and straightforward, with the ability to give and, in turn, receive great loyalty. At the ceremony at which Burgmans received his honorary degree, Westall referred to Burgmans's analytical skill as "formidable"—an ability that allowed him to solve complex problems and define a clear course of action. He noted that Burgmans took time to interview individual consumers in Unilever markets worldwide to keep up with consumer needs and trends and to devise strategies by which the company could best meet those needs. His strategy benefited both consumers and the company. "Antony Burgmans's task has been to provide direction and control, to ensure that this vast operation retains efficiency and focus on consumers' requirements. . . . His objective is to clarify Unilever's activities," said Westall.

CONTINUING EDUCATION PROGRAM

Burgmans made a deliberate effort to keep abreast of the fast-changing world of international business marketing, development, and management. In 1987, while he was still marketing director for Unilever Germany but already had been chosen to become chairman of Unilever Indonesia, he took three months off to attend Harvard Business School's Advanced Management Programme (AMP). The 60 participants in the program worked and studied solidly from 6:00 a.m. until 11:00 p.m. and often until midnight. "The programme was designed to put you in the position of chief executive," he told Della Bradshaw of the *Financial Times* (May 19, 2003). He explained that with the international mix (only 50 percent of the class was American), participant interaction created an ideal atmosphere for learning and broadening perspectives.

More than fifteen years later Burgmans still maintained his association with Harvard through his involvement with the school's European research center in Paris and specifically with the finance professor, Dwight Crane, and the dean, Kim Clark. Bradshaw quoted Burgmans as saying: "These are extremely stimulating people who take a deep interest in business." Because he benefited personally from his experience with Harvard, Burgmans firmly believed that business schools encourage executive development. Each year Unilever sent managers to AMPs conducted by prestigious business schools, including IMD Business School in Lausanne, Switzerland, ranked number two of the top 18 non-U.S. business schools in the world. In fact, at the request of Burgmans and FitzGerald, IMD ran "Enterprise for Growth" workshops for Unilever in which one or the other of the vice chairmen participated.

EXTRACURRICULAR ACTIVITIES

In association with his responsibilities at Unilever, Burgmans helped steer the Global Commerce Initiative, the objective of which was to promote broader international trade while encouraging more universally accepted standards for such trade. Burgmans was committed to promoting a higher and more sustainable quality of life throughout the world. "He cannot see business as sustainable if around it, society is falling apart," said Westall (Lancaster University Management School awards ceremony). On the ecology front Burgmans initiated formation of the Marine Stewardship Council, a charity that promoted international standards for sustainable fishing, through partnership between Unilever and the World Wildlife Fund. "No fish, no fish fingers," Burgmans once said.

His dedication to global ecology was also evident in the fact that he chaired the CEO panel at the World Water Forum in the Hague, the Netherlands, in 2000 and again in Osaka, Japan, in 2003. A criterion for sitting on the 13-member panel was environmental consciousness, and the participating 13 companies placed water consciousness high on their corporate agenda, devoting considerable funds to their objective. Burgmans believed that businesses and governments must work hand in hand and set priorities to address the critical issue of fresh water, particularly in third world countries. He pointed out that Unilever built water-treatment plants at their approximately 350 factories worldwide, noting that many other multinational companies work just as hard to address the water issue. He was not as confident when it came to governmental efforts, however. "When I see how much attention is given to the buildup of armies and the purchase of weaponry, I often wonder if the priorities are set correctly," Ruud Kreutzer quoted him as saying (*Water Forum Shimbun*, March 19, 2003). The panel also developed new concepts, entitled the Sustainable Water Facility, for funding water and sanitation efforts and published protocols for sustainable agriculture. Burgmans said that while only 13 companies participated on the panel, they represented the international business community in general. Kreutzer quoted Burgmans: "Our work is supported by hundreds of people behind the table on the podium. I'm not saying there isn't room for improvement, but I can say with confidence the majority of multinationals are behind us, and want to be part of the solution, not part of the problem."

LOVING LIFE

Burgmans's fascination and respect for wildlife gave him a keen interest in ecology, his interest in 16th- and 17th-century Dutch art led to chairmanship of the supervisory board of the Mauritshuis and Bredius Museum in the Hague, and his love of soccer made him an avid fan of Feyenoord. Burgmans was on the ABN AMRO Bank's supervisory board and the Allianz AG's advisory board, and he cochaired the Global Commerce Initiative. His recreation included golf, skiing, and wildlife expeditions with his wife into the African bush. Apart from his native Dutch, Burgmans spoke German, English, a smattering of French, and Bahasa Indonesian.

See also entry on Unilever PLC/Unilever N.V. in *International Directory of Company Histories.*

SOURCES FOR FURTHER INFORMATION

Bradshaw, Della, "Despite a Career of Achievement, the Unilever Chairman Says He Still Has Much to Learn," *Financial Times* (London), May 19, 2003.

Kreutzer, Ruud, "Corporates Come Together for Water Work," *Water Forum Shimbun* March 19, 2003.

"Our Strategy Is Paying Off, Says Unilever," *Africa News Service* September 4, 2003.

"Planting Seeds of Courage in Workers," *Nikkei Business* January 6, 2003.

"Unilever Chief Receives Honorary Degree," http://www.lums.lancs.ac.uk/news/225.

"Unilever Chief's Anti-Bribe Lines," *BBC News* August 21, 2001, http://news.bbc.co.uk/1/hi/business/1501124.stm.

"Unsettled at Unilever, as Upper Management Works to Restore Momentum," *Delaney Report*, November 24, 2003, p. 1.

—Marie L. Thompson

■■■

James Burke

1925–

Former chief executive officer, Johnson & Johnson

Nationality: American.

Born: February 28, 1925, in Rutland, Vermont.

Education: Holy Cross College, BS, 1947; Harvard Business School, MBA, 1949.

Family: Son of a salesman and a homemaker (names unknown); married; children: two.

Career: Procter & Gamble, toilet goods division, 1950–1953; Johnson & Johnson, 1953–1966, product director; 1966–1970, president; 1970–1971, chairman; 1976–1989, CEO.

Awards: Presidential Medal of Freedom, 2000; named one of the "Ten Greatest CEOs of All Time," *Fortune*, 2002.

■ James Burke led the health-care giant Johnson & Johnson for 13 years. During the Tylenol cyanide scare in the early 1980s, Burke's forthrightness and quick action cost the company millions but ultimately saved its reputation and preserved customer faith in the Tylenol brand. Industry analysts consider his response a model for corporate ethics and responsibility. Under Burke's lead Johnson & Johnson grew to be one of the world's leading manufacturers of consumer health-care products.

THE EARLY YEARS

Burke grew up in Rutland,Vermont. He learned much about intellectual discourse from his father, a salesman, who always encouraged debate among his four children. After completing Harvard's MBA program Burke spent a few years at Procter & Gamble before joining Johnson & Johnson in 1953. He quit after just one year, however, because he found the environment and lack of innovation stifling. When he left, Burke suggested that the company needed a new-products division. Three weeks later he was hired back as the new department's head.

James Burke. © *Bettmann/Corbis.*

Burke focused his attention on developing new products. In the early 1950s he tried to market several new cold-care products for children, but they flopped, and he was summoned to the office of CEO Robert Wood Johnson. "I was full of bravado. I thought I was going to get fired," he recalled to *Fortune* (December 26, 1994). Instead, Johnson said, "I want to congratulate you. Business is about taking risk. Keep doing it."

Burke rose through the ranks of the company. In the 1960s he made the company's first forays into television advertising. He also began marketing Tylenol, which had previously been available only to doctors and hospitals, to consumers. From 1976 to 1989 Burke was Johnson & Johnson's chairman and CEO. He turned the company into a $9 billion empire with some 150 subsidiaries. He also made Johnson & Johnson one of the most employee-friendly and well-respected companies in the country.

FACING A CRISIS

In 1982 Burke faced a corporate crisis of monumental proportions. Someone had tainted bottles of Johnson & Johnson's pain reliever Tylenol with cyanide. The cyanide-laced Tylenol killed seven people in the Chicago area. Rather than trying to cover up the story, Burke quickly put out the word across the media, even appearing on several television programs. He warned the public to avoid all Tylenol products until the company had more information about the tampering.

Johnson & Johnson quickly recalled some 31 million bottles of Tylenol—about $100 million worth of product. Within six weeks Burke had devised a plan to put tamper-proof packaging on all Tylenol products. When tainted Tylenol resurfaced a few years later, Burke decided to do away with capsules entirely. Despite the fact that his decision cost the company as much as $150 million, Burke said at a press conference, "we owe it to customers" (*Time*, March 3, 1986). His bold move restored customer confidence. Just one year later Tylenol had regained 90 percent of its market share. The crisis over, Burke was able to turn his attention back to developing new products, such as the antiwrinkle cream Retin-A and disposable contact lenses.

LEADERSHIP STYLE

Never one to fill his staff with employees who were afraid to state their minds, Burke enjoyed having different viewpoints on board. "My style is to encourage controversy and encourage people to say what they think," he told *Fortune* (October 24, 1988). He always wanted his employees to fight for what they believed in, without fear of repercussions. During his career Burke was also on the board of IBM. He headed up the search for that company's chairman and CEO, placing in the top spot in 1993.

After more than thirty-six years with Johnson & Johnson, Burke retired from the company in the spring of 1989. He quickly found another passion—tackling the nation's growing drug problem. He became chairman, and later chairman emeritus, of the Partnership for a Drug-Free America. For his work with the organization Burke was awarded the Presidential Medal of Freedom, the nation's highest civilian honor. He also became chairman of the Business Enterprise Trust, an association committed to fostering corporate ethics.

See also entries on Johnson & Johnson and Procter & Gamble Company in *International Directory of Company Histories.*

SOURCES FOR FURTHER INFORMATION

Ettorre, Barbara, "James Burke: The Fine Art of Leadership," *Management Review*, October 1996, p. 13.

Koepp, Stephen, "Economy & Business: A Hard Decision to Swallow," *Time*, March 3, 1986, p. 59.

Labich, Kenneth, "The Seven Keys to Business Leadership," *Fortune*, October 24, 1988, p. 58.

O'Reilly, Brian, "Managing: J&J Is on a Roll. The World's Largest Health Care Company Says It Puts Profits Last. So Why Are Its Earnings among the Best in the Industry?" *Fortune*, December 26, 1994, p. 178.

—Stephanie Watson

■■■

Ursula Burns

1958–

First president of Business Group Operations, Xerox Corporation

Nationality: American.

Born: September 20, 1958, in New York, New York.

Education: Polytechnic Institute of New York, BS, 1980; Columbia University, MS, 1981.

Family: Married Lloyd Bean (retired Xerox scientist); children: two.

Career: Xerox Corporation, 1981–1991, various positions in planning and product development; 1991, executive assistant to the chairman; 1992–2000, head of several departments; 1999–2000, corporate vice president; 2000–, senior vice president of Corporate Strategic Services; 2001–2002, president of Document Systems Solutions Group; 2002–, first president of Business Group Operations.

Awards: 50 Most Powerful Black Executives in America, *Fortune*, 2002.

Address: Xerox Corporation, 800 Long Ridge Road, Stamford, Connecticut 06904; http://www.xerox.com.

■ Most people outside of Xerox Corporation had no awareness of the existence of Ursula Burns as of 2004. While remaining relatively unknown, Burns steadily gained ground at Xerox for more than two decades, eventually becoming president of Xerox's Business Group Operations. She and the company CEO Anne Mulcahy together helped bring Xerox through a difficult financial period.

A MATH ACE THROUGHOUT SCHOOL

Ursula Burns was born on September 20, 1958, in New York; she grew up in the projects on Delancey Street in Manhattan with her mother and two siblings. Although her father was not a part of the family, she was able to attend private schools because her mother ran a successful day-care center out of her home while also taking in ironing.

Throughout her schooling Burns was a math ace; she eventually earned an engineering degree from the Polytechnic Institute of New York and went on to earn a graduate degree from Columbia University. Xerox Corporation helped pay for part of her tuition; she also had a summer internship with the company in 1980. After Burns received her master's, she went to work for Xerox, where she would remain for more than 20 years.

Burns began working in various engineering positions in the departments of product development and planning. In 1987 she completed a transition to engineering management, rising through the ranks as the head of several different teams, at one point working as executive assistant to the CEO. For a period of time Burns worked for Xerox's London offices. She held several high-level positions before becoming corporate vice president in 1999 and then senior vice president of Strategic Services in 2000. Her climb up the corporate ladder continued when she added president of the Document Systems Solutions Group to her already-lengthy history of job titles in 2001. Many felt her quick rise was a result of affirmative action. Burns addressed the issue when speaking with Cassaundra Hayes of *Black Enterprise*: "The fact that I did it faster than others has nothing to do with my race and gender. It was my performance" (August 1997). Due to her ascent and undeniable influence at Xerox, Burns was ranked 28th on *Fortune* magazine's list of the 50 Most Powerful Black Executives in America.

HELPED BRING XEROX INTO THE BLACK

In the early 2000s Xerox faced financial difficulties. During this time Anne Mulcahy took over as CEO, and Burns was promoted to first president of Xerox's Business Group Operations, becoming the first woman to hold that position. Burns was responsible for the engineering center and five separate divisions; together her group brought in 80 percent of Xerox's profits.

While Mulcahy crisscrossed the country reassuring employees and shareholders and refining a plan to save the company, Burns began implementing the plan and streamlining the company, hiring an outside contractor, Flextronics International, to make many of its products. She successfully negotiated a contract with union workers. Many at the company placed Burns on the list of Mulcahy's potential successors.

With Burns's streamlining and Mulcahy's finesse, Xerox went from a company in trouble to one poised to become the leader in sales in its industry. Though many believed Burns could become the next CEO, others had their doubts. Many believed she needed to learn to strike a balance between micromanaging and undermanaging; she also needed to hone her listening skills, become more visible to investors and others in the industry, and wait until the appropriate time to make decisions rather than relying on initial reports and moving too quickly. Mulcahy told the *New York Times*, "Every weakness is one she can easily fix" (June 1, 2003).

ROSE THROUGH RANKS IN SPITE OF UNCONVENTIONAL WAYS

Burns accomplished what she did by being smart and fearless in setting goals and moving up the corporate ladder. According to a consultant quoted in the *New York Times*, "Even in her 30s Burns was a smart, unconventional thinker who'd embrace new ideas even while older executives at the table were rejecting them" (June 1, 2003).

In addition to her duties at Xerox Burns was a board member of the Rochester Business Alliance, American Express, Boston Scientific Corporation, and the University of Rochester. She was adamant about spending her weekends with her family and only working at home after the children had gone to bed or early in the morning before they had woken up. Burns was married to Lloyd Bean, a retired Xerox scientist whom she met at the company. The couple resided in Rochester, New York, with Bean's son, Malcolm, and their daughter, Melissa.

See also entry on Xerox Corporation in *International Directory of Company Histories.*

SOURCES FOR FURTHER INFORMATION

Deutsch, Claudia H., "An Apparent Heir at Xerox," *New York Times*, June 1, 2003.

Hayes, Cassaundra, "Life atop the Crystal Stair," *Black Enterprise*, February 1998, pp. 107–112.

———, "Ursula M. Burns, Vice President and General Manager Departmental Copier Business," *Black Enterprise*, August 1997, p. 62.

"Xerox Corporation: Ursula M. Burns Named President of Business Group Operations," *Jet*, July 7, 2003, p. 31.

—Ashyia N. Henderson

■■■

Louis C. Camilleri

1957–

President, chief executive officer, and chairman, Altria Group

Nationality: American.

Born: 1957, in Alexandria, Egypt.

Education: University of Lausanne, Switzerland, degree in economics and business administration, 1976.

Family: Married Marjolyn (maiden name unknown).

Career: W.R. Grace & Co., business analyst; Philip Morris Europe, 1978–1986, business development analyst; Philip Morris International, 1982–1986, director of business development and planning; 1986–1990, vice president of the Eastern Europe, Middle East, and Africa region; 1990–1993, vice president of the Central and Eastern Europe region; 1993–1995, senior vice president of the European Union region; 1995, vice president for corporate business strategy; 1995, senior vice president for corporate planning; Kraft Foods International, 1995–1996, president and chief executive officer; Altria Group, 1996–2002, senior vice president and chief financial officer; 2002–, president, CEO, and chairman.

Address: Altria, 120 Park Avenue, New York, New York 10017-5592; http://www.altria.com.

Louis C. Camilleri. © *Najlah Feanny/Corbis SABA.*

■ As president, CEO, and chairman of Altria—formerly called Philip Morris Companies—Louis Camilleri oversaw the world's largest tobacco firm, with 2004 sales of about $81 billion. Altria controlled about half of the U.S. tobacco market, and the Marlboro name was one of the world's most valuable brands. The company also made the Benson & Hedges, Parliament, and Virginia Slims brands. Tobacco, however, was only one part of the company's business. Its Kraft Foods North America unit was the world's second-largest food company (after Nestle) and the largest in the United States, with leading brands such as Jell-O, Kool-Aid, Maxwell House, and Post cereal. Camilleri took the top spot in the company after earning high marks in positions overseas and in various corporate roles. Despite his long career at Philip Morris, however, Camilleri's leadership style remained an enigma. His understated public persona seemed to suit a company whose employees continued to dodge the persistent question "What is it like to work for a company whose primary product causes terminal illness?"

MULTICULTURAL BACKGROUND PRODUCES A GLOBAL EXECUTIVE

Camilleri was the product of a multicultural background. He was born in Alexandria, Egypt, to Maltese parents and left his native country at age five after the Suez crisis. His father left behind his iron- and steel-trading business but found the money to send his son to boarding school in Britain and, years later, to the University of Lausanne in Switzerland.

That background helped prepare Camilleri for a series of overseas positions with Philip Morris. Two years after graduating with a degree in economics, he launched his career at Philip Morris in Switzerland. That position was followed by a series of other international roles that contributed to the tobacco brand's overseas expansion; as head of Eastern European operations in the early 1990s, Camilleri secured a huge market share in that region. Camilleri's vast international experience became a strong business asset. Robert A. Eckert, the CEO of Mattel and former chief of Kraft, remembered watching in awe as Camilleri interacted with executives of the company's European operations, handling several different languages with ease.

BIG TOBACCO UNDER FIRE

In 1998 Camilleri helped negotiate the state lawsuits that contributed to the company's image as the most reviled corporation in the United States. Philip Morris and three rival companies reached settlements with 46 states amounting to nearly $250 billion, money that would help reimburse the cost of treating smoking-related illnesses. On top of that publicity nightmare, the U.S. government filed a massive lawsuit against the tobacco industry to recover health-care costs and profits allegedly derived from fraud.

In 2000 courts awarded $74 billion in punitive damages to Florida smokers, a verdict that Philip Morris vowed to appeal. As of May 2001 the judgment had been stayed pending the outcome of the company's appeal. This ruling was made possible because the tobacco companies named in the suit agreed to pay at least $709 million in the case regardless of the outcome of the appeal. The company, along with the rest of the tobacco industry, claimed that the original verdict would cause bankruptcy, which is not allowed by Florida tort law. Also in 2001 a Los Angeles jury ruled against Philip Morris, awarding Richard Boeken $3 billion in punitive damages, the largest amount ever awarded to an individual. (Later that year Boeken agreed to accept reduced damages of $100 million, but the company nonetheless appealed the reduced amount.)

On the subject of litigation, Camilleri followed the official line stated by his predecessor: Smoking is a lifestyle choice, not unlike eating a Big Mac, hiking Mount Everest, or spending five out of seven nights per week at the local tavern. Camilleri puffed on Marlboro Lights during his interviews. When asked whether he would advise people not to smoke, he responded: "If they're an adult, it's up to them" (*Financial Times*, January 31, 2003).

AN IMAGE MAKEOVER

In November 2001 Philip Morris announced that it would ask shareholders to approve changing the corporate name to Altria Group in April 2002. Camilleri claimed the move had just one motive: to raise Kraft's profile. "All our research showed that the name Philip Morris was solely associated with tobacco. And I would defy you to find anybody who knew that Kraft was part of Philip Morris. To this day, people are shocked and say: 'Really, you have Oreos? I don't believe it'" (*Financial Times*, January 31, 2003).

Many in the industry believed that the benign, almost altruistic-sounding moniker was clearly an attempt by Camilleri to distance his food division from the constant dark cloud that followed tobacco. After all, Philip Morris ranked 59th out of 60 in a Harris Interactive survey on corporate reputations released by the *Wall Street Journal*. Camilleri contended that the company continued to embrace its hallmark brand. "Most of the attacks [say] we are hiding from tobacco. But the fact is we're pretty proud of the Philip Morris name, and that hasn't disappeared. Philip Morris remains the name of tobacco, but it is confined to tobacco. Our vocal critics have now resorted to attacking our motivations rather than our actions. I see that as progress" (*Financial Times*, January 31, 2003).

In another move to burnish his company's image, Camilleri led Philip Morris's negotiations to divest its beer unit, Miller Brewing, which it acquired in two stages in 1968 and 1970. The division, which marketed the low-performing brands Miller Lite and Miller Genuine Draft, had always been a thorn in the company's side, overshadowing any positive press received by the parent company. In May 2002 Philip Morris agreed to sell Miller Brewing to South African Breweries for $3.6 billion in stock.

A NEW MARLBORO MAN RAISES HIS PROFILE

Camilleri had been one of the most accomplished, yet least visible executives in the company. At Philip Morris's Kraft Foods, he rallied for and then helped oversee the $19 billion purchase of Nabisco Holdings Corporation in 2000, the company's biggest acquisition. The deal added brands such as Chips Ahoy!, Oreo, and Ritz to its food portfolio.

In April 2002 Camilleri was elected president and CEO, succeeding Geoffrey C. Bible, who remained chairman until he retired in August of that year. The pressure on Camilleri was considerable. Apart from replacing a passionate predecessor, Camilleri was charged with making peace with his tobacco critics while maintaining the company's 40-year record of at least 15 percent growth in annual per-share earnings. Said Jane Evans of Opnix, a technology company, and a member of the Philip Morris board since 1981: "It's a tough job. But Louis is probably one of the most brilliant individuals I have ever met" (*BusinessWeek*, April 29, 2002). Despite 25 years at the company, however, Camilleri's management style was a mystery, and he clearly lacked the charisma that marked Bible's reign. Camilleri waited nearly a year to give his first interviews.

PLAYING DEFENSE

A year after his appointment, Marlboro's market share was being attacked from every possible angle. Some of that business went to less expensive brands, such as Rave, Hi-Val, and Roger, which saw their market share rise from 3 percent in 1998 to 10 percent in 2002. Camilleri waged a pricing battle with rival R. J. Reynolds while dealing with such formidable overseas competitors as British Tobacco.

But Camilleri faced considerably less pressure in the courts. A U.S. Supreme Court ruling reduced punitive damages and the Illinois Supreme Court announced that it would hear Philip Morris's appeal without an intermediate appellate court review. Camilleri believed the company would win its appeals and that the litigation onslaught would ultimately fizzle. "The plaintiffs' bar is pretty creative—but at one point they're going to run out of creativity. They'll probably set their sights on some other industry" (*Financial Times*, January 31, 2003). A likely new target is the food industry, which faces increased scrutiny in the wake of an obesity epidemic. Camilleri's food empire is well insulated—Kraft launched several healthier products and announced a campaign to educate the public about healthy eating.

A CLOUDY PORTRAIT

As of early 2004 Camilleri had yet to make a definitive impact on his company and its employees. Said one insider who spoke off the record: "He's unbelievably buttoned up, and there isn't a fact that he doesn't look at because he has a great financial mind. But he hasn't stood up and established himself as a leader yet. A lot of people are wondering whether he's capable of showing he can inspire people and create the pieces to create a bigger puzzle" (*Delaney Report*, April 4, 2004).

Outside the company Camilleri faced other hurdles. The world's first public-health treaty, the Framework Convention on Tobacco Control, placed a spotlight on his leadership. Publicly, Camilleri claimed to support the treaty, but he was criticized for his alleged efforts to undermine it. Nonetheless, Camilleri's quiet leadership style seemed beneficial in the litigious environment that continued to require diplomacy.

See also entries on Philip Morris Companies Inc., Nabisco Foods Group, and Kraft Foods Inc. in *International Directory of Company Histories.*

SOURCES FOR FURTHER INFORMATION

Buckley, Neil, "Food for Thought in Marlboro's New Face," *Financial Times*, January 31, 2003, p. 12.

Byrnes, Nanette, Julie Forster, and Christopher Condon, "A New Kind of Marlboro Man," *BusinessWeek*, April 29, 2002.

"A Little Less Love," *Delaney Report*, April 5, 2004, p. 1.

Sellers, Patricia, "Altria's Perfect Storm," *Fortune*, April 28, 2003, p. 96.

—Tim Halpern

■ ■ ■

Lewis B. Campbell

1946–

Chairman, chief executive officer, and president, Textron

Nationality: American.

Born: 1946, in Winchester, Virginia.

Education: Duke University, BSE, 1968.

Family: Married Mary (maiden name unknown); children: three.

Career: General Motors, 1968–1988, various management positions, including general manager of the Flint automobile division, Buick-Oldsmobile-Cadillac Group, and the GMC Truck Division; 1988–1992, vice president; Textron, 1992–1994, executive vice president and COO; 1994–1998, president; 1998, CEO and president; 1999–2001, chairman and CEO; 2001–, chairman, CEO, and president.

Awards: America's Most Powerful People, *Forbes*.

Address: Textron, 40 Westminster Street, Providence, Rhode Island 02903; http://www.textron.com.

■ Lewis B. Campbell first distinguished himself at General Motors Corporation (GM), where he held a number of top management positions over a 24-year period. His overall experience in market-driven business at GM was broad enough for him to be able to transfer his abilities to the nonautomotive sector; after joining Textron as chief operating officer Campbell played a key role in reshaping the company and cleaning out its attic full of acquisitions.

Textron was founded in 1923 as a traditional holding company, purchasing and selling other companies for investment purposes. In his executive capacity at Textron, Campbell led the Transformation Leadership Team, developing a more focused group of core businesses that could better contribute their respective parts toward the betterment of the whole. By the mid-2000s Textron had become a $10 billion company with over 40,000 employees worldwide. Its diversified holdings included familiar brand names such as Bell Helicopter, Cessna aircraft, and E-Z-Go golf carts.

BIG BUSINESS FROM THE BEGINNING

Born in 1946, Campbell eventually received a bachelor's degree in mechanical engineering from Duke University and became a young management intern at General Motors. He attended the Advanced General Management Program sponsored by GM and was sent to Switzerland to attend the Harvard International School. On the automotive fast track—literally and figuratively—over the next 24 years Campbell mastered management responsibilities in various aspects of manufacturing for the Buick-Oldsmobile-Cadillac Group, as well as for the Chevrolet-Pontiac and GMC Truck Divisions. As general manager of the Flint Automotive Group, Campbell was named a corporate vice president at GM in 1988.

A SHARED VISION

Elsewhere James Hardymon had joined Textron in 1989 as the company's new president, having served for 28 years with Emerson Electric. His vision was to design a focused company that would produce consistent growth in a more well-directed fashion. After being named chairman and chief executive officer in 1992, Hardymon recruited Campbell to come aboard as executive vice president and chief operating officer. Both men shared a vision with regard to where they wanted to take Textron and how they needed to get there.

A WHOLE THAT WAS GREATER THAN THE SUM OF THE PARTS

In 1992 Textron acquired Cessna Aircraft. A market leader in the production of light and medium commercial jets, Cessna complimented Textron's defense-related Bell Helicopter business. Throughout the 1990s Campbell and Hardymon divested Textron of noncore businesses—including military contracting, insurance, and consumer products—and with the raised capital acquired more suitable core businesses, whether aircraft, automotive, industrial, or finance related. Such moves strengthened Campbell and Hardymon's objective to develop complimentary divisions that would all contribute toward Textron's growth.

In 1994 Campbell was elected president of Textron; in 1998 he was appointed chief executive officer and was slated to take over Hardymon's position as chairman in 1999. By that time the two men had succeeded in reshaping Textron's portfolio such that 100 percent of its revenues were generated from core businesses. They had also doubled their company's revenue percentages from non-U.S. operations.

CAMPBELL TAKES OVER

In 1999, following Hardymon's retirement, the CEO Campbell added the title of chairman and relinquished the presidency, as had been planned. Determined to maintain the momentum achieved by his predecessor, Campbell played a key role in developing not only corporate strategy but also cohesive management teams. He was chairman of Textron's Management Committee, which comprised the top six executives of the corporation. The committee forged ahead with refinement plans, earmarking top personnel, reshaping the business portfolio, and organizing the company into complimentary enterprise synergies.

Already recognized for his good judgment and high integrity, Campbell regained the additional title of president in 2001. He continued to build on his vision of better fostering Textron's inter- and intrabusiness relations. Satisfied with restricting core operations to four key groups, he turned his attention inward, cleaning up shop and maximizing existing potential rather than acquiring new businesses with merely speculative potential. He increased the number of personnel transfers and promotions between segments and began to standardize compensation and performance tracking across the board.

THE NEW LOOK OF TEXTRON

Campbell's legacy with Textron was the role he played in integrating and transforming the corporation from a large holding company with a portfolio of unrelated businesses from which it hoped to gain profits to a well-structured parent with four core businesses as progeny. The independent businesses all contributed to the whole and operated more like divisions than separate companies. This unification facilitated the movement of key management personnel between businesses and the commutative leveraging of profits and losses.

See also entry on Textron Inc. in *International Directory of Company Histories.*

SOURCES FOR FURTHER INFORMATION

Campbell, Lewis B., "CEO Outlines the Acquisition Strategy for Textron," interview in *Wall Street Transcript*, November 30, 2000, http://www.twst.com/notes/articles/laf211.html.

Gilman, Xandy, "Alumni Profiles: Lewis Campbell," Duke Univerity, Pratt School of Engineering, http://www.pratt.duke.edu/alumni/profiles_campbell.php.

"History," Company Profile, http://www.textron.com/profile/history.html.

"Lewis B. Campbell," Biographies, http://www.textron.com/newsroom/bios/campbell.html.

Nelson, Brett, "The Soul of a New Machine," *Forbes*, June 11, 2001, p. 66.

—Lauri R. Harding

■ ■ ■

Philippe Camus

1948–

Co-CEO, European Aeronautic Defense and Space Company (EADS)

Nationality: French.

Born: June 28, 1948, in Paris, France.

Education: Institut d'Études Politiques de Paris, BA, 1970; École Normale Supérieure, BS, 1971; actuarial sciences degree, 1980.

Career: Caisse des Dépôts et Consignations, financial management department, 1972–1982, controller; Matra Group, 1982–1992, chairman, finance committee; Banque Arjil, 1992–1993, chairman, supervisory board; Lagardère Group, 1993–1998, chairman and managing director, finance committee; Lagardère SCA, 1998–, general partner; European Aeronautic Defense and Space Company (EADS), 1999–, co-CEO.

Awards: Aerospace Laureate, *Aviation Week*, 1989; Chevalier de la Légion d'Honneur, French government, 2001; Bundesverdienstkreuz, German government, 2004.

Address: European Aeronautic Defense and Space Company (EADS) NV, 37, boulevard de Montmorency, 75016 Paris, France; http://www.eads-nv.com.

Philippe Camus. *AP/Wide World Photos.*

■ Philippe Camus was the French leader of the European Aeronautic Defense and Space Company (EADS) in the early 2000s. He shared the company's chief executive position with Rainer Hertrich, who represented the German half of the Franco-German venture. Founded in 1999, the firm strove to be the worlwide leader in the aeronautics and space industry. EADS was well on its way to achieving its goals in the first decade of the 21st century, ranking in first place worldwide in the commercial launcher systems market, in second place in the helicopter, passenger aircraft, and guided missile markets, and in third place in the field of military transport aircraft. EADS was also a leading global supplier of satellites and military aircraft. The company made waves in the early years of the millennium with the double-tiered Airbus A380, a "superjumbo" airplane scheduled for launching in 2006. Credited with orchestrating the secret talks that were held prior to the EADS merger, Camus later cited the successes he had achieved for EADS in his advocacy of multinational collaborative projects.

EDUCATION AND EARLY CAREER

Philippe Camus was born in Paris on June 28, 1948. From 1967 to 1971 he studied economics and finance at the Institut d'Études Politiques de Paris. He also obtained a degree in physics from the École Normale Supérieure (rue d'Ulm) in 1971. In 1972 Camus entered the financial management department of the Caisse des Dépôts et Consignations as a controller. He completed an actuarial degree in 1980.

Camus joined the general management of the Lagardère Group in 1982 after serving the Caisse des Dépôts for 10 years.

The Lagardère Group held stakes in a variety of industries ranging from media to missiles and motor vehicles. Camus became the chairman of the finance committee of the Matra Group, which focused on the automobile industry. Camus also served as chairman of the supervisory board of the Banque Arjil from 1987 to 1993. In 1993 he was appointed chairman and managing director of the finance committee of the Lagardère Group. In addition to Camus's work at Lagardère, he served from 1996 to 2001 as a member of the Conseil des Marchés Financiers, the French supervisory authority for the financial markets.

In 1989 Camus shared the Aerospace Laureate award given by *Aviation Week* with Jean-Luc Lagardère and Jean-Louis Gergorin. The three men were honored for their teamwork and forward-looking plans to establish a multinational European aerospace company.

Camus became a general partner of Lagardère SCA in 1998, forming a triumvirate with the company's head, Jean-Luc Lagardère, and his son Arnaud. The Lagardère SCA group owned the world's largest magazine publisher, Hachette Filipacchi Medias, held a 15 percent stake in EADS, and operated the Matra Automobile Group. Arnaud Lagardère focused on the media portion of the group, while Camus headed the missiles and automotive divisions.

FROM MATRA TO EADS

Lagardère's Matra Defense Unit, Matra Hautes Technologies, merged with the government-owned Aérospatiale in 1999, in effect privatizing the French government's aerospace company. That year Camus became the leader and chairman of the board of the Aérospatiale Matra group. The French government owned 48 percent of Aérospatiale Matra while the Lagardère Group owned 33 percent. The public held a 17 percent stake. At the time, Aérospatiale Matra was first in the worldwide helicopter market and second on the list of missile companies. Aérospatiale Matra became part of EADS when the company was formed later in 1999. EADS was a trinational conglomerate created by DaimlerChrysler Aerospace (DASA, Germany), Aerospatiale Matra (France), and Construcciones Aeronauticas SA (CASA, Spain).

As *BusinessWeek* reported at the time, "EADS represents a personal triumph for the mild-mannered but intense Camus, who will run the company with DASA CEO Rainer Hertrich. Camus was instrumental in the on-again, off-again secret talks with DaimlerChrysler and the French government late last year, which led to the EADS merger. But Camus, a key figure in French aerospace since joining the Matra missile group in 1982, never lost faith that a deal could be hammered out" (*BusinessWeek*, June 19, 2000).

The French government made Camus a chevalier of the Legion of Honor in July 2000. In 2001 he became a director of the Institut d'Expertise et de Prospective (Institute for Consultant Experts and Futurology) of the École Normale Supérieure as well as the president of Groupement des Industries Françaises Aéronautiques et Spatiales (GIFAS), the French aerospace industries association.

In addition to Camus's work with EADS and GIFAS, he served on the boards of directors of Hachette SA; Hachette Distribution Services; Dassault Aviation; Lagardère Active Broadcast; Hachette Filipacchi Médias; *La Provence*; *Nice-Matin*; and Editions P. Amaury. Camus was also a member of the shareholders and remuneration committees of Airbus as well as the manager of the internal control group of Aero Ré.

AIMING FOR WORLD LEADERSHIP

Camus followed his mentor Jean-Luc Lagardère in having high expectations for EADS. "We want to be the world leader," he said during a discussion of EADS' vision for 2008 (*Financial Times Deutschland*, May 12, 2004). In the civilian aerospace industry, the company projected increased revenues with the future launch of its double-tiered Airbus A380. With regard to defense, Camus said that EADS would pay particular attention to Asia. He also stressed the importance of Russia and the United States as markets for the company's expansion. In the United States, the subsidiary EADS-CASA became the official partner of the U.S. Coast Guard.

With regard to Asia, EADS focused on the history of its member companies in working with Singapore and other markets. "We consider Asia to be a top priority and key export market for EADS' future success," Camus said in 2002 (*AviationNow.com*, [date]). The company planned to invest in local companies and form cooperative projects. EADS purchased a stake in the Chinese aerospace firm AviChina in 2003. Camus also announced plans to work with Japanese airplane manufacturers in developing a supersonic jet to replace the Concorde. He said that the market did not currently support the launch of a commercial program but that a future economic upswing would create a renewed demand for faster travel. Camus reported that working groups in Europe and Japan had already thought about collaborating on designing engines for the jet. The "hypersonic" aircraft that he envisioned would fly seven thousand miles nonstop, carrying three hundred passengers—twice the capacity of the Concorde—between Paris and Tokyo within two hours (*BBC News*, November 23, 2003).

AN ADVOCATE OF TRANSATLANTIC COLLABORATION

In the aftermath of the terrorist attack of September 11, 2001, Camus emphasized the need for transatlantic cooperation and exchange of information in the defense industry, calling for a "strong, healthy, and integrated transatlantic defense industrial base through a framework provided by NATO" (*Vital Speeches of the Day*, November 1, 2002).

"Transatlantic allies should foster an environment in which transatlantic and other international industrial partnerships could focus on delivering the most advanced systems in the most cost-effective manner," Camus said in response to threats of a strengthened Buy American Act (*Aviation Week & Space Technology*, November 11, 2003). The Buy American Act requires public institutions to purchase items made in or from supplies provided by the United States prior to considering goods from other counrties. In 2003 and 2004 bills were submitted to congress to amend the Buy American Act to increase the requirement for American-made content, and to tighten the waiver provisions. Camus cited ongoing initiatives supporting the long-term goal of improved transatlantic cooperation, including EADS's ties with Northrop Grumman covering the Global Hawk, an unmanned aerial reconnaissance vehicle, and the Euro Hawk, a European derivative. Camus also referred to the Medium Extended Air Defense system as a prime example of this kind of cooperation. The initiative was a multinational effort on the part of Germany, Italy, and the United States. Another project involved cooperation between France and Italy in developing a multilayer missile defense system.

LOSS OF A MENTOR

Camus, along with EADS and the Lagardère Group, lost his visionary mentor when Jean-Luc Lagardère died in March 2003. Camus and Hertrich paid tribute to Lagardère in a joint press release: "To the staff of EADS, Jean-Luc has represented the body and soul of European aerospace. He has played a key role in almost all major developments of the European aerospace industry in the last 40 years. He has been a driving force for the launch of the A380, which will be the leading aircraft of the 21st century.... Jean-Luc Lagardère provided great leadership for all of us at EADS. He strongly supported us in steering EADS through its first years.... His name will live on as a legend in European business and commerce. And we all will miss his wisdom and focus (March 15, 2003)."

Camus continued to lead the Lagardère Group together with Arnaud Lagardère while Arnaud assumed his father's position on the EADS board. The Matra Automobile Group was closed in 2003.

CARRYING THE TORCH

In 2004 the German government awarded Camus the Bundesverdienstkreuz, which is given to honor significant achievements in politics, business, or culture. Camus viewed the award as an official recognition of the German-French partnership that EADS represented. "After four years we can state that the EADS is a political, business and industrial success," Camus said. "Today this success of German-French cooperation can be recognized as an exemplary model of Europe and the world" (*Presseportal*, May 18, 2004).

With the impending launch of the Airbus A380 and EADS's continued focus on improving its operations and overall efficiency, Camus' goal for the company— to be a leader in everything that flies—certainly appeared to be within reach.

See also entries on European Aeronautic Defence and Space Company EADS N.V. and Hachette S.A. in *International Directory of Company Histories.*

SOURCES FOR FURTHER INFORMATION

Camus, Philippe, "Toward A Common Defense," *Vital Speeches of the Day*, November 1, 2002, pp. 39–44.

"EADS CEO Philippe Camus mit Bundesverdienstkreuz ausgezeichnet," *Presseportal*, May 18, 2004, http://www.presseportal.de/story.htx?nr=557707&action=bigpic&att=29295.

"EADS Mourns the Death of Its Chairman Jean-Luc Lagardère," March 15, 2003, http://www.eads.net/frame/lang/en/1024/xml/content/OF00000000400004/6/12/504126.html.

"EADS setzt sich ambitionierte Ziele," *Financial Times Deutschland*, May 12, 2004, http://www.ftd.de/ub/in/1084269307790.

Eshel, Tamir, "Camus: Planning For Growth in Asia, Despite Global Slow-Down," *AviationNow.com*, February 27, 2002, http://www.aviationweek.com/shownews/02asia1/topsto19_3.htm.

"Firm Considers 'Son of Concorde'," *BBC News*, November 23, 2003, http://news.bbc.co.uk/go/pr/fr/-/1/hi/business/3231354.stm.

Rossant, John, "Special Report: The Stars of Europe—Challengers. Philippe Camus," *BusinessWeek*, June 19, 2000, p. 190.

Sparaco, Pierre, and Michael A. Taverna, "Perched for Recovery," *Aviation Week & Space Technology*, November 11, 2003, pp. 26–27.

—Maike van Wijk

■■■

Michael R. Cannon

1953–

Chief executive officer and president, Solectron Corporation

Nationality: American.

Born: 1953.

Education: Michigan State University, BS; Harvard Business School, Advanced Management Program.

Career: Boeing Company, 1974–1983, engineer, manager; Control Data Corporation/Imprimis Technology, 1983–1993, senior management in technology-components and disk-drive operations, then vice president of Far East operations; IBM, 1993–1996, vice president of worldwide operations, then vice president of mobile and desktop business unit, then vice president of product design; Maxtor Corporation, 1996–2003, CEO and president; Solectron Corporation, 2003–, CEO and president.

Address: Solectron Corporation, 847 Gibraltar Drive, Milpitas, California 95035; http://www.solectron.com.

■ In January 2003 Michael Cannon was named president and chief executive officer of Solectron Corporation, the electronics-manufacturing and supply-chain services provider, bringing with him over 25 years of manufacturing and operations experience. As president and CEO of Maxtor Corporation he had turned around flagging revenues and built the company into an industry leader. Analysts and colleagues alike expressed confidence in Cannon's leadership abilities and strategic skills, with which he would enhance Solectron's market share and profitability.

BUILDING EXPERIENCE IN THE DATA-STORAGE INDUSTRY

After earning a degree in mechanical engineering from Michigan State University, Cannon was hired by Boeing Company, where he worked as an engineer and eventually as a manager in the manufacturing research and development group. After nine years with Boeing, Cannon began his career in the data-storage industry when he was hired by Control Data Corporation (CDC). Cannon spent the next 10 years with CDC and its spin-off Imprimis Technology in a number of senior management positions, gaining exposure to the technology-components and disk-drive operations areas. He also logged relevant experience in Asian manufacturing, spending four years in Singapore as vice president of Far East operations.

In 1993 Cannon joined IBM's Storage Systems Division and over the next three years held various senior management positions, including vice president of worldwide manufacturing, vice president of the Personal Storage Systems Division, and vice president of product design. His work again took him to the Far East, where he established manufacturing sites in Singapore, Thailand, and China, as well as in Hungary. Cannon left a positive mark on IBM's hard-drive business, returning the struggling unit to profitability.

TURNAROUND AT MAXTOR

Cannon was brought on as Maxtor's president and chief executive officer in July 1996. In *VARbusiness* he said of his decision to take the helm of the troubled company, which had been unprofitable for several years, "I was attracted to the turnaround situation and saw tremendous growth opportunity for the company" (January 19, 1998). Cannon planned to cut costs, introduce efficiencies in manufacturing operations, focus on higher-profit desktop drives, and more quickly bring products to the marketplace. He expected employees to consider themselves accountable for the company's performance. Mark Geenan, the president of the consulting company Trend Focus, said of Cannon in *VARbusiness*, "He pushes people to be on schedule, and everything in the company has sped up. Cannon peeled away businesses that didn't make sense and returned to core competencies" (January 19, 1998).

During Cannon's tenure Maxtor made dramatic improvements in spite of a general downturn in the industry. The company's revenues increased significantly, and its base of businesses became more diversified by virtue of internal growth and acquisitions. In 2001 Cannon arranged a merger between Maxtor and the disk-drive maker Quantum Corporation, creating the world's largest disk-drive company in a deal worth an estimated $2.3 billion.

TAKING THE HELM AT SOLECTRON

In 2003 Cannon replaced Koichi Nishimura as Solectron's president and CEO. From the outset he faced challenging issues: a slump in the electronics manufacturing services industry in the early 2000s had had a serious impact on the company, which suffered several consecutive years of losses. Early on Cannon laid out his recovery plans, which included streamlining operations, cutting expenses, and exploring alternate revenue opportunities.

Financial analysts were generally pleased with Cannon's appointment, describing his candor about the company's financial and organizational problems as refreshing. John McManus, the analyst at Needham & Company, told *EBN*, "he recognizes what he has to do, which is the good news" (May 5, 2003). The IDC analyst Kevin Kane remarked in *EBN*, "Cannon has experience in manufacturing operations, specifically in a low-margin, highly competitive business that can't afford inefficiency" (January 13, 2003). Colleagues soon appreciated the assertive actions that Cannon took in order to meet his goals for the company as well as his open line of communication with Solectron clients and employees around the world.

William Hasler, Solectron's chairman of the board, had only positive things to say about Cannon to America's Intelligence Wire. Hasler referred to him as "an individual who truly knows technology and manufacturing. Mike has broad manufacturing and operations experience and has demonstrated a deep-rooted customer-service mindset. Mike has firsthand knowledge of both the challenges and opportunities that Solectron faces, and he is a seasoned and successful veteran of the hard-disk-drive business." Regarding Cannon's management style, Hasler said, "We are confident that Mike possesses the strategic skills and leadership abilities needed to accelerate Solectron's business and complete the company's return to industry-leading profitability and drive the business through a new phase of growth and development. He is a dynamic leader. Mike has the personal force to build on the great things Ko Nishimura has done for the company and make his own mark" (January 7, 2003).

In Cannon's first year with the company, Solectron was the recipient of numerous accolades, including Teradata's Supplier Excellence Award, Cisco System's Transformation and Integration Supplier of the Year, Brocade's Supplier of the Year Award for Customer Focus, and Sun Microsystem's Meritorious Supplier Performance Award for Electronics Manufacturing. Solectron closed its third quarter of fiscal 2004 with sales of $3.04 billion, up 29 percent from the prior year.

In addition to serving on Solectron's board of directors and remaining on the board at Maxtor, Cannon was a director for the Silicon Valley Manufacturing Group and Adobe Systems.

See also entries on Maxtor Corporation and Solectron Corporation in *International Directory of Company Histories.*

SOURCES FOR FURTHER INFORMATION

Doyle, T. C., "Maxtor: Chapter Two," *VARbusiness*, July 22, 2002, p. 104.

"Michael Cannon Joins Solectron as President and CEO Conference Call," America's Intelligence Wire, January 7, 2003.

Ojo, Bolaji, "Solectron New CEO Promises Major Changes," *EBN*, January 13, 2003, p. 10.

Poole, Jackie, "Hard Drives under the Microscope," *VARbusiness*, January 19, 1998, pp. 93–97.

Serant, Claire, "Solectron Taking Pains to Unite Business," *EBN*, May 5, 2003, p. 3.

—Stephanie Dionne Sherk

■■■

Jim Cantalupo

1943–2004

Former chief executive officer, McDonald's Corporation

Nationality: American.

Born: November 14, 1943, in Chicago, Illinois.

Died: April 19, 2004.

Education: University of Illinois–Champaign, BS, 1966.

Family: Son of James Francis Cantalupo and Eileen Patricia Goggin; married Jo Ann Lucero, 1973; children: two.

Career: Arthur Young & Company, 1966–1971, staff accountant; 1971–1974, manager; McDonald's Corporation, 1974–1975, controller; 1975–1981, vice president controller; 1981–1985, senior vice president controller; 1985–1987, senior vice president and zone manager; 1987–2002, president of McDonald's International; 2003–2004, CEO.

Awards: CEO of the Year, Whitney Tilson of the *Motley Fool* investment letter, 2003.

Jim Cantalupo. *AP/Wide World Photos.*

■ James N. (Jim) Cantalupo was brought up in a working-class Chicago family and eventually became an accountant for Arthur Young. He was hired by his top client, McDonald's, in 1974 and worked his way up through the financial ranks to become a zone manager. A no-nonsense, hands-on manager, Cantalupo ran McDonald's International from 1987 to 2002, turning it into a colossus and the very symbol of American global culture. In the final year of his life, after 28 years with the company, he rescued McDonald's from failing sales.

"I LIKE TO WORK": STARTING A NO-NONSENSE CAREER

Cantalupo's father, James, was an optometrist of Italian descent; his mother, Eileen, was Irish American. Cantalupo grew up in military housing projects in the Austin district on Chicago's West Side and from the beginning embodied a very strong work ethic, enormous drive, and a practical approach to life. He began working part-time after school in laundries and grocery stores, managing one of the latter when he was only 20. He left Chicago to attend the University of Illinois at Champaign, where his hard-nosed practicality guided his decisions. Cantalupo wanted to be an architect but looked first and foremost at the bottom line, and career opportunities for architects were somewhat limited. There existed plenty of opportunities for accountants; Cantalupo majored where the money lay. In 1966 he graduated with a bachelor's degree in accounting and shortly afterward became certified as a public accountant.

DISCOVERING THE ARCHES: A LIFETIME CAREER

In 1966 Cantalupo began working for the accounting firm Arthur Young & Company in Chicago. He audited a number of companies, one of which happened to be the rising fast-food franchise McDonald's Corporation. Throughout the 1960s McDonald's opened outlets along the expanding interstate highway network and in burgeoning suburban shopping malls. Cantalupo and McDonald's were impressed with each other; McDonald's offered the 30-year-old Cantalupo an accounting position that would double his salary. Cantalupo accepted the offer.

Through the 1970s and early 1980s Cantalupo rose through the financial ranks of the company, eventually becoming a high-ranking inventory manager. In 1985 he became the manager of one of several U.S. McDonald's zones, by which time the company had grown exponentially from 228 outlets in 1960 to 1,500 outlets, mostly in the United States. In the early 1970s the first outlets opened in Canada, Australia, and Japan, followed by the United Kingdom, Germany, and France. By 1980 McDonald's was becoming a global company and Jim Cantalupo one of its most able managers. Between 1985 and 1987 he was posted to various districts and regions, wherein he gained an in-depth look at the company's worldwide operations.

BUILDING A GLOBAL BRAND: PRESIDENT OF MCDONALD'S INTERNATIONAL

In 1987 Cantalupo became president of McDonald's International. He transformed McDonald's from an American company supporting international outlets into a global company based in the United States. According to John Love's history, *McDonald's: Behind the Arches*, Cantalupo came into office with one main goal: to open as many international outlets as possible. In the early 1990s he had come to recognize "the potential of McDonald's International," which existed thanks to a global infrastructure that by then could "support faster growth in existing markets as well as handle new markets much more efficiently." Cantalupo planned to accelerate that growth.

Under Cantalupo, McDonald's International grew by an astounding 35 percent annually. According to Andrew Serwer of *Fortune* magazine, the company went global with a vengeance. Before Cantalupo took over, annual international sales amounted to $3 billion, producing revenue of $1.8 billion, or a little over a quarter of company revenues; these figures were brought in by 2,600 outlets in some 40 foreign countries. By 1994 4,700 McDonald's International outlets were grossing $11 billion, for net revenues of $3.4 billion, or fully half of all company revenues. Cantalupo ultimately had charge of over 17,000 restaurants in 160 countries upon his 2002 retirement. The one-time Chicago grocer had forged McDonald's International into the most powerful service franchise on the planet and a symbol of the new global economy—and of American globalization as well.

Thomas Friedman of the *New York Times* developed his Golden Arches Theory of Conflict Prevention based upon Cantalupo's achievement. Friedman sampled McDonald's cuisine from Beijing to Cairo to Jerusalem; he noted in *The Lexus and the Olive Tree* that not only did the food taste the same everywhere but "no two countries that both had McDonald's had fought a war against each other" (2000). Friedman took his rather whimsical theory seriously enough to present it to some of Cantalupo's executives in Oak Brook. They agreed with his premise, which underlined the perception that globalization made war more difficult.

CANTALUPO'S THEOREM: HOW MANY MACS DOES A COUNTRY NEED?

In 1994 Cantalupo boasted that he was seizing the global marketplace. He turned McDonald's into a global brand in a class with Coca-Cola, the difference being that McDonald's represented a service, not just a good. What Cantalupo was truly exporting, many argued, was a way of life—one that, a few anti-American and anticapitalist intellectuals notwithstanding, millions wanted.

Cantalupo focused the greatest expansion in the countries seen to be potentially the most receptive to the McDonald's appeal, which were selected on the basis of Cantalupo's Theorem. The theorem answered the question, How many McDonald's outlets can be built in a given country? Cantalupo first divided the population of the given country by 25,000—there was one McDonald's for every 25,000 people in the United States in 1994. He then multiplied this "people ratio" by a second figure, the "income ratio," which was the per capita income of the country divided by $23,120—the American per capita income. The resulting figure was the "penetration potential."

According to this formula, as of 1994 Japan, the number-two market after the United States, afforded the highest market potential of 6,100 new outlets; Of other Western countries, Germany could handle 3,235; France, 2,237; Canada, 1,023; and Australia, 526. China, Russia, and India could open 784, 685, and 489, respectively. South Africa, Colombia, and Pakistan, none of which had a single McDonald's in 1994, could carry 190, 79, and 90, in that order. By the time Cantalupo stepped down in 2002, in most countries only half of this "penetration potential" had been realized.

Each targeted country presented a different challenge. France presented a long history of strong unions, cultural sensitivity, and labor unrest. Germany had strong governmental restrictions on discounts and special promotions. The more McDonald's became a symbol of Americanization, the more consideration of this too became a factor. Mineral water might be put in a French outlet, kosher beef in an Israeli one, and no beef in an Indian one, and restaurants might close five times a day in Egypt and Jordan; but Cantalupo was only willing to bend so much in compromising McDonald's basic formula, which assumed that people the world over wanted the basic American menu. To a large extent the massive success of McDonald's International demonstrated that Cantalupo was right. In *Fortune* magazine, he remarked, "People are more the same than they are different. I don't think our food is seen as American; it's seen as McDonald's" (October 17, 1994).

Cantalupo's growth strategy involved several stages. In stage one Cantalupo's staff would spend 18 months hashing out details concerning locations, real estate, construction, personnel, business law, and host-government relations. In Canada, Britain, Australia, and Europe, McDonald's operated and expanded via wholly owned McDonald's subsidiaries. In Asia Cantalupo worked through joint ventures such as the highly profitable Japanese operation of Den Fujita, which used the McDonald's logo, returning 50 percent of the profits to McDonald's. In Islamic countries such as Saudi Arabia, Cantalupo was reluctant to risk capital and merely licensed the company name to local providers who would follow McDonald's specifications.

In stage two Cantalupo would deploy the McDonald's brand. In Love's book he boasted, "The McDonald's name and what we stand for opens a tremendous number of doors" (1995). The Golden Arches came to symbolize not just a company but an entire culture. Governments supported McDonald's due to its long-term perspective and because they recognized that Cantalupo was "selling a system and not a trademark" (1995). At one time the company opened three stores a day around the globe.

Some believed that the McDonald's product, service, and management philosophy were not simply American but were calculated to Americanize host countries—triggering the outrage of French nationalists such as Jose Bove. In 2000 Bove pillaged a McDonald's outlet in southern France; the fact that his fellow citizens were flocking to the hated symbol of cultural imperialism in greater numbers than any other Europeans enraged him. Part of Cantalupo's management strategy was, somewhat paradoxically, to make his symbol of globalization-cum-Americanization as self-sufficient and home-grown as possible in the host country. Native managers eventually replaced Americans; the beef and chicken would be raised within the country in question.

BUILDING MCWORLD AND BURYING MARX IN THE GLOBAL 1990S

The 1990s provided tremendous opportunities for Cantalupo, who accelerated his global expansion into high gear. The collapse of Soviet communism fully opened doors that Cantalupo had already been making plans to walk through. In 1988 an agreement had been signed permitting the construction of a score of outlets in Moscow. Thirty thousand Russians lined up on January 31, 1990, when the country's first McDonald's opened. Within a year the outlet had served 15 million customers. McDonald's, serving hamburgers not far from Lenin's tomb, was in Russia to stay and to reap every possible advantage.

Russian success prepared Cantalupo for the next step: entering China. Cantalupo saw long-term potential there for up to eight hundred outlets. While perhaps only 150 million Chinese could then afford a Happy Meal, by the time a McDonald's network was in place from Manchuria to Yunnan, the projected market would be 300 million strong. On April 23, 1991, Cantalupo opened the first Chinese McDonald's near one of the busiest intersections in Beijing. During the China venture he displayed his legendary toughness as a manager. In spite of appeals from his meat supplier, who could not meet his deadlines, Cantalupo refused to move the opening date back a single day, knowing that the firm's brand was at stake. The huge outlet, with almost 30 cash registers set up to handle the expected volume, opened on schedule and served 40,000 on the first day.

Poland came next, in June 1992. Customers flocked to the Warsaw outlet, as did potential employees, who worked much harder than their American counterparts; in a country in which the average annual income was $2,000, a "McJob" was something to be desired, not scorned. Within a year Cantalupo oversaw 20 Polish outlets, and he hoped to establish one hundred by 1998. Poland was a classic example of how Cantalupo was able to use the McDonald's brand in entering new countries with minimal risk. As Love's book quoted him: "We can go in with just one restaurant to test a market from a cultural standpoint, to judge local acceptance, and to determine growth rates" (1995).

At first encouraging the self-sufficiency of McDonald's in each country, by the mid-1990s Cantalupo was integrating global purchasing and other operations. McDonald's Corporation began supplying outlets with foodstuffs, allowing them to cut purchasing costs and to slash menu prices in countries with low incomes, preemptively undercutting potential competitors. In the early 1990s Cantalupo was full of optimism for McDonald's International. The period up to 2010 promised to be very exciting and he saw no limits. Additional regions of anticipated expansion included Spain, Italy, Mexico, Brazil, Indonesia, Taiwan, and Hong Kong, as well as Africa and the Arab world.

Cantalupo's triumphal expansion and his experience in cross-cultural management and global integration and purchasing appeared to make him the prime candidate to succeed Michael Quinlan, who had served as the McDonald's CEO from 1987 to 1998. However, in 1998 the board chose the chief financial officer Jack Greenberg to be Quinlan's successor. Greenberg was a financial man, not a burger man, and purchased a number of unrelated businesses seeking to expand McDonald's into other areas.

"TIME FOR A TRIP TO THE WOODSHED": CANTALUPO'S STYLE AS TURNAROUND CEO

The global prosperity of the 1990s gave way to the global recession and jobless recovery of the early 2000s. The Bush administration's War on Terror and invasion of Iraq as well as its general foreign-policy approach all fed a worldwide upsurge of anti-American sentiment. An organized antiglobalization movement often singled out McDonald's as a target of animosity and negative publicity. Outbreaks of mad cow disease in Britain and Canada and a mad cow scare in the United States futher cut into McDonald's profits. On top of all this, consumers were beginning to desire leaner fast foods and were starting to turn away from McDonald's toward Wendy's and other competitors. The rust on the Golden Arches had actually begun to appear in the mid-1990s, when the American market had become saturated and company growth and profits were increasingly concentrated in Cantalupo's foreign operations.

Cantalupo himself was disillusioned by his failure to be named CEO and retired from McDonald's International in 2002. The retirement did not last long. The McDonald's board of directors quickly grew disenchanted with Greenberg; when in the last quarter of 2002 the company posted its first-ever quarterly loss, the board replaced Greenberg with Cantalupo, effective January 1, 2003.

In the half century of the company's history Cantalupo was the fifth McDonald's CEO. As he remarked in *USA Today*, he knew his company was in trouble: "When I took this job, some people sent me condolences instead of congratulations" (December 23, 2003). His planned remedy for the company was simple: go back to basics. People were deserting McDonald's because they wanted healthier food and healthier service. Cantalupo planned to give the customers what they wanted, as well as to provide clean restaurants, prompt service, and warm food. He would sell off Greenberg's acquired businesses, which ate up time and profits. In April 2003 Cantalupo introduced the Premium Salad Line. He and the Australian-born Charles Bell, his chief operating officer, set up the company's first global marketing campaign, with the slogan, "I'm lovin' it."

Cantalupo, a tough and demanding manager, became an even tougher and more demanding CEO, though he remained personal and involved. His motto was "time for a trip to the woodshed." His hands-on, no-nonsense style stemmed partly from his Chicago roots and partly from the regimented McDonald's culture itself. Bell told the *USA Today*, "Jim and I don't get stressed. We give stress" (December 23, 2003). In the age of the Internet, Cantalupo relied on frequent face-to-face meetings with regional, divisional, and national heads. He and Bell would walk into Chicago area outlets unannounced, often finding dirty bathroom floors and toilets, cold food, and rude, slow service. When they did, the local manager was in serious trouble: "When I see something wrong," said Cantalupo, "someone's gonna hear about it" (December 23, 2003). When Jan Fields, president of the Central Region, told Cantalupo it would take her 18 months to revamp her 4,300 stores, Cantalupo demanded she do it in six. Cantalupo was far from a tyrant, however. He posed the harshest questions in the gentlest way, and his strong people skills allowed him to gently persuade those under him to make the most difficult decisions and perform the most difficult tasks.

Under Cantalupo, sales in early 2003 rose by one-third. Profits at first continued to decline, but by the third quarter had risen by 12 percent. Most of the company's turnaround came in the United States. Sales continued to slump in Europe, Latin America, and especially Asia and Africa. By the end of 2003 Cantalupo was being praised in a number of journals for having sharply turned McDonald's around. Some, such as the consultant Whitney Tilson, deemed him to be CEO of the Year. Others were not so optimistic, insisting that some of the changes had actually been initiated under Greenberg and that the company benefited from a weakening dollar.

In Cantalupo's mind 2004 would be very important. By 2005 he hoped that the company would be growing at a steady rate of 5 to 6 percent. Never again, though, would McDonald's overextend itself by opening three thousand outlets per year. Cantalupo's plan—to turn McDonald's around and then resume his retirement in 2006 or 2007, turning the reins over to Bell—was to be interrupted. On April 19, 2004, Cantalupo had a sudden heart attack and died that day. The board chose Bell as his successor; there was little question that the flamboyant Australian would continue to follow the course Cantalupo had charted for the company.

See also entry on McDonald's Corporation in *International Directory of Company Histories.*

SOURCES FOR FURTHER INFORMATION

Buckley, Neil, "McDonald's Earnings Looking 12 Percent Healthier," *Financial Times* (London), October 23, 2003.

Friedman, Thomas L., *The Lexus and the Olive Tree: Understanding Globalization*, New York, N.Y.: Farrar, Strauss & Giroux, 2000.

Gibson, Richard, "McDonald's Is Recuperating, but Full Recovery a Way's Off?" *Wall Street Journal*, December 9, 2003.

Guy, Sandra, "Running McD an Inside Job," *Chicago Sun-Times*, December 8, 2002.

Horovitz, Bruce, "It's Back to Basics for McDonald's," *USA Today*, May 21, 2003.

———, "McDonald's CEO Could Be One to Copy—or Console," *USA Today*, December 23, 2003.

Love, John F., *McDonald's: Behind the Arches*, New York, N.Y.: Bantam Books, 1995.

Serwer, Andrew E., "McDonald's Conquers the World," *Fortune*, October 17, 1994, pp. 103–104, 106, 108, 112, 114, 116.

Tilson, Whitney, "CEO of the Year," *Motley Fool*, October 17, 2003.

—David Charles Lewis

■ ■ ■

Thomas E. Capps

1935–

Chairman and chief executive officer, Dominion Resources

Nationality: American.

Born: October 31, 1935, in Wilmington, North Carolina.

Education: University of North Carolina, BA, 1958; JD, 1965.

Family: Son of Edward S. Capps Jr. and Agnes Rhodes; married Jane Paden, 1963; children: two; married Sandra Lee Hurley; children: four.

Career: U.S. Coast Guard, 1959–1963; private law practice, 1966–1970; Carolina Power and Light, 1970–1974, senior counsel; Boston Edison Company, 1974–1975, vice president and general counsel; Law Firm of Steel Hector and Davis, 1975–1984; Florida Power and Light, chairman of executive committee and general counsel, 1975–1984; Dominion Resources, 1984–1986, executive vice president of subsidiary Virginia Power; 1986–2003, president; 1990–, chief executive officer; 1992–, chairman.

Awards: Inducted into the Greater Richmond, Virginia, Business Hall of Fame, 2001.

Address: Dominion Resources, 120 Tredegar Street, Richmond, Virginia 23219; www.dom.com.

■ As the long-tenured leader of Dominion Resources, Thomas E. Capps developed the company, based in Richmond, Virginia, from a one-dimensional provider of electricity to a multifaceted utility giant with several major subsidiaries. His primary legacy with Dominion was the role he played in leading the company through a successful merger with Consolidated Natural Gas Company (CNG) of Pittsburgh, Pennsylvania, in 1999, which was finalized in 2000. This made Dominion one of the nation's largest utility providers, serving over five million retail energy customers in nine states. Capps coupled his aggressive business instincts and no-nonsense management style with a relaxed, folksy Southern charm that took root in his Carolina childhood. The combination worked. No other principal in Dominion's history did as much for the success of the company in so few years as Capps.

EARLY INFLUENCES

The son of Edward S. Capps Jr. and Agnes Rhodes, Capps was born on October 31, 1935, in Wilmington, North Carolina, an Atlantic coastal community less than 50 miles north of the South Carolina border. He graduated from the University of North Carolina in 1958 with a bachelor's degree in English literature and served as a lieutenant in the U.S. Coast Guard from 1959 to 1963. Capps went back to the University of North Carolina and earned a law degree in 1965. Upon being admitted to the North Carolina Bar Association in 1966, he practiced law in Winston-Salem from 1966 to 1970.

Capps created his own niche market of legal expertise by serving as counsel for a succession of utility power companies, including Carolina Power and Light (1970–1974), Boston Edison (1974–1975), and (as senior partner at Steel Hector and Davis in Miami) Florida Power and Light (1975–1984). He credited Marshall McDonald, former CEO of Florida Power and Light, and T. Justin Moore Jr., former CEO of Virginia Power, as having been mentors and role models for him.

A MARRIAGE OF LEGAL SKILLS, BUSINESS EXPERIENCE, AND CHARM

Having thus become well versed in the legal issues peculiar to public utility companies, Capps joined Virginia Power in 1984 in the capacity of executive vice president. Virginia Power was the principal subsidiary of Dominion Resources, and it was easy for Capps to immediately envision his future career path. The combination of legal savvy within the utilities industry and a keen sense of calculated risk-taking and clearly defined objectives made Capps a formidable leader from the outset. Within two years he was president of the parent company, Dominion Resources.

Moreover, Capps's degrees in English literature and law provided him with enhanced communications skills, including the art of persuasive argument. He also had a well-honed ability to dissect complex matters and extract the most crucial facts and issues. These talents served him well in a then-public industry (utilities) wrought with convoluted state and federal regulations and other red tape. Articulate, bright, and competitive, Capps channeled these talents into a leadership package that, combined with hard work and dedication, spelled certain success.

But Capps was not all fire and brimstone. He had a heavy southern drawl in his speaking voice that slowed and softened his words and made even the most urgent directives more palatable. He was a visible manager on the job, often making casual stops in the offices of employees to inquire about their work or their concerns. His relaxed style was manifested in both his demeanor and dress. Rather than engaging colleagues and associates in the ritualistic practice of executive golf, he often took them fishing or bird hunting instead. In the corporate boardroom he might appear at an important meeting in a tan business suit when the color of the day was navy blue.

A VISION FOR DOMINION

Early on, Capps wanted to prepare Dominion for the competitive world. At the time he joined Dominion's ranks in 1984, the company was only a few years old. Company president William Berry was an early proponent of electric-utility competition. He took his company, then known as Virginia Power, and transformed it to Dominion Resources in 1983, setting up Virginia Power as its subsidiary. The following year Capps came in as vice president of Virginia Power.

As Dominion began to grow, so did the vision that Capps held for its future. Within his first few years he created a finance company and invested in independent power plants selling electricity to the highest bidders in the new deregulated marketplace. But his most far-reaching plan was to bring electricity and natural-gas services under one roof.

Initially, Capps moved into the natural gas-production business. Then he began to envision expanding from production into the transmission and delivery of natural gas products to retail consumers. In 1990 Capps took over as chief executive officer and made the decision to sell Dominion's natural-gas distribution operations. He then formed joint ventures to develop natural gas reserves. Dominion bought three natural gas companies in 1995 and acquired East Midlands Electricity in 1997, which it sold 18 months later. It also bought an Illinois power station in 1998.

After acquiring several smaller utility independents, Capps might have rested on his laurels. But the biggest risk was yet to come. In 1999 Capps made a bid for the Pittsburgh-based Consolidated Natural Gas Company (CNG). He envisioned selling Dominion electricity to CNG customers, and CNG natural gas to Dominion's electricity customers.

But Oliver G. Richard III, chairman of the Columbia Energy Group, outbid him. (A higher bid usually translates into higher price per share for existing shareholders, and normally carries the day when it comes to selling out.) But Capps managed to convince shareholders and CNG's board of directors that there was more to the deal than just the price tag. He shared with them his vision for the future path of Dominion Resources and what it would mean to shareholders and managers. He won them over, and CNG became the crown jewel in Dominion's holdings, making the new conglomerate one of the top electric and gas energy giants in the United States.

By 2004, with Capps at the helm, Dominion had acquired the Millstone nuclear power complex from Northeast Utilities for $1.3 billion and the Louis Dreyfus Natural Gas Corporation, increasing Dominion's natural gas reserves by 60 percent. The company now had nearly eight thousand miles of interstate natural gas pipeline and operated the nation's largest underground natural gas storage system. It served five million retail energy customers in nine states. Moreover, Dominion's strategy included an expansion designed to serve a potential market of more than 50 million homes and businesses.

NOT WITHOUT CONTROVERSY

As with many top decision makers, Capps often operated in an environment of controversy and dissidence. His vision for Dominion set off a highly publicized battle that polarized the board of directors in 1994 and 1995. The particular disagreement that garnered the attention of the media, as well as Virginia regulators, involved Capps and James T. Rhodes, then president of the subsidiary Virginia Power. At issue was Capps's suggestion that more of the company's legal work be brought in-house. At the time, Dominion and Virginia Power were being billed nearly $5 million annually in legal fees from the law firm of another board member and former chairman, T. Justin Moore Jr. The controversy resulted in several directors creating opposing factions among managers, and Rhodes threatened to retire if he had to continue to work for Capps. The escalating friction eventually triggered the involvement of the Virginia State Corporation Commission as well as the state's General Assembly. The matter was resolved when several board directors created a new position to oversee Rhodes and insulate him from Capps. As part of this resolution, the directors also pressured Capps into agreeing to retire as chief executive when he turned 60, in 1995.

But when one of the rival directors had to resign due to health problems, a replacement was quickly named and ultimately provided the swing vote to expand the number of board members from 12 to 15. The three newly created vacancies were filled with supporters of Capps, and he managed to outlast his rivals and maintain his position with Dominion.

WINNERS IN THE END

As a result of Capps's acquisition skills and adaptability in changing markets, Dominion continued to prosper and make money for its investors, which Capps considered the primary role of any corporation. According to his corporate philosophy, once a corporation has made its money, it then can take on the responsibilities of looking after employees and being a good corporate citizen in the community. To that end, Capps was active in many civic organizations, serving on the boards of the Virginia Foundation of Independent Colleges and the College of William and Mary. He also served on the boards of several other corporations. In 2001 Capps was honored by induction into the Richmond, Virginia, Business Hall of Fame, whose inductees are chosen for their outstanding contributions to free enterprise and society. Looking back on his career and successes with Dominion, Capps told a *Richmond Times-Dispatch* reporter that his only regrets were for the things he didn't do. "It's the things we didn't buy. I don't have any bad feeling about anything we acquired," he remarked (May 11, 2001).

See also entry on Dominion Resources, Inc. in *International Directory of Company Histories.*

SOURCES FOR FURTHER INFORMATION

Edwards, Greg, "Focus on Issues Marks CEO of Richmond, Va.-Based Utility," *Richmond Times-Dispatch,* July 14, 1999.

Kaye, Kenneth, "On Speaking Terms: Boardroom Communication," *Corporate Board,* November-December, 1994, p. 5.

Reference Book of Corporate Management, Dun & Bradstreet, 2004 edition.

"Richmond, Va. Business Hall of Fame Gets Three New Members," *Richmond Times-Dispatch,* May 11, 2001.

Zapinski, Ken, "Pittsburgh Post-Gazette Executive in the Spotlight Column," *Pittsburgh Post-Gazette,* July 12, 1999.

—Lauri R. Harding

■■■

Daniel A. Carp

1948–

Chairman and chief executive officer, Eastman Kodak Company

Nationality: American.

Born: May 4, 1948, in Wytheville, Virginia.

Education: Ohio University, BBA, 1970; Rochester Institute of Technology, MBA, 1973; Massachusetts Institute of Technology, MSM, 1988.

Career: Eastman Kodak Company, 1970-1986, various positions in market research and statistical analysis; 1986–1988, assistant general manager of the Latin American Region; 1988–1991, vice president and general manager of European Marketing Companies; 1991, general manager of European Marketing Companies; 1991–1995, general manager of the European, African, and Middle Eastern Region; 1995–1997, executive vice president and assistant chief operating officer; 1997, president and chief operating officer; 2000–2001, president, chief operating officer, and chairman of the board; 2001–, chief executive officer and chairman of the board.

Awards: Sloan Fellow, Massachusetts Institute of Technology, 1987–1988; Human Relations Award, American Jewish Committee Photographic Imaging Division, 1997; Distinguished Alumni of the Year in Business, Rochester Institute of Technology, 1999; Alumni Hall of Distinction, New York State Commission on Independent Colleges and Universities, 2000; Leadership Award, Photographic and Imaging Manufacturers Association, 2001; named one of the ten chief executives in 2001 who has shown outstanding leadership in the area of workplace diversity, CEO Initiative for Diversity Best Practices and the Business Women's Network; Person of the Year, Photo Manufacturers and Dealers Association, 2004.

Address: Eastman Kodak Company, 343 State Street, Rochester, New York 14650; http://www.kodak.com.

Daniel A. Carp. *AP/Wide World Photos.*

■ In 2000 Daniel A. Carp became the chairman of the board and chief executive officer of the Eastman Kodak Company of Rochester, New York, one of the leading photo-imaging corporations in the world, with annual revenues of more than $13 billion. A career-long Kodak employee, he climbed the corporate ladder gradually, filling positions in both the United States and abroad before entering the elite circle of top management in 1995 and ascending to the top position. Carp's leadership of Kodak was marked by several major initiatives that made him the object of much criticism from some shareholders and financial analysts. He was determined to maintain the company's long dominance in consumer photo-imaging as the industry passed through a radical transition from traditional photography (that is, the exposure of chemically treated film to light) to filmless digital photography (that is, the creation of pixels by computer program). At the same time, he led Kodak in a marketing and manufacturing push designed to make the company dominant in the enormous emerging consumer markets of Asia, especially China, where traditional photographic methods are likely to remain the norm in consumer imaging for decades to come.

A ONE-COMPANY MAN

Daniel Carp was born and raised in Wytheville, Virginia, a town of about eight thousand located in the southwestern corner of the state in the Blue Ridge Mountain region. He attended public schools, graduating from George Wythe High School in 1966. Little is known about his upbringing or family life, subjects he chose not to discuss in public. An early and steady desire for a career in business is evident in his academic record. As a student at Ohio University in Athens, a school known for its broad-based offerings in the liberal arts, he chose to pursue a strictly focused bachelor of business administration degree in quantitative analysis, which he received in 1970. Within months of graduation he secured a job with Kodak as a statistical analyst in Rochester. As an entry-level executive, he continued his studies in business at the Rochester Institute of Technology, earning an MBA. Carp's long climb through the ranks of "Big Yellow," as Kodak is sometimes called, was a gradual one that can be described in terms of three distinct career periods. From 1970 to 1986 he gained hands-on experience and increasing responsibility in market research, business planning, marketing management, and line-of-business management in Kodak's U.S. and Canadian operations, rising through the ranks of middle management to hold such positions as manager of sales for Kodak Canada and general manager of Kodak's Consumer Electronics Division. A second phase, from 1986 to 1995, was international in character. It included stints for Carp in high-level management positions with Kodak's divisions in the Latin American region (1986–1988) and the European, African, and Middle Eastern region (1989–1995).

Carp's success on the world marketing stage in battling Kodak's arch rival, Fuji Corporation of Japan, clearly won the notice of top management and gained him consideration for further advancement. In 1987 he began a year as a Sloan Fellow at the Massachusetts Institute of Technology's Sloan School of Management, where he earned a second graduate degree, a master of science in management, which served as a credential considered appropriate to the huge corporation's highest echelons. A third phase, in which Carp was integrated into Kodak's inner circle of top management, began in 1995 when he was recalled to Rochester from the London regional office and promoted to executive vice president. Within two years he took the positions of president and chief operating officer of the company and was elected to a seat on the board of directors as well. Carp became board chairman on January 1, 2000, thus consolidating his position of optimal executive power in the publicly held company. His predecessor, George Fisher, in handing over power to Carp, praised him for his "expansive focus on customer needs" and his "strategic understanding of growth opportunities" (Deutsch, June 10, 1999). His quick movement to the top in the late 1990s was attributed to the anomalous position in which the company found itself. It was successfully dominating an industry that showed signs of disappearing. Carp was brought in to save the company from a catastrophe attributable to its own success.

ASTRIDE A TECHNOLOGICAL CUSP

Carp was given a mandate to do what he thought necessary to make the venerable company, which had launched the mass market for home photography with its Brownie camera in 1900, into a state-of-the-art imaging corporation capable of achieving similar dominance in the emergent mass market for digital photography. Carp made his intentions clear. Within weeks of taking office he noted in an interview with *Industry Week* that Kodak's founder, George Eastman, had first gained a dominant position for the company by developing new technologies and that he was prepared to follow the founder's example. "R & D [research and development] is at the core of what is going on in our company, probably more so today than at any time in our history," he said (July 17, 2000). He knew that there would be opposition within the company but promised to be a devil's advocate for good ideas, whether or not they made it through the corporate bureaucracy. According to Carp, once an idea had proved viable to him, "it is incumbent on the CEO to find a new way to take [it] to the marketplace" (July 17, 2000). In the broadest sense, the "idea" that Carp had to take to the marketplace was digital photography.

FROM PICTURES TO PIXELS

Though Kodak claims to have invented the digital camera in 1980, the company did little to capitalize on it for almost two decades. When Carp became CEO, Kodak had just completed a record year for traditional silver-halide film production, manufacturing more than one billion rolls in 1999 and utterly dominating the U.S. market with more than a two-thirds share of retail sales, while filmless digital photography accounted for only about 10 percent of the American home-imaging market. Carp, however, saw past those figures to the belief that a mass public switch from film-based to digital photography was inevitable. Given Kodak's heavy investment in the former, the company had no choice, in his view, but to change its core business to meet the demands of this paradigm shift in home imaging. His experience in marketing was likely a factor in this vision.

Whatever else can be said about the two imaging processes, digital offers more convenience to the consumer as well as lower cost at just about every step. Digital requires no purchase of film, nor does it require the time or expense of a developing process. Instead, consumers can view images on a personal computer or other video screen that they probably already own. If traditional photographic finished products are desired, the digital photographer has the option to print or to choose not to. Unlimited numbers of free electronic copies can be produced and delivered by e-mail at no expense. For many households already equipped with a personal computer, digital photography is the logical choice. Longtime Kodak executives, including some who had weathered the storms of previous technology fads, notably, the Polaroid "instant picture," remained skeptical. There was even less enthusiasm from those investors more interested in short-term profits than in seeing the company go through an expensive retooling process to become a primarily digital company, a process that Carp estimated could cost as much as $16 billion.

Carp faced the enormous task of keeping the company astride both sides of this technological cusp in home imaging, even though he had no doubt about the eventual outcome of the struggle between the two technologies. While he was eager to capitalize on the value of the company's history and reputation as the leading force in home imaging, he put sentimentality about the past aside, lest the company be perceived as a doddering old behemoth trapped in a "sunset industry." For example, while Kodak continued to manufacture hundreds of millions of rolls of film each year, the company gradually phased out the use of its Kodachrome film brand in advertising, so as not to be identified as a predigital vendor by consumers switching to digital cameras. Carp liked to describe the change in his industry as an exciting opportunity rather than a threat. "Kodak is convinced that there has never been a better time to be in the picture business. . . . Digital can change the way people take and use pictures. Suddenly there are no boundaries to how often you can take pictures because cost and availability are no longer issues," he said in a 2000 speech to the Advance Digital Photography forum in Boston (April 10, 2000). Rather than wait for the public to make the leap, Carp believed that Kodak should be a driving force in bringing about consumer conversions to digital.

Though the price of Kodak shares suffered and the value of its dividends to shareholders dropped precipitously, Carp mobilized the company to implement his digitalization program. Before 1998 Kodak did not have a digital business to report on. By the end of 2003 it was doing one billion dollars per year of business in digital products and services, including its online photofinishing site, Ofoto.com. In addition to manufacturing its own lines of digital cameras and home-printer docks, Kodak emerged as the world's leading supplier of paper stocks, photofinishing products, and other materials used for commercial and home digital-image printing. Carp struck up corporate partnerships to capitalize on the power of the Kodak brand. Lexmark, for example, licensed the Kodak name for a line of its scanners and printers. Sanyo Electric Company and Kodak launched a joint venture to manufacture active-matrix organic light-emitting diode display screens. In the growing area of medical and dental imaging, Kodak worked on a variety of projects with GE Medical Systems. Retailing partners were outfitted with do-it-yourself Kodak picture kiosks and professional digital minilabs that can conveniently scan traditional pictures into digital documents and and convert digital shots into elegantly printed hard copy. One of Carp's first decisions as CEO was to have Kodak join the International Imaging Industry Association (IIIA), whose members included Fuji and Agfa-Gevaert, its two biggest worldwide competitors. Kodak then entered into an IIIA agreement providing for industry-wide compatibility of digital-imaging products. Kodak's movement from labor-intensive photographic equipment manufacturing to the service-oriented digital imaging industry occasioned sharp reductions in its workforce. In January 2004 Carp announced that Kodak would be cutting between 20 and 25 percent of its worldwide employees.

LEADER OF A WORLDWIDE COMPANY

While the digitalization of Kodak's consumer imaging business was the centerpiece of Carp's strategy, it was by no means his entire plan for Kodak. Emerging industrial societies, such as China and India, where home computers were rare and digital cameras too expensive for all but the wealthy, had large populations of newly urbanized consumers who had never owned a camera or taken a photograph. These countries represented an enormous potential market for traditional photochemical imaging, precisely the product line that Kodak had been delivering best for more than a century. In 2000 Carp journeyed to China and cemented ties between the company and Chinese leaders. Carp served as a member of the U.S.-China Business Council and joined the advisory board of the Tsinghua University School of Economics and Management. Kodak, which did business in China before the Communist revolution of 1949, reentered the Chinese market through its purchase of a stake in Lucky Film, China's largest film company. It provided technological and marketing assistance to Lucky Film in creating a line of entry-level cameras and film products. As consumers "graduate" to more advanced equipment they are sold products bearing the Kodak brand name. In 2003 China became Kodak's second largest market (after the U.S.) in terms of gross sales. Carp wanted Kodak to be there when China was ready to make the leap to digital.

Carp was a strong and vocal advocate for diversity in the workplace. His hiring of Patricia F. Russo as his second in command at Kodak in April 2001 was unprecedented at Kodak, long considered an "old boy" company. He was a trustee of the George Eastman House, the Rochester photography museum endowed by Kodak's founder; a trustee of the Malcolm Baldridge Foundation National Quality Award; a member of the board of directors of Africare; and a member of the Business Roundtable. He served on the Business Steering Committee of the Global Business Dialog on Electronic Commerce and was an executive member of the World Business Council for Sustainable Development. He was known to enjoy watching and playing basketball. Asked by the *Rochester Democrat and Chronicle* how he felt about being in charge of making such radical changes in the company he had been with for most of his life, he said, "I am excited about this being on my watch. I wouldn't want to be anywhere else. I am glad I am here doing this. It's a relief that it is now obvious where the film business is going and we can get on with what we have to do to make the company stronger" (October 3, 2003).

See also entry on Eastman Kodak Company in *International Directory of Company Histories.*

SOURCES FOR FURTHER INFORMATION

Deutsch, Claudia H., "Fisher Will Yield as Kodak's Chief Executive," *New York Times*, June 10, 1999.

"Exclusive Interview: Kodak CEO Dan Carp," *Rochester Democrat and Chronicle*, October 3, 2003.

"Kodak: The CEO vs. the Gadfly," *Fortune*, January 12, 2004, pp. 84–86, 88, 90, 92.

"Kodak Chooses Dan Carp to Succeed George Fisher as CEO," Eastman Kodak, June 9, 1999. http://www.kodak.com.

"Kodak Defines Need to Drive Mass-Market Acceptance of Digital Photography," Kodak press release, June 10, 2000, http://search.netscape.com/ns/boomframe.jsp?query=%22advance+digital+photography+forum%22&page=1&offset=1&result_url=redir%3Fsrc%3Dwebsearch%26requestId%3D7dfd8f69978048b0%26clickedItemRank%3D1%26userQuery%3D%2522advance%2Bdigital%2Bphotography%2Bforum%2522%26clickedItemURN%3Dhttp%253A%252F%252Fwww.dpreview.com%252Fnews%252F0004%252F00041001kodakondigicams.asp%26invocationType%3D-%26fromPage%3DNSBoom%26amp%3BampTest%3D1&remove_url=http%3A%2F%2Fwww.dpreview.com%2Fnews%2F0004%2F00041001kodakondigicams.asp.

"Kodak's Photo Op," *Time*, April 30, 2001, pp. 46–47.

Teresko, John, "Kodak's New Image," *Industry Week*, July 17, 2000, pp. 38–44.

—David Marc

■ ■ ■

Peter Cartwright

1930–

Chairman, chief executive officer, and president, Calpine

Nationality: American.

Born: January 1930, in New York.

Education: Princeton University, BS, 1952; Columbia University, MS, 1953.

Family: Married June (maiden name unknown); children: four.

Career: General Electric, 1960–1979, worked in nuclear plant construction, project management, and new business development; Gibbs and Hill, 1979–1984, engineering consultant; Calpine, 1984–, chairman, chief executive officer, and president.

Address: Calpine, 50 West San Fernando Street, San Jose, California 95113; http://www.calpine.com.

■ Peter Cartwright cofounded Calpine Corporation in 1984 after a long career in engineering that included building nuclear power plants around the world for General Electric. Cartwright established Calpine as a firm that provided management services to independent power generation companies but went on to build Calpine into one of the largest independent power companies in the United States and the largest provider of environmentally cleaner "green power." Considered by many industry analysts as a visionary in the modern power industry, colleagues and employees note that Cartwright fostered the company's growth by rewarding creativity and embracing risk.

SEES OPPORTUNITY

Cartwright served in the U.S. Navy Civil Engineer Corps after receiving his master's degree in engineering from Columbia University. He joined General Electric in 1960 and worked for the company for the next 19 years, spending six of those years overseas. His responsibilities included plant construction, project management, and new business development. He oversaw the company's technology development and licensing programs in Europe and Japan and worked in its nuclear energy division. In 1979 he left to join the New York–based engineering company Gibbs and Hill. He established the company's western regional office, which provided engineering services primarily for power plants.

In 1984 Cartwright and some of his coworkers, believing that natural gas was going to be the wave of the future for power in the United States, decided to start their own company after a series of legislative moves in the course of the preceding decade had created a fertile environment for new start-ups in the energy business. They founded Calpine, deriving the name from the company's location in California and from the word "Alpine" for the Swiss company, Electrowatt, that helped finance their start. Calpine was established with $1 million of seed financing and a team of five, including Cartwright.

In the beginning, Cartwright focused on management services to independent power generators. In 1988 he decided it was time take the next step and establish a power-generation business within the company, which soon owned one megawatt of power. In an article for Princeton University's *E-Quad News,* Cartwright told Sara Peters, "We celebrated everything in those days. So we said, 'Why don't we shoot to have 1000 megawatts by the year 2000?' And we had enough champagne to make it seem feasible to do that" (Winter 2001–2002).

As Cartwright and Calpine started owning and operating power plants, the company began to grow rapidly. Originally, Cartwright focused the company's activities primarily on generating geothermal power, that is, electricity generated by utilizing naturally occurring geological heat sources, such as geysers or hot springs. But the company also became involved in gas-fired projects. From its inception until 1992, Calpine operated as a co-generator. Cartwright had built the company with very limited capital, getting financing from such areas as public equity offerings, public debt offerings, and bank debt. But Cartwright had long been looking to the future and to deregulation to open the door to bigger things. In an interview with Susan Mueller for the *Business Journal,* Cartwright recalled, "It was clear to me, in 1984, that regulation was going to go away and there would be opportunities for an independent company" (September 8, 2000).

By 1992 deregulation had begun in earnest and wholesale generators were able to sell power at prices closer to open market prices to regulated public utilities, like Pacific Gas and Electric in California. Calpine had assets of $21 billion in 1992 and a power plant portfolio of 141 megawatts by 1994. Two years later, Electrowatt wanted to divest of its energy assets, and Cartwright decided to let the public buy out Electrowatt's interest in Calpine. Cartwright then guided Calpine through the largest initial public offering in the history of the power industry to that time. With access to public markets for both debt and equity, Cartwright had placed the company in position to embark on his plan to develop and acquire more geothermal facilities and high-efficiency natural gas.

FOCUSES ON CLEANER ENERGY

Industry analysts considered Cartwright a true visionary in the energy business. He was especially lauded for his ability to both recognize and articulate the tremendous opportunities available in meeting the ever-increasing demands for electricity by building modern power systems that were fuel-efficient and environmentally friendly. Industry experts also noted that Cartwright recognized the need for new generating facilities during the embryonic stages of deregulation and restructuring in the industry.

By 1998 the company, under Cartwright's guidance, had power plants in operation or under development in ten states and was in the process of developing a $250 million, natural gas–fired, 500-megawatt power plant seven miles southwest of Yuba City, California. Cartwright viewed the old power companies and older power-producing plants as very inefficient and a major source of pollution. In contrast, he noted that Calpine's geothermal plants were extremely pollution-free and that the emissions from natural gas–fired plants were insignificant, especially in comparison to coal-powered plants. In an interview with April C. Murelio for *Electric Light & Power*, Cartwright commented on his pet subject of America's outdated and inefficient power generation capabilities: "We don't drive 30-year-old cars, or operate 30-year-old computers, or use 30-year-old telephones, so why do we continue to generate electricity and pollute our air with aging power plants?" (May 1999).

CONTINUES ON GROWTH PATH

In 1999 Cartwright had guided Calpine into place as one of the nation's fastest-growing independent power producers. The company had 5,900 megawatts of capacity in operation, under construction, or in development across 11 states, far exceeding Cartwright's 1998 goal of owning 1,000 megawatts of power by 2000. Much of the growth was based on Cartwright's twofold strategy of expanding and diversifying Calpine's domestic portfolio of power projects and enhancing the performance and efficiency of its existing power plants. Cartwright also oversaw the company's efforts to decentralize its strategic energy program, which allowed the company to integrate the power plants as generating systems with corporate level financing and pooled gas procurement. The strategy allowed Calpine to meet customer needs from the most cost-effective facilities. Instead of operating individual power plants, Calpine operated integrated power systems.

On the heels of the power shortages in California, the company's new goal was to have more than 100 power plants throughout the West, the South, and New England and a total of 40,000 megawatts. Before the end of 2001, Cartwright had established a four-year building-and-buying campaign and had raised about half of the $17 billion needed to pursue his goals. Industry analysts noted that Cartwright and Calpine faced numerous risks in the expansion plan, including a possible initiative by government to re-regulate independent power suppliers like Calpine. Construction delays were another concern. However, industry insiders noted that Cartwright addressed the delays by assigning a roving staff to troubleshoot at every construction site and order parts in bulk, which enabled the company to trim construction costs by 15 percent.

Despite certain risks, investors continued to show confidence in Cartwright's direction for the company as the stock doubled in 2000 to a split-adjusted $47. By 2001 Calpine was the world's ninth-largest electricity producer. The industry analyst Kit Konolige noted in *BusinessWeek*, "These guys were the first to put their money behind a perception that there was going to be a power shortage in the U.S., and it has paid off handsomely for investors" (March 26, 2001).

ADJUSTS TO TOUGH ECONOMIC TIMES

Cartwright faced the nationwide economic downslide that began in late 2001 by scaling back the company's aggressive capital expenditure and plant construction program. He also put 34 advanced-stage development projects on hold in 2002 but continued to move ahead with his ambitions to bring 70,000 megawatts of generation on line by 2005. Although some industry analysts predicted a power supply glut, Cartwright remained bullish on the business and continued to position it to capitalize on improving markets.

Cartwright's strategy to stabilize the company's finances was to assign the net value of Calpine's power contracts over market ($6.5 billion then) and combine it with the value of its gas and power assets ($16.5 billion at the time) and then to back out of Calpine's debt and lease obligations ($15 billion). These moves resulted in the company having a net value of $8 billion, or $21.40 a share. Cartwright also noted in an interview in *Oil Daily*, "We are proud that Calpine achieved a growth rate of 63% even as our nation and industry faced difficult economic conditions" (January 17, 2002).

Cartwright's strategy appeared to pay off as it reported a 57 percent increase in third-quarter profits in 2003. Part of the good result was due to higher realized oil and gas prices that increased Calpine's oil and gas production margins. Industry analysts also noted that gains from debt restructuring helped Calpine report profits of $237.8 million on revenue of $2.7 billion. In the same quarter the previous year, the company had reported profits of $151.1 million on revenue of $2.5 billion.

MANAGEMENT STYLE: NO CHARTS

Cartwright was always noted by industry analysts for his strong vision for the company and his entrepreneurial spirit. He was able find the right deals, make quick decisions, and take prudent risks to achieve success. Cartwright's energy did not wane as he continued to work well into his 70s, and he maintained a clear vision that Calpine would become the largest and most profitable power company in North America.

Cartwright was also known for instilling his entrepreneurial attitude throughout the company. He achieved this by quickly rewarding creativity and accomplishing goals. Cartwright also emphasized promoting from within and letting his employees grow with the company. In an interview with Susan Mueller for the *Business Journal,* Cartwright's friend, the investment banker George Stathakis noted, "Peter is a very decent guy with a lot of integrity. He tells it like it is" (September 8, 2000).

Throughout his years overseeing the company, Cartwright maintained a loose organizational structure and proudly proclaimed that the company had no organizational charts. Instead, Cartwright organized the company so that new projects were done on a team basis that included people from all of the company's various disciplines, such as legal, finance, and insurance. As for his own management philosophy, Cartwright told Bob Schmidt during an interview for the *Sacramento Business Journal,* "We try to give everybody as much authority and responsibility as they can handle, and I try to stay out of their hair" (July 20, 1998).

CALPINE SOARS

Under Cartwright's guidance, Calpine had increased its generating capacity by more than 70 percent in 2002. By 2004, the company had 89 energy centers in 21 states in the United States, as well as in Canada and the United Kingdom. Calpine also had a capacity of more than 22,000 megawatts. Ten new projects were also under construction in 2004, and Cartwright expected the company to have a capacity of more than 29,000 megawatts by the end of 2005. He remained a strong proponent of natural gas as an important fuel in the power industry for at least four decades. In addition to his duties at Calpine, Cartwright served on the board of directors for Catlytica Energy Systems, Cheng Power Systems, the San Jose Symphony, and the California Chamber of Commerce.

See also entries on Calpine Corporation and General Electric Company in *International Directory of Company Histories.*

SOURCES FOR FURTHER INFORMATION

"Calpine Puts Aggressive Power Plans on Hold," *Oil Daily,* January 17, 2002, ITEM02017002.

"The Green Utility That's in the Black," *BusinessWeek,* March 26, 2001, p. 108.

Mueller, Susan, "No Shortage of Energy," *Business Journal,* September 8, 2000, p. 41.

Murelio, April C., "Regional Strategy Catapults Calpine," *Electric Light & Power,* May 1999, p. 1.

Peters, Sara, "Calpine CEO Shares Wisdom, Insight," *E-Quad News,* Winter 2001–2002, http://www.princeton.edu/~seasweb/eqnews/winter_01-02/feature2.html.

Schmidt, Bob (interviewer), "In Depth: Energy," *Sacramento Business Journal,* July 17, 1998.

Wherry, Rob, "Power Surge," *Forbes,* January 22, 2001, p. 99.

—David Petechuk

■ ■ ■

Steve Case

1958–

Director, Time Warner

Nationality: American.

Born: August 21, 1958, in Honolulu, Hawaii.

Education: Williams College, BA, 1980.

Family: Son of Dan (attorney) and Carol (teacher; maiden name unknown) Case; married Joanne Baker (divorced); children: three; married Jean Villanueva.

Career: Procter & Gamble, c. 1980–1982, marketing; Pizza Hut, c. 1982–1983, new product manager; Control Video, which became Quantum Computer Services in 1985, which became America Online in 1991, 1984–1992, various positions including vice president of marketing; 1991–2001, chief executive officer; AOL Time Warner, 2001–2003, chairman; Time Warner, 2003–, director.

Address: Time Warner, 75 Rockefeller Plaza, New York, New York 10019; http://www.timewarner.com.

■ Stephen M. (Steve) Case went from marketing hair care products and pizza to establishing the highly successful online Internet service called America Online (AOL). Unlike other computer and Internet gurus who forged giant companies and made fortunes from the rapidly advancing computer industry, Case did not have a background in technology. Rather, he relied on his marketing expertise to outmaneuver and outperform competing Internet service providers such as Prodigy, Compuserve, and Microsoft. In 2001 Case completed AOL's buyout of the media giant Time Warner and became chairman of the newly named AOL Time Warner. Two years later Case went from being one of the most important media moguls in the world to resigning as chairman of AOL Time Warner as the company's stocks floundered. Despite this turn of events, industry analysts have noted that Case was a true Internet pioneer whose determination and vision helped establish online services as an integral part of the new era of Internet communications and commerce.

Steve Case. *AP/Wide World Photos.*

SHOWS YOUNG ENTREPRENEURIAL SPIRIT

Steve Case was born and grew up in Hawaii. He showed an early entrepreneurial spirit, when he and his brother, Dan, set up a lime juice stand in their neighborhood. In their teens the brothers formed Case Enterprises, a mail-order business that sold watches, seeds, and Christmas cards. For an article in *Fortune*, Case's mother, Carol, told Andy Serwer, "But they were also competitive. They both had typewriters, and you could hear them typing away their ad circulars" (November 22, 1999). Steve also started a number of businesses on his own, including operating an airport shuttle and selling fruit baskets, which helped him make money while he was attending Williams College in Massachusetts. Case even wrote music reviews so he could get free tickets to shows and was a singer in two new-wave rock bands.

After graduating in 1980 Case was dismayed when all his applications to MBA programs were rejected. He applied for jobs at the prestigious New York advertising firm of J. Walter Thompson and at Time's cable-TV network, HBO. Both rejected him. Nevertheless, Case was already thinking big. As reported by Richard Linnett and Kathleen Sampey in *Adweek Eastern Edition*, Case had written in his applications that he envisioned a future when two-way cable systems would make the standard television set "an information line, newspaper, school, computer, referendum machine and catalog" (January 17, 2000).

Case ended up working for Procter & Gamble in marketing. After two years trying to sell items such as Abound hair conditioner, he left and joined Pizza Hut, where he became manager of new pizza development. As he tested new product combinations and offered them to the public, he found that people continued to like the plain old cheese and sauce pizza best. Case noted that he learned to keep it simple, and the lesson would later serve him well.

FROM PIZZA TO HIGH TECH

Developing new toppings for pizza was not exactly Case's idea of being an entrepreneur and he left in 1983 to join Control Video, a video-game specialist company backed by the company where his older brother, Dan, worked. Control Video was pioneering the still-fledgling computer online world and setting up a service for users of Atari computer games. Although Case admitted that he had hated the one computer science course he ever took in college, he had found that communicating via computer was exciting. While working for Pizza Hut he had bought a Kaypro computer, and it took him two weeks to figure out how to hook it into an online service. He told Joel Shore in *Computer Reseller News*, "But when I finally logged in and found myself linked to people all over the country from this sorry little apartment in Wichita, it was just exhilarating" (November 15, 1999). Now he was working for a company that was more aligned with his vision of two-way cable information systems.

Control Video soon encountered financial problems and was re-formed as Quantum Computer Services in 1985. Case was made marketing vice president and set out to establish Quantum's new Q-Link online service for Commodore computer users. The service was successful and Quantum soon expanded to form online deals with Apple Computer and Tandy. When Apple departed company with Quantum, Case's marketing experience told him it was time to give the company a whole new image as it launched a new nationwide online service. Case held a contest to choose a new name for the service and ended up picking his own suggestion of "Online America," which was changed to America Online. In 1991 the company officially changed its name to America Online, and Case took over as the company's chief executive officer the following year.

AOL GOES PUBLIC

On March 9, 1992, Case and AOL went public on the NASDAQ and raised $66 million through an offer of two million shares for $11.50 each. Although many believed that online services were going to be a passing phase and of little use when the Internet and World Wide Web were fully developed, Case saw the future differently. From the beginning, as noted in *Fortune*, he described AOL's mission as building "a global medium as central to people's lives as the telephone or television . . . and even more valuable" (February 7, 2000). Case was not the only one high on the potential of online services. Paul Allen, who was partnered with Bill Gates in Microsoft in 1992, wanted to buy AOL. Case turned him down.

Although Case was confident, AOL only had 181,600 users in 1992. Furthermore, AOL was battling other online services, most of which had more financial backing, for the relatively new and growing market. In addition, within a year major mergers of companies like Time Warner and Turner Broadcasting led many market analysts to predict that Case's smaller online service would be swamped by these behemoths' better offers.

Fortunately for AOL, Case's background in marketing enabled him to make AOL competitive and ultimately to help it come out on top. First and foremost, he recognized that the online service had to be user-friendly, truly useful, fun, and affordable. His goal was to create a medium that anyone, not just computer aficionados, could take full advantage of. Case also recognized that AOL would have to leverage technology and partner with a variety of companies to create that experience. AOL started to send free computer disks in the mail to Americans who owned computers so they could easily load AOL onto their computers and log on to the fledgling World Wide Web. From 1994 to 1996 AOL added five million new customers, more than the *New York Times* and *Washington Post* had added during the previous 50 years. As a result, AOL became the largest online service provider.

THE WEB THREATENS

Despite these successes, Case and AOL were facing several serious problems in 1996. Service blackouts and busy signals on the telephone landlines, because of the high volume that AOL's unlimited usage pricing plan had created, angered many customers. There was also a mounting threat from Microsoft as it created a rival service to AOL, which would eventually become the Microsoft Network. Case's marketing strategy proved too much, however, for even the giant Microsoft to overcome, and AOL would eventually form a partnership with the company. But many market analysts saw the real competition to AOL and all other online service providers as being the Internet and the World Wide Web itself, which computer users could access in a number of ways without a sophisticated Internet service provider such as AOL.

While many saw the Web as a competitor to AOL, Case saw the Web as a niche filled with thousands of disparate home pages with little marketing strategy. The Internet, in Case's view, was just a piece of what consumers would ultimately want. Case was intent on continuing to package AOL in a way that Main Street would find valuable. He proclaimed that the Web was really an opportunity for AOL to expand, emphasizing that the proprietary content service AOL provided was a way to make the broken-up world of Web sites and organizations into a more consumer-friendly entity.

Case realized that the Internet without an organized online service provider would require consumers to buy various software packages, plug-ins, and add-ons in order to take part fully in the experience. Furthermore, they would have to surf the Internet and subscribe to services they wanted on an individual basis. Case told Gene Koprowski in an article for *Forbes* that the approach was fine for those who were technologically astute but was too complicated for the average consumer. He added, "TV would never have gotten a 90 percent market penetration if it had been that hard. If you want to reach a mainstream audience, you have to make it more plug and play. One-stop shopping" (October 7, 1996).

Although in 1997 AOL suffered a $499 million loss that led many to believe the market analysts were right in predicting its fall, Case soon changed their minds. The following year, 1998, AOL garnered $91.8 million in net income on revenues of $2.6 billion. Several factors helped Case to turn things around. First of all, he and the president of AOL, Robert Pittman, continued to rely on old-fashioned marketing campaigns. They increased AOL's direct-mail campaign and flooded American homes with AOL diskettes and CDs, making it easy for consumers to sign up for the service. Case and Pittman also began luring online merchants to advertise and sell their wares to AOL's millions of subscribers. Case saw these e-commerce revenues as perhaps eventually being even more lucrative than subscription fees. By 1999 AOL had 17 million members and Case had turned the company into the first true blue chip Internet stock.

LOOKS TO THE INTERNET CENTURY

By 2000 Case and AOL had accomplished several things that signaled AOL would be one of the leaders of what Case had dubbed the coming "Internet century." Among them was a $4.2 billion deal to buy Netscape Internet portal, which AOL acquired in March 1999 along with Netscape Communications Corporation. The portal was among the most popular destinations on the Web.

Although AOL was nearing 25 million subscribers, Case was facing a threat. High-speed cable Internet access was under development and owned by large corporations, such as AT&T and Time Warner. With the promise of greatly increasing the speed of downloading Internet sites, Case knew the threat to AOL was significant. He had spent much of 1999 lobbying Congress, the Federal Communications Commission, and local governments to force cable companies to open their networks so that AOL and other unaffiliated Internet service providers could bring high-speed access to their customers. But Case also had other plans. He was positioning AOL for the impending broadband explosion by cutting deals with satellite delivery companies and telecommunications companies that offered digital subscriber line services.

In January 2000 Case's next move was clear. He announced that AOL was buying the media conglomerate Time Warner in a merger that would create the new company, AOL Time Warner. The company would combine AOL's online services with Time Warner's vast media and cable assets. Many industry analysts saw it as a coup for Case, who could now pursue his dream to package, distribute, and sell both information and entertainment in radically new ways. Case was made chairman of the new company in January 2001 and was charged with focusing primarily on the technological developments and policy initiatives concerned with the global expansion of the new interactive media. Many industry analysts saw the move as firmly establishing the Internet as a medium for audio and video as well as for traditional text and graphics. In an article on *CNET News.com*, the industry analyst Phil Leigh noted, "It is probably the most significant development in the Internet business world to date" (January 10, 2000).

The purchase was basically an all-stock deal involving about $160 billion. On the day of the deal's announcement, Time Warner's stock soared up $25.31, or 39 percent, to $90.06. But AOL's stock fell 2 percent by the end of the day to $71.88. According to some analysts, AOL's stockholders had good reason to be cautious. Although Case and AOL seemed on the verge of heading a new world that combined online services with media, they still faced many challenges and competitors. Many analysts also thought that Case and AOL had given up an essential and important aspect of the company. Throughout the years Case had been extremely focused on his goals for AOL. He had beaten out Gates and Microsoft in the Internet service provider war because he and the people under him lived, breathed, and dreamed about online services, while Microsoft and other competitors had to pay attention to various non-Internet aspects of their businesses. Analysts noted that with the merger Case and AOL were also going to have to deal with disparate businesses, such as TV networks, cable systems, magazines, books, and movies. At the same time Microsoft was increasing its focus on the Internet. As for Case, he told Jennifer Gilbert in an article for *Advertising Age* that he saw the merger as a way to build bridges among various communications formats. He noted, "The future is more about the PC and the TV and the telephone all connected in a seamless way" (April 17, 2000).

MANAGEMENT STYLE: LOW KEY BUT FOCUSED

Many analysts noted that Case's personal style probably had a lot to do with his ultimate success in taking AOL to the top of the Internet service provider heap. Case had been described as an unassuming and down-to-earth leader who was not boisterous in his managerial style. He understood clearly the need for good PR and the power of the inside strategy of talking one-on-one with people to get what he wanted. For example, he continually met with politicians of all persuasions in Washington, D.C., as he tried to iron out concerns about the Internet, including the availability of pornography. At the same time, he won concessions that virtually eliminated AOL's liability for crimes committed by users of its network and derailed antipornography pressure. He also helped defeat privacy legislation that would have limited online companies' ability to gather marketing information about the Internet habits of teenagers.

Industry analysts noted that AOL became successful because of Case's diligence and vision, values that he ingrained in AOL's corporate culture. For Case, there was no alternative to the Internet and AOL's future domination of it. His stubbornness about building the company was apparent, said analysts, when Case and AOL could have sold out for millions of dollars early on but rejected the deal. They also noted that Case was relentless in reengineering his company around a marketing sensibility that he knew well.

Although coworkers and others observed that Case had a healthy ego, they also said that it never stopped him from hiring people who were more flamboyant and creative. They also said that he did not take a threatening approach to management and worked well with the technological talent he needed to make AOL grow. Writing in *MC Technology Marketing Intelligence*, Michael Schrage commented, "Steve Case was able to attract and retain a conglomerate of truly talented and—in the entrepreneurial sense—effective team of executives" (March 2000).

AFTER THE FALL

Although Case and many industry analysts expected the new AOL Time Warner company to prosper, the market value of the new company had fallen $50 billion by the time of the annual meeting in May 2002. During the meeting, Case took most of the heat for the company's poor performance. Many claimed that Case went from being a visionary to a mere executive. Case himself apologized for setting the company's profit targets too high and sticking with them too long. Further compromising Case's position was a growing AOL accounting scandal that had Securities and Exchange Commission investigators probing into whether AOL had made suspect deals to overinflate its revenue numbers while it had been trying to buy Time Warner with a stock deal.

AOL Online was also presenting many problems for Time Warner because revenues from advertising and subscriptions had decreased $1 billion in one year. Its ad sales were also dying, and AOL could not establish its broadband sales. The debate was heated over whether Case's vision for the company was working. In February 2003 Case stepped down as chairman of AOL Time Warner but remained a director on the board of the newly named Time Warner. Few believed, however, that Case would have much to say in the running of the company.

Although many industry analysts believed that Case's vision was correct, they noted that a number of factors contributed to his departure. First of all, the timing for Case's takeover of Time Warner probably could not have been worse. On the personal front, as the merger took place, Case spent long periods away from the company to spend time with his older brother, Dan, who was dying of cancer.(Dan Case had also become extremely successful as the CEO of Hambrecht and Quist and then chairman of the board of JP Morgan H&Q.) On the national front, the economic recession and the terrorist attacks of September 11, 2001, crippled the new technologies sector. As one of the most outspoken proponents of interactive services, Case's high profile made him an easy target. In addition, once the inflated Internet currency that Case had used to buy AOL finally burst, AOL Time Warner was in dire straits financially. Many insiders also noted that Case's management style and intellect did not transfer well to an established, conservative company like Time Warner. Case had made his name and established his style with a one-time start-up company that did not initially answer to stockholders and remained narrowly focused on its goals. As a result, the corporate cultures of AOL and Time Warner never really meshed.

By the time Case stepped down, nearly $200 billion worth of shareholder value in AOL Time Warner had been lost. As described by Michael Maccoby in *Forbes*, Case was among a number of "chief executives who sold themselves and their companies on innovation and vision, only to be kicked out and quickly replaced by bosses whose immediate goals are cost-cutting, debt reduction and steady and predictable growth" (March 3, 2003). While some analysts thought it would be unwise to cut Case totally loose from the company and that his vision could still serve Time Warner well, others commented that it would be best for AOL to separate completely from the company and bring Case back on board.

Despite his fall, Case remained optimistic about the future. Case commented that the difficult environment in terms of the economy, advertising, and the Internet sector certainly contributed to the company's difficulties. However, he noted that consumer and technology trends were giving consumers more choice, control, and convenience and that these factors were going to ultimately transform media, entertainment, and communications. In an interview with CNN's Paula Zahn, he said, "And our company, AOL Time Warner, is best positioned to ride that wave" (January 14, 2003). After leaving the company, Case spent most of his time concerned with the philanthropic efforts of the Case Foundation.

See also entries on America Online, Inc. and Time Warner Inc. in *International Directory of Company Histories.*

SOURCES FOR FURTHER INFORMATION

"AOL Buys Time Warner in Historic Merger," *CNET News.com,* January 10, 2000, http://news.com.com/2100-1023-235400.html?legacy=cnet.

Cappo, Joe, "A Case of Pioneering in Communications," *Crain's Chicago Business,* November 22, 1999, p. 8.

Gilbert, Jennifer, "Steve Case," *Advertising Age,* April 17, 2000, p. 134.

Koprowski, Gene, "AOL CEO Steve Case," *Forbes,* October 7, 1996, p. S94.

Linnett, Richard, and Kathleen Sampey, "Gray-Flannel Fantasies," *Adweek Eastern Edition,* January 17, 2000, p. 70.

Maccoby, Michael, "The Narcissist-Visionary," *Forbes,* March 3, 2003, p. 36.

"A Scapegoat Named Steve Case," *BusinessWeek,* January 27, 2003, p. 124.

Schrage, Michael, "Mr. Bland," *MC Technology Marketing Intelligence,* March 2000, p. 30.

Serwer, Andy, "Mother Knows Best: The Word on Dan and Steve Case," *Fortune,* November 22, 1999, p. 340.

Shore, Joel, "No. 2: The Gatekeeper," *Computer Reseller News,* November 15, 1999, p. 131.

"Steve Case: Decision 'Right Thing' for Company," *CNN.com,* January 14, 2003, http://www.cnn.com/2003/US/01/13/cnna.steve.case/.

"These Guys Want It All," *Fortune,* February 7, 2000, p. 70.

—David Petechuk

■■■

Cássio Casseb Lima

1955–
President, Banco do Brasil

Nationality: Brazilian.

Born: August 8, 1955, in São Paulo, Brazil.

Education: Escola Politécnica, Universidade de São Paulo, BS, 1978.

Family: Married; children: two.

Career: Banco do Boston, 1976–1979, position unknown; Banco Francês & Brasileiro, 1979–1988, account officer; Banco Mantrust, 1988–1992, vice president of finance and executive vice president; Grupo Vila Romana, 1992–1993, vice president of finance; Citibank, 1993–1997, vice president of finance; Credicard, 1997–1999, president; Banco do Brasil, 2003–, president.

Address: SBS Qd. 01 Bloco C, Edifício Sede III, 24th Floor, 70073-901 Brasília, D.F., Brazil; http://www.bb.com.br.

■ In 2003 the Brazilian president Luiz Inacio da Silva, or "Lula," named Cássio Casseb Lima president of Banco do Brasil. The largest bank in Latin America, Banco do Brasil was the most important financial institution in Brazil and operated branches in every city in the country. While many members of Lula's Workers' Party hoped for a political appointee who would toe the party line, the president instead opted for a professional banker in Casseb. An engineer by training, Casseb had worked for numerous financial institutions in Brazil since 1976. Casseb's long and successful career led Lula to pick him for such an important and powerful position.

EARLY CAREER

Casseb was born in São Paulo, Brazil, in 1955. He obtained an engineering degree from the Polytechnic School at the University of São Paulo in 1978. In 1976 he began his career at the Banco do Boston, where he worked until 1979. Casseb then went to work as an account officer at the Banco Francês & Brasileiro. After nine years, he began a stint at Banco Mantrust, where he worked as vice president of finance and executive vice president. Casseb then spent a year in 1992 and 1993 coordinating the restructuring of the Grupo Vila Romana. He next took a position at Citibank as vice president of finance. In 1997 Casseb became president of Credicard, Brazil's largest issuer of credit cards.

BANCO DO BRASIL

In January 2003 Inacio da Silva appointed Casseb to the post of president of Banco do Brasil, the most important banking job in the country. Created in 1808 the state-owned Banco do Brasil was Brazil's largest bank. When Casseb became the president in 2003, the bank was in good shape because it was well capitalized and well managed. However, such good standing was not always the case. In 1995 and 1996 the bank had posted losses in excess of $10 billion. Banco do Brasil faced a number of problems at the time. It suffered from bad loans and foreign exchange losses. Many Brazilians borrowed from Banco do Brasil to pay their other loans, only to default on the new loan. Government officials excessively interfered in the bank's affairs. An excessive number of employees hurt the bank's finances. Although the bank was weak and running up huge losses, Brazilian law prohibited the liquidation of Banco do Brasil. Instead, the government consistently pumped money into the bank. According to many bank executives, Banco do Brasil was directionless, overstaffed, and demoralized. At the same time, private banks in Brazil were growing larger and stronger.

President Fernando Henrique Cardoso, who governed from 1994 until 2002, turned Banco do Brasil around. In part the government needed a profitable state bank to maintain a flow of revenue into the treasury. The bank reduced the number of employees from 120,000 to 78,000 and adopted a corporate mentality that ended the tradition of favoritism and politicization. The bank implemented a policy of rule by committee whereby the board of directors managed the bank. Directors had to unanimously approve all decisions, meaning that no single person decided bank policy alone. Committee rule also helped to protect the bank from government meddling. The bank's staff was motivated with profit-sharing systems. The bank also implemented stylish marketing campaigns aimed at the young and sophisticated, sponsoring beach volleyball teams and the tennis star Gustavo Kuerten.

When Lula became president, many experts wondered whether the new process would continue or Banco do Brasil would resort to its old ways. There was much discussion within the Workers' Party over whom to pick to lead the bank. Some party members called for a professional banker; others suggested a political appointee. One executive at the bank told John Barham of *Latin Finance* that "it is like this every four years when the government changes. It is like going through a takeover with a completely new owner." Lula surprised many financial observers by implementing relatively orthodox economic policies and selecting Casseb to head Banco do Brasil. Some members of Lula's own party objected to the appointment.

Despite the objections Casseb did not deviate from the bank's new corporate attitude, reducing the concerns of many investors and analysts. His job was not always easy, however. For example, Casseb and the managers at Banco do Brasil were subject to more union pressure than were other bank executives. In October 2003 a strike by bank employees shut down Banco do Brasil. Despite the difficulties Casseb succeeded in continuing the turnaround that had started in the 1990s. In 2003 the bank recorded $596 million in profits, up 64 percent from 2002. Indicative of Casseb's early success was the fact that *Latin Finance* in 2003 selected Banco do Brasil the most improved bank in Latin America.

See also entry on Banco do Brasil S.A. in *International Directory of Company Histories.*

SOURCES FOR FURTHER INFORMATION

Barham, John, "Lean Mean Banking Machine," *Latin Finance*, March 2003, p. 59.

"Government Appoints Bank Executive," *Latin Finance*, February 2003, p. 12.

"A Name to Reckon With," *Latin Finance*, November 2003.

"Solid, Profitable, and Yes, State-Owned," *Latin Finance*, March 2004, p. 50.

—Ronald Young

■■■

Robert B. Catell

1937–

Chairman and chief executive officer, KeySpan Corporation and KeySpan Energy Delivery Corporation

Nationality: American.

Born: February 1, 1937, in Brooklyn, New York.

Education: City College of New York, BME, MME.

Family: Married; children: five.

Career: Brooklyn Union Gas, 1958–1974, junior engineer; 1974–1977, assistant vice president; 1977–1981, vice president; 1981–1984, senior vice president; 1984–1986, executive vice president; 1986–1990, chief operating officer; 1990–1991, president; 1991–1996, president and chief executive officer; 1996–1997, chairman and chief executive officer; KeySpan Energy Delivery, 1997–, chairman and chief executive officer; KeySpan Corporation, 1998–, chairman and chief executive officer.

Awards: Ellis Island Medal of Honor, 1998; named Professional Engineer of the Year by the New York Society of Professional Engineers, 2000.

Publications: *The CEO and the Monk: One Company's Journey to Profit and Purpose* (with Kenny Moore and Glen Rifkin), 2004.

Address: KeySpan Corporation, 175 Old Country Road, Hicksville, New York 11801; http://www.keyspan energy.com.

■ Robert B. Catell became chairman and CEO of KeySpan in 1998 when the company was created through the merger of Brooklyn Union Gas, which Catell headed, and the Long Island Lighting Company. After assuming the reins at KeySpan, Catell developed the company into the largest distributor of natural gas in the Northeast United States and the largest investor-owned electric generator in New York State. Industry analysts have noted that Catell was a prime mover in KeySpan's aggressive efforts to convince many private homeowners in the Northeast to convert from oil to gas heat. Catell also coauthored *The CEO and the Monk: One Company's Journey to Profit and Purpose,* which outlined his corporate philosophy of building a strong company but not at the expense of its customers, employees, or the communities in which it operated.

FROM BASEBALL DREAMS TO ENGINEERING

Born and raised in Brooklyn, New York, Catell dreamed of playing baseball for a living but realized he did not have the talent needed to become a professional. Catell's father died when Robert was young, and he got a job at 14 working in a neighborhood drugstore stocking the shelves. In a profile in *Utility Business,* Catell noted, "I understood what it meant to work for a living. I also learned the importance of getting a good education" (June 1, 2001).

Catell attended City College of New York and admitted that he probably had to work harder at his studies than many of his fellow students. In addition to his studies, he worked to help supplement his mother's disability income after she became sick. He credited these responsibilities with helping him develop a strong work ethic that he maintained throughout his career. Catell eventually received his bachelor's and master's degree in mechanical engineering. Although he would go on to attend Columbia University's Executive Development Program and the Advanced Management Program at the Harvard Business School, Catell noted that his college training in engineering provided an important foundation for his later success in management and business. As he observed in an article in the *Long Island Business News,* "The technical education I received has been helpful. It taught me how to approach problems, and how to solve them" (July 21, 2000).

BECOMES CEO OF BROOKLYN UNION

Catell joined the utility company Brooklyn Union Gas in 1958 and worked in various engineering departments at a variety of jobs that included fixing meters. He eventually advanced to hold management positions in regulation, marketing, and customer service and finance. Catell noted that the opportunity to cross-train in many areas of the company during his early career gave him a comprehensive understanding of all aspects of the energy business.

In 1991 Catell was named president and CEO of Brooklyn Union. He soon began to emphasize the need to promote the use of natural gas and alternatives to other fuels. He stressed that natural gas was the fuel of the future because it was environmentally friendly and economically efficient thanks to its abundant supply. In his 1994 incoming-president's speech to the American Gas Association, as reported by *Gas World International*, Catell noted that he believed environmentalists and businesses could work together and that both were culpable in not trying to come to a middle ground that benefited both the economy and the environment. He told the AGA members, "I believe we must spread the word that natural gas is the primary fuel most able to clean up our environment as well as charge up our economy" (November 1994).

By 1995 Catell had helped turn Brooklyn Union into a $1 billion company. By this time, the energy market was undergoing deregulation, and Catell saw in that the possibility for many new opportunities. The New York company began trading gas and pipeline capacity outside of its territory to customers in 17 states. Catell also oversaw the building of the Grumman and Stony Brook gas-fired cogeneration plants in New York. He then positioned the company as the leader in developing the Iroquois pipeline to bring additional natural gas to the Northeast.

Although the company's business territory had stopped growing, Catell kept Brooklyn Gas thriving. He credited much of his success to the company's intense focus on community support and economic development. The company's most successful effort in this area was the Cinderella program, which worked with local shopping districts and business owners to improve their stores with the help of Cinderella grants and which also helped start a brownstone renovation movement in Brooklyn. Catell saw that fostering growth in the community meant better business for Brooklyn Union.

MERGER CREATED NEW ENERGY POWERHOUSE

By the end of 1997 Catell was strongly supporting a merger between Brooklyn Union and Long Island Lighting Company. He saw the companies as having a strategic fit that would result in numerous economic advantages, including $1 billion in synergy savings during the first ten years of the company's existence. He noted that customers would also benefit. As he told Lisa Josefak for the *Long Island Business News*, "This will be accomplished by eliminating redundant activities and consolidating functions" (August 11, 1997).

The merger took place in 1998, and industry analysts credited Catell as being fundamental to its success by supporting a no-layoff agreement with the union that was crucial to the merger. The merger of the two companies resulted in the creation of the KeySpan Corporation, the holding company formed by the merger of Brooklyn Union's parent company and Long Island Lighting. Brooklyn Union became KeySpan Energy Delivery Corporation, and Catell was elected chairman and CEO of both KeySpan entities.

As chairman and CEO of KeySpan, Catell set out to build the business into a leading company in the Northeast. KeySpan's stock, however, went down 20 percent during the first fifteen months after the merger while the rest of the utility sector flourished. Some analysts blamed the poor stock performance partially on the $1.7 billion in cash that the company had received from the sale of Long Island Lighting assets. The money had been sitting around unused and earning only Treasury bill returns. Nevertheless, investors and analysts remained high on the company's prospects based on Catell's past history in management.

In November 1999, when KeySpan announced it was going to acquire Boston-based Eastern Enterprises, analysts commended Catell for taking an important step in bolstering the company's prospects. The acquisition made KeySpan the largest gas distribution company in the Northeast. It further brightened the growth outlook for KeySpan because many of the households in New England were heated with oil, providing a fertile ground for Catell's efforts to recruit converts to gas heat, thus expanding the company's customer base. In an interview with Philip Lentz in *Crain's New York Business*, the retail energy analyst Ethan Cohen noted, "Regional players in the deregulated energy market need to reach a critical mass to compete, and that's around 2 million customers. That's what KeySpan has accomplished by taking over Eastern Enterprises" (November 15, 1999).

FROM GAS CONVERSION TO COMPANY EXPANSION

Catell and KeySpan Energy also ratcheted up a campaign to convince thousands of homeowners in New Jersey to convert their oil furnaces into natural gas furnaces. Part of this campaign included offering free gas boilers or a $750 credit to homeowners. Growing a customer base, however, meant the need for more gas lines and Catell and KeySpan initially proposed a gas pipeline through the environmentally unique area of the Long Island Pine Barrens. The proposal brought outcries from environmentalists, but Catell was able to defuse the hot-button issue by agreeing to reroute the line to reduce environmental damage.

Catell continued to build KeySpan through acquisitions and partnerships, including acquiring Energy North of New Hampshire and a stake in Houston Exploration. He then took KeySpan into telecommunications by creating a fiber optic network. The market analyst Gordon Howald told Claude Solnik in the *Long Island Business News*, "He's built a great company. He's transformed KeySpan into one of the premier natural gas distribution companies in North America" (December 14, 2001).

Although Catell's efforts at KeySpan were largely successful, the company's track record was not perfect. Unfortunately, KeySpan followed Enron into energy trading and stumbled just as Enron did. However, unlike Enron, Catell and KeySpan maintained their focus on hard assets instead of the "asset light" strategy taken by Enron. As a result, KeySpan came out of the crisis relatively unscathed while Enron collapsed. Catell's efforts at global expansion also did not pan out, and he authorized efforts to sell off much of the company's global assets. In addition, the merger cost of paying $2.5 billion for Eastern Enterprises and Energy North led to a debt load, low rates of return, and negative cash flow. Another misstep was KeySpan's acquisition of Roy Kay, a large contracting firm that had underestimated its costs on completing projects, which led to reduced earning projections for KeySpan in 2001.

MANAGEMENT STYLE: THE CEO AND THE MONK

Catell's career was marked by an unparalleled dedication to his job. His typical routine consisted of leaving home by 6 a.m. and then spending time between his offices in Brooklyn and Hicksville before returning home by 10 or 11 p.m. each night. Industry analysts have also noted that Catell was sensitive to workers' needs and had the ability to compromise with workers, communities, and environmental groups. Even though he was the manager of a large corporation, Catell noted that he saw himself as part of the residential and small business communities and that the company needed to work in groups with these communities.

In the book *The CEO and the Monk: One Company's Journey to Profit and Purpose*, Catell wrote about his views of management and building a better company through employee input, caring, and community service. Coauthored with his company's corporate ombudsman Kenny Moore, a former Catholic clergyman, and the writer Glen Rifkin, the book outlined how KeySpan made it through two major mergers in two years by creating new corporate cultures that were sensitive to its workers needs. Catell described how he and Moore helped the company "hold on to its soul" through various human resources initiatives in which employees meditated, created murals, and vented their feelings in other ways. Catell and Moore also instilled the idea that mistakes happen and that ethics should be a mainstay of the corporate culture. As reported by Claire Poole in the *Daily Deal*, Catell wrote in the book that he had made mistakes and added, "But I do feel extremely comfortable that I will leave behind a very clear set of beliefs about the ethical way to conduct business and treat people" (March 15, 2004).

CONTINUED TO LEAD

Although Catell's term as CEO of KeySpan was slated to end in July 2003, his contract was extended through July 2005. In October 2003, he called for the federal government to reduce regulatory impediments on gas drilling and transportation in order to improve the nation's gas supply while continuing to improve energy efficiency and conservation. In December 2003 KeySpan reaffirmed its 2003 earnings forecast of $2.45 to $2.60 per share for the year and forecast 2004 consolidated earnings of $2.55 to $2.75 per share, driven by what Catell expected to be strong contributions from both its natural gas and electric businesses. In addition to his duties at KeySpan, Catell served on the board of numerous companies, including Alberta Northeast Gas, the Houston Exploration Company, KeySpan Facilities Income Fund, Edison Electric Institute, New York State Energy Research and Development Authority, Independence Community Bank Corp, and J. and W. Seligman.

See also entries on Brooklyn Union Gas and KeySpan Energy Co. in *International Directory of Company Histories.*

SOURCES FOR FURTHER INFORMATION

"AGA Raises the Environmental Stakes," *Gas World International*, November 1994, p. 30.

Josefak, Lisa, "Key Authority Q&A: Robert Catell," *Long Island Business News*, August 11, 1997, p. 34.

"Leading the Charge," *Long Island Business News*, July 21, 2000, p. 5A.

Lentz, Philip, "Investors Await Payoff from KeySpan," *Crain's New York Business*, November 15, 1999, p. 3.

Poole, Claire, "Values 101," *Daily Deal*, March 15, 2004.

"Robert Catell: Chairman & CEO, KeySpan Corp.," *Utility Business*, June 1, 2001, p. 80.

Solnik, Claude, "In the Big Leagues," *Long Island Business News*, December 14, 2001, p. 5A.

—David Petechuk

■ ■ ■

William Cavanaugh III

1939–

Former chairman, chief executive officer, and president, Progress Energy

Nationality: American.

Born: 1939, in New Orleans, Louisiana.

Education: Tulane University, BS, 1961.

Career: U.S. Navy, 1961–1969, rose to the rank of lieutenant commander of the navy's nuclear program; Entergy Corporation, 1969–1986, several management capacities at subsidiaries, became chief operating officer (COO) and director, became group president of Energy Supply; 1986–1992, chairman, president and chief executive officer (CEO) of Entergy Operations; chairman, president, and CEO of System Energy Resources; Carolina Power & Light Company, 1992–1996, president and COO; 1996–2001, president and CEO; Progress Energy, 2000–2004, president, CEO, and chairman.

Awards: Member, National Academy of Engineering, 1993; Thad Eure Jr. Memorial Award, Greater Raleigh Convention & Visitors Bureau, 2002; Outstanding Alumnus Award, Tulane University, 2002.

■ As CEO of Carolina Power & Light Company, William Cavanaugh III forged a merger in 2000 between his company and Florida Progress Corporation to establish Progress Energy as a regional leader in the energy business. While many power and utility companies began to expand quickly after industry deregulation, Cavanaugh and Progress Energy took a more cautious approach, primarily focusing on its core businesses. Cavanaugh's conservative approach helped Progress Energy weather industry scandal, a recession, and the vagaries of deregulation that eventually plagued the more aggressive power companies. Industry analysts subsequently praised Cavanaugh's approach of keeping the company true to its utility roots while taking disciplined steps toward expansion and diversification.

FROM THE HIGH SEAS TO HIGH WIRES

A native of New Orleans, Cavanaugh received his bachelor's degree in mechanical engineering from Tulane University. He then spent the next eight years in the U.S. Navy, primarily serving in the navy's nuclear-powered submarine program. After leaving the navy in 1969 as a lieutenant commander, Cavanaugh joined the Mississippi-based Entergy Corporation, where he spent the next 23 years working in a variety of positions. At first he held management positions with the company's various subsidiaries, including Arkansas Power & Light, Louisiana Power & Light, and Mississippi Power & Light. He went on to serve as group president of Energy Supply; chairman, CEO, and president of Entergy Operations; and chairman, CEO, and president of System Energy Resources.

In 1992 Cavanaugh left Entergy and joined Carolina Power & Light (CP&L) in Raleigh, North Carolina, as president and COO. At the time, the company was a sleepy utility with one of the industry's worst run plants. Over the next eight years, Cavanaugh would guide the company toward establishing facilities that would rank among the best in the industry.

When Cavanaugh was appointed CEO of CP&L in 1996, few industry analysts paid much attention to the change in leadership. Within two and a half years, however, the company had undergone major adjustments; many insiders noted that Cavanaugh sparked more change in the company in that short amount of time than it had experienced in several decades. Cavanaugh oversaw several expansion efforts, including a $354 million acquisition of the North Carolina Gas Company, the building of a $250 million gas turbine plant in Rowan County, and the purchase of the Internet company Interpath Communications, which Cavanaugh integrated with CP&L's Caro-Net Telecommunications. Cavanaugh also made significant changes in senior management and accelerated the company's cost-cutting efforts.

WARY OF DEREGULATION

Early on in his stint at the helm of CP&L, Cavanaugh took a cautious approach to the increasing deregulation of the power industry. Between 1989 and 1994 Congress had passed laws that opened up wholesale power purchasing and energy trading, with utilities sharing their grids and buying and selling electricity from each other. As a result, many companies optimistically saw deregulation as the beginning of a new era of expansion and profits; many states geared up for a more competitive retail market. Cavanaugh and CP&L, on the other hand, remained skeptical. In an article in *Business North Carolina*, the State Utilities Commission Attorney Gisele Rankin told Edward Martin that when a legislative commission began to debate the best method of deregulating retail electricity in North Carolina, CP&L became "known as the just-say-no crowd" (November 2003).

While companies such as Duke Energy, Enron, and others pressed North Carolina for deregulation, Cavanaugh stood firm in his beliefs. Cavanaugh and CP&L were concerned that states with higher electricity rates, like New York, would end up draining power from low-cost states like North Carolina and force CP&L and other electric utilities to raise their prices. He also saw deregulation as removing companies' incentives to invest in power grids and new plants as they focused on becoming the lowest bidders for supplying power. In direct confrontation with Duke Energy, Cavanaugh and CP&L initiated concerted lobbying in an attempt to sway legislators and donated over $60,000 to a pair of groups aligned against deregulation, which assisted two people in attaining appointments to the 23-member commission assessing the issue. Cavanaugh told Martin, "We felt deregulation of electricity was such an important step—fiddling around with something that already worked well—that we should be careful not to put the system in jeopardy" (November 2003).

Cavanaugh rebuffed most offers at expansion and diversification. He was especially wary of Enron, which offered CP&L a 10-year contract for its industrial customers. Cavanaugh later recalled that he couldn't figure how other companies were accomplishing such a great deal of marketing and trading; that is, in spite of high volume, sources of actual profits were unclear. In opposition to these other companies' tactics, Cavanaugh focused his company on the core business of serving wholesale and retail customers. He believed that CP&L was growing and strong, and he was unwilling to go overseas or to any other place where the company would be unfamiliar with the business landscape. Many analysts saw Cavanaugh's philosophy as leaving CP&L out of the ultimately profitable bigger picture.

MAKES A MOVE

While Cavanaugh may have been cautious about deregulation, he was not going to let CP&L be left behind. In 2000 he negotiated the purchase of Florida Progress Corporation, the parent company of Florida Power. The merger of the two midsized companies would allow CP&L to compete in a rapidly consolidating electricity industry and also in a new geographic market. Cavanaugh was named chairman and CEO of the newly formed Progress Energy.

Cavanaugh credited the small financial windfall from the merger with partially offsetting a recent decrease in customer demand for electricity, which had come about as a result of moderate weather, reduced purchases by industrial consumers, and intentional temporary shutdowns at a number of nuclear plants. Taking into account the layoffs of 1,200 employees that had resulted from the merger, the company was on track to notch $100 million in savings through 2001 and an additional $75 million by 2003. Cavanaugh remained optimistic about the company's synthetic-fuel, merchant-generation, and marketing businesses, which sold electricity on the wholesale market. He told Kris Hundley of the *St. Petersburg Times*, "Our plans for solid earnings and dividend growth have not changed" (July 26, 2001).

GUIDES THROUGH TROUBLED TIMES

While Cavanaugh remained optimistic, he faced a struggling economy, which reduced the forecast demand for energy. After the terrorist attacks of September 11, 2001, Cavanaugh saw the future of energy further altered as the economic slowdown deepened. Cavanaugh told Martin in *Business North Carolina*, "We quickly saw that the business of double-digit growth was not going to be possible" (November 2003).

Although Cavanaugh stood on the sidelines during much of the initial activities of deregulation, he had made limited forays into other businesses, not all of which were successful. Expansions of gas-turbine plants in Georgia and North Carolina were halted when wholesale gas prices plummeted in 2002. The company's telecommunications subsidiaries also stumbled.

Cavanaugh proceeded to try to slim down the company by selling such noncore subsidiaries as Progress Rail Services, a rail freight-car lease and repair service. Cavanaugh then reemphasized the company's focus on earning profits through production of regulated electricity. In 2002 the company struggled with less-than-expected earnings of $529 million on gross revenue of $1.9 billion. The company's earnings per share dropped to $2.46 in 2002, compared to $2.64 in 2001. Most industry analysts noted that the company's performance may not have been stellar in 2002, but it consistently outperformed other utilities as it weathered energy-business scandals and the economic downturn.

In a presentation before the company's Annual Meeting of Shareholders in May 2003, Cavanaugh told shareholders, as reported on PR Newswire, "Progress Energy's strategy is to remain true to its utility roots while making strategic investments in related business that can generate higher growth" (May 14, 2003). By the end of the year, Cavanaugh's strategy appeared to be working. The company reported consolidated net income of $782 million, or $3.30 per share, in 2003. In addition, the company made successful efforts to sell further noncore assets—including the North Carolina Natural Gas subsidiary purchased through CP&L in 1999—which helped the company pay down its more than $11 billion of debt. These sales helped reduce the company's capital expenditures and push its leverage (the use of debt to increase returns) to below 59 percent. At the same time, the company raised its dividends for the 16th consecutive year, including the years when it was still CP&L.

MANAGEMENT STYLE: BE COMPETITIVE

Cavanaugh noted that success goes beyond capturing and holding a market share. He stressed that management must comprise good competitors if the company is to be able to pursue and capitalize on opportunities. As reported in *Executive Speeches*, Cavanaugh told attendees of the 23rd National Conference of the American Association of Blacks in Energy that achieving success "also means working with the best suppliers and—at the heart of the matter—attracting and retaining the best employees" (December 2000).

Industry analysts and coworkers noted that Cavanaugh was a high-caliber leader who stressed excellence and ethics. In 2002 Progress Energy was one of only three S&P 500 companies to be recognized by Standard and Poor's for providing the most complete and detailed information possible to investors. As reported by PR Newswire, Cavanaugh observed, "In this post-Enron era, it's more important than ever for corporations to be clear and up-front about their financial condition and business practices. Acting with integrity is very much the Progress Energy way" (May 14, 2003).

DECIDES TO RETIRE

Although Cavanaugh had originally planned to retire on February 1, 2004, the Enron scandal of 2002 and general turmoil in the industry led the company's board to ask him to delay his date of departure. Cavanaugh agreed but said that he would still want to retire close to the initially scheduled date if the financial situation improved. By January of 2004 Cavanaugh and the board believed that the state of the industry had calmed down considerably and that Progress Energy was on firm footing. Cavanaugh retired from his position as CEO in March 2004 and from his position as chairman the following May.

Industry analysts agreed that Cavanaugh turned over the reins of a company with a solid financial foundation. He accomplished this feat by making wise decisions that successfully led Progress Energy through a recession and through the uncertainty of deregulation. In a Progress Energy press release, J. Tylee Wilson, the presiding director, noted, "Bill made Progress Energy a great place to work for employees and an exceptional value for investors" (January 23, 2004).

Upon retirement, in addition to spending more time with his family, Cavanaugh intended to remain involved in nuclear issues for the power industry. He served on the governing board of the World Association of Nuclear Operators as well as the board of directors of Edison Electric Institute, the Nuclear Energy Institute, and the Research Triangle Foundation.

See also entry on Carolina Power & Light Company in *International Directory of Company Histories.*

SOURCES FOR FURTHER INFORMATION

Cavanaugh, William, "Competition as a Springboard for Increased Opportunity," *Executive Speeches*, December 2000, p. 12.

Hundley, Kris, "Progress Enjoys Healthy Growth," *St. Petersburg Times*, July 26, 2001, http://www.sptimes.com/News/072601/Business/Progress_enjoys_healt.shtml.

Martin, Edward, "Watts Up, Doc?" *Business North Carolina*, November 2003, http://www.businessnc.com/archives/2003/11/progress_energy.html.

Price, Dudley, "Progress Energy CEO to Quit in May," *Knight Ridder/Tribune Business News*, January 24, 2004.

"Progress Energy CEO Tells Shareholders the Company Has Demonstrated Its Fundamental Strength and Is Focused on Integrity," PR Newswire, May 14, 2003.

Progress Energy, "Progress Energy Chairman and CEO William Cavanaugh to Retire," press release, January 23, 2004, http://www.progress-energy.com/aboutus/news/article.asp?id=8182.

—David Petechuk

■ ■ ■

Charles M. Cawley

1941–

Former president and chief executive officer of MBNA Corporation; former chairman and chief executive officer of MBNA America Bank

Nationality: American.

Born: 1941, in New Jersey.

Education: Georgetown University, earned degree, 1962.

Family: Married Julie (maiden name unknown).

Career: Maryland Bank National Association, worked primarily in consumer credit; MBNA Corporation, founded in 1982; 1984–2002, president; 2002–2003, president and chief executive officer; MBNA America Bank, ?–2003, chairman and chief executive officer.

Awards: Awarded the Josiah Marvel Cup by the Delaware State Chamber of Commerce; named Person of the Year in 2002 by NJBIZ; awarded President's Medal by Georgetown University, 2002.

■ Charles M. Cawley cofounded the small regional credit card issuer MBNA Corporation in 1982 and developed it into the largest independent credit card issuer and one of the 50 most profitable companies in the United States. Cawley built MBNA largely by adapting affinity marketing to the credit card business. Affinity marketing attracts customers with specific interests, and Cawley used this marketing technique to issue credit cards in association with various organizations, such as universities and their alumni societies, special interest groups, and others. Described by associates and industry insiders as driven, brash, and outspoken, Cawley enjoyed corporate largesse to the full while building a company known for customer service and for being one of the best places to work, as noted by publications as divergent as *Fortune* and *Working Mother* magazines.

DEVELOPS AFFINITY MARKETING FOR CREDIT CARDS

Born and raised in New Jersey, Cawley graduated from St. Benedict's Catholic boys school in 1958 and then from Georgetown University four years later. Early in his career Cawley worked as a door-to-door bill collector in Newark, New Jersey, before beginning his financial services career in 1963. Cawley was working for Maryland Bank National Association in 1982 when he headed a small group of the bank's executives in establishing MBNA. Cawley set up shop in an abandoned A&P supermarket in Ogletown, Delaware, largely because that state had just removed its cap on the interest rates lenders could charge.

Within a year Cawley came up with an idea that would propel the fledgling MBNA to the forefront of the credit card business. Inspired by a program that linked several banks with the American Automobile Association (AAA), Cawley approached Georgetown University's alumni association with an idea. He proposed that the association sponsor a credit card for Georgetown alumni. Cawley believed that people were more likely to choose and use a credit card connected with their alma mater than a card from a company they did not know and with whom they had no connection. Cawley was convinced that such cardholder groups would remain more committed to having MBNA credit cards and less likely to look around for lower rates or to default on their debts. Georgetown's alumni association agreed, and Cawley had given birth to the concept of affinity lending.

Over the next decade following the establishment of MBNA, Cawley developed MBNA into a major marketer of affinity credit cards. In addition to loyalty and nondefault of debts, MBNA's customers also tended to carry a larger balance on their cards from month to month, thus incurring interest charges, further making them ideal customers. Between 1991 and 1992 MBNA Corporation, the holding company of MBNA America Bank, had increased its income14 percent to $149 million. By the end of 1992 MBNA had 8.5 million cardholders and $9.3 billion in card loans. It also was the second-largest issuer of MasterCard and Visa cards in the United States. Furthermore, MBNA continued to be successful while many other credit card issuers were having difficulties finding new customers and facing rates and fees pressures, a faltering consumer confidence, and a barrage of new competitors.

Once again Cawley's success in placing MBNA on firm ground resulted from his marketing of credit cards to 3,000 affinity groups around the country. Industry analysts noted that instead of mass-mail solicitations, Cawley oversaw a campaign that focused on creditworthy spenders by targeting members of its affinity partners. Unlike other credit card issuers, MBNA and Cawley insisted that a credit analyst, and not just a computer program, should screen each individual application. As a result, MBNA's average cardholders were homeowners earning $55,000 annually and who paid their bills on time for an average of 14 years. Cawley explained the approach to Yvette D. Kantrow in *American Banker* this way: "When someone is at the point where he is spending money to be a member of an organization—whether a professional organization, an alumni association, or something else—he has probably settled down. We are giving cards to people who have a high probability of using them properly" (March 2, 1993).

While intelligent marketing to the right customers was the basis of MBNA's growth, Cawley also emphasized customer service and person-to-person marketing. For example, Cawley believed that computers could not routinely make decisions that built loyalty among customers, such as increasing a customer's credit limit. In dealing with different groups, Cawley also hired negotiators that were familiar with or actually associated with the group, such as a former dentist to deal with the American Dental Association and an automobile enthusiast to deal with the transportation sector. To further promote personal contact, Cawley had MBNA salespeople set up booths at more than a 1,000 annual conventions each year.

PURSUES GROWTH STRATEGY

By 1997 the credit card industry was suffering a new set of troubles as charge-offs and delinquency rates climbed and the industry experienced sharply declining growth in new accounts and receivables. Cawley, however, was looking optimistically toward further growth. By year-end 1996 MBNA had $33.8 billion in receivables and stood above other credit card issuers in that its asset quality was well above the industry average. In addition, MBNA's receivables expanded 39 percent over 1996 while other top card issuers experienced a declining or much slower growth. While Cawley and MBNA continued to expand its affinity group cardholders, including signing up 225 new groups over the first quarter of 1997, another factor in the company's success was Cawley's decision to issue a new Platinum card in the spring of 1995. Over the next two years, the card attracted 4.4 million new cardholders.

Cawley's growth plan focused on three areas. On the international front, the company expanded to the United Kingdom and was focusing on establishing itself in Ireland and Canada. Nevertheless, Cawley took a conservative approach to expanding internationally, choosing a wait-and-see attitude to markets in Asia and Latin America. Cawley also began to move MBNA more into consumer financing by setting up a separate division. By 1997, the division had grown into a $4 billion business. Finally, Cawley saw enormous potential in the insurance industry and created a subsidiary insurance agency.

In addition to these growth efforts, Cawley continued to see a growth market in affinity groups despite the claims of many industry insiders that this particular marketing strategy had been mined out. In 1997 he told John W. Milligan for an article in *US Banker*, "Today, 55% of all the physicians in this country carry our card. Well, there's another 45% who don't. Twenty-five percent of all the nurses 36% of all the lawyers . . . and on and on" (July 1997).

ANALYSTS PERCEIVE PROBLEMS

Despite the fact that MBNA had experienced nine straight years of 25 percent earnings growth since the company went public in 1991, industry analysts believed that the juggernaut Cawley had created was beginning to show signs of strain. Seeing indications of an oncoming recession, they were concerned that MBNA would falter because of numerous factors, including recent highly priced acquisitions, a dangerously low leverage, and MBNA's growing emphasis on controversial accounting techniques. Furthermore, getting new accounts was becoming more expensive, costing MBNA $32 per account as opposed to just $14 an account five years earlier. Analysts also noted that, even with a customer base of cardholders who had solid credit histories, a recession could lead to a rash of defaults on credit cards.

For the most part, Cawley shrugged off these concerns, noting that these potential problems were more dangerous for other firms that were not run as well as MBNA. He noted that MBNA had weathered both the recession in the early 1990s and the credit crunch that hurt many lenders in 1998. He told Rob Wherry of *Forbes* magazine, "The reason you don't read a lot about us is that we don't screw things up" (November 13, 2000).

In the end Cawley's confidence proved correct. MBNA not only weathered much of the recession that began in 2001 but also actually prospered. For example, his strategy of giving affinity cards to high-end customers continued to garner a loyal and prosperous cardholder base that included 75 percent of the doctors in the United States by mid-2003. In 2003 the company turned a profit of $2.34 billion and the company's share price by 2004 had grown at a rate of 28 percent a year. Overall, Cawley's leadership led Standard & Poor's to report in 2003 that MBNA had the best five-year annualized return of any bank in the S&P 500.

MANAGEMENT STYLE: BOLD, BRASH, AND EFFECTIVE

Cawley summed up and repeated his philosophy of business and life many times. He related to Stephen Kleege for an article in *American Banker*, "Life by the inch is a cinch; life by the yard is hard" (September 21, 1993). This philosophy was well demonstrated in Cawley's approach in targeting MBNA credit cards to small sectors of the population. Industry analysts praised Cawley for being a focused manager who stuck to his guns. Rather than an indiscriminate mass-marketing approach, Cawley formed regional centers around the country where MBNA marketed to individual states on a very narrow basis.

As for his own personal style, Cawley was described by colleagues as abrupt and temperamental but also as giving and funny. Although shrewd and conservative in his business dealings, he was also somewhat capricious, especially in rewarding himself and other top executives with lavish salaries and perks. On the other hand, Cawley formed a company noted for its good employee relations, which Cawley saw as being good for business. The banking analyst Susan L. Roth told Kantrow in *American Banker*, "They treat their employees so well that they have every incentive to treat their customers well" (March 2, 1993).

Colleagues also noted that Cawley was spontaneous and secure in his decision-making and extremely loyal to those who stood by him. He also had a penchant for order, even going so far as to pull a flower in full bloom from one of the company's flowerbeds because he thought the color was wrong. Michael Auriemma, president of an industry consulting firm, told Jonathan D. Epstein in Delaware's *News Journal*, "He's a visionary that had . . . an idea about how a credit card company should work . . . instilled his culture and his vision in the fabric of that company and has been extremely successful at it" (January 4, 2004).

ALL GOOD THINGS MUST END

After MBNA cofounder Alfred Lerner died in October 2002, Cawley was given the additional title of CEO of MBNA Corporation, retaining his title as president and his position as chairman and CEO of MBNA America Bank, the primary subsidiary of MBNA Corporation. However, despite the company's continued prosperity, Cawley resigned on December 30, 2003. Although the company said that Cawley's retirement was part of a mutually agreed-upon transition, company executives and others eventually revealed that Cawley's departure was the result of an intense disagreement with the board of directors. While other company executives were cutting costs Cawley stubbornly refused to adhere to a new accountability in corporate spending, an issue that had received a great deal of public and federal scrutiny in other companies. Many of the board members believed that Cawley was overusing and perhaps even misusing MBNA's corporate jets and other corporate assets.

With the growing scandals of Enron and corporate leaders bilking company funds for personal use, the board and stockholders became increasingly concerned about what Cawley viewed as a type of executive privilege. As friction between the old and new ways grew, Cawley became upset over the efforts of the board's compensation committee to restructure executives' pay and perks. Ten days after an especially confrontational meeting with MBNA's board in early November 2003, Cawley announced his retirement. An anonymous MBNA director told Lowell Bergman and Patrick Mcgeehan for an article in the *New York Times*, "It probably was time for him to go. Had he been willing to change and do things the way the board wanted him to do, there's no doubt in my mind he would be there today" (March 7, 2004).

Despite leaving his executive positions at the company, Cawley agreed to serve as a consultant. In addition to his financial compensation package, Cawley's retirement package included two full-time personal assistants and access to the company's planes for him and his wife for the rest of their lives. As for Cawley, he told Epstein of the *News Journal*, "Everyone can do things better, but I can't really think of too many things that the company and all of its people have done that in any way I'm not proud to be associated with" (January 4, 2004). Cawley was also noted for his philanthropic efforts. He served on the Board of Regents of Georgetown University and the American Architectural Foundation and on the Executive Committee of the Board of Directors of MasterCard International.

See also entry on MBNA Corporation in *International Directory of Company Histories*.

SOURCES FOR FURTHER INFORMATION

Bergman, Lowell, and Patrick Mcgeehan, "Co-founder of MBNA Meets an Anxious Board and Loses," *New York Times*, March 7, 2004.

Epstein, Jonathan D., "Cawley Sends Out 28,000 Thank Yous," *News Journal* (Delaware), January 4, 2004.

Kantrow, Yvette D., "MBNA's Lerner & Cawley: Masters of Card Marketing," *American Banker*, March 2, 1993, p. 1.

Kleege, Stephen, "MBNA Exploits Affinity for Success in Crowded Card Business," *American Banker*, September 21, 1993, p. 8A.

Milligan, John W., "Defying Gravity at MBNA," *US Banker*, July 1997, p. 35.

Wherry, Rob, "Credit Check," *Forbes*, November 13, 2000, p. 148.

—David Petechuk

■■■

Clarence P. Cazalot Jr.

1951–

President and chief executive officer, Marathon Oil Corporation

Nationality: American.

Born: 1951, in New Orleans, Louisiana.

Education: Louisiana State University, BS, 1972.

Career: Texaco, 1972–1974, geophysicist; offshore division, 1974–1976, various posts; 1976–1977, assistant district geologist; 1977–1979, district geologist; 1979–1981, assistant division geologist; 1981–1984, regional manager of exploration; 1984–1985, staff geologist for exploration and production executive committee; 1985–1987, assistant to vice chairman; frontier exploration department, 1987–1992, general manager; 1992–2000, corporate vice president; 1992, president of Latin America/West Africa Division; Texaco Exploration and Production, 1994–1997, president; Texaco International Marketing and Manufacturing, 1997–1998, president; Texaco Ltd., 1998–1999, president for international production and chairman; 1999–2000, corporate vice president and president for production operations; USX Corporation, 2000–2001, vice chairman; Marathon Oil Company (an operating unit of USX), 2000–2001, president; Marathon Oil Corporation, 2001–, president and CEO.

Address: Marathon Oil Corporation, 5555 San Felipe Road, Houston, Texas 77056–2723; http://www.marathon.com.

■ The oil-industry veteran Clarence Cazalot had already spent more than 25 years in the industry when he was tapped in 2000 to take over the leadership of Marathon Oil Company, which was then operating under the umbrella of the giant steel conglomerate USX. Just a little more than a year later Marathon broke from USX and, in the two ensuing years, reached new levels of profitability under Cazalot's direction. As one of the largest U.S. oil-and-gas companies, Marathon posted net income of more than $1.3 billion for 2003 on total revenue of just over $41.2 billion, a sharp increase from a profit of $516 million on sales of about $31.5 billion in the previous year.

As president and CEO of Marathon Oil Corporation, Cazalot focused much of his energy on expanding the company's asset base through ambitious investments in worldwide exploration and production. In late January 2004 Marathon unveiled a capital spending budget of nearly $2.3 billion for 2004. Roughly 60 percent of the budget was allocated for Marathon's exploration and production operations, while 25 percent was earmarked for refining, marketing, and transportation, with the final 15 percent going to integrated gas and corporate expenditures.

STUDIES GEOLOGY AT LOUISIANA STATE UNIVERSITY

A native of New Orleans, Cazalot enrolled at Louisiana State University (LSU) in Baton Rouge after graduating from high school. As a geology major, he participated in LSU's Geology Field Camp during the summer of 1970. Established in the 1920s, the field camp, located near Colorado Springs, Colorado, was designed to provide LSU students with important field experience in geology, geophysics, and petroleum engineering. (In September 2001 Marathon, under Cazalot's leadership, announced a leadership gift of $100,000 to the LSU Foundation to be used for infrastructure improvements at the camp.) In 1972 Cazalot received his BS in geology.

Shortly after graduating from LSU, Cazalot joined Texaco in Bellaire, Texas, as a geophysicist. Two years later he transferred to the company's offshore division, headquartered in New Orleans. He held a number of posts in the offshore division over the next two years and in 1976 was named assistant district geologist. A year later he was promoted to district geologist, moving to assistant division geologist in 1979 and regional manager of exploration in 1981. Three years later, in 1984, Cazalot was transferred to corporate headquarters in Harrison, New York, and named staff geologist for Texaco's exploration and production executive committee. In 1985 he was named assistant to Texaco's vice chairman, a post he held until 1987, when he became general manager of Texaco's frontier exploration department in Bellaire.

Cazalot was elected a corporate vice president in 1992 and was named president of the company's Latin America/West Africa Division. Under Cazalot, the division, headquartered in Coral Gables, Florida, established three regional centers, all of which reported to Cazalot in Coral Gables. Texaco's center in

Rio de Janeiro was responsible for the company's operations in Argentina, Bolivia, Brazil, Chile, Paraguay, and Uruguay. Another center in Bogota, Colombia, was responsible for the company's activities in Colombia, Ecuador, Panama, Peru, and Venezuela. A separate operations center, also based in Coral Gables, was charged with overseeing Texaco's operations in Central America, the Caribbean, and Canada. In addition, the headquarters operation supervised exploration and drilling in the African countries of Angola, Nigeria, Cameroon, and Togo, the marketing responsibilities for which were transferred to Texaco Europe.

ASSUMES PRESIDENCY OF TEPI

In 1994 Texaco appointed Cazalot, who retained his corporate vice presidency, president of Texaco Exploration and Production (TEPI), headquartered in Harrison, New York. In the fall of 1996 Texaco announced an organizational realignment, effective January 1, 1997, under which Cazalot became president of Texaco International Marketing and Manufacturing and was reposted to London. In 1998 Cazalot was named corporate president for international production and chairman of TEPI. On November 12, 1998, Texaco outlined its plans for a reorganization of its international upstream operations, effective January 1, 1999. The reorganization was designed to focus more sharply on upstream activities in three key areas: the location and acquisition of resources, swift commercial development of such resources, and the optimization of Texaco's global production operations. In this reorganization, Cazalot was named president of production operations and posted to Texaco's offices in White Plains, New York.

In early 2000 USX Corporation, a holding company formed in 1986 to manage operations formerly directed by U.S. Steel Corporation, announced that it had hired Cazalot to run Marathon Oil Company, one of USX's four independent operating units. In accepting his new post as president, Cazalot extolled Marathon, according to a corporate press release, as "a world-class oil company with great potential to grow and prosper." He also stated: "I look forward to working with Marathon's fine management team to take the company to the next level of success." At the same time, Cazalot was named a vice chairman of USX and elected to its board of directors.

Responding to growing pressure from both analysts and investors, USX in April 2001 announced plans to separate Marathon from USX's weaker steel business. In publicizing the spin-off of Marathon, Tom Usher, USX chairman and CEO, said that the move would give the oil company greater flexibility to expand its business through stock-based acquisitions. Under the terms of the breakup, Cazalot became Marathon's CEO as well as its president. Speaking to security analysts in early 2002, Cazalot outlined a business strategy that he said would create sustainable growth in Marathon's value through the pursuit of unique partnerships and innovative energy solutions. Discussing the ways in which Marathon could compete most effectively in a market that put a premium on size, he said that the key to the company's strategy would be to find a way to achieve profitable growth and create value rather than to focus on the company's size. Cazalot said that he hoped to set Marathon apart from its competitors by adopting a business model enabling the company to use its size as an advantage, "linking our technical strength, commercial skills, and international stature with a willingness to do things differently, and to do so with the speed and agility of a small enterprise."

GUIDES MARATHON TO STRATEGIC ACQUISITIONS

Over the next two years Cazalot led Marathon to a number of strategic acquisitions and joint-venture operations, all selected for their fit into the company's overall strategy for the long term. During 2002 Marathon acquired and successfully integrated significant natural gas interests in Equatorial Guinea and laid the groundwork for additional expansion in that tiny West African country. Additional upstream interests were acquired in Norway, and Marathon signed an agreement with XTO Energy, under which the former swapped some of its oil-and-gas properties in Texas and Louisiana for XTO's coal-bed methane assets in the Powder River Basin of northern Wyoming and southern Montana.

In 2003 Marathon reached agreement with the government of Equatorial Guinea and its state-owned oil company, GE-Petrol, to develop a liquefied natural gas (LNG) project on Bioko Island. The joint venture's Bioko LNG plant, scheduled to come onstream in 2007, was forecast to yield an annual output of roughly 3.4 million metric tons of LNG. Marathon also saw significant advances in its Norwegian exploration program, announcing in September 2003 its third Norwegian discovery of the year. After a long absence from the Russian market, where it had played an instrumental role in developing oil-and-gas fields off Sakhalin Island, Marathon in May 2003 acquired Khanty Mansiysk Oil Corporation (KMOC) in a transaction valued at roughly $280 million. In announcing the KMOC purchase, according to a corporate press release, Cazalot said: "This acquisition forms the basis for a new core area with substantial near- and medium-term growth, and is consistent with our strategy of upgrading" the company's upstream portfolio.

In December 2003 Cazalot hinted that Marathon might be interested in buying out Ashland's minority interest in the two companies' joint venture, Marathon Ashland Petroleum (MAP), the fifth-largest oil refiner in the United States. At the time, Marathon owned 62 percent of MAP, which was headquartered in Findlay, Ohio, with Ashland holding a 38 percent stake. MAP operated seven refineries that together were capable of processing more than 900,000 barrels of oil daily. Its refined products were marketed at Marathon's 3,800 service stations and also through its Speedway SuperAmerica retail subsidiary, which operated roughly 1,700 outlets.

MAKES PROGRESS REPORT ON STRATEGY

Meeting with security analysts in Houston in early November 2003, Cazalot expressed satisfaction with Marathon's progress in the implementation of the strategies and business plans he had first outlined in February 2002. He said that the company expected its average daily production in 2004 to total about 365,000 barrels of oil equivalent, reflecting the impact of recent acquisitions and joint ventures. Assessing the energy-industry climate for 2004 and beyond, Cazalot pointed to such key factors as an increasing emphasis on natural gas as a global market commodity, continued volatility in commodity prices, the emergence of heightened competition from state-owned oil companies, and declining output from traditional oil-and-gas basins. Although all factors were sure to have a significant effect on the industry's competitive landscape, Cazalot said that finding "access to profitable new oil and gas resources is perhaps the most critical issue facing international energy companies," according to a corporate press release.

In addition to his responsibilities as Marathon's president and CEO, in the early 2000s Cazalot was deeply involved in both civic and industry-related affairs. He sat on the boards of Spindletop Charities, the Greater Houston Partnership, and the Sam Houston Area Council of the Boys Scouts of America. He also served on the boards of Baker Hughes, the American Petroleum Institute, the Maguire Energy Institute, and the U.S.–Saudi Arabian Business Council and was a member of the National Petroleum Council, National Association of Manufacturers, and the American Association of Petroleum Geologists.

See also entries on Texaco Inc., USX Corporation, and Marathon Oil Corp. in *International Directory of Company Histories.*

SOURCES FOR FURTHER INFORMATION

Antosh, Nelson, "Oil Prices Power Marathon's Profits; Other Majors Likely to Show Large Gains," *Houston Chronicle,* January 28, 2004.

Birger, Larry, "Texaco Planning to Remain in Coral Gables, Fla.," *Miami Herald,* January 16, 1994.

"Cazalot Elected USX Vice Chairman and Marathon President," March 2, 2000, http://www.marathon.com/News_Center/Press_Releases/2000_News_Releases/?releaseid=244652.

Davis, Michael, "Houston-Based Oil Company Leaves Steel Conglomerate," *Houston Chronicle,* April 25, 2001.

Hassell, Greg, "Marathon Oil Names Executive as New President," *Houston Chronicle,* March 2, 2000.

"Marathon Completes Acquisition of Khanty Mansiysk Oil Corporation; Acquisition Establishes Russia as a New Core Area for Growth," May 13, 2003, http://www.marathon.com/News_Center/Press_Releases/2003_News_Releases/?releaseid=411778.

"Marathon Reaffirms Company Strategy and Outlines Plans to Achieve Sustainable Value Growth," November 4, 2003, http://www.marathon.com/News_Center/Press_Releases/2003_News_Releases/?releaseid=466396.

"Marathon Stays with Strategy, Outlines Plans for More Growth," *Houston Business Journal,* November 4, 2004.

—Don Amerman

■ ■ ■

Nicholas D. Chabraja

1942–

Chief executive officer and chairman of the board, General Dynamics

Nationality: American.

Born: November 6, 1942, in Gary, Indiana.

Education: Northwestern University, BA, 1964; Northwestern University, JD, 1967.

Family: Married Eleanor (maiden name unknown; philanthropist).

Career: Jenner & Block (law firm), 1968–1997; 1984–1993, partner; 1986, special counsel to United States House of Representatives; 1992, special counsel to General Dynamics; General Dynamics, 1993–1994, senior vice president and general counsel; 1994–, director; 1994–1996, executive vice president; 1997 (1 January–31 May), vice chairman of the board; 1997–, chief executive officer and chairman of the board.

Address: General Dynamics, 3190 Fairview Park Drive, Falls Church, Virginia 22042-4523; http://www.gendyn.com; http://www.generaldynamics.com; http://www.gd.com.

Nicholas D. Chabraja. *AP/Wide World Photos.*

■ Nicholas (Nick) Chabraja (pronounced cha-*brah*-ya) first made his mark as a lawyer, eventually serving as special counsel to the House of Representatives in 1986 during the Senate impeachment trial of Judge Harry E. Claiburne. For about twenty years he worked on cases for General Dynamics. It was because of his legal services to General Dynamics that he was able to make the shift from lawyer to business executive, becoming both general counsel and vice president for the company in 1993. He revealed an astute understanding of the problems that beset General Dynamics in the 1990s and rose to become the company's chief executive officer. He put the company on a course of expansion after years of cutting away subsidiaries and was so successful that General Dynamics averaged a 19.2 percent annual return on equity from 1997 to 2001, more than double the average for other defense contractors.

FIRST A LAWYER

Chabraja had majored in political science at Northwestern University before earning a degree in law. He was an exceptional legal talent who passed the bar in Indiana in 1967 and in Illinois in 1968. Passing the Illinois bar enabled him to accept a position with Jenner & Block, a prestigious Chicago law firm that also had offices in Washington, D.C. He made his home in Lake Forest, Illinois, a suburb of Chicago, but as he advanced in the law firm, his duties carried him ever more frequently to Washington.

He had worked on the legal affairs of General Dynamics ever since becoming a partner in Jenner & Block in 1984. By the end of the 1980s General Dynamics was losing money. CEO Bill Anders, a former astronaut, sold off problematic divisions, including those making F-16 jets (to Lockheed) and

Tomahawk missiles (to Hughes). By 1993 General Dynamics, which in the 1980s had been the nation's largest defense contractor, had only two divisions left: Electric Boat, which made nuclear submarines, and Land Systems, which made M1 tanks. In March 1992 Chabraja was appointed special counsel to General Dynamics to help with the corporate restructuring.

THEN A BUYER

In 1993 Chabraja joined General Dynamics as senior vice president and general counsel, and in 1994 he became a member of the board of directors, where his sharp mind and astute judgment impressed the other directors. When he became executive vice president in 1994, he began pushing for a new approach for General Dynamics, one of expansion rather than selling off the last divisions of the company. He became Anders's heir apparent, and in quick succession in 1997 he became vice chairman of the board then CEO and chairman. His contract required that he move near to Washington, D.C., and he settled in a suburb in northern Virginia. In 1997 General Dynamics had $4 billion in sales.

General Dynamics faced the choice of dissolving itself by selling what remained or using the capital it had accumulated from the sale of most of its divisions to expand its business. Times were tough for defense contractors, and most were suffering losses in revenue, but Chabraja chose to try to acquire other companies. He looked for companies available at bargain prices that could be improved by better management of their resources, and he tried to acquire companies diverse enough that General Dynamics could make money even when one industry or another was in a slump. Thus, General Dynamics bought Advanced Technology systems, which made fiber optic cables, and Bath Iron Works, which made Aegis destroyers.

In 1999 Chabraja tried his most audacious purchase, the acquisition of Newport News Shipbuilding, makers of nuclear submarines, in a deal agreed to by Newport News management. All seemed well, with shareholders of Newport News happy, but the deal was blocked by the federal government, which wanted to avoid General Dynamics' having a monopoly on the manufacture of America's nuclear submarines. In spite of that setback, Chabraja led the purchase of an ailing maker of private jets, Gulfstream Aerospace Group, concluding the deal on July 30, 1999, for $4.8 billion. Chabraja reduced the size of the company's management and initiated a program of cutting expenses. By 2002 Gulfstream accounted for 40 percent of General Dynamics' profits.

In 2001 General Dynamics bought Motorola's defense unit, which with General Dynamics' fiber optic cable business enabled General Dynamics to improve wiring and communications systems on its ships and in its tanks. In 2002 General Dynamics had $13.8 billion in sales, netting $917 million. On August 8, 2002, the board of directors of General Dynamics extended Chabraja's contract by three years, to 2005.

On March 4, 2003, General Dynamics purchased General Motors' defense division, which made armored vehicles—a good fit with General Dynamics' Land Systems' M1 tank manufacturing. On August 12, 2003, General Dynamics purchased Veridian, an information technologies company that complemented its fiber optics and communications businesses. In 2003 General Dynamics had $16.6 billion in sales, netting $1.004 billion. By 2004 the company employed 67,600 people, up from 9,000 when Chabraja had joined the company.

BUSINESS PHILOSOPHY

Although he was very much admired by coworkers and business journalists, Chabraja was a soft-spoken man who did not care for celebrity status, and he seemed uncomfortable with the public role his leadership of a major defense contractor required. He kept his private life private and his business life focused on the bottom line: "I look at any deal first from the point of view: 'Can I make money?'" he told one reporter (*Forbes*, January 10, 2000) about his acquisitions. During the 1990s, when the defense industry underwent a contraction of business, he looked to investing capital in enterprises that complemented his company's existing businesses and that were only marginally successful or unsuccessful, believing that such companies could be made profitable through prudent cuts in expenses and aggressive marketing. "Generally, we bought businesses at reasonable prices and improved them," he told another reporter (*BusinessWeek Online*, March 27, 2000). He was driven by a belief that good management could solve most problems by focusing on what the marketplace demanded coupled with an understanding that economic reality meant that any business would face temporary downturns in business and therefore should look for long-term profitability.

See also entry on General Dynamics Corporation in *International Directory of Company Histories.*

SOURCES FOR FURTHER INFORMATION

Banks, Howard, "General Dynamics Like a Phoenix," *Forbes*, January 10, 2000, p. 86.

Rubenstein, Bruce, "Back Scratching in the Boardroom: Should Law Firm Partners Sit on Clients' Corporate boards?" *Corporate Legal Times*, January 1995, www.aaronlaw.com/articles/archive%20articles/article01.html.

Serwer, Andy, "General Dynamics: In War and Peace, General Dynamics Is Wall Street's Favorite," *Fortune.com*, November 12, 2001, http://www.fortune.com/fortune/investing/articles/0,15114,373216,00.html.

—Kirk H. Beetz

■■■

John T. Chambers

1949–

Chief executive officer and president, Cisco Systems

Nationality: American.

Born: August 23, 1949, in Cleveland, Ohio.

Education: West Virginia University, BS; JD; Indiana University, MBA.

Family: Son of an obstetrician/gynecologist and a psychologist (names unknown); married Elaine (maiden name unknown); children: two.

Career: IBM, 1976–1983, salesman; Wang Laboratories, 1983–1990, various positions, became executive vice president; Cisco Systems, 1990–1994, senior vice president of Worldwide Operations; 1994–1995, executive vice president; 1995–, CEO and president.

Awards: Lifetime Achievement Award, Smithsonian Institute, 2000; Distinguished Industry Leader Award, IEEE, 2002; Ron Brown Award for Corporate Leadership, The Business Council, 2002–2003; Most Powerful Person in Networking, *Network World*, 2003.

Address: Cisco Systems, 170 West Tasman Drive, San Jose, California 95134; http://www.cisco.com.

■ John T. Chambers rose from the ranks of computer salesmen at IBM to lead Cisco Systems, one of the most innovative and aggressive companies of the technological age. Serving as CEO since 1995, Chambers's tenaciousness and ambition were a major reason why Cisco owned the infrastructure through which over 75 percent of the world's data traveled in 2004. When others shrank in fear during the dot-com collapse of 2000, Chambers's nerves of steel and unflagging optimism allowed Cisco to emerge from the crisis stronger than ever. While many faulted Chambers for his ruthlessness and penny-pinching, none could deny that Cisco Systems would have been a less dominant company at the turn of the century without him at the helm.

John T. Chambers. © *Alan Levenson/Corbis.*

A BORN LEADER

John Chambers was raised in Charleston, West Virginia, in the 1950s, with a background that could hardly be described as provincial. His father was a wealthy obstetrician/gynecologist who delivered all of the children of Governor Jay Rockefeller; his mother was a psychologist. Chambers's family also owned a restaurant in Charleston, and it was there that the boy first thought of someday running his own business. Though Chambers's father recalled him showing leadership skills at a very early age, his study was often made torturous by dyslexia. Although in the 1950s a child could be stigmatized by a learning disorder, Chambers's parents were enlightened, sophisticated people who had faith in their son and obtained the help he needed. The reading specialist they hired, Lorene Anderson-Walters, recalled, "He had this very optimistic attitude about everything. He was just not going to fail. One thing

I notice as I hear him now on TV is that he still has that attitude" (Waters, 2002).

With the single-mindedness for which he would later be famous, Chambers applied himself all the more diligently in school in response to his disability, eventually earning both an undergraduate and a law degree from West Virginia University. His determined, competitive nature showed itself through his participation in intramural sports, his favorite being basketball. Ever the team player, Chamber later remarked that even when he played tennis, he almost always played doubles. He married his high-school sweetheart and frequent doubles partner, Elaine, and for a time thought his life would be centered in his home state. But things had changed in West Virginia since Chambers was a boy. With the government regulating coal mining and chemical plants and the state gaining a reputation as an area of poverty and dissipation, the economy suffered and the population fell. Chambers decided to leave the insular cocoon of his youth and head for Indiana University in Bloomington, where he earned a business degree and lost interest in practicing law.

Knowing that his future would be in business, Chambers accepted a job offer from IBM in 1976. At the time IBM was the giant of the computer industry, massive, powerful, and known as Big Blue. Though the Justice Department was investigating suspected antitrust violations, IBM had just released what would become their most successful computer ever: the System 360. Chambers, who was about to become a father for the first time, claimed he had no desire to become a salesman. But once he started, he found he was quite good at the task; his unrelenting drive was tempered by his smooth Southern gentility, and customers responded. Chambers was aware of IBM's shortcomings, such as its focus on business computers and typewriters while more adventurous start-ups such as Apple led the way into the personal-computer era. In John Waters's book, *John Chambers and the Cisco Way: Navigating through Volatility,* Chambers was quoted as saying, "I learned an awful lot about what not to do. You could see management getting further and further from the customer, telling the customer that they knew what he needed better than the customer did" (2002).

Chambers did well in the sales department but feared his lack of an engineering degree and research experience would prevent him from moving higher up the ladder at IBM. After seven years with Big Blue he decided to move on to Wang Laboratories. Chambers had seen the company's Chinese American founder, An Wang, give a business lecture and came away impressed with his vision for the future of technology. Wang's company was experiencing explosive growth, with so much demand that supply often fell short. Ever ambitious, Chambers soon convinced Wang that he was the right man to lead Wang Labs' Asian sales team. Though at first the assignment might have seemed like a poor fit, Chambers's easygoing Southern manners worked well in the Asian marketplace, where customers could at times be offended by loud, hard-driving American salesmen.

Chambers had a great deal of respect for his boss. In Jeffrey Young's book, *Cisco Unauthorized: Inside the High-Stakes Race to Own the Future,* Chambers remarked, "The most impressive man I've ever known, other than my father, was An Wang. It was the trust he put in me, that he gave me, the belief he had in me, that I'll never forget" (2001). When Wang died of cancer in 1990, the company's prospects took a turn for the worse. In the Chinese tradition Wang had appointed his son, Fred, as his successor, and stock in Wang Labs plummeted as nervous investors jumped ship. In reality the rocky transition was only the straw that broke the camel's back; Wang Labs had continued stubbornly producing expensive office workstations while the rest of the market was moving toward PCs. As executive vice president at the time of Wang's death Chambers was forced to lay off five thousand employees just before the Christmas holidays. He then resigned and began looking for another job.

A NEW BEGINNING AT CISCO

No one in business had been unaware of the fact that Wang had gone from a $2 billion dollar profit in 1989 to a $700 million loss in 1990. Out of dozens of letters Chambers sent out in search of an executive position, only one company even bothered to respond: Cisco Systems. Cisco had been founded in 1983 by the married couple of Len Bosack, the head of Stanford's computer-science department, and Sandy Lerner, who held a master's in business administration from the same school. Bosack and Lerner had begun looking for a way to allow all of the Stanford computer systems to communicate with one another. Bill Yeager, who worked at the Stanford Department of Medicine, had created something he called a "router," a device built around a microcomputer which made it possible for the medical-department system to "talk" to the business-school system and the computer-science system in one language: Internet Protocol (IP).

Bosack and Lerner built their new company around the router, and by 1986 the company was pulling in $10 million a year. When the venture capitalist Don Valentine came aboard with $2.5 million, he was given one-third of the company, and the threesome took Cisco public on February 16, 1990. Just six months later, amid much squabbling with Valentine and the president John Morgridge, Bosack and Lerner quit Cisco and sold their shares back to the company for $170 million. The founders were gone, but their devotion to customer service would live on.

Morgridge, the energetic, no-nonsense veteran of both Honeywell and Stratus, chose John Chambers to be Cisco's senior vice president of Worldwide Operations in the fall of

1990. Chambers was no easy fit in Silicon Valley. In a place where "geeks" in jeans and T-shirts laid sleeping bags next to their desks so that they could work around the clock, the buttoned-up Chambers seemed like a relic of another age in his conservative suits and with his talk about customer service. Yet Morgridge, who had also started out in sales, knew that Chambers's more traditional traits could effectively temper a business sector that at times seemed to be moving so fast that it was out of control. Morgridge and Chambers also shared a thriftiness that most CEOs would balk at: Morgridge was one of the lowest-paid executives in the business, worked in a 12-by-12 office like everyone else at Cisco, and never flew first class.

Chambers proved himself to Morgridge almost immediately by accepting and refining Cisco's policy of "technological agnosticism." Cisco had had incredible success in the router business, but both Morgridge and Chambers believed that any "religious mind-sets" needed to be put aside when making decisions about the future of the company and technology in general. Neither believed that routers were the only game in town; in 1993 Cisco made its first acquisition, that of the switching company Cresendo Communications for $95 million. Switches gave power users and power devices better access to servers and made for easier networking. Analysts were skeptical, since Cresendo at that time had only $10 million in revenue, but Cisco knew that such customers as Boeing and Ford had expressed intense interest in switching products.

The Cresendo takeover proved to be a huge success, initiating an acquisitions strategy that Chambers would continue to use in the future. The former Mergers and Acquisitions leader at Cisco, Barry Eggers, commented in Ed Paulson's book, *Inside Cisco: The Real Story of Sustained M&A Growth,* "Without that first one having a lot of success, it might have slowed down the pace at which they did everything else. When you have one like that to start out with, it makes it a lot easier to do all the others" (2001). Cisco went on to aquire other small switching companies such as Kalpana, Lightstream, and Grand Junction, chipping away at the switching competition piece by piece.

Don Valentine was not happy when in 1993 Morgridge announced his intention to retire in two years. Both Valentine and Cisco's board did all they could to entice Morgridge to stay on with the company, but he had made up his mind. It was no secret that Morgridge wanted his number-two man, John Chambers, to succeed him as CEO; that was what happened in January 1995. Under Morgridge's watch, Cisco had experienced explosive growth, going public and eventually raking in over $1 billion a year. When Morgridge had taken over, the company had 34 employees; 2,260 people were on the payroll in 1995. But Morgridge knew that Chambers was not a man to rest on the laurels of others, and Chambers was determined to leave his own mark and take the company further than many industry analysts thought possible.

TAKING THE REINS

If Chambers had learned one thing at IBM, it was that customers liked the one-step concept of technology. Most executives were grateful for anything that would make their busy lives easier and disliked having to hunt around for various components. Chambers was determined to provide Cisco's customers with a full array of data solutions in order to prevent them from searching out competitors. This meant expanding from routers, packets, and switches and moving into the world of ATM (asynchronous transfer mode). With the telecom market exploding, Chambers felt that ATM, which divided data into fixed-size cells and allowed for faster transmission, would be the key to Cisco's continued growth. Chambers wasted no time in acquiring StrataCom, a company that catered to the wide-area telecommunications transportation market, for $4.5 billion. As he had done in the Cresendo deal, Chambers offered StrataCom's president far more than the company's market value, ensuring as smooth a takeover as possible. As Chambers noted in Waters's book, "Cisco will become the first vendor to provide advanced network infrastructure for the intranet and Internet environments and the only vendor to offer end-to-end connectivity across public, private, or hybrid networks" (2002).

Under Chambers, Cisco began seeking out the best talent in the technology business with a very aggressive recruitment program. Though by the mid-1990s Cisco had a reputation as a vibrant, nurturing workplace, Cisco did not just wait for top people to come to them. Cisco recruiters targeted young, upscale go-getters by hanging out at art fairs, wine-and-cheese festivals, and home-and-garden shows. Also, of course, Cisco used the Internet in new and innovative ways. For example, they set up a Web page that matched each job seeker with their very own "friend" at Cisco—someone who would give the job seeker a personal call and chat about his or her experiences at the company. This not only gave the job hunters an intimate, "insider's" glimpse of Cisco, it provided a way for Cisco employees to earn referral fees and perks. Over one thousand employees took advantage of the program.

The cause that aroused the most passion in John Chambers was education. "There are two equalizers in life," he said many times, "the Internet and education." Chambers saw e-learning as something that could level the playing field for the rich and the poor, for the haves and the have-nots. For the man who told the *San Francisco Chronicle,* "The market always gets it right" (February 2, 2004), the Internet was the ultimate form of what George W. Bush once called "compassionate conservatism." In 1997 Cisco set up the Cisco Networking Academy to train and certify young people in computer design and maintenance. John Morgridge,who had remained on Cisco's board after stepping down as CEO, commented in Waters's book, "It's the first true partnership between schools, government, and business since the days of high-school 'auto shops.'

The difference is, instead of auto mechanics, students learn the conceptual and practical skills necessary to design and manage networks" (Waters, 2002).

Chambers worried about education not only for his own company but for the country as a whole. He felt that the lack of proper computer education in America's elementary schools could spell doom with respect to global competition. With the help of the U.S. Senator Jay Rockefeller and others in the government Cisco contributed $18 million in services and equipment to 57 educational institutions across the country. With the Cisco Networking Academy and its support of such youth programs as Internet Schools CyberFair and the Virtual Schoolhouse grant program, Cisco not only pulled off a major publicity coup but also ensured that it would attract a steady stream of well-trained prospective employees.

LISTENING TO THE CUSTOMER

Chambers believed that the most important thing that the CEO of a technological business could do was to stay ahead of the marketplace; the only way for Chambers to do that was to listen carefully to Cisco's customers. He needed to know not only what they were presently buying but what they would be looking for five, 10, or 20 years down the road. By acquiring as much of his competition as possible, he felt that he could ensure the best response to customers' needs. Since Chambers had always been more of a salesman than a technocrat, it was important that he had the very best talent in research and development. Still, he did not simply expect R&D to create breakthrough products. Rather, he wanted them to integrate the products from acquired companies into Cisco's existing infrastructure. Though he was always looking toward the future, Chambers knew that gobbling up the ideas of other companies would leave his team more time to sell its products.

Though his strategies certainly paid off in the short run, some critics doubted their long-term effectiveness. In *Cisco Unauthorized*, Young argued, "The problem is all about a hollowed-out core of a company and an Elmer Gantry at its head who can talk about a city on the hill, but who can't tell you exactly where it will be pitched without consulting his customer. This kind of reactive leadership works fine when none of the competitors have any idea where the market is going either. But what happens when Cisco hits entirely new technology?" (2001).

Not everything Chambers touched at Cisco turned to gold. The StrataCom deal especially turned off some of the T-shirt-and-jeans "geeks" who had come to Cisco because they wanted to work at an innovative, nonconformist company. With that deal, systems and procedures had to be put into place in order for the companies to mesh; some of Cisco's more free-spirited, brilliant people did not want to even try to fit in with the more buttoned-up, white-collar atmosphere. They knew that with all of Cisco's acquisitions money, their chances of making their mark in advanced engineering—of contributing something truly unique to the market—were slim. In addition, there was no good reason for them to stay, with start-ups and dot-coms exploding throughout Silicon Valley. If one was looking for excitement and risk, one had to look beyond Cisco. Still, most of Cisco's employees were looking for security and stability, and they had found it. In the fast-changing Valley, where the average employee turnover rate was more than 40 percent per year, Cisco's turnover rate held steady at between 4 and 6 percent.

Chambers' biggest challenge at Cisco came on July 20, 2000. For quite some time telecom and network companies had been overvalued; when the market finally turned against them, many analysts predicted a hard road for Cisco. Cisco at first seemed to ride above the fray, announcing its 14th consecutive very strong quarter in August 2000. But in early 2001 the fallout hit; Chambers responded by firing 15 percent of his workforce and cutting his own salary to $1 a year. Chambers stayed the course, continuing with what had worked for him in the past: acquisitions. Cisco acquired Linskys in 2003 for $500 million worth of stock; in 2004 it acquired Latitude Communications, a company that specialized in conferencing systems, for $80 million in cash. Chambers surprised many by leading Cisco to a stronger position than ever, though he cautioned that another tech boom in Silicon Valley might never materialize.

With a rebounded Cisco looking healthy in 2004, Chambers was able to look back at a life filled mostly with success. Asked by the San Francisco Chronicle if his wealth and fame would make him a different person, Chambers replied, "I hope that it does not. Most of my friends would say it does not. My friends that I had when I moved here to Silicon Valley are still my best friends. It didn't change dramatically. The most important thing to me in my life is my family. Money's never been a primary motivator in my life" (February 2, 2004).

See also entry on Cisco Systems, Inc. in *International Directory of Company Histories.*

SOURCES FOR FURTHER INFORMATION

Burrows, Peter, "Cisco's Comeback," *BusinessWeek*, November 24, 2003, pp. 116–118.

Howe, Ken, "Cisco Systems/On the Record: John Chambers," *San Francisco Chronicle*, February 2, 2004.

Maney, Kevin, "Cisco Born Again," *USA Today*, January 21, 2004.

Paulson, Ed, *Inside Cisco: The Real Story of Sustained M&A Growth*, New York, N.Y.: John Wiley & Sons, 2001.

Waters, John K., *John Chambers and the Cisco Way: Navigating through Volatility*, New York, N.Y.: John Wiley & Sons, 2002.

Young, Jeffrey S., *Cisco Unauthorized: Inside the High-Stakes Race to Own the Future*, Roseville, Calif.: Prima Publishing, 2001.

—Kelly Wittmann

■■■

J. Harold Chandler

1949–

Former chairman, chief executive officer, and president, UnumProvident Corporation

Nationality: American.

Born: 1949, in Belton, South Carolina.

Education: Wofford College, BA, 1971; University of South Carolina Graduate School of Business Administration, MBA, 1972; Harvard Business School, Advanced Management Program, 1986.

Career: Citizens and Southern National Bank, 1972–1990; C&S/Sovran, 1990–1991, executive vice president of corporate marketing; 1991, president of Washington, D.C., bank; NationsBank Corporation, 1991–1993, president of Mid-Atlantic Banking Group; Provident Companies, 1993–1999, chairman, CEO, and president; UnumProvident Corporation, 1999–2003, chairman, CEO, and president.

Awards: Young Alumnus of the Year, Wofford College, 1983; Manager of the Year, *Chattanooga Times Free Press*, 2000.

■ J. Harold Chandler was chairman, president, and chief executive officer of UnumProvident Corporation, the leading disability insurer in the United States, from 1999 to 2003. Despite having built a solid career in banking and having been credited with leading the financial turnaround of Provident Companies in the late 1990s, Chandler came under fire in the lead position at UnumProvident for failing to execute strategies to improve the company's performance. He was fired in March 2003.

RISING STAR

Raised in Belton, South Carolina, Chandler was a high-achieving student and talented athlete. He attended Wofford College, the private liberal arts school in Spartanburg, South Carolina, and excelled academically. He graduated summa cum laude with membership in Phi Beta Kappa as valedictorian of his class in 1971. He was also the quarterback for the Wofford football team. He continued his studies the following year at the University of South Carolina, where he earned a master's in business administration. Chandler was awarded Wofford's Young Alumnus of the Year award in 1983.

In 1972 Chandler began working for Citizens and Southern National Bank of South Carolina. He completed Harvard Business School's Advanced Management Program in 1986. In 1990 Chandler's bank merged with Sovran Corporation, and he was named executive vice president of corporate marketing of the newly formed C&S/Sovran. The company sent him to Washington, D.C., in 1991 to act as president of a metro-area bank. Later that year C&S/Sovran merged with NCNB to form NationsBank, and Chandler was named president of the Mid-Atlantic Banking Group. He held that position until 1993, when he announced his resignation and accepted the position of president and chief executive officer of Provident Life and Accident Company of America. Jon Burke, the analyst with Robinson Humphrey Company, said of the move in *American Banker*, "Harold Chandler was a bright and rising star. I'm relatively sure NationsBank will be disappointed that he left" (November 10, 1993).

FROM PROVIDENT TO MERGER WITH UNUM

Chandler had become Provident's ninth president and CEO. The Chattanooga-based company was in a state of financial turmoil, facing significant operating losses. While Chandler's appointment was somewhat controversial given that he had little background in the insurance industry, he soon implemented a number of changes and improvements, instituting new executive management, streamlining the business structure, and changing the name of the firm to Provident Companies. In 1996 Chandler led the acquisition of the Massachusetts-based insurance-company group Paul Revere Corporation, and in 1997 he purchased the national case-management service provider Genex. Those moves reestablished Provident as a profitable company.

Chandler next trained his attention on a merger with the nation's largest group-disability writer, the Portland, Maine–based Unum Corporation. Talks began in 1998; the companies finalized a merger in 1999, creating the nation's largest disability insurer. Chandler was originally instated as chief operating officer of UnumProvident, but the sudden retirement of the chief executive officer James F. Orr III, the former CEO of Unum, just four months after the merger led to Chandler's promotion to the top position.

Chandler had high hopes for the company. He told *Best's Review* that he was "confident that the patience that shareholders have shown will be rewarded in due course. The commitments we've made are all future oriented and are achievable" (August 2002). Analysts and shareholders were initially heartened by the choice of CEO despite the continuing downward trend in UnumProvident's sales and stock numbers; in the *Knight Ridder/Tribune Business News*, David Lewis of Robinson Humphrey called the appointment "a very positive move by the board" (November 7, 1999). In 2000 Chandler was named Manager of the Year by a board of 20 Chattanooga-area organizations.

UNDER FIRE

Over the next year, however, Chandler was barraged by a litany of complaints from claimants, shareholders, and analysts alike. Financial results failed to meet analysts' expectations and the company was hit with negative publicity surrounding several large lawsuits filed by claimants. In May 2002 Chandler was named the third-worst chief executive in the United States by *Forbes* magazine, based on shareholder return and executive compensation.

Many began to question the wisdom of the Unum/Provident merger and of Chandler's installment as CEO. Chandler defended his strategies, claiming that a rising number of claims, low interest rates, and a weak economy were major contributors to sustained disappointing results. Notwithstanding, some began calling for his replacement. Brad McCurtain, the president of the investment firm Maine Securities, told the *Portland Press Herald* with regard to UnumProvident's troubles, "They're earning less money today than they did before the merge. I think it's time for a change at the top or time for the company to be sold. I don't think the management team would accept that kind of performance from employees and I don't think shareholders should accept it from senior management" (February 7, 2003).

In 2003 Chandler's opposition got its wish. On March 27 the UnumProvident board of directors notified Chandler of their intentions to fire him. Lawrence Pugh, a company director, told *SNL Insurance Weekly* that the "announcement was not driven by any specific event—rather the cumulative effect of many things led the board to conclude that a CEO change was in the best interest of the company at this time. It's been the CEO's responsibility, specifically Harold, for the execution of this strategy and we don't think that was performed to the level we wanted it to be" (April 7, 2003). In the same publication the analyst Michelle Giordano of J. P. Morgan Securities was quoted as saying that the change was "long overdue" (April 7, 2003). Thomas R. Watjen, the vice chairman and COO under Chandler, took over the lead role on an interim basis and was later elected as the permanent president and CEO. Chandler received a $17.3 million severance package and later a $2.9 million addendum after he sued the company for not fulfilling the original agreement.

See also entry on UnumProvident Corporation in *International Directory of Company Histories*.

SOURCES FOR FURTHER INFORMATION

Cline, Kenneth, "NationsBank's Mid-Atlantic Region Loses Another Exec as Group President Quits," *American Banker*, November 10, 1993, p. 6.

Murphy, Edward D., "Insurer's Earnings Report Prompts Precipitous Stock Drop," *Portland Press Herald*, February 7, 2003.

Panko, Ron, "Sharpening the Focus," *Best's Review*, August 2002, pp. 74–80.

Parr, Mike, "Chattanooga, Tenn.-Based Disability Insurer Looks for New Chief Executive," *Chattanooga Times Free Press*, April 1, 2003.

———, "Chattanooga, Tenn.-Based Insurance Firm Stumbles after Merger," *Knight Ridder/Tribune Business News*, November 7, 1999.

"Reaction Mixed after UnumProvident Gives Chandler the Boot," *SNL Insurance Weekly Life and Health Edition*, April 7, 2003.

"The Worst," *Forbes*, May 13, 2002, p. 112.

—Stephanie Dionne Sherk

■■■

Morris Chang

1931–

Chairman and chief executive officer, Taiwan Semiconductor Manufacturing Company; chairman, Taiwan Semiconductor Industry Association

Nationality: Chinese.

Born: July 10, 1931, in Shanghai, China.

Education: Massachusetts Institute of Technology, BS, 1952, MS, 1953; Stanford University, PhD, 1964.

Family: Married Christine Chen; children: one.

Career: Texas Instruments, 1958–1983, several management positions, including group vice president in charge of the company's worldwide semiconductor business; General Instrument Corporation, 1984–1985, president and chief operating officer; Taiwan Semiconductor Manufacturing Company, 1987–, chairman and chief executive officer.

Awards: *BusinessWeek* selected Dr. Chang as one of the Top 25 Managers of the Year in 1998; in 1999 he became the first recipient of the Exemplary Leadership Award of the Fabless Semiconductor Association (the award is now named after him); in 2000 he received the Institute of Electrical and Electronics Engineers Robert N. Noyce Medal.

Publications: *The Autobiography of Morris C. M. Chang—Volume 1,* 1998.

Address: Taiwan Semiconductor Manufacturing Company, No. 25, Li-Hsin Road, Science-Based Industrial Park, Hsin-Chu, Taiwan 300, ROC; http://www.tsmc.com/english/default.htm.

■ Morris Chang, founder and CEO of Taiwan Semiconductor Manufacturing Company (TSMC), distinguished himself as a global business leader and a technological innovator. After a 25-year career with Texas Instruments in the United States, he founded TSMC and pioneered the silicon foundry industry. Chang, who is regarded as the father of Taiwan's semiconductor industry, is a hero in his country. "To the Taiwanese, Chang is more than just a successful businessman and

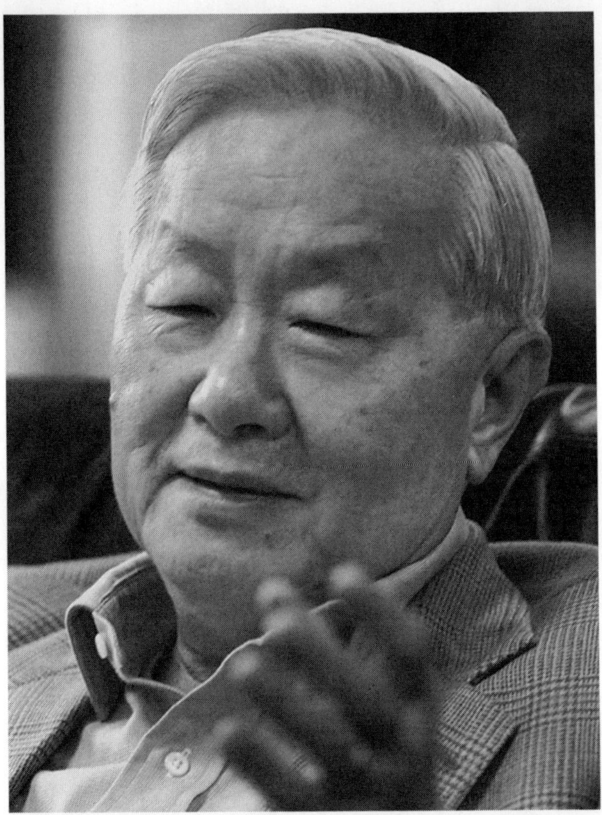

Morris Chang. © *Reuters NewMedia Inc./Corbis.*

engineer. . . . He put Taiwan on the global technology map," Mark Carroll wrote in *Electronic Engineering Times* (September 18, 2000).

ENTERING THE TECHNOLOGY BUSINESS

Chang was born in China but came to the United States with his family in 1949. While he was growing up, he wanted to be a writer, a dream his father strongly discouraged. "My father said to me, 'you will starve as a writer,'" Chang told (*Electronic Buyers' News*, December 21, 1998).

Chang instead wound up in the semiconductor business in the mid-1950s. He spent more than 25 years as an executive with two American technology companies, Texas Instruments and General Instrument. At Texas Instruments he rose from engineering manager to group vice president in charge of the company's worldwide semiconductor business, and he helped groom Texas Instruments into a leader in the integrated circuit market. But when Texas Instruments asked Chang to move into its computer products division in 1984, he turned them down and instead went to General Instrument.

TAIWAN AND THE BIRTH OF TSMC

Only three years later Chang decided on a new venue. He was invited to head up Taiwan's Industrial Technology Research Institute, with the aim of developing the country's semiconductor industry. Even though the job paid less than his position at General Instrument, Chang felt that the opportunity would afford him new challenges. He accepted the offer.

Once in Taiwan, Chang pioneered a new concept in chip manufacturing. At the time most companies did all of their own chip design and manufacturing. The manufacturing end was extremely expensive, while the design was very talent-intensive. Chang proposed the idea of the foundry—a factory (called a "fab," or fabrication plant) contracted out to produce silicon wafers for other chip companies. In 1987 he started the first foundry, TSMC, with $52 million in financial backing from the Taiwanese government and additional support from a Netherlands company, Philips Electronics. Thanks to government subsidies (including healthy tax breaks), an employee base made up of bright young engineers fresh from Taiwan's exemplary educational system, and the growing American demand for integrated circuits, business boomed.

By offering reasonable rates and excellent customer service, TSMC became Taiwan's number-one chip company and the world's leading semiconductor foundry. With TSMC doing the hard circuit work, its clients could concentrate on design, and an explosion of so-called fabless companies followed. The industry was in such a strong upturn that TSMC acquired the rival Worldwide Semiconductor Corporation in 2000 to keep up with the demand.

A FEW SHAKY YEARS

Although business was strong, 1999 was a shaky year for TSMC, literally. In September a magnitude 7.3 earthquake rocked central Taiwan, knocking out power to the company's two plants. While engineers surveyed the damage, Chang sought help from Taiwan's premier. Within 10 days his company was back up and running again.

Chang also helped his company weather a chip crash. The Internet and telecommunications collapse of 2001 hit TSMC hard. Net profits that year fell 78 percent, sales dropped by more than 20 percent, and stock prices plummeted. TSMC also faced increased competition from semiconductor manufacturers in China, Germany, Israel, and Malaysia. By 2003, however, semiconductor demand was once again up, and TSMC was on the rebound. The company dominated the foundry industry, with a solid 55 percent of market share.

A NATIONAL HERO

As TSMC became more successful, Chang's popularity grew. He achieved what can only be described as cult status in Taiwan, his face projecting from billboard ads hawking everything from personal digital assistants to real estate.

Chang is seen as somewhat of an elder statesman at his company. He is known for his intellect, and his employees are often heard repeating his sayings. Chang's sharp mind enticed him to become an expert at the game of bridge; when in America, he was considered one of the country's 1,000 best contract bridge players.

Although Chang valued education, he believed that only innovation can sustain economic growth. In fact, innovation was a cornerstone of Chang's philosophy and shaped many of his business decisions. "We need people with innovative ideas and entrepreneurial spirit," he remarked during an interview with the Central News Agency (February 12, 2001).

Despite the volatility in the technology industry, Chang was optimistic about its future in the early 21st century. He forecasted a 10 percent annual growth rate between 2002 and 2010, and he predicted that foundries like TSMC will turn out 40 to 50 percent of all chips by 2010.

Chang is a member of the MIT Corporation and is on the advisory boards of the U.S. Stock Exchange, Stanford University, and the University of California at Berkeley.

See also entries on Taiwan Semiconductor Manufacturing Company Ltd. and Texas Instruments Incorporated in *International Directory of Company Histories.*

SOURCES FOR FURTHER INFORMATION

Carroll, Morris, "Venerating a Visionary," *Electronic Engineering Times,* September 18, 2000, p. 34.

Chen, Sandy, "Morris Chang—Writing New Chapters in Industry, and in Transformation of Taiwan," *Electronic Buyers' News,* December 21, 1998, p. 46.

Edwards, Cliff, and Pete Engardio, "Taiwan: Betting Big on Chips," *BusinessWeek,* April 30, 2001, p. 54.

"Morris Chang, Microchip Visionary," *Economist,* May 19, 2001, p. 7.

"TSMC Chair Clarifies Myths of New Economy," Central News Agency, February 12, 2001.

—Stephanie Watson

■■■

Chen Tonghai

1948–

Director and chairman, Sinopec Corporation; president, Sinopec Group

Nationality: Chinese.

Born: September 1948, in Huimin, Shandong, China.

Education: Northeastern Petroleum Institute, 1976, bachelor's degree in exploration and oil extracting engineering.

Career: Daqing Research Institute, 1969–1972, geologist; Zhejiang Science and Technology Commission, 1976–1983, staff member, deputy director; Zhenhai Petroleum and Petrochemical General Plant, 1983–1986, deputy party secretary, party secretary; Ningbo City, 1986–1989, acting deputy mayor; Zhejiang Province Planning and Economic Commission, 1989–1991, acting deputy director; Ningbo City, 1991–1992, acting mayor; 1992–1994, mayor; State Development and Planning Commission, 1994–1998, vice minister; China Petrochemical Company Group, vice president, 1998–; president, 2003–; Sinopec Corporation, 2000–2003, director and vice chairman, first board of directors; 2003–, director and chairman, second board of directors.

Address: Sinopec Corporation, No. A6 Hui xin East Street, Chaoyang District, Beijing, China 100029; http://english.sinopec.com/index.jsp.

■ Chen Tonghai began his working life as a geologist, quickly moving into management at the Zhejiang Science and Technology Commission and the Zhenhai Petroleum and Petrochemical General Plant after he earned his degree. He entered the political scene in the mid-1980s, when he served as a deputy party secretary and party secretary. By the late 1990s Chen was a major player in China's petroleum and chemical industry and was quickly becoming known worldwide. As the highly visible director and chairman of Sinopec Corporation, Chen was consistently forceful, progressive, and willing to take a stand when necessary and present positive designs for the future.

POLITICAL CAREER

After working as a geologist and manager early in his career Chen became interested in politics. In 1986 he was named acting deputy mayor of Ningbo City in Zhejiang Province. Chen rose through the ranks of city government in the next few years, ultimately becoming mayor of Ningbo City in 1992. During that time he also served as acting deputy director of the planning and economic commission of Zhejiang Province. In 1994 Chen left city politics to become a vice minister of the state development and planning commission.

PETROLEUM

Chen's background as a geologist led him to the China Petrochemical Company Group. He became vice president of the company in 1998 and president in 2003. He added Sinopec Corporation to his responsibilities in 2000, when he became director and vice chairman of Sinopec's first board of directors. He became director and chairman of Sinopec's second board of directors in 2003.

In China's petroleum and chemical industry Chen had a wealth of knowledge and expertise on which to draw. As head of Sinopec, Chen was considered a senior economist and an experienced senior-level administrator in the petrochemical industry and in macroeconomic control. In 2003 Chen announced plans for three oil-receiving terminals and two pipelines between cities on the east coast of China. The new facilities, set to be operational by 2006 at a cost of CNY 8 billion, would streamline refinery operation, according to Chen. Proving again that he was not hesitant to make crucial decisions, Chen also announced that Sinopec's streamlined operations would allow the company to cut its staff by up to 50,000 jobs over the three-year period of construction.

When concerns about the Chinese economy arose in early 2004, Chen stepped forward with reassurances. Oil consumption would return to its normal rate, he stated, because China's economic development would continue. Addressing the energy shortage that affected two-thirds of China at that time, Chen said fuel supplies to power plants had been increased by one-half million tons to ease the current problem.

WORLDWIDE INFLUENCE

Chen became known and respected worldwide. In early 2004 he visited Gabon, Africa, at the invitation of the Gabonese ministry of mines and energy. Chen and Minister Richard Onouviet made decisions regarding mutual cooperation in the use of energy resources. Along with their respective heads of state, Chen and Onouviet signed a memorandum of understanding outlining future cooperation. Also in 2004 the deputy minister of economic affairs for Iran, Seyed Mohammad Hosein Adeli, offered a vote of confidence to Chen, saying the options China was pursuing in its energy strategy were "proper" and "not aggressive," though China had come late to world energy cooperation. Adeli invited closer cooperation between Iranian and Chinese energy leaders.

At the Boao Forum for Asia in April 2004 Chen delivered an address in which he discussed future challenges to the energy industry, including marine and land transportation and safety and stability issues. He also addressed China's growing dependence on imported oil as its economic growth continued. Peace and development, Chen said, were crucial to a stable world oil market in which there is shared interest and common development. Chen called for increased cooperation and coordination between governments for effective distribution of resources. He especially challenged Asian countries to work together in production, infrastructure, refining, storage and transportation, and research and development.

China, Chen said, was taking positive steps in the fields of oil exploration and production, development of natural gas reserves, and conservation of resources at home and abroad. As the largest refiner and the second-largest oil producer in China, Sinopec had been effective, Chen noted, in its overall energy strategy. Sinopec also worked actively with foreign companies in the development of natural gas resources. Chen cited the good relations Sinopec had developed with African and central and southeast Asian countries and the cooperative efforts it had used with Western oil companies such as Exxon, Shell, and BP. Chen showed himself willing to work with international partners, saying producers should "join hands to maintain the stability of the world petroleum market and create a better tomorrow for the world petroleum and petrochemical industry."

See also entry on China National Petroleum Corporation in *International Directory of Company Histories.*

SOURCES FOR FURTHER INFORMATION

Chan, Elaine, "Sinopec Plans 8b Yuan Infrastructure Spend," *The Standard,* August 27, 2003.

Chen Tonghai, "Jointly Face the Challenge in Petroleum Resources and Market," speech before Boao Forum for Asia Annual Conference, April 2004, http://www.boaoforum.org/boao/2004nh/cd/t20040511_819281.shtml (June 8, 2004).

"Chen Tonghai Paid a Visit to Gabon, Africa," Sinopec Corp. News and Events, http://english.sinopec.com/en-newsevent/en-news/643.shtml (June 8, 2004).

"China Vitae," http://www.chinavitae.com/biography_display.php?id=1458 (June 8, 2004).

Hi, Xiao, "Oil Demand Growth to Maintain Rational Level," *China Daily,* April 26, 2004.

"Slower Economy to Tame Oil Use," *Shanghai Daily,* April 26, 2004.

—Cathy Seckman

■■■

Kenneth I. Chenault

1951–

Chairman and chief executive officer, American Express Company

Nationality: American.

Born: June 2, 1951, in New York, New York.

Education: Bowdoin College, BA, 1973; Harvard University Law School, JD, 1976.

Family: Son of Hortenius Chenault (dentist) and Anne Quick (dental hygienist); married Kathryn Cassell (nonpracticing attorney); children: two.

Career: Rogers & Wells, 1977–1979, attorney; Bain & Company, 1979–1981, management consultant; American Express Company, 1981–1983, director of strategic planning; American Express Travel Related Services Company, 1981–1996, vice president, then senior vice president; 1986–1988, executive vice president of platinum/gold card; 1988–1989, executive vice president of personal-card division; 1990–1993, president of consumer-card and financial-services group; 1993–1995, president; American Express Company, 1995–1997, vice chairman; 1997–2000, president and COO; 2001–, chairman and CEO.

Address: American Express Company, World Financial Center, 200 Vesey Street, 50th Floor, New York, New York 10281-1009; http://www.americanexpress.com.

Kenneth I. Chenault. *AP/Wide World Photos.*

■ One of just four African American CEOs of Fortune 500 companies in 2004, Kenneth I. Chenault was a leader by example and an executive who focused on performance day in, day out. As the head of American Express Company (AMEX) he reenergized his company's brand, increased its market share, and won back many of the merchants who had abandoned the firm because of its high fees. He inspired fierce loyalty in his employees, boosting morale in the aftermath of the September 11, 2001, terrorist attacks. Chenault was designated to succeed the outgoing CEO in 1999 and officially took over the role in January 2001.

With 2003 sales of $25.9 billion American Express was a prominent financial-services firm and the world's number-one travel agency. It issued traveler's checks, published magazines— such as *Food & Wine* and *Travel & Leisure*—and provided financial-advisory services. The company had four units: Global Corporate Services, Global Financial Services, Global Establishment Services and Traveler's Cheques, and U.S. Consumer and Small Business Services. On the Internet AMEX offered online banking and mortgage and brokerage services. Warren Buffett's Berkshire Hathaway owned about 11 percent of the company. Key competitors included Carlson Wagonlit, JTB, and Visa.

BRAINS BUT LITTLE AMBITION AS A YOUNG MAN

Chenault's immense success in corporate America could not have been predicted based on his performance early in life. As a high-school student in a middle-class white community he received a slew of Cs—except in history class, where he typically earned As. His parents knew that he was extremely intelligent but worried about whether he had the focus to maximize his potential. They were certainly good role models: Chenault's father graduated first in his class at Howard University's Dental School, and his mother graduated at the top of her class at Howard's School of Dental Hygiene. While he had an incessant desire to learn, Chenault conceded in *Ebony* magazine with respect to his poor performance in school, "I'm sure it was frustrating for them that I was not applying myself" (July 1997).

Chenault eventually received crucial mentoring from Peter Curran, the head of Waldorf High School—a private school in Garden City, New York—who encouraged the wayward student to apply himself. When Chenault graduated, he did so with numerous honors; he had been class president, an honor student, and the captain of the basketball, soccer, and track teams. He enrolled in Springfield College in Massachusetts, which had offered him a sports scholarship, but craved a more academic experience and thus ended up at Bowdoin College in Maine.

MOTIVATED TO MAKE A DIFFERENCE

At Bowdoin, Chenault realized that he wanted to pursue a profession that would enable him to help other African Americans. He debated the merits of a corporate career with fellow African American students—there were 23 at Bowdoin at the time, as compared with the 950 white students—who warned of a lifestyle that might ultimately force him to abandon his convictions. Chenault disagreed, believing it to be possible for an African American to succeed without selling out. During these often-heated discussions, Chenault displayed his aptitude for debate. Rasuli Lewis, a fellow Bowdoin student who remained a friend, told *Ebony*, "His style was to come in more the middle of the road, to say let's consider both sides here, and to look at it from the point of fact rather than emotion" (July 1997).

Chenault had the ability to elicit respect from African American and white students alike. Geoffrey Canada, another college friend, told *Fortune*, "This was a time when people wanted you to choose sides; he sat with whomever he wanted. What was remarkable was that he could do that and still remain in the mainstream of both worlds. Other people would end up being shunned by one group or the other" (January 22, 2001).

LANDING A COVETED JOB WITHOUT AN MBA

After graduating from Bowdoin and later from Harvard Law School, Chenault spent two years in corporate law at Rogers & Wells and two more years at Bain & Company as a management consultant. W. Mitt Romney, the son of former governor of Michigan who had attended Harvard Law School with Chenault and gone on to Bain, recruited Chenault to the firm. Romney told *Ebony*, "I'll take full credit for hiring Ken. Although Ken lacked an MBA, he was a natural fit for the business world. He was able to process a lot of conflict and frenzy and still be able to cut through the confusion and arrive at very powerful conclusions and recommendations and then see them through to their implementation" (July 1997).

BOOSTING AMEX'S BUSINESS AND HIS STOCK

Recruited by the legendary Lou Gerstner in 1981, Chenault moved to American Express to become a director of Strategic Planning in Travel Related Services. In early 1983 he joined the company's merchandise-services unit, which sold items such as luggage tags and clocks to cardholders through direct mailings and catalogs. Gerstner and other AMEX executives actually discouraged Chenault from joining the unit, which lacked the platform and visibility of other divisions.

Chenault saw the move from an entirely different perspective, however: if he could turn around the struggling division, he thought, people would notice. Instead of luggage tags and clocks Chenault invested in bigger-ticket items such as electronics and home furnishings. He formed partnerships with Panasonic and Sharp, which were eager to expand the distribution channels for their recently released video recorders. In just three years the division's sales skyrocketed from $100 million to $700 million. Tom Flood, who worked under Chenault from 1983 to 1986, remarked in *Fortune*, "The business grew so quickly, and he had made such a quick impact, that his stock really rose after that. It put him on the map" (January 22, 2001).

TURNING AROUND AMEX

By the early 1990s Chenault was overseeing most of the company's travel-related services. It was a challenging period; the economy was weakened by a recession, the company's card business was losing customers to Visa and MasterCard, and merchants began protesting the high fees that they were being forced to pay: AMEX charged a fee of 4 percent of every transaction, while Visa charged less than half that amount. Due to the excessive fees many merchants—including a group of Boston restaurants whose collective decision was tagged as the "Boston Fee Party" by local papers—eventually refused to accept the American Express card. Chenault commented in *Black Enterprise*, "The focus in the early 1990s was frankly one of survival; we were falling off a cliff. But you can't stand still and say the objective is to survive in the long term. You have to say that the objective is to win" (September 30, 1999).

As president of the domestic consumer-card division Chenault was instrumental in turning around the charge-card business. His many accomplishments included expanding the company's customer base beyond the affluent cardholders who paid off their balances each month; signing on an impressive number of gas stations, discounters, and supermarkets as acceptors of the card; establishing the later highly regarded Membership Rewards loyalty program (one of the biggest—if not the biggest—rewards program on the market); and striking partnerships with companies like Delta Airlines, wherein the company expanded its lending business through the issuing of cobranded cards that allowed customers to carry balances.

Additionally Chenault reached a truce with merchants, though not everyone at AMEX agreed with his strategy—particularly his expansion into lower-end businesses like gas stations. Tom Ryder, who rose through the ranks alongside Chenault, said in *Fortune*, "It was an extremely unpopular stance. Ken was the leader of a fairly small group that said unless we made some fundamental changes, we were going to eventually get killed" (January 22, 2001).

RISING THROUGH THE RANKS BASED ON PERFORMANCE

Chenault eventually won dissenters over, gradually transforming AMEX from an uncompetitive, obsolete company into a booming business. The level of interest in the Membership Rewards program surprised even Chenault. Quests for airline miles generated a surge in AMEX charges, and the program helped AMEX woo new merchants as well: the number accepting the card grew from 3.6 million in 1993 to more than 7.2 million worldwide in 1999.

As AMEX's financial performance vaulted forward, so did Chenault's career. In 1993 AMEX's new CEO, Harvey Golub, appointed Chenault as head of U.S. Travel Services, a title that entailed responsibility for the company's entire domestic card business and about half of its revenues. Together Golub and Chenault restructured the company, generating more than $3 billion in savings, and continued an aggressive foray into mainstream businesses. In 1995 AMEX signed on with Wal-Mart—an important win in the fight with Visa and MasterCard for market share.

Between 1995 and 2000 earnings increased every year, reaching $2.8 billion in 2000. The number of American Express cards issued to consumers increased from 25.3 million in 1994 to more than 29 million by 1996. In 1995 Chenault was named vice chairman, and two years later he was named president and chief operating officer. In April 1999 he was named the eventual successor to Golub.

THE SOFTER SIDE OF A LEADER

The public undeniably wanted Chenault to succeed. Anne Busquet, the president of American Express Relationship Services, noted in *Ebony*, "You would go in elevators and hear, 'Isn't it exciting about Ken? Can you believe that Ken got promoted? Isn't it fantastic? Oh, I feel much better about the company now that Ken is president.' People wrote him notes; he was flooded with e-mail; there were flowers and calls from corporate and political leaders" (July 1997).

People inside the company looked up to Chenault—even those who had competed with him for the CEO spot. The intense loyalty that he generated in colleagues was a product of his low-key, caring management style. Rather than being afraid of their leader—as was the relationship between many subordinates and their CEOs—Chenault's employees enjoyed his inspiring presence. The classic axiom states that leaders can lead by fear or by love; Chenault seemed to motivate workers to fear losing his love. Louise Parent, the executive vice president and general counsel for the company, remarked in *Black Enterprise*, "He is the kind of person who inspires you to want to do your best. Part of the reason is his example" (September 30, 1999).

AN AFRICAN AMERICAN PIONEER

When in January 2001 Chenault claimed the top position at American Express—one of the best-known symbols of U.S. capitalism, then with yearly sales of $25 billion—the prospects for African Americans in corporate America had seemed dismal. At General Electric, for example, just one of the top 20 business units was led by an African American. Only two other African Americans headed Fortune 500 companies: Franklin Raines was the CEO of Fannie Mae, and A. Barry Rand was the CEO of Avis. John O. Utendahl, himself a high-ranking African American working in financial services and a close friend of Chenault, told *Fortune*, "When Ken joined American Express 20 years ago, no one would have taken the odds that he would be CEO. But as crazy as this may sound, Ken would have taken that bet. The playing field for minorities may not be level, but when Ken plays, he plays to win" (January 22, 2001).

For his part Chenault did not dwell on racial issues. He understood the social significance of his appointment but wanted people to judge him based solely on his performance. He commented in *Fortune*, "It's a big deal; I won't minimize it. But I want them to say, 'He's a terrific CEO,' not 'He's a terrific black CEO.' Because the reasons why I'm CEO have nothing to do with the social significance of this breakthrough. I've always been focused on performance" (January 22, 2001).

A CEO STUMBLES

Early in his tenure as CEO Chenault sent the message to Wall Street that he had not been completely prepared for the job. After announcing record earnings for 2000, several months later he shocked investors with news of a $182 million write-off on some surprisingly risky assets in the company's money-management division, American Express Financial Advisors. Chenault consequently reduced the company's junk portfolio from 12 percent to about 8 percent and decreased the risks of other investments.

Several months later Chenault caused an even bigger tremor when he announced an additional $826 million charge on the same portfolio; second-quarter earnings sagged 76 percent to $178 million. The central problem was an investment strategy in high-risk junk bonds that had been embarked upon years before Chenault would have his say. While no one could criticize Chenault for operations that had been initiated prior to his watch, critics were troubled by the fact that Chenault appeared to make no effort to understand what the company's rationale at the time had been. When asked in *BusinessWeek* why American Express would put its money into such a risky investment, Chenault responded by simply saying, "I don't know. This is a strategy that was embarked upon seven or eight years ago. I don't know all the rationale and philosophy" (October 29, 2001).

BOOSTING MORALE AFTER SEPTEMBER 11

Chenault showed his true colors as CEO in the aftermath of the September 11, 2001, terrorist attacks on New York City. On the day of the attacks Chenault was stuck in Salt Lake City on a business trip. Still, he was able to make his leadership felt from afar, as he happened to be on the phone with a New York employee when the first plane crashed. AMEX's headquarters were across the street from the former World Trade Center; he asked to be transferred to security and told them to immediately evacuate everyone from the building.

In the hours and days that followed, Chenault made countless decisions that would ease the impact of the attacks on both cardholders and employees. To help the former, millions of dollars in late fees were forgiven, and credit limits were increased. In an effort to comfort the latter, Chenault invited his five thousand employees to New York's Paramount Theater on September 20 for a somber meeting. At that meeting he admitted that his grief had been so strong that he had needed to see a counselor. He announced plans to donate $1 million of the company's profits to the families of AMEX employees who had died on September 11. Charlene Barshefsky, a partner at Wilmer Cutler & Pickering who viewed a video of the event, told *BusinessWeek*, "The manner in which he took command, the comfort and the direction he gave to what was obviously an audience in shock was of a caliber one rarely sees" (October 29, 2001).

After 9/11 American Express committed to keeping its headquarters downtown; it was one of the first major companies to pledge their imminent return to Lower Manhattan. Chenault commented in *New York Voice Inc./Harlem USA*, "Our 152-year history is filled with defining moments—staying open during crises when others close, coming through for our customers all around the world, doing the right things even when it is difficult to do. When we look back on this day several years from now, I believe we will see it as another defining moment that marked the beginning of a new era of growth and opportunity for our company and our city" (May 22, 2002).

FIGHTING FOR MARKET SHARES ON ALL FRONTS

In the first half of the 2000s Chenault continued pumping new blood into the AMEX brand. He pushed hard for the development of the Blue card, a trendy, fashionable card with a microchip allowing cardholders to make secure transactions online. The card appealed to the much-coveted younger demographic.

Further increasing the company's market share, Chenault led AMEX's campaign to build links with banks, changing the company's traditional policy of only issuing cards directly to consumers. He sold banks on the notion that they could increase their profitability by signing on with AMEX, because the company still took higher fees from merchants and because AMEX customers generally charged more money to their cards. Chenault said in *American Banker*, "The leverage that we had as a competitive advantage was a higher merchant discount rate" (June 30, 2000).

Chenault's strategy led to legal disputes with the Visa and MasterCard banking associations, which prohibited their members from issuing AMEX cards. In September 2003 a federal appeals court upheld a lower court ruling requiring Visa USA and MasterCard International to abandon long-held rules prohibiting member banks from issuing cards by American Express and other rivals. Visa and MasterCard said that they would appeal the ruling, while Chenault announced plans to forge partnerships with even more banks by the middle of 2004.

In one of Chenault's proudest accomplishments, he signed Tiger Woods to an AMEX contract. Both Chenault and Woods were leading figures who happened to be African Americans but whose winning appeal was truly universal.

See also entry on American Express Company in *International Directory of Company Histories.*

SOURCES FOR FURTHER INFORMATION

Byrne, John A., and Heather Timmons, "Tough Times for a New CEO," *BusinessWeek*, October 29, 2001, p. 64.

Fickenscher, Lisa, "The President of Amex Depicts It as Victim: Judge Admits Documents about DOJ Talks," *American Banker*, June 30, 2000, p. 1.

New York Voice Inc./Harlem USA, May 22, 2002, p. 19.

Pierce, Ponchitta, "Kenneth Chenault: Blazing New Paths in Corporate America," *Ebony*, July 1997, p. 58.

Schwartz, Nelson D., "What's in the Card for Amex? New CEO Ken Chenault Has No Shortage of Plans for American Express," *Fortune*, January 22, 2001, p. 58.

Whigham-Desir, Marjorie, "Leadership Has Its Rewards: Ken Chenault's Low-Key Yet Competitive Style Has Pushed Him Up the Executive Ladder and to the CEO's Chair," *Black Enterprise*, September 30, 1999, p. 73.

—Tim Halpern

Fujio Cho

1937–

President and chief executive officer, Toyota Motor Corporation

Nationality: Japanese.

Born: 1937, in Tokyo, Japan.

Education: Tokyo University, law degree, 1960.

Career: Toyota Motor Corporation, 1960–1966, apprentice and training employee; 1966–1974, Production Control Division; 1974–1984, manager in Production Control Division; 1984–1986, manager in Logistics Administration and project manager in Production Control Division; 1986–1987, manager in Administration; 1987–1988, manager of Toyota North America Project and executive vice president of Toyota Motor Manufacturing USA; 1988–1994, president of Toyota Motor Manufacturing USA; 1994–1996, managing director; 1996–1998, senior managing director; 1998–1999, executive vice president; 1999–, CEO and president.

Awards: Manager of the Year, Automotive Hall of Fame, 2001; Honorary Doctorate in Engineering, University of Kentucky, 2002; Top Managers, *BusinessWeek*, 2003.

Address: Toyota Motor Corporation, 1 Toyota-cho, Toyota, Aichi 471, Japan; http://www.toyota.com.

Fujio Cho was Toyota Motor Corporation's first director of the 21st century. Bearing a degree in law, he had joined Toyota in 1960 and quickly became one of the company's top production experts. He was personally taught by Taiichi Ohno, author of the system of lean production. Cho spearheaded Toyota's direct investment in production in the United States from 1988 to 1994 and in 1999 succeeded Hiroshi Okuda as the company's president. Under Cho's leadership Toyota became the number-two automotive company in the world and led the industry in the use of hybrid technology and advanced production techniques.

Fujio Cho. *AP/Wide World Photos.*

OHNO'S STAR PUPIL: A LAW GRADUATE LEARNS THE TPS

Fujio Cho was born in Tokyo in 1937. He entered Tokyo University in the mid-1950s, where he studied law—an unlikely discipline for a future industrialist. He graduated in 1960 at the age of 23 and began working for Toyota that same year. He became a member of the Toyota corporate family through "adoption," not birth, as had been the case for his predecessor, Shoichiro Toyoda.

Cho might have remained a minor administrative official in the provincial Japanese company had it not been for Dr. Taiichi Ohno, who would dramatically change the destinies of both Cho and Toyota. Ohno became one of the most revered men in Japan through his formulation of the theory and practice of lean production. In the 1950s and early 1960s Toyota was struggling to make trucks and cars only for the Japanese home market. Eiji Toyoda, the then highest ranking member of the founding family, dreamed of making Toyota a global company and of marketing passenger cars in America. The company, however, was not ready: Toyota vehicles were shoddy and underpowered. Ohno devised a plan for cost-effective production, wherein if the assembly process could be perfectly timed, there would be no need to worry about accumulating expensive inventories. Shoichiro Toyoda, the future heir to the company and the second cousin of Eiji, adopted this procedure in the production division and combined it with a systematic quality-control program.

By the time Cho was rotating through the company as an apprentice, the outlines of the Toyota Production System (TPS) were in place. It worked clumsily at first, but the number of defects on the assembly line soon dropped sharply. Toyota cars were first marketed in America in the mid-1960s. Cho was posted to the Production Control Division in 1966, just as the Toyota Corona began selling in America. There he was thoroughly trained by Ohno, who became his personal mentor.

Ohno made a deep impression on Cho, who become a manager while still in his early 30s. Ohno schooled Cho through lectures, study groups, and hands-on sessions in the factories of Toyota City. Most relevantly he taught Cho the three formulas that were the essence of the TPS: First, top managers needed not only to believe in the system but to convey their commitment to lower-level employees. Second, everyone down to the most menial Toyota worker had to fully participate. Finally, the system needed to be internalized by all employees, who were to be dedicated to its *kaizen*, or constant improvement and ever-increasing efficiency. Cho was given the duty of sharpening the administrative side of the TPS.

The system was designed to keep inventories as lean as possible through "just-in-time" delivery. Parts arrived on the assembly line just as they were needed, a process that required constant communication between dealer, factory, and supplier. In his zeal to keep inventories lean Cho initially engaged in American-style short-term thinking. When Japan was mired in a recession in 1974, Cho cut inventory to the bone and proudly showed the results to Ohno. Ohno, according to Micheline Maynard in her book *The End of Detroit*, exploded: "Are you stupid? We are going to be in a boom. We will need more inventories, not less!" (2003).

Through his humiliation at the hands of Ohno, Cho learned—and would never forget—to look forward to future trends, not back to past or present economic situations. Another important lesson that Ohno impressed upon Cho was that *kaizen* applied to companies and individuals alike; a good professional was ever in need of improvement. Ohno also taught Cho that the TPS was more than just a system: it became, in fact, the guiding philosophy for the entire Toyota firm. Cho continued to manage production and apply his lessons so effectively that he was put in charge of logistical management by 1984.

FUJIO CHO, AMERICAN CORPORATE CITIZEN

More than any other major Toyota official Cho would be shaped by his American experience, of which he was destined to have plenty. The then president Shoichiro Toyoda was so impressed with Cho that he appointed him as general manager of Toyota Motor Manufacturing USA. When the company decided to open its first North American plant in Georgetown, Kentucky, Cho was sent to America to manage it. The plant opened in May 1988; Cho considered this to be the beginning of Toyota's globalization. He directed operations at the plant, which was tremendously successful, until his return to Japan in 1994.

Cho brought to America the same management style that he had practiced in Nagoya and Toyota City. He walked the shop floor and stared for many minutes at the assembly line, asking questions of and listening to answers from Kentuckians as easily as he had with Japanese. Despite his lack of an engineering degree, Cho gradually acquired a thorough practical knowledge of the mechanics of cars and trucks as well as of the buying habits of Americans. One lesson became very important to him: Americans, he discovered, wanted Japanese quality—especially Toyota quality. The oil embargo and consequent rises in gas prices in the 1970s and 1980s persuaded many boomers and yuppies to abandon Detroit-produced automobiles in favor of more reliable, fuel-efficient Corollas and Camrys. Americans also wanted to know that the Camrys made in Georgetown were every bit as good and reliable as those made in Japan. In an interview with Hiroshi Hirai in the *Yomiuri Shimbun*, Cho recalled, "I told workers that U.S. consumers would say, 'I want a Camry made in Japan,' if the quality of our cars was worse than those made in Japan" (October 27, 2003).

Cho would not be disappointed by his American charges. The Kentucky plant began manufacturing Camrys, which Cho had been in charge of turning out at the Tsutsumi plant in Toyota City since 1986. Producing the popular, reliable Camry in the United States would be much less risky than producing an unknown make. American consumers proved just as loyal to American-made Toyotas as they had to imported ones, soon opening the way for additional American Toyota plants. Both Toyota and Cho were very much honored and respected for the prosperity the company's success brought to Georgetown. The company was regarded as an outstanding corporate citizen, and in 2002 Cho was awarded an honorary doctorate in engineering by the University of Kentucky.

No sooner did Cho return to Japan than he was introduced to his next mentor, the new Toyota president Hiroshi Okuda. Okuda was hired in 1995 because no qualified member of the

Toyoda family could be found. Cho continued to serve as senior managing director as he had for Okuda's predecessors. Okuda proceeded to shake up Toyota to ward off the potential threat from Honda, warning Cho that Toyota suffered from "Big Company Disease." He impressed upon Cho the need to hire younger, more creative board members and make Toyota a less formal, more open company.

From Okuda, Cho would learn that cars needed to be designed more quickly and with more freedom given to the designers at the production stage. Toyota was too centralized a company; head officers needed to meddle with designers in the conceptual, not the production stage. Sometimes, Toyota could be too centralized for its own good. Okuda warned Cho that Toyota could one day suffer the fate of American car companies if it lost its awareness of the demands of *kaizen* for perpetual self-evaluation and improvement. The growing competitors Honda and Nissan were small, but they were lean, trendy, and slowly gaining ground.

Okuda left Cho in charge of Toyota's all-important North American operations. The TPS was further refined while Toyota captured 10 percent of the world automotive market and closed in on Ford's number-two global position. The company ambitiously set the goal of dethroning General Motors by 2010 and becoming the world's first truly global automaker.

CHO'S VISION FOR THE NEW CENTURY

In 1999 Okuda retired, and Cho became the second consecutive nonfamily Toyota president. Cho accelerated the pace of growth that had been set by Okuda. In the first three months of 2003 Toyota upstaged Ford in global unit sales for the first time. Much of the credit was given to Cho, who now attracted much media attention. *Fortune* described Toyota as the most respected company in the world, and *BusinessWeek* wondered in the title of a November 17, 2003, article, "Can Anything Stop Toyota?"

While the country of Japan remained in a seemingly endless recession and Japanese management in general was criticized, Cho presided over a company awash in cash reserves and still reaping enormous profits. Writers no longer talked about the Japanese Miracle but of the Toyota Miracle, for which Cho was given his fair share of the credit. When asked by Hisashi Kitahara in the *Yomiuri Shimbun* what the secret of the Toyota Miracle was, Cho pondered for a long time, then gave an astonishing reply. Instead of spouting out a long lecture on *kaizen* or lean production, Cho reduced the essence of Toyota to the ability of its workers to stop the assembly line when the situation demanded, resulting in a total absence of defective cars: "It is that our employees should be courageous enough to bring the production process to a halt, if necessary" (December 3, 2003).

Cho was much more affable, personable, and low-key than the blunt-spoken Okuda. He was, however, no less determined to realize the company vision of capturing 15 percent of the world vehicle market by 2010 and dethroning GM. Cho told Alex Taylor III of *Fortune* that the 15 percent goal was less a fixed target than a vision to motivate Toyota employees to adhere to *kaizen*: "When you achieve an objective, you strive to reach the next objective" (December 8, 2003). One of Cho's favorite slogans was "Beat Toyota."

Cho had a formidable task ahead of him. In order to achieve his stated goal, he would have to sell over nine million cars and trucks against very stiff competition. The potential markets of India and China would not yet be large enough to absorb this production; thus, Toyota's new market would have to come mainly from America and partly from Europe. To compete in those markets, Cho needed to address the issues of styling and image. Many found Toyotas to be reliable but a growing number of young, upscale Japanese were turning to the flashy new models marketed by Nissan and Honda. Cho, worried about Toyota's aging consumer base, felt that the company's cars lacked sex appeal: "Our salespeople are not 100 percent satisfied with styling," Cho said in *Fortune* (December 8, 2003). Consequently, he hired the British-born designer Simon Humphries.

Cho knew that his company was a centralized bastion of traditionalist conformity rooted in the culture of Nagoya, not cosmopolitan Tokyo. As such, he believed that his team could not design smart, global cars while ensconced in Toyota City. Thus, he began to decentralize the design process. Toyota teams located in France and Southern California competed with those in Japan for the best designs. They produced the Toyota Scion, which was geared to appeal to defecting, young, urban Japanese consumers who might have otherwise been tempted to buy Hondas. Recognizing that the somewhat boxlike compact was something of a gamble, Cho intended to first try out the Scion in California in 2003 and then across the United States in 2004. Within a year or two the appeal of the car would be reviewed to determine if sales could reach 100,000.

Cho recognized that engineers and other "car people" alone could not make and sell the vehicles that would push Toyota to number one in the industry. While the safety features, transmission, mileage, and engine were all important, so were the style and total image of the vehicle. Cho knew that he needed to sell all of those aspects in a single vehicle. In addition he wanted Toyota to occupy the leading edge in the sustainable car culture that he and others such as Edouard Michelin and his former superior Shoichiro Toyoda, who had become president of Keidanren, had talked about. The Japanese government provided an extra incentive by setting a deadline by which all Japanese companies would have to be producing cars that used hydrogen and/or electric power. Having huge resources in capital, research, and development, Cho took the lead in marketing the Toyota Prius, one of the world's first hybrid cars. Detroit was several years behind when the Prius was unveiled; the car soon began selling better in America than in Japan. Cho, encouraged, set plans to sell 300,000 hybrids worldwide by 2005. In October 2003 he began selling the second-generation Prius in the United States; by the autumn of 2004 he planned to unveil the hybrid Lexus RX330.

THE *GAIJIN* OF TOYOTA: HIRING AMERICANS

Cho perceived that North America would remain absolutely paramount to the success of his company. In 2002 and 2003 Toyota sold more vehicles there than in Japan, amounting to almost 80 percent of total worldwide profits. Moreover, America was his key test market. If a car, truck, or sport-utility vehicle (SUV) sold well there, Cho and his colleagues could confidently sell it in Japan and around the world as well. The Lexus had first been introduced in America. In beginning to surpass U.S. automotive companies on their home ground, Cho increasingly marketed Toyota Motor Corporation USA as an American company. In June 2003 he promoted James Press to be sales and marketing manager and Gary Convis to be in charge of manufacturing; the presence of two American *gaijin*—a derogatory Japanese term for foreigners—among Toyota's top executives was unprecedented.

Cho had no problem with the hiring of these *gaijin*, considered it to be a wise business strategy; he noted in *Fortune*, "Toyota has been globalized step by step. We are trying to introduce American elements into the company " (December 8, 2003). Cho began to Americanize the Toyota management system as well, although Convis and Press were not the ones in charge of Toyota's American branch. That role fell to the blunt-spoken Yoshi Inaba, a marketer, not an engineer; under Inaba, the American Toyota was slowly moving away from consensus management and toward more rapid decision making.

Cho only took Americanization so far. He was not Carlos Ghosn, the French Brazilian who took over Nissan, and Toyota was not Nissan. Where Ghosn slashed a number of jobs at his then-struggling firm, Cho found no need to do so. For Cho, lifetime employment was not only sustainable in a solvent company with sales worth ¥8 trillion but essential to the continued success of *kaizen.* Cho believed that the jettisoning of lifetime employment in many other Japanese companies was a serious danger to the social stability of his country. Layoffs were a dishonorable practice that Toyota would only consider as a last resort.

Cho maintained a corporate culture that was still highly conservative by Japanese, let alone American standards. Toyota remained centralized and hierarchical and in many ways was the most "Japanese" of major Japanese companies. Nissan, with its new lean structure and French manager, wanted to be aggressive; Toyota, with its commanding position, did not. As a giant company that had conquered Chrysler, overtaken Ford, and was setting its sights on General Motors, Toyota had no desire to risk a direct confrontation with Detroit. Cho proceeded carefully.

Cho continued to dedicate himself to the principles of lean production and *kaizen* that he had learned at the feet of Ohno, whom he quoted consistently. In order for the long-term goals that the company had set to be accomplished, the TPS would have to become ever more nimble and efficient. While Cho and his company were well ahead of most of the competition, they refused to become complacent. Cho knew that in the 21st century consumer wants would be shifting more rapidly than ever; Toyota would need to be able to shift just as rapidly to meet those wants.

Cho gave a high priority to the application of information technology in upgrading the TPS. New models could be developed and their production processes computer generated at the very same time. By 2004 some Toyota plants were using a new technique that allowed them to hold vehicle bodies on assembly lines with one rather than three supports. The streamlined Global Body Line production process made it possible to switch from one model to another on a single line, permitting Cho to place more robots at any given line location. It would soon be possible to custom produce a Lexus, a truck, an SUV, a Camry, or a Prius on the same line on the same day at any plant in the world. This would give Toyota an enormous advantage over less flexible competitors who would constantly have to retool or shift production to other plants to meet customer demand.

Through his example of implementing selective Americanization while remaining deeply Japanese, Cho led the way to a new and revived Japanese management/production model. In contrast to the business writers of the 1990s, scores of whom were pronouncing the death of that Japanese model, the ongoing success of Cho inspired the 2004 book by Jeffrey K. Liker lauding *The Toyota Way.*

See also entry on Toyota Motor Corporation in *International Directory of Company Histories.*

SOURCES FOR FURTHER INFORMATION

Bremner, Brian, and Chester Dawson, "Can Anything Stop Toyota?" *BusinessWeek*, November 17, 2003, pp. 115–120, 122.

Dawson, Chester, et al., "The Americanization of Toyota," *BusinessWeek*, April 15, 2002, pp. 52–54.

Hirai, Hiroshi, "Toyota Boss: Competition Spirit Key to Success," *Yomiuri Shimbun* (Tokyo), October 27, 2003.

Keller, Maryann, *Collision: GM, Toyota, Volkswagen, and the Race to Own the 21st Century*, New York, N.Y.: Currency Doubleday, 1993.

Kitahara, Hisashi, "Few Firms Can Emulate Toyota," *Yomiuri Shimbun* (Tokyo), December 3, 2003.

Liker, Jeffrey K., *The Toyota Way: 14 Management Principles from the World's Greatest Manufacturer*, New York, N.Y.: McGraw Hill, 2004.

Maynard, Micheline, *The End of Detroit: How the Big Three Lost Their Grip on the American Car Market*, New York, N.Y.: Currency Doubleday, 2003.

McKenna, Joseph R., "The Challenger Mindset of Fujio Cho," *Tooling Around*, April 2002, p. 1.

Spear, Steven, and H. Kent Bowen, "Decoding the DNA of the Toyota Production System," *Harvard Business Review*, September–October 1999, pp. 97–106.

Taylor, Alex, III, "The Americanization of Toyota," *Fortune*, December 8, 2003, pp. 165–166, 168, 170.

Togo, Yukiyasu, and William Wartman, *Against All Odds: The Story of the Toyota Motor Corporation and the Family That Created It*, New York, N.Y.: St. Martin's Press, 1993.

Toyoda, Eiji, *Toyota: Fifty Years in Motion; An Autobiography of the Chairman, Eiji Toyoda*, Tokyo: Kodanshi International, 1987.

"Toyota: Japan's Unstoppable Juggernaut," *Automotive Industry*, June 2002, p. 10.

—David Charles Lewis

■■■

Chung Ju-yung

1915–2001

Founder and former chairman of the Hyundai Group

Nationality: Korean.

Born: November 25, 1915, in Asan-ri, North Korea.

Died: March 21, 2001.

Family: Son of Chung Bong-sik and Han Seong-sil; married Byun Joong-seok; children: nine.

Career: 1931–1934, construction laborer; Bokheung Rice Store, 1934–1935, clerk; Kyongil Grain Company, 1936–1939, founder and manager; A-do Service, 1939–1943, founder and manager; Hyundai Motor Industrial Company, 1946–1987, founder and chairman; Hyundai Civil Industries, 1947–1987, founder and chairman.

Awards: Commander of the British Empire, Queen Elizabeth II, 1977; honorary degree, George Washington University, 1982; Olympic Medallion, International Olympic Committee, 1992; Grand Prize, Korea Academy of Business Historians, 1999; listed as one of the 10 greatest persons in Asia in the twentieth century, *Far Eastern Economic Review, 1999.*

Publications: *Born in This Land,* 1992.

■ Born of a peasant family in what is now North Korea during the period when the country was a Japanese colony, Chung Ju-yung showed an early inclination for entrepreneurship. After surviving the Korean War of 1950–1953, he set up two fledgling companies, one dealing in auto repairs and the other in construction. These companies formed the core of a vast industrial empire that became the Hyundai Group, one of South Korea's major *chaebol,* or family-owned business conglomerates. As much a nation-builder as an industrialist, Chung believed that businessmen should serve a larger purpose than the narrow mandate of profit; they were, in his view, also responsible for helping develop the strength of a nation and its people. He gave back to his society by setting up the Asan Foundation, whose philanthropic activities ranged from medical support and social welfare programs to research, development, and scholarship funds. Chung was also active politically, working tirelessly at the end of his life to promote economic development and cultural relations between the two sides of his divided country.

HUMBLE BEGINNINGS

Chung Ju-yung was the first son of a large impoverished peasant family in Asan-ri, a village in what became North Korea after the Korean War ended in 1953. He came of age during the Japanese colonial occupation of Korea, which began in 1910 and lasted until the Allies defeated the Axis powers in 1945. Chung's early education was meager. He attended a primary school in Songjon and learned Chinese literature from his grandfather. His formal education ended when his parents withdrew him from school because they needed his wages to help support the family. Rather than submit to the likelihood of a lifetime of poverty, Chung twice tried to leave his village in search of better prospects in the large city of Seoul. In his first attempt to leave home when he was 16, he financed his journey by selling the family's only cow for a small fee. Chung finally succeeded in leaving his village for good in 1931 at the age of 18, when he found work as a laborer at several construction sites. Chung's construction assignments included Inchon harbor, a professional school in Boseong, and a taffy plant in Poongjeon.

After several years of construction work, Chung obtained a position as a clerk at the Bokheung Rice Store in Gyeonseong, a neighborhood in Seoul. Determined to go into business for himself, he established the Kyongil Grain Company, only to have to close it in 1939 when rice rationing was implemented by the Japanese authorities. The 24-year-old entrepreneur then turned to repairing cars via the A-Do Service, a company that he owned jointly with a Japanese partner. That venture lasted four years but was folded into its Japanese parent company in 1943.

Blessed with natural intelligence and a desire to learn, Chung picked up his education informally by reading business documents and the lectures of better-educated associates late at night. More importantly, he hired educated men who could fill in the gaps in his own schooling.

A DETERMINED EMPIRE-BUILDER

Aware of the business opportunities made possible by the end of World War II and the ousting of the Japanese from Korea, Chung founded two companies in rapid succession after the country's liberation in 1945—the Hyundai Motor Industrial Company in 1946 and Hyundai Civil Industries in 1947. With the former focused on auto manufacturing and servicing and the latter on heavy construction, Chung's business ventures were at the center of Korea's massive postwar drive for reconstruction and industrialization.

Hyundai Civil Industries was responsible for building much of South Korea's transportation infrastructure from the 1950s through the 1970s. It was considered the top company in its industry. Chung won major government contracts, including the Soyang River multipurpose dam in 1967, the Gyeongbu Expressway and a nuclear power plant in 1970, and the Ulsan shipbuilding yard in 1973, among many others. Through the efforts of his younger brother In-yung, who could speak English and was on friendly terms with U.S. Army engineers, Chung won contracts from the American military to build facilities for their personnel.

Hyundai also won major projects overseas. In 1965 Hyundai won the bid to build the Thailand Expressway. In the 1970s the company was granted a major contract in the Middle East. It successfully completed the Jubail industrial port in Saudi Arabia, at that time the largest construction project of the 20th century.

Chung continued to expand his empire into industrial chemicals and shipbuilding, turning Hyundai into one of South Korea's major *chaebol*. With no experience in shipbuilding, he created the Ulsan shipyard, the largest shipyard in the world. What made this project remarkable was that he set about to build both shipyard and vessel simultaneously, reasoning that the two tasks need not be completed sequentially. With orders from an Italian company, Hyundai delivered its first vessel within three years rather than the expected five.

As South Korea continued to industrialize at breakneck speed, Chung dreamed of building a car using only Korean technology and expertise. Setting his automotive company to that task, he introduced the Hyundai Pony Excel in 1986 amid a burst of national pride. Chung continued to explore new technologies during the 1980s and 1990s, incorporating semiconductors and magnetic levitation train technology into Hyundai's automobiles.

SUCCESS AT A PRICE

The relentless pace of building the Hyundai empire, often with limited or no previous experience, came at a heavy cost in terms of human lives as well as finances. The Gogryong Bridge construction project in 1953 nearly bankrupted Hyundai. The Jubail project also suffered from the company's lack of experience. The concrete Soyang River dam encountered several significant problems during its construction and drew much criticism of Chung.

Working conditions in Chung's factories were hazardous and led to visible conflicts with workers. Chung, however, never forfeited a project. Although his determination led to an impressive roster of achievements, Korean factories and plants became known as some of the most dangerous in the industrialized world. It was not until the 2000s that the company guaranteed the safety of its employees. Sensitive to criticism, Chung's successors at Hyundai were quick to document the annual increases in corporate funds dedicated to worker welfare throughout the late 1990s and 2000s.

A SECOND CAREER IN POLITICS

Chung resigned as active chairman of the Hyundai Group in 1987, although he remained its honorary chairman. To everyone's surprise, however, he announced that he was beginning a new career in politics. Chung maintained that economic power was not sufficient to guarantee a nation's strength; it must have wise leadership as well. Ever the nation-builder, Chung declared that South Korea's long-term security and economic competitiveness required unification with Communist North Korea. He thus made the initiation and expansion of economic relations between the two Koreas his short-term project, with national unification as the ultimate goal. Chung's Unification People's Party campaigned under the slogans "Importance of Economy" and "Unified Economy." The Party won 31 seats in the 1992 Korean presidential election, but Chung failed to win the presidency.

Chung retired from political activity after 1992 but decided to work toward his goal through an altogether different channel, namely tourism. The Mount Kumgang Tourism Project and related activities developed tourist facilities around scenic Mount Kumgang in North Korea near the South Korean border. Opened in 1998, the project permitted hundreds of thousands of people to cross the heavily guarded border (the DMZ or demilitarized zone) and visit the site.

Chung also continued his attempts to develop economic relations between the two Koreas. In 1998, at the age of 84, he worked with the government of Kim Dae-jung to stage an economic development summit between North and South Korea, an episode that unfortunately became tainted with scandal. President Kim had determined that relations with the Communist North were best stabilized by offering economic assistance and wanted to provide a $100 million donation as a way to jump-start economic development in North Korea. The problem was that Kim could not find a legal way to transfer the funds. Instead, he turned to his friend Chung, who was himself negotiating a $350 million contract to develop businesses in the North. Kim persuaded Chung to increase his investment by $100 million with money from secret loans provided by the government-controlled Korea Development Bank. The historic South-North summit took place, with Chung traveling across the border in a motorcade of cars containing some 500 "unification cows"—a gift to the North Korean people. But Chung's reputation suffered a severe blow when it was learned that state funds had helped facilitate the event.

Chung also turned to sports to reduce tensions by creating the Unification Basketball Contest, which was held alternately in Seoul and Pyongyang, the respective capitals of South and North Korea. By the mid-2000s, the two sides were holding regular talks on a multitude of issues aimed at reducing tensions in the Korean peninsula. Railway lines and other infrastructure projects linking the divided nation were reestablished. Agreements on various issues ranging from communications facilities to fishing rights were also achieved.

MANAGEMENT STYLE

Chung's management style largely depended on the observer's perspective. His admirers in the Korean business community revered him as a father figure. Westerners, on the other hand, saw Hyundai as a tightly controlled organization whose founder took worker complaints as personal offenses. Chung described himself as an older brother or father, but recurrent conflicts between labor and management characterized his tenure at Hyundai. Although Chung took pains to minimize the impact of these conflicts, he nevertheless came to concede the need to address worker issues.

Chung had an abiding faith in the intelligence and diligence of his workers, holding that Korean human resources are second to none. His attitude was that of *samgo choyeo*, or inviting talented people to do their work patiently before granting them authority and responsibility. Chung's approach was reflected in the core values still held by Hyundai in the early 2000s—diligence, frugality, and love—and implemented by a management policy based on trust. Although Chung was a hard taskmaster, he did not hold himself aloof from his employees. A former laborer himself, Chung enjoyed engaging his men in bouts of Korean-style wrestling and volleyball. He also regularly attended training sessions for new employees.

Chung Ju-yung was widely recognized as one of South Korea's nation-builders. In 1977, he was unanimously elected chairman of the Korea Federation of Industries by his peers. He held that post for a full decade. In 1999 the Korea Academy of Business Historians awarded him its grand prize for establishing businesses. In the 1980s his influence helped reshape the South Korean economy from one dominated by government projects and requirements to a civilian-controlled economy, thus spurring the growth engine that has given South Korea the nickname "Miracle of the Han." The name refers to the Han River, which bisects Seoul from east to west.

PHILANTHROPIC CONTRIBUTIONS

Whereas many Korean businessmen of Chung's generation were focused almost exclusively on industrial development and expanding the assets of their *chaebol* as well as corporate profits, Chung early understood the importance of giving back to the wider community. In 1977 he founded the Asan Foundation, named for the village of his birth. Chung intended to make the scope of its activities comparable to those of the Ford or Rockefeller Foundations.

The Asan Foundation was organized into four major areas of service: medical support, social welfare, research and development, and a scholarship fund. Through its efforts, the Foundation established nine hospitals throughout South Korea, built Ulsan Medical College, and funded the Asan Life Sciences Research Institute. The Foundation also initiated cooperative arrangements between industry and academic institutions by supporting such academic research as the Sinyoung Research Fund.

In terms of sports, Chung lobbied relentlessly over a five-month period for South Korea to host the 1988 Summer Olympics. His success in bringing the Olympics to Korea highlighted the accomplishments of his generation in the eyes of the world and became a source of great pride to the people of Seoul. In 1992 the International Olympic Committee awarded Chung an IOC Medallion for his contributions to sports as a vehicle of international understanding.

Chung fell ill with pneumonia in the first week of March 2001 at the age of 85. He was admitted to the hospital but his condition quickly worsened. He died in his sleep on March 21, 2001. After his death the Hyundai Group was broken up into several smaller companies— the Hyundai Motor Group, Hyundai Heavy Industries, and Hyundai Engineering and Construction.

See also entry on Hyundai Group in *International Directory of Company Histories.*

SOURCES FOR FURTHER INFORMATION

Breen, Michael, *The Koreans*, London: Orion Business Books, 1998.

"Hyundai Founder, Asan Chung Ju-yung: A Giant Who Solidified the Foundation of Korean Economy and South-North Exchange," http://www.asanmuseum.com//english/page/content.asp?main_id=70&sub1_id=10&sub2_id=5&sub3_id=0&sub4_id=0.

Ward, Andrew, "Lunch with the FT: Kim Dae-jung," *Financial Times*, June 18, 2004.

—Carole S. Moussalli

■■■

Carla Cico

1961–

Chief executive officer, Brasil Telecom

Nationality: Italian.

Born: February 21, 1961, in Verona, Italy.

Education: London School of Business, MBA, 1993; University of London, MSE, 1993.

Family: Daughter of Lorenzo Cico and Francesca Provera; single.

Career: Italtel, 1987–1992, representative of Beijing (China) office; IRI, 1993–1994, representative of Beijing office; Stet International, 1995–1999, international director of business operations; 2000–2001, telecommunications consultant for several companies; Brasil Telecom, 2001–, CEO.

Awards: Executive of the Year, Associação Nacional dos Executivos de Finanças, Administração, e Contabilidade, 2002; Businesswoman of the Year, British Chamber of Commerce in Brazil, 2002; Global Influentials, *Time*, 2002; Best CEO in Telecommunications Sector in Latin America, Reuters Institutional Investor Research, 2003; one of Fifty Most Powerful Women in International Business, *Fortune*, 2002 and 2003.

Address: SIA Sul, ASP, Lote D, Bloco B, 71215-000 Brasília, D.F., Brazil; http://www.brasiltelecom.com.br.

Carla Cico. © *Paulo Fridman/Corbis.*

■ In March 2001 Carla Cico became the CEO of Brasil Telecom (BrT). A native of Italy, Cico led the formation of a consortium that won the bidding for the company that operates in nine Brazilian states and the Federal District. She was the first woman to serve as chief executive of a telecommunications company in Brazil. Based on her vast experience dating to the 1980s, Cico came to be regarded as one of the world's top telecommunications executives, as evidenced by her numerous awards and distinctions.

EARLY CAREER

Cico was born and raised in Verona, Italy. After graduating from high school in 1979, she studied at the University of Venice, where she received a degree in oriental languages, specializing in Chinese. In 1984–1985 her language studies took her to Taiwan, where she studied at the Normal Superior University under the auspices of a scholarship from the Taiwanese government.

During the 1980s and 1990s Cico managed a number of Italian telecom ventures in China. From 1987 to 1992 she supervised Italtel projects in Beijing. She was also responsible for accessing new Asian markets, such as Vietnam, Thailand, and the Philippines. Cico continued to work in China until 1994, serving as resident manager for Chong Quing and as principal representative for IRI in Beijing. She then returned to her native Italy to work for Stet International from 1995 until 1999. As international director of business operations, she was responsible for finding investment opportunities in Asia, South America, Eastern Europe, and Africa. Cico's experience had a great influence on her future professional career. She noted that the most relevant person in her business life was her first boss, Idalgo Macciarini, with whom she worked during her first two years in China. He gave her focus and showed her how to approach problems, skills that she used to good effect later in her career.

The BrT CEO's extensive international experience quickly became an asset in the business world. She told *NYSE Magazine* that "in the beginning it was a coincidence, but afterward my diverse background became a skill" (July/August 2002). It seemed to her that working with telecommunications in New York was different from working in China or Brazil. Cico, who had a facility with languages, became fluent in four languages besides Mandarin Chinese. She also discovered that the ability to adapt was invaluable. She told the *Chief Executive*, "Either you adapt or you pack up and go back to a more comfortable life" (February 2002).

EFFICIENCY AND LONG-TERM PLANNING

Cico believed that telecom executives must learn from the mistakes of the 1990s, when too many in the industry were concerned only with short-term results. Instead, she insisted that telecom companies must plan for long-term growth. To achieve this goal, she consistently cut costs to boost efficiency. Cico was known for pushing her managers hard and deploying capital wisely. Her strategy showed concrete results in her first year at BrT, as revenue increased by 65 percent.

Cico and BrT gained recognition in the area of corporate governance. Industry analysts acknowledged that BrT strictly complied with good corporate governance practices, often a rarity in the Brazilian telecommunications industry. Indeed, BrT is the only Brazilian telecom in the Level 1 of the São Paulo Stock Exchange's (Bovespa) corporate governance best-practices program. Cico told *Institutional Investor* that this recognition "demonstrates our commitment to transparency. We were again pioneers. Brasil Telecom is the only company in the sector to be part of this differentiated segment of corporate governance" (September 2003).

Cico looked to attract and continue to train good managers for BrT. She developed a summer internship program to find the best graduates with MBAs from around the world and encouraged her managers to take language-training courses. Furthermore, she believed in creating a culture of quality and competence, often through a job-rotation program. Cico believed in creating good leaders, rewarding those who performed well, and empowering workers by giving them a degree of autonomy. She also emphasized that companies must offer fair and competitive pay to keep good managers.

AN ATHLETE'S MENTALITY

Cico brought the attitude of a well-trained athlete to the business world and thought that her company should contribute to the quality of life of its employees. Thus, BrT provides health-related programs, health clubs in the workplace, and preventative medicine programs. The BrT president practiced what she preached, having run in the New York City marathon with several of her employees. Cico explained to *Time* that "it promotes discipline, preparation, focus, team culture" (November 30, 2002). She also encouraged the company and its workers to become involved in the local community. Such involvement, she thought, reinforced good citizenship, ethical behavior, and solidarity.

See also entry on Brasil Telecom Participaçoes S.A. in *International Directory of Company Histories.*

SOURCES FOR FURTHER INFORMATION

Hanson, Jennifer, "Carla Cico's Circuit," *NYSE Magazine*, July/August 2002, pp. 40–41.

Padgett, Tim, "Carla Cico: TIME 2002 Global Influentials," *Time*, December 2, 2002, p. 55.

Sherwood, Sonja, "Brasil Telecom's Cultural Iconoclast: Career Path Less Traveled," *Chief Executive*, February 2002, p. 6.

Yolen, Steve, and Tom Murphy, "Profiles of CG Programs in Brazil," *Institutional Investor*, September 2003, pp. 20–26.

—Ronald Young

■ ■ ■

Philippe Citerne

1949–

Co–chief executive officer, Société Générale

Born: 1949.

Education: Ecole Centrale de Paris, undergraduate degree in economics, graduate degree in mathematics.

Career: INSEE (French national statistical bureau), 1972–1974, project manager; French Ministry of Finance, Forecast Department, 1974–1979, project manager, then bureau chief of energy, transport, and equipment; Société Générale: 1979–1984, Economic Research Service staff, then 1984–1986, director; 1986–1990, director of financial management; 1990–1995, director of human resources; 1995–1997, Resources and Services Division, deputy chief executive officer; 1997–, co–chief executive officer.

Address: 17 cours Valmy, La Défense, Paris 92972, France; http://www.socgen.com.

■ His education and early career made Philippe Citerne, co-CEO of Société Générale, France's third-largest bank, look like the typical aspiring French bureaucrat. His management style and opinions about the French way of doing business in the global economy, however, told a very different story.

Citerne earned an undergraduate degree in economics and a graduate degree in mathematics from the Ecole Centrale in Paris, a renowned science and engineering school whose graduates include such French luminaries as Eiffel, Michelin, and Peugeot. He began his career in 1972 as a project manager in the Business Department at INSEE, France's institute for statistics and economic studies.

Two years later Citerne began a five-year stint for the French Ministry of Finance, first as project manager and then as bureau chief of energy, transport, and equipment in the Forecast Department. In 1979, at age 30, he left the confines of the French bureaucracy for a position in the Economic Research Department at Société Générale (known in the press and in general parlance as SocGen).

VARIETY OF POSITIONS AT SOCGEN

Over the next 18 years Citerne worked in a number of departments at SocGen, whose strengths are in retail banking and asset management plus the equity derivatives business it developed in the mid-1980s (about 20 percent of the net profit of the bank). His experiences in the research, financial management, human resources, and information technology departments were to serve him in good stead when he became a top executive. A profile of him in *Financial News* (April 1, 2002) quoted Citerne as commenting, "You have to be humble and you have to be best of breed as a good manager. But it does help if you understand what is going on in everybody's business."

In 1997 Citerne became co-CEO of SocGen, sharing the title with president Daniel Bouton. Both men found the arrangement highly workable, although it seemed unconventional to outsiders. Citerne described the relationship as a "kind of chemistry. A case of working in practice and theory" (*Financial Times*, April 1, 2002).

THE BANK WARS

In 1999, despite support from almost half of SocGen's shareholders, the Paribas bank and SocGen failed to merge when Michel Pebereau of the Banque Nationale de Paris (BNP) made a successful offer for Paribas. Four years later, some analysts suggested that a merger between BNP Paribas and SocGen would be an ideal match. The locations of their retail centers and their dominance in differing areas of banking seemed complementary. But bitterness over the past and what some described as a "culture clash" made a merger seem problematic. In the meantime, rumors circulated that SocGen had signed a memorandum of understanding with the pan-European institution Dexia stating that neither of them would consider merging with another bank.

When Xavier Debonneuil, the former CEO of SG, the investment banking division of SocGen, died in an automobile accident in December 2002, Jean-Pierre Mustier replaced him. Mustier's trading background and more active hands-on involvement in day-to-day operations afforded Bouton and Citerne the opportunity to revamp the investment arm of SocGen. Their hiring of several managers who were in their forties was out of the ordinary for a French commercial bank and indicated to global markets that SocGen had become more aggressive and opportunistic. As one *Financial News* analyst favorably commented regarding the identity crisis at SocGen (April 1, 2003), "If you look at the management of the French banks there are a lot of old people with a lot of experience, but I think it is crucial to have younger people to create a new dynamic."

CITERNE LOOKS TO THE FUTURE

In his profile in *Financial News* (April 1, 2002), Citerne expressed confidence that retail branch banking, earning half the profits for SocGen, would survive. Because Internet banking had not proved as popular in France as it had elsewhere in Europe, he believed the "customer-facing business," as it is called, would continue to be solid.

In the same article Citerne expressed frustration over French bureaucracy and the 35-hour work week. Of the latter he said, "It's rational and very French. But if it's so clever why isn't the rest of the world following it? Is this really the best that 50 million people can come up with? It works in practice, but does it work in theory too?"

In addition, Citerne had to factor in his government's tendency to interfere with the banking industry if prospective acquisitions appeared to threaten jobs. The rigid French style of doing business contrasted sharply with the more freewheeling environments he experienced in his dealings with other countries.

Citerne clearly planned to continue supporting innovation at SocGen, and he showed a sense of humor and perspective about the banker's life that distinguished him from many of his counterparts. In an interview over lunch he picked up the menu to make a point: "You see this menu? If I showed it to a banker, he would say: 'What if?', and if I showed it to an investment banker, he would say: 'Let's do the deal.' So the trick is to keep steady through the cyclical nature of the business" (*Financial News*, April 1, 2002).

See also entry on Société Générale in *International Directory of Company Histories.*

SOURCES FOR FURTHER INFORMATION

Chernoff, Joel, "First Step: Citerne, Collas Named to Top Posts at SG Paribas; Merger Creates Europe's 10th Largest Manager," *Pensions & Investments*, February 22, 1999, p. 14.

Morris, Jennifer, "The Crisis of Identity at Société Générale," *Euromoney*, April 1, 2003, pp. 36–42.

Pagano, Margareta, "SocGen's Citerne Laughs Wryly at French Banking," *Financial News Online*, March 31, 2002.

"SG Won't Raise Its KB Stake for Now, Says Citerne," Europe Intelligence Wire, October 8, 2002.

Wrighton, Jo, "Can Citerne Keep the Peace?" *Institutional Investor International Edition*, February 1999, p. 14.

—Anne Lesser

■■■

Jim Clark

1944–

Chairman of Shutterfly; chairman of Neoteris; director of DNA Sciences

Nationality: American.

Born: 1944, in Plainview, Texas.

Education: University of New Orleans, MA, 1971; University of Utah, PhD, 1974.

Family: Married and divorced twice, then married Nancy Rutter; children: two.

Career: University of California at Santa Cruz, 1974–1978, assistant professor; Stanford University, 1979–1982, associate professor; Silicon Graphics, 1982–1994, chairman; Netscape Communications Corp., 1994–1999, chairman; Healtheon/WebMD, 1996–2000, chairman; Shutterfly, 1999–, chairman; DNA Sciences, 2000–, director; Neoteris, 2001–, chairman; Hyperion Development Group, 2003–, co-owner.

Awards: Annual Gold Medal in Physics, Research Society of America, 1971; Computer Graphics Achievement Award, 1984; Entrepreneur of the Year, *Venture Magazine*, 1988.

Publications: (With Owen Edwards) *Netscape Time: The Making of the Billion-Dollar Start-Up that Took On Microsoft*, with Owen Edwards, 1999.

Address: Shutterfly, 2800 Bridge Parkway, Suite 101, Redwood City, California 94065; http://www.shutterfly.com.

Jim Clark. *AP/Wide World Photos.*

■ James H. (Jim) Clark founded two of the most successful and influential technology companies of the 1980s and 1990s. The first, Silicon Graphics (SGI), was cofounded by Clark and six graduate students at Stanford University in 1982, where Clark was employed as an associate professor. SGI revolutionized desktop computing by building high-performance workstations that could create and display 3-D images in real time, thus allowing engineers to model their designs on a computer screen. The second company was Netscape Communications Corporation, which Clark cofounded in 1994 with 22-year-old Marc Andreessen. Netscape is credited with launching the rapid growth of the Internet and World Wide Web in the mid-1990s. The company also initiated the IPO and Internet stock-market boom during this period, making many people, including Clark, millionaires and billionaires overnight. After leaving Netscape, Clark went on to start up a number of other Internet companies, including Healtheon, MyCFO, and Shutterfly. Industry insiders, peers, and competitors considered Clark to be one of the most important figures of the 1990s technology boom.

Though extremely successful as an entrepreneur and risk taker, Clark often failed, by his own admission, as a leader and manager. In his book *The New New Thing: A Silicon Valley Story,* author Michael Lewis describes Clark as a man driven by change and the possibilities of the future, but who was quickly bored with the details of running an established business. According to Lewis, Clark "was keen on things only as they happened, after they had happened he lost interest in them altogether." Even so, the power of Clark's ideas attracted some of the best minds and engineers to his innovative companies. Analysts described Clark as the man who single-handedly rewrote the rules of American business, creating the larger-than-life figure of the entrepreneur and the corporate outsider, rather than the career executive, as the ideal of business success.

UNLIKELY BEGINNINGS

Very little in Jim Clark's youth and upbringing would anticipate his ultimate success as an entrepreneur and technologist. He was born in Plainview, Texas, and grew up in difficult circumstances. His father drank excessively and performed odd jobs for income, while his mother worked in a doctor's office. After his parents divorced when he was still a child, he was raised—along with his brother and sister—by his mother on $225 a month. Clark spoke little of his childhood, describing it bluntly to author Lewis as follows: "I grew up in black and white. I thought the whole world was shit and I was sitting in the middle of it."

As a child, Clark was a nonconformist and a prankster. He was suspended from school for igniting a smoke bomb on a bus, and he once smuggled a skunk into a school dance. He ultimately quit school when he was suspended a second time for telling an English teacher to go to hell.

Determined to escape the confines of Plainview, Clark convinced his mother to sign the permission papers to let him join the Navy. His stint in the military started off badly when Clark, along with other recruits, was given a multiple-choice aptitude test. Having never before taken a multiple-choice test, Clark was confused because he thought most answers to the questions were at least partially true. Instead of picking the one answer that was most correct, he circled them all. His Navy officers accused him of trying to trick the computer that graded the tests, and he was sent, with other "delinquent" recruits, immediately out to sea.

Because of his unfortunate start in the Navy, Clark was given some of the most disgusting chores and was treated badly by other recruits and officers. He recalled officers telling him he was stupid and superiors tossing their plates on the floor, only to watch Clark clean up the mess. The experience hardened him and convinced him that he would never be dependent on anyone again.

When he returned stateside, Clark took a math cxam offered by the Navy and, to his instructors' amazement, scored the highest in his class. Surprised and encouraged by the results, Clark earned his high school equivalency degree and went on to college, where he ultimately earned a BS and MA in physics, and then a PhD in computer science. It was while earning his doctorate from the University of Utah that Clark first saw a high-performance graphics computer. This experience captured his imagination, showing him the potential of computers, and led to the creation of Silicon Graphics.

THE SILICON-GRAPHICS YEARS

While employed as an associate professor at Stanford University, Clark was involved in a project at Xerox's Palo Alto Research Center to enliven computer images with three-dimensional graphics. In 1979 he, along with a number of graduate students under his direction, developed a revolutionary computer chip, which Clark dubbed the "Geometry Engine." The chip was the first to process 3-D images in real time, thus allowing engineers, designers, and other users to model designs in a virtual three-dimensional world. Clark recalled his work on 3-D computer processing as a turning point in his life. He told the author Michael Lewis, "the difference was phenomenal, for me. I don't know how many people around me noticed. But my God I noticed. The first manifestation was when all of these people started coming up and wanting to be part of my project." Three years later, in 1982, Clark left academia and, with a handful of his graduate students and funding from a Silicon Valley venture capitalist, started Silicon Graphics.

SGI became the most successful company in Silicon Valley at the time. The company went public in 1986 and saw its stock rise from $3 a share to more than $30. Even so, SGI's internal affairs were in chaos. Though a visionary and entrepreneur, Clark was no manager. He was not interested in marketing or selling or instituting systems that ensured repetitive results. Clark's idea of leadership was to attract the brightest engineers and people with a passion for changing the world, and then let them figure out the details for making his idea work. His style created considerable tension at SGI between the CEO and executive team brought in by the venture capitalist to run the company and the founding engineers, including Clark. What made matters worse was that Clark and his cofounders were forced to sell larger and larger equity stakes in SGI to Mayfield in order to continue operations. By the time SGI made its first sale, Clark and his engineers owned little of the company they started. The experience left Clark bitter about the workings of American business, and he vowed never to make the same mistake again.

Although Clark retained the title of chairman of SGI, he had little power to influence its affairs. He found himself increasingly marginalized by the company's CEO, who was brought in to run SGI by Glenn Mueller of the Mayfield Fund, and by the corporate board. As the 1990s began, Clark became obsessed with Bill Gates and Microsoft, fearing that it was only a matter of time before the personal computer had enough processing power to replace the more costly and cumbersome SGI workstations. At first Clark tried to convince Ed McCracken,. SGI's CEO, and the board to develop less expensive, commercialized versions of its high-end products. He then turned to the idea of interactive television. McCracken and many of the other SGI executives considered Clark's ideas dangerous and destructive to the future viability of SGI and wanted no part of them. Frustrated and angry, Clark sold out his remaining interest in SGI and left the company in 1994.

THE NEXT BIG THING

It did not take Clark long to begin searching for new, young software talent to help him realize his next idea. His search eventually led him to Marc Andreessen, the 22-year-old graduate student at the University of Illinois who developed the Mosaic Web browser. Still obsessed with the idea of interactive television, Clark convinced Andreessen and a few other UI graduates to join him in developing an application that would transform the ubiquitous TV into the interactive and communication tool of the future. Andreessen, however, was skeptical of interactive television as a business, and he eventually convinced Clark that the Internet, and his Mosaic browser, offered more fertile ground for success. Clark invested $3 million of his own money and started Mosaic Communications Corporation, which was later changed to Netscape Communications.

For Clark success meant creating a product or application that was akin to Microsoft's monopoly in operating systems for personal computers. And he was determined to develop his new business on his terms, not the terms of venture capitalists and corporate insiders whom Clark came to see as "bloodsuckers" (as he told Lewis) to the creative and entrepreneurial spirit. After the formation of Netscape, venture capitalists besieged Clark for a piece of the business. One of these was Glenn Mueller, the original backer of SGI. A Silicon Valley legend claimed that Mueller ultimately committed suicide after Clark told him that he would never be permitted to invest in Netscape. True or not, the incident only fed into the power and mystique of Jim Clark.

Within two months of its introduction, Netscape's Web browser, Netscape Navigator, claimed more than 70 percent of the browser market. One year after its founding, Clark made the audacious decision to take Netscape public. At the time the move was considered reckless; venture capitalists typically waited for a new business to have four consecutive profitable quarters before filing with the Securities and Exchange Commission for an IPO and offering stock to outside investors. In 1995 Netscape showed no profits on its balance sheet, and forecasts for future profitability were vague at best. But Clark believed that Netscape's story was appealing, and that investors would purchase the stock for fear of missing out on a boom that was just beginning to take off. Within three months Netscape's stock rose from $6 a share to $140, making Clark and many other people very rich. Many analysts claim that Netscape's public offering kicked off both the IPO boom and the Internet bubble of the second half of the 1990s.

Netscape's meteoric success sealed Clark's reputation as a genius to many in Silicon Valley and on Wall Street. But Clark knew that Netscape's near monopoly of the browser market would not last for long, given Microsoft's sudden focus on the Internet and launch of its own browser. Though Internet Explorer commanded only a small percentage of the market in 1995, Clark knew that it would not take long for Microsoft to catch up with Netscape, given its dominance in personal-computer operating systems and Bill Gates's personal drive for success. Clark remained actively involved in Netscape, but he left the day-to-day operations and execution to others better suited to building a corporate structure. At the height of Netscape's dominance and market capitalization, Clark was already thinking of his next new company.

FIXING THE HEALTH-CARE INDUSTRY

While he was chairman at SGI, Clark was badly injured in a motorcycle accident that required physical therapy and frequent trips to the hospital. During these visits he was struck by the bureaucratic and inefficient nature of the health-care system, especially the redundant forms and paperwork that doctors, hospitals, and insurers all filled out by hand and exchanged by mail or fax machine. Given the sheer size of the health-care industry—as large as $1.5 trillion, according to some analysts—Clark immediately recognized a business opportunity to streamline and automate all of the paperwork, making the system work more efficiently.

The enormous wealth he amassed from Netscape offered Clark the chance to put his next idea to the test. In 1996, only months after Netscape became a public company, Clark founded Healthscape, which was later renamed Healtheon. More than SGI and even Netscape, Healtheon symbolized Clark's fascination for big ideas and his willingness to follow his instincts into uncharted territory. Neither Clark nor his newly hired engineers understood the U.S. health-care system and its complicated network of doctors, patients, hospitals, and insurers. But the idea of a company at the center of this vast network, using technology and the Internet to streamline and facilitate transactions, made sense. It was a powerful idea, and best of all it was Jim Clark's idea, which meant to many that it had to be a success. As such, the venture capital firms shut out of Netscape came clamoring for a piece of the action. Like SGI and Netscape, Healtheon attracted plenty of investors during the Internet boom years, and it achieved a market capitalization of more than one billion dollars. Thus, Jim Clark became the first entrepreneur to create three different multibillion-dollar technology companies.

LESSONS LEARNED

SGI, Netscape, and Healtheon all fell on hard times. With the growth of the personal-computing industry, as Clark foresaw, SGI no longer dominated high-end computing. Netscape fell victim to Microsoft's dominance—again, as Clark anticipated—and was purchased by AOL in 1999. Healtheon failed to attract the numbers of doctors, hospitals, and insurers that Clark and others had expected; it merged with WebMD in 1999 and became more of a health-information portal than the central clearinghouse for all health-care transactions that Clark had envisioned. Clark abruptly resigned as chairman of the company in 2000. MyCFO, another company Clark founded in 1999, was sold to Harris Private Bank in 2002.

Following the dot-com bust in 2000, Clark's ventures received much less attention. In 2003, he turned to real-estate development, forming Hyperion Development Group in Miami, Florida, with his longtime friend Tom Jermoluk, the former CEO of Excite@Home. In a brief article in *Business Week*, Clark indicated he had left Silicon Valley for good. "We're developers now," he said. "We've gone back to making money the old-fashioned way." In an interview in the *San Jose Mercury News* in July 2000, Clark summed up his business philosophy this way: "Set out to build a long-lasting company. Focus on the market, not the technology. . . . Use the IPO to raise money, not make money. If you want to build a long-lasting, successful company, you'll have to do that. If you want to get quick riches, you won't have a successful company."

See also entries on Netscape Communications Corporation and Silicon Graphics Inc. in *International Directory of Company Histories.*

SOURCES FOR FURTHER INFORMATION

Clark, Jim, and Owen Edwards, *Netscape Time: The Making of the Billion-Dollar Start-Up that Took On Microsoft*, New York: St. Martin's, 1999.

Festa, Paul, "Netscape Founder Sells Start-Up My CFO," *CNET News.Com*, http://news.com.com/2100-1023_3-960749.html.

Hall, Eric A., "Top 10 Most Influential People: No. 4—Jim Clark," *Network Computing*, October 2, 2000, p. 60.

Hamm, Steve, "From Netscape to Seascape," *Business Week*, September 8, 2003, p. 10.

Holson, Laura M., "Healtheon Is Expected to Join Forces with Internet Provider," *New York Times*, May 15, 1999.

Kanter, Larry, "Jim Clark," *Salon.Com*, http://www.salon.com/people/bc/1999/11/24/clark.

Lewis, Michael, *The New New Thing: A Silicon Valley Story*, New York: W. W. Norton, 1999.

Mariano, Gwendolyn, "Jim Clark to Board New Venture, *CNET News.Com*, http://news.com.com/2100-1023_3-872215.html.

Seipel, Tracy, "Business Question and Answer Column: Leading Entrepreneur Clark on Building a Start-Up," *San Jose Mercury News*, July 23, 2000.

Wright, Rob, "The Next Evolution—A Series of New Products Is Pushing Security Technology to New Frontiers," *VARbusiness*, July 22, 2002, p. 41.

—Mark Scott

■ ■ ■

Vance D. Coffman

1944–

Chairman, Lockheed Martin

Nationality: American.

Born: April 3, 1944, in Kinross, Kansas.

Education: Iowa State University, BS, 1967; Stanford University, PhD, 1973.

Family: Son of a farmer and a schoolteacher (names unknown); married Arlene (maiden name unknown); children: two.

Career: Lockheed Corporation, 1967–1985, guidance and control systems analyst in Space Systems Division; 1985–1987, vice president; 1987–1988, corporate vice president and assistant general manager of Space Systems Division; 1988–1992, president of Space Systems Division; 1992–1995, corporate executive vice president; Lockheed Martin, 1995–1996, president of Space and Missiles; 1996, executive vice president and director of Space and Missiles; 1996–1997, president and COO; 1997–1998, CEO; 1998–2004, chairman and CEO; 2004–, chairman.

Awards: Professional Progress in Engineering Award, Iowa State University, 1989; Fellow, American Astronautical Society, 1991; Fellow, American Institute of Aeronautics and Astronautics, 1996; Distinguished Achievement Citation, Iowa State University, 1999; John J. Bergen Industry Award, New York Council of the Navy League, 2000; Chester W. Nimitz Award, Navy League of the United States, 2001; Executive of the Year, Washington Techway, 2001; Bob Hope Distinguished Citizen Award, National Defense Industrial Association, 2002; Executive of the Year, National Management Association, 2002; National Reconnaissance Pioneer Award, National Reconnaissance Office, 2002; Industrial Leadership Award, American Astronomical Society, 2003; CEO Diversity Leadership Award, Business Women's Network, 2003; Woodrow Wilson Award for Corporate Citizenship, Woodrow Wilson International Center for Scholars, 2003; Corporate Citizenship in the Arts Award, Americans for the Arts, 2003; Washington Center Leadership Medal, Asia Society, 2003.

Address: Lockheed Martin, 6801 Rockledge Drive, Bethesda, Maryland 20817-1877; http://www.lockheedmartin.com.

Vance D. Coffman. *AP/Wide World Photos.*

■ Vance D. Coffman was one of America's foremost astronautical engineers and business leaders. He developed new techniques for guiding satellites and was responsible for developing communications satellites for the Space-Based Infrared System that formed part of America's early-warning defense system. As a leader of Lockheed Martin, he pressed for openness in dealing with friendly nations and envisioned an age of cooperation among allies that would include sharing of defense technology and the cooperative development of defense systems so that all countries would be equally capable of participating in mutual military obligations.

FROM AN IOWA FARM

Coffman was raised on a soybean farm near Winthrop, Iowa, where the launching of Sputnik first inspired him to study science. He took five years to earn a bachelor's degree in aerospace engineering from Iowa State University in 1967 due to the lack of mathematics coursework available at his high school. In 1973 he received a doctorate in aeronautics and astronautics from Stanford University.

In 1967 he took a job as an analyst of guidance and control systems for Lockheed Corporation's aircraft and spacecraft manufacturing. He established himself as worthy of upper management's attention by devising a way for satellites to precisely position themselves using distant stars as references. As his responsibilities increased, he studied books on management, turning himself into an engineer with business qualifications as well.

SECRET OPERATIONS FOR THE MILITARY

In 1988 Coffman was appointed president of Lockheed's Space Systems Division, where he was responsible for the development of the Hubble Space Telescope and the MILSTAR communications satellite. Coffman eventually became involved in secret defense projects such as the Space-Based Infrared System, and because he could not talk in public about much of his work he gained a reputation for being subdued. Meanwhile, he pushed Lockheed toward becoming more involved in commercial enterprises, especially telecommunications satellites.

In March 1992 a new job was created specifically for Coffman: that of corporate executive vice president. In 1995 Lockheed merged with Martin Marietta Corporation, and during the reshuffling of management positions Coffman became president of the Space and Missiles division of the new Lockheed Martin. As part of the corporate consolidation, he closed two of Lockheed's missile manufacturing plants. On January 10, 1996, he was elected to the board of directors; on July 1, 1996, he was appointed president and chief operating officer. That year, Lockheed Martin amassed $27 billion in revenue.

IN THE HOT SEAT

On August 1, 1997, Coffman became chief executive officer and vice chairman of the board at Lockheed Martin. He was well liked because of his friendly, honest manner and had big plans for the company, wanting to boost space-systems and information-systems technology. He quickly became an outspoken advocate for his views. Yet, problems were brewing thanks to poor communication between Lockheed Martin's top management and its division leaders. The F-22 fighter aircraft under joint development with Boeing was $2.1 billion over budget, and Theater High Altitude Area Defense missiles being developed for the U.S. Army failed to function properly. In spite of these setbacks, Lockheed Martin netted $1.2 billion in 1998. That year, Coffman became chairman of the board.

By the end of 1999 rumors were rife that Coffman was about to be replaced. Sales for the C-130J military transport aircraft were far below projections; defense projects were beset by overrunning costs; and Titan and Athena rockets exploded at launch, destroying three $100 million spy satellites. From January 1 to June 10, 1999, Lockheed Martin cut eight thousand jobs. From May to November, its stock value declined 55 percent; the company was $11 billion in debt. In June, Coffman was called to the Pentagon to explain Lockheed's failures. For the first time since the 1960s, Lockheed lost a spy-satellite contract; the $6 billion project instead went to Boeing.

Not all news was bad news, however. Lockheed Martin quickly forged a partnership with DaimlerChrysler Aerospace (of Germany) and Alenia (of Italy) to build the Medium Extended Air Defense System (MEADS), designed to protect front-line troops. Coffman was an advocate of open cooperation among defense allies, and this project was a highlight of his efforts. The company netted $575 million and by the end of the year had $50 billion in back orders.

In 2000 Coffman reorganized Lockheed Martin, consolidating its manufacturing into three divisions: electronic, aeronautical, and astronautical. He expanded his company's commercial operations by purchasing Comsat for $2.7 billion, the cost of which was largely responsible for Lockheed Martin's posting a net loss of $519 million in 2000. On the positive side, Lockheed Martin's Patriot Advanced Capability–3 missile was chosen for MEADS, and the company added $39 billion in new orders. Throughout Lockheed Martin's successful business dealings, Coffman continued to be a passionate public advocate for his vision of a NATO alliance that offered equal access to all member nations' defense projects.

In 2001 Lockheed Martin had 20 successful rocket launches, and it landed a $7 billion contract for 80 F-16s from the United Arab Emirates. That year Lockheed Martin also landed the F-35 Joint Strike Fighter contract for $200 billion, to be spent over the next two decades. In 2003 Lockheed Martin had a company-record $32 billion in revenue, 25 percent of which came from information technology. Yet, the company's stock declined by 11 percent, part of a worldwide decline in technology stocks. Although the board of directors wanted him to remain, Coffman planned to leave the CEO post on August 6, 2004, and he planned to retire as chairman of the board in April 2005, citing a desire to begin a new stage of his life.

See also entry on Lockheed Martin Corporation in *International Directory of Company Histories.*

SOURCES FOR FURTHER INFORMATION

Banks, Howard, "Not Rocket Science," *Forbes*, April 16, 2001, p. 140.

Crock, Stan, "Can This Farm Boy Keep Lockheed in Orbit?" *BusinessWeek Online*, October 27, 1997, http://www.businessweek.com/1997/43/b3550131.htm.

Muradian, Vago, "Great Impact Not Expected from Augustine's Departure," *Defense Daily*, April 21, 1997, pp. 122–124.

—Kirk H. Beetz

■ ■ ■

Douglas R. Conant

ca. 1952–

President, chief executive officer, and director, Campbell Soup Company

Nationality: American.

Born: ca. 1952, in Chicago, Illinois.

Education: Northwestern University, BA, 1973; MBA, 1975.

Family: Married (wife's name unknown); children: three.

Career: General Mills, 1976–1989, marketing department; Kraft General Foods, 1989–1992, director of strategy; Nabisco Foods Group, 1992, vice president and general manager of Fleischmann's division; Nabisco Biscuit Co., 1992–1994, senior vice president of marketing; 1994–1995, sales and integrated logistics unit executive; Nabisco Food Company, 1995–2000, president; Campbell Soup Company, 2001—, president, chief executive officer, and director.

Address: Campbell Soup Company, 1 Campbell Place, Camden, New Jersey 08103-1799; http://www.campbellsoupcompany.com.

■ Beginning his career with General Mills, Douglas R. Conant worked in management and executive positions in the prepackaged food industry in the United States. During his stops at Kraft and Nabisco, he earned a reputation for developing new brands, revitalizing faltering brands, and marketing both; his strategies often resulted in growth and profit. Though he had no CEO experience, Conant was hired in 2001 as president and CEO of Campbell Soup Company and named a director. Conant faced many challenges in the position but worked to reinvigorate the condensed soup brand.

A native of Chicago, Illinois, Conant attended Northwestern University for both undergraduate study and graduate school. An undergraduate political science major, he was also a star tennis player on the university's tennis team. After graduating, Conant considered playing professional tennis but instead went to graduate school, earning an MBA. Conant then began his professional career in 1976, when he was hired by General Mills.

While Conant was employed at General Mills, he held a number of positions in marketing, strategy, and product management, primarily for food products. Over the next 10 years he worked variously as the marketing assistant for Betty Crocker potatoes, assistant product manager for new products, assistant product manager for Nature Valley granola bars, and product manager for Betty Crocker desserts. Conant left General Mills in 1986 to join Kraft.

WORKED IN STRATEGY AND MARKETING AT KRAFT

Conant was hired by Kraft as the vice president of strategy for Kraft USA—the company created when Kraft merged with Philip Morris—and vice president of marketing and strategy for Kraft's Grocery Products Group. In 1989 he was promoted to director of strategy of Kraft USA. While Conant was at Kraft USA, the company enjoyed record-high sales, earnings, and return levels in 1988 and 1989. In early 1992 Conant left Kraft to work for Nabisco.

When Conant went to Nabisco, his skills in enhancing brands began to shine. His first position was as the vice president and general manager of the Fleischmann division. Conant was in charge of Fleischmann brand margarines and spreads, Blue Bonnet margarines and spreads, and EggBeaters (an egg substitute). In December 1992 he was promoted to senior vice president of marketing for Nabisco Foods Group in charge of Nabisco's cookie and cracker brands, including Chips Ahoy!, Oreos, Fig Newtons, and Ritz crackers. In this post Conant helped aggressively to build these brands when they were facing stiff competition from store brands, which were often cheaper but of similar quality. In 1993 the company's sales increased by 7 percent, and Nabisco was having one of its best years in the past 20 or so, despite the fact that the market for such products was stagnant.

MADE NEWTONS POPULAR, LAUNCHED SNACKWELLS

Conant scored several major successes at Nabisco. With his team he came up with new ideas for branding Newton cookies, including introducing such new flavors as strawberry and apple, that doubled the volume of sales. Using Nabisco's research and development capabilities, Conant also helped create and market Snackwells, a new brand of cookies that capitalized on the low-fat craze of the early 1990s. The various Snackwells brands reached $100 million in sales in 1993.

In December 1994 Conant was promoted to the head of the Sales and Integrated Logistics unit in Nabisco as part of the company's policy to rotate jobs among top executives. This division focused on efficiency in the selling and distribution of all of Nabisco's products that were distributed in warehouses. Within a year Conant was promoted again. In 1995 he was named the president of Nabisco Food Company, which covered snacks and condiments.

Under Conant's leadership, Nabisco dominated the snack market in the late 1990s and early 2000s. Nabisco managed double-digit growth each year for five years through 2001. One reason for Conant's success was his use of a cross-functional team approach to branding. By using people of different backgrounds, he was able to develop new products and integrate ways to market them. Employees were as important to him as brands. He hired a number of the company's top managers and worked hard to retain them. Conant was able to retain 90 percent of the managers he hired. An avid reader, Conant often gave books to others, primarily biographies that were inspirational.

One way Conant emphasized growth was by building brands through the improvement of existing products and their packaging. Through this strategy, he helped Nabisco rejuvenate several core products, including Planters nuts, Life-Savers candies, and Milk-Bone dog biscuits. New products using these names were also successfully launched. They included LifeSavers Creme Savers and Ice Breakers, a gum bearing the LifeSavers brand name.

HIRED AS CEO OF CAMPBELL SOUP COMPANY

In 2001 Conant was hired by the Campbell Soup Company as its president and CEO and was named a director of the company. Campbell was the largest soup company in the world. In addition to soup, Campbell also manufactured other products, such as Pepperidge Farm cookies and crackers, Prego pasta sauce, V8 vegetable drinks, Goldfish crackers, and Godiva chocolates. Conant was expected to turn around the company, in part by using his success with branding. When he took over, soup sales were falling and Campbell was losing market share in that area, though its cookie and cracker sales were on the rise.

One of Conant's first acts as CEO was to reorganize the North American arms of the company into two distinct business entities with their own executives—North American Soup and North American Beverages and Sauces. The latter included cookies, crackers, and other prepared foods. Conant made the move to help improve Campbell's soup sales because it allowed for focused strategy and marketing to consumers on the company's primary brand while also giving the company's other products their own emphasis. As part of his three-year plan announced in 2001, Conant increased the amount of money spent on U.S. advertising and laid out new marketing ideas. He also revitalized the company's products—for instance, changing how cream soups were manufactured—and improved the company's technology and its factories.

By 2002, under Conant's leadership, Campbell had expanded soup offerings to include more convenience foods, such as Soup at Hand, which was microwavable, and new soup flavors under the Chunky and Select lines. Despite Conant's best efforts, sales of soup continued to fall through 2003, though stock prices were on the rise in early 2004, primarily because Campbell's snack foods were doing well.

See also entries on Campbell Soup Company, General Mills, Inc., Kraft Inc., and Nabisco Food Group in *International Directory of Company Histories.*

SOURCES FOR FURTHER INFORMATION

DeNitto, Emily, "Doug Conant Nabisco Cookies," *Advertising Age*, July 4, 1994, S16.

"Douglas Conant: In the Soup," *BusinessWeek*, January 22, 2001, p. 46.

"SN's Power 50 (Part Eight) Manufacturers," *Supermarket News*, July 21, 2003, p. 64.

"What Campbell's New Chief Needs to Do Now," *BusinessWeek*, June 25, 2001, p. 60.

Winter, Greg, "Campbell Soup Picks Chief, Playing Down Talk of Sale," *New York Times*, January 9, 2001.

—A. Petruso

■ ■ ■

Phil Condit

1941–

Retired chief executive officer and chairman of the board, Boeing Company

Nationality: American.

Born: August 2, 1941, in Berkeley, California.

Education: University of California, Berkeley, BS, 1963; Princeton University, MS, 1965; Massachusetts Institute of Technology, Sloan School of Management, MS, 1975; Science University of Tokyo, PhD, 1997.

Family: Son of Daniel Harrison Condit and Bernice C. Kemp; married Madeleine K. Bryant (divorced); married (wife's name unknown, divorced); married Janice Condit (divorced); married (wife's name unknown); children (first marriage): two.

Career: Boeing Company, 1965–1968, aerodynamics engineer; 1968–1971, lead high-speed configuration engineer for the 747; 1971–1973, lead performance engineer for the 747; 1973–1974, marketing manager for the 727; Massachusetts Institute of Technology, 1974–1975, Sloan Fellow; Boeing Company, 1975–1976, manager of new program planning; 1976–1978, director of program management, 707/727/737 Division; 1978–1981, chief project engineer for the 757; 1981–1983, director of engineering for the 757; 1983, vice president and general manager, 757 Division; 1983–1984, vice president of the Renton Division; 1984–1986, vice president of sales and marketing, Boeing Commercial Airplane Company; 1986–1989, executive vice president, Boeing Commercial Airplane Company; 1989–1992, executive vice president and general manager, New Airplane Division (later renamed the 777 Division); 1992–1996, president; 1996–1997, chief executive officer; 1997–2003, chief executive officer and chairman of the board.

Awards: Edward C. Wells Technical Management Award, 1982; American Institute of Aeronautics and Astronautics (AIAA), aircraft design award, 1984; elected to the National Academy of Engineering, 1985; *Aviation Week & Space Technology* magazine, Laurels Award, 1990; Wright Brothers Lectureship Aeronautics award, 1996; *Financial World*, Chief Executive Officer of the Year, 1996, 1997; Japan America Society, Kokusai Shimin Sho (International Citizens Award), 1997; Ronald H. Brown Standards Leadership Award, 1997; University of California, Berkeley, Distinguished Engineering Alumnus Award, 1998; Peter F. Drucker Strategic Leadership Award, 1998; United Negro College Fund, Frederick D. Patterson Award, 1999; Air Command and Staff College, Distinguished Eagle Award, 1999; Aerospace Historical Society, International von Karman Wings Award, 1999; Boy Scouts of America, Los Angeles Area Council, Aerospace Industry Distinguished Good Scout Award, 1999.

Phil Condit. *AP/Wide World Photos.*

■ Philip (Phil) Murray Condit was a visionary engineer who helped shape the aircraft designs that would dominate the world. He was a problem solver, brilliant, a good listener, amiable, self-effacing, and willing to give credit to others. But some considered him to be indecisive and self-indulgent. As a chief executive officer he often seemed aloof and isolated. His greatest contributions to aeronautics may have been his elegant solutions to aircraft design problems.

BRILLIANT ENGINEER

As a child Condit liked watching aircraft take off and land at San Francisco's airport; airplanes filled his imagination. With his grandfather's help, he earned his pilot's license at age 18. Condit received a BS in mechanical engineering at University of California, Berkeley, and was offered a job at McDonnell Douglas. He turned the job down. On January 25, 1963, Condit married Madeleine K. Bryant, but his relentless dedication to work soured this and his subsequent marriages.

In 1965 Condit received an MS in aeronautical engineering from Princeton University and accepted a job at Boeing in Seattle. He made his presence felt by designing a flexible wing called the "sailwing," which improved the durability and maneuverability of jet aircraft. He received a patent for the wing design. In the late 1960s there was much concern at the Federal Aeronautics Administration (FAA) about the effect on smaller aircraft of turbulence created by the new jumbo jets such as the 747. Condit calculated the forces in the vortexes created by any size aircraft and the effects of the resulting turbulence on following aircraft, enabling the FAA to make rules for safely spacing takeoffs and landings of various aircraft, rules that remained in effect forty years later.

In 1974 Condit won a fellowship to the Sloan School of Management at MIT, where he earned an MS in management in 1975. The combination of graduate degrees in engineering and business management made Condit a force to be reckoned with at Boeing, but his long hours at work cost him his marriage to Madeleine, which ended in divorce in 1982. In 1983 he was appointed vice president of the Renton Division, responsible for the design and manufacturing of the 707, 727, 737, and 757 airplanes.

In 1989 Condit put his intelligence, creativity, and management skills to work as executive vice president and general manager of the New Airplane Division, which was later renamed the 777 Division. He wanted to create not only the preeminent jet of the twenty-first century but also a new manufacturing process for building jet aircraft. Boeing budgeted $6 billion for development of the 777 wide-body airliner, but it may have cost as much as $12 billion (poor accounting meant that no one knew how much for sure). Condit introduced numerous new manufacturing techniques and aircraft designs that later resulted in huge savings in manufacturing all of Boeing's aircraft. Among Condit's innovations was the replacement of models with computers, which reduced design costs and created parts that fit precisely. By using lasers to guide parts into place, Condit halved the number of workers required to assemble a fuselage. Parts fit together so well that the noise of the aircraft was greatly diminished. He solicited suggestions from airline companies for the 777, and thousands of ideas came in, which computer software turned into numerous customer-satisfying features in the aircraft. To improve the assembly process Condit studied Japanese automobile manufacturers, trying to imitate the efficiency with which Toyota and others manufactured soundly designed vehicles.

Boeing executives had a tradition of living modestly, but Condit was flamboyant. In the early 1990s he built a medieval-style mansion. For it he designed a small railroad that would carry drinks from room to room. He partied lavishly. He may have been burning the candle at both ends because he had much to absorb him at work. Boeing had 450 computer programs that did not talk to each other. As president from 1992 to 1996, he tried to unify the computer programs into one set of simplified off-the-shelf software that all Boeing's employees could use.

In 1991 Condit married for the third time, this time to his first cousin Janice Condit. His fifteen-hour-plus workdays were hard on her. In May 1995 the first 777 came off the assembly line and was delivered, and the following month it took its first commercial flight. That same year Boeing, which usually had good labor relations, endured a 69-day strike by 32,000 members of the International Association of Machinists. The strike seemed as though it was not going to end soon, so Condit put on his wool sweater and walked into the picket lines and talked with picketers. He helped to find compromises that brought the strike to an end, and he won the enduring respect of the union members and of Boeing's engineers as well. He would always be seen by labor as a friend. Heavy competition from Europe's government-subsidized aircraft manufacturer Airbus and others cut into Boeing's sales in 1995, and Boeing began lowering its prices to undersell its competitors. In the past, Boeing had relied on its superior quality to attract buyers.

THE ENGINEER'S CEO

In April 1996 Condit became chief executive officer (CEO), replacing Frank Shrontz. He acted decisively to fix problems he perceived in the company. He cancelled Boeing's program to design and build a super jumbo-jet to compete with Airbus's A380. Airbus claimed it could sell 1,400 A380s over 20 years, a rate almost double what Boeing's 747 had achieved in its manufacturing lifetime. Condit believed that there was not enough of a market to make a super-sized airliner profitable, and he predicted that Airbus would give up on the A380. In that he was mistaken.

Of greater concern to Condit was the boom-and-bust cycle of commercial aircraft manufacturing, something that bothered Wall Street investors as well. In 1996, 80 percent of Boeing's income came from manufacturing commercial aircraft, which meant that its stock value would swing wildly as sales rose and fell with each new cycle of demands for aircraft from airline companies. He tried to ease the impact by diversifying Boeing's holdings. Previous CEOs had tried to do this by investing in furniture manufacturing and other nonaeronautical businesses. Condit instead went looking for complementary matches to Boeing's core business of commercial aircraft.

When he became CEO Boeing had three corporate jets, but Condit built a fleet of jets, eventually including his own personal 737, which was decorated in the style of an English library. He logged hundreds of hours in corporate jets as he put together his deals. He had Boeing buy Rockwell's space-related manufacturing business, and in December 1996 he engineered Boeing's takeover of McDonnell Douglas. Many McDonnell Douglas executives were absorbed into Boeing's headquarters, and as a group they resisted some of Condit's efforts to create an open atmosphere of cooperation among employees; they were used to the stern discipline of Harry C. Stonecipher, former CEO of McDonnell Douglas, who became Boeing's president. Michael M. Sears was another McDonnell Douglas manager who joined Boeing.

Boeing's assembly lines were very inefficient, with a parts-distribution system that left large portions of shop floors covered by bins of parts. Condit tried to introduce a system in which parts were delivered when they were needed. This would eventually result in improved efficiency, but in 1997 it collided with a huge upsurge in orders from customers. In 1997 Condit became chairman of the board as well as CEO. He strove to integrate McDonnell Douglas's defense-contracting business into Boeing's operations, hoping to use defense business to offset commercial-airline down cycles. By the end of 1997 Boeing had become the world's largest manufacturer for both commercial and military aircraft. That year Condit imitated the corporate structure of General Electric by establishing three divisions—commercial, defense, and space—and naming their leaders CEOs in the hope that each division would function as an independent company. In early 1997 Boeing had a $79 billion backlog of orders, and in April Boeing's stock rose to $104 per share.

All was not well, however. Longtime Boeing employees complained of a reverse takeover, bitterly joking that McDonnell Douglas had purchased Boeing with Boeing's own money. They did not like Stonecipher's harsh style, and they wanted Boeing to remain a company with its goals set in technological advances, not stock returns. Condit had hoped that Stonecipher's style would complement his own style of visionary innovation. In August 1997 Boeing spent $1.4 billion to shut down McDonnell Douglas's aged, outmoded assembly lines.

To meet the huge backlog of orders, Condit pressed his divisions to speed up their manufacturing processes, but the assembly lines were still in the process of reconciling his new software with the old software, and the assembly lines backed up. In October 1997 two of Seattle's commercial-aircraft assembly lines had to be shut down completely, costing Boeing $2.6 billion to fix. The backlog of orders became a nightmare as Boeing missed commitments to customers, and the company lost $178 million in 1997, its first annual loss in 50 years. The fallout from this fiasco included the loss of many jobs; between 1997 and 2001 Boeing laid off over 48,000 employees.

CRISIS MANAGEMENT

During 1998 Boeing lost many of the orders it did not fill because the global market for commercial aircraft declined. Condit won high marks from Wall Street analysts and journalists that year for successfully using McDonnell Douglas's defense contracts to soften the impact of the decline in commercial business. But when Boeing was caught illegally using proprietary information taken from Raytheon Company to win a contract to build antimissile warheads, the contract was taken from Boeing and given to Raytheon. In August 1998 a Boeing-built Delta rocket exploded, destroying a $225 million communications satellite. This highlighted quality-control problems that threatened Boeing's rocket and defense programs. That month Condit met with Wall Street analysts and was excoriated for Boeing's seeming to have overpaid for McDonnell Douglas and for Rockwell's space business, as well as for the falling value of Boeing's stock. On August 5, 1998, Condit assembled his top executives and told them he had been humiliated and wanted them to tighten their control of expenses. A few weeks later, when nothing had been undertaken to solve the problems, Condit fired 80 of his top executives. Meanwhile, Boeing held on to 35,000 pages of proprietary Lockheed documents that had been used in a failed joint venture and were supposed to be returned to Lockheed. These documents gave Boeing an edge in bidding on rocket contracts, winning a $1.37 billion contract in 2003 with the ill-gotten information. This would eventually contribute to Condit's downfall. To make the year even worse for Condit, he and Janice divorced, and she got to keep the medieval-style mansion.

In 1999 Condit sold Boeing's information-services and electronics-warfare projects. He instituted the Managing for Value Program, trying to make his employees more conscious of the desires of the marketplace. This made many long-time Boeing employees even more restive; they felt Boeing's strength lay in innovating and leading the marketplace, not in following the marketplace's sometimes-unimaginative desires. It was another sign, some believed, that the corporate culture of McDonnell Douglas was taking over and ruining Boeing. Yet the Managing for Value Program more likely came out of Condit's studies of Japanese manufacturing and his own desire to make Boeing focus on improving the quality of the goods it sold. It was a sour time for Condit; due to continuing manufacturing glitches, Boeing lost over $4 billion in 1998 and 1999.

CONDIT TRIED TO BE BOLD

Condit was criticized for being timid and having Stonecipher do most of the tough, unpleasant work of disciplining employees and setting standards of behavior that Condit himself should have been doing, he was still the man who had revolutionized aircraft manufacturing with his 777 work in the 1980s. In 2000 Condit spent 584 hours in the air in his 737, striving to pull the pieces together that would keep Boeing dominant in an industry in which Airbus, whose losses were covered by government, was rapidly gaining ground. Boeing bought the Space & Communications Division of Hughes Electronics Corporation for $3.75 billion and the Tribune Company's flight mapmaker and pilot services company Jeppesen-Sanderson for $1.5 billion. These further diversified Boeing's business while keeping the company anchored in the aerospace industry. The hope was that the new businesses would help Boeing achieve steady growth for many years in a row. Since about 85 percent of the world's airliners had been built by Boeing, Condit began a new business dedicated to maintaining the aircraft for their owners, a business that had the potential to earn $74 billion a year. Another positive development was that Condit's innovations in assembly-line efficiency finally took hold, with the labor hours required to build a 737 dropping from a high of 30,000 to 6,500.

Condit had to spend much of his time on damage control. Employee morale had plummeted: An internal survey had shown 69 percent positive feelings about Boeing among employees in 1998, while a survey the next year drew a 31 percent positive response. Boeing's white-collar engineers were angry over the lack of creativity in their work, and they affiliated with the AFL-CIO. In February 2000 they went on strike for 40 days, which delayed the completion of 50 aircraft. Union leader Charles Bofferding later said, "We weren't fighting against Boeing. We were fighting to save Boeing" (*Fortune*). Only when Condit spoke directly with the strikers did they come to a settlement. Other problems included continued rocket failures and the loss of $323 million by the space business acquired from Hughes.

On March 12, 2001, Condit announced that he was moving Boeing's headquarters out of Seattle. He said he wanted to keep management out of day-to-day business operations, an explanation that would seem nonsensical to many hands-on CEOs. On May 10 he announced that the corporate headquarters would be moving to Chicago, and he took the opportunity to cut headquarters staff from one thousand to five hundred. Condit wanted to give the heads of Boeing's divisions more independence, but increasingly decisions were bogged down in committees and corporate bureaucracy now far removed from the core commercial business in Seattle.

Boeing developed Connexion, a system that allowed individual passengers to combine phone calls and Internet surfing while in flight, but there were no buyers. But Condit's maintenance services unit had a big boost when it won a contract to upgrade the Pentagon's five hundred C-130s, aircraft that had been built by Lockheed Martin. Condit worked a punishing schedule, but the hard work seemed to be paying off. He secured a deal to supply Italy with 767 air tankers, which opened access to a potential international market of $50 billion for new tankers.

MOUNTING PROBLEMS

In 2002 some shareholders sued Boeing, accusing the company of using accounting tricks to mislead people about the effects of the 1997 assembly-line disaster. Boeing gave them $92.5 million to settle the suit. Meanwhile, Boeing's share of the commercial-airliner market was shrinking, from 70 percent in 1996 to 50 percent in 2003.

In January 2003 former Pentagon procurement officer Darleen A. Druyun was hired by Boeing. In November it was revealed that she had given Michael M. Sears a copy of Airbus's rival bid for an $18 billion Air Force contract for one hundred new tankers. Boeing used the information to outbid Airbus, winning the contract. In response, Congress reduced the contract to 20 tankers, then chose to delay the contract indefinitely. Condit fired Sears and Druyun. In July 2003 the Pentagon suspended Boeing indefinitely from bidding on rocket contracts after Boeing's illegal use of Lockheed's documents was finally revealed and took $1 billion in contracts away from Boeing and gave them to Lockheed. Thirty-eight women employees filed a class-action lawsuit against Boeing, alleging that women had been paid less than male equals and had been denied promotions in order to inflate Boeing's bottom line; the case went to trial in April 2004. In 2003 Boeing had to write down a $1.1 billion loss on its Hughes acquisition, $1 billion on Jeppesen-Sanderson, and $1 billion in operational losses.

In November 2003 Condit offered to resign if asked to do so by the board of directors. After meeting twice a day to wrestle with Boeing's mounting disgraces, on December 1 the board demanded and received Condit's resignation as CEO and chairman of the board. The board, dominated by old McDonnell Douglas directors, then hired Stonecipher as the new CEO and director Lewis E. Platt, once the chairman of the board for Hewlett-Packard, as nonexecutive chairman. Condit stayed on to help with the transition of power until officially leaving Boeing in March 2004.

See also entry on The Boeing Company in *International Directory of Company Histories.*

SOURCES FOR FURTHER INFORMATION

Holmes, Stanley, "Boeing: What Really Happened," *BusinessWeek*, December 15, 2003, pp. 32–37.

Osterland, Andrew, "Philip M. Condit of the Boeing Company," *Financial World*, April 15, 1997, pp. 66–71.

Serling, Robert J., *Legend & Legacy: The Story of Boeing and Its People,* New York: St. Martin's Press, 1991.

Useem, Jerry, "Boeing vs. Boeing: America's Export Champion Is Going Head-to-Head with a Company Even Tougher than Airbus: Itself," *Fortune*, October 2, 2000, pp. 148–160.

—Kirk H. Beetz

■ ■ ■

Terence Conran

1931–

Chairman, Conran Holdings Ltd.

Nationality: British.

Born: August 4, 1931, in London, England.

Education: Attended Central School of Arts and Crafts, 1949–1950.

Family: Son of Rupert Conran and Christine Halstead; married Brenda Davison (architect), 1954 (divorced 1955); married Shirley Ida Pierce, 1955 (divorced 1962); married Caroline Herbert (writer), 1963 (divorced 1966); married Victoria Davis (design-business manager), 2000; children: five (second marriage, two; third marriage, three).

Career: Rayon Centre, 1950–1951, textile designer; Dennis Lennon Studio, 1951–1952, interior designer; Conran and Company, 1952–1956, freelance furniture designer; Conran Design Group, 1956–1971, director; Habitat, 1964–1971, director; Habitat Mothercare Limited, 1982–1990, chairman; Conran Roche Architectural and City Planning, 1982–1993, director; CD Partnership, 1993–1999, chairman; Conran Holdings Ltd., 1990–, chairman.

Awards: Duke of Edinburgh Awards for design management, Royal Society of Arts, 1968 and 1975; Design Medal, Society of Industrial Artists and Designers, 1980; Bicentenary Medal, Royal Society of Arts, 1982; knighthood, Queen's New Year Honors, 1983; honorary fellow, Royal Institute of British Architects, 1984; President's Award for outstanding contribution to British design, Design and Art Direction (DA&D), 1989; Commandeur des Arts et des Lettres, government of France, 1992; Design Award, *House Beautiful*, 2002.

Publications: *The House Book,* 1974; *The Essential House Book: Getting Back to Basics,* 1994; *Terence Conran on Design,* 1996; *Terence Conran Q&A: A Sort of Autobiography,* 2001.

Address: Conran Holdings Ltd., 22 Shad Thames, London SE1 2YU, England; http://www.conran.com.

■ Terence Conran became one of the most successful and influential figures in the design world in the latter half of the 20th century. His business empire encompassed a furniture-making business, an architecture and planning group, a design company, a book publishing company, a hotel, and restaurants. He sought to create a wide range of accessible products whose simple forms would be both pleasing to the eye and a reflection of their function, and he used his various endeavors to expound this design philosophy.

EARLY LIFE AND CAREER

Conran was born in 1931 in London. In 1952, after studying textile design in London and working at the Rayon Centre, Conran established his own furniture-making business, Conran and Company. In 1953 he opened his first restaurant, Soup Kitchen. He founded the Conran Design Group in London in 1956 and Habitat furnishing stores in 1964.

Conran was perhaps best known for the Habitat stores, an offshoot of which was the more upscale Conran Shop chain. Habitat's streamlined, functional designs had wide international appeal, making high-quality, modern furniture, and housewares affordable to the middle class. His other retail holdings included the Mothercare shops, selling clothing for mothers and babies, and Hepworth stores, specializing in men's wear. In 1986 Habitat and Mothercare merged with British Home Stores; the merged entity became known as the Storehouse Group. Conran retired from Storehouse in 1990, and the Habitat stores were sold to Ikea. The Conran Shop chain, however, continued into the 21st century.

OTHER BUSINESS INTERESTS

In 1982 Conran cofounded Conran Roche Architectural and City Planning. In 1993, with the incorpation of several interior designers, this business morphed into CD Partnership, and in 1999 the entity changed its name to Conran and Partners. The Great Eastern Hotel in London, a joint venture between Conran and Wyndham International, opened in 2000.

Following his retirement from Storehouse Group, Conran founded Conran Associates, which became one of the largest design consultancies in Europe. Through this entity, Conran expanded his design empire to encompass clothing, office products, and graphic design projects. Both Conran Associates and Conran and Partners were subsumed under the umbrella name Conran Holdings, of which Conran was chairman.

The designer incorporated his interest in cooking and fine food into his career by opening a series of restaurants in London and other major European cities. Following Soup Kitchen were restaurants including Bibendum, Mezzo, the Zinc Bar, Bluebird, and Alcazar.

To reach an even broader market for his design concepts, Conran published his first of many books, *The House Book*, in 1974. Originally intended as an in-house training manual for Habitat employees, the work evolved into an influential manual for planning and designing the modern home. Following its success, Conran wrote several more design books before founding Conran Octopus publishing in 1983. His books covered a broad range of topics, from home decor to gardening to cooking, and gained him a measure of celebrity. Conran also wrote an autobiography, *Terence Conran Q&A*, chronicling his lengthy, multifaceted career, in which he describes himself as a "hard-working hedonist."

GAINING WIDESPREAD RECOGNITION

Conran's contributions to design and architecture won him recognition from numerous professional organizations and governments. He received awards from the Royal Society of Arts, the Society of Industrial Artists and Designers, and the Association for Business Sponsorship of the Arts, among others, and was honored with a knighthood in 1983.

SOURCES FOR FURTHER INFORMATION

Bailey, Stephen, ed., *Conran Directory of Design*, New York: Villard Books, 1985.

MacCarthy, Fiona, "The Emperor Strikes Back," *Guardian*, July 8, 1995.

Nadelson, Reggie, "Terence Takes Manhattan," *Vogue USA*, December 1999.

Phillips, Barty, *Conran and the Habitat Story*, London: Weidenfeld & Nicholson, 1984.

Williams, Alex, "Welcome Back, Conran," *New York Magazine*, http://www.newyorkmetro.com/nymetro/realestate/urbandev/features/1592/.

—Lisa Wolff

■■■

John W. Conway
1945–
Chairman, president, and chief executive officer, Crown Holdings, Incorporated

Nationality: American.

Born: 1945.

Education: University of Virginia, BA; Columbia Law School, JD.

Career: Continental Can International, served in various positions and then as president; Crown Cork & Seal (established as Crown Holdings in 2003), various management positions leading to president and COO, 1991–2001, then president, chief executive officer, and chairman, 2001–.

Address: Crown Holdings, Incorporated, 1 Crown Way, Philadelphia, Pennsylvania 19154-4599; http://www.crowncork.com.

■ John W. Conway became the CEO of Crown Cork & Seal in early 2001. The company was later established as Crown Holdings in 2003. In 2001, however, he faced a series of challenges in placing the century-old bottling and packaging company on a stronger financial basis. In addition to dealing with a recession coupled with rising prices for raw materials, energy, and transportation, Crown had to contend with the possibility of bankruptcy due to asbestos-related court claims. Conway's approach to strengthening the company's financial foundation combined aggressive cost cutting and conservative expansion.

EDUCATION AND EARLY CAREER

Conway graduated from the University of Virginia and then earned a law degree from Columbia Law School. He went on to hold a series of management positions both in the United States and abroad with the Continental Can International Corporation, a metal can manufacturing company, before he became Continental's president. Crown Cork & Seal Company acquired Continental Can in 1991.

Conway joined Crown's board of directors in 1997 and became the company's president and chief operating officer the following year. He assumed the position of CEO in January 2001 after the retirement of his predecessor, William J. Avery. A press release reprinted by PR Newswire quoted Avery as saying, "With John Conway's experience and his leadership abilities so clearly demonstrated, I think this is the time for me to step aside and let John and his management team guide this great company" (November 14, 2000). A few months later, Conway also succeeded Avery as chairman of the board.

CROWN FACES BANKRUPTCY

Conway took charge of Crown just as an economic slowdown began to affect the company. Ranked among the two hundred largest companies headquartered in the United States, Crown was the leading supplier of packaging products to consumer marketing companies around the world. In spite of the company's market share, however, its stock performance deteriorated as its packaging business slumped.

Conway decided to use a conservative financial strategy while improving the company's balance sheet. His strategic plan included a heavy emphasis on cost structure and positioning Crown as a low-cost producer. Conway's cost-cutting measures included the closing of 10 plants in North America and Europe and the reduction of Crown's salaried work force. He also realigned the production capacity of Crown's plant in Weston, Ontario. The Canadian plant converted two of its existing four aluminum beverage can lines to the manufacture of two-piece steel food cans, thus substantially reducing its beverage can capacity. PR Newswire quoted Conway as saying, "Converting underutilized manufacturing capacity . . . will help capture sales for our Food Can Division and at the same time trim capacity in the beverage can industry" (February 27, 2001).

THE ASBESTOS CRISIS

In addition to a slow economy, the major challenge facing Conway and Crown was the threat of asbestos-related litigation. The lawsuits were related to Crown's 1963 purchase of a company called Mundet, which had produced cork bottle caps in addition to insulation that contained asbestos. Crown was interested only in Mundet's bottle division and sold off its insulation business 93 days after it had purchased Mundet.

Nevertheless, Crown eventually paid dearly for its brief period of ownership, paying out millions of dollars by mid-2001 to settle some 70,000 asbestos-related claims. As industry analysts observed, other large companies involved in these cases such as Owens Corning and Armstrong Holdings were forced to declare bankruptcy, causing a ripple effect that left the remaining companies like Crown facing an increased share of liability payments.

Settling the legal claims eventually put Crown on the verge of bankruptcy. Conway had the company suspend its quarterly dividend in order to set aside money for payouts. The combination of legal claims and packaging business problems led to the company's stock falling over the course of a year from $36 per share to $4 per share by April 2001. The legal difficulties were mitigated in December 2001, when the governor of Pennsylvania signed a law limiting the asbestos-related liabilities of Crown and other Pennsylvania-based companies. Conway thought that the General Assembly and the governor had made the right decision, saying, "Crown does not discount the problem of serious asbestos-related disease, but rather sees the new legislation as a demonstration of fundamental fairness in allocating liability" (PR Newswire, December 17, 2001).

CROWN GOES GLOBAL

While dealing with the asbestos crisis, Conway sought out new markets for Crown as part of his strategy for maintaining the company's global presence. He oversaw the opening of the first beverage can production facility in Seville, Spain, as part of Crown's efforts to meet steadily increasing market demand in Europe. Conway also signed a long-term agreement to supply Nestlé Russia with cans for Nescafé products. In an interview with a reporter from *Beverage Industry*, Conway remarked, "Crown is committed to supporting customers throughout Europe" (October 2002).

By the end of 2002, Conway was able to report that the company was on track with its 24-to-30-month plan for achieving profitability. Crown's operating income in 2002 had increased 53 percent to $481 million. Its net income from continuing operations was $0.49 per share compared to a $0.74 per share in 2001. Conway had also increased the company's free cash flow to $300 million from $142 million.

LOOKING AHEAD

Conway continued to focus on reducing Crown's costs while improving the productivity of its operations and taking a careful and conservative approach to investing. He also remained committed to debt reduction. Crown reported losses of 33 cents a share for the fourth quarter of 2003, which was an improvement from the $1.71-per-share loss it had reported in the fourth quarter of 2002. Another good sign was that net sales for the quarter were $1.59 billion, up 3 percent from a year earlier. Nevertheless, net sales for the year were down to $6.63 billion, 2.4 percent lower than the previous year's sales.

Although industry analysts remarked that Conway had taken some positive steps to putting the company back on track, they also observed that Crown was not yet out of the woods. The Pennsylvania Supreme Court struck down the state's asbestos reform law in March 2004, which meant that Crown was once again faced with paying out higher legal claims at the state level and the federal level.

In addition to Conway's duties at Crown Holdings, he also served as a director of West Pharmaceutical Services and PPL Corporation.

See also entry on Continental Can Co., Inc. in *International Directory of Company Histories*.

SOURCES FOR FURTHER INFORMATION

"An Affair to Remember," *Forbes*, June 11, 2001, p. 54.

"Crown Cork & Seal Comments on New Pennsylvania Asbestos Law," PR Newswire, December 17, 2001, http://stg.syndnet.thomsonfn.com/InvestorRelations/PubNewsStory.aspx?partner=10390&storyId=107838.

"Crown Cork & Seal Major Capacity Change at Facility," PR Newswire, February 27, 2001, http://stg.syndnet.thomsonfn.com/InvestorRelations/PubNewsStory.aspx?partner=10390&storyId=64338.

Greenberg, Allen, "Asbestos Drills Crown Cork, *Philadelphia Business Journal*, August 10, 2001, p. 51.

McLeod, Douglas, "Pennsylvania Keeps Door Open on Asbestos Successor Liability," *Business Insurance*, March 1, 2004, p. 3.

"Supplier Profile," *Beverage Industry*, October 2002, p. 89.

"William J. Avery to Retire as CEO of Crown Cork & Seal; John W. Conway, President and COO to Succeed Him," PR Newswire,November 14, 2000, cached as http://216.239.41.104/search?q=cache:tUfFJ1dh5fwJ:www.findarticles.com/cf_0/PI/search.jhtml%3Fnav%3Dadv%26key%3D%2522Bill%2BAvery%2522%26magR%3D+%22William+J.+Avery+to+Retire%22&hl=en&ie=UTF-8.

—David Petechuk

John R. Coomber

1949–

Chief executive officer, Swiss Re

Nationality: British.

Born: February 7, 1949, in England.

Education: Nottingham University, BS, 1970.

Family: Married (wife's name unknown).

Career: Phoenix Insurance Company, 1970–1973, actuarial trainee; Swiss Re (UK), 1973–1974, actuarial trainee; 1974–1983, reinsurance; 1983–1987, appointed actuary; 1987–1990, head of life division and general manager; 1990–1993, deputy chief executive officer; 1991, director; 1993–1995, managing director and chief executive officer; Swiss Re, 1995–2003, member, executive board; 2003–, chief executive officer.

Awards: Fellow, Chartered Insurance Institute, 2002; one of the one hundred most powerful people in the insurance industry, Insurance NewCast, 2003.

Publications: *The Private Role in Social Insurance,* 2001.

Address: Swiss Re, Mythenquai 50/60, Zurich, Switzerland; http://www.swissre.com.

John R. Coomber. *AP/Wide World Photos.*

John R. Coomber was named the first non-Swiss CEO of Swiss Re effective January 1, 2003. Coomber was regarded as a "hard man of business . . . a safe pair of hands," a cost-cutter, and a risk-taker by Roland Gribben in the *Daily Telegraph* (November 11, 2002).

BACKGROUND

Coomber's education was in mathematics. He graduated from Nottingham University in 1970 with a degree in theoretical mathematics. He took a position immediately after graduation with the Phoenix Insurance Company in London as an actuarial trainee. Three years later, however, Phoenix began to transfer its staff to Bristol, United Kingdom. Coomber, who preferred to stay in London, resigned from Phoenix and began to work for a Swiss insurance company, Swiss Re, at its British office on Cannon Street in London. He continued training and in 1974 passed the actuarial examinations and became Swiss Re UK's appointed actuary.

SWISS RE UK

In 1987 Coomber was appointed general manager of Swiss Re UK and head of its life insurance division. His world expanded from pure insurance work to include administration and management. In 1991 Coomber was appointed a director of the UK operations and in 1993 he became its managing director. During Coomber's tenure, revenues and earnings increased more than 30 percent per year, and the overall percentage of the company's earnings from life and health insurance increased to 42 percent from 18 percent. Another hallmark of Coomber's years with the London office was his policy of expansion through acquisition, especially in North America. In January 1993 Coomber was named managing director and CEO of Swiss Re UK and was given responsibility for the firm's property casualty businesses. This marked addition to his responsibility prompted criticism that Coomber had little or no experience in property casualty, which was Swiss Re's core business.

SWISS RE

While Coomber was advancing in the United Kingdom, there was turmoil at the Swiss Re headquarters in Zurich. The firm's CEO, Walter B. Kielholz, wanted to rescue Credit Suisse, a large Swiss bank, and he believed that he could handle the top positions of both companies together. In September 2002, however, both Swiss Re and Kielholz realized holding the two positions would be impossible, and Kielholz resigned from Swiss Re. In a move that surprised the business world, Swiss Re appointed Coomber the first non-Swiss CEO in the company's 129-year history. At the time Swiss Re was the second largest reinsurance group in the world. It consisted of three business groups: property and casualty insurance, life and health insurance, and financial services. As described in its annual reports, Swiss Re used a strategy of diversification, allocating resources that reflected a beneficial risk-return ratio.

Coomber faced a formidable task. The insurance industry was hit hard by heavy losses after September 11, 2001, by the ensuing decrease in investment earnings, and by a general decline in profits. Furthermore, a series of natural disasters in 2002, especially flooding, were extremely expensive to insurers. The company announced a net loss for the year 2001. Coomber and Swiss Re met these problems with resolve. Periodic press briefings were held, and Coomber was accessible to members of the news media. Reporters, however, complained that his speeches were "a fluidity of obfuscation," according to Ronald Gift Mullins.

Early in 2003 Swiss Re posted a net loss for 2002, and Coomber blamed the year's losses on depression in the capital markets. However, the renewal rate of insurance policies increased 10 percent for January 2003. Confronted with this continuing negative picture, Coomber and Swiss Re ceased to emphasize the traditional framework of long-term value creation and reassessed corporate strategy.

CHALLENGES

By 2004 Coomber saw that the future of the insurance industry was going to be based on three criteria: climatic change, increasing threats to health, and increasing threats to the economy because of terrorism. World leaders in the fields of business, government, and science met in late 2003 and in the spring of 2004 to discuss, define, and strategize. Among those present were representatives of Swiss Re, the Allianz Group, AON, Goldman Sachs, JP Morgan Chase, Johnson & Johnson, BP, and the Association of British Insurers. This roundtable was part of a partnership of Swiss Re, the Center for Health and the Global Environment of Harvard Medical School, and the United Nations Development Programme. As a result of the discussions the participants stated that they would work to increase their knowledge of these new risks to identify proactive responses. They agreed to work individually and in concert. The Rüschlikon Compact—named for the location of the meeting, the Swiss Re Center for Global Dialogue in Rüschlikon, Switzerland—targeted the areas in which the group believed it could be the most proactive: ecological degradation caused by climate change and increased health risks. Extreme weather events had caused damage projected to cost $150 billion per year in the coming decade, and at least 30 new diseases had emerged in the past 30 years. In addition, many existing diseases were believed to be on the increase because of climate change; for example, malaria in Africa was reducing gross national products approximately 6 percent.

The *Financial Times* reported on April 27, 2004, "For a self-confessed optimist, John Coomber, head of Swiss Re, has a sober vision of the future. Crops will fail; floods will intensify; life-threatening diseases will spread across the world." Coomber and Swiss Re earned the approval of the "green" community because of the company's stated intention of becoming "greenhouse neutral." That is, the company announced a 10-year program to combine emission reduction measures with investment in the World Bank Community Development Fund. GreenBiz reported that this plan made Swiss Re the world's largest financial services company to set itself this goal. All locations were to participate and to offer the program to Swiss Re clients.

Coomber pursued a straightforward path from actuarial trainee who did not want to move to Bristol, England, to global corporate leader. His personal and professional strategy was risk management. Coomber was a member of the supervisory board of Euler Hermes and a member of the boards of the Association of British Insurers and the IMD Business School.

SOURCES FOR FURTHER INFORMATION

"Businesses Pledge Action on Threats from Climate Change, Biodiversity Loss," United Nations Development Programme, http://allafrica.com/stories/200406150765.html.

"Coomber's Challenge: People," *Financial Times*, November 12, 2002.

Gribben, Roland, "'Hard Man' Scales Swiss Re Summit," *Daily Telegraph*, November 12, 2002.

Mullins, Ronald Gift, "Swiss Re Nurtures Media with Barren Content," August 7, 2003, http://www.insfolks.com/article.php?cmd=1&id=10.

"Swiss Re Appoints Briton," *The Times*, November 12, 2002.

"Swiss Re Changes the Climate," *Financial Times*, April 27, 2004.

"Swiss Re to Become Climate-Neutral Company," *GreenBiz.com*, http://www.greenbiz.com/news/news_third.cfm?NewsID=25918.

—Barbara Gunvaldsen

Roger Corbett

1942–

CEO and managing director, Woolworths

Nationality: Australian.

Born: 1942, in Sydney, New South Wales, Australia.

Education: University of New South Wales, BA; Stanford University, MBA.

Career: Grace Brothers, 1963–1984, started on loading docks but soon moved into management, serving as merchandise director and stores director; David Jones, 1984–1990, director of operations; Big W, 1990–1997, managing director; Woolworths, 1997–1998, managing director, retail; 1998–1999, chief operating officer; 1999, CEO and managing director.

Address: Level 5, 540 George Street, Sydney, NSW 2000, Australia; http://www.woolworthslimited.com.au.

Roger Corbett, chief executive officer and managing director of Woolworths, Australia's leading supermarket chain and its most successful retailer, began his career on the Grace Brothers loading dock. Over the years, he picked up marketing know-how from some of Australia's leading retailers, including David Jones (Australia) and Grace Brothers. Corbett also developed a keen understanding of technology and the supply chain, knowledge he used to give Woolies—as Woolworths is affectionately known Down Under—a strategic advantage in its battle for market share.

MARKETPLACE COMPETITION AND CORBETT'S STRATEGIES

Under Corbett's direction, Woolies surpassed its chief rival, Coles Myer, in the food-retailing market. In addition to supermarkets, both Woolworths and Coles Myer operate a variety of other retailing outlets, including general and specialty merchandise stores, discount outlets, and liquor stores. Although Coles Myer's retail empire continued, as of 2004, to be the biggest in Australia, Woolworths was slowly but steadily closing in on its rival and, perhaps more important to its shareholders, had managed to post consistently higher profits than Coles in the preceding few years.

Roger Corbett. © *Reuters NewMedia Inc./Corbis.*

The supermarket rivalry between Woolworths and Coles Myer—Australia's two largest food retailers, with an estimated 75 percent of the market between them—had begun long before Corbett took the helm of Woolies. At the outset of the 1980s Woolworths had been the undisputed leader in Australian food retailing, but it fell on hard times by the middle of that decade, even posting a loss in 1986. Coles soon moved into the lead and stayed there for several years. Woolworths, which had built a reputation for its wide variety of fresh produce and other foods, finally overtook its rival and, by the early 2000s, had a solid lead over Coles.

With competition for Australians' food dollars already sharp, the entry of the German grocery retailer Aldi into the mix, beginning in 2001, further complicated the market outlook. Corbett acknowledged Aldi as a serious competitor, but he also said that he doubted that the German company would substantially cut into Woolworths' market share. Aldi, said Corbett, offered a very limited number of grocery items—approximately six hundred to eight hundred—compared with the 25,000 to 35,000 different branded products available on the shelves of the typical Woolworths supermarket. "I think Aldi is a nice operator that seeks a market around the world," Corbett told Richard Salmons of the *Age*. "It's a very focused and narrow offer."

Next, Corbett faced a significantly reinvigorated Coles, which seemed determined to hold on to its leadership in Australian retailing. However, for every initiative mounted by Coles to steal market share from Woolies, Corbett came up with an innovative counterstrategy not only to protect Woolworths' market share but also to propel Woolies into the lead. When Coles Myer struck a deal with Shell to take over nearly six hundred Shell gasoline outlets across Australia, Corbett struck back. The Woolworths CEO set up a joint venture with Caltex to market gasoline at 450 co-branded Caltex/Woolworths service stations. The Caltex deal expanded the gasoline marketing share of Woolworths, which also marketed gasoline through its 280 Plus Petrol outlets.

In still another round of the continuing face-off between Woolworths and Coles Myer, Corbett in 2003 announced a plan to introduce pharmacies into selected Woolworths supermarkets. These in-store pharmacies, he said, would be operated by licensed pharmacists. The plan immediately drew fire from Australia's Pharmacy Guild, which pointed to the obvious conflict between pharmacists' efforts to discourage smoking and the supermarkets' earnings from tobacco products. However, by year's end, Coles Myer had announced that it was seriously considering following Woolworths' lead.

CORBETT'S EDUCATION AND PROFESSIONAL DEVELOPMENT

Corbett, a native of New South Wales, attended Shore School in North Sydney. While at Shore, he was a member of school's rugby team and thereafter remained a big fan of the game. A passionate supporter of Shore, which was also known as the Sydney Church of England Grammar School, Corbett served in 2003 as chairman of the school's council. He later attended the University of New South Wales, where he earned his BA in business administration. Corbett also earned an MBA from Stanford University in Palo Alto, California.

Corbett's career in retailing began in the mid-1960s on the loading docks at the Grace Bros. department store in Sydney's Chatswood neighborhood. He was hired to unload pallets, "unbelievably hard" work as he told a June 2003 seminar sponsored by the *Financial Review BOSS* magazine. "There was no motorization of the pallets; you just had to pull them, and they were really heavy." It was not long, however, before Corbett's potential as a manager was recognized, and he moved quickly up through the ranks at Grace Bros. Over the next couple of decades he held positions as merchandise director and stores director. It is something of an irony that Corbett's first stop in his long retailing career later became part of the retailing empire of Coles Myer, Woolworths' chief rival. Grace Brothers Holdings was acquired in 1983 by Myer Emporium, which two years later merged with Coles to form Coles Myer.

Corbett in 1984 joined the board of David Jones as director of operations. David Jones, which first opened its doors in May 1838, was Australia's oldest department store and the oldest department store in the world to be still trading under its original name. Corbett remained with David Jones until 1990, when he was hired to serve as managing director of Big W, the discount department store division of Woolworths.

Corbett was an unapologetic adherent to the discount retailing gospel according to the late Sam Walton, the Arkansan who created Wal-Mart, the world's largest retailer. Using some of the same strategies Walton employed to transform Wal-Mart into a retailing giant, Corbett successfully guided Big W into the big time during the 1990s. To help ensure that Big W made no missteps in its efforts to recreate the Wal-Mart magic Down Under, Corbett brought in the American Jack Shewmaker, a former Wal-Mart president. By the late 1990s Big W sales were outpacing those of its biggest rivals—Kmart and Target, both of which operated in Australia under the corporate umbrella of Coles Myer. Corbett generously gave much credit for Big W's success to Shewmaker.

Impressed by Corbett's accomplishments at Big W, top management at Woolworths in July 1997 named Corbett managing director, retail, for the entire group. A year later he became Woolworths' chief operating officer. In January 1999 he became CEO and managing director.

MANAGEMENT PHILOSOPHY AND RECORD OF SUCCESS

A central tenet in Corbett's management philosophy was the importance of creating a corporate culture that embraced egalitarianism and fostered teamwork. Corbett put a high priority on caring for other people, a concept that he defined as essentially following the golden rule of doing unto others as you would have them do unto you. His strict adherence to this concept helped create a fiercely loyal workforce at Woolworths. Of the importance of teamwork, Corbett told the June 2003 *Financial Review BOSS* seminar, "Colleagueship is a terribly important part of that process. It's got something to do with what I like to call the aggregate of the whole, that people feel that they belong."

Under Corbett, Woolworths' revenue and net income improved significantly. In fiscal 2000, which ended June 30, 2000, the company posted net income of $176.4 million on revenue of nearly $12.3 billion. Reflecting the worldwide recession in fiscal 2001, revenue dropped to $10.9 billion, but Woolies managed to end the year with a bigger profit ($242.6 million) than in the previous year. Fiscal 2002 brought net income of $317.3 million on sales of nearly $13.8 billion. In fiscal 2003 revenue jumped more than 27 percent, to $17.5 billion, and Woolworths posted a profit of $433.8 million. In addition to shepherding Woolworths to greater profitability, Corbett worked wonders for the company's stock. In 1998 the year before Corbett took over as CEO, Woolies stock, traded on the Australian Stock Exchange under the stock symbol WOW, languished at about A$4.20. In early 2004 the stock was trading just under A$12 a share.

Elaborating on what he saw as the key ingredients to a formula for business success, Corbett told the *Financial Review BOSS* seminar that in addition to knowing their business and being willing and able to do their homework, business executives must undertake reasonable business management. "You need to have good administration. You need to be able to measure your business. You need to be able to manage your risk."

Central to Corbett's success at Woolworths had been Project Refresh, a business strategy he introduced six months after taking over as CEO in January 1999. Although the company was riding high at the time, firmly entrenched as Australia's leading food retailer, he cautioned Woolworths employees and shareholders against the dangers of becoming complacent. Corbett said that when things were going relatively well was "precisely the best time to refresh ourselves, to reinvigorate the businesses, and to increase momentum," according to a company press release. He called upon employees at all levels to examine closely what the company was doing and to try to come up with ways of doing it better. In the years after the strategy was first unveiled, Project Refresh teams explored virtually every aspect of Woolworths's operations, including human resources, information technology, logistics, organization structure, and the cost of doing business. Tangible byproducts of Project Refresh were major overhauls of the company's technology and supply chain systems.

Speaking to shareholders in November 2003, Corbett predicted that the Project Refresh strategy would generate savings of A$4 billion over the following few years. He also reaffirmed the company's commitment to pursuing its successful low-cost strategy. In an interview with the Sydney newspaper the *Age*, he said that in the long run the outcome of the ongoing competition for Australians' food dollars would depend upon which company operated the "the most cost-efficient business." Corbett said that while the costs of Woolworths's leading competitors had increased during the first quarter of fiscal 2004, Woolies had managed to cut its costs significantly. He promised that the company's costs would continue to be reduced, saying "the competitive advantage of being a low-cost operation is where Woolworths' future lies, and that will give us our strength in the marketplace."

See also entries on Aldi, Wal-Mart Stores, Inc., and Coles Myer Ltd. in *International Directory of Company Histories.*

SOURCES FOR FURTHER INFORMATION

"AFR BOSS CLUB Transcript," June 4, 2003, http://www.afrboss.com.au/events/transcript.asp?eventid=371.

"Aldi Invades Australian Market," *MMR*, April 16, 2001.

Downie, Stephen, "Profile: Woolworths' Chief, Roger Corbett," *Daily Telegraph* (Sydney, Australia), August 27, 2003.

Hedge, Mike, "Vic: Aldi Opens in Victoria," *Australian Associated Press*, May 14, 2003.

Maiden, Malcolm, "Shedding Light on the Corbett Deal," *Sydney Morning Herald*, September 22, 2003.

McCombie, Helen, "Woolies Still Going Strong," *Business Sunday* (television show), November 16, 2003.

Mitchell, Peter, "Woolworths Wins Back Lost Ground, Says Corbett," *Sydney Morning Herald*, October 17, 2003.

Salmons, Richard, "Corbett Stays at the Helm," *Age* (Sydney, Australia), July 9, 2003.

"Top 10 Mass Retailers: Excellent, Exciting," *MMR*, May 28, 2001.

Turnbull, Jeff, and Jonathon Moran, "Fed: Woolworths Strikes Back Hard in Petrol War," *Australian Associated Press*, August 21, 2003.

Wavish, Bill, "Woolies' Exec Move," *MMR*, May 12, 2003.

"Woolies Sales 'Excellent,'" *Sunday Times* (Perth, Australia), December 31, 2003.

"Woolworths Joins Pacesetters," *MMR*, May 28, 2001.

"Woolworths Momentum Grows," *MMR*, September 8, 2003.

"Woolworths Strategy Saves 'Billions,'" *Age* (Sydney, Australia), November 21, 2003.

"Woolworths to Meet Its Projections," *MMR*, October 20, 2003.

—Don Amerman

■■■

Alston D. Correll

1941–

Chairman of the board and chief executive officer, Georgia-Pacific Corporation

Nationality: American.

Born: April 28, 1941, in Brunswick, Georgia.

Education: University of Georgia, BS, 1963; University of Maine, MS, 1966; University of Maine, MS, 1967.

Family: Son of Alston Dayton Correll Sr. and Elizabeth Flippo; married Ada Lee Fulford; children: two.

Career: Westvaco, 1963–1964, technical service engineer; University of Maine, 1964–1967, instructor; Weyerhaeuser Company, 1967–1977, various pulp and paper management positions; Mead Corporation, 1977–1980, division president; 1980, group vice president of paperboard; 1981, group vice president of paper; 1981–1983, group vice president of forest products; 1983–1988, senior vice president of forest products; Georgia-Pacific Corporation, 1988–1989, senior vice president of pulp and printing paper; 1989–1991, executive vice president of pulp and paper; 1991–1993, president and COO; 1993, president and CEO; 1993–2002, president, CEO, and chairman of the board; 2002–, CEO and chairman of the board.

Awards: Named one of the 25 Most Influential Georgians, *Georgia Trend*, 1996–1998; named one of the One Hundred Most Influential Georgians, *Atlanta Business Chronicle*, 1994, 1995, and 1999–2002; received the Institute of Human Relations award, American Jewish Committee, 1995.

Address: Georgia-Pacific Corporation, 133 Peachtree Street, Atlanta, Georgia 30303; http://www.gp.com.

■ In 1993 Alston Dayton (Pete) Correll became chairman of the board and chief executive officer of Georgia-Pacific Corporation, one of the world's top manufacturers of paper and building products. In that position, Correll focused his efforts on repositioning the company from a forest-industry building-materials manufacturer to a consumer-products company. He took the company through a very difficult financial period in the late 20th and early 21st centuries. During that time stock prices fell and the company was shadowed by millions of dollars worth of asbestos-related legal claims. Despite these setbacks, Correll remained upbeat, showing continued commitment to his company and staunch support for his industry; he referred to himself proudly as the "king of toilet paper." In the *National Review*, Jay Nordlinger referred to Correll as "a southerner whose sweet drawl can't conceal an exceptionally sharp mind."

THE EARLY YEARS

In the 1950s Correll's family owned a men's store in Brunswick, Georgia. When he was just 12, Correll and his mother were forced to take over the business when his father suddenly passed away. Correll had to learn the business from the ground up, including how to sew hems when his mother was forced to let go of the company's seamstress.

After graduating from the University of Georgia, Correll was accepted into Harvard University's MBA program, but he decided instead to attend the University of Maine, from which he earned a master's degree in paper and pulp technology and another in chemical engineering. Correll spent the first ten years of his career at the Weyerhaeuser Company, working in various positions. He then joined Mead Corporation in 1977 as a division president. He was with Mead for 11 years, eventually rising to the position of vice president of the forest-products division, when he left to join Georgia-Pacific.

A NEW FACE AT GEORGIA-PACIFIC

When Correll arrived at Georgia-Pacific in 1988 as senior vice president of pulp and printing paper, he found a company steeped in the old ways. In the more than 60 years that the company had then been in operation, it had not ventured far from its roots as a lumber wholesaler. As Correll moved up the ranks—to executive vice president in 1989, president and chief operating officer in 1991, and chief executive officer in 1993—his aim was to move the company away from traditional forest products, such as timber, pulp, and chemicals, and into more high-value consumer products, such as tissue. He believed that the move would strengthen Georgia-Pacific's earnings and improve its market share. In August 1993 Correll was appointed to the President's Council on Sustainable Development. He was part of a group of 25 business leaders who were chosen to help the government develop policies to encourage economic growth and protect the environment.

In 2000 Georgia-Pacific moved closer to Correll's goal of becoming a consumer-oriented company when it acquired Fort James Corporation, the manufacturer of Dixie Cups, Quilted Northern toilet paper, and Brawny paper towels. The acquisition cemented Georgia-Pacific as the world's leading manufacturer of tissue products. In 1999 Correll led the company through the $7 billion acquisition of another paper giant, Unisource Worldwide, the leading distributor of paper products and packaging supplies in North America.

DIFFICULT YEARS AT GEORGIA-PACIFIC

But the company faced several debilitating setbacks. Consumer paper-goods rivals Kimberly-Clark and Procter & Gamble began to eat away at Georgia-Pacific's share of the market, and the company faced millions of dollars in liability from asbestos-related lawsuits. The liabilities stemmed from the company's production in the 1960s and 1970s of wallboard joint compound containing asbestos fibers. (Georgia-Pacific stopped using asbestos in 1977.) Furthermore, a new-construction slowdown had reduced the demand for building materials and dropped the prices on timber and other construction products.

In 2001 the company faced a run of bad luck. A $400 million deal to sell a Mississippi pulp mill to Enron Corporation fell through when the latter company went through its much-publicized financial meltdown. Then, Williamette Industries considered joining with Georgia-Pacific's building-products division, an arrangement that would have netted $3 billion in much-needed income for Georgia-Pacific. But Williamette turned down the deal because of concerns over asbestos liability, and it was acquired instead by rival Weyerhaeuser.

In 2002 Correll sought to reduce the company's debts and increase shareholder value by splitting Georgia-Pacific into two separate publicly traded companies—a consumer-products and packaging company (Brawny, Coronet, Dixie, Quilted Northern), and a building-products and distribution company. He was going to head up the new consumer-products company. There was some talk that the move was an attempt to shield certain divisions from the asbestos liability. The separation never went through, however. Georgia-Pacific withdrew its proposed $1 billion stock offering in early 2003, citing poor market conditions and slow sales on building products.

Also in 2002, for the second year in a row, Correll did not get his promised $2 million bonus. The board cited as its reasons disappointing earnings and the continued decline of the company's stock prices. Georgia-Pacific stocks had dropped 42 percent in 2002, and the company was nearly $12 billion in debt, in large part because of the Fort James acquisition. Late that year Standard & Poor's announced that it was downgrading Georgia-Pacific's debt from BBB- to BB+, or junk status.

In the midst of this difficult period, Correll experienced health problems. In October 2002 he was hospitalized with chest pains, and he required angioplasty to open a blocked artery. Just over one week after his hospitalization, however, he was back in the office for a conference call, and he returned to work full time within a month. In early 2003 Moody's Investors Service further downgraded Georgia-Pacific's credit rating, citing rising asbestos liabilities, high debt level, and uncertainty surrounding the future of the company's building products. In a conference call with investors that year, Correll admitted, "We're in the worst possible of all worlds for Georgia-Pacific right now" (Associated Press, January 22, 2003). But he was confident that his company would recover as soon as the market rebounded.

In an effort to reduce debt and shift the company's focus to its consumer-products divisions, Correll began selling off many of the company's building-products businesses. In 2002 Georgia-Pacific sold a controlling 60 percent of its Unisource Worldwide distribution segment. Two years later it unloaded its building-products distribution business to a new company owned by the investment group Cerberus Capital Management. In early 2003 the board of directors met to discuss the company's rising debt. There was reportedly some discussion of removing Correll from his position, which the board would not corroborate.

THE TIDE SHIFTS AGAIN FOR GEORGIA-PACIFIC

Later in 2003 the company's luck began to turn. Georgia-Pacific reported better-than-expected earnings, especially in its packaging and building-materials divisions. Its stock soared, and the junk-bond market experienced a resurgence, earning the company much-needed revenue against its debt.

Correll continued to shift the company's strategic focus to its consumer products. In 2003 and 2004 Georgia-Pacific spent millions revamping its Brawny and Quilted Northern products. The company developed a new drying technology, which made Brawny paper towels soft on one side and tough on the other. To promote the new technology, the company rolled out a series of ads with a new "Brawny man." In January 2004 Georgia-Pacific released what it touted as the "softest ever" incarnation of Quilted Northern toilet paper, complete with a new ad campaign and redesigned packaging. By 2004, with Correll still at the helm, Georgia-Pacific boasted annual sales of more than $20 billion, and the company employed more than 60,000 people throughout North America and Europe.

In addition to his duties at Georgia-Pacific, Alston Correll served on a number of corporate and association boards, including Norfolk Southern Corporation, SunTrust Banks, American Forest and Paper Association, and the Institute of Paper Science and Technology. He once served as chairman of the Atlanta Chamber of Commerce, and he has been on the boards of several charitable organizations, including the Nature Conservancy, the Atlanta Symphony Orchestra, the Carter Center, Keep America Beautiful, and the Robert W. Woodruff Arts Center.

See also entries on Georgia-Pacific Corporation, The Mead Corporation, SunTrust Banks Inc., and Weyerhaeuser Company in *International Directory of Company Histories.*

SOURCES FOR FURTHER INFORMATION

Associated Press, "GP Posts Wider Loss," January 22, 2003, http://www.wluk.com/common/article.shtml?article_id=1043242107079898.

Berman, Phyllis, "Brawny—Lucky Too," *Forbes,* February 2, 2004, p. 60.

Jordan, Meredith, "Georgia-Pacific's Correll Feels Heat Over Results," *Atlanta Business Chronicle,* January 24, 2003.

Ligos, Melinda, "For Toilet Paper King, a Constant Question and a Simple Answer," *New York Times,* January 4, 2004.

Nordlinger, Jay, "Davos Journal, Part IV," *National Review Online,* http://www.nationalreview.com/impromptus/impromptus200401270838.asp

—Stephanie Watson

■ ■ ■

Alfonso Cortina de Alcocer

1944–

President, chairman, and chief executive officer of Repsol YPF

Nationality: Spanish.

Born: March 13, 1944, in Madrid, Spain.

Education: Madrid University; Higher Technical School of Industrial Engineers, Madrid.

Family: Son of Pedro Cortina Mauri (foreign minister during government of Carlos Arias Navarro); children: two.

Career: Banco de Vizcaya Group, 1968–1982, various positions including engineer, vice chairman, and managing director; Portland Valderrivas, 1984–1990, vice president; 1990–1996, president; Repsol YPF, 1996–, president, chairman, and CEO.

Awards: Businessman of the Year, Madrid Chamber of Commerce and Industry, 1995.

Address: Repsol YPF, Paseo de la Castellana, 278, 28046 Madrid, Spain; http://www.repsol-ypf.com.

■ After serving for more than a decade as vice president and president of the Portland Valderrivas cement company, Alfonso Cortina de Alcocer became president of the Spanish oil firm Repsol in 1996 despite his lack of experience in the petroleum industry. Under Cortina de Alcocer's leadership Repsol invested heavily abroad, particularly in Latin America. Notable among its investments was the purchase of the Argentine oil company YPF. Cortina de Alcocer's aggressive investments brought Repsol YPF both great profits and major financial problems.

EARLY CAREER

Cortina de Alcocer was born in the Spanish capital of Madrid. He remained in Madrid for his higher education, receiving a degree in economics from Madrid University. He also obtained a degree in industrial engineering from the Higher Technical School of Industrial Engineers in Madrid before beginning his professional career. He spent his early career working in various positions for the Banco de Vizcaya Group from 1968 until 1982. In the 1980s he joined the Construcciones y Contratas Group along with his brother Alberto Cortina and his cousin Alberto Alcocer. He served as vice president of the Portland Valderrivas cement company, and he became president of the same firm in 1990. By the end of his tenure at Portland Valderrivas in 1996, Cortina de Alcocer had become one of Spain's wealthiest and most successful businessmen.

JOINS REPSOL

Cortina de Alcocer became president of Repsol in 1996, a result of both his successful business career and his political maneuverings. He became a member of the board of directors of the Banco Bilbao Vizcaya (BBV) in 1995 and soon was the bank's largest shareholder. BBV, in turn, was a major shareholder in Repsol, which allowed Cortina de Alcocer to use his connections to become a favorite to replace Repsol's president, Oscar Fanjul. Furthermore, the new center-right Spanish government of the Popular Party sought to remove Fanjul, who had been appointed by the previous Socialist government. The state owned 10 percent of Repsol at the time, giving the government a degree of influence in company decisions. In June 1996 Cortina de Alcocer joined Repsol's board of directors and then was named chairman of the company. The move was not without controversy, as Fanjul had built Repsol into a successful corporation and was regarded as one of Spain's top executives.

AGGRESSIVE EXPANSION IN LATIN AMERICA

After Cortina de Alcocer took over at the helm of Repsol, he largely continued the strategies of his predecessor, such as becoming more involved in the electricity sector. A notable change, however, was that the company expanded significantly overseas, especially in Latin America. Between 1995 and 2003 Repsol invested $44.5 billion, two-thirds of which went to Latin American countries. Cortina de Alcocer saw many opportunities in the region. He told the *New York Times*, "There was good stability in South America, good opportunities and liberalization. Of course, too, these opportunities were much cheaper than European investments" (June 29, 2003).

His boldest move was the acquisition of the Argentine oil company YPF. In January 1999 Repsol bought the 15 percent of YPF still owned by the Argentine government. Many experts saw the $2 billion purchase as a risky maneuver, as Argentine nationalists were sensitive to foreign ownership of a former state-run monopoly. Also, oil prices were low at the time, potentially limiting profits. Then, in May 1999, Cortina de Alcocer bought the remaining 85 percent of YPF for more than $13 billion. Despite some resistance in Argentina the generous cash offer persuaded YPF shareholders to sell.

Cortina de Alcocer explained that his audacious takeover would make the newly created Repsol YPF into a major force in the world petroleum industry. Indeed, the purchase made Repsol YPF the eighth-largest oil company in the world. The merger combined Repsol's expertise in marketing and refining with YPF's large reserves and production capacity. Cortina de Alcocer told the *Financial Times* that "Repsol and YPF are a prefect strategic fit, forming a powerful international oil company with a balance of upstream and downstream earnings" (May 12, 1999). He rejected claims that Spanish companies were simply trying to reconquer a region that was once part of the Spanish Empire. He believed that Spanish investment in Latin America helped support local communities there.

Cortina de Alcocer did not foresee the dramatic downturn in the Argentine economy that occurred soon after his company purchased YPF. A major scandal in the Argentine government in late 2001 that included bribes being paid to senators led to protests against President Fernando de la Rua. De la Rua resigned, and at one point Argentina had five different presidents in a two-week period. This political crisis soon developed into a severe economic crisis. The Argentine government devalued the peso and defaulted on its foreign debt, and the country suffered through record unemployment and poverty. The value of Repsol YPF shares in Madrid decreased significantly in 2001 and 2002, leading to many questions and criticisms about the company's expansion in Latin America.

LOW-KEY STYLE

Cortina de Alcocer was not a charismatic leader. His voice was monotone, he possessed little sense of humor, and he was sensitive to criticism. Some described him as evasive. He had minimal contact with the public, and his communication style was dry and laconic. Cortina de Alcocer told the Spanish newspaper *El Mundo*, "I think you should come out only when there is something important to communicate; if not, you run the risk of boring people. I don't think the president has to tell everything he does all day. That is my nature, I don't like to be at the podium" (February 21, 1999).

Cortina de Alcocer was extremely loyal. He continued working despite having amassed great wealth. With the onset of the Argentine economic crisis in 2002, however, he chose to remain at the helm of Repsol YPF despite many calls for his removal. One source close to Cortina de Alcocer told *El Mundo* that "Alfonso is not going to leave things half done. YPF was the apple of his eye and he is not going to throw in the towel" (May 5, 2002).

See also entry on Repsol-YPF S.A. in *International Directory of Company Histories.*

SOURCES FOR FURTHER INFORMATION

"El Reto," *El Mundo*, May 5, 2002.

Tagliabue, John, "With Capital in Hand, Spain Revisits Empire," *New York Times*, June 29, 2003.

Tizón, Alvaro, "Alfonso Cortina, del 18 al 10," *El Mundo*, February 21, 1999.

Warn, Ken, "YPF Board Backs Merger with Repsol," *Financial Times*, May 12, 1999.

—Ronald Young

■ ■ ■

David M. Cote

1952–

President, chief executive officer, and chairman, Honeywell International

Nationality: American.

Born: 1952.

Education: University of New Hampshire, BS, 1976.

Family: Married twice; children: two from first marriage, one from second marriage.

Career: General Electric, 1974–1976, factory laborer; 1976–1996, manager; 1996–1999, senior vice president, president and CEO of Appliances; TRW, 1999–2001, president and COO; 2001, president and CEO; 2001–2002, president, CEO, and chairman; Honeywell International, 2002, president and CEO; 2002–, president, CEO, and chairman.

Awards: Honorary Juris Doctor, Graziadio School of Business at Pepperdine University, 2001.

Address: Honeywell International, 101 Columbia Road, Morristown, New Jersey 07962; http://www.honeywell.com.

■ In a speech at Pepperdine University in April 2001, David M. Cote outlined four areas in which businesspeople should focus: recognizing the importance of people and one's own behaviors; getting out of one's comfort zone; having goals and being results oriented; and enjoying life. Cote's success in managing people may have stemmed from his understanding the needs of others. His shifting from tough job to tough job certainly reflected his continuous desire to extend beyond his comfort zone. Throughout his career, he developed a reputation for being very goal oriented. As for happiness: as a driven man, devoted to performance, he derived profound enjoyment in meeting and overcoming challenges.

GENERAL ELECTRIC

When he graduated from high school, Cote seemed to have no goals, belying the driven temperament that would eventually propel him to the apex of his profession. He decided to skip university, instead using his college money to buy a car, and worked as a manual laborer; after a couple of years he realized that he would not excel in that field. Thus, he entered the Wittemore School of Business at the University of New Hampshire. His studies were protracted by his full-time night job in a General Electric jet-engine manufacturing plant, as well as by a period during which he also purchased a boat with a friend and worked as a lobster fishermen. He graduated from college after approximately six years.

After receiving his bachelor's degree in business administration, Cote worked as a manager in the consumer-electronics, jet-engines, and plastics divisions at General Electric. The company was noted for its goal-oriented style of operations, and Cote readily absorbed its management doctrine. In 1996 the business world learned what upper management at General Electric seemed to already know—that Cote was an innovator who could aptly refine the company's business practices, cutting costs and improving sales. That year, he was named corporate senior vice president and also became the president and CEO of the $6 billion Appliances division.

Cote soon became the leader of General Electric's "smart bomb" technique for generating sales in Asia. Instead of creating a marketing plan for the entire continent, he formed bubble teams of sales representatives, engineers, and cultural experts to study each Asian nation individually, with the teams eventually creating bundles of appliances suited to the cultural groups of each individual nation. General Electric Appliances registered profits of about $100 million in each of the years Cote ran the division, and other General Electric divisions copied the "smart bomb" techniques. Cote also led one of General Electric's first joint-venture efforts, forming a partnership with Culligan to manufacture refrigerators with built-in water filtration. In what would be a hallmark of his management, Cote streamlined the appliances division by emphasizing the specific goals that needed to be achieved.

TRW

When it became evident that Cote would not be the one to replace the retiring CEO Jack Welch, Cote looked elsewhere for new challenges, eventually finding them at TRW. In November 1999 he became TRW's president and COO, with the understanding that he would replace the CEO Joseph Gormanin 2001. At TRW, Cote introduced the Six Sigma management system, a doctrine that focused the production process on reducing defects in products to less than 3.4 per million opportunities; "opportunities" were defined as occasions when a defect could occur, and "defects" were defined as any results outside of customer specifications. As a whole, the Six Sigma system made the manufacturing process especially responsive to customer needs.

In February 2001 Cote became CEO as well as president of TRW; in August 2001 he added chairman of the board to his title. Cote led the creation of the TRW subsidiary Velocium, which manufactured ultra-high-speed semiconductors and was just beginning to make itself felt in the marketplace when Cote departed from TRW.

HONEYWELL INTERNATIONAL

Honeywell International had earlier tried to merge with General Electric, only to have the merger rejected by antitrust authorities in the European Union; having reorganized to become part of General Electric, the company had trouble reorienting itself to remaining an independent entity. The former chairman Lawrence A. Bossidy was brought in to save Honeywell from collapse, and when he retired for a second time he selected Cote to be his replacement.

On February 19, 2002, Cote was named president, CEO, and a member of the board of directors for Honeywell. On July 1, 2002, Cote was elected chairman of the board after Bossidy retired. Cote had his hands full: although Honeywell grossed $24 million in 2001, the company faced mounting debts, settlements for lawsuits stemming from employees' exposure to asbestos, a stock that would fall 31 percent in 2002, and demoralized management. Cote knew that running the huge company, with 115,000 employees in 95 countries, would prove challenging. He quickly applied his goal-oriented management philosophy to Honeywell, making cash, growth, people, productivity, digitization, and Six Sigma the focuses of his administration.

Honeywell lost $220 million in 2002, partly because of asbestos-suit payouts, the purchase of the sensors business Invensys for $416 million, and slow sales. However, by selling other Honeywell units and cutting costs—partly by sending some American jobs abroad to Romania and Singapore, where labor costs were lower, and partly by reducing defects in production—by the end of 2003 Honeywell had amassed about $2 billion in cash reserves. Cote was heavily criticized in the press for the $32 million in compensation he received in 2002, although he explained that the amount was intended to cover options that he had lost at TRW as a result of moving to Honeywell.

See also entries on TRW Inc. and Honeywell Inc. in *International Directory of Company Histories.*

SOURCES FOR FURTHER INFORMATION

Barrett, Amy, "In the Credibility Penalty Box: Can Honeywell CEO Cote Restore Investors' Confidence?" *BusinessWeek*, April 28, 2003, p. 80.

Cote, David M., "Keynote Commencement Address: The Graziadio School of Business and Management," Pepperdine University, April 14, 2001, http://www.pepperdine.edu/PR/NotableSpeeches/cote.htm.

Grant, Linda, "GE's Smart Bomb Strategy," *Fortune.com*, July 21, 1997, http://www.fortune.com/fortune/subs/article/0,15114,380002,00.html.

Murphy, Tara, "Honeywell's New CEO Is the Right Man," *Forbes.com*, March 5, 2002, http://www.forbes.com/2002/03/05/0305bigcap.html.

—Kirk H. Beetz

■■■

Robert Crandall

1935–

Former president, chief executive officer, and chairman of the board, AMR Corporation

Nationality: American.

Born: December 6, 1935, in Westerly, Rhode Island.

Education: Attended William and Mary College, 1953–1955; University of Rhode Island, BS, 1957; Wharton School, University of Pennsylvania, MBA, 1960.

Family: Son of Lloyd Evans Crandall (insurance salesman) and Virginia (Beard) Crandall (homemaker); married Margaret Jan Schmults; children: three.

Career: Eastman Kodak, 1960–1962, credit supervisor; Hallmark Cards, 1962–1966, computer programming division supervisor; Trans World Airlines, 1966–1970, assistant treasurer; 1970–1971, vice president of data services; 1971–1973, vice president and controller; Bloomingdale's, 1973, senior vice president and treasurer; American Airlines, 1973–1974, senior vice president of finance; 1974–1976, senior vice president of marketing; 1980–1985, president and chief operating officer; AMR Corporation, 1985–1998, president, chief executive officer, and chairman of the board.

Awards: Horatio Alger Award, 1997.

■ Robert Crandall earned a reputation as the toughest executive in the airline industry by mercilessly pursuing the best return possible for the shareholders of American Airlines and AMR Corporation. He drove his management employees relentlessly and would fire a friend as readily as a foe if he thought that doing so would benefit his company. He had a passion for new technology and was responsible for revolutionizing travel of all kinds. Crandall introduced the first computer system for use by travel agents to make reservations and used data on passengers to create the "yield management system" that saved his airline millions of dollars. In addition, he introduced "supersaver" fares and other innovations that became standard practice throughout the airline industry.

Robert Crandall. *AP/Wide World Photos.*

CLIMBING THE CORPORATE LADDER

In the beginning Crandall had no social or financial advantages, but he had a good education, and he was driven to succeed. He also had a remarkably flexible mind that could adjust quickly to new economic realities as they arose. It was while working at Hallmark in 1962 that he began developing theories about how computers could revolutionize the ways in which businesses marketed themselves. While working for Trans World Airlines from 1966 to 1973, he implemented his ideas for applying computer technology to improve profits for airlines. It was Albert V. Carey who gave Crandall the authority to put his innovations into practice. Carey had been named president, chief executive officer, and chairman of the board of American Airlines in 1974. While he and Crandall were interviewing candidates to run American's marketing department, Carey realized that Crandall knew more about marketing than did the interviewees; as a result, he appointed Crandall senior vice president of marketing.

INNOVATIONS

In 1975 Crandall founded the Semi-Automatic Business Research Environment (SABRE), a program codeveloped with the IBM Corporation to provide travel agencies with a unified computer reservation system that would allow them to book reservations with any airline, not just American. Being able to make flight reservations immediately rather than having to wait for confirmation by mail transformed airline travel; it enabled travelers to make reservations at the last minute rather than having to plan weeks ahead. On April 24, 1977, Crandall introduced the supersaver plan in New York and California; in 1978 it was expanded to all routes. The supersaver plan offered discounts on tickets purchased months in advance; this program offered American Airlines a cash flow that it could use to cover overhead and factor into its spending plans.

Crandall bitterly opposed the deregulation of the airline industry. When deregulation came in 1978, it hit American Airlines hard. Small, low-fare airlines popped up, taking passengers away from established airlines. The low-fare airlines used nonunion labor to keep costs down, but American was locked into long-term union contracts. When Crandall was made president and chief operating officer, American Airlines was losing money. After American Airlines transferred its corporate headquarters from New York City to Dallas–Forth Worth, Texas (and Crandall moved from New Jersey to North Dallas), he began reshaping the company to suit the new marketplace by cutting low-yield routes, adding seats to aircraft, and trimming the number of employees from 41,200 to 37,000.

In 1981 Crandall introduced the concept of the frequent-flier program, calling it "AAdvantage" and rewarding repeat customers with free flying miles. American Airlines also introduced "AAirpass," which offered travelers long-term fixed-rate contracts for five years to life. On May 19, 1982, a holding company for American was formed, called AMR. It was in that year that Crandall had his greatest personal crisis; he telephoned the chairman of the board of Braniff Airlines, Howard Putnam, and declared, "Raise your goddamn fares 20 percent. I'll raise mine the next morning" (*Texas Monthly*, August 1993) Putnam taped the conversation, and the Justice Department used the tape as the basis for filing an antitrust lawsuit against Crandall. In October 1983 Judge Robert M. Hill dismissed the lawsuit, saying that no violation had actually occurred.

On December 12, 1983, AMR Services was created to sell services to other airlines. In that year Crandall temporarily solved his labor problems by implementing the two-tier wage system in a deal with unions that enhanced job security while allowing American Airlines to pay newly hired workers lower wages than established workers. From 1983 to 1988 American spent $7 billion for more fuel-efficient and quieter aircraft. In 1984 American retired its Boeing 747 cargo carriers and switched to using passenger jets to carry cargo as well as travelers.

By 1985 approximately 10,000 travel agencies were using SABRE, and AMR had become a service company for the airline industry as well as an airline company. When Carey retired, Crandall became president, CEO, and chairman of the board of AMR while retaining the same positions at American Airlines. From 1986 to 1989 AMR grew from 50,000 employees to 78,000. In 1987 SABRE was made accessible by personal computers. In 1988 AMR netted $806 million, and in 1989 Crandall bought the Latin American routes of Eastern Airlines and ordered $9 billion in new jets. That year American Airlines grossed $10.6 billion and netted $535 million.

In 1990 AMR lost $40 million. Even though it had 20 percent of the domestic airline market of the United States, AMR lost $935 million in 1992. Crandall responded by creating "value pricing," which featured an easy-to-understand four-level pricing system based on the individual needs of travelers. It failed because discount airlines undercut even the plan's lowest price level. That year the AMR Consulting Group was formed as part of Crandall's vision of a diversified, service-oriented company. It offered management help and maintenance services to other airlines. In July 1993 AMR Consulting Group became AMR Training and Consulting Group, and AMR formed SABRE Technology Group. In 1994 American Airlines created First Call, which focused on making travel arrangements for group travels. These innovations helped pull AMR out of the red. In 1997 American Airlines grossed $16 billion. On May 20, 1998, Crandall retired. In retirement Crandall served as a spokesman for the airline industry. In 2003 he was appointed to the Federal Aviation Administration Management Advisory Council.

See also entries on American Airlines and AMR Corporation in *International Directory of Company Histories.*

SOURCES FOR FURTHER INFORMATION

"Crandall, Robert," *Current Biography*, ed. Judith Graham, New York, H. W. Wilson, 1992, pp. 138–141.

Pedersen, Daniel, "One Tough [Expletive]," *Newsweek*, June 1, 1998, p. 50.

Rubin, Dana, "Bob Crandall Flies Off the Handle," *Texas Monthly*, August 1993, pp. 98–108.

—Kirk H. Beetz

■ ■ ■

Mac Crawford

1949–

Chairman, chief executive officer, and president, Caremark

Nationality: American.

Born: 1949.

Education: Auburn University, BS, 1971.

Family: Married Linda (maiden name unknown); children: two.

Career: Arthur Young & Company, 1971–1981; GTI, 1981–1985, CFO; Oxylance Corporation, 1985–1986, CFO; Mulberry Street Investment Company, 1986–1990, president; Charter Medical Corporation, 1990–1992, executive vice president of hospital operations; 1992–1993, president and COO; 1993–1995, chairman, CEO, and president; Magellan Health Services, 1995–1997, chairman, CEO, and president; MedPartners, 1997–1998, president and CEO; Caremark, 1998–, chairman, CEO, and president.

Address: Caremark, 211 Commerce Street, Nashville, Tennessee 37201; http://www.caremark.com.

■ Mac Crawford has been praised as one of the most successful turnaround CEOs in the health-care industry. His earning of a reputation as an expert in saving floundering companies began in 1993 when he was appointed chairman and CEO of Charter Medical Corporation; a year later Charter emerged from Chapter 11 bankruptcy and was struggling to return to profitability. At the time, Charter owned and operated nearly one hundred psychiatric and acute-care hospitals across the United States. Under Crawford's leadership, Charter (which later changed its name to Magellan Health Services when it acquired that company in 1995) sold off its psychiatric and acute-care hospitals to focus on its managed-care business. The move paid off, and Magellan returned to profitability in the late 1990s, eventually becoming the nation's largest managed behavioral health-care firm.

Because of his success with Magellan, Crawford was picked to be chairman and CEO of MedPartners in 1998. MedPartners was also struggling with the massive changes in the health-care industry in the 1990s. Once the leader in the physician-practice management business—with more than 11,000 affiliated physicians and $3 billion in net revenues—the company imploded in early 1998, when it began reporting losses from its Western U.S. operations and was struggling with debt obligations in excess of $1.8 billion.

Crawford took over the helm at MedPartners in March 1998. Once in charge he began selling off the company's physician practices and shifted its focus to its small but growing pharmacy-benefits management business. At this time MedPartners changed its name to Caremark. During the next six years, Crawford transformed the company into the largest mail-order pharmaceutical business and the fourth-largest pharmacy-benefits management company in the United States. In an interview in the *Tennessean*, Crawford described his experience at Caremark as "one of those stories where when you start out you don't have a clue what it will look like. But today, it's been a real success" (February 22, 2004).

PROSPERS AT CHARTER MEDICAL CORPORATION

After graduating from Auburn University in 1971, Crawford received a license as a certified public accountant and worked for Arthur Young & Company for 10 years. During this early period of his career he developed his strong financial management skills and general knowledge of business. After his years at Arthur Young, Crawford served as chief financial officer for a number of companies and in 1986 became president of Mulberry Street Investment Company, where he managed real-estate, venture-capital, oil- and gas-tax, and shelter investments.

In 1990 Crawford joined Charter Medical as executive vice president of hospital operations—his first experience with the health-care industry. By 1990 Charter was already experiencing serious legal and financial problems. In 1989 it had come under investigation for allegations of Medicare and Medicaid fraud and was involved in a lawsuit between Charter's then CEO and the company's employee stock ownership plan. Charter's psychiatric and acute-care hospital businesses were also in trouble, as cost controls in the health-care industry—driven by the growth of managed care—pushed psychiatric and chronically ill patients into less expensive treatments, such as outpatient and home-care programs. Despite these trends

Charter continued to build or acquire inpatient facilities, accruing deeper loses.

In a 1995 article in *Hospitals & Health Networks*, Crawford recalled his early experience at Charter: "I didn't have a health-care background. I came to Charter to financially restructure the company"; after a short time there, he realized that the company could no longer "continue to deliver behavioral health care in the same way. We needed a new model to continue to provide good-quality care on a more cost-effective basis" (February 5, 1995). Crawford won praise from analysts and industry insiders for reining in Charter's operational costs and improving relations with insurers and payers. He led Charter through a major financial restructuring and a Chapter 11 bankruptcy, from which the company emerged in 1992.

Crawford's success and leadership during this difficult period in Charter's history led to his appointment as president and COO in 1992, then as chairman and CEO in March 1993, replacing Fickling. Crawford quickly refocused Charter on its core business of managed behavioral health-care operations, selling off its general hospitals and many of its psychiatric facilities. The company also began offering outpatient and home-care services, and it aggressively sought out partnerships with large health-care systems to either provide or manage their behavioral-health services. In 1995 Charter purchased Magellan Health Services and took on that name. Magellan, too, owned and operated a number of psychiatric hospitals before it was acquired by Charter; in 1997 these facilities were sold to Crescent Operating, the money being used to purchase two more behavioral-health companies. By the late 1990s Crawford had succeeded in transforming Charter into the country's largest managed behavioral health-care company.

In 1995 Crawford discussed the management and leadership issues he confronted during his years at Charter. Speaking of the transformation of Charter from an owner and operator of psychiatric hospitals to a managed-care company, he said: "Internally, it's been very difficult. Many of our people are traditional hospital people, and convincing them that we are not a hospital company anymore isn't easy. Cultural issues were the most difficult part of the transaction" (February 5, 1995).

Crawford further emphasized the importance of instilling a value system in an organization, especially during times of change, and in making those values very clear. "If the value system is in place, it's fine to have cultural differences on how certain facilities will be run." He also stressed the importance of empowering employees to take risks: "I've got 104 CEOs throughout my facilities. We've told them that we are going to take chances while we build linkages. They have my assurance that I won't fire them for making a mistake" (February 5, 1995).

TRANSFORMING MEDPARTNERS

In March 1998 Crawford left Magellan to become president and CEO of MedPartners. MedPartners was the country's largest physician-practice management company and was in turmoil following a failed takeover by smaller rival PhyCor and larger-than-expected losses of nearly $841 million in the fourth quarter of 1997. The company also faced debt obligations totaling $1.8 billion.

A few months after joining MedPartners, Crawford went to the company's board of directors with a solution: sell off most of the company's 240 physician practices and concentrate instead on Caremark, its pharmacy-benefits management division. Pharmacy-benefits management firms, or PBMs, are essentially intermediaries that negotiate discounts with pharmaceutical companies for large employers and managed-care insurers or health plans. Because of the growing pressure on employers to hold down increases in health-care costs, Crawford saw promise in the growing role PBMs could play in providing a solution. By the following year MedPartners had sold off all but 12 of its physician practices across the United States and had laid off several thousand workers in order to focus exclusively on its PBM business. It also changed its name to Caremark in order to reflect this change.

Crawford recounted this turbulent time at Caremark in a February 2004 article in the *Tennessean*: "You can't be successful doing turnarounds if you don't walk in from day one and believe you're going to fix it. But we didn't exactly know what we were going to do" (February 22, 2004). Crawford was drawn to Caremark's PBM business for more than its growth potential: the division had revenues of $2.4 billion and generated large amounts of cash. According to Crawford, such cash flows are the key to turning around any struggling business. "Any time you're doing a restructuring, you need cash flow. Cash is a valuable commodity" (February 22, 2004).

Under Crawford's leadership Caremark thrived. In 1998 its revenues were $2.4 billion; by 2003 they had grown to nearly $9 billion. In spite of the difficult decisions he was forced to make—especially the layoffs of thousands of workers—Crawford won the respect of employees, analysts, investors, and creditors for saving MedPartners and transforming it into one of the country's most successful businesses. In 2004 the company had nearly paid off its debt and had acquired the nation's second-largest PBM firm, AdvancePCS. The merger made Caremark the second-largest pharmacy-benefits management company, with annual revenues of more than $23 billion and 600 million prescriptions filled per year.

See also entry on Caremark International Inc. in *International Directory of Company Histories.*

SOURCES FOR FURTHER INFORMATION

Cerne, Frank, "Capital Decisions," *Hospitals & Health Networks*, June 5, 1995, p. 33.

Cooper, Helene, and Glenn Ruffenach, "Charter Medical's Board Ousts Fickling, Firm's Founder, Chairman, Top Officer," *Wall Street Journal*, March 5, 1993.

Crawford, Edwin, "Finding the Right Niche," *Hospitals & Health Networks*, June 5, 1995, p. 38.

———, "The Wake-Up Call," *Hospitals & Health Networks*, February 5, 1995, p. 48.

Evans, Carol Muse, "Caremark Has Forged a Drastic Turnaround," *Birmingham Business Journal*, June 9, 2000, p. 11.

Freudenheim, Milt, "Merger of Drug-Buying Companies Has Some Doubting Purchase Price," *New York Times*, September 4, 2003.

"The Leadership," *Hospitals & Health Networks*, February 20, 1995, pp. 30–33.

"Mac Crawford: Changes Have Only Begun at Charter," *Alcoholism & Drug Abuse Week*, August 15, 1994, p. 3.

Ruffenach, Glenn, "Charter Medical Taps New Manager to Run Hospitals," *Wall Street Journal*, October 24, 1990.

Russell, Keith, "Caremark Triumphs in Fight for Profitability," *Tennessean*, February 22, 2004.

Seligman, Phill, "Good Medicine at Caremark," *BusinessWeek Online*, January 13, 2004.

Sharpe, Anita, "MedPartners Loss Exceeds Its Forecast," *Wall Street Journal*, March 19, 1998.

Yu, Roger, "Antitrust Issues Surround Merger of Pharmacy-Benefit Managers," *Dallas Morning News*, September 3, 2003.

—M. Scott

■■■

Carlos Criado-Perez

1952–

Former chief executive officer, Safeway PLC

Nationality: Argentinian.

Born: 1952, in Buenos Aires, Argentina.

Family: Children: three.

Career: SHV Makro, 1976–1990, international roles; 1990–1997, executive director; Wal-Mart, 1997–1999, COO of International Division; Safeway, 1999, COO; 1999–2004, CEO.

Awards: Retail Personality of the Year, Retek, 2001.

■ Carlos Criado-Perez, a charismatic Argentinian and one-time executive with Wal-Mart, was hired as chief operating officer and quickly became chief executive officer of the United Kingdom's Safeway retail food chain in order to help revitalize the ailing company. His impressive management style and unusual marketing tactics, which led to the chain's quick turnaround, attracted much attention from the company's executive management team, investors, and the general public. In a bitter—and according to Criado-Perez and others, unfair—takeover bid, Safeway was sold in March 2004 to a smaller competitor, and the outgoing chief executive remained uncertain about his plans for the future.

WORKED HIS WAY FROM RAGS TO RICHES

When Criado-Perez left Safeway in early 2004, his annual income was around £100,000, and his compensation package was upward of £4 million. Life had not always been so lucrative, however. Born into a middle-class family in Buenos Aires, Criado-Perez left the Argentinian university where he was studying civil engineering after his parents separated and his mother moved to Spain. There, bereft of immigration papers, he cleaned a bar by night and pushed supermarket carts by day. Within a year, however, the man who described himself as a doer was managing a supermarket store. In 1976 he joined the Dutch-based SHV Makro, a job that took him to Portugal, Brazil, and Taiwan, where he learned Mandarin. He became an executive director in 1990, where he remained until Makro was sold in 1997.

Criado-Perez next found himself in the United States as COO of Wal-Mart's International Division. An independent thinker, he disagreed with the company's "one strategy fits all countries" philosophy. He told Sarah Cunningham on the Safeway Web site that his 14 months with the world's biggest retailer taught him a great deal, including "not to be too in awe of the company" (May 24, 2000). He joined the United Kingdom's Safeway (which bore no relation to the U.S. retailer) as COO in 1999 and three months later had become chief executive. Coincidentally, Wal-Mart owned Asda, one of Safeway's major competitors.

OUTGOING PERSONALITY AND UNIQUE MANAGEMENT STYLE

Criado-Perez—with a reputation of being charismatic, creative, outspoken, personable, enthusiastic, and frank—had been brought on board specifically to revive the ailing Safeway. Sarah Ryle wrote in the *Observer* on November 25, 2001, that a colleague called him "dynamic—one of those people who jollies everybody along"; an analyst said of him, "This is somebody with a vision, and there isn't much of that in this sector." Ryle said that during their interview, Criado-Perez was "answering questions with a fullness that visibly disconcerts his chairman, David Webster, who is perhaps more used to the tight-lipped style of chief executives trained in Anglo-Saxon business." In spite of his outgoing nature, Criado-Perez was uncomfortable with all the attention he attracted, insisting his accomplishments depended on the efforts of his team.

Criado-Perez brought an entirely new marketing style to the United Kingdom's retail food industry. His first tactic was to "buy" customers with what observers called guerrilla tactics. He made deep price cuts on selected products, having heavily invested in extra stock so stores could meet customer demand. In a vision statement on the company's Web site, he wrote, "It was clear to me that we had to deliver these deals in a way which both motivated our store managers and their teams and made it difficult for competitors to respond" (May 24, 2000). He therefore strategically grouped certain stores; ran different promotions in each group for limited periods, which made competition more difficult; and gave individual stores incentives and resources to advertise promotions through distribution of flyers to homes.

When stunned competitors engaged in the inevitable price war, Criado-Perez was prepared with hit squads that descended on rival-supermarket parking lots distributing fliers that urged consumers to demand the advertised discounts. Competitors ran out of stocks within hours. "The tactics achieved legendary status in British retail circles," said Ryle, who noted that the move was merely a business strategy to Criado-Perez (November 25, 2001). Safeway's customer base grew by around 750,000 shoppers every week, and sales volume soared.

PEOPLE-ORIENTED PERSPECTIVE

While impressed, analysts declared that Criado-Perez needed to do more than just cut prices in order to develop a loyal customer base; Criado-Perez agreed. In his vision statement, the highly customer-oriented chief executive explained that his short-term "best deals ever" tactic was just the beginning. Longer-term ambitions were to be the "best at fresh, best at availability, and best at customer service" (May 24, 2000).

Criado-Perez believed success would come only through his staff. He noted in his vision statement that he intended to create an environment in which employees were "passionate about our products, our stores, and everything we do; have an unbreakable will to compete; and have the skills, knowledge and resources to do their best, every day" (May 24, 2000). He gave store managers more autonomy to fine-tune selections to suit their customer base and provided them with crucial store information such as daily profit and loss statements. He decentralized authority to area teams and felt that managers were better informed as a result, with businesses being discussed more openly. He also insisted that members of headquarters management enter stores to see just what shoppers wanted. As a chief executive who actually spent time at the ground level, he said he was impressed and humbled when talking to his staff in their own environment. "They'll make any sacrifice for the company if they are taken care of," he told Cunningham. "British people are very talented but very process-driven. I'm creative and can push. And here if you push, things do happen" (2000).

Criado-Perez's push naturally focused on another group of people as well: shoppers. His long-term goal was to turn shoppers into loyal customers by developing a dialogue with them, responding quickly to their needs, and building their trust, such that Safeway would become customers' first choice for local shopping. He noted that while Safeway was smaller than its three major competitors, scale of operations played no part in this strategy. He believed that leveraging skills and assets drove sales, and doing so had nothing to do with size. His ideas were working: in a statement in Safeway's 2000 preliminary results, Chairman Webster indirectly acknowledged Criado-Perez's influence on the chain's turnaround when he commented, "Safeway has regained its confidence. It is now positioned to grow profits and value for shareholders" (May 17, 2000).

CREATING A SENSUAL SHOPPING ENVIRONMENT

To further gain and retain customers, Criado-Perez aimed to liven up their shopping experience. In 2001 Safeway launched a new-concept store that embodied his vision of that experience. Nigel Cope of the *Independent* said Criado-Perez had never hesitated to express his view that British supermarkets were sadly lacking in "visual merchandising and retail theatre" (January 2001). In this instance, Criado-Perez's idea was to take fresh produce out of its sweaty plastic wrapping, create a continental marketplace, and give customers a more sensual shopping experience.

The innovative prototype store was a success. In a fresh-to-go department at the front of the store, chefs cooked up Chinese meals in woks and threw pizza dough in the air, to the delight of customers. A pasta machine made fresh noodles while shoppers chose their favorite sauces. Lighting and color became a major feature: there was softer lighting in the food-to-go section and spotlights on visually attractive products, giving certain areas the feeling of being a shop within a shop. The beer and liquor section sported dark floor tiles and a vaulted ceiling and offered a broadened selection. "The range extended from £2.99 plonk to a £36.99 Penfolds," wrote Cope (January 2001). In keeping with the "best at fresh" tactic, fruit and vegetables were set off in blocks of color—freed of their plastic wrapping—and upmarket breads as well came out of plastic bags and were put into wicker baskets. Criado-Perez even employed actors to help build staff members' confidence in their ability to interact with customers.

One retail analyst said that the single store in itself was not that important, but it did allow insight into the company's intentions. Cope quoted the analyst as saying, "If Carlos can reproduce this elsewhere then Safeway can become a growth story as well as a recovery story" (January 2001). Safeway's pretax profits increased 10 percent over the last half of 2000 to £166 million. By May 2001 those numbers had increased 30 percent over the previous year to £320 million. Cope commented: "Safeway has achieved a remarkable renaissance since Mr. Criado-Perez joined little more than a year ago" (January 2001). To Criado-Perez, the rennaissance was just the beginning. He planned to add 50 "sensual" stores and seventy "hypermarkets" that would sell everything from TVs to bed and bath goods. He told Cunningham: "I have a great knowledge of retail. And because I have seen so much I often know what will happen next. I can see opportunities" (2000). In the chairman's statement in the 2000 annual company report, Webster wrote, "Since Criado-Perez's arrival he has proven time and again that he is a first-class international retailer with outstanding leadership skills."

BITTER TAKEOVER BATTLE CHANGED OUTLOOK ON LIFE

By the end of 2002, Safeway still lagged behind its three major competitors, Tesco, J. Sainsbury, and Asda. There was also speculation of takeover bids, which became a reality in January 2003 with a bid from Safeway's smaller rival, William Morrison. Not to be left behind, the three rich and powerful competitors and one private investor entered what became a bitter bidding war, which Alex Brummer of the *Daily Mail* called a "web of intrigue that became more complex by the day" (January 17, 2003). Safeway management eventually acknowledged that they could no longer compete independently, and 14 months later Morrison won a £3 billion bid with the help of the Competition Commission, which disallowed bids by the three largest groups on competitive grounds. The ruling had left Morrison as the only truly viable bidder.

Criado-Perez was highly critical of the commission's decision, as were Webster and shareholders. "Ever since I started here," Criado-Perez told Julia Finch of the *Guardian*, "Asda was like a sword of Damocles. We were always wondering when they would jump. We always thought that if we did something, Asda would bid for us" (March 6, 2004). One long-standing shareholder commented that once Asda had been banned from bidding, Morrison was able to get Safeway for a bargain price; another added that the chain had been left with little alternative after the commission's decision. In fact, while waiting many months for the commission to decide on whether the three big companies could bid, Criado-Perez attempted to raise funds to place a buyout bid himself and thus force Morrison to raise its bid.

After the Morrison deal was completed, an emotional Webster told stockholders that they had received the best deal possible under the circumstances, commenting that the regulatory commission had put Safeway in a straitjacket. Some analysts believed, however, that selling the Safeway chain to Morrison may have been Webster's intent all along, as he had obviously brought Criado-Perez on as chief executive to make the chain more desirable. Richard Wachman, reporting for the *Observer*, commented, "The resulting marriage with Morrison is hardly a surprise. Webster and Sir Ken Morrison have often talked about a tie-up over the years. Rivals such as Sainsbury and Asda never had a snowball's chance, as any reading of competition policy would have told them" (February 15, 2004). Wachman noted that hundreds of Safeway employees would lose their jobs in a merger that would make Webster "a millionaire many times over."

Following the close of the deal, Finch reported that a tearful Criado-Perez said, "This has been a life-changing job for me. Until 14 months ago it was a straightforward turnaround job, like others I had done. But since the bidding began, it has taken on a personal dimension. I have learned so much about myself, and I have changed" (March 6, 2004).

Criado-Perez was an excellent tango dancer, a maker of his own bread and soap, a lover of Mozart and Homer, a runner of marathons, and a speaker of seven languages. Most relevantly to the business world, he was a manager who executed maverick strategies while exuding Latin enthusiasm; after Safeway was sold, he left the United Kingdom for the edge of the Atacama Desert in northwest Argentina to ponder his future. "I am very emotional at the moment," he told Finch. "My thinking is all upside down and I need some time and space. I don't think I will retire, but it may be time to do something completely different" (March 6, 2004). His immediate objective was to write a book about his life experiences—not for publication, but for his children.

See also entry on Safeway Inc. in *International Directory of Company Histories.*

SOURCES FOR FURTHER INFORMATION

Brummer, Alex, "Safeway Tangle," *Daily Mail*, January 17, 2003, http://www.thisismoney.com/20030117/nm57976.html.

Cope, Nigel, "Safeway Spices Up Grocery Shopping," *Independent*, January 2001, http://www.accaglobal.com/publications/corpsecrev/35/20590.

Criado-Perez, Carlos, interview by Sarah Cunningham, 2000 Safeway annual report, May 24, 2000, http://www.gardenshed.net/clients/safeway/04_passion_people.html.

———, "Passion, People, Product," 2000 Safeway annual report, May 24, 2000, http://www.gardenshed.net/clients/safeway/04_passion_people.html.

Finch, Julia, "Emotional, Humbled, and £4m Richer, Carlos Makes a Tearful Exit," *Guardian*, March 6, 2004, http://www.guardian.co.uk/supermarkets/story/0,12784,1163551,00.html.

Ryle, Sarah, "Safeway Dances to Latin Beat," *Observer*, November 25, 2001, http://observer.guardian.co.uk/business/story/0,6903,605422,00.html.

Safeway, "Preliminary Results 1999/00," press release, May 17, 2000, http://www.hemscott.com/scripts/AFXnewstory.dll/text?EPIC=SFW&SerialNumber=902&NewsType=AFR&Indate=17/05/2000.

Wachman, Richard, "Don't Get Too Excited, the Boom Isn't Back Yet," *Observer*, February 15, 2004, http://observer.guardian.co.uk/business/story/0,6903,1148167,00.html.

Webster, David, "Embracing Change," 2000 Safeway annual report, May 24, 2000, http://www.gardenshed.net/clients/safeway/02_embracing_change.html.

—Marie L. Thompson

■■■

James R. Crosby

1956–

Chief executive officer, HBOS PLC

Nationality: British.

Born: March 14, 1956.

Education: Attended Brasenose College, Oxford, 1977–1980.

Family: Married; children: three.

Career: Scottish Amicable, 1977–1983, fund manager; 1983–1994, investment director and head of overseas equities; Halifax Building Society, 1994–1996, managing director; Halifax PLC, 1996–1998, director of financial services and insurance; HBOS PLC, 1998–, CEO.

Address: P.O. Box 5, The Mound, Edinburgh EH1 1YZ, Scotland; http://www.hbosplc.com.

■ James R. Crosby attended the Lancaster Royal Grammar School from 1967 to 1974 and studied mathematics at Bransenose College, Oxford, from 1977 to 1980. While at college he worked at Scottish Amicable, a life-insurance company in Glasgow. This educational background and work experience allowed Crosby to become a fellow of the Faculty of Actuaries in 1980. In 1994 he was employed by Halifax Building Society as a managing director and in 1996 became the financial services and insurance director of Halifax. In 1998 he was selected for the post of chief executive officer of HBOS. Although his appointment was initially viewed in neither a positive nor a negative light by the business community in the United Kingdom, many later came to appreciate his creative talents in strategically positioning HBOS to become a leader in the financial sector. In July 2003, HBOS was ranked as the top firm in European financial sales, with revenues of 30.3 billion euros.

THE ROAD TO THE TOP AND THE MAKING OF HBOS

An actuary by training, Crosby applied his considerable skills of persuasion and sound business judgment in acquiring various financial corporations to create a corporate empire that began with Halifax and, with the 2001 merger with the Bank of Scotland, became HBOS. Crosby was a rich, self-made man and an astute, tireless business leader. He was also very well connected socially and, in recognition of his excellent business skills, was asked to join various committees and boards in UK's elite business world. A family man, he was as comfortable helping his wife give birth to one of their children as he was at mediating major business deals, takeovers, and marketing promotions for HBOS.

Crosby was hired at Halifax to set up the life insurance arm of the mortgage bank. His successes at Halifax included the acquisition in 1996 of Clerical Medical, a mutual insurer. According to the *Times*, "James Crosby, the virtually unknown insider, who will ascend into Mr. Blackburn's role, is said to have won his spurs during that acquisition" (London; October 23, 1998). He also successfully battled General Electric to acquire Equitable Life in 2001. The end result of the various acquisitions and business partnerships put together by Crosby transformed Halifax from a successful mortgage bank into a leading financial-services firm with a diversified portfolio that included life insurance, mortgages, and other financial products.

Crosby followed these impressive acquisitions with the defining achievement of his helm, the 2001 merger of Halifax with the Bank of Scotland to create HBOS. This merger created one of the top four banking conglomerates in the United Kingdom. Its chief competitors in the UK included the Royal Bank of Scotland, Lloyds TSB, and JP Morgan Fleming.

LOWS AND HIGHS ALONG THE WAY TO CONTINUED SUCCESS

Europe Intelligence Wire reported in October 2002 that HBOS was in financial trouble, due to some bad loans. The bad loans tarnished the bank's credibility but did not reduce the business influence of its chief executive. For example, in late October 2002 the Financial Services Authority (FSA) appointed Crosby to its panel. According to the *Financial Adviser*, "the practitioner panel was established in November 1998, comprising senior figures from a cross-section of the financial services industry, to provide a high-level body available for consultation on policy by the FSA and able to communicate views and concerns of the regulated industries to the FSA."

Also in November 1998 Crosby was appointed as non–executive director of Granada. Granada is the UK's biggest commercial television broadcaster.

In a matter of a few years, Crosby rose from relative obscurity in the UK's financial world to become one of its wealthiest and most successful bankers. The merger between Halifax and the Bank of Scotland that created HBOS enabled the new corporation to access the mortgage and retail banking markets, respectively, as these were the markets in which the two initial companies were competing in before the merger. Because HBOS gained access to two markets, revenue could be generated from sales across both markets. Cross-selling and also portfolio diversification, or the ability to rely on a variety of products for revenue generation, became emblematic of the way HBOS conducted business after the merger.

STYLE OF MANAGEMENT

Crosby's successes through the years, at HBOS and elsewhere, were due to his strong and well-developed leadership style. He was an energetic and ambitious man. His actuarial background kept him focused on the numbers side of the business, but his successful deal-making skills showed him to be a man of vision, energy, and social acumen. As Jill Treanor reported in the Guardian Unlimited, "Crosby is a bundle of energy as he rushes into an ultramodern meeting room. . . . He refuses to admit fatigue after arduous talks to clinch the purchase of a mutual insurer [Equitable Life] almost very other potential bidder has refused to touch."

Energy, persistence, and intelligence can be sufficient for success, but vision is the added ingredient that can propel a leader and his company to great heights. Even as he apologized to customers over the disruption caused during the merger of the Bank of Scotland and Halifax, Crosby's vision for the future was clearly evident. "We are in the course of achieving a significant extension of the reach and presence of Bank of Scotland as a financial services and business brand in the UK," he remarked (BBC News/Scotland).

Crosby had a strong commitment to customer relations. He criticized other banks, especially the major competitors of HBOS, for taking their customers for granted by offering low interest rates for customer accounts. HBOS was itself criticized for its treatment of its own customers, but this did not diminish Crosby's focus on the needs of his customers and his understanding that the success of HBOS depended on creating and maintaining a strong and loyal customer base.

SOURCES FOR FURTHER INFORMATION

"FSA Rearranges Industry Panel," *Financial Adviser*, October 31, 2002.

"HBOS Boss Apologizes to Customers," *BBC News/ Scotland.* Retrieved from http://news.bbc.co.uk/1/low/scotland/3392217.stm.

"HBOS's Crosby Named Director of UK Finance Watchdog," Reuters, http://uk.biz.yahoo.com/031218/80/ehdvp.html.

Hosking, Patrick, "HBOS Admits to Losses through Lending to Splits," *European Intelligence Wire*, October 7, 2002.

"James Crosby, CEO, HBOS Leads an HRH The Prince of Wales's Seeing Is Believing Visit in Leeds," Business in the Community, http://www.bitc.org.uk/news/news_directory/260603sibnews.html.

Merrell, Caroline, "Halifax Takes the Banking Revolution to Heart," *Times* (London), March 24, 2001.

Miles, Richard, "Blackburn To End 16 Years in Halifax Hot Seat," *Times* (London), October 23, 1998.

Treanor, Jill, "Actuarial Artistry: James Crosby, Chief Executive, Halifax," *Guardian Unlimited*, http://www.guardian.co.uk/business/story/0,3604,435999,00.html.

—Anastasis D. Petrou

■■■

Adam Crozier

1964–

Chief executive, Royal Mail Group

Nationality: British.

Born: January 26, 1964, in Falkirk, Isle of Bute, Scotland.

Education: Heriot-Watt University, BA, 1984.

Family: Married Annette (maiden name unknown); children: two.

Career: Mars Pedigree, 1984–1986, graduate trainee; *Daily Telegraph*, 1986–1988, media salesperson; Saatchi & Saatchi, 1988–1992, media executive; 1992–1994, media director; 1994–1995, vice chairman, joint managing director; 1995–1999, joint chief executive; Football Association, 1999–2002, chief executive; Royal Mail Group, 2003–, chief executive.

Address: Royal Mail Group, 148 Old Street, London, EC1V 9HQ, United Kingdom; http://www.royalmailgroup.com.

Adam Crozier. *Mike Hewitt/Getty Images.*

■ Between 1988 and 1999 Adam Crozier steadily moved up the ranks at Saatchi & Saatchi, a renowned and expanding international marketing and advertising agency. He survived a major shake-up in 1995 caused when the company's founders resigned under pressure and then created a rival agency. Crozier ended his career at Saatchi & Saatchi holding the position of joint chief executive, having helped stabilize, rebuild, and expand the company's client base, despite analysts' predictions of disaster. Starting late in 1999 Crozier served as chief executive of the Football Association, one of Great Britain's two national soccer leagues. At the Football Association, Crozier met with controversy as he successfully began modernizing and reorganizing the institution. By the time he was forced to leave, Crozier had dramatically increased revenue and brought in the first non-English coach of the national England team.

In 2003 Crozier was hired by the Royal Mail Group to provide leadership in its transition from a floundering government monopoly mail and package delivery service to a competitive, modern institution that would be prepared for the government-mandated deregulation that would open the primary British postal market to competing international carriers in 2007. Crozier's strategy and leadership met with as much controversy at the Royal Mail Group as they had at the Football Association and for much the same reason—resistance to change. Crozier was consistently described by coworkers and journalists as well mannered, affable, and low-key in outward demeanor but a tough change agent underneath who valued fairness, pragmatism, and success.

RISING STAR

Crozier came from a tight-knit family. He was the second of three children and the only boy. He played soccer in high school and studied business organization in college at Heriot-Watt, not sure of his career path. Crozier's first noted business experience started at Mars Pedigree pet food, where he worked as a graduate trainee. He later told Andrew Davidson of *Management Today* that it was at Mars that "he learnt about the importance of deciding clear objectives, and plotting how you can achieve them, before leaping into a project." Deciding to try something new, in 1986 Crozier joined the sales division of the Telegraph newspaper group, which had recently been acquired by the Canadian Conrad Black and was undergoing reorganization. Crozier was subsequently rebuked for exaggerating his sales figures, almost losing his job. In the long run Crozier considered the experience a useful lesson in humility. After two years Crozier was hired in 1988 as a low-level media executive by the successful and growing international advertising group Saatchi & Saatchi, then headquartered in London. He took to the work and was promoted repeatedly.

By later accounts Crozier enjoyed his media work and worked hard to acquire new business. Working on a new Sky TV account, he met his future wife, Annette. Together they acquired the account. Although seemingly quiet in demeanor, Crozier was drawn to magnetic personalities at Sky TV and Talk Radio, and they were responsive and friendly.

Clients liked Crozier and, because he was calm, charming, rational, and reassuring during negotiations, requested him in person. Eventually Crozier supervised 35 major international advertising accounts. He rose to the positions of media director in 1992 and vice chairman in 1994. After they were forced out by internal conflict, the company's founders and namesakes created a rival agency that took a substantial portion of the staff and clientele with them. Crozier stayed at the original company and was appointed joint chief executive with Tamara Ingram. He was only 31 years old. "Everyone thought we would collapse like a pack of cards," he later told Lisa Campbell of the trade journal *Campaign*. "No-one predicted that we would come back as London's second largest agency." Crozier and Ingram succeeded by patiently rebuilding the company and restoring its profitability by carefully working with existing clients and adding new ones. Crozier left for a new position in late 1999, less than a year before the French-owned Publicis Groupe bought out Saatchi & Saatchi.

A GOOD KICKING

While at Saatchi & Saatchi, Crozier advised the Football Association on its potential bid for the 2006 World Cup. He loved football (soccer) and often played for fun with the Saatchi clubhouse team. Not too surprisingly, given his success at Saatchi, Crozier was offered the opportunity of leading the English Football Association, which according to its own assessments was in dire need of a competitive marketing strategy and general modernization, especially in light of successes by the Premier League, the rival soccer organization in the United Kingdom.

When he became chief executive of the Football Association in 1999, earning a £300,000 salary, Crozier acted quickly. In his first year he presented a three-year reorganization plan and had it approved; relocated the association headquarters from Lancaster Gate to Soho Square; and replaced more than half of the existing staff, the average age of staff members decreasing from 55 to 32. Crozier replaced the 91-member oversight board with a 12-member committee. Within three weeks of the resignation of Kevin Keegan, the manager of the national England soccer team, Crozier found a replacement: Sven-Goran Eriksson, a successful coach, but from Sweden. Eriksson's appointment met with resistance, but he proved a winner, taking England to the World Cup quarterfinals against Brazil, which eventually won the championship. Crozier also proceeded with plans for the new Wembley National Stadium. As a fellow Saatchi & Saatchi associate predicted to Campbell before Crozier took the job, Crozier also initiated detailed market research and "treated the fan as a customer." Crozier set up the Football Association's first marketing department. Profits from marketing, merchandise, and television and other revenue shot up from an estimated £3 million in 1999 to £125 million in 2001. But Crozier had several critics, such as the Chelsea chairman Ken Bates, who angrily resigned from the Wembley National Stadium board and aired his opposition in the press. Even successful change came at a cost, and under fire by some of the old guard but having done most of what he had set out to do under the reorganization plan, Crozier resigned. He then took on, along with Allan Leighton, the new chairman of the board, the even more daunting task of leading the restructuring of Royal Mail Group.

ROYAL MAIL GROUP

Crozier and Leighton's overall task at Royal Mail Group was to streamline and galvanize the government-affiliated mail and delivery service so that it could meet the challenge of deregulated competition mandated to begin in 2007. The huge organization, operating at or near monopoly status for three centuries, had been losing money. When Crozier took over as chief executive, Royal Mail Group was emerging from the failed experiment of renaming itself "Consignia" and had already announced layoffs of 32,000 employees. Crozier's challenge was daunting: implement a three-year renewal plan affecting more than 200,000 employees while making a profit. Crozier reached out to his employees and began his first week on the job doing postal delivery rounds starting at 4:30 a.m. and explaining the importance of restructuring. "They are absolutely up for change but nobody likes change, change is difficult," Crozier told the Glasgow *Sunday Herald* (June 20, 2004).

At the end of his first full year at Royal Mail Group, Crozier and his management team oversaw a profit. However, with only a 2.5 percent profit margin, the impact of layoffs, and more changes underway, Crozier deferred contractual bonuses for a year. In addition to increasing profit, Crozier emphasized better marketing, streamlining, and improvements in delivery service. As with the United States Postal Service, regular mail deliveries were reduced from two to one per typical day; carrier pricing was changed to reflect the size of envelopes as well as weight; and incentives were planned to give postage discount incentives to businesses that presorted their direct marketing and billing mailings. Crozier and Leighton also negotiated carefully with employee unions, arguing that out of necessity, wage raises and cost-of-living adjustments had to be held to a minimum to retain competitiveness and viability. As with his stint at the Football Association, Crozier's leadership came under criticism, but by mid-2004 many of the changes he had sought were beginning to take effect, well before the 2007 deadline for deregulation.

See also entry on Saatchi & Saatchi plc in *International Directory of Company Histories.*

SOURCES FOR FURTHER INFORMATION

BBC News, "Profile: Adam Crozier," September 17, 2003, http://news.bbc.co.uk/1/hi/business/3115098.stm.

Campbell, Lisa, "Saatchi's Man for a Crisis Accepts the Ultimate Test," *Campaign*, October 29, 1999, p. 18.

Darroch, Valerie, "Post's Modern Male: For the Man at the Helm of the Royal Mail, Experience of a Good Kicking Comes in Useful," *Sunday Herald*, June 20, 2004.

Davidson, Andrew, "Adam Crozier," *Management Today*, December 2000, p. 78.

Lawton, James, "The Monday Interview: Adam Crozier, Chief Executive, Football Association," *The Independent*, August 12, 2002.

Morgan, Oliver, "Can the Suit Deliver?" *The Observer*, September 28, 2003.

—Erik Donald France

■ ■ ■

Alexander M. Cutler

1951–

Chairman, president, and chief executive officer, Eaton Corporation

Nationality: American.

Born: May 28, 1951, in Milwaukee, Wisconsin.

Education: Yale University, BA, 1973; Dartmouth College, MBA, 1975.

Career: Cutler-Hammer, 1975–1977, financial analyst; 1977–1979, business group controller; Eaton Corporation, 1979–1980, division controller; 1980–1982, assembly plant manager; 1982–1985, manager of U.S. Power Distribution Division; 1985-1986, general manager of U.S. Industrial Control and Power Distribution Operations; 1986–1989, president of Industrials Group; 1989–1991, president of Controls Group; 1991–1993, executive vice president of Operations; 1993–1995, executive vice president and COO of Controls; 1995–2000, president and COO; 2000–, chairman, president, and CEO.

Address: Eaton Corporation, Eaton Center, 1111 Superior Avenue, Cleveland, Ohio 44114-2584; http://web.eaton.com.

■ In less than 20 years with Eaton Corporation, Alexander M. Cutler became president, chairman, and chief executive officer of the company that had become the second-largest manufacturer of hydraulic equipment and the largest maker of truck transmissions in the United States. Eaton started out as a provider of automotive parts; Cutler's vision and his ability to act upon that vision made him highly instrumental in the diversification of the company into the multinational manufacture of fluid power systems; distribution and control systems; automotive parts; aerospace equipment; and electrical power quality, distribution, and control systems.

COMPANY GROWTH THROUGH MERGERS, ACQUISITIONS, AND DIVESTITURES

Cutler began his career in 1975 as a financial analyst with Cutler-Hammer. Created in Milwaukee, Wisconsin, in 1893 by Harry T. Cutler (who bore no relation to Alexander Cutler), Franklin S. Terry, and Edward West Hammer, the company first patented a starting box for motors. Through an acquisition, it added rheostats and light dimmers for theaters to its product line and eventually became a pioneer in electricity control. Through further acquisitions and the development of 54 patents, Cutler-Hammer's sales soared from $193,000 in 1900 to $12 million in 1920.

The young Eaton Corporation, which began in 1911 in Bloomfield, New Jersey, when J. O. Eaton, Henning O. Taube, and V. V. Torbensen started the Torbensen Gear and Axle Company, also grew largely through acquisitions. In its first year the company manufactured seven truck axles by hand; six years later it produced 33,000 axles. By 1970 it had undergone more than a dozen mergers and acquisitions, vastly expanding its line of automotive products.

Eaton acquired Cutler-Hammer in 1979—and along with it, Cutler, who became a division controller. He was promoted to manager of the Power Distribution Division in 1982 and general manager of the Industrial Control and Power Distribution Operations for the United States. Before long, Cutler had his eye on Westinghouse, the electric-industry giant that in the late 1800s developed the component that led to alternating current surpassing direct current as the world standard in electricity delivery. In the 20th century, Westinghouse became a nuclear-energy powerhouse, supplying nuclear-generated electricity to the navy, national defense systems, television companies, and the general populace.

Cutler was looking to make Eaton a major player in the electrical-distribution and control industry and was impressed with the strategic directional change Westinghouse had made in that sector during the late 1980s and early 1990s. In January 1994 Eaton merged Westinghouse into its Cutler-Hammer division in what became one of the biggest acquisitions in the electric industry's history. Throughout the 1990s Eaton made 50 acquisitions while divesting itself of 48 less profitable divisions. In 2000 Cutler was named chairman, CEO, and president of the company. By 2004 Eaton boasted 48,000 employees and had manufacturing facilities in more than 20 countries and product sales in more than 50.

A MAN OF ACTION

A brief description of Eaton on the National Leadership Council's Web site declared, "Eaton plays for keeps—if it can't win, it doesn't play," a philosophy clearly evident in Cutler's management style. Robert Sherefkin wrote in *Crain's Cleveland Business*, "Alexander Cutler, the new chief executive officer of Eaton Corporation, has wasted little time shaking up the supplier" (September 11, 2000). After rising to the head of the company, he almost immediately announced plans to sell off Eaton's cockpit-switch business, which manufactured switches used in automobile door locks, mirrors, seats, and windows. Cutler made the decision to sell the business while it was still profitable; its sales the previous year had totaled $330 million. Proceeds from the sale were used to pay off debt or reinvested in the company, allowing Eaton to focus more heavily on its engine and drive-train divisions. Sherefkin wrote that, according to analyst Kent Mortensen of Robert W. Baird & Company of Milwaukee, the probable reason for Cutler's decision was that Eaton had not developed the "critical mass to lead the consolidation of vehicle interiors, where its switches are used. 'So it was fish or cut bait, and they decided to cut bait'" (September 11, 2000).

In his CEO message on Eaton's Web site, Cutler wrote, "Eaton has changed. We have transformed our company from a manufacturer of vehicle components into a diversified industrial enterprise." Cutler always searched for the most lucrative mix of products, acquiring and divesting appropriately in order to achieve that goal. As the demand for cars and trucks decreased, he focused more heavily on the industrial and commercial controls divisions. He led Eaton to take advantage of two huge challenges that the auto industry faced: improving both gas mileage and emission controls. He also readily positioned the company to avail itself of the opportunity that was presented, and missed by many electric companies, when the industry deregulated and the demand for power surged. In an article in *Tirekicking Today*, Cutler was reported as saying, "It's necessary to know what adds true value to a product, and what does not. Who are the value creators and who are the value destroyers?" (September 1998).

GROWTH UNDER HIS LEADERSHIP

After Cutler became chairman and CEO, Eaton spun off its semiconductor-equipment business, which became Axcelis Technologies and of which Cutler became a board member. In a series of moves that evoked images of a game of Monopoly on an international scale, in 2001 Eaton purchased Sumifomo Heavy Industries' 50 percent share in a fluid-power joint venture, which became Eaton's first wholly owned Japanese business. Eaton then sold its Switch/Electronics Division for $300 million and later became Lockheed Martin's primary fluid-power system supplier for the billion-dollar Joint Strike Fighter program. The subsequent additions of several other such contracts brought Eaton's aerospace-industry sales to almost $2 billion within a six-month period. Cutler noted that the Joint Strike Fighter contract in particular was a major win for Eaton, proving that they were forerunners in the research and development of high-pressure fluid-power systems for aircraft.

Attesting to Cutler's vision for streamlining Eaton's product line, the company sold its Navy Controls business in 2002 for $92.2 million; bought the remaining 40 percent interest in its Jining Eaton Hydraulica Company in China; acquired the hose, tubing, and fluid-power systems connector division of Dana Corporation for $130 million; and bought Mechanical Products' line of aerospace circuit breakers. Eaton later won an $84 million contract with the Boeing Company to provide high-pressure hydraulic and other systems for the U.S. Air Force. In 2003 it acquired Commonwealth Sprague Capacitor's power systems and the electrical division of London-based Delta.

When introducing Cutler to a class of students at the Tuck School of Business at Dartmouth College, instructor Sydney Finkelstein noted that one of the major principles in mergers and acquisitions (M&A) was that they must "augment, regenerate, or create new competitive advantages." Finkelstein pointed out that, spearheaded by Cutler, Eaton had done just that and, "as such, represents a great opportunity to see the M&A principle in action."

PERSPECTIVE ON PEOPLE, PRINCIPLES, AND PARTNERSHIPS

In an interview with *Design News*, Cutler stressed the importance of teamwork among design engineers and the need for those engineers to get out of the lab, into the marketplace, and around customers. He said that people who design products for a consumer must know what the consumer wants and understand his problems, and that meeting with customers was not just necessary, it was mandatory. "That's really how you get the creative juices running, and it's how you ensure that you're solving the problems your customers really need solved," he said (March 6, 1995).

During the interview, Cutler said that the rapidly changing environment "puts a tremendous premium on employee speed and flexibility." His philosophy, however, was "simplify first, automate second." Rather than using technology to replace employees, he preferred to use technology as a way to help them become more productive and flexible. When asked by the interviewer how such a huge company could remain efficient, Cutler commented that the most important factor was communication, which meant moving away from the traditional management style and becoming "a facilitator, a coach, a communicator, whatever word you want to use" (March 6, 1995).

Cutler wrote in his CEO Web-site message that while Eaton's business had changed, their principles had not. He noted three fundamental principles he believed helped Eaton grow as a business and its employees grow as individuals: innovation—"We value innovation and change as a source of strength"; impact—"High-performance products, employees, and operations make a positive impact on the world around us"; and integrity—"We care about how we get results." He wrote: "Eaton values, Eaton people, and the power of one integrated operating company are what make us strong. They're also what drives our success."

MANAGING ASSETS AND EDUCATION

Cutler believed that to keep his company on the cutting edge, it was essential to provide its employees with continuing education and efficiently manage its assets. With the goal of transforming his workforce in mind, he was a major proponent of the Eaton Business System, an extensive and sweeping program to systematically monitor the company's assets and employees. Cutler's idea was to remove what he called the "silos," or barriers, from between each business unit in order for managers to learn from each other's experiences.

Eaton University was launched shortly after Cutler's rise to chairman and CEO. It began as an instructor-based management-training program but soon became an e-learning facility. Quickly added to the original e-library was a wealth of material acquired from an outside organization, and general business courses were later added that trained managers to set performance goals, reward employee performance, develop coaching skills, and provide general career development. On the *Alchemy* Web site, Cutler commented that the program was about "capturing the benefits of diversity, scale, and rapid transfer for best practices and turning that into the 'power of one'" (December 3, 2002).

TRIM TO SURVIVE

In the process of keeping Eaton profitable and on the cutting edge, Cutler had the unpleasant responsibility of cutting jobs. Between 2001 and 2002, Eaton closed 34 factories and slashed 12,000 jobs. Even though the cockpit-switch works was only a small part of Eaton's huge Automotive Components Group, its sale eliminated more than four thousand employees in eight plants in North America, South America, and Europe. While Cutler did what he felt was necessary for his company's overall health, he remained aware of the effects it had on individuals. The *Taipei Times* reported that Cutler said in an interview, "When you go through the kind of human trauma that organizations go through when they downsize, there's a very natural tendency to be very, very careful about how you add back resources" (November 4, 2001).

After the general downturn of the U.S. economy in the early 2000s, Cutler announced in 2004 that the previous year had been a very good one. Fourth-quarter earnings in 2003 surpassed expectations, with sales growth of 17 percent and a net-income increase of 70 percent—from $67 million in 2002 to $114 million in 2003.

See also entry on Eaton Corporation in *International Directory of Company Histories.*

SOURCES FOR FURTHER INFORMATION

Cutler, Alexander, "From the CEO," http://web.eaton.com/NASApp/cs/ ContentServer?pagename=EatonCom%2FPage%2FEC_T_ArticleFull&c=Page&c=1007421202658.

———, "Simplify First, Automate Second," *Design News*, March 6, 1995, http://www.designnews.com/index.asp?layout=searchResults&content=all.

Davis, Dan, "Special Online Feature: Learning Lessons, Enterprises Increasingly Turn to E-learning Technology as Part of Strategic Efforts to Broaden Workforce Skills," *Alchemy*, December 3, 2002, http://www.software-strategies.com/Web_First/ss.nsf/ArticleID/DDAS-5F6RYE?OpenDocument&click=.

"Eaton Corporation Molds a Century of History into a $2.4 Billion Electrical Distribution and Control Giant," http://www.eatonelectrical.com/NASApp/cs/ContentServer?pagename=C-H/Common/AssetTemplateLink&c=Apubarticles&c=993227143100&sec=company&uid=Variables.uid.

Finkelstein, Sydney, "Mergers and Acquisitions," http://oracle-www.dartmouth.edu/dart/groucho/tuck_mba_program.syllabus?p_id=MMA.

Flammang, James M., "Automakers Search for Efficiency," *Tirekicking Today*, September, 1998, http://www.tirekick.com/sep98/EFFICIENCSEP98.HTM.

National Leadership Council, http://www.business-linc.org.

Sherefkin, Robert, "New CEO Moving Fast at Eaton," *Crain's Cleveland Business*, September 11, 2000, p. 20.

"Unemployment Rate Soars, Payrolls Fall," *Taipei Times*, November 4, 2001, p. 11.

—Marie L. Thompson

■ ■ ■

Márcio A. Cypriano

1943–

President, Banco Bradesco

Nationality: Brazilian.

Born: November 20, 1943.

Education: Universidade Mackenzie, JD, 1967.

Career: Banco da Bahia, 1967–1973, bank clerk; Banco Bradesco, 1973–1984, branch manager; 1984–1986, department manager; 1986–1988, associate executive officer; 1988–1995, managing director; 1995–1999, executive vice president; 1999–, president.

Address: Banco Bradesco, Avenida Ipiranga 282, 10 andar, CEP 01046-920 São Paulo, Brazil; http://www.bradesco.com.br.

■ A lawyer by training, Márcio A. Cypriano began his banking career in 1967. In 1973 he started working for Banco Bradesco, one of Brazil's most important banks. After more than 25 years of loyal service, Cypriano became president of Bradesco in 1999. Despite expectations that he would not make significant changes at the bank, Cypriano did in fact implement a number of important innovations. Among the key changes were making the bank more open, improving online banking, acquiring stakes in other financial institutions, and increasing the company's profits.

MOVING UP THROUGH THE RANKS

Cypriano did not intend to make banking a career. He graduated with a law degree from the Universidade Mackenzie in São Paulo. He studied law mainly because his father encouraged him to do so. In 1967 he became a bank clerk at the Banco da Bahia in the city of São Paulo. Cypriano told *Euromoney* that "I entered banking provisionally, and I have just reached thirty-one years in the business" (March 1999).

In 1973 Banco Bradesco bought the Banco da Bahia, and Cypriano became manager of a new branch in the old downtown section of São Paulo. He recalled for *Euromoney* that "I got to the branch at five o'clock on a Sunday afternoon and we needed to open on Monday morning. The branch was dirty. Where are you going to get people at 5 p.m. on Sunday to clean a branch that is going to be inaugurated at 7 a.m. the following day?" (March 1999). In order to open on time, Cypriano enlisted his wife and some of the branch employees to clean up.

After becoming branch manager, Cypriano began slowly but surely to work his way up through the company's ranks. In 1984 Bradesco promoted him to department manager, and by 1988 he had become managing director. In 1995 the company rewarded his years of service and hard work by making him executive vice president.

CYPRIANO ASSUMES THE PRESIDENCY

In January 1999 Lázaro Brandão stepped down after 18 years as president of Banco Bradesco. While Brandão stayed on as chairman, he appointed Márcio Cypriano as the new president. Cypriano said that he did not mind sharing power with Brandão, stating that the board of directors would give the bank direction, and as president he would execute the wishes of the board. The outgoing president picked Cypriano in part to his success in running Banco de Crádito Nacional, a Bradesco subsidiary since 1997. Cypriano was the first Bradesco president to hold a university degree.

Because Cypriano had spent so much of his career at Bradesco, most analysts expected him to largely continue the strategies and style of Brandão by concentrating on the middle-banking market, expanding the company's insurance business, and developing a portfolio of minority shares in industrial companies. Cypriano did not change the overall corporate strategy that Brandão had established. He continued Bradesco's emphasis on the middle-to-low-end retail-banking sector rather than going after large corporate clients. As he told *Latin Finance*, "you get more profit from personal business than in corporate business where the spreads are very small." Along with this emphasis on retail banking, he wanted to increase the number of Bradesco customers, setting a goal of 10 million clients by the end of 2000. "Broadening the client base is very important for the bank because we a have a broad range of products for this group. We want to make sure that each client uses all of our products," Cypriano explained to *Latin Finance* (March 2000). Cypriano also continued the Bradesco tradition of emphasizing lifelong ties with both retail and corporate clients. He argued that this long-term support benefits the bank in the end. Customers will return to do all of their banking with Bradesco in appreciation of the bank's loyalty.

Despite expectations that there would be little deviation from tradition, Cypriano instituted a number of significant changes. One of his most important cultural changes was to make Bradesco a more open company. It had a reputation of being secretive, and Brandão had avoided almost all contact with the media and investors. Furthermore, the fact that Bradesco's headquarters were located in a 1950s-style office complex known as Cidade de Deus (City of God) in a distant and unfashionable suburb of São Paulo contributed to the company's reputation for aloofness.

In contrast to his predecessor, Cypriano and his top managers met more than two hundred times with investors and analysts in 1999. Conference calls with analysts became commonplace. The Bradesco president told *Latin Finance* that "the bank did not show itself much before because the market did not demand it. But once the market began to demand it, we reacted and adapted" (March 2000). With Cypriano at the helm, analysts were now able to question senior company officials and look at Bradesco's inner workings. Along with other factors, this new openness contributed to a rapid rise in the value of Bradesco's shares in 1999. Cypriano also applied a personal touch within the bank. He traveled around Brazil to meet the managers at Bradesco's 2,200 branches. He told *Euromoney* that "if you are locked up in your office, you don't know what is happening out there" (March 1999).

Another innovation that Cypriano emphasized after becoming president at Bradesco was online banking. Bradesco was the first Latin American bank to offer Internet banking services. In 1995 the company had about 50,000 online customers. By 2001, 3.2 million clients used Bradesco's Internet banking services. In 2002 Cypriano could boast that one-third of the company's customers used the Internet services, accessing Bradesco's Web site more than one million times everyday. He told *Latin Finance* that "people don't have the time to waste going to banks" (November 2001). In addition to satisfying the needs of clients, the spread of Internet banking also helped Bradesco reduce operating costs.

Cypriano and Bradesco were at the forefront of a wave of online banking that made Brazil a world leader in the area. The bank had put the technology in place in the mid-1990s when the Internet became popular. Then, economic problems in the country led many Brazilian banks to develop electronic systems to clear checks quickly so that customers would not lose money due to inflation; there were times in the 1990s when the Brazilian currency could lose 3 percent of its value in a single day. Cándido Leonelli, a Bradesco executive in charge of Internet banking, told the *New York Times* that "we built up Internet banking not because it was fashionable like in the U.S., but because it created serious value to the customers and thus the bank" (March 25, 2001).

GREATER PROFITS AND ASTUTE ACQUISITIONS

Many analysts and journalists compared Banco Bradesco to a supertanker because it was so big in terms of assets but often slow to change or react. Many investors complained that the company historically was more concerned with size than profits. Indeed, profits had declined in the years prior to Cypriano's appointment as president. Other investors disliked Bradesco's involvement in the insurance business and its heavy investment in industrial assets. By making Bradesco more efficient and making numerous key acquisitions, however, Cypriano helped the bank earn healthy profits.

Cypriano made a number of important acquisitions after taking over at Bradesco. As in the United States and Europe, in Brazil asset management concentrated in fewer banks, with larger institutions buying out their noncompetitive smaller rivals. Cypriano orchestrated the purchase of the Banco Mercantil de São Paulo, the asset-management unit of Deutsche Bank, and the financing business of Ford Brasil. The 2003 acquisition of the asset-management unit of J. P. Morgan placed Bradesco nearly even with the Banco do Brasil as largest bank in terms of asset management. The acquisition of Banco Mercantil in 2001 was especially significant. Banco Mercantil was a small, family-owned bank that catered to Brazil's wealthy. Before Cypriano became president, Bradesco had largely ignored this select clientele. By purchasing Banco Mercantil, Cypriano brought new upper-class retail and corporate clients to Bradesco, marking yet another break with the past. In addition to adding new, high-end customers, Cypriano also made an effort to serve low-income Brazilians. Bradesco opened numerous minibranches in post offices around the country that offered loans to poorer Brazilians, often those involved in the informal economy.

When not working on changes at Bradesco, Cypriano escaped to his large cattle ranch more than 300 miles from São Paulo. Of his cattle-ranching hobby, Cypriano told *Euromoney* that "it only gives emotional return, no financial return" (March 1999).

See also entry on Banco Bradesco S.A. in *International Directory of Company Histories.*

SOURCES FOR FURTHER INFORMATION

Adese, Carlos, "No. 1 Wants More," *Latin Finance*, April 2002.

"Banco Bradesco Grows Sharper and More Nimble," *Latin Finance*, November 2001, p. 38.

Barham, John, "Brazilian Banker Steps Down," *Financial Times*, January 28, 1999.

———, "Stuffy Bradesco Turns on the Charm," *Latin Finance*, March 2000, p. 47.

"Bradesco Expands with Agility," *Latin Finance*, November 2002, p. 24.

Hieronymus, Bill, "Brazil: Sizing up the Competition," *Banker*, April 2003.

———, "Márcio Cypriano," *Euromoney*, March 1999, p. 23.

Lipschultz, David, "Advanced Online Banking, Born of Necessity," *New York Times*, March 25, 2001.

"Modernizer: Márcio Cypriano," *Latin Finance*, July 2003, p. 40.

—Ronald Young

■ ■ ■

David F. D'Alessandro

1951–

Former chairman, chief executive officer, and president, John Hancock Financial Services; former president and COO, Manulife Financial Corporation

Nationality: American.

Born: January 6, 1951, in Utica, New York.

Education: Utica College of Syracuse University, BS, 1972.

Family: Son of Dominick D'Alessandro and Rosemary Pallaria; married Jeannette (maiden name unknown), 1996; children: three.

Career: Daniel J. Edelman, 1972–1974, account supervisor; Control Data Corporation, 1974–1977, information programs manager in service bureau; 1977–1979, commercial manager of data services; Citibank Commercial Services, 1979–1980, assistant vice president; Muir, Cornelius, Moorecq, 1980, marketing representative; Citibank Commercial Services, 1980–1984, general manager of commercial credit; John Hancock Financial Services, 1984–1985, vice president for communications and marketing; 1985–1988, senior vice president for communications and marketing; 1988–1991, president of corporate sector; 1991–1996, executive vice president of retail sector; 1996–2001, CEO and president; 2001–2004, chairman, CEO, and president; Manulife Financial Corporation, 2004, president and COO.

Awards: Marketer of the Year, *Ad Week*, 1986; 50 Best CEOs, *Worth*, 2001; Four Best New CEOs, *Money*, 2001; 100 Most Powerful People in Sports, *Sporting News*, 2002.

Publications: *Brand Warfare: Ten Rules for Building the Killer Brand* (with Michele Owens), 2001; *Career Warfare: Ten Rules for Building a Successful Personal Brand and Fighting to Keep It* (with Michele Owens), 2004.

■ David F. D'Alessandro served as the chairman, chief executive officer, and president of John Hancock Financial Services from 2001 to 2004. He had joined John Hancock's communications and marketing team in 1984, where he successfully revitalized the company's image. Over his 20-year career with the firm he applied his marketing skills in unique ways, increasing the company's growth and competitive positioning in the financial services sector. In April 2004 D'Alessandro spearheaded the merger of John Hancock Financial Services with the Canada-based financial services group Manulife Financial Corporation. Coworkers and analysts described D'Alessandro as a passionate, nontraditional manager who rewarded his employees for innovative ideas, honesty, and integrity.

GAINING EXPERIENCE

D'Alessandro learned the importance of an innovative marketing plan in his first position out of college at the Daniel J. Edelman public-relations firm. As an entry-level employee D'Alessandro felt that the only time an executive noticed him was when he vomited on one of them during a meeting. After realizing that he did not want to be associated solely with such unpleasant experiences, he developed a plan to be recognized for more positive accomplishments.

D'Alessandro studied corporate management structure and found that as an entry-level employee one needed to carve a niche for oneself through the development of a personal marketing plan. At Daniel J. Edelman, D'Alessandro found that his personal marketing plan would center around his development of innovative ideas about tough client problems. For example, one of his early accounts was with Mobil Travel Guides. In order to increase the guides' prestige and recognition, D'Alessandro looked for a unique feature to market—which he found in their often-overlooked practice of giving awards to restaurants that received their highest ranking of five stars.

D'Alessandro expanded the awarding of the prize into a publicity opportunity for the travel guides as well as for the restaurants they honored. By releasing press statements and asking local television food critics to interview the award-winning chefs, D'Alessandro led the award, the restaurant, and the travel guides to become more valuable and glamorous. By extension D'Alessandro himself developed a reputation as an innovative thinker—and was always able to get reservations at the honored restaurants. He expanded the concept of a personal marketing plan for success into the development of a marketing campaign for companies that needed to develop positive reputations among current and potential customers.

In addition to the important lesson learned about the strength of a good marketing plan, D'Alessandro learned a second lesson about truth in the business environment. When applying for a position at Control Data Corporation in 1974, D'Alessandro lied about his age on his resume, making himself two years older. When he was offered the position, he realized that he had to put his true birth date on multiple personnel forms. He admitted to his lie to his new supervisor; the company somewhat reluctantly still hired him on probation.

Through this experience he learned a valuable business lesson: the earlier one admits to a falsehood, the less time it has to increase in size and destroy one's reputation. He found applications of this principle for corporations as well as individuals when looking at the development of "emergency cleanup plans" following the exposure of corporate wrongdoings. In the 1990s D'Alessandro applied this lesson at John Hancock when it was revealed that some agents had used deceptive practices in selling insurance policies. Adhering to the strategy he had conceived, he quickly acknowledged the agents' deceptive sale practices, created an ethics board to review questionable cases, settled the lawsuit filed by irate policyholders, and changed the agents' commission structures.

ALTERING A STODGY IMAGE

D'Alessandro's reputation as a successful advertiser had led John Hancock to hire him to revitalize its corporate image in 1984. In order to develop a successful marketing campaign, D'Alessandro took a close look at the overall goals of the company and developed two strategies with which to convey those goals to John Hancock's existing and potential customers. He directed the marketing team to think of real-life situations that could convey the company's goal of connecting with clients; the team created a marketing campaign referred to as "Real Life, Real Answers." In this campaign short, realistic dramas—such as a brief clip of two brothers talking—were used to convey John Hancock's understanding of clients. The underlying message was that through the development of relationships with individuals, John Hancock could better help with personal financial needs. In 1986, the first year of the ad campaign, Hancock's life insurance sales rose 17 percent, and *Ad Week* magazine named D'Alessandro its Marketer of the Year.

To further boost John Hancock's image, D'Alessandro looked for an event to sponsor; in 1986 he chose the Boston Marathon. In order to attract more world-class runners, the marathon needed to offer prize money to race winners. D'Alessandro pushed John Hancock to back the marathon knowing that the action would make the company somewhat of a hero for its support of a city tradition. John Hancock signed on as a sponsor for 10 years, and the resulting positive press served the firm well.

SHIFTING FROM MARKETING TO MANAGEMENT

In 1988 D'Alessandro was invited to lead John Hancock's group insurance business, which provided insurance plans to companies and organizations. Although he did not have traditional management experience, his capacities to learn and quickly solve problems would make him a successful executive. One New York advertiser who worked with D'Alessandro noted in *Boston Globe Magazine*, "He knows what people want, and it's scary, beyond intuition; his ability to read people is Martianlike, their aspirations, goals, what they hope to attain" (April 16, 2000). Coworkers saw D'Alessandro as a strong, focused leader who worked with his employees to develop and implement innovative ways to increase corporate profits.

By 1991 D'Alessandro had become executive vice president of John Hancock's retail sector, which focused on selling insurance, annuities, and mutual funds to individuals. From 1991 to 1998 net profits in the division increased from $117.3 million to $337.8 million. D'Alessandro helped increase profits through expansion of sales outlets and enhanced comprehension of client needs. He understood that more customers wished to work directly with John Hancock and eliminate local agents as middlemen. Thus D'Alessandro ensured that customers could communicate with the company in a variety of ways, including through direct mail, over the telephone, and on the Internet. When John Hancock's chief executive officer retired in 1996, D'Alessandro took on the title, becoming John Hancock Financial Services' youngest CEO.

SHARING THE EXPERIENCE

In keeping with his background, D'Alessandro found multiple ways to apply his practical knowledge about developing marketing skills. The most visible examples of his outreach were his two books, which were coauthored by Michele Owens. The first book, *Brand Warfare: Ten Rules for Building the Killer Brand*, discussed the need to create and protect a company's image. The second book, *Career Warfare: Ten Rules for Building a Successful Personal Brand and Fighting to Keep It*, served as a primer instructing individuals in navigation through the business world.

APPLYING HIS PRINCIPLES

D'Alessandro's books, public statements, and actions underscored his willingness to speak out about his concerns and offer concrete solutions to solve problems. In 1998 he voiced his deep concern over the scandal involving bribes paid to members of the International Olympic Committee (IOC), cancelling John Hancock's scheduled television advertising for the Olympic Games in Atlanta. In 1998 and 1999, when financial improprieties continued at both the IOC and the

United States Olympic Committee (USOC), D'Alessandro wrote letters in which he provided several concrete suggestions on how to eliminate the IOC's and USOC's financial problems, such as by initiating structural changes and making alterations to business operations. D'Alessandro requested financial audits of IOC and USOC operations and offered funding to help defray the costs, threatening to discontinue John Hancock's sponsorship of Olympic events unless the correct changes to business operations occurred.

D'Alessandro was criticized by the NBC Sports president Dick Ebersol as an attention-seeking bully because of his demands and the accompanying threat of financial withdrawal. D'Alessandro rebutted critics by noting in *Boston Globe Magazine* that he did not want John Hancock associated with the Olympics if the allegiance would conjure up visions of "financial improprieties, questionable business practices, and perpetual instability" among consumers (April 16, 2000). By the conclusion of the battle in 1999 the IOC had made major changes to the ways in which members of the committee could conduct themselves and in which money was spent. Additionally a "Hancock clause" was added, which stated on behalf of the company, "If the Olympic movement conducts itself in a manner that is detrimental to our brand, we can cancel our contract at any time" (April 16, 2000).

MERGERS AND TRANSITION

In 1998 D'Alessandro transformed John Hancock into a publicly traded business, leading its initial public offering. He believed that this move would help the company to stop losing money. By 1999 John Hancock had $126 billion in assets under management and annual revenues of $10.1 billion. Along with the company's increased profits D'Alessandro increased his own salary, making himself one of the highest-paid executives in financial services. His compensation of more than $21 million in 2003 placed him 79th on *Forbes*'s list of best-paid CEOs and increased debate at John Hancock over discrepancies between CEO compensation and shareholder returns.

In 2002 D'Alessandro perceived his company's size to be a vulnerability and began a search for a merger partner that would allow John Hancock to grow from a medium-sized company into a large one, such that it might avoid being marginalized or taken over by industry giants. In 2004 D'Alessandro spearheaded the merger of John Hancock Financial Services with the leading Canada-based financial-services group Manulife Financial Corporation. Upon completion of the merger D'Alessandro became chief executive officer of Manulife, with his stated position being to help lead the integration team. Late in 2004, in order to help smooth the merger of the two companies, D'Alessandro retired as chief operating officer and president of Manulife. He continued to serve as the chairman of John Hancock's advisory board and as a member of the Manulife board of directors in order to oversee John Hancock's charitable and philanthropic activities and to continue to provide strategic direction to Manulife.

See also entry on John Hancock Financial Services, Inc. in *International Directory of Company Histories.*

SOURCES FOR FURTHER INFORMATION

D'Alessandro, David, *Brand Warfare: Ten Rules for Building the Killer Brand,* with Michele Owens, New York, N.Y.: McGraw-Hill, 2001.

———, *Career Warfare: Ten Rules for Building a Successful Personal Brand and Fighting to Keep It,* with Michele Owens, New York, N.Y.: McGraw-Hill, 2004.

Mehegan, David, "Doing It His Way," *Boston Globe Magazine,* April 16, 2000.

—Dawn Jacob Laney

■■■

Eric Daniels

1951–

Group chief executive, Lloyds TSB Group

Nationality: American.

Born: 1951, in Dillon, Montana.

Education: Cornell University, BA, 1973; Massachusetts Institute of Technology, MSc, 1975.

Family: Married (wife's name unknown); children: one.

Career: Citibank Panama City, 1975–1980, corporate banker; Citibank Argentina, 1980–1982, chief financial officer and branch manager; Citibank Chile, 1982–1985, business manager; Citibank Argentina, 1985–1988, country head; Citibank Private Bank of London, 1988–1991, divisional executive; Citibank, 1992–1996, president of West Coast consumer franchise; Citibank Consumer Bank, 1996–1997, regional head; 1998, chief operating officer, consumer finance; Travelers Life & Annuity, 1998–2000, chairman and chief executive officer; Zona Financiera, 2000–2001, chairman and chief executive officer; Lloyds TSB Group, 2001–2003, group executive director, United Kingdom retail banking; 2003–, group chief executive.

Address: Lloyds TSB Group, 25 Gresham Street, London EC2V 7HN, United Kingdom; http://www.lloydstsb.com.

■ Eric Daniels was appointed group chief executive of Lloyds TSB Group in 2003, after spending a year as group executive director of U.K. retail banking. In 2004 Lloyds TSB was one of the largest banks in the United Kingdom, with nearly 80,000 employees and operations in 27 countries. Daniels's extensive banking experience, coupled with his commitment to offering superior value to customers and shareholders, led to early success in his tenure with the company.

CLIMBING THE CORPORATE LADDER

Born in 1951 in Dillon, Montana, Daniels spent his youth in the state, gaining affection for the sports of fly-fishing and shooting. His parents were first-generation immigrants, his mother from China and his father from Germany. Daniels attended Cornell University in Ithaca, New York, and graduated in 1973 with a bachelor of arts degree in history. Two years later he earned a graduate degree in management from the Massachusetts Institute of Technology.

Daniels began his career with Citibank in 1975 and moved steadily up the corporate ladder. He first worked in corporate banking in Panama City, Panama, and then became chief financial officer and branch manager of 15 Citibank branches in Argentina in 1980, business manager of Citibank Chile in 1982, and country head of Citibank Argentina in 1985. Daniels was transferred in 1988 to London, where he acted as divisional executive of Citibank Private Bank, and in 1992 to San Francisco, California, where he was president of Citibank's West Coast consumer franchise. In 1996 Daniels returned to Europe, where he was regional head of Citibank Consumer Bank, based in Brussels, Belgium. Two years later Daniels was promoted to chief operating officer of consumer finance, a position that took him to New York City.

In 1998 Daniels was named president and chief executive officer of Connecticut-based Travelers Life & Annuity, a unit of Citibank formed by the merger of Citicorp and Travelers Group. Daniels's expertise in marketing and building consumer franchises was believed to be an excellent fit to the needs of the organization, despite his limited background in the insurance industry.

Daniels' next move was considered unconventional, considering his 25 years with a well-established banking firm. In 2000 he left Citibank to head Zona Financiera, an Internet start-up company designed to provide financial services information to the Latin American market. "It's never an easy decision to leave a place you've been a part of for a long time," he told David Reich-Hale of *American Banker*, "but I really believe this company is going to succeed" (May 18, 2000). By 2001, however, the company was falling short of Daniels's expectations, and the timing was right for his recruitment by Lloyds TSB Group, which was headquartered in London.

CHIEF POSITION AT LLOYDS TSB

Daniels began his tenure at Lloyds TSB in the role of group executive director of U.K. retail banking. He kept a relatively low profile, however, and thus his installment as chief executive of the company in 2003 took some by surprise. To European analysts and investors Daniels was somewhat of an unknown entity; analysts nicknamed him "the invisible man." The powers that be at Lloyds, however, were well aware of Daniels's extensive financial services background. Maarten van den Bergh, the chairman of Lloyds TSB, told Joanne Hart of *The Times*, "Eric is a fantastic combination of a good manager, with excellent analytical skills, a tremendous sense of reality, a highly developed imagination, and [is] a great leader of people" (December 21, 2002).

The new chief wasted no time in implementing his strategy to improve performance at the company. "Since joining Lloyds, I have refocused the bank around the customer so there is a better balance between shareholder needs and customer needs," Daniels told Hart (December 21, 2002). Daniels's customer-centric approach, along with a series of strategic changes that included selling off operations in New Zealand and Brazil and reducing the number of staff members, led to a 66 percent improvement in annual profits for Lloyds. By the end of 2003 Daniels was optimistic about the company's progress and had "an increasing sense of confidence that we are now building on the foundations that have been put in place for the group to deliver improved performance in 2004 and beyond," he told the *Evening Standard* (December 15, 2003).

PERSONAL QUALITIES

Daniels was described by colleagues and analysts as analytical yet imaginative, realistic yet optimistic, reserved yet charming. Hart and Caroline Merrell of *The Times* wrote, "Daniels appears the most cerebral leader within his industry, with few of the conventional hallmarks of a mainstream UK bank director" (July 4, 2003). Daniels hung a "No Whining" poster in his office, evidence of his uncompromising approach to getting the job done. He received greatest enjoyment from spending time with his wife, who was originally from Panama, and his son, who was born in the United Kingdom. Daniels told Hart and Merrell his ambition was "to be a good person, a good parent, and a good member of society" (July 4, 2003).

See also entries on Citigroup Inc. and Lloyds TSB Group plc in *International Directory of Company Histories.*

SOURCES FOR FURTHER INFORMATION

Chase, Brett, "Citibank Veteran Will Lead Travelers Insurance Division," *American Banker*, March 25, 1999.

Hart, Joanne, "Lloyds Recruits 'Invisible Man' as New Chief," *The Times*, December 21, 2002.

Hart, Joanne, and Caroline Merrell, "New Stage for a Son of the Wild West," *The Times*, July 4, 2003.

"Lloyds TSB Banking a GBP4.35bn Profit," Europe Intelligence Wire, March 8, 2004.

Reich-Hale, David, "CEO of Unit at Citi Quits to Lead Latin Web Firm," *American Banker*, May 18, 2000.

"US Banker Takes Over as CEO at Lloyds TSB," *Euroweek*, January 10, 2003.

"Wary UK Financial Giant Lloyds TSB Shuns Higher-Risk Mortgage Deals," *Evening Standard*, December 15, 2003.

—Stephanie Dionne Sherk

■■■

George David

1942–

Chairman and chief executive officer, United Technologies Corporation

Nationality: American.

Born: April 7, 1942, in Bryn Mawr, Pennsylvania.

Education: Harvard University, BA, 1965; University of Virginia Darden Business School, MBA, 1967.

Family: Son of Charles Wendell (history professor) and Margaret (maiden name unknown); married Barbara Osborn (divorced); children: three.

Career: Boston Consulting Group, ?–1975, management consultant; Otis Elevator Company, 1975–1976; United Technologies Corporation, 1976–1977, position with Otis Elevator Company (subsidiary of UTC beginning in 1976); 1977–1981, general manager of Latin American operations for Otis Elevator; 1981–1986, president of North American operations for Otis Elevator; 1986–1992, president and chief executive officer for Otis Elevator; 1989–1992, executive vice president as well as president of Commercial and Industrial Division; 1992–1994, chief operating officer; 1992–1999, president; 1994–, chief executive officer; 1997–, chairman.

Awards: Order of Friendship for contributions to the Russian economy, Russian Federation, 1999; John R. Alison Award for contributions to national defense by an industrial leader, Air Force Association, 2001; Legion of Honor, government of France, 2002; one of the 50 Best CEOs, *Worth*, 2002; CEO of the Year, *Industry Week*, 2003; Transatlantic Business Award, British American Business, 2003; one of America's Most Powerful People, *Forbes*, 2000–2001.

Address: United Technologies Corporation, United Technologies Building, Hartford, Connecticut 06101; http://www.utc.com.

■ As chairman and CEO of United Technologies Corporation (UTC), an aerospace and building services company based in Hartford, Connecticut, George David broadened the company's holdings, improved its overall financial outlook, increased the value of its shares, and established UTC as a global business leader. He implemented a company-wide commitment to pioneering technology, performance, employee development, social responsibility, and shareholder value. Over David's decade-plus run as chairman and CEO, UTC exceeded many of its rivals, including General Electric, in overall earnings and shareholder return. David was well known for his competitive spirit, but he was just as well known for his philanthropy and for his support of education and the environment.

INTELLECTUAL DEVELOPMENT

David's father, a professor at the University of Pennsylvania and one of America's first Rhodes scholars, was 58 years old when David was born. Although David may not have had the opportunity to partake in the traditional father-and-son outings, his father did share with him his rich intellect. However, despite his abilities, David at first showed no proclivity for learning. He earned only average grades in his first two years at Harvard University. After his second year he took a year off (at Harvard's request) from the physics and chemistry program to work as a technical writer. He returned with greater focus, and his grades rebounded.

After graduating from Harvard and the University of Virginia Darden Business School, David began his career at Boston Consulting Group. One of his clients was Otis, the legendary elevator manufacturer. Hubert Faure, then president of Otis, was so impressed with David that he wooed him away from Boston Consulting in 1975.

MOVING UP THROUGH THE RANKS AT UTC

Otis was acquired by UTC just one year later, and David thought he was out of work. "I was overtitled, overpaid and underexperienced," he recalled to the *New York Times* (November 19, 2000). But he prevailed. In 1977 he became general manager of Otis's Latin American operations. In 1981 he moved up to become president of its North American operations, and in 1986 he was named Otis CEO. That year *Fortune* magazine publicly recognized David's talents, calling him a rising star. Over the next few years David also rose through the ranks of UTC. He served as senior vice president and executive vice president before becoming CEO of UTC in 1994. In 1997 he succeeded Robert F. Daniell as chairman.

Although it is the world's largest elevator producer, Otis is just one of UTC's many corporate holdings. The company's numerous divisions also include Carrier, the number-one manufacturer of heating and air conditioning systems; the aircraft engine manufacturer Pratt & Whitney; and Sikorsky, maker of Blackhawk helicopters.

PUSHING UTC INTO NEW MARKETS

Until David came along, UTC lagged behind in its industry. In the mid-1990s, David initiated a significant restructuring program, ridding the company of secondary businesses and slashing thousands of jobs to cut costs. He also pushed the company into the global arena, seeking opportunities abroad, especially in Russia and China. He expanded the company into Russia in 1995, supplying elevators and aircraft engines to the former Communist country. David spent much of his time traveling between Russia, China, Europe, and Southeast Asia, fostering potential UTC partnerships. Not bound by politics, he visited China just weeks after the government's much-criticized student crackdown in 1989.

In February 1999 David led UTC through a significant restructuring. The company began to move away from the automotive business and increased its concentration in the aerospace industry. To that end, UTC acquired the aerospace-components maker Sundstrand Corporation for $4.3 billion. In March 1999 it sold its automotive-parts business to Lear Corporation for $2.3 billion.

That same year, battered by the declining aerospace industry, David was forced to cut 10 percent of the workforce, or 15,000 jobs. Forty percent of the layoffs were in the company's Pratt & Whitney division. The company also closed 8.5 million square feet of manufacturing and other company space. David said the cuts would save $750 million a year starting in 2002 and would help maintain the company's competitive edge in a difficult economic climate.

The terrorist attacks on the World Trade Center in New York City on September 11, 2001, dealt UTC a serious blow. The downturn in the airline industry that resulted from the attacks hit the aerospace-heavy company squarely in its bottom line. David said the attack truly saddened him, even though he had not known any of the victims. From a business perspective, however, he was determined to do everything he could to win back confidence on Wall Street.

In late 2001 David announced that the company was cutting another five thousand jobs, primarily in the Pratt & Whitney and Sundstrand units. Because UTC was the largest private-sector employer in Connecticut, repercussions from the job cut were felt throughout the state. David faced a lot of criticism. In a letter to David, the Machinists Union decried the move, pointing to the already anxiety-ridden climate in the United States following September 11. "Our children no longer feel safe. How can you decree at such a time that loyal workers from Pratt & Whitney and Hamilton Sundstrand go home and tell these same children, 'I no longer have a job'?" (*Airline Industry Information*, October 17, 2001).

Critics argued that the job cuts were unfair. UTC's profits were up, they said, not to mention the fact that David had just the year before pocketed $22.6 million, mostly from exercising stock options. Some accused him of being emotionless during the massive layoffs, but those who knew him said his coolness was merely a facade. "He dislikes all the trappings of false warmth. He shows his compassion in deeds, not words," Hubert Faure told the *New York Times* (November 19, 2000).

IN PURSUIT OF EDUCATION

One of David's most notable good deeds was to set up a landmark $60 million-a-year employee scholarship program in 1996. The program pays for college tuition, books, and fees (and gives time off) for each UTC employee who wants an education. David even extended benefits for four years to laid-off workers who had been relocated. He also added another incentive: $5,000 worth of company stock to all employees who complete associate degrees and $10,000 worth of company stock to those who complete bachelor degrees or higher.

In the first three years of the program, UTC spent more than $100 million on tuition, fees, and books. As of 2003, 12,000 employees had taken advantage of the program. David said the employee scholarship program was designed to meet his goal of having "the best educated workforce on the planet" (*Chief Executive*, June 1, 2000). The program was also a move to empower employees in an unstable economic climate (as evidenced by UTC's own rounds of layoffs). When David first proposed the program in 1995, other executives thought he was crazy. They believed employees would take their new degrees and use them to benefit other employers. Evidence suggests, however, that employees who go through the program actually become more loyal to UTC, as the turnover rate for these employees has been about one-half that of the overall workforce.

David may have been generous, but he also expected a lot from employees. For example, he constantly asked questions. "He's like a college professor, and you'd better have done your homework," one UTC senior executive told *Industry Week* (January 1, 2003). "It's not that I want to know everything myself about everything. It's that I want to cause others to know everything," David explained in the same article.

Although he was famous for his brevity and clarity, David had an uncanny ability for intellectual discourse, perhaps inherited from his father. He was known to break into erudite discussions of various subjects. At one UTC board meeting, for example, he related Boyle's law, the 17th-century mathematical equation governing the behavior of gases, to the development of fuel-cell technology used in some of the company's products.

David was always highly competitive. "Someone once said that business is bloodless warfare. I confess that I like to compete and I like to win," he is quoted as saying on the United Technology Web site. Given his nature, it is no surprise that he was an avid sailboat racer. In 1999 David and his 50-foot sailboat, *Idler*, led the U.S. team in competition for the America's Cup, coming in third. When asked by the *New York Times* in 2000 whether he ever just went for a cruise in a sailboat, he replied with one word, "Boring." David was also a proficient golfer, making *Golf Digest*'s list of Top 200 Golfing CEOs in 2000.

PUSHING FOR UTC STOCK GROWTH

David was accused of being overly focused on the company's shareholders and, admittedly, stock prices were one of his biggest focuses. During his tenure, he improved the company's products, executed share buybacks, cut costs, and acquired several synergistic businesses because he wanted to maintain a yearly 15 percent growth in earnings per share. In 2002 David boasted that the company had provided a 448 percent total return to shareholders since he had taken over. UTC had even beaten out General Electric.

Part of the success of UTC can be attributed to its strategic acquisitions. In October 2000 David put in a $40 billion bid to acquire the aerospace and materials company Honeywell International. The merger would have significantly enlarged UTC's business and provided a much-needed boost to its aviation-parts business. But David was outbid (by $5 billion) by Jack Welch, General Electric CEO (although the deal was later rejected by European regulators). Never one to be a sore loser, David was reportedly nothing but gracious when he ran into Welch in Florida just a few days after his failed bid.

In August 2004 David launched another acquisition bid, this one successful. UTC acquired Chubb, the London-based electronic security and fire-protection company, for $1 billion. David said Chubb would fit well within UTC's other building services ventures.

In 2003 the commercial aerospace industry was still suffering the repercussions of September 11. However, thanks to the success of its elevator and other service divisions, UTC was able to meet its earnings projections, and David remained ever hopeful that the aerospace industry would make a comeback.

DAVID THE CEO

David always shunned the spotlight, and he complained that CEOs get too much publicity. "You put your head down, do good work, and good things will happen," he told *BusinessWeek* (January 12, 2004). His quotes were rarely big news, and David shied away from the headline-grabbing theatrics of some of his fellow CEOs. David also passed on the traditional corporate monarchy. Instead, he favored a more decentralized structure in which every employee has a voice and openly encouraged disagreement among the ranks.

In the early 2000s, when the CEOs of Tyco, Enron, and other large corporations were facing legal troubles for serious violations, David earned respect for his firm commitment to corporate ethics. In January 2003 *Industry Week* recognized David as CEO of the Year. He insisted that his company keep a spotless record, making no exceptions. In fact, his motto regarding UTC's financial statements was "What you see is what you get" (London *Sunday Times*, April 28, 2002).

David was also a staunch advocate of social responsibility, stating that despite his interest in shareholder value, he was more concerned that his employees work in a safe and healthy environment. He was also a firm believer in corporate responsibility when it came to environmental protection. In 1998 he announced a UTC global conservation program that planned to cut the company's energy and water consumption by 25 percent within a decade. The move was a reflection of the company's commitment to reducing greenhouse emissions at its facilities worldwide.

MOVING INTO THE FUTURE

As 2004 got under way, David described business as good. During the company's annual meeting, he said, "You can hear the cash go by the door" (*Milwaukee Journal Sentinel*, March 22, 2004). At that time UTC was operating at more than two thousand locations in 180 countries, with revenues of $28.2 billion.

However, as UTC moved forward, the 62-year-old David was forced to contemplate another venture, his own retirement. According to company rules, he would have to retire at age 65, but first he would have to find a successor. As of 2004 he was working with the company board to identify an internal candidate. David once told *Worth* magazine that he planned to learn Spanish and French after he retired.

OTHER INTERESTS

As chairman of the U.S.-ASEAN Council of Business and Technology, which promotes trade with Southeast Asian countries, David consistently promoted his belief that international growth depends upon continuing foreign investment. In 1996 he was even prepared to defy U.S. sanctions against Burma because he believed financial involvement would be more effective than sanctions in bringing about change in the Southeast Asian country.

David was a member of the board of directors of Citigroup and the board of trustees of Carnegie Hall. He also sat on the boards of the National Minority Supplier Development Council and the Institute for International Economics and was a member of the Business Council and the Business Roundtable.

A longtime supporter of the arts, David sat on the board of the Bushnell Center for the Performing Arts in Hartford, Connecticut. He was president of the board of trustees at Hartford's Wadsworth Atheneum Art Museum until he resigned in December 2002 because of a disagreement over organizational leadership. David continued to support his alma mater, the University of Virginia, acting as chairman of the Darden School Foundation Trustees and donating $10 million to the graduate school, one of the biggest donations in the school's history.

See also entries on The Boston Consulting Group, Otis Elevator Company, Inc., and United Technologies Corporation in *International Directory of Company Histories.*

SOURCES FOR FURTHER INFORMATION

"The Best and Worst Managers of 2003—The Best Managers: George David," *BusinessWeek,* January 12, 2004, p. 60.

Deutsch, Claudia H., "Even His Soufflés Can't Relax," *New York Times,* November 19, 2000.

McClenahen, John S., "UTC's Master of Principle," *Industry Week,* January 1, 2003, pp. 30–33.

O'Connell, Dominic, "Giant U.S. Engineer Sees No End to Growth," *Sunday Times* (London), April 28, 2002.

Torres, Carlos, "Demand for Durable Goods," *Milwaukee Journal Sentinel,* March 22, 2004.

United Technologies, "Executive Bio: George David, Chairman and Chief Executive Officer." http://www.utc.com/profile/facts/executives/david.htm.

"United Technologies Axes Jobs at Several Units," *Airline Industry Information,* October 17, 2001, p. 60.

—Stephanie Watson

■ ■ ■

Richard K. Davidson

1942–

Chairman and chief executive officer, Union Pacific Corporation

Nationality: American.

Born: January 9, 1942, in Allen, Kansas.

Education: Washburn University, BA, 1965.

Family: Son of Richard Davidson (farmer) and Thelma Rees; married Trish (maiden name unknown); children: three.

Career: Missouri Pacific Railroad, 1960–1966, brakeman and conductor; 1966–1975, assistant trainmaster and various operating department positions; 1975–1976, assistant to vice president of operations; 1976–1982, vice president of operations; Union Pacific Railroad, 1982–1986, various management positions; 1986–1989, vice president of operations; 1989–1991, executive vice president of operations; 1991–1997, president, CEO, and chairman; Union Pacific Corporation, 1997–, CEO and chairman.

Awards: Inducted into Kansas Business Hall of Fame, 2001; Horatio Alger Award, Horatio Alger Association, 2001; named Railroader of the Year, *Railroad Age*, 2003.

Address: Union Pacific Corporation, 1416 Dodge Street, Omaha, Nebraska 68179; http://www.up.com.

■ After a career in the railroad business spanning almost 40 years, Richard K. Davidson became chairman and CEO of Union Pacific Corporation, the United State's leading railroad freight carrier, in 1997. Davidson strove to maintain the railroad's heritage while continuing to modernize and move the company into the future. In 1997 he brought Union Pacific through a much-publicized shipping crisis. As a result of Davidson's investment in technology and focus on customers, the company not only recovered but also thrived. A straightforward Midwesterner with humble roots, Davidson's philosophy centered around the concepts of continuous improvement and solid customer service.

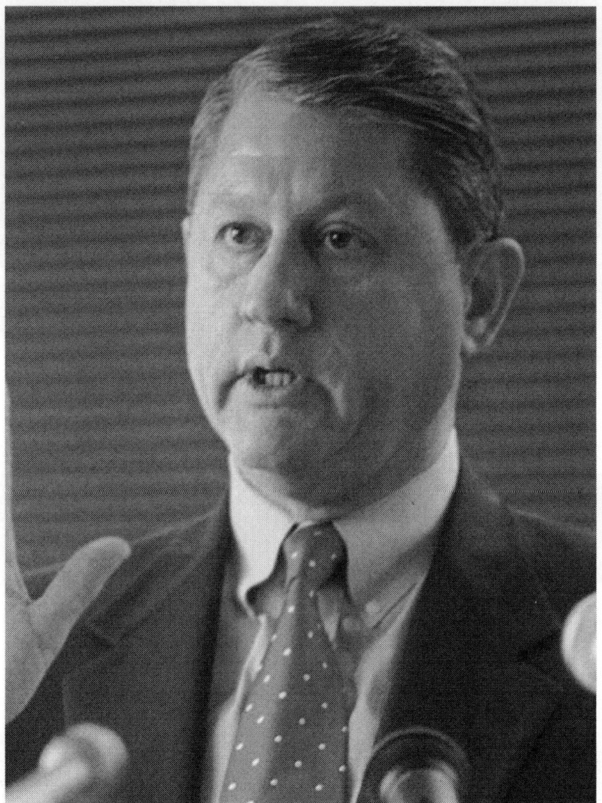

Richard K. Davidson. *AP/Wide World Photos.*

WORKING ON THE RAILROAD

Davidson began his railroad career in 1960. His father had died in 1948, when Davidson was six years old, leaving the family with little money. To pay for college, Davidson took a night and weekend job as a brakeman at a Missouri Pacific railyard.

One of Davidson's most influential mentors was Downing Jenks, the Missouri Pacific chairman. After a huge flood hit Texas, Davidson was up to his waist in water, trying to fix a piece of washed-out track, when Jenks came and stood by his side. "That really set a tremendous leadership example of how you get out and just prove to everybody that you're willing to work as hard as or harder than anyone else in the company," Davidson recalled in *Chief Executive* (January 1, 2004).

In 1966, after graduating from Washburn University in Topeka, Kansas, Davidson accepted a position as an assistant trainmaster with Missouri Pacific in Shreveport, Louisiana. At the time, the railroad was trying to modernize. Davidson helped oversee the railroad upgrade, which was completed in 1971. Davidson was transferred to the company's headquarters in St. Louis in 1975 to assist the vice president of operations, Jim Gessner. When Gessner left in 1976, Davidson, age 34, was promoted to his position. He joined Union Pacific in 1982, when the company merged with the Missouri Pacific and Western Pacific railroads.

In 1987 the Union Pacific president, Mike Walsh, asked Davidson to oversee the implementation of a new corporate philosophy based on the tenets of customer satisfaction and continuous improvement, a philosophy Davidson carried with him throughout his career. He was appointed president and CEO of Union Pacific Railroad in 1991. Only seven weeks later he was named chairman and CEO.

A TRAIN WRECK

In 1997, just after he was named chairman and CEO of Union Pacific Corporation, Davidson was faced with a massive shipping crisis. Labor and locomotive shortages, a string of accidents, and a messy takeover of the ailing Southern Pacific railroad had left Union Pacific trains in gridlock. Coal was not transported to utilities, grain sat rotting in the Midwest, and cars bound for Texas wound up in California. The situation was called, aptly enough, a "train wreck" and was one of the worst transportation crises in U.S. history. All in all, the logjam cost Union Pacific customers $2 billion. The company's stock dropped by nearly half between 1996 and 2000. But Davidson was not afraid to face his critics. He traveled around the country, assuring investors and Wall Street analysts that the company would recover and, even thrive, when people began to realize the benefits of the merger.

Such straight talk was a hallmark of Davidson's persona. A simple man with straightforward values, he preferred hunting quail to attending cocktail parties. "You look at the other CEOs out there and a lot of them are accountants or lawyers," Davidson told *Chief Executive.* "I think it's just my good fortune that I know what I am—a son of toil."

BRINGING ABOUT A UNION PACIFIC RECOVERY

To deliver his promised recovery, Davidson knew that he had to lure back customers. He spent $2.8 billion updating the company's computers and other information technology systems and funneled hundreds of millions of dollars into capital projects. He also decentralized the company, transferring operational power from Union Pacific headquarters to three regional offices and 22 service divisions reporting to those offices. As part of his commitment to customer satisfaction, Davidson rolled out dozens of new services, including the 1-5 Corridor, which expedites freight along Interstate 5 from Seattle to Los Angeles. For a man accused by many of having no vision, Davidson did a lot of forward thinking.

In 1998, just one year after the crisis, Union Pacific cars were rolling smoothly again. In 2002, although the U.S. economy continued to falter, the company had one of the best years in its history. The "33,000-mile factory—with no roof," as Davidson referred to his company in *Railway Age* (January 1, 2003), was growing steadily. By the end of 2003 Union Pacific stock was back up to $65 a share.

Despite his rise to the top of the railroading industry, Davidson never forgot what brought him into the business in the first place. "I still get emotional when I get on a locomotive and listen to those turbochargers kick in," he told *Time* magazine (August 23, 1993). Davidson was due to retire in 2006, and by 2003 he had already started the search for his successor.

In addition to his positions at Union Pacific, Davidson served as the chairman of the Greater Omaha Chamber of Commerce, as a director at Creighton University, and as a member of the boards of the Kroger Company, the Boy Scouts of America, and the Capitol Visitors Center. He also served as chairman of President George W. Bush's National Infrastructure Advisory Board.

See also entry on Union Pacific Corporation in *International Directory of Company Histories.*

SOURCES FOR FURTHER INFORMATION

Frailey, Fred W. "Union Pacific and Its Comeback Kid," *Trains,* November 1, 1998, pp. 24–27.

Galuszka, Peter. "Back on Track," *Chief Executive,* January 1, 2004, pp. 53–55.

Sidey, Hugh. "Hugh Sidey's America: Back at Full Throttle—Leaner, Cleaner, Tougher and Better Managed, America's Freight Train System Is Becoming Competitive Again," *Time,* August 23, 1993, p. 52.

Vantuono, William C. "Railroader of the Year: Union Pacific's Dick Davidson—Managing a 33,000 Mile Factory—with No Roof," *Railway Age,* January 1, 2003, pp. 29–41.

—Stephanie Watson

■■■

Julian C. Day

1952–

President, Kmart Corporation

Nationality: British.

Born: May 14, 1952, in Scarborough, England.

Education: Oxford, BA, 1974; Oxford, MA, 1979; London University, MS, 1979.

Family: Son of Stephen Bradshaw and Gwendoline Adams; married Kathleen Lynn Healy; children: two.

Career: McKinsey & Company, 1980–1985, senior engagement manager; Chase Manhattan Bank, 1985–1987, European development manager, then vice president; Kohlberg, Kravis, Roberts & Company, 1987–1993, executive management consultant; Safeway, 1993–1998, CFO, then executive vice president; Sears, Roebuck and Company, 1992–2002, CFO and executive vice president; Kmart Corporation, 2002–, COO, then president, CEO, and director.

Address: Kmart Corporation, 3100 West Big Beaver Road, Troy, Michigan 48084; http://www.kmart.com.

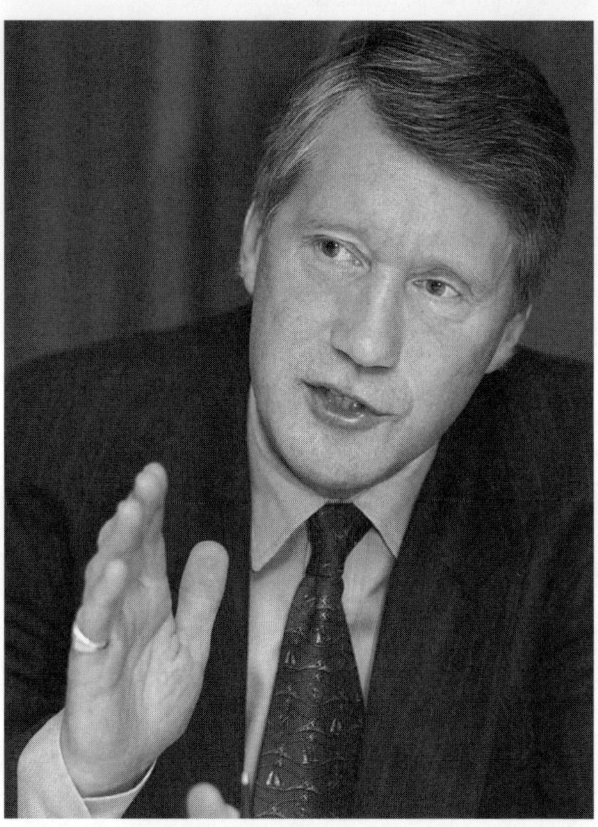
Julian C. Day. *AP/Wide World Photos.*

■ Julian C. Day was appointed as president and chief executive of Kmart Corporation in January 2003 when the board of directors sought their sixth CEO in an eight-year period. With Day at the helm Kmart emerged from bankruptcy through refinancing and store closures. He used back-to-basics strategies to improve the corporate culture, streamline inventory management, and decentralize merchandising decisions in order to tackle the logistical and accounting problems that had caused the largest-ever retail bankruptcy. Stock analysts were hopeful that the surfing, marathon-running, rugby-playing executive would have the discipline needed to whip Kmart back into shape, a task he had accomplished for other companies.

DEVELOPING ENTREPRENEURIAL SKILLS

Day was considered one of the best financial consultants in the retail industry. He developed his reputation after he left Kohlberg, Kravis, Roberts & Company and went to work at the struggling Safeway, whose stock was worth $5 a share when he started and over $40 when he left. His get-it-done attitude and ability to make tough decisions helped him create one of the best performing supermarket chains through the implementation of simple solutions such as the cutting of office costs and the streamlining of the data-processing system. Day stated in *CFO* magazine that he felt that "getting things right in the company is an amalgamation of getting a lot of small things right in the right places" (May 1999).

Day took this attention to detail to Sears, Roebuck and Company, where he was recruited as a turnaround specialist. His work at Safeway had been noticed by James Drury of the chief-executive search firm Drury Partners, who tipped the Sears board off that Day would be "their man"; as reported in the *Detroit Free Press*, Drury called Day an "off the chart smart guy who is able to take his intellectual brilliance into a tough setting and draw upon it" (March 12, 2002). At Sears, Day proved that his grocery-retail skills could be transferred to a company with an assortment of business lines, from clothes to credit cards. While there he created and developed the GlobalNetXchange, which allowed retailers and manufacturers to use the Internet more efficiently as a business-to-business marketplace for buying and selling goods. He also directed cost reductions for the chain of 860 department stores and 2,100 retail outlets. His reputation for "saving the day" was well established by the time he decided to leave. His shared office of chief executive was eliminated by the new president, Alan Lacy; he was ready to test his strength on another challenge.

RESCUING KMART

His reputation led him to be highly demanded by Kmart, which had once been larger than Wal-Mart and would prove to be Day's next renewal project. When he took over, two former Kmart vice presidents were facing federal indictments for overstating the company's revenues by $42.3 million; in May 2002 it was revealed that the 2001 earnings were inflated by improper bookkeeping of rebates and supplier discounts. Through court hearings, shareholders learned that the corruption had spread to the top. The former president Charles Conway had concealed Kmart's sinking finances from the board of directors, had taken part in a plan to cheat vendors, and had been one of 25 large-loan recipients, providing himself with $28.9 million of the company's money.

The company was reeling and by January 2002 had no choice but to file for Chapter 11 bankruptcy. Over three hundred stores were closed in order to liquidate $1.5 million; more than 35,000 workers lost their jobs. Kmart's creditors anxiously pushed for litigation against the corrupt executives. Financial institutions received 40 cents on the dollar against the $1.8 billion in loans, while shareholders received nothing. Everyone hoped that Day would revitalize if not reinvent Kmart's remaining 1,500 stores.

Those remaining locations included many unprofitable stores that Day projected he could turn around within the first year of Kmart's rebirth. He planned to draw on his financial strength to achieve three priorities: The first was to drive same-store sales while keeping a close eye on the overall company profit margin. Monitoring same-store sales was critical because it allowed Day to assess the strength of the stores that had survived the bankruptcy sell-off.

Day also planned to cut expenses while maintaining a high level of customer service and to use inventory and other assets more effectively. He perceived that the company had a solid information system but was not putting it to good use. Ten years had passed since the company had last done a stock-keeping unit rationalization to obtain assortment recommendations and analyze the special-products inventory. Of existing stock 10 percent was thinned out, freeing space for the best-selling products—poor supply-chain management had given Kmart an out-of-stock reputation that could not be afforded in a fierce retail marketplace where customers could easily turn to Wal-Mart and Target.

Part of Day's plan to help the company switch gears was to move away from a top-down management style toward a store-level approach. The new executive management team granted more purchasing power to store-level management, allowing them to customize inventory for their particular communities; they chose from lists of high-volume items in order to match their stores' stocks with local needs. Putting more decision-making power in the hands of individual managers helped keep shelves full and merchandise out of the back rooms, reversing the out-of-stock reputation that had haunted the chain.

While Day's customized approach made sense, critics from Kmart's earlier days were quick to point out that such strategies had been tried in the past. When Super Kmart centers had been planned, attempts had been made to create a new operating culture and shed the out-of-stock stigma; decision making had been decentralized and more choices had been put in the hands of store managers. But in the early 1990s upper management had been stricken with shortsightedness, and support for the changes had been insufficient. Day felt that he was in a position to buck old trends with his new management style. In the first year his performance was closely watched and judged by the price of the company's stock.

Midway through Day's first year as president, Kmart's sales were still falling and its rivals Wal-Mart and Target were still growing. Antsy investors traded the new stock, which had started at $15, when the price dipped to $14.35 so that they could get back money lost in the bankruptcy. Yet Day showed himself to be a long-term thinker—a characteristic that had been lacking in previous Kmart presidents—emphasizing that the company was ahead of its core earnings goal of $75 million for that year. Day offered extra bonuses to encourage demoralized executives to beat the forecasted core earnings. The 2003 adjusted EBITDA (earnings before interest, taxes, depreciation, amortization, reorganization costs, fresh-start valuation charges, restructuring, impairment, and other charges and bankruptcy-related items) was $164 million. This performance helped to earn back investor confidence in that it proved that Day's management abilities were indeed restoring the chain's profitability.

MANAGEMENT STYLE

Kmart's process of recovery was relatively successful due in large part to Day's solid financial grounding. When he took over he announced, "Gone are the days when this company was operated by the seat of its pants with a lot of merchant flair"; he told employees to "picture an internal memo with an image of a cowboy on it with a line through it" (March 2003). He made sure to fill executive openings that had resulted from the scandal following the bankruptcy with new hires that had "financial literacy."

Day worked to build a new culture in the upper management of Kmart that was based on honesty, integrity, discipline, and leadership. He seemed to target the executive level in order to overcome the corruption that had led to the company's downfall. The move away from top-down management was a bold effort to pay closer attention to details at the individual-store level. He stated, "Operating retail stores is all about details. It doesn't matter how smart we are or how good the concept is if we can't execute it" (March 2003). It was his goal to make the chain "customercentric" to woo shoppers back from Wal-Mart.

Cutting costs did not mean cutting the company's support of local communities and national charities. Day continued Kmart's two-decade tradition of sponsoring fundraising campaigns with the March of Dimes. Each year store employees participated in WalkAmerica events; in 2003 Kmart raised $3.5 million to help the volunteer health agency prevent birth defects.

While Day's strategies appeared pragmatic, Drury, who had watched Day's career since Sears, as quoted in the *Detroit Free Press,* saw "real flashes of strategic balance" (March 12, 2002). As president, chief executive, and even chief merchant, Day filled many roles in leading Kmart's recovery.

Listed as one of the top executives in the country in making physical fitness a priority, Day brought his sense of personal discipline into the work environment. He reenergized companies by proving that good discipline created good business habits and a strong company. In addition to his duties at Kmart, Day was also the advisor to several other companies and a member of the board at Petco.

See also entries on Safeway Inc., Sears, Roebuck and Co., and Kmart Corporation in *International Directory of Company Histories.*

SOURCES FOR FURTHER INFORMATION

Bennet, Jeff, "Tough Pro Will Run Kmart," *Detroit Free Press,* March 12, 2002.

"Business: Kmart Ex-VPs Indicted over Accounting," *Facts on File World News Digest,* March 13, 2003.

Hoffman, Gene D., "Will Julian Save the Day?" *Retail Merchandiser* 43, no. 4 (April 2003), p. 38.

Jacobson, Greg, "Day's Turn at Kmart," *Mass Market Retailers* 20, no. 6 (March 24, 2003), p. 1.

"Julian Day Exits Sears," *Women's Wear Daily,* September 25, 2000.

"Kmart and March of Dimes Kick Off 2004 Campaign," Business Wire: Yahoo Finance, March 17, 2004, http://biz.yahoo.com/bw/040317/175698_1.html.

"Kmart's Day, On the Record," *DSN Retail Fax* 10, no. 10 (March 10, 2003), p. 1.

"A New Day for Sears," *CFO,* May 1999.

Tierney, Christine, "Kmart's Toughest Sell," *BusinessWeek Online,* May 5, 2003.

—Margaret E. Gillio

■■■

Henri de Castries

1954–

Chief executive officer, AXA Group

Nationality: French.

Born: August 15, 1954, in Bayonne, France.

Education: HEC School of Management, 1976, undergraduate business degree; law degree; École Nationale d'Administration, graduate, 1980.

Family: Married; children: three.

Career: French Finance Ministry Inspection Office, 1980–1984, auditor; French Treasury, 1984–1989, deputy secretary of the Interministerial Committee on Industrial Restructuring; AXA, 1989–1991, trained in many areas of insurance and then joined the corporate finance division; 1991–1993, corporate secretary; 1993–1997, senior executive vice president; 1997–2001, chairman, AXA Financial (known as The Equitable Companies until September 1999); 2001–, chief executive officer.

Awards: Chevalier de Ordre National du Mérite, 1996.

Address: AXA, 25 avenue Matignon, Paris 75008 France; http://www.axa.com.

Henri de Castries. *AP/Wide World Photos.*

■ In 2001 Henri de Castries, groomed by his dynamic, well-known predecessor Claude Bébéar for over a decade, became chief executive officer (CEO) of AXA, the world's biggest insurer by income and the third-largest investment manager. Clearly de Castries's challenge was to distinguish himself from his former boss as well as to lead his company at a time when the once predictable insurance business was facing challenges from both new technologies and new rivals.

TRADITIONAL BEGINNINGS

De Castries, a descendant of Louis XVI's naval commander, was born in Bayonne in the Basque region of southwestern France to an old noble family whose men had served in the military for several generations. His maternal grandfather and his father played significant roles in World War II and in Algeria and Korea, respectively. De Castries himself served as a paratrooper during his military service. After his preparatory studies at a lycée in Paris, de Castries earned both a business and a law degree. He then graduated at the top of his class at the École Nationale d'Administration, the prestigious school for senior civil servants in Paris whose alumni are known as *énarques*, a term derived from the acronym ENA.

De Castries launched his career in a traditional way at the Finance Ministry Inspection Office, where he audited various government agencies from 1980 to 1984. Then he became deputy secretary of the Interministerial Committee on Industrial Restructuring, overseeing companies that were struggling financially. In 1986 he played a role in privatizing several entities, including TF1, the French national television network. De Castries also supervised the balance of payments for the French Treasury, a notable achievement for a man only in his thirties.

ENTERS THE PRIVATE SECTOR

In 1989, after nine years working for the French government and tiring of the bureaucracy, de Castries met the head of AXA, Claude Bébéar, who was searching for new talent to help him in his ambitious plans for the company. De Castries spent two years training in the field and then became part of AXA's corporate-finance division. With his appointment to the position of corporate secretary in 1991, he managed the legal issues involved in AXA's merger and reorganization with the Compagnie du Midi. Other promotions followed as de Castries assumed greater roles in the numerous acquisitions of the company. While he was the senior executive vice president from 1993 to 1997, his responsibilities began to extend outside France, and he played key roles in AXA's operations in Germany and central Europe.

EXECUTIVE ROLES AT AXA

In 1997 de Castries became chairman of AXA Financial (known as The Equitable Companies until 1999) and led the negotiations for AXA's acquisition of Guardian Royal Exchange. His participation in AXA's global operations increased, and he began to emerge from the inevitable comparisons with the charismatic Bébéar as an important leader in his own right. That year he also played a vital role in acquiring UAP, the second-largest French insurance company, which doubled the size of AXA.

De Castries received praise from many of his colleagues for his problem-solving skills and clear legalistic thinking. His management style was described as consensual, and in an article in *Banker*, Sylvain Hefes, an executive at Goldman Sachs, commented, "Things are achieved by consensus but he [de Castries] is not afraid of being questioned and in that way he is very different from the French establishment." Criticism of the French legal system also contributed to de Castries's reputation as outspoken.

NAMED CHIEF OF AXA

In 2001 de Castries become CEO of AXA, and he was eager to put his own mark on the company. His tenure came at a challenging time for the insurance industry, however, and de Castries stated in an article in *BusinessWeek* that "In a field that has already been leveled by deregulations, we're seeing an entire industrial revolution in financial services."

Although he was quoted in the media as saying he would like to continue building the AXA empire, de Castries acknowledged that his first priority had to be growing the firm internally to make the revenues necessary for more acquisitions. Competition was fierce from companies offering online financial services and others that were gearing up to take advantage of deregulation and woo AXA's key clients in insurance and asset management. So de Castries had to count on his firm's sales force, its greatest asset, to sell high-margin products like mutual funds to AXA's present insurees.

De Castries maintained his stamina by horseback riding on his estate in Anjou in the Loire valley, playing tennis and golf, and hunting and shooting with his family and friends. He also did his share of charitable work as treasurer of AXA Atout Coeur, which encourages employee involvement in community service, and as a board member of the Association pour l'aide aux jeunes infirmes, an organization that helps youth who are disabled.

See also entry on AXA Group in *International Directory of Company Histories.*

SOURCES FOR FURTHER INFORMATION

"A Blue Blood Leading AXA into Battle," *BusinessWeek*, January 31, 2000, p. 25.

Capon, Andrew, "Noblesse Obliged," *Institutional Investor*, January 2001, p. 35.

Clow, Simon, and Charles Fleming, "AXA Chief Sees a Silver Lining," *Wall Street Journal—Europe*, September 17, 2002.

———, "AXA Chief Vows More Acquisitions as Sector Revives," *Wall Street Journal—Europe*, August 13, 2003.

"The Difficulty of Being Dauphin," *Economist*, September 4, 1999, p. 64.

Robinson, Katrina, "Talking Down the Disbelievers," *Banker*, May 1, 2003.

—Anne Lesser

■ ■ ■

Michael S. Dell

1965–

Chairman, Dell Inc.

Nationality: American.

Born: February 23, 1965, in Houston, Texas.

Education: Attended University of Texas, Austin, 1983–1984.

Family: Son of Alexander (orthodontist) and Lorraine D. (stockbroker) Dell; married Susan Lieberman (fashion designer, boutique owner), 1989; children: four.

Career: Dell Computer Corporation, Dell Inc., 1984–2004, chief executive officer; 1987–, chairman.

Awards: Customer Satisfaction Award, J. D. Power and Associates, 1991; CEO of the Year, *Financial World*, 1993; CEO of the Year, *Industry Week*, 1998; Entrepreneur of the Year, *Inc.*, 1998; Chief Executive of the Year, *Chief Executive*, 2001.

Publications: *Direct from Dell: Strategies That Revolutionized an Industry,* 1999.

Address: Dell Inc., 1 Dell Way, Round Rock, Texas 78682-0001; http://www.dell.com.

Michael S. Dell. *AP/Wide World Photos.*

■ Michael Dell defied conventional wisdom—that consumers would not purchase computer equipment over the telephone—and built a billion-dollar company doing just that. Through his direct method of offering low-cost, custom-configured personal computers direct to customers, Dell changed the competitive dynamic of the computer industry. Notable for a natural business talent coupled with a willingness to share power, Dell carried the company through rapid growth and economic difficulties. He innovated operating processes, took risks, learned through his mistakes, and built Dell Inc. from a college dormitory operation to a global corporation. Along the way Dell became one of the wealthiest Americans and the youngest CEO of a company on the Fortune 500 list of largest American companies.

ENTREPRENEURIAL ABILITIES EMERGE

Dell understood the meaning of "business opportunity" early in life, as his mother's profession, stockbroker, frequently raised discussions of business and economic affairs at the family dinner table. So when he began to collect stamps at age 12 and noticed prices rising, Dell recognized a business opportunity. He determined the most profitable way to sell stamps would be to bypass the auctioneer and sell direct to collectors. He compiled a 12-page catalog of his and his friends' stamps and advertised in a stamp collectors' magazine. In this first business venture Dell earned $2000.

Dell further developed his business acumen at the age of 16, when he sold newspaper subscriptions for the *Houston Post.* The inefficiency of cold-calling prompted Dell to find better marketing methods. He determined that the people most likely to subscribe were newly married couples and people who had moved. He obtained lists of marriage license applicants and mortgage applicants then used his Apple II computer to address sales letters to people on these lists. The approach succeeded so well that Dell earned $18,000 the first year and had bought a BMW automobile by the time he went to college. In the back seat of that BMW, Dell carried three personal computers, the seeds of PC's Limited and Dell Computer Corporation.

Dell's fascination with computers began with exposure to a data processor in junior high school then to computers at the local Radio Shack store. After much persuasion, Dell's parents allowed him to use savings to buy an Apple II computer at the age of 15. To the fury of his parents, upon arriving home Dell dismantled the computer to see how it operated. The following year, in 1981, Dell bought an IBM desktop computer and learned how to upgrade and add new components. With insight that IBM-compatible computers would become the choice of business, Dell began to buy, upgrade, and resell personal computers for friends and acquaintances, eventually purchasing components at wholesale rates from distributors. Exposure to the computer industry fostered Dell's desire to start a computer business. In June 1982 he skipped classes for most of a week to attend the National Computer Conference. After saving money to buy a hard disk drive (not standard equipment at the time), Dell communicated with other computer enthusiasts on a bulletin board system and learned how the industry operated. He found dealers sold computers for $3,000 and made $1,000 gross profit, yet he could purchase components for less than $700.

FOUNDING DELL COMPUTER CORPORATION

Dell determined that he could compete with retail computer dealers by selling direct to consumers at a lower price and offering better technical service, but his parents had another idea—that Dell should become a physician. Dell went to the University of Texas at Austin in fall 1983. While he attended to premed studies, Dell continued to upgrade and resell computers, finding customers among students and local businesspeople through word-of-mouth. By the time his parents made a surprise visit in November to address poor class attendance, Dell knew he wanted to compete with IBM. An attempt to be the good son and study premed lasted approximately three weeks, then Dell returned to upgrading computers. In early 1984 Dell registered PC's Limited with the state of Texas and moved to a two-bedroom condominium. Between word-of-mouth referrals and a small advertisement in the local newspaper, PC's Limited sold between $50,000 and $80,000 per month in computers, add-on components, and upgrade kits. The week before final examinations in May 1983 Dell incorporated the company as Dell Computer Corporation with the state-required minimum of $1,000 capital. He never returned to college.

PC's Limited moved to a 1,000-square-foot office, and Dell hired a few people to take and fill orders and upgrade basic machines. Computer sales increased so rapidly that the company outgrew that facility and two larger ones in one year. When the company moved into a 30,000-square-foot facility in 1985, Dell believed the space would never be used. But that year the company began to design and build computers with purchased components. Dell hired an engineer to develop a 286 microprocessor from chip sets, a strategy that simplified computer design. In spring 1986 Dell introduced the fastest personal computer of the time, a 12-megahertz 286 processor. The price of $1,995 compared favorably with IBM's price of $3,995 for a 6-megahertz 286 processor. The machine caught the attention of the news media and garnered excellent performance reviews and a cover story in *PC Week*. Sales exploded to $60 million that year.

Despite speculation that consumers would not want to purchase a technologically complex product over the telephone, Dell succeeded. From the start Dell emphasized a customer focus. Another company could compete on price, but quality products and excellent service would make Dell Computer sustainable over the long term. The advantage of custom configuration and a direct relationship with customers meant that Dell did not have to guess what a customer might want then attempt to inventory and sell preconfigured computers, as the competition tended to do. Parts inventory and computer manufacturing processes were designed for rapid configuration and product delivery in a matter of days. Because the direct model did not allow the customer to see or handle the product, however, in 1986 Dell began to offer a 30-day money back guarantee, a first in the industry. When the company began to pursue corporate business, Dell initiated another industry first in 1986, next-day, on-site service for personal computers in the customer's home or office.

BUSINESS AS AN EXPERIENCE IN HANDS-ON LEARNING

Rapid growth challenged Dell's abilities as a businessman. Although he made many mistakes, Dell credited those mistakes with helping him learn quickly. It was ironic that when Dell made big mistakes, those mistakes conflicted with his most cherished ideas: to manage inventory, to focus on the customer, and to sell direct to the customer.

The first major mistake involved excess parts inventory and led to innovation in high-tech production. Growing at a rapid pace, the company bought as many parts as it could. When technology changed in 1989, however, the company was left with memory chips that could not be used or sold. The company had to raise prices to compensate for the loss, slowing growth. Taking an unconventional approach to problem solving, the company implemented supply process in partnership with vendors. This strategy limited parts inventory, so that when technology changed, Dell Computer could adopt the new technology quickly. During the late 1990s Dell refined supply chain management to less than an eight-day lead, whereas competitors maintained inventory of preconfigured computers for more than 60 days. The vendor relationships worked because Dell shared information and helped vendors stay abreast of technological change.

The second major mistake involved development of the Olympic computer, introduced in 1990 with technology that far exceeded anything in the industry. Customers said they did not need that much technology. While certain elements of the new technology were applied elsewhere, Dell realized he had not communicated with his customers before product development. He learned that slow, incremental change served the customer better.

The third problem involved entry into the retail market in 1990. Once profit and loss analysis by business segment was put into place, Dell discovered that the company lost money in retail. Although retail sales accounted for 10 percent of total sales, and retail sales were growing more than 15 percent industrywide, Dell risked an exit from retail in 1994 and refocused on the direct model. Dell launched www.dell.com that year, introduced online pricing in 1995, and initiated online sales in 1996. Internet sales quickly reached $1 million per day and increased to $50 million per day in 2000. Dell Computer entered the market for servers in 1996 and storage products in 1998, passing the cost savings of the direct model to customers. Again, Dell's direct method, selling servers and storage products directly over the telephone and then via the Internet, defied conventional wisdom.

SEEKING COUNSEL AND SHARING POWER

Unlike many entrepreneurs, Dell learned to relinquish responsibility and share power when he could no longer handle responsibilities himself. He sought the wisdom of experienced executives early in the company's history. In 1986 Lee Walker, a venture capitalist and consultant, joined Dell Computer and established a mentoring relationship with Dell. Dell matured as a businessman when he accepted Walker's decision to fire or demote most of the senior management staff, recognizing the need to find people who could grow into positions of increasing responsibility as the company expanded. Walker encouraged Dell to overcome his shyness as well as his reluctance to take a public role. He persuaded Dell to use his name for the company and its computer brand, a change that took place in 1987 in conjunction with the company's first international foray, to the United Kingdom. Walker brought two high-profile executives to the board of directors, George Kozmetsky, the cofounder of Teledyne, and Bobby Ray Inman, the former chairman, president, and chief executive of Westmark Systems. These executives provided Dell executives with sound advice, particularly as the company made its first offerings of stock—a private placement in October 1987 and a public offering in June 1988.

When rapid growth surpassed the company's ability to provide quality products and service and operate profitably in the early 1990s, Dell sought objective perspectives. First he hired Thomas J. Meredith of Sun Microsystems as chief financial officer in November 1992. Rather than simply pursue rapid growth as a goal, Dell adapted to the need to include data about cash liquidity and profitability into daily decision making. When the company failed to launch quality laptop computer products in 1993, Dell hired John Medica, who had led development of the Apple PowerBook computer. Medica focused on a single product, the Latitude XP computer, which gave Dell Computer its first significant share of the laptop market in 1994. Aware that even a CEO-founder can be removed from position in a public company, Dell approached the board of directors in August 1993 with an outline for improving operations and profitability. He hired Bain & Company to assist with profit and loss analysis and to develop measurements that created responsibility and accountability at the level of each business unit.

In May 1994 Dell hired the former Motorola executive Morton L. Topfer as vice chairman. Topfer's experience in product cycles and management restructuring fit well with Dell Computer's needs for executive leadership. Dell handled products, technology, and general strategy and took a more public role, that of customer relations, dealing with the press, and giving speeches. Topfer handled budget, day-to-day operations, sales, and marketing. The change allowed Dell to spend more time with his growing family, and Topfer brought ideas and discipline to a new emphasis on detailed, long-range planning. A three-year goal of achieving $10 billion in revenue by the end of 1997 was exceeded by $2 billion.

Kevin Rollins, a Bain & Company consultant credited with recommending that Dell Computer cease retail operation, joined the company in 1996 and began to work with Dell and Topfer in the office of chairman in 1997. The three men shared the responsibilities until Topfer left in 1999. Afterward, Dell and Rollins shared responsibilities, working from adjoining offices divided by a glass wall and a glass door that never closed. In 2004 Dell relinquished the CEO title to Rollins, a recognition that Rollins was already functioning in that role, rather than of a change in responsibilities.

MAINTAINING THE ENTREPRENEURIAL SPIRIT IN A GLOBAL CORPORATION

During the company's early years of rapid growth, unconventional thinking and new ideas pervaded the decision-making process at Dell. A simple, informal business process was the consequence and the facilitator of rapid expansion. Employees frequently handled any task needed, such as taking orders when the telephone lines were busy. That salespeople had to set up their own computers cultivated customer service through hands-on experience with the product from the point of view of the user.

As sales rose from the millions into the billions, Dell sought to maintain an entrepreneurial company culture while addressing the needs of a publicly owned, global corporation. Involving more facts and data in the decision-making processes constituted a major adjustment to the free-spirited, entrepreneurial culture of the company. A careful approach involved not pursuing every business opportunity but prioritizing, because growth can occur too quickly and threaten the existence of the company. Rather than pursue every idea, Dell chose to examine ideas more closely in relation to the whole of the company and to develop chosen ideas to their full potential.

While he learned to apply facts to intuitive knowledge and an awareness of risk, Dell encouraged all of the attitudes embodied in the company culture from the start. Open communication and exchange of ideas across all levels of the organization contributed to a flexible, nonhierarchal structure that allowed for quick responses in a constantly changing environment. Dell found employees' spontaneous interactions and candid comments more helpful than planned presentations. A learning attitude accepted failure as essential to the process of taking unconventional approaches to problems, and open-minded self-criticism provided the foundation for innovation.

One way that Dell strove to maintain the intimacy of a small company involved creating manageable business units, beginning in the mid-1990s. Corporate sales divided into small and large companies, then medium-sized companies. International divisions divided into specific markets as sales increased. In 2003 sales to educational institutions segmented into kindergarten through grade 12 and higher education. Segmentation allowed executives to move into positions of manageable, if fewer, responsibilities. The challenge of segmentation involved sustaining a sense of common goals. To unify a large organization of people with diverse responsibilities, Dell believed that each individual needed to understand his or her role in contributing to overall success. Communication throughout the company via e-mail newsletters and posters as well as compensation incentives furthered this goal.

COMPETITIVENESS EXPANDS MARKET SHARE

Although Dell was known to be friendly and approachable, these qualities belied the competitiveness that helped his company become the leading manufacturer of personal computers worldwide. Although he designed the direct method with the intention of competing on price and service, Dell used that competitive edge whenever necessary. In 1992, when industry consolidation threatened smaller operations, Dell initiated a price war. When he introduced servers in 1996 Dell knew that Compaq used high profit margins in servers to offset low margins in desktop computers. He also knew the direct model gave Dell a price advantage.

When economic downturn negatively affected sales of personal computers, Dell initiated another price war, beginning in January 2001, adding aggressive advertising and cost cutting to the strategy. Dell restructured earlier than the competition, reducing the company's workforce by 1,700 in February 2001 and by another 3,000 jobs later that year. Dell also reduced inventory lead time to several hours. Supply trucks held inventory at the dock until needed on the factory floor when the customer paid for the computer. In 18 months the company rose from number five in worldwide personal computer sales to number one. Dell competed directly with Hewlett Packard (HP) by initiating printer sales in 2001. Taking advantage of the atmosphere of uncertainty surrounding the merger between Compaq and HP, Dell cut prices and captured market share. When HP implied possible price increases to offset low profits in 2003, Dell cut prices again and captured market share.

Dell's entry into any product market or geographical market caused prices to decline, a process referred to as "the Dell effect." Industry observers noted that competition on price hindered innovation, as other companies cut research and development costs to remain profitable while Dell relied on suppliers to innovate technology. For Dell, focusing on the customer meant value at low cost with excellent service. While Dell emphasized a focus on the customer rather than the competition, he and his executive team kept their attention on both.

See also entry on Dell Computer Corporation in *International Directory of Company Histories.*

SOURCES FOR FURTHER INFORMATION

Anderson Forest, Stephanie, et al., "The Education of Michael Dell," *BusinessWeek*, March 20, 1993, p. 82+.

"Dell, The Conqueror," *BusinessWeek*, September 24, 2001, p. 92+.

Goldstein, Mark L., "An Industry Legend—At 21," *Industry Week*, April 20, 1987, p. 72+.

Pellet, Jennifer, "Who's Afraid of Michael Dell?" *Chief Executive*, July 2001, p. 29+.

Pletz, John, "Dell Founder Still Hones Instincts 20 Years Later," *Palm Beach Post*, May 16, 2004.

—Mary Tradii

■ ■ ■

Guerrino De Luca

1952–

President and chief executive officer, Logitech International

Nationality: Italian.

Born: September 1952, in Lanciano, Abruzzo, Italy.

Education: University of Rome, BS.

Family: Married Daniela (maiden name unknown); children: one.

Career: Olivetti, 1977–1988, research and development; manager of product development and sales for networking unit; Apple, 1988–1995, vice president of business marketing; 1995–1997, president and CEO of Claris Corporation (subsidiary of Apple); 1997, corporate executive vice president of marketing; Logitech International, 1998–, president and CEO.

Address: Logitech International, 6505 Kaiser Drive, Fremont, California 94555; http://www.logitech.com.

■ Guerrino De Luca had the experience that Logitech needed when he became its president and chief executive officer in 1998: he was an engineer who knew marketing. Under his direction, sales of Logitech products exploded. In 1999, after 19 years in existence, the company sold its 200 millionth mouse; it sold its 300 millionth mouse in 2000, its 400 millionth in 2001, and its 500 millionth in 2002. De Luca led Logitech into new markets such as those of Webcams and game-console controllers, rivaling IBM and Microsoft in the worldwide sales of computer peripherals.

Guerrino De Luca. *AP/Wide World Photos.*

APPLE

De Luca received a bachelor's degree in electrical engineering from the University of Rome. He began his career at Italy's Olivetti, working in research and development and eventually becoming the manager of product development and sales for Olivetti's networking unit. After 11 years at Olivetti, he took a job at Apple, spending most of his time in Paris, where he took charge of Apple's European marketing. In April 1995 he was appointed president of Claris Corporation, a subsidiary of Apple that developed personal software. In the mid-1990s Apple was suffering from net losses and demoralized management, and in February 1997 De Luca was appointed executive vice president of marketing and made responsible for directing Apple's worldwide sales efforts. He worked 18-hour days, seven days a week trying to repair Apple's sales efforts, until he quit out of exhaustion, leaving the company on September 17, 1997.

LOGITECH

Logitech had had problems in the 1990s: when personal-computer sales dipped in 1992, Logitech mouse sales dipped as well, because the company sold its mice primarily to computer manufacturers. Logitech proceeded to sell its European and American factories in order to pay debts, leaving most of its manufacturing to be carried out in China. The then CEO Daniel Borel decided to try to separate Logitech sales from computer sales by emphasizing direct retail markets, producing peripherals that computer owners would buy independently in order to enhance their technological experiences. In spite of Borel's efforts, Logitech continued to suffer from poor marketing strategies until De Luca joined as president and CEO in February 1998, with Borel becoming chairman of the board.

De Luca brought to his work an ebullient personality and a mischievous streak, as well as a talent for mixing comfortably with his employees, which enabled him to learn from workers what was working well and what was not. He quickly made his presence felt at Logitech by reorienting the corporate culture to being consumer rather than technology directed—meaning the company would tout style and special features instead of merely pushing out the latest technological advances. De Luca pushed wireless and optical computer interfaces; he also engineered the purchase in November 1998 of the QuickCam division from Connectix for $25 million, thus increasing Logitech's worldwide share of Webcam sales from 4 to 50 percent. That year Logitech introduced the first computer video camera with a built-in microphone.

From 1998 to 2000 Logitech's stock price quadrupled, and sales grew 30 percent annually. In 1998 Logitech shares were worth $8 each; in August 2000 they were worth $33 each after briefly hitting a high of $39. For fiscal 1999 Logitech grossed $470.7 million, while netting $7.1 million. In 1999 Logitech pressed into the Internet market by introducing iTouch software that enhanced keyboard functionality in navigating the Web. In 2000 Logitech provided Apple with a new mouse to ship with its Macintosh computers; Logitech was in possession of 30 percent of the computer-mouse market worldwide. "You have your hand on your mouse 50 percent of the time you're using the PC. It's about time people paid attention to it," De Luca told *Forbes.com* (August 28, 2000). For fiscal 2000 Logitech grossed $615.7 million, netting $30 million.

In 2001 personal-computer sales dropped 14 percent during a global downturn in the high-tech industry; yet Logitech stock increased 60 percent on sales of $944 million and profits of $75 million. De Luca remarked on *Forbes.com*, "We are in the PC industry but we are not influenced by PC sales" (November 5, 2001). That is, his marketing strategy had successfully persuaded retail consumers to buy Logitech products not as necessary components of new computers but as enhancements for computers they already owned. In 2001, 85 percent of Logitech's income resulted from retail sales, the remaining 15 percent being earned through personal-computer manufacturers. In January 2001 De Luca dyed his hair fuschia before a meeting with Zurich bankers, which he had promised to do if his sales staff met their goals for 2000. The incident solidified his reputation as a good-natured leader. His daughter told him his pink hair was "cool." In 2001 Logitech expanded into the game-console market by introducing a cordless joystick and a steering wheel for Sony's PlayStation 2. In addition, De Luca directed the purchase of Labtech, the manufacturer of computer speakers and headsets.

In 2002 industry analysts and journalists expressed worry over Logitech's expansion into accessories for game consoles and handheld computers, as well as into the manufacture of trackballs, wireless and optical mice, and computer video cameras during a period of lagging computer sales. Yet Logitech achieved a 37 percent gross margin in 2002 while capturing 45 percent of the world computer video camera market and 55 percent of the world trackball market, and it sold over 3 million units of a new line of cordless keyboard-mouse combination. Financial analysts had trouble understanding how Logitech's optical-mouse sales remained strong; De Luca noted that his company's own survey indicated that consumers liked the way the optical mice glowed. He had hired a European design firm to create mice that were not only comfortable in the hand but looked sleek and stylish. Logitech ads showed him smiling and toying with mice that were both functional and beautiful.

In 2003 Logitech reached $1 billion in revenue for the first time. For the fiscal year 2003, Logitech netted $94 million. Still, in *Business Week* De Luca insisted, "We can never afford to think we walk on water" (June 17, 2002), reminding himself that any success could be fleeting. But he seemed to have tapped into an essential truth in marketing: people want beauty in their lives, even in everyday tools such as mice and keyboards, and will pay for it.

See also entry on Logitech International SA in *International Directory of Company Histories.*

SOURCES FOR FURTHER INFORMATION

DiCarlo, Lisa, "Logitech Under the Radar," *Forbes.com,*, November 5, 2001, http://www.forbes.com/2001/11/05/1105logitech.html.

Einstein, David, "Logitech, the Mousemaker That Roared," *Forbes.com,* August 28, 2000, http://www.forbes.com/2000/08/28/feat2.html.

Kanellos, Michael, "Inside Logitech's House of Style," News.com, April 11, 2003, http://news.com.com/2010-1071-996567.html.

Rocks, David, "Company Closeup," *BusinessWeek Online,* June 17, 2002, http://www.businessweek.com.

—Kirk H. Beetz

■ ■ ■

Hebert Demel

1953–

Chief executive officer, Fiat

Nationality: Austrian.

Born: 1953, in Vienna, Austria.

Education: Technical University of Vienna, 1971–1978; PhD, 1981.

Family: Married (wife's name unknown); children: four.

Career: Institute for Combustion Engines and Automotive Engineering, 1978–1984, scientific/engineering assistant; Robert Bosch, 1984–1990, senior manager of ABS/ASR applications and quality assurance; Audi, 1990–1995, senior manager, then CEO; 1994–1997, chairman of the management board; Volkswagen, 1997–2002, president of Brazilian affiliate; Magna Steyr, 2002–2003, CEO and president; Fiat, 2003–, CEO.

Address: Fiat, Via Nizza 250, Turin, 10126, Italy; http://www.fiat.com.

Hebert Demel. *AP/Wide World Photos.*

■ Hebert Demel became the first non-Italian to be hired as the chief executive officer of Fiat in 2003. Demel worked in the automotive industry throughout his entire career, meeting with success at both Audi and Volkswagen before moving on to Fiat. He was able to turn Audi around by turning the company into a key luxury-car producer; there he was known as a team player and a manager who did not give up when problems arose.

AN EARLY START WITH CARS

Demel was born in 1953 in Vienna, Austria, where from an early age he was interested in cars and racing. His parents sent him to a racetrack to do lube jobs for three months in the hopes of turning him away from the automotive industry; their plan backfired, with Demel only growing more interested in car engines and racing. He attended the Technical University of Vienna from 1971 to 1978, earning a mechanical engineering degree. In 1981 he earned his doctorate.

In 1984 Demel gained employment with Robert Bosch in Stuttgart, Germany, where he worked for six years in many different areas, including traction control and transmissions. He also worked on the development of antilock brakes and in quality control.

MOVES TO AUDI, VOLKSWAGEN

In 1990 Demel was hired by Audi to work in Ingolastadt, Germany, as a manager for the development of engines and transmissions. He worked his way up through the ranks, eventually being promoted to president, chief executive officer, and in 1994 chairman of the management board. His work led to Audi's transformation into a manufacturer of premium automobiles.

In 1996 Demel left Audi to become the president of Volkswagen's South American operations in Brazil, where he was responsible for the company's interests in both Brazil and Argentina. He was able to lead the company successfully through an economic crisis in the late 1990s, learning much about the Brazilian automobile market that would prove helpful when he worked for Fiat. While in Brazil, Demel altered management and product structures and was able to uphold Volkswagen's market share through a two-year recession.

MOVES TO MAGNA STEYR

In August 2002 Demel was hired to be the chief executive of Magna Steyr, the Austrian automotive-parts producer; he had wanted the position because he would have the chance to run a company the way he wanted. Magna Steyr hoped that Demel would be able to increase their contract manufacturing, design, and assembly for other car companies. *Time* magazine noted, "Demel brings the expertise of a major car company to what was a mere supplier of drive trains and other components" (December 2, 2002). Demel stayed with Magna Steyr for less than a year before moving to Fiat.

CHIEF EXECUTIVE

Demel became Fiat's CEO in 2003. As noted in *Automotive News Europe,* the company felt confident in hiring Demel "because he had broad experience in the two most important markets for the Italian carmaker: western Europe and Latin America" (October 3, 2003). Upon taking over, Demel faced many challenges; he needed to alleviate debt problems, reorganize the company, and create better business models for the future.

Demel did not bring executives with him from Magna Steyr in order to assist in his restructuring efforts at Fiat. He remarked in *Automotive News Europe,* "I don't conquer companies taking people with me, because I work to get the best out of their own organization"(October 20, 2003). Demel made some immediate changes with respect to positions and company structure but did not comment on his broader ideas when he first began the job.

MAKES CHANGES TO FIAT

Before long Demel made further strategic changes at Fiat. He created new management positions that would report directly to him; he also let some of Fiat's previous top executives go. He hoped that these changes would result in a more cohesive structure and enhanced communication within the company. He wanted all of the top managers to deal directly with him so that he could offer support and immediately learn of any problems.

Demel faced the challenge of leading Fiat into the production of appealing cars with improved function and style by 2007, hoping to introduce up to 20 new models to increase profits. He was confident that he would be able to transform Fiat much as he had previously done with Audi. Demel was a team player who worked through problems to make his companies more successful.

See also entry on Fiat SpA in *International Directory of Company Histories.*

SOURCES FOR FURTHER INFORMATION

Ciferri, Luca, "Demel Won't Take Steyr Team to Fiat," *Automotive News Europe,* October 20, 2003, p. 1.

———, "Fiat Selects Demel for Top Auto Position: Ex-VW Brazil Boss Chosen for Troubled Italian Automaker," *Automotive News Europe,* October 6, 2003, p. 1.

Purvis, Andrew, "Herbert Demel: Chief of Magna Steyr," *Time,* December 2, 2002, p. 67.

—Deborah Kondek

■ ■ ■

Roger Deromedi

1953–

Chief executive officer, Kraft Foods

Nationality: American.

Born: 1953, in California.

Education: Vanderbilt University, BA, 1975; Stanford Graduate School of Business, MBA, 1977.

Family: Married Sandra (maiden name unknown); children: three.

Career: General Foods, 1977–1988, brand manager; Kraft Foods, 1988–1989, vice president, corporate development; 1989–1992, vice president, marketing, grocery products and retail cheese; 1992–1993, executive vice president and general manager, specialty products; 1993–1995, executive vice president and general manager, U.S. cheese division; 1995, executive vice president and area director for France, Iberia, and Benelux; Kraft Foods International, 1995–1998, executive vice president; Kraft Jacobs Suchard, 1995–1998, president, Western Europe; Kraft Foods International, 1998–1999, group vice president and president, Asia Pacific; 1999–2003, president and chief executive officer; Kraft Foods, 2001–2003, co-chief executive officer; 2003–, chief executive officer.

Address: Kraft Foods, Three Lakes Drive, Northfield, Illinois 60093; http://www.kraft.com.

Roger Deromedi. © *Reuters NewMedia Inc./Corbis.*

■ Roger Deromedi worked his way up in the food industry to become CEO of Kraft Foods, the largest food company in North America and the second largest in the world. As co-CEO in 2001 he helped the company go public. When he became CEO in 2003 Deromedi moved quickly to restructure the organization, increase marketing, and streamline its manufacturing processes. A sharp finance man and strategic planner, Deromedi implemented cost-cutting measures using data analysis.

CLIMBING THE FOOD LADDER

Born and raised in California, Deromedi was graduated from Vanderbilt University with a degree in economics and mathematics and earned his master of business administration degree at the Stanford Graduate School of Business. He began his career as an entry-level brand manager at General Foods. When Kraft acquired General Foods in 1988, Deromedi became vice president for corporate development. He was in charge of formulating a strategy for fat-free products.

Founded in 1916 when J. L. Kraft obtained a patent on processed cheese, by 2004 Kraft Foods was operating in 68 countries and had more than 100,000 employees. Kraft products were sold in more than 150 countries and could be found in 99 percent of American households. Cheese remained Kraft's biggest product, automated production facilities producing more than two billion pounds annually.

In the early 1990s Deromedi made his name in Kraft's specialty products and cheese divisions. He began marketing dairy products to niche markets, particularly older consumers, women working outside the home, and children. He boosted sales with low-investment alterations. Deromedi told Sarah Ellison of the *Wall Street Journal*, "We've had great success just slicing our chunks of cheese, or adding reclosable packaging" (May 21, 2004). When low-carbohydrate diets became the fashion, Deromedi changed the cheese labeling. He told Ellison, "The products have always been low in carbs. It's not like we've had to create a whole new something to get at that."

BECOMING CO-CEO

In 1995 Deromedi moved to Kraft Foods International, becoming president and CEO in 1999. He expanded Kraft's overseas operations and integrated more than 30 newly acquired European businesses. In 2001 Deromedi became co-CEO of Kraft Foods along with Betsy Holden. Although their salaries were equal, Holden, as CEO of Kraft North America, was responsible for approximately three-fourths of the company's business. As CEO in charge of Kraft International, Deromedi was responsible for $9 billion in sales and more than 53,000 employees. The management arrangement was unusual, and many analysts considered it unstable. Dennis E. Logue, a management professor at Dartmouth College's Tuck School of Business, told Theo Francis and Shelly Branch of the *Wall Street Journal*, "I think it's a nutso idea. Guys don't get to be CEOs because they like to share" (April 11, 2001). In one of the largest initial public offerings (IPOs) in history, Deromedi and Holden led Kraft's IPO of 16 percent of the company. Kraft's parent company, the Altria Group (formerly Phillip Morris Companies), retained control with 84 percent of the shares.

Kraft had trouble keeping up with the rapidly changing American diet. Betting on the popularity of high-fat snack foods, Kraft bought Nabisco in 2000, just as concerns over obesity and other food-related health issues came to the fore. Consumers demanded more healthful, better-tasting, and more sophisticated foods and were increasingly suspicious of processed foods. Kraft began to buy its way into the gourmet and organic food markets. In July 2003, in response to the threat of obesity lawsuits, Kraft announced that it would promote healthier lifestyles, change some recipes, reduce some single-serving portions, and stop promoting snack foods in schools.

PROMOTED TO SOLE CEO

Kraft continued to lose market share and miss its earnings projections. Holden took the blame. On December 16, 2003, the chairman of the Altria Group demoted her, and Deromedi became the sole CEO of Kraft. In January 2004 Deromedi announced his four-point sustainable growth plan for a leaner, more efficient company. He would invest heavily in "new and improved" brand-name products and advertising while readjusting Kraft's product line to match consumer and demographic trends and expand globally. He would cut costs and improve asset utilization to fund growth and acquire new companies. He announced that over the next three years Kraft would cut six thousand jobs and close 20 of its 197 plants. He also lowered the targets for long-term profit growth.

Deromedi also announced a major restructuring of the company, designed to improve international operations and expand global marketing. The separate international and domestic businesses were reorganized into global product units. Deromedi also launched a new Kraft product line—a special coffeemaker with coffee packets. Many analysts remained skeptical about Deromedi's ability to turn the company around.

MANAGEMENT STYLE

Despite his low-key manner, Deromedi was direct and blunt. Kraft insiders referred to him as "Skeletor" because of his stern and succinct style and his sharp physical features. Deromedi was passionate about work. During his progression to the top, Deromedi was flexible and took advantage of opportunities but was not overly career oriented. As a manager Deromedi rewarded those who focused more on the company than on their careers. He treated employees with integrity and recognized the importance of balancing work and family, particularly when moving executives globally. In 2003 Deromedi told Vic Bhatia and Dyasmin Zarolia of the Stanford Graduate School of Business that the most important thing was to love the job, love the organization, and have fun.

Deromedi defined leadership for Bhatia and Zarolia as "the ability to communicate a vision and gain commitment to it." The vision must be both inspiring and well-grounded in the business. It required effective oral and written communication and listening skills to adapt leadership to employee, supplier, and customer needs. Deromedi believed in supportive mentoring and leadership by example. While respecting local culture, Deromedi claimed that an international business leader was required to promote change. Deromedi was known for attention to detail. James Kilts, his former boss and mentor, told Delroy Alexander of the *Chicago Tribune*: "What he is very good at is taking those complexities and simplifying them so the organization can understand where he's headed. Roger has the ability to see the big picture but to drive right down to the execution level and get it done" (February 10, 2004).

See also entries on General Foods Corp. and Kraft Foods Inc. in *International Directory of Company Histories.*

SOURCES FOR FURTHER INFORMATION

Alexander, Delroy, "Kraft Skipper Making Waves," *Chicago Tribune*, February 10, 2004.

Bhatia, Vic, and Dyasmin Zarolia, "Leadership and Vision Are a Big Part of the Job," *Alumni Profiles*, Stanford Graduate School of Business, http://www.gsb.stanford.edu/news/profiles/deromedi.shtml.

Ellison, Sarah, "Eating Up: As Shoppers Grow Finicky, Big Food Has Big Problems," *Wall Street Journal*, May 21, 2004.

Francis, Theo, and Shelly Branch, "Amid Weak IPO Market, Kraft Is a Big Cheese," *Wall Street Journal*, April 11, 2001.

—Margaret Alic

■■■

Thierry Desmarest

1945–

Chairman and chief executive officer, Total

Nationality: French.

Born: December 15, 1945, in Paris, France.

Education: Ecole Polytechnique, graduate; Ecole des Mines, graduate.

Career: Corps des mines, 1971–1975, engineer; Ministry of Industry, 1975–1978, engineer; Ministry for Economic Affairs, 1978–1980, engineer and technical adviser; Total compagnie française des pétroles (renamed Total in 1992), 1981–1983, director of Algerian operations; 1983–1988, director of Total Exploration and Production (TEP) for Latin American and West Africa; 1988–1989, manager and economic director; 1989–1995, director general of TEP and senior executive vice president; 1995–1998, president and chief executive officer; 1998–, chairman of the board and chief executive officer.

Address: Total, 2 Place de la Coupole, La défense, Paris 92078, France; http://www.totalfinaelf.com.

Thierry Desmarest. *AP/Wide World Photos.*

■ Through his audacious and bold leadership, which many described in compliments as distinctly "un-French," Thierry Desmarest, chief executive officer (CEO) of the oil giant Total, acquired both the Belgian company PetroFina and the French company Elf Aquitaine to make Total the world's fourth-largest oil company in 1999. True to his nickname, *le petit prince* (the little prince), that is, short in stature and big on ideas, Desmarest's next move was rumored to be the creation of a European-based oil company to compete with the big three: Exxon Mobil, Royal Dutch/Shell, and BP Amoco.

EARLY CAREER YEARS

Desmarest graduated from the Ecole polytechnique and the Ecole des mines in his native Paris. For the first 15 years of his career, he worked as an engineer, including a series of technical-adviser posts in New Caledonia for the ministries of economics and industry. After the Socialist François Mitterand became president, Desmarest, who did not care for Mitterand's politics, left the civil service and went to work in 1981 in the exploration and production division of Total compagnie française des pétroles, which shortened its name to Total in 1992.

Desmarest spent his first two years directing the company's Algerian operations. Most noteworthy during his tenure was the addition of oil reserves to the company's assets. In 1983 he became director of Total Exploration and Production (TEP) in French West Africa and Latin America. Five years later he was rewarded for his hard work in those challenging parts of the world with a promotion to director of TEP for both North and South America, France, and the Far East.

JOINS EXECUTIVE TEAM AT TOTAL

After a series of other promotions, Desmarest become president and CEO of Total in 1995. His job was challenging because at the time Total seemed to be losing ground to the other oil giants. But the profile of the company changed when Desmarest made the first bold move of his executive career: a $2 billion deal with Iran to develop the South Pars natural-gas fields. Since the shah was toppled from power in the 1970s, no company in the West had done any serious business with Iran. Desmarest's move was criticized sharply in the United States and elsewhere, although he had the support of the French government.

Desmarest did not back down from his stance, arguing that the United States was hypocritical in its refusal to do business with Iran on human rights grounds while simultaneously pursuing a trade relationship with China and other countries where the same issues were at stake. Total's reputation as an astute and resourceful force in global markets began to grow, and in 1998 Desmarest was named chairman of the board in addition to his title of CEO.

ORCHESTRATES MERGERS WITH PETROFINA AND ELF

The merger of Total with the Belgian oil company PetroFina was only the first part of a scenario that displayed Desmarest's boldness as a leader. Total succeeded in acquiring PetroFina, in which Elf Aquitaine, a French oil company previously owned by the government, also had an interest. According to an article in *Fortune International*, "What followed speaks volumes about the audacity, ruthlessness, and acute sense of timing hiding behind Desmarest's bland exterior."

Desmarest faxed an offer to Philippe Jaffre, the CEO at Elf, in July 1999, only three days after the PetroFina deal was completed. He offered to buy out Elf as well. Stunned by this hostile takeover bid, which was definitely not in the French tradition, Elf board members attempted a counteroffer. By the fall, however, the shareholders had voted for the merger, and Robert Alexander, a former banker and Total board member, admiringly described Desmarest as a "modern chief executive," rather than merely a civil servant who had been handed a top position. According to a *Washington Post* article, Desmarest "is a model of the tough new executives who are now emerging in Europe after decades of genteel corruption and corporate sleepwalking. Friends describe him as a low-key, soft-spoken man whose manner hides a determined, risk-taking approach to business."

DESMAREST PONDERS EFFECTS OF WAR IN IRAQ

Before the U.S.-led war with Iraq began in 2003, it seemed likely that Total would profit hugely from its dealings with the oil-rich country. But France's opposition to the war complicated matters, and Desmarest denied reports that he had made any deals with Saddam Hussein or signed contracts with the Iraqis. The general consensus in the press was that Desmarest was, according to an article in the *Economist*, "one of the best managers in the oil business . . . [who] stresses shareholder value and capital discipline." With Britons and Americans making up one-third of Total's shareholders and the firm's excellent capital returns, Desmarest's leadership of Total seemed secure.

See also entry on TOTAL S.A. in *International Directory of Company Histories.*

SOURCES FOR FURTHER INFORMATION

"Desmarest: Less Acquisitive," *Weekly Petroleum Argus*, February 25, 2002, pp. 8–10.

Ignatius, David, "Rival Tycoons," *Washington Post*, July 14, 1999.

"It's Not Easy Being French; Face Value," *Economist*, April 5, 2003.

"Oil CEOs Discussing New Guidelines on Booking Reserves," *Oil Daily*, February 23, 2004.

"Thierry Desmarest," *BusinessWeek*, June 11, 2001, p. 32.

Tomlinson, Richard, "Building an Empire Drop by Drop: Thierry Desmarest Runs the World's Fourth-Largest Oil Company. He Wants to Be a Supermajor. The Last Thing He Needs Is a War in the Middle East," *Fortune International* (Asia edition), October 15, 2001, p. 76.

—Anne Lesser

■ ■ ■

Michael Diekmann

1954–

Chairman and chief executive officer, Allianz

Nationality: German.

Born: December 23, 1954, in Bielefeld, Germany.

Education: Göttingen University, 1982.

Family: Married; children: three.

Career: Diekmann/Thieme, 1983–1988, CEO; Allianz, 1988–1989, executive assistant to the head of the Hamburg regional office; 1990, head of sales at the Hamburg Harburg office; 1991–1992, head of the Hannover office; 1993, head of customer relationship management for private customers; 1994–1995, head of sales for the North Rhine–Westphalia region; 1996–1997, director of insurance management for the Asia-Pacific region; 1998–2003, member of the Allianz management board; 2002–2003, responsible for Central and Eastern Europe, the Middle East, Africa, the Americas and group human resources; 2003–, chairman and CEO.

Publications: *Wildnis Privat—Der Ratgeber für Kanutouren in Kanada*.

Address: Allianz AG, Königinstraße 28, D-80802, Munich, Germany; http://www.allianz.com.

Michael Diekmann. *AP/Wide World Photos.*

■ Michael Diekmann headed up the Asia-Pacific and North America business arms of Allianz until 2003, when devastating losses at the German insurance giant led to the resignation of the CEO, Henning Schulte-Noelle. Diekmann stepped into the position and moved quickly to fix the ailing company. He cut noncore businesses, reduced staff, and raised capital. Within a year Allianz was back in the black and poised to become a world leader in the insurance market.

EARLY ADVENTURES IN PUBLISHING

Michael Diekmann studied law and philosophy at Göttingen University in Germany. After graduating in 1982, he headed up his own publishing business, Diekmann/Thieme, which produced adventure travel books. He wrote and published his own book describing his experiences on canoe trips through the Canadian wilderness. But in 1988, tired of competing with the big publishing houses, he left Diekmann/Thieme and took a job with Allianz as executive assistant to the head of the company's Hamburg office.

STARTING OUT WITH ALLIANZ

Diekmann rose quickly in the company, becoming head of the Hamburg Harburg sales office in 1990 and head of sales for the region of North Rhine–Westphalia in 1994. In 1996 he moved to Singapore to head up Allianz's Asia-Pacific region. Two years later he was given a seat on the Allianz management board. In the Pacific he turned losing subsidiaries into profitable businesses through acquisitions and through the introduction of a new infrastructure and new pricing models.

In 2002 Diekmann became head of Allianz's insurance businesses in the Americas. In the United States he faced a huge challenge with the consistently underperforming U.S. Fireman's Fund. Diekmann slashed thousands of jobs and cut relations with unprofitable vendors. He also centralized and streamlined operations and pumped more money into the ailing subsidiary. He then focused on insuring more profitable clients, such as commercial and marine properties, agribusinesses, and wealthy homeowners. Although the Fireman's Fund was not completely healed, Diekmann put it on the road to recovery.

"Michael was instrumental in allowing us to get traction," Jeff Post, Fireman's Fund CEO, told *Institutional Investor* magazine (February 2004). "He puts the right people in place and then makes sure that they deliver. If they don't, he will take action." But even as Diekmann was turning around Allianz businesses, the company as a whole was struggling. In 2002 Allianz was hit hard by big losses from recently acquired Dresdner Bank's investment division. Also devastating were the September 11 terrorist attacks, destructive flooding in Europe, and huge asbestos claims from the U.S. Fireman's Fund. Altogether, Allianz lost $1.45 billion, its first loss since World War II.

RISE TO CEO

In 2003 the company underwent a great deal of turnover. In March, the Dresdner Bank CEO Bernd Farholz stepped down from his post in the midst of significant losses and severe job cutting. Then in April the Allianz CEO Henning Schulte-Noelle stepped down, turning over the reins to Diekmann. Diekmann, a much more aggressive manager than his predecessor, introduced several radical changes to bring his company back. He slashed costs by cutting employees (more than 15,000 at Dresdner Bank), eliminated noncore businesses, increased capital through a $5 billion rights issue, and established tough profitability targets to turn around the company's subsidiaries. In less than a year Diekmann was able to bring Allianz back into the black (profits neared $2 billion in 2003) and increase share prices significantly.

Diekmann's charm and open management style won over Allianz employees, many of whom had grown weary of the closed-door approach of his predecessor. Analysts also praised his track record in turning around underperforming subsidiaries, as he did in the United States and Australia.

A Frankfurt senior investment banker well acquainted with Diekmann said that the word describing his colleague best was "Schonungslosigkeit" (ruthlessness). "It is an unbending, uncompromising bloody-mindedness, and it is very much regarded as a virtue," he told *Institutional Investor* magazine (February 2004).

As of 2004 Diekmann was still trying to fix Dresdner Bank while moving closer to his goal of making Allianz a global force in the insurance industry and a serious rival to the insurance leader American International Group. In addition to his responsibilities at Allianz, Diekmann was a member of the boards of BASF, Linde (deputy chairman), and Lufthansa.

See also entry on Allianz AG in *International Directory of Company Histories.*

SOURCES FOR FURTHER INFORMATION

Capon, Andrew. "Back to Basics: Tough, Disciplined, Intensely Focused, Allianz's CEO Michael Diekmann Is Putting His Haus in Order," *Institutional Investor*, February 2004, pp. 20–28.

Fairlamb, David, "Can Diekmann Plug the Leaks in Allianz?" *BusinessWeek Online*, December 30, 2002, http://www.businessweek.com/magazine/content/02_52/b3814065.htm.

Tomlinson, Richard, "Insurance for Dummies: It Doesn't Take a Genius to Figure Out that Allianz Has a Big Problem. Now It Is New CEO Michael Diekmann's Turn to Come Up with a Solution," *Fortune International* (Asia Edition), May 26, 2003, p. 42.

—Stephanie Watson

■■■

William Dillard II

1945–

Chief executive officer and chairman of the board, Dillard's

Nationality: American.

Born: June 16, 1945.

Education: University of Arkansas, BSBA, 1966; Harvard University, MBA, 1968.

Family: Son of William T. Dillard (deceased founder of Dillard's) and Alexa (homemaker; maiden name unknown); married Mandy (maiden name unknown).

Career: Dillard's, 1968–1973 (position unknown); executive vice president, 1973–1977; president and chief operating officer, 1977–1998; chief executive officer, 1998–; chairman of the board, 2002–.

Address: Dillard's Department Stores, 1600 Cantrell Road, Little Rock, Arkansas 72201; http://www.dillards.com.

■ William Dillard II began his career in 1967 at Dillard's, the company his father, William T., had founded in 1938 in Little Rock, Arkansas. Dillard's is known as an upscale department store chain and by 2004 ranked number three in the United States, with Dillard family members owning 99 percent of the voting stock and electing two-thirds of the company's directors.

William Dillard II was named executive vice president in 1973, rising to the position of chief executive officer by 1998. He made his mark on the company almost immediately through the introduction of computers in the 1970s. Dillard took the company through its largest acquisition with the $3 billion purchase of Mercantile Stores Company in 1998. Despite criticism from industry analysts that they risked becoming a discount chain, Dillard's also initiated its own brand of clothing in 2002 to help reduce debt while increasing sales. Dillard was criticized for not being aggressive enough in slashing prices when inventory did not sell and possessing a weaker management style than his father. He and his younger brothers adamantly refused to sell the company despite falling sales and stock prices and open criticism from nonfamily stockholders.

INHERITING THE GOOD AND BAD FROM A FAMILY-OWNED BUSINESS

Dillard grew up as the oldest son of a retailing pioneer. At the time of his birth, Dillard's had been operating for seven years. Dillard's father ran the company with an iron fist and groomed all five of his sons to take over management roles as they came of age. After receiving degrees in business from the University of Arkansas and Harvard, Dillard immediately began working for the family business, where he received all of his retail training under the watchful eye of his father.

Many critics of Dillard's noted the family's penchant for keeping the status quo and not allowing anyone else into the family's inner circle of running the business. In 1991 *Forbes* referred to the family as insulated and private.

Even though the company went public two years after Dillard began working there, its structure remained a dual-class stock, where the family owned the majority of voting stock yet retained a small percentage of the company. In 2000 the Dillard family owned 10 percent of the company but held 99 percent of the voting stock. They also kept control of the board by placing family members on it. The elder Dillard held the chairman's position until 1998, when he turned over the reins to his eldest son.

As the retailing market changed in the 1990s, Dillard remained loyal to his father's example of holding on to inventory and waiting too long to mark down out-of-season items. When the company began losing profits steadily each quarter by the end of the decade, however, Dillard began to introduce new strategies in an effort to reduce debt and bring Dillard's back to the retail giant once dubbed in 1991 a company with "profit margins that would knock your eyes out" (as quoted in *Forbes*, September 18, 2000).

DILLARD MAKES STRIDES WITHIN THE INDUSTRY

Dillard made his mark in the company by introducing data processing as early as 1973, when he became the executive vice president. Dillard's was at the forefront of computerizing purchase orders. Dillard was also praised for being a computer whiz long before other companies began using computers.

In 1998 Dillard made a surprising move for the company, which had typically bought stores on the cheap. He made a bid for Mercantile Stores in 1998 for $3.1 billion in cash. Dillard won the bid, but analysts claimed the company paid too much, which caused Dillard's to accumulate a high level of debt. Dillard ended in-store promotions and stopped an easy-going return policy at Mercantile Stores. Both of those customer-friendly policies had been the hallmark of Mercantile. By 2002 *Arkansas Business* noted that the acquisition was disappointing and resulted in damaging the company's stock price. Dillard blamed the poor performance on losing time to consolidating Mercantile Stores into Dillard's.

Dillard began in 2002 to make up for the Mercantile purchase by selectively buying one store at a time in malls where businesses had exited or closed. In some locations, this gave Dillard's two anchor stores within one mall, each one specializing in different departments. Dillard called this "a doubleheader." Dillard's led the industry with these doubleheader stores, with two anchor stores in 50 different malls by May 2002.

The ownership of real estate by Dillard's continued to be the company's strong point as it struggled to keep pace with the changes in the retail industry. Analysts noted that investors seemed more interested in the land holdings than in sales when profits plunged in 2002 and 2003. Experts noted not only that Dillard has continued to make wise decisions on real estate but also that the location of the properties has been a positive for the company. By 2001 Dillard's owned 75 percent of its stores, making it a company with a strong book value, unlike other chains that lease most of their stores.

DILLARD STARTS A PRIVATE LABEL

With discount retailers taking business away from the mall-oriented stores such as Dillard's by the end of the 1990s, Dillard began making decisions that seemed aggressive compared with the strategies previously employed by the company. Developing a private brand of merchandise led to a rise in sales by 2002. When the brand was first introduced, many thought it would hurt Dillard's by making the stores more of a discount chain; others felt the move would improve sales. One industry insider said that Dillard's started its private-label program before many other chains, which helped them get a boost on the competition. Dillard was praised for offering customers a choice between the core brands and their own brand, which was discounted. Other analysts said that consumers are obsessed with known brand-name labels and criticized Dillard's for attempting to give consumers something they did not want to buy.

Dillard told shareholders in 2002 that the company sought the perfect balance between the known labels and private ones. By 2003 the strategy had paid off, with the private label steadily increasing its profits to 18.2 percent of total store sales. However, the old problem left over from the elder Dillard continued to plague the company. Large amounts of inventory and huge markdowns hit the gross profit margins hard. Insiders said the markdowns were so drastic because Dillard waited too long to make the decision to discount the overabundant inventory at the end of the season. Dillard's became desperate to move the merchandise and slashed prices too low. Despite increasing sales of the private label, this other strategy left the company in a sales slide by mid-2003.

Along with its private label, Dillard also instituted a policy to help move merchandise faster at the end of the season. The movement of items out of the store helped stabilize the profit margins. Dillard increased the private-label merchandise and negotiated up-front vendor allowances. *Forbes* noted in 2000 that Dillard's had made strides with these decisions. Dillard closed unprofitable stores while reducing staff. *Arkansas Business* said in 2002 that these new strategies had finally taken hold to improve the net income despite dropped net sales. Dillard said in a press release, "We consider our accomplishments in the fourth quarter [fiscal year 2002] to be solid affirmation that we are on the right track with our strategies" (March 11, 2002).

PRIVATE EVEN WITH STOCKHOLDERS

Dillard's career cannot be separated from the successes and failures of the company. Critics often lambasted the man and the company for the lack of communication with the media, industry analysts, and shareholders. *Forbes* noted in an article in 2000 that Dillard refused to be interviewed for the story. He made it a policy never to comment on criticisms and speculations regarding the company.

One of the shareholders did speak to *Forbes* for the article, complaining about management's lack of response to written requests for information. Thomas Jackson, a managing director of Prudential Investment Corporation, was the second-largest shareholder in 2000, owning 9.2 percent of Dillard's stock. Jackson told *Forbes* that even though he was disgusted with what he perceived as arrogance, he held on to his stock, hoping Dillard would make the decision to sell the company.

When the founder of Dillard's died in 2002, many insiders speculated that his son would make the decision either to sell or to make significant changes in the policies governing the company. The speculation occurred because the elder Dillard was seen as the spiritual guide of the company despite his son's appointment as CEO in 1998. An editorial in *Arkansas Business* in 2002 said that even Wall Street was betting the heirs would sell the company. Dillard, although reticent to speak to the media, had sent word through friends that the family remained committed to Dillard's and entertained no ideas of selling.

Dillard said he kept shareholders informed on the company's status at the annual meetings and held conference calls with investors and any other interested parties, the media included, on a regular basis. He issued a statement after the *Forbes* piece came out, noting that what some refer to as "snubbing" he called "fair disclosure." By 2003, however, investors were concerned that Dillard had not participated in the last four conference calls held, despite the investors' request that Dillard be present. Robert Buchanan, an analyst for A. G. Edwards, told the America's Intelligence Wire on September 9, 2003, "In the interest of the shareholders he [Dillard] should sell the company." Analysts blamed Dillard's lack of forthrightness as one of the reasons that forecasting the earnings of the company was nearly impossible. This secretiveness kept Wall Street wary.

MANAGEMENT STYLES

Analysts praised Dillard and his hands-on style of management during his early years as president. Nothing reached the floor for sale until Dillard had made a decision about it. In 1983 Dillard was praised for creating market dominance for the company through his computer system, which led to higher efficiency. However, criticisms regarding management's conservative approach to change began to surface despite the innovation in tracking merchandise through computerized files.

What had once worked for Dillard's in the 1980s no longer helped, because the nature of retail stores changed in the 1990s. Dillard made some adjustments, but he remained steadfast to his father's original strategies even with dire predictions from industry analysts as of 2004.

As Dillard began to change strategies toward private-label brands and real-estate acquisition, profits fluctuated for the decade from 1994 to 2004. When the elder Dillard died in 2002, speculation that Dillard and his brothers would sell the company created ups and downs in stock valuations. While the changes Dillard instituted did help profit margins, some of the same criticisms of management's style remained.

Forbes magazine charged in 2000 that Dillard hung on stubbornly to the belief that the family could handle the downturn in sales. The magazine said Dillard lacked his father's business sense. In 2003 analysts said that sales fell because the company had waited too long to lower prices on summer stock. By 2004 Moody's Investors Services expressed anxiety over the value of Dillard's performance and its ability to recover.

See also entry on Dillard Department Stores, Inc. in *International Directory of Company Histories.*

SOURCES FOR FURTHER INFORMATION

"Dillard's Dogged by Charges of Dull Management Style: Founder's Son Told to Sell the Company," America's Intelligence Wire, September 9, 2003.

Friedman, Mark, "Dillard's Brand Strategy Has Supporters, Critics," *Arkansas Business,* November 25, 2002, p. 1.

Halkias, Maria, "Chief of Dillard's Says Company Not for Sale," *Dallas Morning News,* May 21, 2002.

Kroll, Luisa, "Bargain Bin," *Forbes,* September 18, 2000, p. 52.

Whitsett, Jack, "Dillard's Strategy Begins to Show," *Arkansas Business,* March 11, 2002, p. 10.

—Patricia C. Behnke

■■■

Barry Diller

1942–

Chief executive officer and chairman, InterActiveCorp

Nationality: American.

Born: February 2, 1942, in San Francisco, California.

Education: Attended University of California, Los Angeles, 1961.

Family: Son of (a store owner) and Reva Addison (a receptionist); married Diane von Furstenberg (a clothing designer), 2001.

Career: William Morris Agency, 1961–1966, began in mailroom and became junior agent; American Broadcasting Company (ABC), 1966–1968, assistant to the vice president in charge of television programming; 1968–1969, executive assistant to the vice president in programming and director of feature films; 1969–1971, vice president for feature films and program development; Circle Entertainment (a division of ABC), 1971–1973, vice president (feature films, miniseries, and movies of week); ABC Entertainment, 1973–1974, vice president for prime-time TV; Paramount Pictures Corporation, 1974–1984, president and chairman of the board; Gulf & Western Entertainment and Communications Group, 1983–1984, president; Twentieth Century–Fox Film Corporation, TCF Holdings, 1984–1985, chairman and CEO; Fox, 1985–1992, chairman and CEO; QVC Network, 1992–1995, chairman and CEO; Silver King Communications, 1995–1998, chairman of board of directors and CEO; Home Shopping Network, 1996–1998, chairman of board of directors and CEO; InterActiveCorp (formerly USA Networks), 1998–, chairman and CEO; Vivendi Universal Entertainment, 2002–2003, chairman and CEO.

Address: InterActiveCorp, 152 West 57th Street, New York, New York 10019–3310; http://www.iac.com.

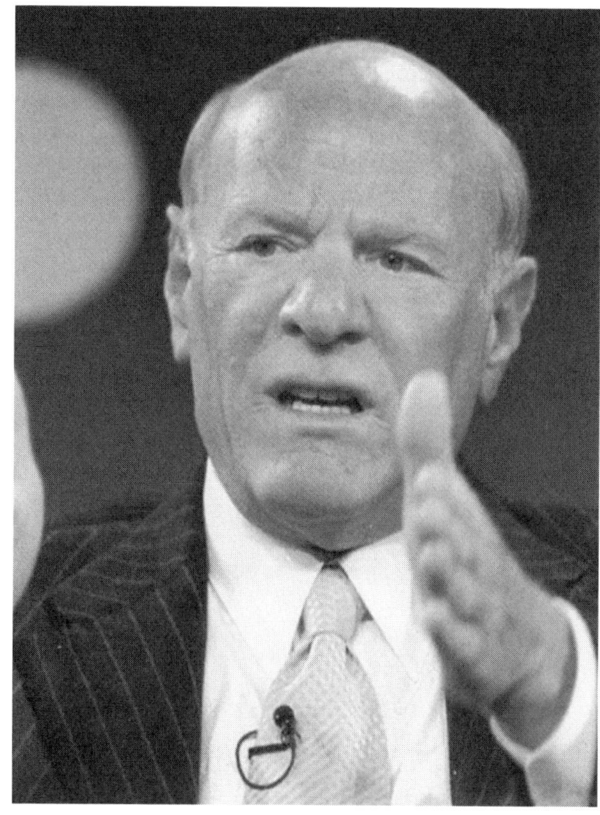

Barry Diller. *AP/Wide World Photos.*

■ As of the early 2000s Barry Charles Diller was a communications executive with InterActiveCorp, a multibrand interactive commerce company that transacted worldwide business through the Internet, television, and telephone. Diller's accomplishment was remarkable considering that his company's chief source of income was the risky Internet. During his career Diller was credited with creating such groundbreaking television concepts as the made-for-TV movie and the miniseries and even the debut of *The Simpsons* on Fox Television. The mogul had made a revolutionary career of extending the traditional boundaries of the media industry. Diller saw opportunities where competitors first saw failures and later copied his work. A rebel on many occasions, Diller was quoted on AskMen.com as having said, "I've not conducted my life in the service of smallness."

GROWING UP IN HOLLYWOOD

Diller was exposed early to the realities of business, real estate development, and the entertainment world. The Diller families, headed by Barry's father, Michael, and his uncle,

Richard, formed a home-construction business, which eventually spread into many construction and real estate development companies in and around Beverly Hills, California. Diller found formal education to be boring. After completing high school, he attended one year of college at the University of California, Los Angeles, before dropping out to enter the business world.

LEARNING THE TRADE

Like many business people who successfully climbed the corporate ladder, Diller began his career with an entry-level position. He worked in a mailroom at the William Morris Agency, a powerful Hollywood talent agency. There, Diller received the education he never got in college. He read all the contracts, memos, and correspondence that came through, in order to learn how the agency operated within the entertainment industry.

Diller was promoted to secretary and later to junior agent, in which capacity he continued to absorb job details, learning how to handle telephone calls, talk to buyers, and make deals. The message he valued was to follow through on promises and to have integrity in business dealings. During his time at the William Morris Agency, Diller developed the passion that characterized his subsequent professional career.

THE ABCS OF MOVIES

During a heated argument in 1966 with Leonard Goldberg, who was about to be named head of programming for the American Broadcasting Company (ABC), Diller impressed Goldberg with his knowledge. At the age of twenty-four, Diller secured a job as personal assistant to Goldberg. Within a few years Diller had impressed ABC upper management with his talent and ability to obtain desired results, mostly with a style of demand, pressure, and intimidation. Diller was promoted in 1968 to the position of executive assistant to the vice president in programming and director of feature films. One year later Diller was made vice president for feature films and program development. Diller was promoted again in 1971, this time to vice president in charge of prime-time feature films and program development for Circle Entertainment (a division of ABC). His tough negotiation style worked well, and he was given an enormous amount of power. Diller quickly learned how to separate good offers from bad ones.

One of Diller's early accomplishments was the premier in the fall of 1969 of the prime-time 90-minute series *ABC's Movie of the Week*. Under his direction, the series—which concentrated on stories drawn from news headlines, melodramas, mysteries, and controversial issues targeted to young, urban audiences—became the most popular TV movie series. The program raised viewership at ABC and elevated Diller's status so that he controlled advertising, direction, and promotion of the project. Two of his young producers were Aaron Spelling, who eventually became a prolific television producer, and Steven Spielberg, who would go on to fame as a feature film director.

Diller discovered the miniseries concept while on a trip to England. The British Broadcasting Company (BBC) had developed novels and plays into episodes that were being shown on television over three or more nights. Realizing that it was less expensive to produce one eight-hour miniseries than eight one-hour programs, Diller elaborated the concept. He soon was producing such miniseries as *QB VII* (by Leon Uris), *Roots* (by Alex Haley), and *Rich Man, Poor Man* (by Irwin Shaw).

MANAGEMENT AT PARAMOUNT

In October 1974 Diller was hired by Charles Bluhdorn to run and revitalize Paramount Pictures, a division of Gulf & Western Industries. Diller became chairman in 1975. For ten years, under the direction of Diller, Paramount produced such blockbuster films as *Saturday Night Fever* (1978), *Raiders of the Lost Ark* (1981), *48 Hours* (1982), and *Terms of Endearment* (1983), along with television series, including *Taxi* and *Cheers*. Having become a force in Hollywood, Diller saved Paramount from financial disaster by cutting costs and raising income with better promoting and merchandising of movies. He also revolutionized the method that studios used to acquire scripts, by forcing executives to find good movie projects rather than waiting for scripts to be offered to them. But in 1984 Diller quit Paramount after a continuing bitter conflict with the company's new leader, Martin S. Davis.

TRANSFORMS TWENTIETH CENTURY–FOX

Almost immediately, oil magnate Marvin Davis hired Diller to revive his financially ailing movie studio, Twentieth Century–Fox Corporation (TCF). Diller turned around the nearly bankrupt motion-picture division of TCF with brutal cost-cutting measures. Later, he was placed in charge of developing the studio's new TV network, Fox Broadcasting Company, which Davis hoped to turn into the fourth major U.S. television network. Most experts predicted its demise, believing that only three networks were needed. However, Diller ignored such dire predictions while working with the Australian media entrepreneur Rupert Murdoch, who had bought Fox in 1984 after seeing signs of life in the company with Diller at the helm.

With only a limited number of programs on the schedule, Diller knew that he had to develop other programs quickly, so that the fledgling Fox network could compete against the established networks, ABC, CBS, and NBC. Needing big-name stars to give validation to the new network, Diller persuaded Joan Rivers to leave her permanent guest-hosting job with *The Tonight Show Starring Johnny Carson.* Diller's first program was *The Late Show Starring Joan Rivers,* which debuted in 1986 but was canceled after several months because of conflicts between Rivers and Diller.

In 1987, working under the premise of less bureaucracy and more creativity, Diller introduced a limited prime-time television schedule on weekends with such series as *Married with Children.* After two years of operation, Fox had monetary losses of $136 million. During this time, however, Diller acquired more than 100 affiliate stations and developed a rapidly growing audience of 18- to 34-year-old viewers. Fox first earned a profit in 1990, the same year that *The Simpsons,* an animated situation comedy that became extremely successful, premiered. Diller's instincts did not fail him as he continued to concentrate on providing low-cost "reality" shows, such as *Cops* and *American's Most Wanted,* and offbeat shows, such as *In Living Color, The Tracey Ullman Show,* and *21 Jump Street.* Diller had his failures, too. At the end of 1987 *The North Wilton Report* debuted, receiving disastrous criticism from the media while being almost completely ignored by viewers.

Under Diller's guidance, Fox developed the successful scheduling strategy of debuting new programs in August, when the other networks traditionally programmed reruns. Diller also created an atmosphere of conflict and confrontation, business manipulations, and power struggles. George Mair, a person who regularly interacted with Diller and who later wrote a biography of Diller, summed him up with this comment: "Barry's very willful, very success-oriented. I think that in pursuit of his goals he was very wasteful on a human scale. He cared not for the body count that he created in his wake" (Mair, p. 189).

USING THE COMPUTER TO ENVISION NEW PROGRAMS

Diller left Fox in April 1992. After working constantly since the age of nineteen, he decided to buy an Apple PowerBook laptop computer and learn how to use it. He was amazed by how it stimulated his imagination and caused him to think in a new way about network and cable television programming, interactivity, and information services. Diller set off across the United States on what he called his "odyssey," to talk with the big names in computer technology, such as Bill Gates of Microsoft and Steve Jobs of Apple. During this time, Diller and his friend Diane Von Furstenberg traveled to West Chester, Pennsylvania, to visit the headquarters of the QVC Shopping Network. Diller was impressed with the mostly automated and effective sales operations of the company.

Through his company Arrow Investments, Diller bought into a partnership with QVC in 1993, to use it as a springboard for future investments. According to Mair, where critics saw an "electronic flea market selling jewelry and beanbag chairs," Diller saw a "money machine, and a place from which he could control his own destiny" (p. 231). Diller proceeded to buy other broadcasting properties and serve as their chief executive. After failing to succeed in merging QVC with CBS in 1994, Diller brokered a successful deal with Comcast and then left QVC about $100 million richer.

SILVER KING AND INTERACTIVITY

Then, in 1995, Diller purchased Silver King Communications, acquired Savoy Pictures Entertainment, and gained controlling interest over the media company USA Interactive, which owned the Home Shopping Network (HSN) and Ticketmaster Online. He transformed the company into the interactive commerce company InterActiveCorp. Diller expanded the company to include not only home shopping but also a variety of successful companies that dealt with interactive business on the Internet, such as Expedia, Hotels.com, Match.com, and Ticketmaster Online-Citysearch. He also oversaw more traditional enterprises, such as USA Networks (which included such television properties as the USA Network, the Sci-Fi Channel, and HSN), and numerous local television stations. Diller also bought controlling interest in the Internet portal Lycos as a way to turn the site into an outlet for the direct marketing of his own ventures. The travel sites Expedia.com and Hotels.com were models for Diller's strategy for revolutionizing the online travel-agency business. Because of their dominant positions, they were able to demand wholesale prices, which they resold for a 25–30 percent markup, rather than the traditional 10 percent commission.

In 2003 Diller bought LendingTree, a top online mortgage intermediary. With Internet mortgage companies possessing only 5–7 percent of the total consumer lending market and with LendingTree having less than 1 percent of that market, Diller expected to grab more market share with his new acquisition by using the company's cost-effective strategy to attract potential consumers and to present them with a variety of qualified lenders from which to choose their final loan. Diller used his tried-and-true techniques at Expedia.com and Hotel.com to expand LendingTree. He discovered that LendingTree actually rejected many lenders that applied for admission because the demand was so high and its screening requirements so strict. Diller expected a 70-percent annual earnings growth rate at least until 2007.

QUINTESSENTIAL BUSINESSMAN

Diller was often praised for his ability to choose winning projects and reject losing propositions at the same time that he was sometimes criticized for his direct, aggressive management style. According to Mair, Diller acknowledged being a difficult person: "I think difficult is good, especially if you're dealing with the 'creative process,' in which you have to make editorial choices. . . . All you really have to contribute is what you think. There is no rightness involved, only being true to oneself" (p. 7).

As CEO of InterActiveCorp, Diller continued to work to maintain the company's low-debt-to-high-cash ratio and continued to acquire functioning companies with sound business plans that were already on or ready to move onto the Internet. Diller's goal for the business was for it to become the world's largest and most profitable interactive commerce company by pursuing a multibrand growth strategy through its operating businesses. With a 2002 market value of around $12.5 billion, InterActiveCorp was a distant second to Ebay's $22 billion but above the figures for Yahoo! and Amazon, at $10 billion and $8 billion, respectively. In the early 2000s Diller commanded 26,000 employees in 26 nations around the world.

Even though he possessed a soft-spoken voice and kindly physical features, Diller earned a reputation as a tough negotiator and an imposing, highly motivated presence. He parlayed his perfectionist nature, abrasive temper, and often emotionally abusive personality into a business empire.

See also entry on USA Interactive, Inc. in *International Directory of Company Histories.*

SOURCES FOR FURTHER INFORMATION

"Barry Diller," http://www.askmen.com/men/business_politics_60/65c_barry_diller.html.

Block, Alex Ben, *Outfoxed: Marvin Davis, Barry Diller, Rupert Murdoch, and the Inside Story of America's Fourth Television Network,* New York: St. Martin's Press, 1990.

Mair, George, *The Barry Diller Story: The Life and Times of America's Greatest Entertainment Mogul,* New York: John Wiley and Sons, 1997.

—William Arthur Atkins

■ ■ ■

John T. Dillon
1938–
Former chairman and chief executive officer, International Paper Company

Nationality: American.

Born: September 7, 1938, in Schroon Lake, New York.

Education: University of Hartford, BA, 1965; Columbia University Graduate School of Business, MA, 1971.

Family: Married Mary Catherine (maiden name unknown); children: one.

Career: International Paper Company, 1965–1987, sales trainee, then head of Asian operations; 1987–1995, executive vice president of packaging; 1995–1996, president and COO; 1996–2003, chairman and CEO.

■ After a 38-year-career at International Paper Company (IP), the world's largest forest-products company, John T. Dillon retired on October 31, 2003, at the age of 65. Dillon would be remembered as a product of his times—a low-key executive who recognized the forces of consolidation and led two major mergers. Dillon was all business. While most CEOs routinely led a board outside company life, Dillon instead became head of an industry trade group and used that role to create a more favorable business climate for his firm and those of his peers.

Dillon helped build International Paper into an enormous multinational corporation with 2003 sales of $25.2 billion. IP produced plywood, paper, pulp, and packaging; the company also processed chemicals such as crude tall oil and crude sulfate turpentine, which were byproducts of the papermaking process. The subsidiary Arizona Chemical produced resins and inks. IP controlled about nine million acres of forest in the United States and 1.5 million in Brazil and also held interests in 810,000 acres in New Zealand. About 75 percent of the company's sales were registered in the United States. Unfortunately for Dillon, the tail end of his career was marked by soft demand for his company's products.

A COMPANY MAN MAKES HIS MARK

John Dillon joined International Paper in 1965. One of his earliest management roles—leading International Paper's operations in Asia—prepared him to ultimately make his mark on the global stage. In his words, as quoted by the Associated Press, "In the last 10 years developing nations such as Indonesia, Russia, and Brazil have become important markets. When I got my start in the business, IP had about 25 competitors in the U.S. Soon, there will be just four or five companies competing worldwide" (December 5, 2000).

While leading IP's Asian operations, Dillon also served as a director of Carter Holt Harvey, the New Zealand paper and forest products company of which 51 percent was owned by IP. Dillon soon rose through the ranks at International Paper, attaining a series of high-profile positions. He served as executive vice president of packaging, as which he oversaw the company's industrial and consumer packaging businesses as well as its corporate engineering and technology staffs. He was then appointed president and chief operating officer in 1995.

A FOCUS ON ACQUISITIONS

One of Dillon's most important contributions to IP was his directing of the accumulation of market share—along with massive debt—through two key mergers. As recorded by CNBC, Dillon framed both mergers, which proved economically controversial, in historical terms: "Consolidation in the paper and forest products industry—indeed, in many of the basic industries—has been going on forever. In fact, our company was formed by consolidation. And I expect it to continue" (January 7, 1999).

In 1999 Dillon purchased Union Camp Corporation for $5.86 billion, a deal that he said promised huge savings. He noted on CNN, "One of the leverage factors of the Union Camp merger is a huge amount of productivity that we'll be able to get out of the combination of two companies, in the simple sense, as a result of the overhead reduction" (October 29, 1999).

Dillon's next deal would be even bigger. In April 2000 International Paper paid $7.3 billion in cash and stock to acquire its rival Champion International, besting an offer from the Finnish paper company UPM-Kymmene. In announcing the acquisition, Dillon noted that the headquarters of the two firms were just a few miles apart and that the cultures were similar and would be easily integrated. He commented on CNBC, "Champion strengthens each one of our core businesses. It's accretive to earnings. It's above the cost of capital, on an acquisition basis, so it not only is financially attractive, but it also continues the march to improve our core businesses" (May 12, 2000). Dillon predicted the merger would yield annual cost savings of $425 million from consolidations in manufacturing—but as part of the deal IP incurred about $2.3 billion in Champion debt.

TIMING IS EVERYTHING

By March 2001 most economists agree that the global recession had started. Within one year of a retirement that could have been his crowning glory, Dillon was focused on paying down the debt from the Champion acquisition amid a brutal business climate. Demand for the company's paper and packaging grades had fallen to dismal levels. On CNBC he noted with regard to 2001, "The first quarter was perhaps one of the weakest quarters in fundamental demand that this industry has seen way back into the 1980s" (May 10, 2001).

BUSINESS LEADER AND ADVOCATE

During the period of dismal finances Dillon was outspoken about the U.S. government's role in sustaining the economy. CNBC quoted him as saying, "The strength of the U.S. dollar is a major problem for our industry. The size and the balance of trade deficit is a major problem and those are two areas that, from a public-policy perspective, we've also got to focus on" (May 10, 2001).

In May 2001 the Business Roundtable, a leading business association comprising the chief executives of leading U.S. corporations, named Dillon its new chairman, as such he would be an advocate for the fostering of economic growth, a strong global economy, and a competitive workforce. Bob Burt, the outgoing chairman of the Roundtable and the chairman and chief executive officer of FMC Corporation, was quoted by PR Newswire as saying, "John will provide a robust vision for the Roundtable as we grapple with a fluid economy and a changing workforce. We could not have chosen a better advocate for global leadership in today's world" (May 10, 2001).

DO AS I SAY, NOT AS I DO

But taking on such a public role for the normally discreet Dillon was not without its risks. In August 2002 the Business Roundtable took out a full-page ad in response to the accounting scandals that were contaminating corporate America: "Enough is enough," the ad said. In a scathing rebuttal piece in *Fortune*, a reporter instructed the group to "look in the mirror" (August 12, 2002). Despite advocating financial reform in the ad, the group failed to acknowledge how exorbitant CEO compensation packages—including those of its own members—contributed to the problem. It went on to list what 10 of the group's leaders had earned in 2001. According to the piece, Dillon's 2002 pay was an alarming $5.9 million.

AN ANTICLIMACTIC ENDING TO A LONG CAREER

Thanks to the weakened economy Dillon's billion-dollar acquisitions failed to translate into solid earnings in the final years of his career. Around the time of his October 2003 retirement Standard & Poor's cut short-term ratings on International Paper; Deutsche Bank followed suit, citing "continued industry malaise," as reported by the *Wall Street Journal* (October 8, 2003).

International Paper was not alone in its struggles, nor was it entirely complicit. Commodities such as paper were subject to market cycles, where solid demand kept prices and shares soaring, but weakened demand led to oversupply and falling prices; paper felt the brunt most of all. In fact in early 2004 the Dow Jones Industrial Average removed International Paper from its index; the company had been factored into the index for 48 years.

The company's removal from the Dow Jones average was all the more noteworthy considering that the old-economy peers Alcoa and Caterpillar still remained. Of the three names, International Paper had had the smallest market capitalization and the most discouraging performance record over the preceding several years. Since 1990 Alcoa's and Caterpillar's stocks had generated annual returns of more than 11 percent and 15 percent respectively; International Paper had reported mere 6 percent gains.

Jeremy J. Siegel, the professor of finance at the Wharton School at the University of Pennsylvania and the author of *Stocks for the Long Run*, told the *Wall Street Journal*, "It's my guess that with International Paper, the index people feel that they are pruning from the bottom" (April 1, 2004). Time will tell whether history will view John Dillon's career positively or not.

See also entry on International Paper Company in *International Directory of Company Histories.*

SOURCES FOR FURTHER INFORMATION

Ahlberg, Erik, "International Paper Seen as Weakest of 'Old-School' Names in the DJIA," *Wall Street Journal*, April 1, 2004.

Defterios, John, and Deborah Marchini, "International Paper Will 'Continue to See a Very Good Market Condition and

Very Good Opportunities,'" *Ahead of the Curve*, CNN, October 29, 1999.

Gural, Natasha, "International Paper CEO Speaks at Alma Mater," Associated Press State & Local Wire, December 5, 2000.

Haines, Mark (anchor), and Don Hays (reporter), *Squawk Box*, CNBC News Transcripts, January 7, 1999.

Haines, Mark (anchor), and Nanette Hansen (reporter), *Squawk Box*, CNBC News Transcripts, May 10, 2001.

Herera, Sue (anchor), "John Dillon, the Head of International Paper Talks about His Company's Deal to Acquire Champion International," CNBC News Transcripts, May 12, 2000.

"John Dillon, Chairman and CEO of International Paper Company, Elected New Chairman of the Business Roundtable," PR Newswire, May 10, 2001.

Reigber, Beth Demain, "International Paper Is Poised for Rally," *Wall Street Journal*, October 8, 2003.

Schlosser, Julie, "What the Roundtable Doesn't Talk About," *Fortune*, August 12, 2002, p. 44.

—Tim Halpern

■■■

Jamie Dimon

1956–

President and chief operating officer, J. P. Morgan Chase & Company

Nationality: American.

Born: March 13, 1956, in New York City, New York.

Education: Tufts University, BA, 1978; Harvard Business School, MBA, 1982.

Family: Son of Theodore Dimon (broker) and Themis (maiden name unknown); married Judith Kent; children: three.

Career: Goldman Sachs, 1978, intern; Management Analysis Center, 1978–1980, consultant; American Express Company, 1982–1985, vice president and assistant to the president; Commerical Credit Group, 1986–1989, executive vice president and CFO; 1989–1991, president and CFO; Primerica Corporation, 1991–1993, president and CFO; Smith Barney, 1990–1993, chief administrative officer; 1993–1995, COO; 1996–1997, chairman and CEO; Salomon Smith Barney Holdings, 1997–1998, cochairman and co-CEO; Citigroup, 1998, president; Bank One, 2000–2004, chairman and CEO; J. P. Morgan Chase & Company, 2004–, president and COO.

Address: 270 Park Avenue, New York, New York 10017; http://www.jpmorgan.com.

Jamie Dimon. *AP/Wide World Photos.*

■ In 2004 James Dimon—well known as Jamie—an executive who spent most of his career under the tutelage of Citigroup's Sandy Weill, finally emerged from the tycoon's shadow, doing so as a viable threat to his once revered mentor. The most interesting chapter of Dimon's life remained to be written after he resurrected the struggling midwestern Bank One by cutting costs and administering financial discipline. Effective June 15, 2004, J. P. Morgan Chase & Company acquired Bank One for about $58 billion in stock, forming the second-biggest U.S. bank, with loans and assets of $1.1 trillion. Dimon was expected to succeed the J. P. Morgan chair and CEO William Harrison in 2006.

By 2004 Bank One had become the sixth-largest U.S. bank, with assets of $320 billion. Its businesses, which spanned the United States and about a dozen other countries, comprised consumer, corporate, and institutional banking; lease financing; investment management; and brokerage, insurance, and consumer finance, including mortgages and student loans. The company had some 1,800 branches in 14 mostly midwestern and southeastern states. Bank One also managed the One Group mutual-fund family and was one of the largest issuers of credit cards in the world, with nearly 52 million cards in circulation and $74 billion in managed receivables. Early in 2004 the company bought most of the business of the U.S.-based Zurich Life from Zurich Financial Services.

A CHILD OF THE INDUSTRY

Dimon's career in the brokerage business seemed preordained by his lineage. His grandfather, a Greek immigrant from Smyrna, was a broker and passed on his knowledge of the business to his son and partner, Theodore Dimon. Jamie Dimon's father and grandfather worked together for 19 years, and Dimon worked summers in their New York office.

SHAPED BY A MENTOR

In 1978 Dimon graduated cum laude from Tufts University. He worked for the Management Analysis Center, a consulting firm in Boston, for several years and then enrolled in Harvard Business School. The Harvard professor Jay O. Light noted in *BusinessWeek*, "He was generally perceived as one of the very brightest guys in finance in that class" (October 21, 1996).

While a student at Harvard, Dimon interned at Goldman Sachs and was offered a job there after graduation in 1982. He declined, instead going to work for the mentor who would profoundly shape his career: Sandy Weill. The two men had met six years earlier; Weill knew Dimon's father and the two families had formed a close relationship, convening annually for Passover dinners. Dimon's mother gave Weill a copy of the college thesis her son had written about the 1970 merger of the two brokerage firms Shearson Hammill and Hayden Stone—a union engineered by Weill, who had been running Hayden at the time. Impressed, Weill offered Dimon a summer job. Recalled Weill in the *New York Times*, "After a week he was telling me how we could do things better" (July 13, 1995).

BUILDING FROM THE GROUND UP

From 1982 to 1985 Weill and Dimon teamed up at American Express, where Dimon signed on as vice president and assistant to the president. Dimon's abilities to crunch numbers meshed well with Weill's people skills. When Weill was forced out of American Express, he made Dimon his second in command at the little-known consumer-lending outfit that he bought called Commercial Credit Company. That tiny firm was the beginning of what would eventually become Citigroup; as quoted by the *New York Times*, when asked about his decision to stay with Weill, Dimon replied, "I love the idea of being in on the ground floor" (July 13, 1995).

RESTRUCTURING AN ULTIMATE WINNER

Dimon was a key member of the team that launched and defined Commercial Credit's strategy. He served as the company's chief financial officer and an executive vice president and then later as president. Through the course of Dimon's time at the firm, Commercial Credit was completely restructured and made numerous acquisitions and divestitures, substantially improving its profitability. The most significant transaction was the 1987 acquisition of Primerica Corporation, which included Smith Barney. Commercial Credit then assumed the Primerica name. In 1983 Primerica had acquired the Travelers Corporation (of which Smith Barney was a part), which had then been renamed Travelers Group. Between 1987 and 1994 the Travelers unit of Primerica touted compound annual growth of 21 percent in per-share earnings—an achievement that executives credited to Dimon's staunch financial discipline.

EMERGING FROM MERGER AFTER MERGER

At Travelers, Dimon was named chairman and CEO of its Smith Barney subsidiary in January 1996, having previously served as COO and chief administrative officer. Dimon's father had once worked at Smith Barney, so the younger Dimon knew the firm well; he would help transform Smith Barney from a small brokerage into a major Wall Street player. He was put in charge of integrating Smith Barney with Shearson, the brokerage business that Smith Barney purchased in 1993. Dimon recalled the difficulty of extricating Shearson from Lehman Brothers, its former sister company, and from American Express, its old parent—comparing the process in the *New York Times* to "splitting apart Siamese twins" (July 13, 1995). Elsewhere he stumbled trying to build the company's investment-banking business, luring bankers from Morgan Stanley with exorbitant pay packages that robbed colleagues of a substantial portion of the bonus pool. Morale declined and dozens of bankers left the company. In January 1996 Dimon apologized to his team, as quoted by *BusinessWeek*: "I know I made mistakes, and I'm sorry. Let's move forward" (October 21, 1996).

A PRECOCIOUS PERFORMER

Dimon quickly rebounded and in 1996 became the chairman and CEO of Travelers' Smith Barney subsidiary—at age 40 he was the youngest CEO of a major securities firm. His achievements included spearheading the firm's arrival on the Internet, making Smith Barney the only brokerage to tie into the widely used personal-finance software program Quicken, and pushing the company to become the first brokerage to offer no-load mutual funds to customers. As Dimon emerged from his mentor's shadow with the confidence to make his own decisions, tensions between the two began to surface. One insider who wished to remain anonymous noted in *BusinessWeek*, "Jamie's riding high on Smith Barney's success. He can hold stronger views than ever before" (October 21, 1996).

NUMBERS ARE NOT EVERYTHING

A bullish market—along with Dimon's unrelenting focus on keeping costs down—continued to fuel Smith Barney's strong performance. In 1996 the company's return on equity was among the highest in the industry; in the second quarter of that year it was a record 36.7 percent. In the fall of 1996 Smith Barney contributed 30 to 40 percent of its parents' earnings. Dimon's only demerit throught that period of time was his lack of people skills; during one meeting with 20 employees, as reported by *BusinessWeek*, Dimon openly disparaged one underling, saying, "That is the stupidest thing I ever heard" (October 21, 1996). An employee who witnessed the exchange noted, "It wasn't personal or mean spirited, but he would be more effective if he would lighten up" (October 21, 1996).

TOO MANY MERGERS COMPROMISE QUALITY

In November 1997, with the merger of Smith Barney and Salomon Brothers, Dimon became cochairman and co-CEO of the combined firm. In 1998 Weill and Dimon engineered a $73 billion deal: Travelers Group, the brokerage and investment-banking and insurance giant they had created from humble beginnings, purchased the retail market leader Citicorp to form Citigroup. Their aim was nothing less than to transform the financial-services landscape by creating the first comprehensive financial-services behemoth with dealings in both the consumer and corporate banking markets.

For half a year after the $73 billion 1998 merger of Citicorp and Travelers, Dimon, Sir Deryck Maughan, and Victor Menezes were all given co-CEO status to supervise the investment-banking segment of Salomon Smith Barney (SSB). Under their watch SSB lost hundreds of millions of dollars in overseas markets and other risky bond investments.

POWER STRUGGLES DESTROY A RELATIONSHIP

Concurrently the tension between Dimon and Weill reached a boiling point when Dimon refused to appoint Weill's daughter, Jessica Bibliowicz, as chief of asset management at Travelers and as well to turn over Salomon's bond business to Weill's son, Marc. A $1.3 billion trading loss in Dimon's Salomon division further exacerbated the situation. On November 1, 1998, the man Dimon had once referred to as a second father asked him to resign. Dimon said several years later in *Money* magazine, "It was a surprise. And yes, it was hard, because that company was my baby, my family" (February 2002). Dimon had been forced out. Given the choice between his own children and his "adopted" son, Sandy Weill had favored his blood. Ironically both of Weill's children wound up leaving their father's firm.

The news of Dimon's departure seemed to stun Wall Street, which had expected Dimon to become chairman of Citigroup after Weill's retirement. Sally Krawcheck, the analyst at Sanford C. Bernstein & Company, told the *Washington Post*, "I was shocked, followed by terror about his resignation. I went through mourning, denial, all that stuff. This is a man who is tremendously respected" (November 3, 1998). In fact Dimon was so well respected that when he stepped onto the Salomon Smith Barney trading floor after handing in his resignation, one thousand traders responded by giving him a standing ovation. In the *Washington Post* a Salomon investment banker said, "We all wanted to hate him, but he turned out to be a real quality guy. He was thoughtful and always willing to spend time explaining" (November 3, 1998). In a coincidental twist, in 2003 Krawcheck joined Citigroup as director of research for its Smith Barney Division—the unit Dimon had helped build.

As far as Dimon was concerned, Weill's motivation in forcing out his right-hand man and protégé of 17 years was transparent. He compared the situation to a Shakespearean tragedy, casting himself as the Earl of Kent, who paid the price for challenging the authority of King Lear.

TIED TO THE BANKING INDUSTRY

On March 27, 2000, after an 18-month break from the financial-services industry, Dimon became the chairman and CEO of Bank One, the fifth-largest bank in the country. Dimon said he turned down top jobs at Amazon.com and other coveted employers because banking was an inextricable part of his life. As he told *Money* magazine, he came to his decision after taking more than a year off: "I just took out that old white pad: Maybe I want to be an investor. Maybe I want to be a teacher. Maybe I want to write books. Maybe I want to stay home and be with my kids when they're growing up. I thought about all of that, and I was very open-minded about it, and what I came to is: My craft is financial services. Right or wrong, that's what I know, and I'm pretty good at it" (February 2002).

Dimon had been hired to turn around the ailing Bank One, which had been hit by a series of management missteps and earnings shortfalls beginning in 1999 that left the bank with a $511 million net loss in 2000. Dimon told the *Lafayette* (IN) *Journal and Courier*, "I want to make the company strong so it's a predator, not the prey" (April 3, 2000). Dimon backed up his words with cash, buying two million shares of his new company. He remarked in *Money* magazine, "Ownership is a critical thing. Even if you run a retail store, you think, 'Hey, it's my store, my company,' and you run it like it's your own. And I learned that from Sandy" (February 2002).

A FOCUS ON COSTS BEGETS A TURNAROUND

In his first year at Bank One, Dimon strengthened the management team and fortified the corporation's balance sheet, saving more than $1 billion through waste-reduction efforts. He severed relationships with corporate borrowers that failed to purchase the company's more profitable services, such as money management and stock underwriting, and closed the much-hyped but unprofitable online division, Wingspan-Bank.com. Each of the company's 1,800 offices were ordered to post profit-and-loss statements, and branch managers were compensated based on net revenues, not sales. Dimon scrutinized every dollar the company spent. As reported by *Money*, when a high-level executive informed him of the numerous subscriptions held by the company, Dimon said, "You're a businessman; pay for your own *Wall Street Journal*" (February 2002).

During this period Dimon's conservative side emerged. After taking the reins at Bank One, he immediately implemented a complex risk-management system that left the company with a more diversified investment portfolio. The procedure put in place by that system led Bank One to reduce loans to WorldCom and other risky firms by billions of dollars—before the technology market tanked; Dimon's leadership was prescient. Effective May 2004 Dimon's former employer Citigroup agreed to pay $2.65 billion to settle a lawsuit brought by WorldCom investors, opening an expensive new chapter in the company's efforts to clean up after various corporate scandals.

Dimon judiciously turned down several possible deals. Household International, the struggling consumer-finance company based in the Chicago area, went up for sale in 2002. Dimon was more than familiar with the firm's core business: like Commercial Credit, the outfit he had developed with Weill, Household offered loans to consumers with poor credit. But Dimon passed; Household was later sold to HSBC. Dimon told London's *Financial Times*, "I don't think we are ready to take on whole other business lines" (March 28, 2003).

A CAREER-BOOSTING MERGER

In January 2004 Dimon negotiated a deal to merge Bank One and J. P. Morgan Chase & Company of New York. Both banks needed each other in order to truly compete globally—and especially to keep up with Citigroup, the world's largest financial-services firm in 2003 with more than $100 billion in revenues. The merged entity would be headquartered in New York but would base certain retail operations in offices in Chicago.

J. P. Morgan Chase described the transaction as a merger of equals; it had acquired Bank One for about $58 billion in stock, forming the second-biggest U.S. bank, with loans and assets of $1.1 trillion. Following the merger both of the companies' U.S. consumer and commercial banking businesses would operate under the Chase brand. The transaction combined Bank One's strength in consumer financial services with J. P. Morgan's formidable hold on the corporate-banking market. The combined network of branch banks comprised 2,300 outlets—three times as many as were run by Citigroup. Thomas Brown, the independent analyst with Bankstocks.com, said in *Fortune*, "Their strengths and weaknesses match up almost perfectly" (February 9, 2004).

When asked if he was bothered by the fact that the new entity would have no retail brokerage network—a hallmark of Weill's various companies dating back to the 1960s—Dimon's response, as reported by the *New York Times*, was telling: "My dad is still a stockbroker; but we have to get this done and then dream about the next thing" (January 18, 2004).

Under the agreed-upon terms at the new J. P. Morgan, Dimon would succeed William Harrison as CEO in 2006—until that time he would remain president and chief operating officer, and the board would evenly comprise Bank One and J. P. Morgan directors. While the advantages to both Bank One and Dimon were evident, Dimon recalled feeling extremely anxious about making the deal official. He said in *Fortune*, "It's terrifying. Do you push the button or not? But if you don't and this opportunity is gone when you want it later, you've made a horrible mistake. So I pushed the button" (February 9, 2004).

MANAGEMENT STYLE MATTERS

The J. P. Morgan deal provided Dimon with the career opportunity of a lifetime and the chance to directly challenge his one-time mentor. Whether or not he would excel in his new position was said to be largely dependent on his ability to keep his hallmark intrusiveness in check. At Bank One, Dimon spent half of each day drilling employees from the top of the management chart on down about the tiniest details of the business. He disliked being caught off guard and went to incredible lengths to amass and digest huge amounts of information. Linda Bammann, Bank One's chief risk officer, noted in *Fortune*, "God help you if you go on vacation. He'll meet with your people and start changing things" (February 9, 2004).

In early 2004 Dimon claimed that he would take a more laid-back approach in the future at J. P. Morgan. *Fortune* quoted him as saying, "After the merger I won't say, 'I want A, B, or C.' I will try it their way. I'll put out ideas and let them work it" (February 9, 2004).

See also entries on Bank One Corporation and J. P. Morgan Chase & Co. in *International Directory of Company Histories*.

SOURCES FOR FURTHER INFORMATION

"Bank One Hopes Kid Wonder's Game Plan Works," *Journal and Courier* (Lafayette, Ind.), April 3, 2000.

Day, Kathleen, and Ianthe Jeanne Dugan, "Clash of Corporate Cultures Shakes Citigroup Management," *Washington Post*, November 3, 1998.

Kurson, Ken, "Jamie Dimon Wants Respect," *Money*, February 2002, p. 46.

Silverman, Gary, "I Am Not Restless in Chicago," *Financial Times* (London), March 28, 2003, p. 15.

Spiro, Leah Nathans, "Whiz Kid," *BusinessWeek*, October 21, 1996, p. 96.

Thomas, Landon, Jr., "Dimon's Bank Deal: Big, but Maybe Not His Last," *New York Times*, January 18, 2004.

Truell, Peter, "Becoming His Own Man," *New York Times*, July 13, 1995.

Tully, Shawn, "The Deal Maker and the Dynamo," *Fortune*, February 9, 2004, p. 76.

—Tim Halpern

■ ■ ■

Peter R. Dolan

1956–

Chairman, chief executive officer, and president, Bristol-Myers Squibb Company

Nationality: American.

Born: January 6, 1956, in Salem, Massachusetts.

Education: Tufts University, BA, 1978; Dartmouth College, MBA, 1980.

Family: Son of John Ralph Dolan and Lois Burkhart; married Katherine Helen Lange (former executive director of Saint Joseph's Hospital); children: two.

Career: General Foods, 1983–1984, associate product manager; 1984–1985, product manager; 1985–1986, senior product manager; 1986–1987, general product manager; Bristol-Myers Squibb Company, 1988–1993, vice president of marketing; 1993–1995, president of marketing; 1995–1996, president of Mead Johnson Nutritional Group; 1996–1997, president of Nutritionals and Medical Devices Group; 1997–1998, president of Pharmaceuticals Group in Europe; 1998–2000, senior vice president for strategy and organizational effectiveness; 2000–2001, president; 2001–2002; CEO and president; 2002–, chairman, CEO, and president.

Address: Bristol-Myers Squibb Company, 345 Park Avenue, New York, New York 10154-0037; http://www.bms.com.

Peter R. Dolan. *AP/Wide World Photos.*

■ With 2003 sales of $20.8 billion Bristol-Myers Squibb Company at the start of the 21st century was one of the top pharmaceutical firms in the United States. The company specialized in anticancer, cardiovascular, and anti-infective pharmaceuticals; it was also active in the area of AIDS research and treatment, particularly through protease inhibitors, and was increasing its efforts to find genetic remedies for diseases—particularly infections—often in collaboration with other researchers. Although most of Bristol's sales came from perscription pharmaceuticals, the company also marketed Excedrin and Bufferin over the counter and, through its Mead Johnson subsidiary, sold infant formula. The company focused on creating product franchises by manufacturing several leading products within each of its core markets; for example, as the manufacturer of TAXOL, Paraplatin, Platinol, and VePesid, Bristol was a leading producer of anticancer drugs. The chairman, CEO, and president Peter R. Dolan had a personal interest in cancer, as several members of his family suffered from the disease.

Dolan was the seventh CEO in the corporation's 114-year history. A 15-year veteran of the company, his ascent to the top was particularly quick—some said too quick—as at 45 Dolan became one of the youngest chief executives of any of the largest drug makers. As of 2004 Dolan's standing with the company was tenuous due to a series of poor management decisions and an accounting scandal that made him the target of a federal investigation.

LIKE MOTHER, LIKE SON

Dolan acquired his first job delivering newspapers at age nine, which led to employment at the local fruit stand, a job prized by neighborhood boys. Among his memories from the dinner table at home were those of conversations between his mother and father about his father's job. Each night Dolan's mother would drill her husband about his company's inner workings and its key players; she mapped out her husband's climb to the top of the corporate ladder through so much repeated minutia that Dolan never forgot the names and titles of certain employees at his father's company.

The youngest of five children, Dolan inherited his mother's insatiable drive for success. At Tufts he was president of his fraternity, and at Dartmouth's Amos Tuck School of Business, where he earned his MBA, he was president of his class. As a first-year graduate student he cleaned tables in the cafeteria—a year later he was helping to run it. When recruiters came to the school, Dolan was sure of himself and his plans. In the *New York Times* he recalled saying, "I'm either going to be a United States senator or I'm going to be head of a packaged-goods company" (May 12, 2002).

FROM JELL-O TO EXCEDRIN

Dolan's instincts were almost on target. He got his start marketing Jell-O and other desserts for General Foods; but after Philip Morris acquired the company, Dolan quit, telling the *New York Times*, "I decided I wanted to work at a health-care company, rather than a tobacco company" (February 8, 2001).

Not long after Dolan began working at Bristol-Myers Squibb Company, and by 1993 he was in charge of Bristol-Myers Products, the firm's over-the-counter drug business. He played an important role in the company's push to invest more heavily in Excedrin, which in 1998 became the first over-the-counter drug approved to treat migraines. Sales increased by 17 percent under Dolan's leadership.

HOW TO SUCCEED IN INTERNATIONAL BUSINESS

As president of Bristol's Nutritionals and Medical Devices Group, Dolan had responsibility for the Mead Johnson Nutritional Group, which produced infant formula. Under Dolan, Mead Johnson made international business a top priority. The company opened manufacturing facilities in four countries and international sales climbed to 40 percent of the corporation's revenue by 1996.

Dolan spearheaded a number of initiatives emphasizing new-product development and international marketing, establishing the 70-employee Global New Business Development Team. He set up what were affectionately referred to as the "Big Hairy Audacious Goals," which included making Mead Johnson number one in the world in infant formula; operating companywide on a global level; launching a new product with sales of $100 million; garnering 30 percent of business from new products; and cutting operating costs by $100 million. While Dolan's unit did not meet all of those goals by the 1997 target date, Mead Johnson did become the world's largest infant-formula manufacturer; by 1986 the subsidiary controlled 23.6 percent of the world market. Also during Dolan's tenure Mead relaunched Sustacal, positioning it toward active seniors as opposed to the institutional market.

RACE TO THE TOP

In November 1998 Bristol reorganized its senior management, signaling the start of a race for the company's top jobs for when the executive vice president Kenneth Weg and the chairman Charles Heimbold would retire in 2000 and 2001, respectively. Weg and Heimbold formed the office of the chairman, which would groom their successors. Dolan was mentioned as a second-tier candidate for the CEO job and was promoted to senior vice president for strategy and organizational effectiveness, heading a council to consider strategic alternatives for the company.

A PERSONAL STAKE IN CANCER TREATMENT

Dolan's mother had died of ovarian cancer, and his sister had both ovarian and colon cancer, which eventually went into remission. In 2000 he was the creative force behind advertisements for Taxol featuring Lance Armstrong, the American cyclist who won the Tour de France after his own battle with cancer. Bristol-Myers Squibb and Armstrong teamed up to launch the Cycle of Hope, a national educational campaign for people with cancer or at risk of developing the disease. Dolan noted in the *New York Times*, "The company's mission of extending and enhancing life is very personal to me" (February 8, 2001).

A CEO STUMBLES

Somewhat surprisingly Dolan proved to be on the fast track; he was named CEO in February 2001 and chairman in 2002. Heeding calls from Wall Street, he quickly jettisoned auxiliary businesses—selling Clairol, the number-one hair-color brand and a longtime anchor product, for example—and focused on pharmaceuticals. He set audacious goals for the company, vowing to double the company's sales and earnings within five years—a promise he would later come to regret. In 2002, his first full year at the top, sales totaled $18.1 billion, down 1 percent from 2000.

Sagging sales, however, would be the least of Dolan's problems. In 2001, amid much scrutiny, he negotiated a $2 billion deal with Imclone Systems, the company notorious for its involvement in the Martha Stewart insider-trading scandal. The guiding principle had been to join forces to develop and promote the long-anticipated cancer drug Erbitux. But in 2002 Imclone received a "refusal-to-file" letter from the U.S. Food and Drug Administration, signaling a shortfall of convincing data with regard to the drug's efficacy. Investor outrage over the fact that Dolan had invested in the partnership without solid reassurance resulted in a write-down of $367 million—most of Bristol's investment in Imclone.

DRIVEN, ON THE TRACK AND IN THE BOARDROOM

Analysts speculated as to whether Dolan was truly the right executive for the top job at Bristol-Myers. They didn't like the fact that he had climbed the corporate ladder so quickly and said that he lacked the character-building experiences that would have taught him how to deal with adversity. Dolan said in the *New York Times* that he took such criticism seriously but added, "I may be at my best when I'm underestimated" (May 12, 2002). Dolan evidenced his determination through athletic feats. In his 20s his inability to swim was not enough to thwart his plans to compete in a triathlon—he simply taught himself the crawl. At age 40 he ran two marathons in three weeks, in one beating the personal marathon record he had set 15 years earlier. Dolan and his wife were also competitive cyclists.

INVESTIGATING MANAGEMENT IMPROPRIETIES

Most damaging to Dolan's reputation may have been the restatements of sales and earnings from previously issued financial statements from 1999 through 2001. During that time period, the company later admitted, Bristol had lied, inflating sales by as much as $3.35 billion and earnings by at least $900 million. The restatements were thought to have been the result of a commonly used—albeit morally questionable—tactic known as "stuffing the sales channel." Bristol conceded that in its quest to meet unrealistic growth expectations, the company had used sales incentives to entice distributors to buy more products than their pharmacy customers reasonably needed. As a result, Bristol seemed to be selling large quantities of its drugs, when in fact the products were sitting untouched on distributors' shelves.

The restatements spiraled into a widespread investigation of the company's business practices. The Sarbanes-Oxley Act, passed in 2002 as part of an aggressive federal attempt to rein in corporate abuse, required that top company officials swear to the truth of their companies' financial data and provided stiff penalties for those who knowingly engaged in deception. In August 2002 Dolan swore to the accuracy of the company's statements—and proceeded to deny any responsibility for them only a few months later.

OUT OF HIDING

After laying low through one of the darkest periods in the company's 147-year history and dealing with a deluge of criticism, Dolan emerged from the shadows. As reported by the *New York Times*, in a conference call on April 29, 2003, he struck an optimistic note, saying he hoped the company would soon move into the "business-as-usual period" (May 18, 2003).

Analysts were skeptical—especially since federal prosecutors were still in the midst of their investigation. Barbara A. Ryan, the analyst at Deutsche Bank Securities who was among those interviewed by prosecutors, noted in the *New York Times*, "You're listening to him on the one hand and thinking on the other that he's the subject of a major criminal investigation. That certainly doesn't help rebuild credibility" (May 18, 2003).

A BELEAGUERED EXECUTIVE TRIES TO BOUNCE BACK

In 2003 Bristol's board of directors approved the five-year plan Dolan had put forth to save the company. In addition to implementing management controls that would prevent corporate abuses from resurfacing, Dolan vowed to bolster the company's research and development efforts and strengthen its product pipeline.

With many of the company's drugs nearing the end of patent protection, the pressure to roll out new blockbusters was immense—losses from patent expirations were estimated at about $1 billion in annual net sales. Instead of relying on partnerships and alliances, Dolan shifted focus to developing more products internally; he aimed to produce two-thirds of new drugs in the company's own laboratories.

NEW DRUGS SIGNAL A TURNAROUND

In the first half of 2003 two major drugs were approved: Abilify, an antipsychotic, and Reyataz, the first once-daily protease inhibitor for the treatment of HIV/AIDS. In addition limited clearance was given to Erbitux, the sidelined cancer drug licensed from Imclone. Analysts at SunTrust Robinson Humphrey estimated that Erbitux sales could peak at more than $700 million.

The promising drugs signaled a potential new beginning for the company. Morningstar projected an average revenue growth rate of 3 percent through 2007. The Morningstar analyst Todd Lebor observed in *Med Ad News*, "Bristol isn't the cash machine of the past, but we think its future cash flows justify a $27 stock price. We think Bristol will pull out of its death spiral and reward patient investors" (September 1, 2003).

A COMPETITOR MEETS HIS MATCH?

While Bristol had the chance to pull itself out of its slump, the competitive Dolan found himself in one race he would possibly prove unable to finish. Bristol's board temporarily left him in control, but with the investigation into the company's accounting practices looming in the background, their continued loyalty was by no means assured. Although Dolan had only been named CEO in 2001, he had been an executive since 1998, making it impossible to indemnify him for any penalties resulting from accounting improprieties. Lebor noted in *Med Ad News*, "He's hanging on to his job by a very thin thread, and we think the accounting shenanigans, misguided focus, and poor investments under his watch will catch up to him soon" (September 1, 2003).

See also entry on Bristol-Myers Squibb Company in *International Directory of Company Histories.*

SOURCES FOR FURTHER INFORMATION

Abelson, Reed, and Greg Winter, "The Optimist Leading Bristol-Myers," *New York Times*, May 12, 2002.

Boersing, Charles, "Time to Heal: Management Issues and Generic Competition Continue to Plague Bristol-Myers Squibb, but the Company Has Promising New Products and a Strong Start in 2003," *Med Ad News*, September 1, 2003, p. 68.

Harris, Gardiner, "Will the Pain Ever Let Up at Bristol-Myers?" *New York Times*, May 18, 2003.

Petersen, Melody, "Bristol-Myers Squibb Names Marketing Official as Chief Executive," *New York Times*, February 8, 2001.

—Tim Halpern

■■■

Guy Dollé

1942–

Chairman and chief executive officer, Arcelor

Nationality: French.

Born: 1942, in France.

Education: École Polytechnique.

Career: Irsid Steel Research Center, 1966–1980; Usinor, 1980–1984, head of plates and tubes division; 1985, chair of GTS Industries; 1986, executive vice president of Unisor Aciers; 1987–1993, vice president of industrial affairs for Solca; 1993–1995, chairman and CEO of Unimetal; 1995–1997, executive vice president of strategy, planning, and international affairs; 1997–1999, head of stainless-steel and alloys division; 1999–2001, senior executive vice president; Arcelor, 2002–, chairman and CEO.

Address: Arcelor, 19, avenue de la Liberté, L-2930 Luxembourg; http://www.arcelor.com.

■ Guy Dollé became the CEO and management-board chairman at Arcelor's inception in February 2001 when the industry giants Aceralia Corporation Siderurgica (of Spain), Arbed (of Luxembourg), and Usinor (of France) joined forces to create the world's largest steel business. Dollé, who spent his entire career in the steel industry, was a longtime senior executive with Usinor; his last position with the company prior to the merger was senior executive vice president. He was active not only within Arcelor but in the international steel trade in general, believing that consolidation among international companies—as was the case with the inception of Arcelor—was the best way for steel corporations to survive in an industry that he saw as suffering from overcapacity.

Arcelor was officially formed on February 19, 2001; the consolidation became fully effective when the company's shares were first listed on several stock exchanges on February 18, 2002. The company functioned under four core business operations: the production of flat carbon steel, such as coated steel sheets and cold and hot coils; the production of long carbon steel, such as beams, merchant steel, sheet piling, concrete reinforcement, and public transport rails; the manufacture of stainless steel, for the appliances, construction, packaging, mechanical-engineering, and automotive industries; and the management of steel distribution, transformation, and trading.

INTERNATIONAL INFLUENCE

Dollé's experience with Usinor as executive vice president of the strategy, planning, and international-affairs department made him not only a valuable member of Arcelor's senior management team but a respected player in the global steel arena. During the last decades of the 20th century and into the 2000s the steel industry worldwide had been experiencing upheavals. In particular the United States saw many of its gigantic steel conglomerates struggle and collapse one by one as steel from other countries increased in quality, quantity, and affordability. Japan's Nippon Steel and JFE Holdings became major players, and by 2004 Arcelor had a 30 percent stake in the Brazil-based Companhia Vale do Rio Doce, the biggest and one of the least expensive of the world's iron-ore suppliers. The Luxembourg-based Arcelor was producing 9 million of its annual 44 million tons of steel in that country.

On March 6, 2002, under Section 201 of the Trade Act of 1974, President George W. Bush imposed stiff import tariffs on steel products, with duties ranging from 8 to 30 percent. European steel producers angrily denounced the imposition, though analysts could not agree on exactly how badly the tariffs would affect European producers. A BBC News reporter quoted one analyst as saying, "As Asian producers redirect exports to Europe, there will be increased competition and the potential for disproportionate price pressure on companies in the already weak market"; downplaying the possible effects, another commented, "Europe produces 160 million tonnes of steel a year, of which only four million are exported to the United States" (March 6, 2002).

Of the 4 percent of Arcelor's exports going to the United States, approximately 70 percent were lost as a result of the imposed tariffs. Dollé attacked the importation taxes, saying, "This decision is unfair and incompatible with laws of international trade" (March 6, 2002). The tariffs created such anger that the Anglo-Dutch group Corus asked the European Commission (EC) to retaliate against the United States; the EC immediately announced it would take the issue to the World

Trade Organization (WTO), the acting court for international trade disputes. The EC's top trade official Pascal Lamy said, "The U.S. decision to go down the route of protectionism is a major setback for the world trading system." In the *New York Times* Dollé was outspoken about the issue: referring to the health and retirement benefits due to retired workers, he said, "The big problem in the United States is the legacy costs of the integrated steel companies" (March 6, 2002). He believed the U.S. government imposed the tariffs in order to "safeguard" the U.S. steel industry from increased imports, not because foreign producers were competing unfairly—as such he believed the action was taken on shaky legal grounds.

PROMOTES NEGOTIATION RATHER THAN CONFRONTATION

By September 2002 major unrest still existed among Asian and European steel producers over the tariffs, though the U.S. government agreed to exempt more than 700 steel products—a move many U.S. steel producers said could only harm the local industry. Japan, which had been strongly in favor of retaliation, softened its stance after the United States added more of the country's products to the exemption list. Dollé commended Japan's flexibility and urged the EC to follow suit; Nancy Kelly of *American Metal Market* quoted him as saying, "Retaliation on exports of Florida orange juice will not help solve the problems of the steel industry" (September 5, 2002). He believed that negotiation, as oppposed to confrontation, would be a far more effective way of dealing with the tariff issue and instituting further exemptions.

In early 2003, however, Dollé attacked the United States further, accusing the superpower of operating under a double standard: the government continued to impose tariffs under Section 201 even while U.S. steel producers had increased exports to Europe. In *American Metal Market* he wondered, "They take 30 percent duties and the advantage of a dropping dollar and export to Europe—is that fair?" (March 7, 2003).

ADVOCATES CONSOLIDATION TO ADDRESS OVERCAPACITY

Though he would not rest easy with respect to Section 201, Dollé indicated that he would concentrate on addressing what he saw as the longer-term problem in the industry—global overcapacity—by initiating a debate on the matter prior to the October 2003 International Iron and Steel Institute in Rome and the high-level multilateral talks scheduled for December. Dollé was adamant about the need for industry consolidation; Arcelor, the largest steel producer in the world following the consolidation of the three independent companies, still only accounted for 4.5 percent of world production. Andrew Sharkey, the president of the American Iron and Steel Institute, agreed with Dollé on the consolidation issue. Kelly of *American Metal Market* reported Sharkey as commenting, "It is appropriate that opponents of the tariffs are shifting their attention to the hard work of reducing excess capacity and instituting new government disciplines. Dollé's personal commitment to those goals can only help" (September 5, 2002).

In November 2003, as the guest of honor at the National Association of Steel Stockholders' annual dinner, Dollé noted the difficulty of achieving success in the steel industry due to the high capital-investment requirements and costs associated with keeping substantial inventories for the typical four to six months. He said that while distribution was one way of creating value, service innovations were necessary in order to reduce capital costs, particularly in inventory. He reiterated his philosophy of consolidation, which would necessarily, he believed, involve intercontinental mergers.

WORLDWIDE STRATEGY FOR ARCELOR

One-fourth of Arcelor's revenue was earned outside the European Union (EU), and Dollé was developing a worldwide strategy to further exploit the company's global influence. One strategy focused on the automotive industry—and was driven by that industry's own globalization—in which Arcelor built partnerships with manufacturers in Italy and Spain and with Nippon Steel in Japan, forming their Global Steel Alliance. He looked into the possibility of forging a joint venture with Baosteel in Shanghai in order to gain access to China's auto industry. In *Metal Bulletin Monthly*, referring to the highly successful global alliance initiated by Lufthansa in the airline industry, Dollé was quoted as saying, "So we have a worldwide strategy for automotive—mainly focused outside of Europe, on joint ventures and partnership. It's like the Star Alliance with more shareholder links" (June 2003).

Another line of attack was the institution of low-cost production. Dollé noted, "For the moment, there are two regions in the world where you can produce very cheap steel: the first is Brazil; the second is Russia." He planned to increase the company's already significant presence in Brazil, particularly in the production of carbon steel, and establish operations in Russia by partnering with Severstal. Dollé's first goal in that country was to deliver products to Russia's auto industry, which he said was a medium-to-long-term goal because of the industry's relative weakness; Arcelor would also help Severstal deliver Russian products to the rest of the world. Dollé noted that J&L Steel, Arcelor's stainless-steel producer in the United States, had yet to break even.

Dollé believed that while having a global strategy in place was beneficial, mustering the resources necessary to implement that strategy required an entirely unique approach. He stated that although the company's balance sheet was not weak, he would concentrate on debt reduction before focusing on growth. He told *Metal Bulletin Monthly*, "In this business you must be a low-debt company if you want to be consistent" (June 2003).

CAUTIOUS ABOUT CAPITAL

To gain footing in the U.S. market, Dollé had been negotiating with Bethlehem Steel Corporation, the third-largest steel producer in the United States, for a stake in their Burn's Harbour, Indiana, steel mill; Bethlehem had filed for Chapter 11 bankruptcy protection the previous year. By mid-2002, however, Dollé announced that he would not pursue the deal because Arcelor was unwilling to shoulder the burden of Bethlehem's health-insurance and pension-plan liabilities. He was quoted in *Stainless Steel World* as commenting, "We cannot take over this risk" (July 10, 2002).

In early March 2003 Dollé announced 2002 operating earnings of EUR 780 million for Arcelor, compared to its 2001 operating loss of EUR 200 million. While commenting that the company was open to cooperation with Japan's Nippon Steel to supply coated material to China, Dollé said that the company was still not delving into the acquisitions market due to the need to improve cash flow before spending capital. He had no definite intentions to act at that time, but Dollé certainly had a plan of action if the necessity arose: Arcelor would consider selling its more than 50 percent stake in the Germany-based Dillinger Hutte if ultimately unable to restructure its heavy-plate business. Dollé noted, "We don't want mere financial participation in our balance sheet and, if we can't find the industrial synergy, we will sell our stake in Dillinger." As he told *American Metal Market*, he was unwilling to make any commitment that would put the company in a high-risk financial situation: "In the next two years there might be a larger cash operation, but not in the U.S. Concentration in the U.S. has only begun, and only they themselves can handle the necessary adjustments to benefit plans" (March 7, 2003).

After reviewing Arcelor's progress at the company's Ordinary General Meeting on April 25, 2003, Dollé said that, despite the difficult economic and global environment and a marked slowdown in growth in the steel industry, Arcelor's operating performance measured up to management's ambitions and expectations. He noted that the group had increased its selling price by more closely tailoring supply to demand and making profit margins a higher priority than volumes. As reported by Business Wire, he stated, "2002 was a year of integration; 2003 will be a year of consolidation. It is now up to us to confirm over the longer term the good start Arcelor has made" (April 25, 2003).

SOURCES FOR FURTHER INFORMATION

Andrews, Edmund L., "Angry Europeans to Challenge U.S. Steel Tariffs at WTO," *New York Times*, March 6, 2002.

"Arcelor Chief Slams U.S. Steel 'Double Standards,'" *American Metal Market*, March 7, 2003, p. 5.

"Arcelor Ends Talks with Bethlehem Steel," *Stainless Steel World*, July 10, 2002, http://www.stainless-steel-world.net/projects/news_detail.asp?NewsID=1839.

"Arcelor Ordinary General Meeting on April 25, 2003," Business Wire, April 25, 2003, http://articles.findarticles.com/p/articles/mi_m0EIN/is_2003_April_25/ai_100604008.

Barrett, Richard, "Global Influence," *Metal Bulletin Monthly*, June 2003, p. 32.

Kelly, Nancy E., "Steel Exec: EC Should Follow Japan 201 Stay," *American Metal Market*, September 5, 2002, p. 1.

"Steel Shares Recover Early Losses," BBC News, March 6, 2002, http://news.bbc.co.uk/1/hi/business/1857850.stm.

—Marie L. Thompson

■ ■ ■

Tim M. Donahue

1949–

President and chief executive officer, Nextel Communications

Nationality: American.

Born: 1949.

Education: John Carroll University, BA, 1971.

Career: MCI Communications Corporation, 1984–1986; McCaw Cellular Communications (now AT&T Wireless Services), 1986–1989, president of paging division; 1989–1991, president of U.S. central region; 1991–1994, president of northeast region; AT&T Wireless Services, 1994-1996, president of northeast region; Nextel Communications, 1996–1999, president and COO; 1999–, president and CEO.

Awards: Networking and Communications Entrepreneur of the Year, Ernst & Young, 2003; Greater Washington Master Entrepreneur of the Year, Ernst & Young, 2003.

Address: Nextel Communications, 2001 Edmund Halley Drive, Reston, Virginia 20191; http://www.nextel.com.

■ As of 2004 Tim M. Donahue was the president and chief executive officer of the Reston, Virginia–based Nextel Communications, a unique cellular-phone company with a network of private mobile-radio systems favored by the group of customers considered by industry experts to be the most highly coveted: business clientele. From companies employing delivery drivers, construction workers, and taxi drivers to those involved in government and security contracts, the backbone of the Nextel market is willing to pay the highest prices for communications products and services in order to be assured of the utmost reliability.

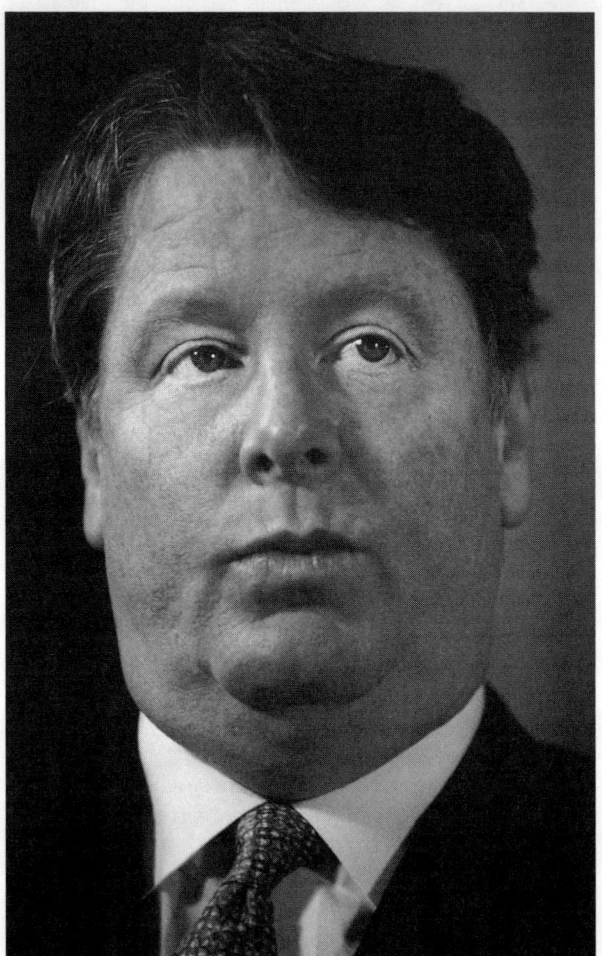

Tim M. Donahue. © *James Leynse/Corbis.*

TALKING BUSINESS AT NEXTEL

In the mid-2000s Nextel Communications—a company that went public under the name Fleet Call in 1992, becoming Nextel in 1993—was a major provider of fully integrated wireless-communications services and had built one of the largest all-digital wireless networks in the United States. Under the leadership of Donahue, Nextel was providing service to 95 percent of Fortune 500 companies—as of February 2004, 90 percent of its 12.3 million users were business customers. Corporations and government organizations thrived thanks to communication provided by Nextel Wireless Business Solutions and Customer Network Solutions. Nextel Communications and its affiliate Nextel Partners were serving 293 of the 300 major U.S. markets where approximately 250 million people worked and lived.

Nextel's customers made use of Digital Cellular, a service providing high-quality calls and guaranteed message delivery in the protected, secure environment available throughout the Nextel network. The software code used in the Nextel system was based mostly on Java and Wireless Application Protocol, providing specialized data applications for business markets such as construction and building trades, education, field sales and service, financial services, government, health care, manufacturing, real estate, emergency services, and transportation and distribution.

SHAKESPEAREAN SCHOLAR GOES WIRELESS

The educational and early work background of Donahue bore no relation to either telecommunications or technology. Upon his father's insistence Donahue studied English literature and Shakespeare at John Carroll University in University Heights, Ohio, graduating in 1971. A few decades later Donahue attributed much of his business success to his education, which had given him the confidence to speak in public in a variety of situations, honed the skills he would need to become a leader, and evoked his ability to make personal connections with people.

Little is known about Donahue's early career. He entered the telecommunications industry in 1984, when he gained employment with MCI Communications Corporation. He started his wireless career with the company now known as AT&T Wireless Services—formerly McCaw Cellular Communications—in 1986 as president of the paging division. In 1989 he was named president of the U.S. central region; from 1991 to 1996 he served as the northeast regional president. Donahue began his career with Nextel in January 1996 when he was appointed to be the company's president and chief operating officer; he became Nextel's president and chief executive officer in 1999.

BASIC PHILOSOPHY

When Donahue began his term of employment at Nextel, the company was not meeting the standards set by the competition. While other wireless operators were flying high on the technology bubble of the mid-1990s, Nextel was almost deflated. The company had concentrated on production of push-to-talk cellular phones, which were popular in the early 1990s but less so a few years later. Push-to-talk technology allowed users to connect to each other with only a push of a button—that is, with no dialing, ringing, or waiting. At this time Donahue first stated the philosophy that he would continue to use at Nextel for years to come: "Be first, be better, be different" (March 24, 2004). Donahue hoped to ascertain the market segment in which Nextel would most reasonably specialize by asking such pointed questions as, "Who are our customers?" "How do we attract them?" and "How do we keep them?"

AIMING TO BE UNIQUE

The questions were answered when Donahue decided to target the underserved commercial and enterprise (business-to-business) markets. In 1996 Donahue put forth high-end specialized data applications along with a variety of top-of-the-line communications services aimed specifically at corporations with extensive, nonstationary work forces. The intent was for businesses to realize that with Nextel services, waste management supervisors, for instance, could locate all of the company's garbage trucks at any given time; swimming pool contractors could use Nextel technology to determine the number of gallons of water in a spa; and carpenters could calculate the rise and run of a staircase.

Donahue arranged for software developers such as Etrieve and Mobilesys to sell or rent their software (usually on a monthly basis) directly to Nextel customers (with Nextel receiving a percentage of the profits). He formed alliances with such industry leaders as IBM, EDS, Microsoft, and Sun Microsystems in order to provide unique services that customers could only receive through Nextel products. In addition, Donahue made it a priority for his sales force to understand and be trained in the use of the specific applications and products its customers needed.

UNIQUE PRODUCTS AND SERVICES

Under the direction of Donahue, Nextel implemented a digital technique invented by Motorola called iDEN (integrated digital enhanced network), which was unique from other wireless techniques such as TDMA (time division multiple access), CDMA (code division multiple access), and GSM (global system for mobile communications). Nextel's iDEN, which was introduced in 1996, was an integrated digital-technology platform providing superior transmission and audio quality for such services as regular dialed calls, two-way radios and instant messaging, data terminals, and dual capabilities with other companies' wireless platforms.

Donahue chose to use Direct Connect (an exclusive Nextel feature where every Nextel phone has a special button that lets the owner connect instantly and reliably to any Nextel customer in the local coverage area) for three reasons in particular. First, the technology was capable of establishing connections in about one second, compared with the two- to nine-second connection time found with other services. Second, Direct Connect allowed the largest number of characters to be sent per message: five hundred (in 2002) versus the average of 160 allowed by competitors. Third, Direct Connect would allow businesspeople to communicate with associates, family, and friends without placing actual phone calls. Most financial and telecommunication analysts agreed that the service Donahue created at Nextel was superior to that of the competition.

WALKIE-TALKIE PHONES

Nextel became especially well known for its Direct Connect walkie-talkie phones. Donahue expanded Nextel's operations by ensuring that its communication devices were technologically superior to the competition and by identifying and concentrating on niche business users who traditionally spent more time using mobile communications than the average customer. As of February 2004 the average Nextel customer paid $71 per month before taxes and most additional fees, as compared with the industry average of $50.

The Direct Connect system, offered by Nextel since the middle of the 1990s, was especially popular with companies and government agencies involved in natural security thanks to its private, exclusively owned technology that was impossible to illegally access. Donahue expected its importance to grow well beyond the 10 percent of Nextel customers with high-security needs as of February 2004; among these customers were the Central Intelligence Agency, the Federal Bureau of Investigation, and the U.S. Senate.

Donahue completed nationwide Direct Connect service in 2003, such that a user on the East Coast, for example, would receive the same performance whether talking to someone on the West Coast or down the street. In 2004 Donahue planned to introduce new features to Direct Connect, improving voice quality, adding video functions, and setting up Web-based directories for dynamic conference lines. While Donahue advanced Nextel's established push-to-talk features, the competition still struggled to introduce push-to-talk for the first time. Donahue was also developing plans to use satellite technology to deploy Direct Connect globally, which was very appealing to the fastest-growing customer sectors of government and public safety.

THREE YEARS OF PREPARATION PAY OFF

Before 2002 Nextel was just another company in the wireless phone business. By that year, with the competition struggling, Nextel's accomplishments over the preceding years became evident. Donahue felt that Nextel had become the leader in the United States with regards to data services in the wireless arena, pointing out that in 2001 Nextel, in conjunction with Motorola, was the first wireless company to launch Java-technology-enabled wireless phones in the United States. Mobile professionals could personalize and improve their phones with the latest business tools and network applications as well as improve the quality of their professional lives.

Later in 2001 Donahue had launched the Motorola iBoard, which let Nextel customers compose e-mail, organize address books and calendars, and work with Java-enabled applications—all from a wireless phone and a full-sized, foldaway keyboard. In late 2002 Donahue directed the successful launch of the handheld, wireless BlackBerry device, created by Research in Motion. The device offered a suite of Nextel wireless mobile solutions, including all-digital cellular service, e-mail, Direct Connect digital walkie-talkie service, numeric and text messaging, Nextel Online service, and Java technology.

FUNDAMENTAL STRENGTH

By the end of 2002 Nextel had one million Java-capable handsets on the market. At this point Donahue saw Nextel's fundamental strength as its ability to initially sell cost-effective walkie-talkies to businesses, later upgrading services to include a wider range of data transmission capabilities.

Domestic revenues for Nextel in 2003 were $10.8 billion; the company had 12.9 million domestic digital subscribers and about 17,000 U.S. employees. Though Nextel was ranked fifth among the six national U.S. wireless carriers, it had been growing at the fastest rate of all six operations. As a result of Donahue's efforts Frost and Sullivan, a New York City consulting and market-research organization, named Nextel the 2003 Mobile Communications Company of the Year, and *BusinessWeek* ranked Nextel first in its 2003 Information Technology 100 list. Paralleling such honors for Nextel, Donahue was named the 2003 Entrepreneur of the Year in the Networking and Communications category and the 2003 Master Entrepreneur of the Year in the greater Washington area, both by Ernst & Young.

RESULTS SPEAK FOR THEMSELVES

With Nextel focusing primarily on the business customer, Donahue found the company's average revenue per user to be the best in the industry; the company itself was profitable since 2001, unlike rivals such as Sprint PCS Group and AT&T Wireless Services. Overall, Nextel experienced record-setting financial results, with six straight quarters of positive net income as of the last quarter of 2003. Donahue built Nextel into a Fortune 300 company with a significantly reduced debt load and a subscriber base that had more than tripled between 1996 and 1999.

Donahue stayed focused on the business customer, developing products and services that others could not provide or quality that others could not match. Even during the very significant economic downturn during 2000 and 2001—which hit the telecommunications industry especially hard—Nextel did well. Nextel made its first full-year profit in 2002 with a net income of $1.66 billion. Donahue made a point of cutting debts during this time; in that year debt was reduced by $6 billion, from $16 billion in the last quarter of 2000 to $10 billion in the last quarter of 2002. Donahue expected that debt would decrease to $7.4 billion by the end of 2004. He emphasized that the company accomplished these financial feats thanks to quality products that increased productivity, most especially Direct Connect and its ability to link users nationwide almost instantaneously.

SERVICE OVER PRICING CONCENTRATION

Donahue demonstrated value and return on investment to be important Nextel traits within the worldwide wireless-business market by concentrating on service over pricing. Nextel had a termination rate of 1.4 percent, the lowest in the industry—in the third quarter of 2003 AT&T Wireless had a termination rate of 3.3 percent. Donahue believed that Nextel could continue maintaining and adding to its customer base for many years to come. About four million users were added to Nextel's customer base each year from 2000 to 2002, and Donahue expected about 1.6 million more users in 2004. He stated that the company was nowhere near market saturation, as it had acquired business from only about 32 percent of construction companies, 19 percent of manufacturing companies, and 7 percent of service companies. Donahue expected the transportation and service industries to be two especially strong growth segments.

Donahue did not rest on past successes: in 2004 he guided Nextel to sponsorship of NASCAR auto racing. Donahue felt that hugely loyal racing fans would be attracted to Nextel's dedicated style of operations.

OTHER DUTIES

Donahue was a member of the board of directors of Eastman Kodak Company and NII Holdings. He was the chairman of the board of directors of Cellular Telecommunications and the Internet Association.

See also entry on Nextel Communications, Inc. in *International Directory of Company Histories.*

SOURCES FOR FURTHER INFORMATION

Hamerly, David, "Nextel Communications, Inc." Hoover's Online, http://www.hoovers.com/nextel/—ID__10950—/free-co-factsheet.xhtml.

"Keynote Sessions: Timothy Donahue, President and CEO, Nextel Communications," CTIA Wireless, March 24, 2004, http://www.ctiawireless2004.com/keynotes/keynote.cfm?calID=284.

—William Arthur Atkins

■■■

David W. Dorman

1954–

Chairman and chief executive officer, AT&T Corporation

Nationality: American.

Born: 1954, in Georgia.

Education: Georgia Institute of Technology, BS, 1975.

Family: Married Susan (maiden name unknown); children: three.

Career: Sprint, 1981–1990, manager; 1990–1994, president of Sprint Business; Pacific Bell, 1994–1997, president, CEO, and chairman; SBC Communications, 1997, executive vice president; PointCast, 1997–1999, president, CEO, and chairman; Concert Communications, 1999–2000, CEO; AT&T Corporation, 2000–2002, president; 2002–, chairman and CEO.

Address: AT&T Corporation, 1 AT&T Way, Bedminster, New Jersey 07921-0752; http://www.att.com.

■ David W. Dorman had a relaxed style and spoke with a Georgian drawl; his keen wit and considerable charm put fellow workers at ease and enabled him to speak easily with the people he supervised. He gained a reputation for being able to build businesses when he increased Sprint Business's revenue from $4 million in 1990 to $4.5 billion in 1993. The greatest challenge of his career came in 2000, when he took on the task of rebuilding AT&T, a company whose total stock value had fallen from a high of $110 billion to a low of less than $11 billion in the late 1990s.

SPRINT

Dorman graduated with a bachelor's degree in industrial management from the Georgia Institute of Technology in 1975, just three years after entering college. His big break came in 1981, when he became the fifty-fifth employee hired by the company that would later become Sprint. He worked various management positions for the company until he was appointed as president of Sprint Business, where careful marketing led to rapid growth; the division eventually comprised 10,000 employees.

David W. Dorman. *AP/Wide World Photos.*

PACIFIC BELL AND SBC

In 1994 Dorman was hired away by Pacific Bell, a division of Pacific Telesis Group, one of the Baby Bells spun off from AT&T in the early 1980s. At the age of 39 Dorman was the youngest leader ever at any of the Baby Bells, having become Pacific Bell's president, chief executive officer, and chairman of the board. The company was quite large, with 50,000 employees, 10 million household customers, one million business customers, and $11 billion in annual revenue.

In 1997 SBC Communications bought Pacific Telesis Group, and Dorman lost his exalted position, becoming SBC's executive vice president. Many observers thought that his move to PointCast in late 1997 was motivated by his frustration with having to answer to corporate leaders who did not share his management views, as well as by his desire to be the leader of a company. But Dorman stated that his wife and three children had not wished to move to SBC's corporate headquarters, demanding instead to stay put in California; his family's wishes motivated him to accept the position of president, CEO, and chairman of PointCast, an Internet information provider. Dorman received a $1.5 million signing bonus from PointCast and a $250,000 salary in 1998. He found PointCast to be confused, pushing too many different kinds of data; he gave the company focus by instituting an emphasis on news reporting. In spite of Dorman's efforts, however, PointCast ran short of capital in 1999, and in April of that year Dorman accepted the position of CEO at Concert Communications.

AT&T

Concert Communications was a joint venture by AT&T and British Telecommunications. The companies' hope was to build Concert into a worldwide telecom service, but the project was doomed by unrealistic expectations from the management at both AT&T and British Telecommunications; in 2000 Concert failed. In December 2000 Dorman was named president of AT&T, becoming responsible for customer services, AT&T labs, network services, and global business ventures. AT&T had been without a president for over a year.

In 1998 AT&T's market capitalization was $110 billion, and the company was growing in new directions, having become the country's sixth-largest provider of Internet services. In 2000 AT&T carried more data traffic than voice traffic for the first time. On October 25, 2000, AT&T began reorganizing itself into four segments: AT&T Wireless, AT&T Broadband, AT&T Business, and AT&T Consumer. When Dorman became president, the company was chaotic, with communication between departments sorely deficient; in one instance, sales representatives were selling goods that the divisions responsible for production did not have.

Dorman spent much of 2001 fostering cooperation among those departments. He devoted his time to clarifying the motivation behind the changes AT&T was undergoing, such as the May 25, 2001, purchase of NorthPoint Communications, a network service provider, as well as the spinning off of AT&T Wireless to become an independent company. The revenue from Dorman's responsibilities totaled $40 billion, out of $66 billion altogether for AT&T; in all Dorman supervised over 82,000 employees.

In February 2002 Dorman was appointed to AT&T's board of directors, a step toward his becoming the company's CEO. During 2002 Dorman strove to modernize AT&T by replacing 48 "legacy" telecommunications switching systems with up-to-date systems that used Internet protocol. He hoped to use the Internet for routing voice telephone calls as well as data communications, thus eliminating the need to pay local telephone companies access fees in order to use their lines. Additionally Dorman directed the marketing of bundled services to customers, which proved especially attractive to businesses that wanted a wide variety of services and could find them all available at AT&T. The company sold these bundles of services to corporations such as Hyatt Hotels, MasterCard, and Merrill Lynch. AT&T introduced ultra-accurate voice-recognition software that would replace operators at some companies. Dorman spent $200 million to develop new customer services, and he had all 4,300 customer-services personnel retrained to be more helpful. On November 18, 2002, AT&T Broadband merged with Comcast Corporation, and the AT&T CEO and chairman C. Michael Armstrong left AT&T to run the new Comcast; that day Dorman became CEO and chairman at AT&T. For the year Dorman was paid $6.5 million.

In 2003 AT&T became the largest provider of Internet services and doubled its total number of local-service customers to 28 million. Another 52 "legacy" systems were replaced. The company introduced software called "underware" to handle basic computer tasks, and Dorman puckishly suggested that customers should not leave home without their underware. He negotiated a merger with BellSouth that would have put him in a position to become CEO when BellSouth's leader F. Duane Ackerman retired; however, the merger talks fell apart on October 28, 2003, when Ackerman decided the $25 apiece price for AT&T shares was too steep. That year Dorman cut 8,500 jobs, or 12 percent of AT&T's workforce.

In 2004 some observers still expected AT&T to fail, but its situation was looking up. Dorman had carefully paid down AT&T's debts, giving the company a good debt-to-income ratio. Furthermore, the company's stock was once again increasing in value, giving AT&T $15 billion in stock capitalization.

See also entry on AT&T Corp. in *International Directory of Company Histories.*

SOURCES FOR FURTHER INFORMATION

Backover, Andrew, "Laid-Back AT&T Chief Looks for '90 Percent Substance,'" *USA Today*, December 24, 2003, http://www.usatoday.com.

Rosenbush, Steve, "New Honcho, New AT&T? David Dorman's Big Plans May Not Save the Phone Giant," *BusinessWeek*, May 20, 2002, pp. 130–131.

Woolley, Scott, "'I'm Just Dave,'" *Forbes*, May 26, 2003, p. 76.

—Kirk H. Beetz

■■■

Jürgen Dormann

1940–

Chairman, ABB

Nationality: German.

Born: January 12, 1940, in Heidelberg, Germany.

Education: University of Heidelberg, master's degree, 1963.

Family: Married Lizbeth (maiden name unknown); children: four.

Career: Hoechst, 1963–1964, management trainee; 1964–1973, head of fiber-sales department; 1973–1974, member of corporate staff; 1975–1979, overseer of all international personnel; 1980–1985, head of international department; 1986–1987, overseer of special-chemicals division and dyes operations and North American division; 1987–1993, CFO of information technology and head of Hoechst Celanese; 1994–1999, chairman and CEO; Aventis, 1999–2002, chairman of management board; 2002–, chairman of supervisory board; ABB, 2001–2002, chairman, 2002–2004, chairman, CEO, and president; 2004–, chairman.

Awards: Manager of the Year, *Manager*, 1995.

Address: ABB, Affolternstrasse 44, 8050 Zurich, Switzerland; http://www.abb.com.

■ Jürgen Dormann admitted that he would never run from a challenge; the two biggest challenges of his business career were rescuing both the chemical manufacturer Hoechst and—at a stage when most senior executives would have been contemplating retirement—the engineering company ABB from almost certain death following dramatic shifts in the economy, overexpansion programs, and poor management. He identified and developed the corporations' core strengths, focused their Byzantine structures into clearly defined divisons, divested noncore businesses and underperformers, demanded honesty and openness from his managers, and persevered through adversity.

Jürgen Dormann. *AP/Wide World Photos.*

FOCUS, FOCUS, FOCUS

Dormann began his almost 40-year career with Hoechst in 1963 immediately after obtaining his master's degree in economics from the University of Heidelberg. In 1987 he was placed in charge of American Hoechst, which that year merged with the American Celanese Corporation to create Hoechst Celanese, the fourth-largest chemical manufacturing company in the United States. The company underwent several years of solid financial growth under Dormann's leadership. When he was chosen in 1994 to head Hoechst's entire operations, Dormann became the first company chairman never to have been trained as a chemist. Hoechst had been struggling financially as a result of international market shifts and the enormous changes in the German economy that followed the fall of the Berlin Wall in 1990; Dormann's first priority would be to help resuscitate the company.

Dormann immediately made drastic changes at Hoechst, giving a speech entitled "New Beginnings" to the company's 170,000 employees indicating that henceforth the company would be less bureaucratic, more shareholder friendly, and more profitable, and that management would become more international—he soon appointed the first-ever non-German board member. He divested the company of its remaining industrial divisions, low-profit chemical divisions, and cosmetics business to concentrate on what he identified as Hoechst's core strengths: agricultural and pharmaceutical products. Managers were given a four-year time frame in which to turn their individual sectors into viable businesses that could compete in their respective fields; some companies were spun off to create independent entities. English was instituted as the company language to improve communication between international entities, and policies fostering corporate openness were put into place. Tens of thousands of jobs were cut in Germany, and the head offices were moved to a more modest location.

In the ensuing years Dormann rebuilt Hoechst by focusing almost solely on pharmaceuticals and agriculture. The company acquired other pharmaceutical giants, including Marion Merrell Dow for $7 billion, creating a new pharmaceutical division named Hoechst Marion Roussel (HMR). Dormann mandated that the division release several new products each year; HMR hit on a winner in the late 1990s with the nonsedative allergy medication Allegra. Dormann also initiated the manufacture of crop-protection chemicals in conjunction with the Berlin-based pharmaceutical manufacturer Schering; the joint venture was named AgrEvo.

As a result of the restructuring, the value of Hoechst shares nearly doubled between 1994 and the end of 1998. In 1999, in what was heralded as the most successful cross-border merger since World War II—though it was not entirely popular with his German colleagues—Dormann united his venerated German company with the French rival Rhone-Poulenc to form Aventis, the world's sixth-largest pharmaceutical company. He became the new company's chairman and divested it of its gases, fibers, and industrial-chemicals holdings in order to focus on its life-sciences operations, which included AgrEvo and HMR, becoming the world's second-largest life-sciences company. Dormann consequently earned a reputation as one of Europe's corporate superstars. Richard Tomlinson wrote in *Fortune*, "He was one CEO, investors on both sides of the Atlantic agreed, who got it" (November 18, 2002).

RISE AND FALL OF A GIANT

In the late 20th century ABB, once known as Asea Brown Boveri, was created when the two electrical engineering and equipment giants ASEA of Sweden and BBC Brown Boveri of Switzerland joined forces. In the unusual merger ASEA (which became ABB AB) and BBC (which became ABB AG) continued operating and trading as separate entities while equally sharing ownership of the parent ABB. Percy Barnevik became the company's CEO and began an aggressive expansion program, acquiring the American company Combustion Engineering in 1990. Within six years ABB gobbled up more than 150 companies worldwide; many began drawing comparisons between the successful ABB and General Electric (GE). However, many of the acquired businesses ultimately became drains on the company, and ambitious projects in Asia had excessively high risk and low profit margins; ABB was overextended.

Amid what Dormann described in *Fortune* as "a lot of friendly and less friendly questions" (November 18, 2002), Barnevik retired as CEO in 1997; he would stay on as chairman until 2001. He was succeeded as CEO by Goran Lindahl, an engineer who had worked his way up the ASEA ladder. Profits continued to drop, however, and Tomlinson summarized in *Fortune* what happened next: "Lindahl, the new CEO, led ABB into its ill-advised—and in retrospect ludicrous—attempt to reinvent itself as a high-tech services company" (November 18, 2002). Costs spiraled until Lindahl was pushed out in 2000; Dormann, who had been recruited to ABB's board by Barnevik in 1998, wielded significant influence in that move. Lindahl was replaced by the head of ABB's automotive business, Jörgen Centerman, in 2001.

The company soon faced serious economic slowdowns in its key markets and in July 2001 declared that it would cut its workforce by 8 percent—which amounted to 12,000 jobs—within 18 months. Then an unforeseen catastrophe hit: claims were made against Combustion Engineering, ABB's U.S. subsidiary, due to asbestos exposure from products supplied prior to the mid-1970s—well before the company's 1990 acquisition by ABB. A total of $952 million was set aside for asbestos-related litigation, significantly contributing to ABB's record net loss of $691 million in 2001. Amid the furor Barnevik resigned from his post as chairman.

To add to ABB's woes, a major controversy erupted surrounding the $88 million pension awarded to Barnevik and the $55 million received by Lindahl without full board approval. Although the awards were not technically illegal, they were most certainly disproportionate and seriously damaging to the company's reputation. Dormann quickly announced that the board had determined the approval procedures permitting the awards to have been unsatisfactory, and the company demanded restitution; the two former leaders agreed to pay back about $82 million. But the financial woes were still mounting: amid continuing industry slumps, the company found itself $4.4 billion in debt. ABB sold a portion of its financial-services unit to GE Commercial Finance for $2.3 billion, which Dormann noted should have kept the company afloat until the sale of its oils, gas, and petrochemicals division, which was slated for 2003.

INHERITS A MESS

The day following the GE deal Centerman resigned; as he had with Lindahl, Dormann played a key role in Centerman's departure. As reported by *Fortune*'s Tomlinson, in the only public remark about his retirement Centerman told a Swedish radio station, "My decision to resign is totally connected to Jürgen Dormann" (November 18, 2002). Dormann himself was subsequently chosen as CEO, taking office on September 9, 2002; though he had not expected to take over the helm at ABB, the board could find no one else they felt to be up to the job. Dormann remarked in *Fortune*, "I'm not saying I was the best candidate, but the best available candidate" (November 18, 2002).

Upon taking over, Dormann was still unaware of the full extent of the company's troubles. A month after his instatement he expressed complete confidence that ABB would hit their earnings targets and averred that liabilities surrounding the asbestos cases were under control. However, two weeks later he issued a warning that the company would not hit its earnings goals and would possibly need to seek bankruptcy protection for Combustion Engineering because of skyrocketing liability claims. Following a downgrading of ABB's debt by Moody's to the lowest possible rating, the company's shares plummeted by more than 40 percent. Dormann apologized to shareholders, but their confidence in ABB and its CEO had dropped as quickly as the company's share prices. The analyst Andreas Riede of Sarasin Bank in Zurich told *Fortune*, "He has lost our trust within one month" (November 18, 2002).

Amid concerns as to whether Dormann could regain that trust were questions as to why he had been deluded about the full extent of the company's problems. The answer he gave to *Fortune* was, "If you are the chairman, you do not have regular contact with the people doing the day-to-day business" (November 18, 2002). He further noted that just one week after becoming CEO he had called on his senior management team to justify their positive forecasts, and they had done so: "How could I say, 'Hey, guys, I don't believe you?'" (November 18, 2002). Dormann was in a tough spot. By February 2003 ABB's shares had dropped from the $33 of three years earlier to $2.86, and the company was carrying a debt load of $23 billion against market capitalization of only $3.2 billion. *BusinessWeek* reporters wrote, "If Dormann is over his head, then one of Europe's largest companies, with some $23 billion in sales and close to 150,000 employees, will probably be broken up" (February 10, 2003). When asked why, at the age of 62 and after a successful career with Hoechst, he had wanted to accept the job of trying to resurrect ABB, he replied without hesitation, "The way I was raised and trained, you don't run away from a challenge" (February 10, 2003).

RESUSCITATING THE FALLEN

Dormann wasted no time in taking up that challenge. He wrote to his managers informing them that he no longer wanted to be inundated with flashy PowerPoint presentations when he asked for information; he wanted the facts, plain and simple. As quoted by Tomlinson, he wrote, "I don't want to be sold to when we are discussing real-life business issues within the company. I don't want self-promotion; I want someone to lay out the issues at hand so we can examine them and find solutions." Tomlinson noted: "It's a measure of ABB's dire straits that Dormann is losing his patience with those in the company who don't match his exacting standards" (November 18, 2002).

As he had done at Hoechst, Dormann focused. He had already sold off the structured-finance business for $2.3 billion, and in the following five months he identified ABB's high-producing areas and reorganized the previously sprawling corporation into two operating divisions: power and technology. He embarked upon a $1.3 billion cost-reduction program, filed for Chapter 11 bankruptcy for Combustion Engineering in order to protect the rest of the company from further litigation, and negotiated a $1.2 billion settlement that, if approved by all parties, would bring an end to the asbestos issue. By the end of the year he had reduced the company's debt by $1.5 billion, and the two core divisions combined showed 38 percent growth. However, net losses totaled $783 million—more than the $691 million of the year before that had primarily been due to the asbestos negotiations.

As quoted in the *Guardian*, ABB's finance director commented, "When I came here the debt mountain looked like the Himalayas to me. Now it's like the Matterhorn: still high, but it can and will be climbed"; in somewhat of an understatement Dormann attempted to reassure shareholders: "It's been a difficult year, but we've put the worst behind us. I am confident we can deliver on our growth targets and return to profitability in 2003" (February 28, 2003). Investors remained unconvinced, however, and share values dropped another 10 percent. Earlier in the year Dormann had indicated that the coming 12 to 18 months would determine whether ABB could remain independent; as seen by analysts, he had yet to improve the company's junk credit rating, sell the remainder of its noncore businesses, or boost the low revenue-per-employee ratio—all of which could lead to cuts of 30,000 jobs.

By February 2004, under Dormann's ongoing comeback plan, while ABB's worldwide workforce had been halved to 115,000, its two core units had turned in stronger-than-forecast returns, and the stock price had grown steadily, reaching $6.55. Despite a net loss of $767 million over 2003, first-quarter results in 2004 showed that Dormann's plan was taking effect: the company posted a net income of $4 million, as compared to the $388 million loss from the final quarter of

2003. Dormann said that 2003 was the company's turnaround year and that he expected to see continued growth through 2004. Indeed, in June 2004 ABB announced that it had won a bid worth upwards of $40 million to deliver process automation, drives, quality-control systems, electrification, and related services to China's Asia Pulp and Paper Company as well as a $390 million order to build a key power link to Shanghai from China's Three Gorges hydroelectric dam; the latter order was the world's largest power-transmission project in several years. As of June 2004 the company was still awaiting a ruling by the U.S. judge who had run the hearing over the asbestos issue; Dormann felt confident that his settlement proposal would be accepted.

Beneath his photograph on ABB's Web site, Dormann stated, "Two of ABB's enduring strengths are technology and the ability to innovate. These great assets are at the core of our customer relationships, and we should be proud of them." He announced that he would retire as CEO at the end of 2004 but would remain with ABB as chairman.

See also entry on Hoechst A.G. in *International Directory of Company Histories.*

SOURCES FOR FURTHER INFORMATION

"ABB Group Executive Committee," ABB Web site, http://www.abb.com/global/abbzh/abbzh251.nsf!Open Database&db=/global/abbzh/ abbzh252.nsf&v=76C6&.e=us&c=4E94D980FFFD6725C125670C003E0FAD.

Milner, Mark, "Asbestos Contributes to ABB's Record Loss," *Guardian* (UK), February 28, 2003.

Reed, Stanley, and Michael Arndt, "Work Your Magic, Herr Dormann ABB Faces Meltdown—So This CEO Isn't Wasting Any Time," February 10, 2003, *BusinessWeek*, p. 46.

Tomlinson, Richard, "Mission Impossible?" *Fortune*, November 18, 2002, p. 147.

—Marie L. Thompson

■■■

E. Linn Draper Jr.

1942–

Former chairman, chief executive officer, and president, American Electric Power Company

Nationality: American.

Born: February 6, 1942, in Houston, Texas.

Education: Rice University, BA, 1964; BS, 1965; Cornell University, PhD, 1970.

Family: Son of Ernest Linn Draper and Marcia L. Saylor; married Mary Deborah Doyle, 1962; children: four.

Career: University of Texas, 1970–1979, faculty; Gulf States Utilities, 1979–1987, nuclear technician, then senior management; 1987–1992, CEO and president; American Electric Power Company, 1992, president and COO; 1993–2003, chairman, CEO, and president; 2004, chairman.

Awards: Individual Leadership Award, *Energy Daily*, 1997; Distinguished Eagle Scout Award, Boy Scouts of America, 1998; Columbus Award, Greater Columbus Chamber of Commerce, 2002; Roy Family Award for Conservation, Harvard University John F. Kennedy School of Government, 2003.

■ E. Linn Draper Jr. became the president of American Electric Power (AEP), the electric-utility holding company headquartered in Columbus, Ohio, in March 1992. In April 1993 he was named chairman, president, and chief executive officer of AEP and all of its major subsidiaries, which positions he held until December 31, 2003. He continued to serve as chairman until his retirement in April 2004.

As the head of AEP Draper led the company through the uncertainties of several events: the deregulation that followed the 1992 Energy Policy Act; the Enron collapse of 2001, which shook the entire energy industry; and the largest blackout in North American history, which occurred on August 14, 2003. By 2002 AEP was America's largest electricity generator—with more than 22,000 U.S. employees—and a world energy leader with operations in Europe and 7.3 million customers worldwide. The company ranked thirty-fifth on *BusinessWeek*'s 2002 list of the 50 top-performing companies. In May 2003 *Public Utilities Fortnightly* recognized Draper as one of the five best power-industry CEOs "for his leadership in restoring the reputation of a great utility name" (May 14, 2003).

EARLY CAREER HIGHLIGHTS

Draper began his career as a faculty member at the University of Texas, where he taught until 1979. During his time there Draper at one point served as the director of the Nuclear Engineering Program. Between 1979 and 1992 he was employed by Gulf State Utilities, continually moving into positions of increasing responsibility. He started out as a nuclear technician and by the mid-1980s held senior management positions. Between 1987 and 1992 Draper served as the president and chief executive officer of Gulf States Utilities.

Draper joined American Electric Power as president and chief operating officer in 1992. In 1993 he was appointed chairman, president, and chief executive officer of the company.

NAVIGATING DEREGULATION

By 1997 AEP served in excess of three million customers in Ohio, Virginia, West Virginia, Indiana, Kentucky, Michigan, and Tennessee. The company owned all or a portion of 21 major generating plants, 19 of which were coal-fired, one a nuclear station, and one a pumped-storage hydroelectricity facility.

In response to external pressures Draper soon began realigning AEP's organization and cutting the workforce to adapt to an increasingly competitive marketplace. In anticipation of the onset of a radically different electric industry in which the generation, transmission, and sale of electric power could all potentially become separate businesses, he appointed individual presidents at the state levels. In preparation for the transition from public monopoly to mere player in the competitive marketplace, Draper determined that the company's core business should remain power generation. Although some of his decisions were viewed as aggressive and were unpopular among employees, Draper ensured that the financial security of the firm remained solid.

In late 1997 AEP acquired Central & South West Corporation, the Dallas, Texas–based public-utility holding company.

According to Draper, the merger created a company that was "diverse in its fuel, its generation, and in the workplace—a link between the Midwest and Southwest, reaching from Canada to Mexico" (Brown, December 28, 1997). Following the acquisition AEP concentrated on wholesale customers—companies that purchased power for resale to residential and commercial customers. Draper made clear that AEP had no plans to expand its distribution business and had no intentions of competing at the retail level. The separation of generation, transmission, and distribution assets was a key factor in preserving AEP's shareholder value during this period. Draper noted in the Stockholder's Letter 2000 Annual Report, "AEP is a utility that thinks like a growth company. This growth will come from our strengths in power generation and related wholesale marketing and energy trading."

INDUSTRY SHAKE-UP: THE ENRON COLLAPSE

By 2001 AEP rivaled the industry leader Enron in the volume of electricity and natural gas traded. The subsequent collapse of Enron shook confidence in AEP as well, but under Draper's leadership AEP management was able to reassure investors that its bookkeeping was credible and its balance sheet sound. Industry analysts reported that AEP could sustain a $50 million write-off, had recorded a net income of $971 million in 2001 on revenues of $61.2 billion, and carried debt with investment-grade ratings. In addition analysts predicted that with Enron out of the picture AEP would be able to garner a larger share of the wholesale energy market. As the largest producer of electricity in the United States, with a capacity of 38,000 megawatts, and as much more than a trading house, AEP was able to emerge unscathed by the exposures of accounting scandals and corporate malfeasance throughout the energy industry following the Enron meltdown.

In response to economic conditions and the pressures that resulted from operating in a restructured, competitive marketplace, AEP began downsizing its trading and wholesale-marketing operations, divesting itself of noncore assets, and cutting dividends in order to raise capital and shore up its balance sheet during 2002 and 2003. Following a credit-rating downgrade that was based on the company's risk profile, Draper refocused AEP on its core utility operations and made solid progress toward improved performance. By mid-2003 Draper was able to claim that AEP's ability to weather the economic downturns of 2001 and 2002 had been possible because the company "never left the basics. We stuck to our core strategy throughout the restructuring of our industry. We took a look at the restructured industry early on and decided where our expertise lay and recognized that we have been a distributor of electricity for many, many years" (*Public Utilities Fortnightly*, May 14, 2003).

BLACKOUT 2003

On August 14, 2003, much of New York and the northeastern United States and southeastern Canada experienced the most widespread blackout in history. Testifying before the House Committee on Energy and Commerce less than three weeks following the power outage, Draper stated, "From the outset, let me be clear, we did it right. The AEP system held together—a point of pride for us" (September 4, 2003). AEP managed to isolate itself from the cascading blackout because, according to Draper, "our protective systems performed automatically, our operators performed and communicated as they should, and our load and generation remained in balance" (September 4, 2003).

By December 2003 many of the nation's largest electric utilities were experiencing major changes in leadership, and AEP would be no exception. Draper announced in April 2003 that he would step down as president and CEO at the end of the year. When asked how he would like to be remembered, Draper said that he hoped people would say that he left AEP "a strong company that was noted for providing reliable and affordable service to its customers. That it was an environmentally responsible entity, and that the employees, customers, and shareholders found AEP an attractive place to work, take electric service, and invest in" (*Public Utilities Fortnightly*, May 14, 2003).

PROFESSIONAL MEMBERSHIPS AND AFFILIATIONS

Draper was elected to membership in the National Academy of Engineering—one of the highest distinctions for a professional engineer—in 1992 for "significant contributions to nuclear-power development through research, engineering innovations, and overall management" (www.nae.edu Member Directory). In 1998 he was elected to the Cornell University Council Board and in 1999 was appointed to the University of Chicago Board of Governors for the Argonne National Laboratory. He was president of the American Nuclear Society and chairman of the Nuclear Energy Institute, the Institute of Nuclear Power Operations, the National Coal Council, and the Edison Electric Institute—the trade association of investor-owned electric utilities. He was a registered professional engineer in the state of Texas.

From 1984 to 1985 Draper served on a U.S. Department of Energy advisory panel charged with the study of the management of radioactive waste. He was appointed to the President's Council on Sustainable Development, a group comprised of government, business, labor, and environmental leaders assembled to recommend a national economic strategy for the protection of the environment. He served as chairman of the Electric Power Research Institute and of the Utility Nuclear Waste Management Group, a consortium of 43 electric utilities.

In 1999 Draper was elected to serve on the board of The Nature Conservancy, an international nonprofit organization that protected plants, animals, and natural communities by protecting the lands and waters that they need to survive. He also served on the board of the Ohio chapter of The Nature Conservancy.

While living and working in Columbus, Draper was involved in numerous community-service activities and organizations, including the Columbus Technology Leadership Council, the Ohio Business Roundtable, the Simon Kenton Council of the Boy Scouts of America—as president—and education-related causes such as Battelle for Kids and Education 2000. He served on the boards of Cellnet Data Systems, Borden Chemicals and Plastics, Sprint Corporation, and Temple-Inland.

See also entries on American Electric Power Company and Gulf States Utilities Company in *International Directory of Company Histories.*

SOURCES FOR FURTHER INFORMATION

"American Electric Power to Divest Utility End of Business," *Fort Wayne (IN) News-Sentinel,* October 31, 2000.

American Electric Power 2003 Summary Report to Shareholders, American Electric Power, 1 Riverside Plaza, Columbus, OH 43215-2373, www.aep.com.See also http://www.world-gen.com/class2/draper.html.

"The Best of the Best: Five Electric Utility Chiefs Are Showing True Leadership for Their Companies and for an Entire Industry," *Public Utilities Fortnightly,* May 14, 2003, p.28+, Richard Stavros, executive editor.

Brown, Wesley, "Diversity Seen in AEP-C&SW Utility Merger," *Tulsa World,* December 28, 1997.

"Chamber Honors Global Energy Leader Dr. E. Linn Draper Jr.," Greater Columbus Chamber of Commerce, February 20, 2002, http://www.columbus-chamber.org/newsroom/newsreleases/2002/pr020220a.html.

Draper, E. Linn, Jr., "Blackout 2003: How Did It Happen and Why?" witness testimony read before the House Committee on Energy and Commerce, September 4, 2003.

———, "Q&A with AEP's E. Linn Draper Jr.," *BusinessWeek Online,* March 25, 2002, http://www.businessweek.com/bw50/content/mar2002/a3776038.htm.

Martz, Michael, "American Electric Power Prepares for Competition with Restructuring," *Richmond (VA) Times-Dispatch,* August 14, 1995.

Reddy, Sudeep, "Energy Industry Changes Prompt CEO Searches," *Knight Ridder/Tribune Business News,* December 18, 2003.

—Virginia Finsterwald

■ ■ ■

John G. Drosdick

1943–

Chairman, chief executive officer, and president, Sunoco; chairman, Sunoco Logistics Partners

Nationality: American.

Born: August 9, 1943, in West Hazleton, Pennsylvania.

Education: Villanova University, BS, 1965; University of Massachusetts–Amherst, MS, 1968.

Family: Married Gloria J. Shenosky; children: four.

Career: Exxon USA, 1968–1973, engineer; 1973–1974, crude-oil coordinator; 1974–1976, planning manager for ocean operations; 1976–1978, manager of development department; 1978–1981, analysis manager; 1981–1983, manager of refinery operations; Tosco Corporation, 1983–1985, vice president of refining; 1985–1986, senior vice president of refining; 1986–1987, executive vice president; 1987–1989, president and COO; Tosco Refining Company, 1989–1992, CEO and president; Ultramar, 1992–1996, president and COO; Sun Company, 1996–1998, president and COO; Sunoco, 1998–2000, president and COO; 2000–, chairman, CEO, and president; Sunoco Logistics Partners, 2001–, chairman.

Awards: J. Stanley Morehouse Memorial Award, Villanova University Alumni Association, 1999.

Address: Sunoco, 10 Penn Center, 1801 Market Street, Philadelphia, Pennsylvania 19103-1699; http://www.sunocoinc.com.

■ At Tosco and Ultramar, John G. Drosdick built a reputation for reforming corporate culture as well as for cutting costs; at Sunoco he demonstrated an ability to rebuild a company. His employees responded well to his straightforward directions, and he had a knack for making his goals plain to his managers. Although he made tough decisions as a leader, Drosdick had a sense of humor and a relaxed manner that translated not only into his flashy suits but into a cheerful corporate atmosphere.

BUILDING A CAREER

Drosdick earned a bachelor's degree from Villanova University in 1965 and a master's degree from the University of Massachusetts at Amherst in 1968, both in chemical engineering. In 1968 he was hired by Exxon USA and moved to Houston, Texas; in 1976 he moved to Baton Rouge to manage Exxon's department of facilities development; and in 1981 he became manager of Exxon's refinery operations. Tosco Corporation hired Drosdick away in 1983 in order to obtain his help with their failing refinery business, making him vice president of that division; he moved to Santa Monica, California. As corporate executive vice president in 1986 he helped restructure Tosco's debt: the company sold $150 million in bonds and issued $250 million in preferred stock to pay off loans from 19 banks. While president and chief operating officer of Tosco, Drosdick engineered the sales of three of the company's four refineries, keeping one in California, where he cut costs and improved production.

When he moved to Ultramar in Long Beach, California, Drosdick took over the operations of another petroleum company in decline. There he cut costs and set up a merger with Diamond Shamrock, creating Ultramar Diamond Shamrock Corporation; the merger occurred soon after he left to join Sun Company, another petroleum company that had endured tough times in the 1990s.

RESTRUCTURING SUN COMPANY INTO SUNOCO

In November 1996 Drosdick became the first person from outside Sun Company to be named president. Corporate headquarters lay in Philadelphia, Pennsylvania, and he moved to Bryn Mawr. The CEO Robert H. Campbell had already begun restructuring Sun Company through the selling of its international operations, and as president Drosdick oversaw the final stages of reorganization. His day-to-day presence was quickly felt among coworkers in Philadelphia, where he created a notably upbeat atmosphere. He remarked in the *Philadelphia Business Journal*, "I don't think you can be too clear with people" (May 2, 1997), as he made sure his managers knew exactly what was expected of them.

In 1997 Sun Company's net income rose $270 million, and Drosdick was paid $560,000 in salary; he was promised bonuses of up 90 percent of his base salary if the company continued to improve. On November 6, 1998, Sun Company became Sunoco, a name intended to signify happier times at the company, but 1999 proved to be a very tough year. Gasoline prices went into a slump, and Drosdick was forced to oversee layoffs of refinery employees. Still, he earned a $73,200 bonus on top of his year's salary of $610,012.

MAKING SUNOCO A STAR

On May 4, 2000, while remaining president, Drosdick became CEO and chairman of the board at Sunoco, replacing Campbell. His vision was to make the company resistant to the up-and-down cycles of the petroleum industry. In 2000 Sunoco's biggest move was the acquisition of one hundred gas stations owned by Coastal Mart in the eastern United States. The stations and their convenience stores were renamed Sunoco and APlus. That year Sunoco netted $438 million.

In January 2001 Sunoco purchased Aristech Chemical Corporation of Pittsburgh, Pennsylvania, from Mitsubishi Corporation for $674 million. The purchase included a research center and five chemical plants, with totals of 1,100 employees, and gave Sunoco the capacity to produce nine billion pounds of petrochemicals. Further, the deal was expected to give Sunoco economic "balance," as Drosdick explained, because chemical-sales cycles tended to oppose gasoline-sales cycles; chemical sales would cushion Sunoco during periods of poor gasoline sales. Unfortunately, for the first nine months of 2001 Sunoco's chemical business lost $21 million—$9 million by Aristech—on sales of $1.1 billion. Still, Drosdick had bought Aristech from the cash-strapped Mitsubishi for only half of its worth, and the purchase was intended to be a long-term investment.

In 2001 Sunoco dropped its Kendall lubricant line and shut down its Yabucoa, Puerto Rico, refinery and three related lubricant plants in California, Oklahoma, and Pennsylvania. Drosdick searched for buyers for the facilities without success. At the end of 2001 Sunoco possessed 3,900 gas-station and convenience-store outlets and 35 terminals for petroleum-products storage. The company netted $390 million for the year.

In June 2003 Sunoco purchased 193 gas stations and convenience stores in Florida, Georgia, South Carolina, and North Carolina from Speedway SuperAmerica—a subsidiary of Marathon Ashland Petroleum—for $140 million. By the end of the year Sunoco owned over 4,300 retail sites, and the convenience stores were helping keep the bottom line steady. The company bought the Eagle Point refinery from El Paso for $130 million—the price was considered low because few companies were interested in buying the plant. Sunoco's refining capacity grew to 730,000 barrels per day; it began the year as America's ninth-largest petroleum company and finished as the eighth–largest.

During this period, as Sunoco had come under fire from environmentalists as well as Congress for polluting the air at its manufacturing plants, the company undertook the installation of new pollutant-capture technology at its facilities. The most dramatic environmental effort came in 2004, when Sunoco built a new manufacturing plant for the solid fuel coke, used in making high-grade metals, in Haverill, Ohio, for $140 million. The plant included a special heat-recovery system that would produce steam to be piped to a Sunoco chemical plant, thus reducing pollution as well as recycling recovered energy. That year Sunoco's retail empire grew to 4,600 sites.

See also entries on Sunoco, Inc., Tosco Corporation, and Ultramar PLC in *International Directory of Company Histories.*

SOURCES FOR FURTHER INFORMATION

Bishop, Todd, "Drosdick to Become Top Gun at Sunoco," *Philadelphia Business Journal*, April 28, 2000, http://philadelphia.bizjournals.com/philadelphia/stories/2000/05/01/story6.html.

Reisch, Marc S., "Buying at the Low Point," *Chemical & Engineering News*, November 5, 2001, pp. 18–19.

Webber, Maura, "Sun 'Outsider' Drosdick Is Shaking Things Up," *Philadelphia Business Journal*, May 2, 1997, http://philadelphia.bizjournals.com/philadelphia/stories/1997/05/05/story4.html.

—Kirk H. Beetz

■ ■ ■

José Dutra

1957–

President and chief executive officer, Petrobrás

Nationality: Brazilian.

Born: April 11, 1957, in Rio de Janeiro, Brazil.

Education: Universidade Federal Rural do Rio de Janeiro, BA, 1979.

Career: Geologia Sondangens, 1980–1981, geologist; Petrobrás Mineradora, 1983–1990, geologist; Companhia Vale do Rio Doce, 1990–1994, geologist; Brazilian Government, 1995–2003, senator; Petrobrás, 2003–, president and CEO.

Awards: Geologist of the Year, Geologist Association of Sergipe, 1988.

Address: Petrobrás, Avenida Chile 65-20031-912, Rio de Janeiro, RJ, Brazil; http://www2.petrobras.com.br/ingles/index.asp.

■ In 2003 Brazilian President Luiz Inacio da Silva appointed José Dutra as president and CEO of Petrobrás, the country's partially government-owned oil company. At the time, Petrobrás was Brazil's largest corporation, with some 48,000 employees, 10,000 miles of pipeline, nearly eight thousand service stations, and close to two million barrels of oil production per day. A geologist by training, Dutra had previously worked in geological planning for several firms in Brazil during the 1980s and 1990s. He also became heavily involved in politics as a member of the Workers Party, serving as a senator from the state of Sergipe starting in 1995.

EARLY CAREER

Dutra was born in Rio de Janeiro, Brazil. After graduating with a degree in geology from the Universidade Federal Rural do Rio de Janeiro in 1979, he worked for the next 15 years as a geologist. He spent two years doing geological mapping in the state of Rio de Janeiro and mining research in the state of Bahia for the Geologia Sondagens company. He then went to work for Petrobrás Mineradora (Petromisa) from 1983 until 1990, where his main duties were related to geological planning in the Taguari-Vassouras potassium mine in the city of Rosário do Catete in the state of Sergipe. Dutra was rewarded for his work with Petromisa when the Geologist Association of Sergipe selected him as Geologist of the Year in 1988. Dutra worked as a geologist for four more years, from 1990 to 1994, with the Companhia Vale do Rio Doce, the world's largest iron-ore exporter.

While living and working in the state of Sergipe, Dutra became involved in the labor movement and in politics. From 1988 to 1990 he was the national director of the Centro Unico de Trabalhadores, and between 1989 and 1994 he served as president of the Miners Union of the State of Sergipe. Dutra also became a member of the Workers Party, running for office in Sergipe in 1990 and serving as president of the state's Workers Party Regional Board. In 1994 the people of Sergipe elected him to the Brazilian legislature for the 1995–2003 period. In 1997 and 2001 Dutra served as the leader of the opposition block in the Brazilian Congress. He was a member of many congressional committees, including the Justice and Citizenship, Constitution, Economic Affairs, Infrastructure, and Education committees.

AT THE HELM OF PETROBRÁS

During the Brazilian presidential campaign in late 2002 many Petrobrás investors worried about the possible election of the left-wing Workers Party candidate Luiz Inacio da Silva, known simply as "Lula." Petrobrás had won much autonomy in the 1990s, but the Brazilian government retained 56 percent of the company's voting shares and the rights to appoint top management. In his campaign speeches Lula's rhetoric regarding Petrobrás was very nationalistic and interventionist. He asserted that large contracts to build oil platforms should be awarded not to foreign companies but only to Brazilian firms. Some investors worried that giving contracts would become a political tool to reward domestic supporters even if their bids were higher or they were less qualified to carry out the required work. Panic among investors over the rise of the Workers Party and a possible Lula victory forced Petrobrás to cancel a planned $200 million bond issue, even though the company offered political-risk insurance.

After he won the election, Lula toned down much of his radical rhetoric. Among his first actions as president of Brazil was to appoint Dutra as the new president of Petrobrás. Some investors expressed lingering concern about the future direction of the company, believing Dutra to be a political appointee with no experience in the petroleum industry. Many investors would have preferred someone with more technocratic rather than political experience. Dutra also faced the unenviable prospect of replacing the former CEO Francisco Gros, a well-respected and market-friendly executive.

In spite of these initial doubts in the corporate community, Dutra seemed to convince investors of his ability to run Petrobrás, offering toned-down, financially sound talk. He promised to respect the company's existing strategies, insisting that Petrobrás would continue a four-year, $32 billion investment plan set in motion under the previous leadership and that he would seek private participation in the company. In contrast to Lula's campaign comments, Dutra insisted that all contracts should be based on technical value, and that if the government forced Petrobrás to contract with Brazilian firms, the company should be reimbursed. He reported to the *Gazeta Mercantil* that "Petrobrás is not a government agency. It is the biggest Brazilian company, which must yield results and will be administered as such" (February 17, 2003).

Following Dutra's initial actions, Petrobrás was seen to be one of the world's best-run state oil companies, and by 2003 investors who avoided Petrobrás during the 2002 presidential campaign scrambled to purchase bonds. Dutra told *Petrobrás Magazine,* "The reopening of international markets and the positive evaluation of Petrobrás are both due to the results of good political-economic management by the government, and naturally Petrobrás's credibility with investors" (2003). Almir Barbossa, a long-time executive at Petrobrás, told *Latin Finance,* "The management has changed but we do not expect that there will be different goals for the company. Petrobrás will keep investing in the growth of production and that is it" (April–May 2003).

THE FOUR PILLARS OF PETROBRÁS

Dutra's main challenge as head of Petrobrás was to balance the company's need to remain profitable and efficient while at the same time staying true to its vision of social responsibility. He told *Petrobrás Magazine* that "the focus of Petrobrás will be the development of the country, without wavering from its commitment to shareholders" (2003). To achieve this dualistic goal, the company's overall strategy was to center on four basic pillars.

First, Petrobrás would continually seek to expand the exploration and production of oil. Dutra succeeded in this area early in his term as CEO, with the company breaking records for both daily and monthly production levels. He set a goal of establishing Brazilian oil self-sufficiency by 2006. Dutra also wanted Petrobrás to continue to be a world leader in deepwater oil exploration and production technology. The company already held the world record for deepwater extraction at 1,800 meters; it once explored as deep as 2,700 meters and had a program in place to probe beyond three thousand meters. Petrobrás intended to invest $800 million in research and development in oil exploration and production between 2003 and 2005.

Second, Dutra wanted Petrobrás to continue its leadership in the Brazilian downstream market, including the refining, marketing, and distribution of petroleum products. He hoped to maintain a competitive advantage by investing in the quality of Petrobrás's products and also updating the company's refining units to increase output.

Third, the company would consolidate its position in the natural-gas and energy market, emphasizing the provision of fuel for collective transport in cities and generating thermoelectric power for the industrial and commercial sectors. Brazil had traditionally depended on hydroelectric power; however, in the years before Dutra's arrival at Petrobrás the country suffered through severe electrical shortages, increasing the attractiveness of alternative forms of electricity production.

Finally, the Brazilian oil company would selectively expand into international operations. Such plans came on the heels of the 2002 purchase of the Argentine company Pérez Companc, which was renamed Petrobrás Energia. Dutra reported to *Petrobrás Magazine,* "Priority is to consolidate this acquisition, exploiting the synergies in our businesses both inside and outside Brazil" (2003). The company was active throughout South America, investing in oil and gas projects in Argentina, Bolivia, Colombia, Cuba, Mexico, and Venezuela. Dutra also wanted Petrobrás to implement its deepwater expertise globally, in such locations as the Gulf of Mexico and West Africa.

STRESS ON CORPORATE GOVERNANCE

Another of Dutra's goals as the leader of Petrobrás was to raise the company's corporate-governance standards. While the Brazilian government was Petrobrás's controlling shareholder, the company needed to answer to many minority shareholders as well. Petrobrás was traded on both the São Paolo Stock Exchange (Bovespa) and the New York Stock Exchange, such that stressing corporate governance would be a key part of its investor-relations strategy.

In Brazil the company was considering entering the stringent second level of Bovespa's standards for corporate governance. On the international front Petrobrás complied with the Sarbanes-Oxley Act of 2002, a U.S. bill enacted to protect investors by improving the accuracy and reliability of corporate disclosures. Adhering to the U.S. requirements would be worth the costs, according to Dutra, as it sent a clear message about Petrobrás's commitment to investors. In *Institutional Investor*, Dutra insisted that Petrobrás would follow a path that included "perfecting the transparency process within the company, adhering to Bovespa Level 2, and increasingly respecting the interests and rights of minority shareholders" (September 2003).

ENVIRONMENTAL CONCERNS

Another key issue facing Dutra was that of the environment. The Petrobrás CEO stated that the company placed an emphasis on upholding a culture giving the utmost attention to health, safety, and the environment. This had been the case at Petrobrás since a large oil spill in Guanabara Bay off the shore of Rio de Janeiro in 2000. Between 2000 and 2003 Petrobrás invested $1.3 billion in accident prevention, bringing its pipeline system up-to-date, installing Environmental Defense Centers, and acquiring environmental certification for all units of the company.

In an interview for *Petrobrás Magazine*, Dutra said that such investment allowed the company "to concentrate on improving the reliability of our systems, seeking new technologies and perfecting management methods, with emphasis on training and deviations correction" (2003). He stressed that his aim was to disseminate the culture stressing health, safety, and the environment throughout the company, with the goal of reducing accidents and leakages.

SOURCES FOR FURTHER INFORMATION

Collitt, Raymond, "State Tones Down Its Rhetoric on Petrobrás," *Financial Times*, January 13, 2003.

Conceicão, Claudio R. Gomes, "Petrobrás Must Make a Profit," *Gazeta Mercantil*, February 17, 2003.

"Efficiency and Social Responsibility," *Petrobrás Magazine*, 2003, pp. 6–11.

Myers, Randy, "The Global Stance on Sarbanes-Oxley," *NYSE Magazine*, September 4, 2003, pp. 30–33.

O'Brien, Maria, "Oil on Troubled Waters," *Latin Finance*, April–May 2003, pp. 12–16.

Yarm, Mark, "The Deepwater Front," *NYSE Magazine*, January 2, 2004, pp. 34–35.

Yolen, Steve, and Tom Murphy, "Profiles of CG Programs in Brazil," *Institutional Investor*, September 2003, pp. 20–26.

—Ronald Young

■ ■ ■

Tony Earley Jr.

1949–

Chairman and chief executive officer, DTE Energy

Nationality: American.

Born: July 29, 1949, in Jamaica, New York.

Education: University of Notre Dame, BS, 1971; MS, 1979; JD, 1979.

Family: Son of Anthony Francis Earley and Jean Ann Draffen; married Sarah Margaret Belanger, 1972; children: four.

Career: U.S. Navy, 1971–1976, lieutenant; Hunton and Williams, 1979–1985, associate; 1985, partner; Long Island Lighting, 1985–1989, general counsel; 1988–1989, executive vice president; 1989–1994, president and COO; The Detroit Edison Company, 1994–1996, president and COO; DTE Energy, 1996–1998, president and COO; 1998–, chairman and CEO.

Awards: Michiganians of the Year, *Detroit News*, 2003.

Address: DTE Energy, 2000 2nd Avenue, Detroit, Michigan 48226; http://www.dteenergy.com.

■ As of 2004 Anthony Francis (Tony) Earley was the chairman and CEO of DTE Energy, the Detroit-based diversified energy company involved in the development and management of energy-related businesses throughout the United States. Its largest operating units were Detroit Edison, an electric utility serving 2.1 million customers in southeastern Michigan, and MichCon, a natural-gas utility serving 1.2 million customers in more than 550 communities throughout the state. In 2003 the largest blackout in U.S. history left seven northern U.S. states, including most of Michigan, in the dark for three August days. In a strategy that was considered risky for a CEO, Earley became the public face of DTE during the crisis, winning accolades for his performance from employees, government officials, and anxious customers alike.

LEARNING TO REMAIN CALM UNDER PRESSURE

After earning a degree in physics from the University of Notre Dame, Earley embarked on a five-year career in the U.S. Navy during the latter part of the Vietnam War. He served as the chief engineer officer aboard the USS *Hawksbill*, a nuclear submarine. The experience of serving in the military gave Earley many of the skills that would make him an effective leader during the blackout crisis. He credited working on a Soviet torpedo exercise in particular with giving him poise under stress. Paul Hillegonds, the president of Detroit Renaissance, the group of chief executives promoting redevelopment that Earley chaired, would later say, "What he exuded during the blackout was the real Tony Earley. He has the kind of quiet confidence that gives others inspiration at times and a sense of calm when the times demand it" (*Detroit News*, May 9, 2004).

Upon leaving the service, Earley took advantage of the GI Bill to complete degrees in engineering and law at Notre Dame. He then worked as an attorney for the Virginia law firm of Hunton and Williams as a member of its energy and environmental team. As such Earley participated in the licensing of both nuclear and nonnuclear generating plants and represented a substantial number of nuclear utilities in rule-making actions before the Nuclear Regulatory Commission. He then became general counsel to the large New York energy company Long Island Lighting (LILCO) in 1985. He worked his way up to eventually become LILCO's president.

As a LILCO executive Earley became known as the spokesman who, in a series of television advertisements, pledged to freeze electric rates for two years; the power company made this move after abandoning, under political pressure, plans to operate a $5.3 billion nuclear plant. The episode badly soured relations between LILCO and its customers. Earley would later categorize his efforts to restore LILCO's reputation as great training for the 2003 blackout.

HEADING AN OLD-ECONOMY ELECTRIC COMPANY

Earley joined The Detroit Edison Company in March 1994 as president and chief operating officer. He was responsible for a broad range of utility operations, such as the development of the workforce skills and culture needed by Detroit Edison in order to be successful. After being repeatedly sued for race-based discrimination—and threatened with a class-action lawsuit—under Earley DTE Energy would come to be recognized as one of the best companies for minorities by *Fortune* magazine.

As government regulation was the largest concern facing energy companies in the 1990s, Earley's background in law and public service helped him to lead Detroit Edison through various bureaucratic webs. The company needed a friendly regulatory environment, and Earley put his legal skills to use by aiding Michigan's efforts to restructure the electric-utility industry.

Detroit Edison established the DTE Energy holding company in 1996, naming Earley as chairman and CEO in 1998. At DTE Earley was a major factor in the company's evolution from an old-fashioned, electric-only business into one that provided both gas and electricity. Despite his nuclear background Earley stayed away from that particular energy source, probably because of the inevitable surrounding controversy as well as bad memories from the LILCO debacle. DTE's change in focus away from electricity did not impress the financial community, however; Earley experienced considerable trouble raising DTE's stock price, blaming the lackluster performance on Wall Street's fascination with technology stocks over old-economy companies.

To resolve this problem, Earley continued to diversify DTE and pursue new businesses for the holding company; by 2004 more than 40 percent of DTE's earnings were derived from nonregulated ventures. Investment in emerging technology appeared to be reaping rewards for the energy giant. Plug Power, the Latham, New York–based company that developed residential fuel cells, was one of Earley's success stories. Created in 1997, the company went public in October 1999 and had a market capitalization of more than $4 billion by January 2000; DTE's investment in the company was worth $1.3 billion.

With his attention centered on the emerging technology favored by Wall Street, Earley had temporarily pushed Detroit Edison to the back burner. To later improve the subsidiary's performance, he stressed such fundamentals as trimming trees more attentively and increasing the number of meter readers—nevertheless, he appeared to pay comparatively little attention to the already mature business. Possibly as a result in late 2001, in an episode that would come to be called the "customer storm," DTE botched bills and service for 690,000 customers. Earley blamed the miscues on technology-transfer difficulties resulting from the merger between Detroit Edison and MichCon. State regulators ordered DTE to overhaul its billing, and Earley acknowledged that as of 2003 the company's customer-service department was still under construction.

RESPONDING TO THE LARGEST BLACKOUT IN U.S. HISTORY

The 2003 blackout crisis gave Earley the opportunity to prove himself amid the worst situation that could befall any energy-company chief executive. In August Earley was sitting in his office on the top floor of DTE's Detroit high-rise when the lights flickered; before long the power went out and stayed out. Lights, air conditioners, refrigerators, gas stations, and ATMs throughout Detroit had fallen victim to a massive shutdown. Earley then began to hear the phones in his 24th-story office ringing, as acquaintances reported that they had lost power and wondered what Earley planned to do about it. Earley thoroughly recognized how crucial the situation would be for both himself and DTE: "You realize that this is a bet-the-company operation. Either the company is going to survive or not survive depending on how well it performs. Leadership has to step up in those situations" (*Detroit Free Press*, August 20, 2003).

Earley had prepared for the emergency of a massive blackout but never expected to actually experience one. After learning that the blackout stretched far beyond downtown Detroit, he realized that he needed to personally reassure Detroit Edison's customers about the situation. He held seven press conferences in the following three days, stressing that life would soon be back to normal and asking those with restored power to be conservative until the system could be stabilized. Earley was one of the most visible utility officials anywhere during the shutdown; his response earned him praise from numerous officials, including Michigan Governor Jennifer Granholm, who called Earley a "calming presence" and described him as exactly the person she would want to be leading during a crisis (*Detroit Free Press*, August 20, 2003). The *Detroit News* later honored Earley for his "leadership and calm" (May 9, 2004).

The blackout gave Earley further impetus to promote new energy technology. He suggested transforming the local substations that distributed power around neighborhoods into electricity-generating islands; such a strategy would circumvent the huge legal and environmental obstacles to building new transmission towers as well as bring back power much more quickly in the event of any future massive losses of electricity.

Despite DTE's diversification Earley continued to stress the importance of the basics. In 2004 he stated that his formula for success was a simple one, based on a strategy linked to the core skills and assets of the utility as well as to conservative financial policies. Earley aggressively cut costs and sought to modify Michigan's Electric Choice program, which sapped a substantial chunk of Detroit Edison's electric margins by permitting customers to choose alternative suppliers. He expressed concern that the continuation of the Electric Choice program could lead to severe consequences for DTE.

See also entries on The Detroit Edison Company, DTE Energy Company, and Long Island Lighting Company in *International Directory of Company Histories.*

SOURCES FOR FURTHER INFORMATION

Boschee, Pam, "DTE Energy Tops Growth Targets, Leverages Energy Technologies, and Expands Business Portfolio," *Electric Light and Power,* July 2000, pp. 17–19.

Bunkley, Nick, "Anthony F. Earley, Jr.: The Spotlight Reflects Well on the Man with the Power," *Detroit News,* May 9, 2004.

Earley, Anthony F., "The New Job Security Model: From Employment to Employability," *Executive Speeches,* October/November 1996, pp. 13–19.

Rios, Brenda, "Detroit-Based Electric Utility's Stock Continues to Sink," *Detroit Free Press,* April 15, 2000.

Webster, Sarah A., and Jeff Bennett, "DTE Energy CEO's Skills Shined During Blackout," *Detroit Free Press,* August 20, 2003.

—Caryn E. Neumann

■ ■ ■

Robert A. Eckert

1954–

Chairman and chief executive officer, Mattel, Incorporated

Nationality: American.

Born: August 14, 1954, in Elmhurst, Illinois.

Education: University of Arizona, BS, 1976; Northwestern University, MBA, 1977.

Family: Married Kathie (maiden name unknown); children: four.

Career: Kraft Foods, 1977–1987, held several marketing positions (specific job titles unknown); 1987–1989, vice president for strategy and development, grocery products division; 1989–1990, vice president for marketing, refrigerated products; 1990–1993, vice president and general manager, cheese division; Oscar Mayer Foods Corporation, 1993–1996, president; Kraft Foods, 1996–1997, group vice president; 1997–2000, president and chief executive officer; Mattel, Incorporated, 2000–, chairman and chief executive officer.

Awards: Listed among the Top 25 Managers of the Year, *BusinessWeek*, 2001; Executive of the Year, University of Arizona, 2001; Lifetime Achievement Award, Eller College of the University of Arizona, 2002.

Address: Mattel, Incorporated, 333 Continental Boulevard, El Segundo, California 90245; http://www.mattel.com.

■ Robert Eckert rose from lower management positions to attain a series of leadership positions at Kraft Foods during the late 1980s and 1990s. After revitalizing the cheese division at Kraft as well as the company's Oscar Mayer unit, Eckert was appointed group vice president in 1996. He became Kraft's president and chief executive officer in 1997. His success continued when he moved to Mattel in 2000 to become its chairman and chief executive officer. He experienced significant success at Mattel during his first three years with the company through a low-key but assertive leadership style.

LOW-PROFILE BEGINNINGS

Eckert was a modest child, which largely shaped his leadership style in the years to come. He grew up in Elmhurst, Illinois as the son of a dentist and did little to stand out in his early years. His personality during his high school years was described as "low wattage," according to an article in *Forbes*. Eckert agreed. "[Y]ou never would have predicted that I'd be a CEO someday," he said (November 18, 2002).

Eckert left his home state of Illinois to attend the University of Arizona. He graduated with a bachelor's degree in business administration in 1976 and returned to Illinois, where he enrolled in the Kellogg Graduate School of Management at Northwestern University. He received his MBA in marketing and finance in 1977.

CLIMBING THE CORPORATE LADDER AT KRAFT

Eckert began his career at Kraft Foods immediately after receiving his MBA. For the first 10 years of his career, he held a variety of marketing positions within the company. In 1987 he was promoted to vice president of strategy and development within Kraft's grocery products division. Phillip Morris Companies acquired Kraft during the following year, though it did not affect Eckert's assent into top management. In 1989 he was moved to the position of vice president for marketing for refrigerated products. In the following year he became the vice president and general manager of the company's cheese division.

Eckert was credited with turning around Kraft's cheese division by reducing product prices. His success with the division led to a new appointment as president of Oscar Mayer Foods, another company owned by Philip Morris. At Oscar Mayer, Eckert introduced ambitious plans for pricing and successfully introduced new product lines. During his tenure as president of the unit, Oscar Mayer introduced a line of fat-free meals as well as the popular Lunchables® prepackaged food combinations. These items combined to bring in an estimated $400 million in sales during Eckert's time as president.

Eckert's achievements in the cheese division and at Oscar Mayer propelled him to the second-highest executive position at Kraft in 1996. He retained responsibility for Oscar Mayer as group vice president but also took charge of the company's foodservice group as well as five operational staff groups.

During the following year, Kraft's president and chief executive officer, Robert Morrison, resigned to take over as head of the Quaker Oats Company. After Morrison's departure, Eckert was named as Kraft's new president and CEO in October 1997. "He is representative of the depth and talent we have in the company and is well-prepared to provide the seamless leadership that has been a cornerstone of Kraft's success," said William Webb, the chief operating officer of the Philip Morris Companies (*Chicago Sun-Times*, October 24, 1997). Under Eckert's guidance, Kraft continued to grow. The company launched aggressive marketing campaigns while sales continued to increase. By 1999 the company had 32 product brands that each earned more than a hundred million dollars in annual revenue, and the company's total revenue reached an estimated $17.5 billion.

TAKING CHARGE OF A TROUBLED MATTEL

Kraft continued to make gains through 2000. After 23 years with the company, Eckert remained loyal to it even though his leadership abilities had made him an attractive prospect for recruiters of top executives. Mattel Incorporated targeted Eckert in its search for a new leader at the turn of the new millennium. In May 2000, Eckert resigned from Kraft to become the new chairman and chief executive officer at Mattel. He replaced Jill Barad, who had had a difficult three-year tenure at Mattel. Stock prices had fallen from a high of $46 per share in 1998 to approximately $10 around the time that Eckert joined the company.

Eckert had to quickly resolve what were perceived as Barad's mistakes. One of the major thorns in Mattel's side was the $3.5 billion that Barad had spent in the late 1990s to acquire the Learning Company, a software producer. By the time that Eckert took charge, the Learning Company was costing Mattel an estimated $1 million per day. At Mattel's annual meeting in June 2000, Eckert faced a group of disgruntled shareholders who grilled him with questions about the company's future. Eckert remained optimistic, displaying a positive attitude despite the shareholders' agitated behavior.

A MODEST MANAGEMENT STYLE

Eckert's leadership style was described on one occasion by the *Chicago Tribune* as "the picture of Midwestern sobriety," especially when compared with the flamboyant behaviors of other chief executives (January 28, 2001). During Eckert's first year as the head of Mattel, he sold the Learning Company, terminated an expensive licensing agreement with the Walt Disney Company, and cut jobs and other expenses. His management of Mattel earned him recognition as one of the "Top 25 Managers of the Year" by *BusinessWeek* in 2002.

Mattel continued to benefit from Eckert's sound leadership, as its net income in 2003 rose to $487 million from $362 million in 1999. Mattel's stock during Eckert's first two years with the company nearly doubled in price. Mattel suffered some setbacks in the latter part of 2003, when the toy industry as a whole endured a period of weak sales. Under Eckert's guidance, however, Mattel responded in 2004 by focusing attention on its line of Barbie dolls as well as its electronic learning unit.

Eckert was a member of several company boards and civic organizations. He served on the board of McDonald's Corporation, the Advisory Board of the Kellogg Graduate School of Management, and the Board of Visitors of the Anderson School of Management at the University of California at Los Angeles.

See also entries on Kraft Foods Inc., Mattel, Inc., The Learning Company, Inc., Oscar Mayer Foods Corp., and Philip Morris Companies Inc. in *International Directory of Company Histories.*

SOURCES FOR FURTHER INFORMATION

Lublin, Joann S., and Lisa Bannon, "Mattel Taps Kraft Chief Robert Eckert to Succeed Jill Barad as CEO," *Wall Street Journal*, May 17, 2000.

Pauly, Heather, "Kraft Promotes Veteran to Fill Vacant Top Spot," *Chicago Sun-Times*, October 24, 1997.

Pollack, Judann, "Eckert's Enterprise Crafts No. 2 Slot at Kraft," *Advertising Age*, August 12, 1996.

Sachdev, Ameet, "Recipe for CEO Success Includes a Dash of Kraft," *Chicago Tribune*, January 28, 2001.

Sellers, Patricia, "The New Breed," *Fortune*, November 18, 2002, pp. 66–70.

Tippit, Sarah, "Toymaker's New Chief Doesn't Break Under Shareholders' Assault," *Chicago Tribune*, June 8, 2000.

—Matthew C. Cordon

■ ■ ■

Rolf Eckrodt

1942–

Former president and chief executive officer, Mitsubishi Motors Corporation

Nationality: German.

Born: June 25, 1942, in Gronau, Westphalia, Germany.

Education: University of Bochum, ME, 1966.

Family: Married; children: two.

Career: Daimler-Benz, 1966–1968, member of quality assurance for passenger cars; 1968–1981, manager in Passenger Car Division; 1981–1983, leader of production components for passenger cars; 1983–1986, vice president of axle production for passenger cars; Mercedes-Benz (subsidiary of Daimler-Benz), 1986–1987, executive assistant to president of Passenger Car Division; Daimler-Benz, 1987–1989, director of planning and production for passenger cars and components; Mercedes-Benz, 1990–1992, director of worldwide marketing for passenger cars; Mercedes-Benz do Brasil (subsidiary of Mercedes-Benz), 1992–1996, president; Adtranz (subsidiary of Daimler-Benz and ABB Daimler-Benz Transportation), 1996–1998, deputy chief executive officer and chairman of the board; Adtranz (to become Adtranz-DaimlerChrysler Rail Systems in 1999), 1998–2000, president and chief executive officer; Mitsubishi Motors Corporation, 2001–2002, executive vice president and chief operating officer; 2002–2004, president and chief executive officer.

■ Rolf Eckrodt was the epitome of the company man, someone who devoted his life to the prosperity of his corporation. His reputation was built on turning failing subsidiaries of Daimler-Benz (eventually DaimlerChrysler) into profitable companies. He did so through his emphasis on innovation, budget cuts, analysis of the market for products, and effective sales strategies. With infectious enthusiasm, he motivated employees and attracted buyers. He favored what Europeans called the "American style" of corporate leadership, meaning leadership that focused on profits rather than on stability.

Rolf Eckrodt. *AP/Wide World Photos.*

MERCEDES-BENZ DO BRASIL

Eckrodt began as an engineer at Mercedes-Benz and slowly gained broader responsibilities as he demonstrated his skills. His early work in quality assurance seems to have influenced his business decisions throughout his career because wherever he went, he made quality a high priority. As director of planning and production for passenger cars and components, 1987–1990, he showed a capacity for organizing complex lines of products. His buoyant personality and thorough knowledge of Mercedes-Benz automobiles made him a good choice for director of worldwide marketing for Mercedes-Benz passenger cars. The most enduring legacy of his years at Mercedes-Benz in Germany was his shift in focus from reliance on the company's reputation for great engineering to aggressive sales tactics to sell cars.

Edzard Reuter, then CEO of Daimler-Benz (owner of Mercedes-Benz), tapped Eckrodt to salvage the fortunes of the foreign subsidiary Mercedes-Benz do Brasil. Mercedes-Benz had a long history in Brazil, going back to 1914, when Daimler automobiles were first marketed there. Mercedes-Benz's long-term strength in Brazil had been its heavy trucks.

When Eckrodt arrived in São Paulo, Brazil, both the nation and the company were in hard times. What Eckrodt found at Mercedes-Benz do Brasil was overcapacity—the company was paying too much in overhead to maintain facilities that were not producing because the market for their products was too small. Eckrodt began by closing a manufacturing plant and cutting 1,800 workers, mostly through attrition. He then created the Centro de Desenvolvimento Tecnológico (Center of Technological Development), making it the biggest automobile research and development facility in Latin America. One quick payoff from this investment was a new truck cabin with high headroom and improved visibility of the road, achieved by elevating the driver's seat and windows. This innovation was the first of several changes in design to three lines of heavy trucks that would prove popular in Brazil.

In 1993 Eckrodt was elected vice president of the Germany-Brazil Chamber of Commerce, a post he held until 1996. During this period, Eckrodt not only directed the improvement of heavy trucks but also led an expansion into the manufacture of buses. In addition, he helped develop a complex interrelationship among a components plant in Argentina, manufacturing plants in Germany, and plants in Brazil to produce cars and trucks that shared components with Mercedes-Benz vehicles manufactured elsewhere in the world, even while developing automobiles unique to South America, based on what he and his employees had learned about what local customers wanted. His use of market studies probably influenced the creation of a state-of-the-art plant in Juiz de Fora; the plant cost $400 million and was completed after he left in 1996. In 1996 Mercedes-Benz do Brasil accounted for 20 percent of Mercedes-Benz's global sales.

Given a chance to spread his wings while in Brazil, Eckrodt displayed some of the passions that would become hallmarks of his leadership: aerodynamic designs for vehicles, fuel-efficient vehicles, and the exploitation of such alternative fuels as natural gas, which was introduced in Mercedes-Benz do Brasil's buses. He also preferred streamlined management in which new ideas did not have to percolate through several layers of executives but could be proposed, approved, and developed quickly.

ADTRANZ

In 1996 Eckrodt was offered a new challenge: Adtranz (short for ABB Daimler-Benz Transportation). Adtranz was a manufacturer of railroad equipment and had been created when the Swedish manufacturer Asea Brown Boveri and Daimler-Benz formed a fifty-fifty partnership between their railroad manufacturing divisions. Adtranz's primary concern was the building of "rolling stock," that is, railroad cars and engines. During Eckrodt's tenure at Adtranz, rolling stock would be expanded to include people movers, such as buslike vehicles. For instance, in 1999 Adtranz would introduce the Innovia people mover, a rubber-tired vehicle that would follow prescribed electronic pathways, moving people around large areas, such as airports. The Innovia was aerodynamic and used the Flexiblok electronic guidance system that integrated vehicle manufacture, electronics, and software.

Eckrodt initially held the post of deputy to the CEO and chairman of the board of Adtranz; his experience with juggling international sources of supply while in Brazil may have helped him in his awkward new position, which involved satisfying two different corporate owners. In that same year, Jürgen Schrempp became CEO of Daimler-Benz, and he did not tolerate partnerships well. He pushed to have Daimler-Benz control Adtranz, a move that resulted in Eckrodt's becoming president and CEO of Adtranz in 1998.

Upon taking his new positions, Eckrodt immediately began reshaping Adtranz. For instance, he reorganized its manufacturing structure, creating seven distinct product lines. One line was that of the Innovia, which used composite bodies and featured a modular design. Another line was Crusaris, based on Adtranz Flexliner railroad passenger cars. The Crusaris line produced heavy electrical and diesel-powered trains for intercity travel and quickly became popular in the United States, with sales in Pennsylvania, Texas, and Washington State. The Incentro line consisted of light-rail trains and featured low floors for easy boarding and disembarking; the Itino line filled the gap between Incentro's light-rail and Crusaris's heavy cars, marketed for local and regional transportation; the Movia line produced high-capacity cars; and the Octeon line produced electric locomotives. The Blue Tiger line united Adtranz in partnership with General Electric to produce diesel locomotives.

These lines consisted of about 80 percent standard designs that could be modified by a host of accessories. The idea was to cut costs by minimizing the kinds of body shapes through standardization while allowing customers to specify components that suited their particular needs. This strategy, coupled with vigorous sales tactics, enabled Adtranz to expand into new markets, the most important of which may have been China, which ordered hundreds of cars for its Canton subway system. Adtranz called this a "market-driven" plan, with Adtranz manufacturing in response to consumer needs. The reorganization of Adtranz, with the standardization of car bodies, resulted in a 30 percent reduction in manufacturing costs over the first 18 months. A portion of the savings was passed on to customers, making Adtranz more cost competitive.

Even so, Adtranz continued to lose money; it lost $111 million in 1997. Asea Brown Boveri set a deadline of 1999 for Adtranz to make a profit, and even though the company's revenues increased, surpassing $3.7 billion in 1998, managers at Asea Brown Boveri were not satisfied. Under Eckrodt's leadership, Adtranz said that it expected to turn a profit in 2000, but this was not soon enough. Adtranz's financial situation, coupled with Schrempp's wish for total control of Adtranz, resulted in Asea Brown Boveri's selling its 50 percent share of Adtranz to Daimler-Benz in 1999 for $472 million. That very year, Daimler-Benz merged with the Chrysler Corporation in America, becoming DaimlerChrysler, resulting in Adtranz's being renamed Adtranz-DaimlerChrysler Rail Systems. By then Eckrodt's stature was such that he was elected chairman of the Union of European Railway Industries, a position he held until 2001.

Asea Brown Boveri may have made a wise move, because Adtranz's revenues declined to $3.2 billion in 2000. That year Eckrodt sold Adtranz's electrical business to Balfour Beatty, a construction company in the United Kingdom, moving about 1,400 employees to Balfour Beatty. Greenbrier Companies, which owned the Polish company WagonySwidnica, a manufacturer and exporter of railcars, purchased Adtranz's Freight Wagon Division and formed a partnership with Adtranz's Customer Support Division to maintain and market railcars. Eckrodt shopped around Adtranz's signaling technology but found no buyers. Meanwhile, he made a purchase, buying the British company Railcare from Babcock International (which had owned 60 percent of Railcare) and Siemens Transportation Systems (which had owned 40 percent).

Adtranz was then the second-largest manufacturer of locomotives and railcars in the world, with about 20,000 employees and a projected gross of $7.2 billion for 2000. Yet it was still losing money, if less than in 1996. Bombardier of Canada offered to buy Adtranz from DaimlerChrysler. Bombardier was a manufacturing giant, already the world's third-largest producer of airliners as well as a major manufacturer of railroad equipment. The purchase of Adtranz would make it the world's largest manufacturer of railroad gear. Despite Adtranz's losses, Eckrodt made the purchase tempting: Bombardier could sell a couple of divisions and make back its investment; in addition, Adtranz had $14.5 billion in outstanding orders, offering hope for future profits. Bombardier bought Adtranz for $771 million, considered a bargain at the time. A year later Bombardier would file a grievance with the International Chamber of Commerce, asking that DaimlerChrysler be required to pay Bombardier over $900 million for misleading the company about Adtranz's financial problems.

MITSUBISHI MOTORS

By then Eckrodt had been posted to another financially troubled company, Mitsubishi Motors Corporation. With the purchase of Chrysler to form DaimlerChrysler, Schrempp had added the manufacturer of medium-priced cars to the Daimler empire and had created a strong presence in the United States as well. As part of his vision of creating a global company, he wanted to establish a strong presence in Southeast Asia and to add the manufacture of small, low-priced cars to his company. Mitsubishi, the fourth-largest automobile manufacturer in Japan, was ripe for purchase.

The company had just gone through a very embarrassing period during which it was forced to reveal that since the 1970s it had covered up design flaws that had caused many of its automobiles to malfunction. It had used intimidation to silence people who complained about accidents that had resulted from the flaws. Sales dropped dramatically in Japan because of a loss of consumer confidence in Mitsubishi products. The company was forced to recall over two million vehicles in Japan alone. DaimlerChrysler bought 37.4 percent of Mitsubishi Motors for about $2 billion, with the option to buy all of Mitsubishi after three years, and sent Eckrodt to oversee the company's return to profitability.

Eckrodt was named executive vice president and COO of Mitsubishi Motors Corporation, and he would be responsible for overseeing the company's marketing, production quality, research and development, and supply system. The leader of Mitsubishi's American operations, Takashi Sonobe, was named president and CEO; his success at keeping Mitsubishi's American operations profitable while the rest of Mitsubishi declined offered hope that he could lead the manufacturer to a recovery at home. Eckrodt and Sonobe faced a daunting task: Mitsubishi had accounted for 11.4 percent of Japan's automobile market in 1995, but that share had declined to 8 percent. In 2000 Mitsubishi lost $750 million on sales of $31 billion and was on its way to losing between $2.21 billion and $2.5 billion for 2000 and 2001 combined.

Eckrodt quickly set about cutting costs. When he first arrived, he gave chunks of the Berlin wall to each of the top 25 Mitsubishi executives, with each rock labeled "Leave no stone unturned" as a reminder of the company's need to seek out every possible way to cut expenses. One way was to cut the number of employees, and 12 of the top 38 executives were let go, including 11 of the top 25. Eckrodt set goals of cutting costs by 15 percent and trimming jobs by 9,500 in three years. Mitsubishi surpassed both, reducing costs by 16 percent and jobs by 12,000 through early retirement and attrition.

One of Eckrodt's most difficult tasks was to straighten out Mitsubishi's *keiretsu*, a complex system of interrelated suppliers that were partly owned by Mitsubishi and that, in turn, partly owned Mitsubishi. It was an arcane system built up over several decades, reflecting the Japanese custom of close relationships among major corporations and small companies as well as the tradition of diffusion of manufacturing throughout the society rather than centralization. Eckrodt managed to carve out direct lines of supply, a ruthless process that left some members of the *keiretsu* without a buyer for their products, Mitsubishi having been their only customer. The bulk of the savings realized by Eckrodt came from streamlining lines of supply.

Mitsubishi suffered from overcapacity: it could manufacture far more automobiles than it had customers. Whereas a manufacturer of large vehicles could weather a period of low demand because its profit margins were big, Mitsubishi manufactured mostly small cars, which had slim margins of profit, and the overhead required to maintain underutilized plants ate deeply into the company's revenues. Eckrodt closed one Japanese manufacturing plant and cut others to reduce Mitsubishi's production capacity by 20 percent.

While cutting these costs, Eckrodt doubled Mitsubishi's outlay for research and development. He brought in Olivier Boulay to head Mitsubishi's design team. In a 2003 article in *BusinessWeek*, Boulay explained his approach: "We're trying to be serious but fun" (February 10, 2003). Market research showed that Mitsubishi had an edge among young consumers, so cars were designed to appeal to them. Eckrodt wanted to gain a greater share of the urban market, so he sent his designers to Tokyo to experience firsthand what people in Tokyo wanted from their cars. Others brought in by Eckrodt included the research and development leader Ulrich Walker and the finance expert Joachim Coers. The Mitsubishi board of directors was expanded from 10 members to 11, four of whom were from DaimlerChrysler, including Eckrodt.

By the end of 2001 most of the bloodletting was over, with 6,400 jobs already cut. Eckrodt and Sonobe had engineered a remarkable turnaround for Mitsubishi; for the 2001–2002 fiscal year, Mitsubishi had for the first time in three years realized a profit, $93.8 million. Most of this profit came from the United States; sales in Japan still lagged. Matters in Japan were still tough in 2002. In March, Mitsubishi recalled 340,000 buses and trucks to repair flawed parts. Nine models of automobile were recalled during the year. In March, Eckrodt was named president of Mitsubishi, and he brought in Eiji Iwakuni to become the senior vice president of marketing; Iwakuni was hired away from the Japanese unit of Ford Motor Company. The hiring of a Japanese marketing expert was somewhat unexpected, because DaimlerChrysler had a history of heavy-handedly replacing executives of the companies it bought with German managers, but Eckrodt explained, "Japanese integration is necessary. There are a few expatriates here but they cannot run the company" (*Detroit News*, May 22, 2002).

On June 24, 2002, the Japanese shareholders approved the elevation of Eckrodt to CEO, and on June 25 he officially replaced Sonobe, who became the chairman of the board. Sonobe had seemed to be doing an excellent job, but his move first from the presidency and then from the CEO position may be explained by his death in October 2003—he may already have been in failing health. Eckrodt stated that he planned a three-year tenure as CEO of Mitsubishi. One of his first moves as CEO was to eliminate Mitsubishi's traditional system of promotion, which was based on seniority. In its place he installed a system of rewards for good performance.

For the fiscal year 2002–2003 Mitsubishi realized $28.3 billion in sales and a $316.7 million profit, but much of this profit came from strong sales in the United States, and 2003 would prove to be a disaster for Mitsubishi's American operations. Not all was gloomy, however; Mitsubishi's sport-utility vehicle, launched in March 2003, was a hit in the United States. In February the Colt subcompact was launched in Japan to much fanfare, with Eckrodt taking a public role as the genial salesperson reaching out to Mitsubishi's loyal customers who had been put off by the company's fiascoes of the 1990s. Iwakuni created an advertising campaign that promoted the "German-Japanese" roots of the Mitsubishi lineup.

Still, American sales were down 20 percent overall for 2003. In the United States, Mitsubishi had created a popular "0, 0, 0" credit program: zero money down, zero payments for one year, and zero interest for one year. This offer attracted young buyers; 16.4 percent of American buyers of Mitsubishi vehicles in 2003 were under 25 years old. Disaster threatened to overwhelm Mitsubishi's American operations when buyers, especially young ones, defaulted on these generous loans. This meant not only that Mitsubishi had received no money for a year on cars that it had sold, but also that it had a host of used vehicles that were not worth the cost of manufacturing them. On August 31, 2003, Eckrodt hired Finbarr O'Neill away from Hyundai Motor America to take charge of American operations and repair the damage to what had been Mitsubishi's best market.

For the fiscal year 2003–2004, Mitsubishi lost between $650 and $946.8 million (sources are uncertain as to the exact amount), between $375 million and $420 million of this loss in bad American loans. In 2004 rumors were rife that Eckrodt would resign because of the 2003 disaster, but he said that he would leave his positions only if Mitsubishi's shareholders asked him to do so. There were rumors that Schrempp would dispatch a replacement for Eckrodt from Germany, placing all the blame for the losses of 2003 on Eckrodt. Yet the American loan fiasco was a onetime problem, not to be repeated, and it did not reflect any lasting problems for Eckrodt's innovations in Mitsubishi.

Indeed, in 2003 and 2004 Eckrodt continued to pursue new markets and new ways of making profits for Mitsubishi. He retained ties to Brazil and in 2003 arranged for Mitsubishi to collaborate with Mercedes-Benz do Brasil on the design and manufacture of automobiles for the South American market. There was the prospect of building a new factory in the United States because sales of the Endeavor were very strong there. Mitsubishi and DaimlerChrysler finalized plans for building a joint factory in Holland, where they would manufacture a compact automobile.

In February 2004 DaimlerChrysler gave Mitsubishi $490 million to stabilize it after its American losses from defaulted loans, and Eckrodt negotiated for another $1.8 billion investment in Mitsubishi. However, DaimlerChrysler surprised him in April 2004 by declaring that it would give Mitsubishi no more financial support. As a consequence, Eckrodt abruptly resigned on April 26, 2004. Mitsubishi was $6.4 billion in debt and looking for a bailout from the Japanese government.

PROSPERITY THROUGH INNOVATION

A consistent hallmark of Eckrodt's leadership was innovation. In Germany, he changed the way Mercedes-Benz marketed its automobiles. In Brazil he turned a subsidiary into a creator of its own line of vehicles. In Japan his recipe for recovery included not only cost-cutting strategies and creative marketing but also the independent development of new automobiles, based on careful market research. He was willing to take chances, not all of which were successful, but his ability to coordinate large groups of resources into coherent wholes made Mitsubishi Motors into a fundamentally sound corporation.

See also entries on DaimlerChrysler AG, Daimler-Benz A.G., and Mitsubishi Motors Corporation in *International Directory of Company Histories.*

SOURCES FOR FURTHER INFORMATION

"Bombardier Gets Adtranz for a 'Bargain,'" *Railway Age,* September 2000, p. 36.

Dawson, Chester, and Katie Kerwin, "Mitsubishi Moves into High Gear: Eckrodt's Sales Savvy Is Sparking a Turnaround," *BusinessWeek,* February 10, 2003, p. 16.

Dawson, Chester, et al., "Mr. Fix-It?" *BusinessWeek,* May 14, 2001, pp. 22–24.

Gibbs, Edwina, "Mitsubishi Motors Reports First Profit in 3 Years," Reuters, May 13, 2002.

Whipp, Lindsay, and Kae Inoue, "Mitsubishi's Eckrodt Plans Three-year Tenure," *Detroit News,* May 22, 2002, http://www.detnews.com/2002/autosinsider/0205/22/index.htm.

—Kirk H. Beetz

■ ■ ■

Michael Eisner

1942–

Chief executive officer, The Walt Disney Company

Nationality: American.

Born: March 7, 1942, in Mt. Kisco, New York.

Education: Denison University, BA, 1964.

Family: Son of Lester Eisner and Margaret Dammann; married Jane Breckenridge; children: three.

Career: NBC, 1963, page; 1964, FCC logging clerk; CBS, 1964–1966, commercial slotter for programming department; ABC, 1966–1968, assistant to the national programming director; 1968–1969, manager of specials and talent; 1969–1971, director of program development for the East Coast; 1971–1975, vice president of daytime programming; 1975, vice president for program planning and development; 1976, senior vice president for prime-time production and development; Paramount Pictures, 1976–1984, president and COO; The Walt Disney Company, 1984–2004, chairman and CEO; 2004–, CEO.

Publications: *Work in Progress* (with Tony Schwartz), 1998.

Address: The Walt Disney Company, 500 South Buena Vista Street, Burbank, California 91521; http://www.disney.com.

Michael Eisner. *AP/Wide World Photos.*

■ With an entertainment career spanning three decades, Michael Eisner had a tremendous impact on popular culture. As one of the most powerful people in the media industry, he was the target of both lavish praise and intense criticism, as Disney first defied and later fell short of expectations under his reign. His leadership was so significantly polarizing that the executive once credited with breathing new life into Disney might ultimately be remembered as a mercurial manager who robbed it of its magic.

LITERATURE, NOT THE LION KING

Michael Eisner was raised in affluence. His maternal grandfather was the cofounder of the American Safety Razor Company, and the family amassed a fortune selling military uniforms and razor blades. As was consistent with the family business, Eisner's childhood was filled with much discipline. His parents strictly rationed the children's visual consumption of both television and movies, requiring two hours of reading for every hour of TV watching.

ENTERTAINMENT COMES CALLING

Eisner enrolled in Ohio's Denison University as a premed student but quickly found that his true interests lay in English literature and the theater. In a 1998 interview with Larry King he said, "I just stumbled from one thing to another. I had a kind of a general feeling that I loved the entertainment business; I loved the creative business; I loved the fun of doing things, but I didn't grow up saying, 'I am going to be a movie executive'" (October 10, 1998).

After trying to woo a girl in his college's theater department by writing a play for her, Eisner was hooked. He worked his first industry job during the summers of his college years as a page at NBC studios in New York. He answered phones for Johnny Carson and gave out the restaurant gift certificates that Carson awarded to contestants.

A BREAK IN THE TV BUSINESS

After graduating in 1964 Eisner returned to New York to work at NBC as an FCC logging clerk—by his own admission merely a fancy way of saying that he wrote down the times the commercials came on. Within six weeks he had moved to the programming department at CBS, where he was responsible for placing commercials in the most appropriate slots during children's programs. Dissatisfied with this work, he mailed out hundreds of résumés, receiving exactly one response—from Barry Diller in the programming department at ABC, himself a mogul in training. Diller lobbied for Eisner to be hired as assistant to ABC's national programming director, a post which Eisner held from 1966 to 1968. While he and Eisner were of the same age, Barry Diller's career started sooner, and as such he was a boss, rival, and friend to Eisner ever since they met.

Eisner produced his first television special, *Feelin' Groovy at Marine World*, in 1967. In 1968 he was promoted to manager of specials and talent and within a year became director of program development for the East Coast. In this capacity the young executive was responsible for Saturday-morning children's programming. Among other projects he oversaw the production of animated programs based on the popular singing groups The Jackson Five and The Osmond Brothers.

In 1971 Eisner became ABC's vice president of daytime programming, where he helped sell the popular soap operas *All My Children* and *One Life To Live*. In 1975 he became ABC's vice president for program planning and development and was next made senior vice president in Prime Time Production and Development in 1976. In these posts he fostered programs such as *Happy Days*, *Welcome Back Kotter*, *Barney Miller*, and *Starsky and Hutch*. During Eisner's years in the programming department, ABC moved from a perennial third place to first place among the three major television networks.

HIS MENTOR CREATES AN OPPORTUNITY

In 1974 Barry Diller moved on to become chairman of Paramount Pictures. In 1976 Eisner's mentor offered Eisner the post of president and chief operating officer at Paramount, giving him an opportunity to learn the movie business. At Paramount, Diller and Eisner applied the lessons they had learned in network television to keep the studio's costs down. During Eisner's tenure as COO the average Paramount film cost only $8.5 million to produce, while the industry average was $12 million. Paramount soon moved from last to first place among the six major movie-production studios.

In October 1978 half of the top 10 box office attractions belonged to Paramount. Films produced at the studio during Eisner's reign included *Raiders of the Lost Ark*, *Saturday Night Fever*, *Grease*, *Heaven Can Wait*, *Ordinary People*, *Terms of Endearment*, *An Officer and a Gentleman*, *The Elephant Man*, *Reds*, *Flashdance*, *Footloose*, *Trading Places*, *Beverly Hills Cop*, *Airplane*, and the first three installments of the *Star Trek* series.

A PRINCE AWAKENS SLEEPING BEAUTY

Charles G. Bluhdorn, the chairman of Paramount's parent company, died and his successor Martin Davis disliked Eisner. Eisner told Larry King, "I was on the way out" (October 10, 1998). Fortunately, around the same time Roy Disney, Walt Disney's nephew, asked Eisner to run his family's company. Since Walt Disney's death in 1966, the studio had enjoyed periodic box-office successes and continued to earn profits from theme parks and merchandising, but many in the industry felt the company was suffering from a lack of direction. In September 1984 Eisner left Paramount to become the chairman and CEO of The Walt Disney Company.

Within a few years Eisner transformed Disney into the industry leader. In rapid succession, the studio turned out a new cycle of animated features such as *The Little Mermaid*, *Beauty and the Beast*, *Aladdin*, *The Lion King*, and *Pocahontas*. Each proved to be a box-office blockbuster and a merchandising bonanza. At the same time Disney diversified, releasing films for a wider audience through its Hollywood Pictures subsidiary and acquiring the independent Miramax to produce more offbeat films for the specialized urban market. As the value of Disney stock soared, market watchers described Eisner as the prince who had awakened Sleeping Beauty.

As quoted in the *Philadelphia Inquirer*, Nell Minow, the editor of The Corporate Library, an independent investment-research firm in Portland, Maine, said of Eisner, "He thinks about things in a richly textured, multilayered way. He's extremely smart" (March 1, 2004). Barry Diller noted in London's *Guardian*, "Michael has a genuine creative sense and is a genuinely great businessman. You could count the number of people with that combination on one hand. I don't care who you put him in a room with—his ideas, his judgment, are pure pitch" (April 10, 1999).

A TRAGIC DEVELOPMENT

In 1994, after a decade of contributions to the company, Disney's second in command Frank Wells was killed in a helicopter crash. Wells was known for handling the details of Disney's day-to-day operations but was often overshadowed in the public eye by the colorful Eisner. From 1984 to 1994 Wells and Eisner helped to increase annual revenues from $1.5 billion to $8.5 billion, and the company's market capitalization leapt from $2 billion to $22 billion, as revenue from theme parks and resorts tripled. Wells and Eisner had together reestablished Disney's dominance in animated feature films with a series of hits. Not only had Wells been instrumental to Eisner's success, but the two had been personally close. In his autobiography Eisner said: "If I was the rudder, he was the keel. For 10 years we never had a fight or a disagreement. I never once felt angry at him—not until he died instantly. Even then I felt angry only because Frank was not around to help me out with a very difficult situation, as he had so many times before. But mostly what I felt was an overwhelming sense of sadness and loss" (1998).

Wells's death marked the beginning of a decade of misfortune for Eisner and the Magic Kingdom. Less than 36 hours after losing his number-two man, Eisner found himself being aggressively lobbied by the head of Disney's film studio, Jeffrey Katzenberg, who felt he was next in line to head Disney's day-to-day operations. Katzenberg was in fact fired six months later, and five years of lawsuits began. The settlements were complicated by the long and controversial professional and personal relationship between Katzenberg and Eisner. Hearings brought to the surface years of animosity on both sides, culminating in embarrassing testimony by a visibly shaken Eisner in which he was confronted with disparaging statements he had made about Katzenberg to Tony Schwartz, the coauthor of his autobiography; as reported by *Time* magazine, one of the statements was, "I hate the little midget" (July 19, 1999).

In 1994 Eisner discovered he had severe cardiac disease and underwent bypass surgery. In a letter to the Pulitzer Prize–winning author Larry McMurtry, which was reproduced in his autobiography, Eisner called the experience a formative one: "Something happened to me that was a big deal. My life has a finite sense to it, and there is certainly a hollowness that comes with such realizations. Although I fear the ceiling of death, at the same time I accept death for the first time and even look at it without fear" (1998).

ANOTHER KEY RELATIONSHIP FAILS

After facing his own vulnerability and having become concerned about his lack of a successor, in 1995 Eisner orchestrated the hiring of the Hollywood super agent Mike Ovitz as Disney's president. Hoping to push Disney's assets even further into the entertainment landscape, Eisner announced in 1996 that the company would acquire Capital Cities, the owners of the ESPN and ABC television networks—the latter being Eisner's old employer.

Ovitz's management got the ABC merger off to a dismal start, however, and his 16-month tenure scarred the company. Just five weeks after hiring Ovitz, Eisner believed that his friend needed to be fired. Yet he hesitated out of the fear that Ovitz would commit suicide. A little more than a year after joining Disney, Ovitz left with a severance package that included a $38.9 million cash payout and stock options valued at more than $100 million.

While temporarily hurting profits, the $19 billion merger with Capital Cities appeared strategically sound. The principle of the deal was to marry typical Disney content with ABC's broadcast and cable distribution; the challenge lay in the execution. While ESPN and other cable properties grew, no unit of the company was as besieged as ABC, which lost money for the first time in a decade in spite of a fantastic advertising marketplace because audiences were splintering and programming costs kept climbing. Under competitive pressure Disney agreed to spend a whopping $9.2 billion for the rights to televise National Football League games on ABC and ESPN through 2008. In one particularly bad year following the acquisition, operating income for the company's broadcasting segment—which included ABC, 80 percent of ESPN, the Disney Channel, ABC Radio, and stakes in Lifetime, A&E, the History Channel, and E! Entertainment—grew by just 3 percent.

ABSORBING A MERGER

Throughout the rest of the 1990s Disney seemed less able than ever to cope with adversity. Some analysts said that the company had grown so big and its problems so far-reaching that they could not be counteracted by a couple of hit movies or TV shows or additional Disney stores. Some were troubled by Eisner's persistent failure to designate a clear successor to himself as the head of the company.

While Disney's 1998 net income surpassed that of its three major competitors combined, all other key indicators were down—some shockingly so. For the first nine months of fiscal 1999, excluding a one-time gain from an asset sale, Disney reported declines in operating income of 17 percent, net income of 26 percent, and earnings per share of 27 percent. Some Wall Street analysts cut their fiscal 1999 earnings estimates as many as five times, and 13 of 25 analysts issued a "hold" on the stock, according to Zacks Investment Research. The company had simply stopped growing, and the stall was not merely a momentary dip: Disney was not expected to match its fiscal 1997 earnings until 2001 at the earliest—a major setback for a company that for the decade after Eisner took over in 1984 had delivered annual increases in both profit and returns on equity of 20 percent.

In *Fortune* magazine Eisner defended what he saw as a premature burial of his company: "We're in a transition period.

I would rather have every quarter be up. It was for 13 years. Everybody loves you. But you can't manage a company like ours quarter to quarter, maniacally, so that the media will write good things about you. I don't think our problems are in the fabric of our company. And I don't have my head in the sand. The criticisms of me and Disney today are as shortsighted as were the praises of me and Disney in the high economic times" (September 6, 1999). In 1999 Jeffrey Katzenberg and Disney finally settled a bitter breach-of-contract lawsuit which analysts estimated paid Katzenberg $250–275 million, including the $117.5 million that he had received in late 1997 when the case had been partially settled.

RULING THE MAGIC KINGDOM WITH AN IRON FIST

Eisner's critics contended that for all his creativity, charisma, and grand plans, he presided over an insular and arrogant corporate culture where the acting authority was hierarchical, centralized, and slow. According to popular wisdom Eisner insisted on making too many decisions himself, clogging the decision-making process. Working with Disney was notoriously difficult—so much so that a group of partners, including Coca-Cola, AT&T, Delta, and Kodak, used to meet informally to trade tips on how to cope.

Yet Eisner had a powerful defense. As he told *Fortune*, "If there's an area where I think I can add value, I dive in. I heard from a friend that the cast members at Disneyland Paris weren't as helpful as those at Walt Disney World; he recommended better training. Is that meddling or is that insisting on a high standard of excellence? Yes, at certain times I paralyze people. I'm never satisfied. It gets people crazy, I know that. But I leave my best executives alone. There's no brain drain. We have unbelievably strong management" (September 6, 1999).

As the lions circled, Eisner's fellow mogul and longtime peer Barry Diller stood firm. Diller told the *Guardian*, "He's developed into the most potent executive of them all. The deeper you dig with Michael Eisner, the better it gets. On the way there he will drive you crazy, though. Why? He's a complex character. He's paranoid. Michael is very suspicious of motives" (April 10, 1999).

Another Eisner criticism was that he did not truly value other people and ousted anyone who gained too much power, as with Katzenberg and Ovitz. Other strong executives left the Disney fold of their own volition, among them the former CFOs Stephen Bollenbach and Richard Nanula, the Internet guru Jake Winebaum, and the former ABC executives Geraldine Laybourne and Steve Burke. Still, to Eisner's credit, as of early 2004 many talented executives remained, including the ESPN president George Bodenheimer and the consumer-products chairman Andy Mooney.

A PLUMMETING APPROVAL RATING

Three years after the terrorist attacks of 2001 Disney's theme parks were still recovering, offering discounted prices in order to keep attendance figures up. The $5.2 billion purchase of Fox Family Channel in 2001, which became ABC Family, was proving to be a failure. During the recession, when advertisers tightened belts, ABC stumbled to last place in ratings among the four major broadcast networks. While Disney films generated a record $3 billion at the box office in 2003, the company could only take part of the credit for the star performer *Finding Nemo*, which had been coproduced by Pixar. Critics said that the fabled Disney theme parks were losing their luster.

The knocks against Eisner's survival tactics were plentiful. He was accused of undermining the company's creativity by dismembering much of its vaunted feature-film animation unit. Critics said he had manipulated a board that had been constantly reshuffled to remain beholden to him. In a final blow the last link to the company founder Walt Disney—his nephew Roy—resigned from the Disney board in 2004 to voice his displeasure with Eisner. As quoted in the *New York Times*, in his resignation Roy Disney blamed Eisner for creating among employees, shareholders, and customers alike a "perception that the company is rapacious, soulless, and always looking for a quick buck rather than creating long-term value, which is leading to a loss of public trust" (February 15, 2004).

THE MOUSE THAT ROARED

The grumbling over Eisner's mismanagement came to a boiling point at a March 2004 shareholder meeting in Philadelphia. In front of three hundred livid shareholders, Eisner gave a ninth-inning plea regarding his personal turnaround and commitment to the company: as reported by *Newsweek*, he said, quite simply, "I love this company" (March 15, 2004). Investors did not care. In an unprecedented showing 43 percent voted against his reelection as chairman. Although the former Senator George Mitchell was named nonexecutive chairman and the vote was clear evidence of public opinion against him, Eisner vowed to stay on at Disney until his contract ended in 2006 and not be forced out.

Considering that Disney had just started to regain some of its magic—stock value and profits were rebounding, and the company anticipated double-digit earnings growth through 2007—the shareholder meeting showed just how low Eisner's standing had sunk. Disney diehards believed Eisner had sacrificed the company's soul for synergies and profits; for example, to cut costs Eisner had eliminated the street sweepers at Disney Land. In *Newsweek* the shareholder Roxann Grzetich of Chicago said, "The deterioration in the appearance of the parks is awful" (March 15, 2004).

The week after the fateful meeting Eisner turned 62; still, he had yet to name a successor. Eisner insisted on staying while everyone else wondered when the chief Mouseketeer would finally lose the keys to the kingdom.

See also entry on Walt Disney Company in *International Directory of Company Histories.*

SOURCES FOR FURTHER INFORMATION

Bates, James, and Michael Cieply, "As Spender, Ovitz Was $6 Million Man," *Los Angeles Times*, February 28, 2004.

Berenson, Alex, "The Wonderful World of (Roy) Disney," *New York Times*, February 15, 2004.

Corliss, Richard, "Enough Is Enough!" *Time*, July 19, 1999, p. 76.

Eisner, Michael, *Work in Progress*, with Tony Schwartz, New York, N.Y.: Random House, 1998.

Gunther, Marc, "Eisner's Mousetrap," *Fortune*, September 6, 1999, p. 106.

Hattenstone, Simon, "Michael Eisner: Master of the Mouse," *Guardian* (London), April 10, 1999, p. 6.

Jefferson, David J., and Johnnie L. Roberts, "The Magic Is Gone," *Newsweek*, March 15, 2004, p. 52.

King, Larry, "*Work in Progress*: Michael Eisner on His Life at the Helm of Disney," CNN Larry King Weekend, October 10, 1998.

Tanaka, Wendy, "Eisner Put Stamp on U.S. Pop Culture," *Philadelphia Inquirer*, March 1, 2004.

—Tim Halpern

■ ■ ■

John Elkann

1976–

Vice chairman, Fiat

Nationality: American.

Born: 1976, in New York, New York.

Education: Turin Polytechnic, BS, 2001.

Family: Son of Alain Elkann (writer) and Margherita Agnelli; married Princess Lavinia de Borromeo-Arese, 2004.

Career: Fiat, 1994–1995, intern; Magneti Marelli, 1996, manager; Fiat Auto, 1997, assembly-line manager; 1998, sales and marketing manager; Fiat/General Electric, 1998–2001, e-business project manager; General Electric, 2001, analyst for Corporate Initiatives Group; 2001–2002, corporate audit staff; Fiat, 2002–2003, manager in charge of company reorganization; IFIL Group, 2003–2004, operational officer in Development and Control Department; Fiat, 2004–, vice chairman.

Address: Fiat, 250 Via Nizza, 10126 Turin, Italy; http://www.fiat.com.

John Elkann. *AP/Wide World Photos.*

■ Heir to Italy's leading business, the company that made Fiat, Alfa Romeo, Maserati, Ferrari, and Lancia brand automobiles, John Philip Elkann was a member of the clan that was once seen as Italy's uncrowned royal family. The deaths of his grandfather, the flamboyant Fiat patriarch Giovanni "Gianni" Agnelli, in 2003 and his great-uncle Umberto several months later propelled Elkann into the vice chairmanship of the Fiat board as well as into control of the Agnelli family's 30 percent stake in Fiat. While the Agnellis had long been preparing Elkann for a leading role in the family business, he was considered too young to yet fully take over.

Part of Elkann's expected strength as a manager lay in his international outlook and background. After attending primary school in New York, he earned a scientific secondary-school diploma at the Victor Duruy Lycée in Paris. While his inclinations appeared to be scientific, Elkann was nevertheless pushed by family tragedy into a life in the automotive business. Gianni Agnelli had designated his son to be his successor, but the younger Agnelli died of cancer at the age of 33 in 1997; Elkann then became heir apparent. He began to sneak away from his university studies in Italy to complete incognito stints at Fiat operations in Europe. He worked at a headlight plant in England, on a Fiat 500 assembly line in Poland, and in the Fiat sales and marketing department in France.

Named to Fiat's board at the age of 21 in 1997, Elkann's youth sparked rumors of a succession crisis that Agnelli quieted with the reminder that he had also been young when he joined the Fiat board in 1943 at the age of 22. After earning his bachelor's degree in 2001, Elkann found a job on General Electric's corporate-audit staff with the aid of the fellow Fiat board member and General Electric Company chairman Jack Welch. Elkann then joined Fiat's investment group, IFIL; the holdings of that firm included the San Paolo bank, Rinascente department stores, Club Med resorts, the top daily newspapers Corriere della Sera of Milan and La Stampa of Turin, and

Italy's most successful soccer team, Juventus. When in 2003 Gianni Agnelli died and his brother Umberto succumbed to cancer shortly thereafter, Elkann inherited the family voting rights in the Fiat Group.

A studious and determined man, Elkann possessed both poise and elegance, but as of 2004 it was not yet clear whether he had the toughness of his grandfather—and the ability to lead Fiat. Elkann would have considerable responsibility for adapting Fiat to a more competitive environment. The Italian automaker had been unable to lure consumers with new models; meanwhile its vehicles had become saddled with such a reputation for needing frequent repair that a popular joke declared that Fiat stood for what owners would tell mechanics: "Fix It Again, Tony." To survive, Fiat needed to reaffirm its brand at home while expanding abroad. Elkann was put in charge of developing the direction of that brand.

The marketing problem facing Elkann would determine whether the Agnelli family remained in the automobile business. Fiat saw its share of the Italian auto market fall from 60 to 40 percent in the late 1990s before striking a stock-swap deal with General Motors in 2000. The arrangement gave 20 percent of Fiat to the American company, with the Italians given the option to force General Motors to buy the remaining 80 percent between 2004 and 2009. The sale would rescue the Fiat Group, which continued to lose money on the 40 percent of the firm comprising Fiat Auto. Other family members, notably the late Umberto Agnelli, had recommended diversification through the sale of Fiat Auto.

See also entry on Fiat SpA in *International Directory of Company Histories.*

SOURCES FOR FURTHER INFORMATION

Edmondson, Gail, and Kate Carlisle, "Who'll Take Over from the Patriarchs?" *BusinessWeek*, May 13, 2002, p. 60.

Israely, Jeff, "With the Grace of Grandpa," *Time Canada*, December 1, 2003, p. 50.

Owen, Richard, "Can 'The Boy' Rescue a Dynasty?" *Times* (London), January 25, 2003.

Rachman, Tom, "Heir Force," *Sunday Mail* (Queensland, Australia), October 20, 2002.

—Caryn E. Neumann

■ ■ ■

Larry Ellison

1944–

Chief executive officer, Oracle Corporation

Nationality: American.

Born: August 17, 1944, in New York, New York.

Education: Attended University of Illinois, 1962–1964; attended University of Chicago, 1964–1966.

Family: Son of Louis (accountant) and Lillian (maiden name unknown; bookkeeper) Ellison; biological son of Florence Spellman (biological father unknown); married (first two wives' names unknown; divorced); married Barbara Boothe (divorced); married Melanie Craft (writer), 2003; children: five (third marriage, two; fourth marriage, three).

Career: Precision Instruments, 1976–1977, vice president, research and development; Software Development Laboratories (Oracle Corporation), 1977–, chief executive officer; Oracle Corporation, 1978–1996, president; 1990–1992, 1995–2004, chairman.

Awards: Entrepreneur of the Year, Harvard Business School, 1990; Science Applications International Corporation Information Technology Leadership Award, Smithsonian Institution, 1994.

Address: Oracle Corporation, 500 Oracle Parkway, Redwood Shores, California 94065; http://www.oracle.com.

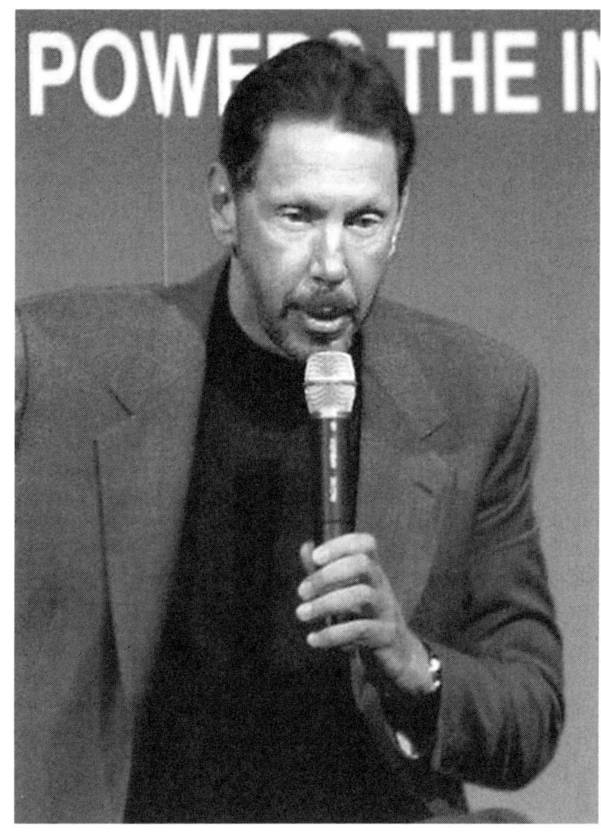

Larry Ellison. *AP/Wide World Photos.*

■ Lawrence (Larry) Joseph Ellison was regarded one of the most visionary leaders in the information technology industry. In 1977, with two colleagues, he founded a company that created the world's first commercially viable relational database. This technology revolutionized the way businesses were able to access and use data. Owing to Larry Ellison's drive and competitive spirit, Oracle databases eventually dominated the market, and Oracle grew to become the second largest independent software company in the world. With a personal fortune estimated at $18.7 billion in 2004, Ellison became one of the world's richest people. Ellison's remarkable foresight and willingness to take risks were demonstrated in his early recognition of the significance of the Internet. Ellison's interests outside the software business, such as his love of yacht racing and his profound interest in Japanese culture, also attracted a great deal of attention from the news media. His lavish lifestyle contributed to an image of Ellison as a flamboyant and charismatic personality.

Ellison also faced harsh criticism for his management style. His arrogance and recklessness at times put the company and his personal fortune in jeopardy and drove many talented executives out of the company. Oracle gained a reputation for having a ruthless and unethical corporate culture. In addition, Ellison's credibility was often damaged by his tendency to exaggerate the performance of Oracle and its products. Many observers believed Ellison's involvement in other projects, such as the Oracle America's Cup campaign in 2002, were serious distractions that were detrimental to his business. One of

America's most controversial business leaders, Ellison excited strong emotions—ranging from loyalty and admiration to bitter hatred—from those who worked with him.

EARLY LIFE

Ellison was born in New York to a single mother, who gave him up for adoption to her aunt and uncle. Raised in Chicago in a lower-middle-class Jewish family, Ellison had a difficult relationship with his adoptive father. Ellison later cited his father's lack of faith in his son's abilities as an important factor in his own desire for recognition and success. However, the drive and ambition for which Ellison was to become notorious did not appear until he was well into adulthood. After graduation from South Shore High School in 1962, Ellison enrolled in courses at the University of Illinois but left without completing his degree when his mother died of cancer. He then enrolled as a physics and mathematics major at the University of Chicago but again left without graduating. Ellison later blamed his failure to complete his college education on his short attention span, lack of discipline, and lack of respect for authority.

Ellison's experience at college was valuable in one respect. As part of a course in physics, he taught himself computer programming. He started doing contract programming and discovered a work culture that suited his temperament and his lifestyle. In *Softwar*, Matthew Symonds quoted Ellison as saying, "My short attention span didn't work against me because I could get programs written very quickly. I ended up making quite a lot of money, and I only had to work a few days a week. It was fun and it was easy. And nobody cared if you were a Ph.D. from MIT or had never finished high school." In 1966 Ellison left Chicago and headed for California. For most of the next decade, Ellison moved from company to company as a programmer. His main motivation was earning enough money to finance hiking and rock-climbing trips in the Yosemite Valley.

SOFTWARE DEVELOPMENT LABORATORIES

In 1976 Ellison worked for a small company called Precision Instruments, which changed its name to Omex. The company was working on a mass storage concept, and Ellison was hired as vice president of research and development. His experience at Omex led Ellison to believe that he could do a better job of running a technology company than most of the managers he observed around him. The independence of being his own boss also was appealing to Ellison's nonconformist temperament. When Omex needed software for the project, Ellison persuaded two friends, Edward A. Oates and Robert N. Miner, to join him in establishing a company to successfully bid for the contract. In 1977 Software Development Laboratories was founded with $2000, and Ellison, as architect of the idea, held majority ownership.

The company was conceived as a consultancy business. However, the three men soon decided to go into the fledgling software business instead. As computer hardware technology developed, business demand was growing for prepackaged software programs that were ready to use. The three men needed to develop a useful program that could be sold repeatedly to different companies. The key would be coming up with the right product.

RELATIONAL DATABASES

In 1970 an IBM researcher named Edgar H. Codd published a paper on relational databases. His paper was highly theoretical and not widely understood, but it conceived of a new way of organizing large amounts of data so that information could be accessed easily. The potential in Codd's theory was enormous, because it meant that companies could manage and retrieve data in ways that had never been previously possible. However, with the current state of technology, the relational database, as Codd's model was known, would be very slow. It was widely accepted that the idea had no immediate commercial viability. In the mid-1970s IBM Research built a prototype relational database and developed a special programming language called SQL, which allowed easier interaction with the database.

For a variety of reasons, IBM was slow to move on the progress it had made with the database. It was up to a young upstart company with nothing to lose in the way of reputation or market share to take the technology and turn it into a viable product. Ellison was one of many who had read the papers that were published on IBM's work with the relational database. However, he was one of few willing to risk everything in making the effort to produce the world's first commercially viable relational database. Over the next two years Software Development Laboratories changed its name to Relational Software Inc. and developed the technology. The U.S. Central Intelligence Agency (CIA) had been interested in the concept of relational databases for several years and provided the company with money to help get the software ready for commercial release. When Oracle Version 2 was launched for the market in 1979, the CIA was one of the first customers, along with several other government intelligence agencies. The small company had snatched the technology out from under the noses of IBM and put the first relational database, albeit one that did not work very reliably, on the market.

BUILDING ORACLE

In 1983 with the launch of Oracle Version 3, the company changed its name to Oracle. In establishing his company, Ellison exhibited the fanatical determination and aggression that were to make him legendary in the industry. His task was not only to get customers to buy Oracle databases but also to persuade them that relational databases in general were the way of the future. To overcome customers' initial reservations, Ellison was required to exercise all his powers of persuasion to captivate and dazzle his audience. According to Symonds in *Softwar*, Donald L. Lucas, a company director, described Ellison as "like a spiritual leader, an evangelist for the relational database model." In the early days of the company Ellison developed one of his key skills—his ability to communicate his vision for the future of the information technology industry to those around him.

Completely focused on gaining market share for the product, Ellison became notorious for his wildly exaggerated claims about what the software could do. In the race to gain market share before rivals in the industry could launch their own versions, Ellison was willing to take incredible risks. The first versions of Oracle were notorious for their unreliable performance, and customers complained of late deliveries and broken promises. But the aggressive sales strategy seemed to work. In 1986, one day before Microsoft did, Oracle went public at $15 a share, closing the day at $20.75 a share, a market value of $270 million. Ellison's 39 percent stake was valued at $93 million. In 1987 Oracle posted revenue of $131 million, and Ellison predicted it was going to become the largest software company in the world.

Determined to maintain the company's growth, Ellison developed a reputation for pushing his employees extremely hard. In 1985 he declared that the company would double its revenue every year. For a couple of years his boast seemed to be coming true. Ironically, however, Ellison's arrogance and recklessness, which partly accounted for the company's success, resulted in business practices that nearly led to the downfall of the company. In 1988, facing intense competition from companies with superior products, Ellison decided to release Oracle Version 6 before it had been properly tested. The ensuing problems were disastrous for Oracle's reputation and its credibility with customers.

The decrease in revenue resulting from the problems with Version 6 was exacerbated by Oracle's aggressive sales force. Spurred by the demands of their ambitious CEO, Oracle salespeople were willing to offer almost anything to close a deal, including huge discounts, and were selling to companies that did not have the money to pay. Because of these problems as well as a chaotic accounting system, by 1990 Oracle had lost control of its finances and faced a serious cash-flow crisis. In 1991 Oracle announced losses from the previous year of nearly $36 million, which severely affected the company's share price and nearly led to its demise.

MATURITY

While many of the company's problems could be traced to Ellison's own shortcomings as a CEO, it was also apparent that the company's future depended on Ellison's visionary brilliance and drive. However, the entrepreneurial spirit that had launched the company and driven it through the early years needed to be tempered with more solid and professional business practices. Jeffrey O. Henley and Raymond J. Lane were brought into the company, taking on the roles of chief financial officer and chief operating officer, respectively. Ellison himself refocused and paid more attention to the details of running the company in a professional manner, aspects he had previously ignored. With the positive impact of the new management team and the launch of a new product, Version 7, which was superior to anything else on the market, Oracle was able to return to profit. By 1994 Oracle had clearly triumphed over its competitors and was dominating the database market.

THE INTERNET REVOLUTION

Despite its success Oracle was still a small player in the technology industry and was far from achieving Ellison's goal of being the largest software company in the world. To his chagrin Ellison was far short of the wealth and influence wielded by the Microsoft cofounder William Henry (Bill) Gates III. Considerable foresight and vision on Ellison's part were needed to propel Oracle into the forefront of the industry. In 1995, while the rest of the world was dazzled by the launch of Microsoft Windows 95, Ellison was predicting the eventual decline of the personal computer, which was the basis of Microsoft's computing concept. Although most experts dismissed Ellison's comments as ludicrous, few could have predicted the impact that the rise of the Internet would have on the information technology industry.

From the mid-1990s Ellison focused his business strategy on the Internet. Because of Ellison's foresight Oracle was ideally positioned to take advantage of the dot-com boom. By contrast, Microsoft, among others, was slow to recognize the significance of what was taking place in the business world. Oracle's powerful databases became an essential platform of business on the Internet, transforming Oracle into one of Silicon Valley's most powerful companies. In 2000 Ellison even briefly overtook Gates as the world's richest person. This position was mainly achieved through the force of Ellison's visionary leadership. As David J. Roux, a former manager at Oracle, explained to Andy Serwer, Julia Boorstin, and Jessica Sungin of *Fortune*, "Is he a great technologist? No, there are 100 guys in the Valley as good as he is. Is he a great manager? No, but he's been smart enough to get them. What he is is a great leader. His great strength is to make exceptional employees do the impossible."

Despite success Ellison's dedication to the vision of computing via the Internet was a high-risk strategy for the company. Ellison was convinced that the old client-server paradigm of computing, whereby the software was shared between the desktop personal computer and the server computer, was a technological dead-end. Therefore he announced in 1997 that all the company's software would be written for the new Internet environment. This move was dangerous, because it risked alienating customers who were not prepared to make such a dramatic change to their business software platforms. Ellison also wanted to change the company's core business. Because of the limited growth potential in Oracle's traditional database market, Ellison looked to Internet applications as the way of the future for Oracle. This software was used to carry out a company's major business operations, such as sales, finance, and customer relations management. Most software companies focused on developing applications for one area of business, an approach known as "best of breed." Ellison's ambitious strategy was to develop a completely integrated e-business package, which he believed would dominate the industry the way Microsoft Windows had dominated the world of operating systems.

Ellison launched a massive shake-up of Oracle with the aim of transforming it into an e-business. This internal restructuring was intended to serve as an advertisement for what Oracle technology could do to improve business efficiency. While the strategy saved the company approximately $1 billion, it also had a severe impact on the management team at Oracle. The e-business restructuring centralized control in Ellison's hands, often at the expense of his senior executives. Lane, the chief operating officer who had been generally regarded as Ellison's second in command and eventual successor, was forced out of the company.

DOWNTURN

The departure of Lane in 2000 and of several other executives in the following years left analysts worried about the stability of Oracle. It was feared that Ellison's apparent unwillingness to share power with his executive team was creating a management vacuum. In addition, problems occurred with the e-business suite launched in 2000. The product was intended to establish Oracle's dominance in the Internet applications software market, but the software fell short of the expectations Ellison had created, and his strategy looked shaky. Then the collapse of the dot-com and telecommunication industries, economic recession, and the September 11, 2001, terrorist attacks reduced technology spending. As a result, Oracle's growth was severely curtailed. Ellison's personal fortune dropped from $58 billion in 2000 to $18.7 billion in 2004. In 2002, when his leadership was most needed, Ellison spent months at a time away from the company, focused instead on the America's Cup race in Auckland, New Zealand. Business analysts pointed to declining revenue—$10.9 billion in 2001 to $9.5 billion in 2003—as a sign of a company in trouble.

Ellison remained dedicated to his vision of shifting Oracle's focus onto the Internet applications market. Oracle caused a furor in the industry in 2003 by launching a hostile $7.7 million bid for the takeover of the application software company PeopleSoft. The CEO of PeopleSoft, Craig Conway, a former Oracle employee, accused Ellison of trying to ruin his company. Others claimed the bid was just another Ellison ploy to gain attention. The U.S. Department of Justice investigated the proposed takeover and filed a lawsuit to block the deal for being anticompetitive. The Department of Justice claimed that only three companies—PeopleSoft, SAP, and Oracle—operated in this market and that merging two of the companies would reduce the chance for competition. In its defense Oracle claimed that the Department of Justice's definition of the market was too narrow and that many other firms were producing different types of software and could provide adequate competition. In addition, Oracle pointed to the likelihood of Microsoft's entering the market, which was part of the reason Oracle wanted to consolidate by purchasing PeopleSoft.

As of 2004 analysts continued to express doubts about Ellison's egocentric management style and about his long-term commitment to the company. As Ellison approached his 60th birthday, there were suggestions that he might leave Oracle to pursue his interest in the biotechnology industry. However, in mid-2004 Ellison remained firmly ensconced in the role of CEO, focusing on the legal battle over the PeopleSoft bid and the task of extending Oracle's market share in the Internet application software industry.

See also entry on Oracle Systems Corporation in *International Directory of Company Histories.*

SOURCES FOR FURTHER INFORMATION

Hamm, Steve, Jay Greene, and David Rocks, "Oracle: Why It's Cool Again," *BusinessWeek*, May 8, 2000, pp. 114–122.

"Larry Ups the Ante: Why Oracle Wants PeopleSoft," *The Economist*, February 7, 2004, pp. 59–60.

Serwer, Andy, Julia Boorstin, and Jessica Sung, "The Next Richest Man in the World," *Fortune*, November 13, 2000, pp. 98–110.

Symonds, Matthew, *Softwar: An Intimate Portrait of Larry Ellison and Oracle*, New York: Simon and Schuster, 2003.

Wilson, Mike, *The Difference Between God and Larry Ellison: Inside Oracle Corporation*, New York: Harper Business, 1997.

—Katrina Ford

■ ■ ■

Thomas J. Engibous

1953–

Chairman, Texas Instruments Incorporated

Nationality: American.

Born: January 31, 1953, in St. Louis, Missouri.

Education: Purdue University, BS, 1975; MS, 1976.

Family: Son of James (research scientist) and Emma Buck; married Wendy (maiden name unknown); children: three.

Career: Texas Instruments, 1976–1980, design engineer, semiconductor group; 1980–1986, department manager, semiconductor group; 1986–1991, vice president, semiconductor group; 1991–1993, senior vice president, semiconductor group; 1993–1996, executive vice president, semiconductor group; 1996–1998, president and chief executive officer; 1998–2004, president, chief executive officer, and chairman; 2004–, chairman.

Awards: Distinguished Engineering Alumnus award, Purdue University, 1990; honorary Doctor of Engineering degree, Purdue University, 1997; listed among the Top 25 Executives of the Past 25 Years, *Electronic Business*, 2000; listed among the Top 25 Managers, *BusinessWeek*, 2000.

Address: Texas Instruments Inc., 12500 TI Boulevard, Dallas, Texas 75266; http://www.ti.com/.

■ Thomas J. Engibous developed his reputation as a top leader in the semiconductor group at Texas Instruments Incorporated (TI). He became the company's president and chief executive officer in 1996 and its chairman in 1998. Under his direction, TI changed from a broad-based conglomerate into a semiconductor company with a major worldwide presence. Engibous, who stepped down as the company's president and CEO in 2004, was known for his aggressive business strategies and plain-spoken management style.

A COMPETITIVE SPIRIT

Engibous grew up in Mount Prospect, Illinois, a suburb of Chicago, as the son of a research scientist. He developed his competitive spirit in such sports as baseball and wrestling and remained an avid sports fan as an adult. Engibous discovered an interest in engineering in high school when he constructed a digital computer that could add numbers.

Engibous enrolled at Purdue University in West LaFayette, Indiana, after graduating from high school. He continued to participate in athletics as an undergraduate by playing on the Purdue hockey team. He graduated with a bachelor of science degree in electrical engineering in 1975. Engibous then enrolled in Purdue's graduate school, earning a master of science degree in electrical engineering in 1976. In 1997, nearly two decades after concluding his formal education, Purdue awarded Engibous an honorary doctorate in engineering in recognition of his success at Texas Instruments.

Engibous learned early in his career that leadership skills are as important in engineering as technical abilities. When he was designated a Distinguished Engineering Alumnus by Purdue in 1990, Engibous told the graduate students, "Remember that once you've graduated you will be required to make decisions—and there's a big difference between having a sound technical background and having the capacity to make sound technical decisions. The first doesn't necessarily lead to the second. It's the decision-making aspect that takes time to learn after graduation" (February 24, 1997).

WORKING AT TEXAS INSTRUMENTS

Texas Instruments hired Engibous immediately after he received his graduate degree from Purdue in 1976 and assigned him to the semiconductor group as a design engineer. Four years later he was promoted to department manager, a position he held until 1986. As department manager, he oversaw the worldwide operations of the semiconductor group, including the development of new technologies. He continued his rise within the company in 1991, when he was appointed vice president of the semiconductor group. He was later promoted to the position of senior vice president.

After Engibous had spent 17 years in various management positions in the semiconductor group, his leadership qualities were further rewarded when he was named executive vice president in charge of the group. He quickly developed a reputation as a fierce competitor. His years at the head of the semiconductor group were highly successful, as Texas Instruments gained market share each year while the group produced record profits for the company. Engibous improved the semiconductor group's efficiency by focusing on the development of specialized computer chips rather than the production of standard memory chips to make money for TI.

A SURPRISING CHOICE

Texas Instruments underwent troubling times in 1996, when chip prices fell and caused the company's net income to drop sharply. In addition, the company lost its leader that June when James R. Junkins, the company's president, chief executive officer, and chairman died suddenly. Unfortunately, the company had not groomed an immediate successor at the time of Junkins's death. Two vice chairmen, William P. Weber and William B. Mitchell, assumed Junkins's duties. Both candidates resembled Junkins in their management styles; moreover, TI was considered a conservative and cautious company.

The company thus made a bold move when it promoted Engibous, who was then 43 years old, to serve as its president and chief executive officer. Engibous's ambitious and intense style stood in stark contrast to that of Junkins, who favored a more easygoing approach. The company named James R. Adams, a former group president of SBC Communications, as the board president. Adams maintained that Engibous was the right choice to lead TI. "He is the right man to be leading Texas Instruments into its long-term future," Adams said of Engibous (June 21, 1996).

REFOCUSING THE COMPANY

Engibous was widely credited with shifting the focus of Texas Instruments. The company had been known as a broad-based conglomerate prior to 1996, but Engibous turned TI into a semiconductor company. Texas Instruments sold several of its divisions between 1996 and 1998, including its custom manufacturing and notebook computer businesses, its defense electronics operation, and its enterprise applications software. The company's semiconductor business soared throughout much of the late 1990s. By 2000 Texas Instruments controlled nearly half of the $4.4 billion worldwide market for digital signal processors, which were used for such devices as modems and cellular phones.

Engibous was hailed for his assertive management style. In addition to constant travel, he was known to rise before 4 a.m. in order to address business matters with employees and customers. He took advantage of his background in athletics by using sports metaphors in his speeches. Although his plans were often bold, he maintained a straightforward personal manner and generally avoided wearing neckties.

Although TI benefited from Engibous's style of leadership, the market for memory chips fluctuated. The company's income fell off during several quarters in the late 1990s and early 2000s, leading to a series of layoffs. At the same time, however, TI's growth had a significant positive impact on the economy of the Dallas area, as the company constructed a state-of-the-art semiconductor factory north of the city.

STEPPING DOWN

After eight years as the head of Texas Instruments, Engibous stepped down as president and chief executive officer in 2004, much to the surprise of industry analysts. The transition from Engibous to his successor, longtime company employee Richard K. Templeton, was planned although it came sooner than analysts had expected. Engibous remained as chairman of the board. In addition to his position at Texas Instruments, he served as chairman of the board of Catalyst Semiconductor Incorporated as well as a trustee of Southern Methodist University, a member of the Purdue University Visiting Committee, and a member of several civic and company boards, including the board of directors of the J. C. Penney Company.

See also entry on Texas Instruments Incorporated in *International Directory of Company Histories.*

SOURCES FOR FURTHER INFORMATION

Goldstein, Alan, and Jim Mitchell, "TI Names President, Chairman," *Dallas Morning News,* June 21, 1996.

Harrison, Crayton, "Swap at Top for TI," *Dallas Morning News,* January 16, 2004.

McWilliams, Gary, "A 20-Year Man for Texas Instruments," *BusinessWeek,* July 8, 1996, p. 42.

Myerson, Allen R., "Texas Instruments Passes Over Two in Picking Chief," *New York Times,* June 21, 1996.

"1990 Distinguished Engineering Alumni: Thomas J. Engibous," Purdue University, http://www.ecn.purdue.edu/ECN/DEA/1990/Thomas_J_Engibous.

"Special Report: The Top 25 Managers," *BusinessWeek,* January 10, 2000, p. 74.

—Matthew C. Cordon

Gregg L. Engles

1957–

Chairman and chief executive officer, Dean Foods Company

Nationality: American.

Born: August 16, 1957, in Durant, Oklahoma.

Education: Dartmouth College, AB, 1979; Yale University, JD, 1982.

Family: Married Cindy (maiden name unknown; divorced).

Career: United States Court of Appeals, 1982–1983, law clerk; 2M Companies, 1983–1984, analyst; 1985–1988, real estate investor (self-employed principal); Reddy Ice, 1988–1995, chairman and chief executive officer; Engles Capital Corporation, 1988–1992, president; Engles Management Corporation, 1993–1994, president; Suiza Puerto Rico, 1993–1995, chairman; Velda Farms, 1994–1995, chairman; Suiza Foods Corporation, 1994–2001, chairman and chief executive officer; Engles, Urso, Follmer Capital, 1994–, chairman; Dean Foods Company, 2001–2002, vice chairman and chief executive officer; 2002–, chairman and chief executive officer.

Address: Dean Foods Company, 2515 McKinney Avenue, Suite 1200, Dallas, Texas 75201; http://www.deanfoods.com.

Gregg Engles presided over a consolidation of the dairy industry, first as head of Suiza Foods Corporation and then as chairman and chief executive officer of Dean Foods Company. Dean Foods Company became the largest processor and distributor of milk in the United States.

EARLY YEARS IN COLORADO

Although born in Oklahoma, Gregg Engles grew up in the Denver, Colorado, area. He attended Dartmouth College and studied law at Yale University. After graduation in 1982 Engles worked as a law clerk for Judge Anthony Kennedy, who at the time was serving on the United States Court of Appeals, Ninth Circuit, and later became an associate justice of the United States Supreme Court. In 1983 while a clerk, Engles attempted to form a time-share business for corporate aircraft but was unable to raise funds. Engles was ahead of his time, because jet time-shares later became a huge business.

Engles was admitted to the Colorado state bar in 1982 and to the state bar of Texas in 1984, but he decided not to practice law. While pursuing his unsuccessful aircraft time-share venture, Engles had met "entrepreneurs who impressed him as being fully engaged in their work. In contrast, many of the young lawyers seemed unenthusiastic about their jobs, even though they were buying new cars and homes. Engles decided that his biggest personal risk was getting hooked on a lifestyle that would handcuff him to a job," according to June Eichbaum and Victoria Reese of *Chief Legal Officer* (2002).

PURSUES ENTREPRENEURIAL CAREER

Engles went to work for an investor in Dallas, Texas, who made investments in private companies. Through the business he met a partner, Bob Kaminski, and began investing in real estate in 1985. Again Engles's timing was off. The Texas real estate market was poised for a major downturn. The ventures went so poorly that Engles and his partner were almost bankrupt. In 1988 the Southland Corporation, which later became 7-Eleven, had excessive debt because of a management buyout and needed to raise cash. Engles and Kaminski paid $26 million, almost entirely borrowed, for the Southland subsidiary Reddy Ice Group, a producer of packaged ice.

Using Reddy Ice, Engles and his partners began acquiring other ice companies and consolidating the local ice industry. Gayle Beshears, who had led the ice operations for 7-Eleven, advised Engles. By 1990 Reddy Ice had acquired 15 ice plants. Beshears's brother, Cletes "Tex" Beshears, was a semiretired veteran of the dairy industry. He suggested that the larger dairy industry could be consolidated as Reddy Ice had consolidated the ice business.

ACQUIRES SUIZA DAIRY

In 1993 Engles and his partners acquired Suiza Dairy in San Juan, Puerto Rico, as the first step in their dairy consolidation plan. Engles's strategy was to buy the leading producer in a region, acquire other nearby producers, and then consolidate operations to capitalize on the economies of scale and increase profit. In the dairy industry Engles's timing was right. Engles had an advantage in the consolidation of the dairy industry because his customers in the grocery industry were going through a similar consolidation. The large grocery companies wanted to reduce the number of vendors and preferred dealing with a large dairy that had a national presence. In addition, changes in processing and transportation technologies increased the shelf life of dairy products, and processors became able to ship greater distances.

In 1994 Engles Management Corporation bought Velda Farms, another dairy, and in 1995 Engles merged Reddy Ice into the dairy acquisitions to form Suiza Foods Corporation. In 1996 Suiza Foods Corporation went public, providing additional capital for growth and spurring further acquisitions. Suiza Foods reached sales of $1 billion in 1997. Suiza Foods sold Reddy Ice in 1998 to focus on the dairy operations. Suiza Foods made more than 40 more acquisitions from its initial public offering through 2000, when Suiza Foods became the nation's largest dairy processor and distributor. That year Suiza Foods was named dairy supplier of the year by Wal-Mart because of a large sales increase, a 99.5 percent on-time delivery record, and innovative marketing programs.

At the acquired companies Engles attempted to preserve the entrepreneurial spirit of the local management and made bonuses dependent on performance. Joining Suiza Foods was an attractive option for many local and family-held businesses. The family and employees could continue in the dairy business yet have greater access to capital, new technologies, and branded products.

SUIZA FOODS CORPORATION BECOMES DEAN FOODS COMPANY

In December 2001 Suiza Foods Corporation acquired Dean Foods Company, and Suiza Foods Corporation changed its name to Dean Foods Company. After the Dean Foods acquisition, the new company had a 30 percent share of the milk market. Engles became chairman when Howard Dean retired in April 2002.

Dean Foods Company sold dairy products under more than 50 different brands, including Country Fresh, Medal Gold, Alta Dena, and Garelick Farms, and was the only milk company that could serve as a sole supplier to national retailers. The company also encompassed Silk soy milk, Horizon organic dairy products and juices, International Delight coffee creamers, and Marie's dips and dressings. The company licensed the brands Hershey's, Land O Lakes, and Folgers for use on its milks and milkshakes, creamers, and milk and coffee beverages. Dean Foods Company was also one of the nation's largest pickle processors.

Engles's transformation of the dairy industry was "analogous to what Herb Kelleher's Southwest Airlines accomplished in air transportation and what Sam Walton's Wal-Mart did in retailing. The dairy business will never be the same," wrote Shad Rowe of *D—Dallas/Ft. Worth*. William Heuslein, writing for *Forbes*, quoted food analyst William Leach describing Engles as a visionary.

After the acquisition of Dean Foods Company, Engles and the company entered a new phase. Much of the plan for consolidation of the dairy industry through acquisitions had been completed. Dean Foods Company's strategy turned toward increasing branded products and producing higher margins.

MANAGEMENT STYLE

In addition to his full-time role at Dean Foods Company, Engles remained a partner in Engles, Urso, Follmer Capital, formed in 1995. Engles served as a director of one of the group's portfolio companies, Evercom, which provided pay phones in prisons. In 1998 Engles, Urso, Follmer Capital purchased the vacuum cleaner company Electrolux, and Engles served as a director of that private company.

Engles continued to seize opportunities despite poor timing and missteps in his early endeavors. He told Eichbaum and Reese, "Many lawyers let knowledge of risk paralyze them. They focus exclusively on risk, while entrepreneurs focus primarily on opportunity. The person who can simultaneously perceive the opportunity and the risk has a competitive advantage." Rowe described Engles's career path as follows: "A smart, capable person becomes consumed by a business opportunity so big that both the business and the individual grow to levels unimaginable once even to him." Rowe also noted, "People who meet Engles frequently describe him as 'scary smart'." Engles himself saw his strengths as doing deals and attracting well-qualified people.

Engles served on the boards of directors of a number of charitable and industry organizations, include the Grocery Manufacturers of America, Southern Methodist University, and Students in Free Enterprise. He was a trustee of the Boys and Girls Clubs of America and the Southwestern Medical Foundation. He served on the School of Business Administration Advisory Council for the University of Texas at Arlington.

See also entry on Dean Foods Company in *International Directory of Company Histories.*

SOURCES FOR FURTHER INFORMATION

Cook, Lynn J., "Got Growth?" *Forbes*, May 12, 2003, pp. 102–103.

Eichbaum, June, and Victoria Reese, "The Lawyer-CEO: Role Model for a Strategic Business Partner," *Chief Legal Officer*, Summer 2002, pp. 37–40.

Forgrieve, Janet, "Cream of the Crop," *Rocky Mountain News*, April 10, 2004.

Heuslein, William, "Suiza Foods Milkman," *Forbes*, January 10, 2000, pp. 136–137.

Lee, Steven H., "Head of the Herd: Suiza Foods Becomes One of the Largest Dairy Processors through Steady Stream of Acquisitions," *Dallas Morning News*, August 15, 1999.

Rowe, Shad, "Milkman to the Nation," *D—Dallas/Ft. Worth*, September 1, 2001, p. 52.

—Jean Kieling

■ ■ ■

Ted English

1954–

President and chief executive officer, TJX Companies

Nationality: American.

Born: 1954.

Education: Northeastern University College of Business Administration, BA, 1976.

Family: Married Maureen (maiden name unknown).

Career: Filene's Basement, 1983, buyer; T. J. Maxx, 1983–1995, various merchandising positions; 1995–1997, senior vice president of merchandising; Marmaxx Group, 1997–1998, executive vice president of merchandising, planning, and allocation; 1998–1999, senior vice president and group executive; TJX Companies, 1999–2000, president and chief operating officer; Marmaxx Group, 1999–2000, chairman; TJX Companies, 2000–, president and chief executive officer.

Awards: Honorary doctor of laws degree, Framingham State College, 2002; Sir Ernest Shackleton Award, Shackleton Schools, 2002; named Business Leader of the Year, MetroWest Chamber of Commerce, 2003; named one of America's Most Powerful People, *Forbes*, 2000.

Address: TJX Companies, 770 Cochituate Road, Framingham, Massachusetts 01701–4672; http://www.tjx.com.

■ Edmond "Ted" English served as president and CEO of the TJX Companies, a leading discount retailer of apparel and home fashions. His intense focus and constant implementation of new and innovative ideas kept TJX profitable through times of economic downturn. English directed the successful acquisition of several off-price retail companies that increased TJX's assets and holdings without diminishing financial growth. Coworkers and analysts described English as a focused, innovative, and compassionate manager.

DEVELOPING SKILLS

English devoted his career to the merchandising and growth of TJX Companies. As an entry-level employee, he had a keen eye for customer shopping behavior and generated ideas to attract repeat customers, which helped him move up the corporate ladder. In 1995, as senior vice president of merchandising, English played a key role in the consolidation of T. J. Maxx and Marshalls, the two largest off-price clothing chains in the United States, to form the single operation Marmaxx. To keep the stores profitable, he preserved the names and individual characters of the stores. Both stores carry brand-name clothing and home decor, but Marshalls carries a large selection of shoes and costume jewelry, while T. J. Maxx offers more fine jewelry. In demonstration of his ability to predict customer desires, English carefully researched individual community markets to learn which store, T. J. Maxx or Marshalls, had the competitive edge and should remain open in a specific community, if a community's particular market appeared to be oversaturated by the presence of both stores. Through the merger of T. J. Maxx and Marshalls into Marmaxx, TJX continued to reap the benefits of both stores' reputations; the merger also boosted TJX's purchasing power and reduced expenses through TJX's augmented ability to negotiate in bulk with clothing distributors.

INTENSE FOCUS ON STRATEGY

Based on his success in the Marmaxx organization, English was made president and CEO of TJX in 2000. English's strengths as a CEO included his ability to focus on merchandising, produce innovative ideas, predict customer shopping habits, and direct ongoing growth. English managed TJX with the primary goal of "captur[ing] customers during hard times and then keep[ing] them when times get better" (*Home Textiles Today*, June 10, 2002). In order to bring in new customers and retain repeat customers while increasing profits, English continuously analyzed and applied new and innovative merchandising principles to the store's operations.

English found success through advertisement and creation of a store with constantly changing brand-name merchandise. TJX found this model to be successful, since customers shop at a store with daily-changing merchandise more frequently than they would in a store that varies merchandise only seasonally. Beyond standard clothing sales, English found that the quick turnover of goods was a very effective merchandising technique during the holiday season, as customers returned to the stores several times for holiday shopping over the course of one or two months. As a way to maximize profits and minimize expenses, English optimized the variety of merchandise, decreased stock on hand by buying close to need, and sent specific merchandise to targeted stores or markets in which he believed they would sell best. English's strategies had the net effect of keeping customers shopping at TJX's stores during times of economic downturn and low consumer confidence.

GROWTH THROUGH ACQUISITION AND EXPANSION

After becoming CEO in 2000, English directed TJX's acquisition of A. J. Wright in the United States and both Winners and HomeSense in Canada. TJX also expanded into Europe by opening more than 100 T. J. Maxx retail stores. Despite the financial toll that large acquisitions and new stores could have had on the company, TJX had a 2002 annual growth rate of 11 percent, and by 2004 TJX's first quarter earnings had increased over 20 percent.

The application of the TJX store model to the virtual marketplace was unique, in that English wanted to reflect the fast turnover of merchandise in local stores in the virtual T. J. Maxx and Homegoods stores. Growth into new markets and new bricks-and-mortar stores without large profit loss gave TJX the luxury of three years for researching and evaluating possible business plans before directing their own virtual expansion.

English's growth expansion model proved to be very profitable for TJX Companies. From 2002 to 2003 TJX revenues increased 11 percent, to $13 billion. As a bonus, in the Fortune 500 ratings, TJX ranked 11th for return on assets, 23rd for return on equity, and 47th for 10-year EPS (earnings projected statement) growth. TJX was also ranked fifth among the specialty retailers on *Fortune* magazine's Most Admired Companies list of 2003.

SOCIAL PROGRAMS AND PHILANTHROPY

In 1997 there was low unemployment in the United States, and TJX had increasing difficulty finding retail employees. To solve their unemployment issue and help the community, TJX joined the national nonprofit Welfare to Work (WTW) program to move workers off public assistance and into jobs in the private sector. Under the guidance of English and then-CEO Bernard Cammarata, TJX not only hired employees from the welfare lists but also took great pains to make sure the employees were trained in merchandising and given all the resources needed to be successful in their jobs. In 1998, recognizing that some people needed more training than others, English and Cammarata developed the First Step program, with Morgan Memorial Goodwill Industries, to train potential employees. Those persons who tested at the eight-grade level or lower and did not have a high school diploma (or GED) entered into three weeks of retail-specific classroom training and then participated in a one- to five-week internship at a store. Those who completed the classroom training and internship were guaranteed a full-time job.

The training program helped TJX bring more trained and long-term employees into the company. As an added benefit to the employees, TJX and Goodwill Industries provided ongoing case management to solve child-care and transportation issues as they arose and helped employees become more aware of government aid programs, such as the Children's Health Insurance program, food stamps, and the Advance Earned Income Tax Credit. Beyond the Goodwill training program, TJX also identified employees who needed assistance in learning English and created English as a Second Language classes. TJX became a national model for the WTW program by hiring five times as many workers as the five thousand required by program guidelines. A 2000 *Forbes* article found that 61 percent of welfare workers had stayed with their TJX jobs after one year.

GRACE UNDER PRESSURE

Seven TJX employees on their way to a meeting were killed in the terrorist attacks of September 11, 2001. English's quick, compassionate corporate leadership set the standard for other corporate CEOs and presidents facing the same situation. English not only sent personal notes to family members offering condolences but also offered family members the use of TJX lawyers, accountants, and other professionals; established college scholarships for the employees' children; created a TJX Family Memorial Trust Fund; and offered financial assistance for memorial services. Beyond helping the families cope with the immediate impact of a loss, English also brought together a committee driven by family members to develop a September 11th Memorial Garden at TJX and dedicated a new learning center to the honor of the slain employees. Through his compassion and assistance, English earned the loyalty and respect of his employees and the community. In recognition of his kindness, English was awarded an honorary doctor of laws degree from Framingham State College.

TEACHING THE NEXT GENERATION OF BUSINESS LEADERS

English also forged close links with local students. For example, he worked as a volunteer with the Shackleton School, a nonprofit, Boston-based, experience-focused school, to help students learn leadership skills. English also had a particularly close relationship with his alma mater, the Northeastern University College of Business Administration (CBA). At CBA, English participated in the Executive MBA Alumni lecture series, chaired the CBA Board of Visitors, entered TJX in CBA's corporate partners program, and helped CBA try a newly designed Introduction to Business Course that focused intensively on TJX. As a result of his work with programs at the Shackleton School and other educational ventures, English was awarded the Sir Ernest Shackleton Award "for his commitment to leadership, education, and serving deserving young people."

See also entry on The TJX Companies, Inc. in *International Directory of Company Histories.*

SOURCES FOR FURTHER INFORMATION

Bock, Linda, "Framingham State Grads Urged to 'Strike Out Boldly'; 999 in Class of 2002 Told of Keys to Success," *Worcester Telegram and Gazette,* May 28, 2002.

Goodison, Donna, "TJX Seen as National Model for Welfare-Work Initiative," *Boston Business Journal* March 8, 2002, p. 7.

Lillo, Andrea, "TJX Maps Out Expansion Plans," *Home Textiles Today,* June 10, 2002, p. 1.

"Newsmakers 2001: Ted English," *Boston Business Journal,* December 28, 2001, p. 7.

—Dawn Jacob Laney

■ ■ ■

Roger Enrico

1944–

Former chairman and chief executive officer, PepsiCo

Nationality: American.

Born: November 11, 1944, in Chisholm, Minnesota.

Education: Babson College, bachelor's degree, 1965.

Family: Married Rosemary Margo, 1969; children: one.

Career: General Mills, 1970–1971, marketing assistant; Frito-Lay, beginning in 1971, associate production manager; Pepsi-Cola International, vice president of southern Latin America unit; Pepsi-Cola Bottling Group, 1980–1981, senior vice president of sales and marketing; Pepsi-Cola USA, 1982–1983, executive vice president; PepsiCo Beverages & Foods, 1983–1986, president and CEO; PepsiCo Worldwide Beverages, 1987–1991, CEO; Frito-Lay and PepsiCo Foods International, 1991–1993, chairman and CEO; PepsiCo Worldwide Restaurants, 1994–1995, president and CEO; PepsiCo, 1996, CEO; 1997–2001, vice chairman and CEO; 2001–2003, chairman.

Awards: Soft Drink Hall of Fame, *Beverage World*, 1990; 48th Annual Public Service Award, Advertising Council, 2001.

Publications: *The Other Guy Blinked: How Pepsi Won the Cola Wars* (with Jesse Kornbluth), 1986.

■ Roger Enrico spent almost his entire career working under PepsiCo, eventually serving as CEO of each of its three primary business divisions—beverages, foods, and restaurants—before becoming chairman and CEO of the entire corporation. During his stint in the 1980s as CEO of the beverage division, he guided Pepsi-Cola's rise to a share in the cola market that was essentially equal to that of its major competitor, Coca-Cola. When Enrico took over as chairman and CEO of PepsiCo in 1996, he revitalized a slumping company through the initiation of a comprehensive restructuring campaign and a focus on entering new markets. Described by industry analysts as action oriented, Enrico is known as a corporate leader with vision who made his name as a maverick marketer.

Roger Enrico. © *Robert Maass/Corbis.*

TWO EARLY LESSONS

One of the first business lessons Enrico learned—and never forgot—came from his father, who was a maintenance man at an ore-smelting plant in Minnesota. The senior Enrico often commented to his son that he couldn't understand why management did not pay attention to ideas coming from the people who actually worked in the shop. According to Karen Benezra, writing in *Brandweek*, the future PepsiCo CEO's father told him, "They pay for my muscle and get my mind and brain for free" (October 7, 1996). Years later, the younger Enrico would carry that lesson with him as he reached beyond the boardroom to seek the advice of the people who had the closest relationships with the customers.

Enrico's second lesson came in the late 1960s when he was a navy supply officer in Vietnam during the war. Enrico marveled at his commanding officer's ability to combine resourcefulness and a penchant for not "going by the book." Throughout his subsequent career, Enrico would incorporate both traits into his management philosophy, sometimes raising the ire of his superiors but ultimately winning them over as he championed new ideas and products.

ENTERS THE COLA WARS

After he left the service, Enrico worked for a brief time for General Mills before joining PesiCo's Frito-Lay division as an associate brand manager for Funyuns, an onion-flavored snack. Enrico quickly established himself as a brash newcomer; some of his superiors even saw him as impudent. One production chief for Frito-Lay at the time, James H. O'Neal, recalled in a *BusinessWeek* article, "He was just more aggressive and more pushy than anybody else" (April 10, 2000).

Enrico was more than just aggressive, however. His flair for marketing was evident, and he obtained results. Following the traditional grooming of managers at PepsiCo, Enrico was introduced into the beverage business. In the late 1970s he served as vice president of Pepsi-Cola International's southern Latin America unit, and he later became senior vice president of sales and marketing at the Pepsi-Cola Bottling Group.

In 1983 Enrico was named CEO of Pepsi-Cola. That same year, as part of an effort to revamp the soft drink's image and better compete with archrival Coca-Cola, Enrico sought a company spokesperson to whom the younger generation could relate. In what has become a part of marketing history, Enrico landed the pop singer Michael Jackson, who was the hottest and most popular recording artist at the time, to do a series of television commercials for Pepsi-Cola. The commercials garnered a wide range of media coverage for Pepsi and its new marketing slogan, "The Choice for a New Generation." Despite the success of the strategy, Enrico once again angered his superiors by neither informing them of his plan nor asking for their approval before implementing it.

Throughout the rest of the 1980s Enrico broadened Pepsi's profile and established the company as a strong competitor in many of the markets that Coca-Cola had traditionally dominated. Enrico's brash style once again came to the forefront when Coca-Cola announced a new version of its product. Enrico and many industry analysts interpreted the move as one in which Pepsi's rival was trying to market a soft drink that matched the taste of Pepsi. In response, Enrico placed an ad in many of America's major newspapers that, according to Greg W. Prince in *Beverage World*, started out this way: "It gives me great pleasure to offer each of you my heartiest congratulations. After 87 years of going at it eyeball to eyeball, the other guy just blinked" (January 1998). Enrico went on to write the book *The Other Guy Blinked: How Pepsi Won the Cola Wars*, with coauthor Jesse Kornbluth. In 1987 the Pepsi-Cola beverage division had increased its market share by 10 percentage points to 32 percent, just 0.8 percent behind Coca-Cola. That same year, Enrico was made CEO of PepsiCo Worldwide Beverages.

TURNS ATTENTION TO FOODS AND RESTAURANTS

In 1990 Enrico had to temporarily relinquish the day-to-day operations of Pepsi's beverage business after suffering a mild heart attack on a dance floor in Turkey. According to Enrico and some of his colleagues, the episode had a profound effect on him, as he began to question his all-consuming desire to succeed. Some in the industry said that after the heart attack Enrico became more sensitive to people, rather than focusing solely on the bottom line.

Enrico was soon able to return to work, and in 1991 he became the chairman and CEO of Frito-Lay. He quickly set out to reorganize the division, cutting 1,800 jobs and instilling a new sense of competitiveness in the remaining employees. Once again, Enrico turned to his knack for attracting the attention of consumers and orchestrated several successful marketing blitzes, like "Doritos D-Day."

In 1994 Enrico was appointed chairman and CEO of PepsiCo Worldwide Restaurants, where he oversaw the PepsiCo divisions of Pizza Hut, Taco Bell, and KFC. Enrico recognized that these entities were often competing with one another and had become obsessed with growth to the point of losing sight of operations and letting supply outstrip demand. Enrico's strategy was to shift from hypercompetitive divisiveness to a system of cooperation. Within two years, the restaurant-industry analyst Jennifer Solomon of Salomon Brothers was able to tell Steve Brooks in an interview for *Restaurant Business*, "The businesses really operated as autonomous units. Now they're operating as a restaurant division" (August 10, 1996). Enrico continued to make changes, his growth plan based on same-store sales boosts, margin increases, and additional franchising.

Although PepsiCo's restaurant businesses made a much-touted recovery in 1995 with a $508 million increase in domestic revenues and a $94 million gain in operating profits, Enrico decided to take a sabbatical from the business side of PepsiCo and spent the next 14 months thinking about his future. During that time, he set up what he called a "war college," where he mentored and coached PepsiCo's most promising executives at his Cayman Islands retreat and Montana ranch.

LURED BACK TO THE BATTLEFIELD

It did not take long for PepsiCo to recruit Enrico back to a hands-on position within the company. The PepsiCo CEO D. Wayne Calloway was suffering from cancer, and the company wanted Enrico to take over the entire operation. Enrico, however, remained reluctant. He was quoted in *BusinessWeek* as saying, "It was sort of like running the same show over again, rather than moving on to the next act" (April 10, 2000).

Eventually, Enrico's sense of duty to the company won out, and he assumed the position of CEO at PepsiCo on April 1, 1996. When Enrico took over, the company was suffering from a sluggish restaurant business and growing troubles in competing with Coca-Cola in overseas markets. Returning to his roots, Enrico immediately made a marketing coup by landing the coveted George Lucas franchise in a multiyear promotional alliance designed to begin with the February 1997 re-release of the original *Star Wars* science-fiction movie, which was to be followed by the re-releases of the remaining two movies in the trilogy. As noted by Karen Benezra in *Brandweek*, the move was estimated to have a $2 billion promotional value and showed Enrico's strong belief that it was important to "get some points on the board early" (October 7, 1996).

Enrico proceeded to introduce cost-cutting and resource-sharing measures to the company's operations. He initiated a spin-off of PepsiCo's restaurant group of Taco Bell, Pizza Hut, and KFC into Tricon Global Restaurants, a move that analysts saw as a perfect fit with the company's focus on chips and soda. As described by George W. Prince in *Beverage World*, Enrico explained his move in a letter to PepsiCo shareholders, "The reason for the spin-off is focus. And the best performing companies are those that devote all their energy to what they do best" (January 1998).

In 1998 Enrico acquired the fruit-drink company Tropicana to further broaden PepsiCo's soft-drink lineup. Rather than continuing to stress direct competition with Coca-Cola in established markets, he refocused the company's efforts on emphasizing growth in emerging markets like China and Russia. In December 2000 Enrico announced PepsiCo's acquisition of Quaker Oats for $13.4 billion in stock, once again beating out rival Coca-Cola, which was also vying for the company. Later adding the popular Gatorade to its fleet of noncarbonated beverages gave PepsiCo the dominant brand in the $2.5 billion sports-drink category.

Industry analysts generally applauded Enrico's restructuring and acquisition efforts at PepsiCo. In 1999 the company met or exceeded expectations on earnings and profit margins in each quarter. By early 2001 Enrico's management efforts had helped boost PepsiCo stock by 36 percent. In the spring of 2001 Enrico stepped down as CEO and became one of two vice chairmen on PepsiCo's board.

MANAGEMENT STYLE

Described by market analysts as a deadly earnest competitor, Enrico's deal-making prowess and marketing savvy were the foundations of his success. After landing Michael Jackson as a Pepsi spokesperson and making various promotional deals involving blockbuster movies as well as the Internet company Yahoo!, he established a reputation as a manager who was willing to make bold and dramatic marketing deals.

Although once noted for his flamboyance and swaggering management style, Enrico eventually developed a more personal and less arrogant approach to management, which in part involved giving credit to others in the company for its success. Part of this change was reflected in his dedication to teaching up-and-coming PepsiCo executives through leadership programs. According to analysts, Enrico believed teaching to be a vital aspect of the CEO's job, an aspect that gave him the chance to shape the executives that would prove to be the corporation's most important contributors. Enrico was noted for his ability to communicate well with investors and with the media. In an interview with George Prince for *Beverage World*, James Lee Jr., the chairman of Buffalo Rock (a privately owned Pepsi bottling company), summed up Enrico's managerial attributes this way: "He's a trench fighter. He's got plenty of guts. He's got flexibility and he moves with speed. He's not a committee man" (January 1998).

MOVING ON

In February 2003 Enrico stepped down from PepsiCo's board of directors. Nevertheless, he continued to mentor PepsiCo executives at annual gatherings at his Montana ranch. He also taught business leadership courses and seminars at Yale School of Management and at Southern Methodist University's Cox School of Business. Enrico discussed both business and personal ethics with students, recommending that they envision how they wanted to be regarded by their peers and those who worked for them. With respect to the possibility of reentering the business world, Enrico told Patricia Sellers for an interview in *Fortune*, "I've done that. Now I have the opportunity to do other things" (November 18, 2002).

See also entries on PepsiCo, Inc. and Frito-Lay Company in *International Directory of Company Histories*.

SOURCES FOR FURTHER INFORMATION

Benezra, Karen, "Roger Enrico," *Brandweek*, October 7, 1996, p. S56.

Brooks, Steve, "The Artful Roger: What Will Enrico Do with PepsiCo's Restaurants?" *Restaurant Business*, August 10, 1996, p. 58.

"Leadership Lessons from Roger Enrico," *BusinessWeek Online*, http://www.businessweek.com/bschools/content/oct2003/bs2003107_0453_bs001.htm.

"Pepsi Regeneration: Roger Enrico Looks to Snack Foods to Put Some Pop in His Stock," *Money*, March 1, 2000, p. 48.

"Pepsico's New Formula," *BusinessWeek*, April 10, 2000, p. 172.

Prince, Greg W., "PepsiCo-Star," *Beverage World*, January 1998, p. 113.

Sellers, Patricia, "Gone Fishin'?" *Fortune*, November 18, 2002, p. 156.

—David Petechuk

Charlie Ergen

1953–

Chairman and chief executive officer, EchoStar Communications Corporation

Nationality: American.

Born: March 1, 1953, in Oak Ridge, Tennessee.

Education: University of Tennessee, BS, 1975; Babcock Graduate School of Management, Wake Forest University, MBA, 1976.

Family: Son of William K. (Oak Ridge National Laboratory scientist) and Viola (business manager of the Children's Museum of Oak Ridge, Tennessee; maiden name unknown); married Cantey (cofounder of Echostar; maiden name unknown); children: five.

Career: Frito-Lay, 1976–1978, financial analyst (certified public accountant); EchoStar Communications Corporation (formerly EchoSphere), 1980–, chairman and CEO.

Awards: Star Award, Home Satellite TV Association, 1988; Master Entrepreneur of the Year for the Rocky Mountain region, *INC.*, 1991; Space Industry Business Man of the Year, *Aviation Week*, 2000; CEO of the Year for the Satellite Industry, Frost & Sullivan, 2001; 400 Richest Americans, *Forbes* 1998 and 2001.

Address: 5701 South Santa Fe Drive, Littleton, Colorado 80120; http://www.dishnetwork.com/.

Charlie Ergen. © *Reuters NewMedia Inc./Corbis.*

Charles W. ("Charlie") Ergen is somewhat of a legend in the satellite business. A onetime professional gambler, he launched the EchoStar Communications Corporation with practically nothing, bet large, played for high stakes, and became a major figure in the television communications industry.

Ergen originally called his company EchoSphere; it started in 1980, selling C-band full-size satellite-television dishes in rural Colorado. By 2004 EchoStar had 15,000 employees and nine satellites circling the earth and bringing hundreds of channels of television, audio, and other data to nine million direct-to-home (DTH) subscribers. EchoStar, through its DISH Network, was the second-largest satellite broadcast provider in the United States (after DirecTV), and Ergen was the largest EchoStar shareholder, owning about 51 percent of the corporate stock and more than 85 percent of voting shares. (Rupert Murdoch's News Corporation held about 12 percent of the company, even though Murdoch and Ergen were fierce competitors and business foes.)

Chairman and CEO Ergen developed the company's DTH products and services, which included direct broadcast satellite (DBS) television dishes, integrated receivers and descramblers, programming, installation, and third-party consumer financing for the company's products and services. In the early 2000s EchoStar operated nine U.S. distribution centers that served an independent network of DTH retailers, distributors, and consumer electronics outlets. EchoStar also partnered with Microsoft Corporation to provide WebTV access though EchoStar's DBS system.

Ergen first glimpsed a satellite when his father took him out to a field near their home to watch Sputnik, the pioneering Russian satellite, pass overhead in the autumn of 1957. After graduation from business school in 1976 Ergen became a certified public accountant for the snack maker Frito-Lay. He left Frito-Lay in 1978 to spend time investing in the stock market, hoping that he would later go into business for himself.

STORMY BEGINNINGS

In 1980 Ergen and Jim DeFranco, a gambling buddy, tried their luck at the blackjack and poker tables in Las Vegas, Nevada—they were both considered professional gamblers at the time. Both men were ejected from the town after being accused of counting cards at blackjack; while looking for something else to do, they saw a truck carrying a huge satellite-television dish. Like shrewd card players attracted to games of risk, they impulsively decided to jump into the new business of satellite television.

Ergen, DeFranco, and Ergen's future wife, Cantey, pooled their savings of $60,000 and started their company. They bought two satellite dishes and set out in a truck to drive one of the dishes to Colorado, judging that the mountainous state with its poor TV reception was an obvious market for satellite television. Unfortunately, a strong wind blew the trailer off a highway, destroying the equipment, but the one functioning satellite dish they still owned was all they needed to display their wares. Operating on a shoestring budget, they drove around small towns and rural areas in the Denver area selling full-size satellite dishes from the back of their truck.

The company prospered by keeping up with the rapid technological changes in the industry and offering new services as soon as they were available. In 1990 Ergen brought EchoStar into the small-dish satellite business by raising $335 million in junk bonds, buying orbital slots for satellites, and going head to head with his much larger competitors. In 1992 the Federal Communications Commission granted EchoStar a DBS license and assigned the company its own satellite orbit.

In November 1994 Ergen began construction on his DISH Network's first uplink center in Cheyenne, Wyoming, and on December 28, 1995, he directed the launching of the company's first satellite, EchoStar I, from Xichang, China. That allowed EchoStar to provide its own DBS service, which began three months later, and in another three months the network was serving served 100,000 subscribers and had become the fastest-growing DBS television service.

Ergen's expanding company opened a second customer service center and sent a second satellite into orbit later the same year. Following Ergen's successful launch of the company's third high-power satellite, EchoStar III (this one from Cape Canaveral, Florida), on October 5, 1997, the company signed up its millionth customer. In 1998 Ergen sued Rupert Murdoch's News Corporation for $5 million when Murdoch backed out of a merger in 1997 between Murdoch's ASkyB satellite service and Ergen's company. Ergen eventually forced News Corporation to turn over satellite assets after alleging misconduct by Murdoch regarding the planned merger. That year probably marked the beginning of Ergen's long-standing public feud with Murdoch.

A GAMBLER PERSONALITY

Ergen, the onetime professional gambler, was often described by friend and foe as unpredictable, wily, mercenary, renegade, daring, dueling, combative, ironfisted, or scrappy. Known to everyone as "Charlie," he earned a reputation as a fierce and respected competitor. He was also accused of penny-pinching—requiring employees to double up in hotel rooms and take cheap airplane flights in order to save company money. (He followed those cost-saving rules himself.) Ergen's passion for winning was once noted by Jimmy Schaeffler, chairman of a media and technology research firm: "If people won't deal with him at the table one on one, they'll deal with him in front of their shareholders or in the courtroom" (*Time*, August 20, 2001).

The employees of EchoStar often called Ergen "Elvis"—but never to his face—to describe how he could sway his audience to his way of thinking. Ergen frequently starred in his own TV show *Charlie Chat*, which consisted of infomercials and calls from DISH Network subscribers. On one occasion Ergen made a heartfelt pitch for pay-per-view movies, then quickly changed the subject to offer a free trip to Ireland and free installation for equipment upgrades, and then switched the subject again to express his staunch views on a particular matter of federal legislation. To top it off, Ergen described his feud with the owner of a small group of television stations who had forced him to drop two stations from his network, and then he suggested that his viewers call the station owner to complain about it.

For two decades Ergen forcibly battled with larger and more powerful rivals. Using junk bonds, cut-rate prices, and outrageous decisions, Ergen often triumphed over such media giants as John Malone (Liberty Media Corporation) and Rupert Murdoch (News Corporation). One of Ergen's favorite tactics over the years was to give away satellite dishes and receivers to customers who agreed to long-term contracts. He once gave away free dishes to the entire town of Boulder, Colorado, to lure customers away from a competitor.

ERGEN VERSUS MURDOCH

In the early 2000s Ergen clashed frequently with Rupert Murdoch, whose News Corporation was trying to buy Direc-

TV from General Motors' Hughes Electronic Corporation. Although Ergen himself attempted several times to put together a group of investors to buy DirecTV, Murdoch outmaneuvered him. Ergen, however, continued to place obstacles in the way of Murdoch's GM deal. While all that was going on, the management of DirecTV became so distracted with the on-again, off-again negotiations that its operations suffered and Ergen was able to pick up large pieces of its market share. Although Ergen ultimately lost DirecTV to Murdoch in 2002, he maneuvered through some of the roughest power plays ever seen in the media industry.

In 1988 Ergen received the Star Award of the Home Satellite TV Association, and in June 1991 *INC.* magazine named him Master Entrepreneur of the Year for the Rocky Mountain region. In 2000 *Aviation Week* named him Space Industry Business Man of the Year, and in 2001 he was the Frost & Sullivan CEO of the Year for the Satellite Industry.

Ergen, a cofounder of the Satellite Broadcasting Communications Association, helped gather support for the passage of the Satellite Home Viewer Improvement Act of 1999, which permitted satellite broadcast of local TV channels. He also testified often before the U.S. Congress regarding TV competition issues. In his off hours, Ergen climbed mountains, played poker, and played basketball.

Under Ergen's direction EchoStar was the first company to sell a satellite receiver for less than $200 and the first to develop a UHF (ultrahigh frequency) remote control. Other EchoStar innovations included a nationwide installation network dedicated solely to satellite TV systems and satellite receivers with built-in video recorders.

See also entry on EchoStar Communications Corporation in *International Directory of Company Histories.*

SOURCES FOR FURTHER INFORMATION

Cohen, Adam, "Satellite Showdown: EchoStar's Daring, Dueling Charlie Ergen Won't Let Rupert Murdoch Buy DirecTV without a Fight," August 20, 2001, *Time,* http://www.time.com/time/archive/preview/0,10987,1101010820-170853,00.htm

Heary, Donald F., *Cutthroat Teammates: Achieving Effective Teamwork among Professionals,* Homewood, Ill.: Dow Jones-Irwin, 1989.

—William Arthur Atkins

■■■

Michael L. Eskew

1949–

Chief executive officer and chairman, UPS

Nationality: American.

Born: June 28, 1949, in Vincennes, Indiana.

Education: Purdue University, BS, 1972; Wharton School of Business, Advanced Management Program, 1993.

Family: Married Molly (maident name unknown); children: four.

Career: UPS, 1972–1982, industrial engineer; 1982–1984, manager of the northwest region; UPS Airlines, 1984–1991, industrial engineering manager; UPS, 1991–1993, district manager for central New Jersey; 1994, corporate vice president for industrial engineering; 1996–1999, group vice president of engineering; 1999–2000, executive vice president; 2000–2002, vice chairman; 2002–, chief executive officer and chairman.

Awards: Schools of Engineering, Purdue University, Distinguished Engineering Alumnus Award, 1998; Jet, Corporate Leadership Award, 2003.

Address: UPS Inc., 55 Glenlake Parkway NE, Atlanta, Georgia 30328-3474; http://www.ups.com.

Michael L. Eskew. *AP/Wide World Photos.*

■ Michael Eskew was an engineer with a flair for organization: processes preoccupied him, and his assignments as he climbed the corporate ladder at the United Parcel Service (UPS) involved everything from reorganizing parking spaces to the logistics of opening service to hundreds of millions of Chinese customers. His hobbies included golfing, but most significant for his place in history may have been his avidly reading nonfiction books, because he developed exceptional writing skills that he put to use in speeches and official documents. His skill at coining apt descriptions made "synchronization" a catchword for organizing businesses to meet the challenges at the beginning of the 21st century and made "constructively dissatisfied" a favorite of journalists for describing his management style. By going out into the field and listening to what customers said they wanted, he developed the principle that global markets should be run by the desires of the end customers in transactions. He was a gifted speaker, eloquent and quotable, who became an outstanding advocate of the globalization of business and of the free market system: "No development in the history of mankind has brought greater opportunity, greater prosperity, greater understanding, and greater hope for peace in the world than democratic market trade," said Eskew in a speech at the Town Hall of Los Angeles (April 10, 2002).

INDUSTRIAL ENGINEER

In 1972 Eskew received a BS in industrial engineering from Purdue University, and he sought employment in his native Indiana. He found work with UPS and was first assigned the job of redesigning parking lots so that more trucks could fit in them. He next conducted time-motion studies, working out the efficiency of the processes that brought parcels to, through, and out of UPS. At the time UPS served only 37 states and was working through complex legal requirements to serve more.

In 1976 UPS began internal service within West Germany, and Eskew was sent there to oversee the development of the company's business in that country. In Germany he learned how to coordinate aircraft and truck parcel transfers while developing the skills he would need to establish guaranteed, on-time delivery to customers. In 1984 UPS created UPS Airlines and made Eskew its industrial engineering manager. He organized the airline's systems to make deliveries reliable, eventually creating UPS's Next Day Air service, which became a large part of the company's business. It was during his time at UPS Airlines that Eskew began developing his ideas for coordinating and tracking individual parcels. In the 1980s UPS packed parcels randomly in its delivery trucks, and drivers had to hunt through them to find which package to deliver at each address; Eskew eventually changed this costly procedure with supply-chain management. Probably of greater concern for his bosses during his time at UPS Airlines was the selection of aircraft; they trusted Eskew's judgment and put him in charge of buying the planes as well as of strategic planning and technology. By 1989, thanks in part to Eskew's efforts, UPS service was available in 180 countries and territories.

Eskew completed the advanced management program at Wharton School of Business of the University of Pennsylvania in 1993, which gave him academic qualifications that may have helped him win promotions; it demonstrated his dedication to management. Also in 1993 UPS began offering logistics management to business customers, which was the beginning of its development of supply-chain management services. In 1994 Eskew was promoted to corporate vice president in charge of industrial engineering for UPS, as well as of logistics management services for clients.

OPENING THE WORLD FOR UPS

Eskew was named group vice president of engineering in 1996. He was in charge of all of UPS's engineering worldwide, and he supervised all development and maintenance of UPS sites and buildings. Already skilled at coordinating airline and truck pickups and deliveries, Eskew took on the responsibility of coordinating all of UPS's air and ground operations around the world. He was also given accountability for making UPS more environmentally friendly, and under his leadership the company's engineers experimented with schemes for cutting pollution from UPS's vehicles, including developing an engine that could run on corn oil; eventually new, cleaner diesel technologies won out over the other alternatives for engine design. Eskew focused much attention on finding ways to reduce the number of miles driven by UPS trucks, cars, and motorcycles, reasoning that fewer miles driven meant less pollution, as well as savings in fuel costs. In 1996 UPS grossed $22.4 billion and netted $1.15 billion, up from a gross of just $1 billion in 1972.

A tough year followed 1996 because in August 1997, the International Brotherhood of Teamsters (IBT), representing about 200,000 UPS employees, went on strike for 15 days. The president of the IBT, Ron Carey, was up for reelection that year, and he called the strike as a way to rally union members behind him. UPS's business suffered as a result of the strike. Many customers switched their business to Federal Express and the United States Postal Service (USPS); UPS had won customers by claiming greater reliability than the USPS, but many former customers did not return after the strike. UPS lost $350 million in revenue to their two competitors.

Eskew was elected to the board of directors for UPS in 1998, and he found himself in charge of UPS Capital, which provided financial services to clients. UPS's logistics coordination enabled company loan officers to know how much inventory a client had and to use that knowledge to secure loans with the client's inventory. It was a quick and efficient process that enabled businesses to get loans tailored to their immediate needs and to pay those loans back swiftly.

SYNCHRONIZED COMMERCE

In 1999 UPS created a new post especially for Eskew, that of executive vice president. Eskew remained in charge of engineering for UPS, and he was given new responsibilities, including corporate strategic planning. He also developed UPS's information services; he vigorously pursued the company's entry into Internet commerce. Further, he took charge of the UPS Logistics division. By being accountable for all these areas, Eskew had an overview of UPS's vast and diverse operations and saw links among them, inspiring him to add freight hauling and document delivery to the company's portfolio of services and to develop a new way of coordinating his various responsibilities into what he called "synchronized commerce."

Synchronized commerce involved arranging all of UPS's processes so that each matched the others in perfect timing. The vision for the existing system had a UPS truck picking up a parcel at a given time, then delivering it for sorting at exactly the time there would be space for it. Next it would be put on a UPS aircraft just before the aircraft took off and then picked up by a truck at exactly the moment the aircraft landed. Finally, it would be delivered at a prearranged time. This process had had an enormous amount of waste in it because none of the elements had meshed with the others. Using the Internet, Eskew led the development of tracking services that enabled clients and UPS to know exactly where a parcel was at any given moment. This system saved clients millions of dollars in inventory costs because they did not need to store property for extended periods. They could arrange with UPS to have what they needed delivered to them just when they needed it, not earlier, and manufacturers could arrange through UPS to produce exactly what was needed, with nothing extra, for when they had buyers.

In 1999 UPS went public with what was then the largest initial public offering in history. Its shares were inflated at $73 apiece because speculators overestimated UPS's initial value as an Internet company. The company grossed $29.8 billion for the year. When he was selected to be vice chairman in 2000, Eskew became the heir apparent to the CEO and chairman, James P. Kelly.

With Eskew in charge of developing UPS's information systems, the company had spent between $11 billion and $15 billion on information technology between 1985 and 2000. Eskew wanted to use this infrastructure to interconnect businesses around the world. He wanted a small businessperson in Africa to be able to discover clients on other continents through UPS; he reasoned that such businesspeople would then use UPS to ship what they sold.

Essential to Eskew's ambitions for UPS was the opening of Asian markets to the company's services, especially mainland China. He believed that world commerce was undergoing an epochal upheaval that would change how everyone did business and that globalization was an essential part of this revolution. He argued publicly that the changes would be the inevitable result of a universal human aspiration to be connected to other people. "Only elastic, adaptable corporations—and people—can survive this once-in-a-lifetime upheaval," asserted Eskew in a press release (March 30, 2000). This belief led him to pursue what he called the "consumer-pull business model," in which end customers drove the marketplace through their demands for goods, which meant UPS would be best served by making sure that their end customers received what they wanted when they wanted it.

During 2000 Eskew lobbied the United States Congress and the Chinese government to allow UPS Airlines to fly between the United States and China. In a rare convergence of interests, both Eskew and James P. Hoffa, the president of the IBT, lobbied Congress to approve the flights. Hoffa realized that expanding UPS business into China would result in more jobs for his membership. The lobbying worked; China and the United States granted UPS Airlines air rights for the transport of American and Chinese goods between the two nations. In 2000 UPS grossed $29.8 billion, while netting $2.93 billion. Eskew was paid $857,348 in salary and bonuses.

The next year began well for Eskew and UPS. After years of working on the project, Eskew finally led UPS into hauling freight, using its synchronized commerce system to help manufacturers keep track of their inventories and to reduce the overhead incurred by storing unneeded items. On January 10, 2001, UPS ordered 60 planes from Airbus for flying to Asia. In August Kelly announced that he would retire from UPS on January 1, 2002, and UPS's board of directors quickly named Eskew as Kelly's successor. Although Eskew noted that the world economy was flatlining, depressing sales of UPS's services, the creation of new business lines had so far enabled UPS to continue growing. This changed on September 11, 2001, when terrorists flew airliners into the World Trade Center in New York City, destroying the buildings and killing thousands of people.

"I've learned to stay out of the way and let our folks run the system" (October 1, 2001), Eskew later explained to account for why Manhattan District UPS employees were able to organize themselves within a few hours after the disaster. Eskew and other executives had developed a corporate culture in which local managers were given the authority not only to respond to emergencies but to suspend UPS rules when they needed to. Within hours of the attack, UPS's tracking system accounted for all of their New York City employees and vehicles; four trucks had been crushed, but all employees, including those who worked in the towers, were accounted for and were put to work sorting parcels by hand.

Eskew was now on top of UPS's worldwide operations and almost immediately began rearranging the company's services. There were many UPS Airlines craft in the air over America when the United States government ordered all aircraft grounded. The UPS airplanes landed in many unexpected places, their cargo far from where it was supposed to go. Normally, at any given moment, UPS delivered 13.6 million parcels, carrying 7 percent of America's gross national product, making its delivery services important to the functioning of America's economic engine. Using the tracking systems he had helped create, Eskew had his employees identify parcels and reorganize delivery schedules according to the availability of UPS trucks and other vehicles; those packages that could be delivered on the ground within three days were given top priority. Eskew reasoned that the government would allow UPS Airlines flights within one week and that they could then quickly transport the remaining parcels to their destinations. He proved to be correct. Meanwhile, workers in UPS's Manhattan District filled 27 tractor trailers with parcels that could not be delivered to seven Manhattan zip codes. (Two of the zip codes no longer existed, and five others were inaccessible.) Using its synchronized system information, UPS identified intended recipients who had been murdered in the attack and then tracked down people or businesses who had legitimate claims to the Manhattan parcels; remarkably, all of them were delivered. UPS grossed $30.6 billion, while netting $2.4 billion for the year, a decline from 2000 mostly attributable to a decrease in commerce because of the destruction of the World Trade Center. Eskew was paid $953,864.

SUPPLY-CHAIN MANAGEMENT

On January 1, 2002, Eskew became UPS's chairman and its ninth CEO. That year the company opened an aircraft hub in the Philippines to serve Asia; UPS had spent $200 million on the hub and on new aircraft to serve the distant continent. The company served 451 markets in over 200 nations and territories around the world.

Eskew initiated a $45 million ad campaign, the biggest in UPS's history. He hoped to expand the company by offering new services to existing customers. UPS Capital began collecting payments for business clients from their clients' customers. This helped clients expand their businesses, which in turn meant more shipping business for UPS. The company put its synchronized commerce skills to good use in contracts with computer manufacturers to pick up and repair their customers' broken computers with as little as a 24-hour turnaround. In addition, UPS managed the inventories for many clients, decreasing their overhead costs. In an era of mistrust of corporations because of the misdeeds of the management at Enron, WorldCom, and other companies, Eskew took pride in maintaining transparent corporate finances, where anyone could find out where UPS's money was going.

Eskew pushed hard for UPS to expand its supply-chain management, which he believed was a $3 trillion global market waiting to be tapped. UPS's strengths in shipping, parcel tracking, and synchronized commerce enabled it to find ways to reorganize client companies' supply chains, making them more efficient and enabling them to focus on their core businesses while UPS took care of the delivery of supplies and the transportation of their manufactured products. Eskew saw this as an important service to the business world because it could enable clients' expansions into new markets. UPS's supply-chain services were expected to grow 20 percent to 30 percent annually.

Eskew became an outspoken proponent of global business, and he insisted that globalization was inevitable. To him, globalization satisfied a basic human need to be connected to other people, as well as the desire for economic opportunities and individual empowerment. He believed businesses should clarify what they meant by globalization and should help people hurt by the changes in old economies wrought by globalization. Further, he advocated regulation, believing businesses should be held accountable for their actions. For instance, the destruction of local environments because of business activity should not be tolerated.

In January 2002 UPS and the IBT began negotiating a new contract. The issues were common ones: wages, benefits, and retirement funds. The IBT president, James P. Hoffa, did not wish to send business to nonunion companies such as Federal Express, but he did not wish to appear soft on UPS's management, either. The union represented 230,000 of UPS's 370,000 workers; that 60 percent of the drivers owned stock in the company was a strong point for UPS. Even so, Hoffa bargained hard. On July 16, 2002, UPS and the IBT agreed on a contract to be submitted for a vote to UPS's union members that gave them a 22 percent wage increase over the contract's six-year duration.

In 2003 UPS invested $600 million to reorganize its delivery network in the United States. UPS Airlines had 265 aircraft, making it the ninth largest aircraft fleet in the United States and the eleventh largest in the world, carrying 1.2 million parcels per day of their total of 13.3 million. The company grossed $31.3 billion.

Eskew was appointed to the President's Export Council in 2002, and in 2004 he was elected chairman of the United States-China Business Council. On February 11, 2004, Eskew submitted his written recommendations for USPS reform to the Committee on Government Reform Special Panel on the Postal Service of the United States House of Representatives. Eskew worried about competing against a government-supported monopoly. He argued that the USPS should focus on delivering standard mail, first-class mail, and periodicals and leave most other services to public competition. Further, he wanted the USPS to have financial transparency so that its spending could be tracked and made more effective, that it not be allowed to use its subsidies to the detriment of private businesses, and that regulators be given more authority over how it conducted business.

As for UPS, Eskew wanted the company to emphasize solutions instead of products; clients should be shown how UPS could solve some of their problems. Eskew believed that UPS was no longer best characterized as a delivery company but as a global commerce company because of the diverse services it offered. He said that UPS relied on the flow of orders, the flow of goods, and the flow of money; how well it managed these flows would affect how much it prospered. Even though the company's supply-chain services alone sorted 350,000 parcels per hour, he still wanted each parcel to be treated as if it were the only one UPS was caring for rather than as if it were one of many.

See also entry on United Parcel Service of America Inc. in *International Directory of Company Histories.*

SOURCES FOR FURTHER INFORMATION

Barron, Kelly, "Logistics in Brown," *Forbes*, January 10, 2000, pp. 78–83.

Eskew Michael, "The 'I' in the Middle: Finding Common Ground in the Global Divide," *Vital Speeches of the Day*, June 1, 2002, pp. 493–497.

———, "Statement for the Record," United States House of Representatives, February 11, 2004, http://www.postcom.org/public/2004/eskew.pdf.

Haddad, Charles, "How UPS Delivered Through the Disaster," *BusinessWeek*, October 1, 2001, p. 66.

"Quantum Shift," company press release, March 30, 2000, http://www.pressroom.ups.com/.

Shook, David, "UPS Is 'Constructively Dissatisfied,'" *BusinessWeek Online*, May 13, 2002, http://www.businessweek.com/bwdaily/dnflash/may2002/nf20020513_5458.htm.

"UPS CEO Champions Global Trade," company press release, April 10, 2002, http://www.pressroom.ups.com/.

"UPS Chairman and CEO Jim Kelly to Retire," company press release, August 16, 2001, http://www.pressroom.ups.com/.

—Kirk H. Beetz

■ ■ ■

Matthew J. Espe

1959–

Chairman, president, and chief executive officer, IKON Office Solutions

Nationality: American.

Born: 1959.

Education: University of Idaho, bachelor's degree; Whittier College, MBA, 1984.

Family: Married; children: four.

Career: General Electric, 1980–1992, sales and marketing management; 1993, general manager, marketing, GE Plastics-America; 1994, sales and marketing management and general management assignments, Europe; 1996–1997, director, commercial operations, GE Plastics-Europe; 1998–1999, president, GE Plastics-Asia; 1999–2000, president, GE Plastics-Europe; 2000–2002, president and chief executive officer, GE Lighting; IKON Office Solutions, 2002–, president and chief executive officer; 2003–, president, chief executive officer, and chairman.

Awards: Received the Partnership Award from Ricoh Corporation, 2004.

Address: IKON, 70 Valley Stream Parkway, Malvern, Pennsylvania 19355-0989.

■ During his successful 22-year career with General Electric (GE) in Europe, Asia, and the United States, Matthew J. Espe developed effective management and product-implementation skills and a strong customer-oriented perspective. These qualities led to his being chosen in 2002 to head up IKON Office Solutions, a business that provided a channel to connect customers and suppliers in the total-business-solutions industry. IKON could continue to grow as a leader in the industry only if customers on both ends of the channel were satisfied. IKON board members saw Espe as the perfect candidate to lead their company into the future.

MANAGEMENT STRATEGY AT GE

Espe began with GE in 1980 and worked on his master's degree while working his way through progressively more responsible positions in sales and marketing management. After several years with the company's plastics operations in Europe, he was made president of plastics in Asia and, a year later, of plastics in Europe. In 2000 he was appointed president and CEO of GE's entire lighting operations, which at the time had $2.7 billion in annual sales. Shortly after his appointment, the U.S. and world economies took a plunge. GE Lighting's sales dropped 6 percent and profits declined 32 percent in 2001. "You have to go back 20 years to see this kind of softness," Espe was quoted as saying by Jim Lucy (*Electrical Wholesaling*, June 1, 2002).

Experience had taught Espe that in tough times it was important to return to the basics. He instituted a cleanup of inefficiencies and paid particular attention to customers' feedback. By June 2002 Espe had led GE into its largest-ever new-product launch with a multimillion-dollar marketing campaign to promote the Reveal light bulb. The lamp produced a crisp white light that was more appealing than the yellowish light produced by all previous light bulbs. Espe was quoted in a GE press release as commenting that people would now be able to see their world in a "whole new light" (press release, June 2001). He also noted that 85 percent of trial users preferred the new bulb, which filtered out the yellowish tint through a natural-earth element, neodymium, that GE added to the glass. Improvements in efficiency and color of halogen and fluorescent lamps were predicted to encourage growth in GE's industrial and commercial lighting sector.

Espe's 13 years in supply and sales management were important in helping him define his strategy. "I have a lot of empathy for inside salespeople and outside salespeople. We are always soliciting advice from our distributors. Just like anything else, it starts with listening to the voice of the customer," he said (*Electrical Wholesaling*, June 1, 2002). After listening to requests from GE's distributor-advisory council, Espe focused on improving GE's digitized online-sales tools to help salespeople audit customers' existing lighting systems and suggest cost-efficient alternatives. One such tool was the GE Lighting Auditor (GELA), which Espe used—among other applications—to target the relatively untapped education market. The tool would help teachers and students measure the efficiency of a school's energy use and calculate potential savings. In a kickoff to the program with Vanguard Middle School in Los Angeles late in 2001, GE Lighting retrofitted the school's entire lighting system, changing it from fluorescent T12s to the new T8 product. Over the life of the new product, the school would save $75,000 in energy costs. Customers could also access online a virtual-design tool that would allow them to compare the effect various lamp types would give to a room. At the same time, Espe was focusing on LED lighting technology that he believed would become the holy grail of the lighting arena due to its increasing capacity to replace almost any white-light application in industry, business, or residential settings. GE Lighting applied for a patent after developing a special phosphor for its LED lamps, which improved the life span by more than 100,000 hours over a conventional bulb life, increased durability, and dramatically decreased energy consumption.

Espe, however, would not see the results of his strategy come to fruition as the head of GE Lighting. After Jeffrey Immelt took over as GE's new CEO in 2001, he came under pressure from investors to simplify GE's structure. Because the lighting and appliance arms were growing more slowly than other GE divisions, primarily due to a sluggish economy and competition, Immelt merged them. "Both of these product lines have had pretty tough pricing environments," Jonathan Berr quoted analyst Mark Demos of Fifth Third Investment Advisors as saying (*Detroit Free Press*, August 30, 2002). The day the two divisions were merged, Espe announced he would leave GE and become head of IKON Office Solutions effective September 9, 2002.

FROM BULBS TO BUSINESS SOLUTIONS

IKON, based in Malvern, Pennsylvania, was the world's largest independent-distribution channel for printers, copiers, faxes, and other office-equipment technologies, with two of its largest brands being Ricoh and Canon. As well, IKON represented the broadest document-management service in the entire industry. As a total-business-solutions provider for offices of all sizes, it provided production and outsourcing requirements, facilities management, legal-document solutions, network integration, and similar services. The company also provided complete support through seven thousand service professionals worldwide. In fiscal year 2003 revenues reached $4.7 billion and IKON employed more than thirty thousand people in six hundred locations.

THE BEST MAN FOR THE JOB

When Espe was chosen to replace 67-year-old James J. Forese as IKON's CEO, the company had already undergone several years of restructuring and layoffs. Between 1999 and 2001 revenues and profits declined, and between April 1998 and early 2001 shares fell from $35 to below $5. Following the announcement of Espe's instatement, shares rose 6¢ to $9.11. He traveled to company offices to assure employees that IKON would not change its direction and would retain its centralized structure with support from its large branch-office network, which he believed was an excellent model through which to solicit business worldwide. He said Forese had done a commendable job and he would build on that foundation.

Lead independent director of IKON, Richard A. Jalkut, said the board searched for a leader with discipline, talent, proven skills, appropriate experience, integrity, and dedication to the highest principles of IKON's governance. After a comprehensive internal and external search, they chose Espe. "As a rising star at one of the most successful companies in America today, Matt has proven again and again, at a variety of GE business units, that he has an outstanding ability to build and lead great businesses," Jalkut said. Forese explained that their six-month, methodical search for the ideal person followed a plan to execute a smooth transition to maintain stability and continuity. He was impressed with Espe's range of operational experience and exceptional background in sales, marketing, and global distribution. "He is customer-focused and adept at introducing and building on new products and services. His success in increasing revenue and controlling costs while growing a variety of different businesses fits precisely with IKON's strategy of establishing sustained growth for this Company," he said (*Business Wire*, August 29, 2002).

Five months after Espe joined IKON, directors remained impressed. New lead director Thomas R. Gibson said Espe's experience, ability, energy, innovation, and integrity were boons to the company, and he expressed confidence that Espe would lead the organization to further successes: "Matthew Espe is an executive of exceptional caliber. He is a strong leader dedicated to the highest principles of corporate governance, ethics, and organizational development that are essential to this critical role and to building long-term value for our shareholders" (press release, February 25, 2003).

A WINNING STRATEGY

Enhancing IKON's niche in bringing the service provider and the customer together remained the major focus for Espe. As 2003 drew to a close, Espe assessed IKON's position. He said in an interview with CNNfn that, as document management was clearly in the early stages of its maturity, the "channel" to the customer was of utmost importance. He said IKON was well positioned to offer both productivity to customers and to suppliers of their key services as well. He noted that IKON was Canon's leading independent channel in North America, generating more than 40 percent of their revenue, and that they generated more than 20 percent of Ricoh's revenue. In June 2004 Ricoh honored Espe with its Partnership Award. "Over the past year and a half Matt Espe has helped define the word partnership," said Tom Salierno, president of RICOH U.S., a division of Ricoh Corporation. "Our

2004 Partnership Award depicts the mutually beneficial relationship of IKON and Ricoh working as teammates" (*PRNewswire*, June 2, 2004.) Combine that success with having become HP's exclusive distributor, and IKON was able to provide an extensive suite of products that could facilitate customers from the smallest office to Fortune 500 companies. Espe noted that because distribution was IKON's business, their suppliers could therefore focus their investments on research, development, and manufacturing productivity.

In December 2003 IKON sold IOS Capital, IKON's profitable Georgia-based financing arm, to GE in what Espe called "a hell of a deal." GE acquired approximately $1.9 billion in assets and liabilities and took over the function of financing IKON's customers. "We never considered ourself a finance company. We were a document-management firm that provided financing as a service," Espe commented (*Knight Ridder/Tribune Business Wire*, December 12, 2003). He noted that IOS was getting large and loading up its balance sheet with debt. Under the deal, GE agreed to hire all four hundred IOS employees, IKON would keep a portion of the lease portfolio, and the companies signed a five-year agreement that could be renewed for a further three or five years in which IKON would continue to earn fees on leased copiers financed by GE. This would provide a positive income stream for IKON. Espe noted that GE would "have the motivation to run the business as we did." Creating an income source while eliminating debt load was especially favorable for IKON, since the weak economy created a drop in revenue in the entire document-management industry of 10 percent over the year and another 5 percent in early 2004. The strategic move created an immediate 20 percent increase in IKON's stock prices, taking them to a 52-week high.

FOCUSES ON THE FUTURE

Going forward, Espe saw affordable color copying becoming a prime generator of revenue from the equipment side and, on the services side, felt document work-flow solutions and onsite and offsite document outsourcing would produce increasingly greater returns: IKON was already the second-largest provider of document-outsourcing services in North America. At the 2004 annual shareholder's meeting, Espe said the market was at the point where service and support quality was as important as product quality. Drawing on his extensive customer-service experience, he added: "Utilizing a consultative approach that blends best-in-class technologies with value-added services provides IKON a tremendous advantage in our ability to offer customers a choice of cost-effective, reliable solutions that help create efficiencies at every phase of the document lifecycle" (*Business Wire*, February 24, 2004).

In May 2004 Espe outlined the company's strategic priorities to drive long-term growth: expanded product and customer opportunities; the emergence of IKON Enterprise Services, which combined its professional services, managed services (onsite and offsite outsourcing), and customer-service operations; and opportunities in Europe, which the company estimated as a $35 billion market. Espe said the company's refined business model would focus more on customers' requirements for "immediate and longer term document management services. With an improved revenue mix emphasizing services, we have also enhanced our cash profile and continue to create operational leverage within our infrastructure. As we look ahead, we are optimistic about IKON's future as an industry leader" (*Business Wire*, May 26, 2004).

See also entries on General Electric Company and IKON Office Solutions, Inc. in *International Directory of Company Histories.*

SOURCES FOR FURTHER INFORMATION

Berr, Jonathan, "GE Set to Combine Appliance, Lighting. Move Under Pressure Expected to Cut Costs," *Detroit Free Press*, August 30, 2002.

"CNNfn 'The Money Gang' Stock of the Day Interview with Matthew J. Espe," http://www.ikon.com/about/ir/financial_info/downloads/transcript_stockoftheday.pdf.

Fernandez, Bob, "Chester County, Pa., Copier Firm to Sell Financing Arm for $1.5 Billion," *Knight Ridder/Tribune Business News*, December 12, 2003, p. 1.

"GE Lighting Reveals a Light That Will Change the Way People See Their World. GE Reveal Represents Largest Light Bulb Launch In Its History," press release, June 2001, http://www.gelighting.com/na/pressroom/pr_reveal.html.

"IKON Leadership Highlights Strategy for Investors: Matthew J. Espe and Other Senior Executives Discuss IKON's Strategic Priorities to Drive Long-Term Growth," *Business Wire*, May 26, 2004, p. 5484.

"IKON Names Matthew J. Espe President and Chief Executive Officer," *Business Wire*, August 29, 2002, http://www.businesswire.com/webbox/bw.082902/222412059.htm.

"IKON Office Solutions Names Matthew J. Espe Chairman of the Board," press release, February 25, 2003, http://www.shareholder.com/ikon/releaseDetail.cfm?ReleaseID=122272.

"IKON's Chairman, Matthew J. Espe, Recaps Company's Strategy at 2004 Annual Shareholders Meeting," *Business Wire*, February 24, 2004, p. 5920.

Lucy, Jim, "Lighting The Way—GE Lighting's CEO Matt Espe Discusses Management Strategies," *Electrical Wholesaling*, June 1, 2002, http://articles.findarticles.com/p/articles/mi_m3720/is_2002_June_1/ai_88681899.

"Ricoh Honors Matt Espe of IKON Office Solutions With Partnership Award," *PRNewswire*, June 2, 2004, http://news.corporate.findlaw.com/prnewswire/20040602/02jun2004135147.html.

—Marie L. Thompson

■■■

Robert A. Essner

1947–

Chairman, chief executive officer, and president, Wyeth

Nationality: American.

Born: October 26, 1947, in New York, New York.

Education: Miami University, bachelor's degree; University of Chicago, master's degree.

Family: Son of Arthur Essner and Charlotte E. Levy; married Rosalind (maiden name unknown; divorced); married Anne (maiden name unknown); children: five (first marriage, two; second marriage, three).

Career: Sandoz Pharmaceuticals Corporation, 1978–1986, various management positions; 1986–1987, vice president; 1987, corporate vice president and COO for business management; 1987–1989, president of Sandoz Consumer HealthCare Group; Wyeth-Ayerst Laboratories, 1989–1991, senior vice president for sales and marketing; 1991–1993, executive vice president; 1993–1997, president; Wyeth-Ayerst Global Pharmacueticals, 1997, president; American Home Products Corporation, 1997–2000, executive vice president; 2000–2001, president and COO; 2001–2002, CEO and president; Wyeth, 2002, CEO, president, and COO; 2003–, chairman, CEO, and president.

Awards: Prix Galien Suisse, 2003; Science/Technology Medal, Research and Development Council of New Jersey, 2003.

Address: Wyeth, 5 Giralda Farms, Madison, New Jersey 07940; http://www.wyeth.com.

■ After a decade of climbing the corporate ladder at Sandoz Pharmaceuticals, Robert Essner joined Wyeth-Ayerst Laboratories. He eventually became president, chief executive officer, and chairman of the board of directors at Wyeth, one of the world's largest producers of over-the-counter and prescription medications. Essner guided the company's transition from conglomerate with an assortment of consumer products back to focused drug developer and producer. His steady management style led Wyeth through years of legal entanglements, including the fen-phen diet-pill scandal of the 1990s.

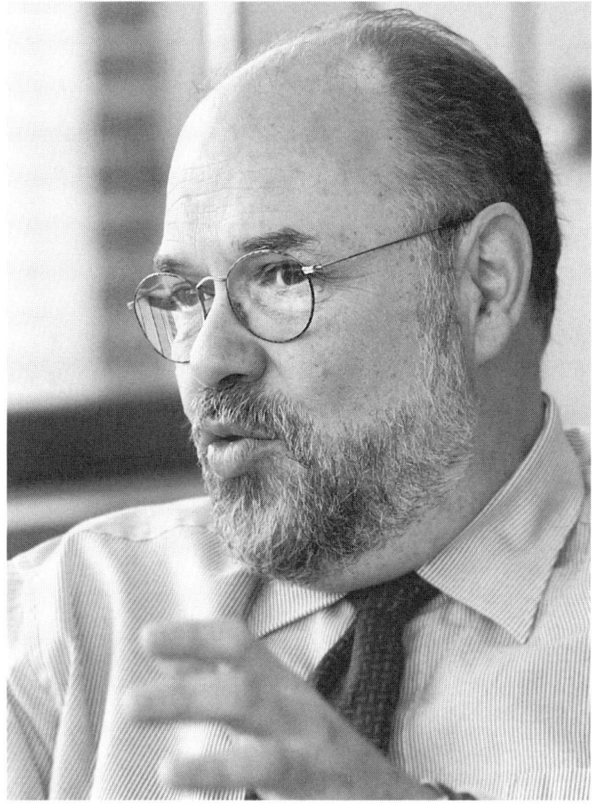

Robert A. Essner. *AP/Wide World Photos.*

UP THE CORPORATE LADDER

Born and raised in New York City, Robert Alan Essner graduated from Miami University in Oxford, Ohio, and earned his master's degree from the University of Chicago. In 1978 he joined Sandoz Pharmaceuticals Corporation, the manufacturer of over-the-counter and prescription medicines based in East Hanover, New Jersey. By 1987 Essner was president of the Sandoz Consumer HealthCare Group in Parsippany, New Jersey.

In 1989 Essner moved to Wyeth-Ayerst Laboratories, the subsidiary of American Home Products Corporation (AHP), as senior vice president for sales and marketing. AHP was one of the world's largest research-based producers of pharmaceutical and health-care products. In 1993 Essner became president of Wyeth-Ayerst, responsible for the company's U.S.-based pharmaceutical business. In March 1997 Essner was named president of Wyeth-Ayerst Global Pharmacueticals.

Later in 1997 Essner became executive vice president and a member of the board of directors of the Madison, New Jersey–based AHP. In 2000 he was elected president and chief operating officer, with responsibility for all of AHP's three divisions: Wyeth-Ayerst Pharmaceuticals, Whitehall-Robins Healthcare, and Fort Dodge Animal Health. In March 2001, while remaining president and a member of the board, Essner replaced Jack Stafford as CEO. Stafford was quoted by PR Newswire as saying, "The appointment of Bob Essner as the next CEO of AHP provides for continuity of our strategic direction as a first-tier pharmaceutical company" (March 6, 2001). Essner undertook a complete reorganization of the company. On January 1, 2003, he replaced Stafford as board chairman.

GUIDED AHP THROUGH GROWTH AND SCANDAL

AHP grew under Essner's leadership, introducing new products and increasing its drug-manufacturing capacity. Although its nasal flu vaccine FluMist proved disappointing, the anti-depressant Effexor became AHP's biggest seller. The company's over-the-counter brands—including Advil, Centrum vitamins, Preparation H, and Robitussin cough suppressant—remained steady.

On the other hand, under Essner AHP was plagued by scandal and faced thousands of lawsuits. The company was forced to recall Duract, a short-term pain reliever, as well as a new rotavirus vaccine. The company settled thousands of lawsuits from women suffering side effects from the implantable contraceptive Norplant.

Most of the lawsuits faced by the company, however, involved the popular—but potentially lethal—diet drug known as fen-phen. In 1997, in the largest consumer drug recall to date, the U.S. Food and Drug Administration (FDA) yanked AHP's diet pills off the market. Court testimony indicated that AHP used temporary, undertrained employees to review and process adverse-effects reports and failed to notify the FDA of its actions. Furthermore the company had resisted the packaging of warnings with the drugs. Essner denied all charges but nevertheless instituted a new computer-tracking system for adverse-event reports. The *Wall Street Journal* quoted Essner as remarking, "We're going to fight the things that are wrong with diet-drug litigation tooth and nail, and we intend to win" (October 26, 2003). By 2004 the company had paid out $13 billion and set aside another $16.6 billion for diet-drug claims while continuing to struggle toward a final resolution. Having opted out of the original class-action settlement, some 78,000 people were eligible to sue Wyeth on individual bases.

RESPONDED TO SCANDAL WITH NAME CHANGE

The business practices of Wyeth-Ayerst and AHP had come into question, and the company was accused of putting its own interests, and those of its stockholders, above public safety. In March 2002 Essner changed the company's name to Wyeth, claiming that this name better reflected the company's increasing global presence, its emphasis on research-based pharmaceuticals, and its divestitures of other products, including herbicides, candy, food, household products, and medical devices. Most observers assumed that Essner was attempting to erase the public's association of AHP with fen-phen.

In the summer of 2002 the National Institutes of Health reported that Wyeth's top-selling hormone-replacement-therapy (HRT) drug Prempro increased the risks of breast cancer and heart disease. Sales of Wyeth's line of HRT drugs—known as Premarin and accounting for 14 percent of company revenue—fell. Essner told the *Philadelphia Inquirer*, "We believe that, once the media sensation subsides, hormone replacement therapies will remain an important part of women's health care" (July 24, 2002). Wyeth's HRT drugs also became a target of animal-rights groups because they were produced from the urine of pregnant horses. When Wyeth announced a cutback in Premarin production—an action that would send about 40,000 mares and foals to probable slaughter—animal-advocacy groups began a letter-writing campaign directed at Essner.

INCREASED RESEARCH AND DEVELOPMENT

Essner's growth philosophy focused on the development of innovative products; the company had previously licensed many more drugs than it discovered. Essner told the *Wall Street Journal*, "Innovation is the most important, scarcest, and most fragile asset in the industry today" (June 3, 2004). With 34 new drugs in the pipeline Wyeth invested more than $2 billion in research and development in 2002. In June 2003 Essner announced that he was spending an additional $100 million to investigate a single lead for an Alzheimer's vaccine. He also signed new partnership agreements with Japan's largest drug company, reinforcing his expansion into the world's second-largest pharmaceutical market.

In 2003, after introducing Prevnar, the only vaccine against meningitis in young children, Essner accepted the Prix Galien Suisse—the "Pharma-Oscar"—for the most innovative preventive therapy of the year. After the Centers for Disease Control and Prevention recommended that all children receive four doses of Prevnar before the age of 15 months, production could not keep up with demand.

Essner garnered both good and bad press in 2003. Wyeth was named one of the 100 Best Companies for Working Mothers by *Working Mother* magazine for the sixth consecutive year and was selected as a Workplace Model of Excellence by the National Healthy Mothers, Healthy Babies Coalition. However, along with CEOs from other drug companies, Essner informed Canadian companies that they could no longer buy drugs at wholesale prices for marketing to American consumers.

In 2004 Essner announced that beginning in 2006 Wyeth would introduce two new drugs per year. Since 2000, 12 new drugs per year had been moved into full development. In 2004 research spending increased more than 10 percent over the $2.1 billion spent in 2003.

See also entry on Wyeth in *International Directory of Company Histories.*

SOURCES FOR FURTHER INFORMATION

Hensley, Scott, "Wyeth Is Upbeat about Innovation at Its Drug Laboratories," *Wall Street Journal*, June 3, 2004.

Hensley, Scott, and Peter Landers, "Drug Companies Report Pain: Results for 3rd Quarter Diagnose Industry's Flagging Health," *Wall Street Journal*, October 26, 2003.

Loyd, Linda, "Wyeth's Profits Grew by 26 percent in 2nd Quarter," *Philadelphia Inquirer*, July 24, 2002.

"Robert A. Essner Named Next CEO of American Home Products Corporation," PR Newswire, March 6, 2001.

—Margaret Alic

■■■

John H. Eyler Jr.

1948–

Chairman of the board, president, and chief executive officer, Toys "R" Us

Nationality: American.

Born: 1948, in Seattle, Washington.

Education: University of Washington, BS, 1969; Harvard University School of Business, MBA, 1971.

Family: Son of John Sr. (engineer) and Ell Dora (nurse and homemaker); married Dolores (journalist); children: three.

Career: May Department Stores, 1980–?, chief executive officer of May D&F division; Federated Department Stores, dates unknown, chairman and chief executive officer of MainStreet division; Hartmarx Corporation, ?–1992, chief executive officer of retail subsidiaries; FAO Schwarz, 1992–2000, chairman and chief executive officer; Toys "R" Us, 2000–, president and chief executive officer; 2001–, chairman of the board.

Address: Toys "R" Us, 1 Geoffrey Way, Wayne, New Jersey 07470-2030; http://www.toysrus.com/.

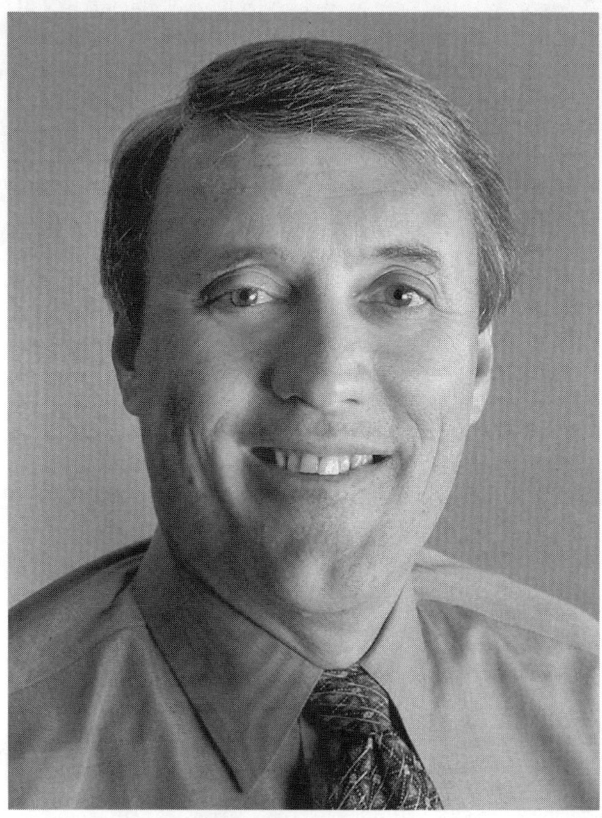

John H. Eyler Jr. *AP/Wide World Photos.*

■ John H. Eyler Jr. quickly made Toys "R" Us a friendlier and more accessible store for consumers—after the longtime model for toy retailers had settled near the bottom in customer-service rankings. As chairman of the board, president, and chief executive officer of one of the world's largest toy retail chains, Eyler oversaw more than 1,500 Toys "R" Us stores in the United States and abroad. He also guided the company's Web sites (run by Amazon.com) toward a new look and feel.

Before joining Toys "R" Us in January 2000, Eyler served as chairman and chief executive officer of FAO Schwarz. He began building his retail merchandising career with the May Department Stores Company, becoming chief executive officer of its May D&F division at age 32. Later he was chairman and chief executive officer of Federated Department Stores' MainStreet division and then chief executive officer of Hartmarx's retail subsidiary before moving to FAO Schwarz in 1992. He also served as a director of Donna Karan International.

DEVELOPING RETAILER SKILLS

Eyler was born in Seattle and grew up on nearby Mercer Island. His father, an engineer for Boeing, played significant roles in the Apollo 11 space mission and the Minuteman missile program. The younger Eyler attended the University of Washington as a finance major and later received an MBA from Harvard University. While writing a paper about eliminating middlemen from the distribution process, he discovered his interest in retailing. Specifically, he became aware that the computer revolution would allow for measurement of the effectiveness of each link in the retail chain and could lead to consolidation. Realizing that this effect would spark opportunities for young executives, after graduation he decided to try his hand as a trainee in management with May Department Stores. Although it seemed a natural course for a young businessman, the move was well thought out and not a coincidence.

Eyler's early career had both high and low points. Among his best-known accomplishments was beginning MainStreet, a chain of lower-priced stores for Federated Department Stores. According to Eyler, MainStreet was on an annual pace of $300 million in sales in 1988 and just about to become profitable when Federated's new owner, Robert Campeau, sold the chain to reduce debt. Following that, Eyler switched gears and oversaw the retail arm of Hartmarx, an upscale suitmaker. Unfortunately, after the market shifted toward the office-casual style, the stores were eventually closed. Forever the optimist, Eyler believed that this experience of failure enabled him to excel in future undertakings because it made his assessment of reality more acute. In 1992 he signed on as CEO at FAO Schwarz, where he made his name by emphasizing attractions such as in-store toy demonstrations and products such as Schwarz-only giant stuffed animals.

JOINS TOYS "R" US

In 1948 Charles Lazarus, only 25 years old and just finished with a tour of duty in the U.S. Army, founded the company that would become Toys "R" Us. Lazarus is credited with introducing "toy supermarkets" in approximately 1952. The new concept in toy retail quickly caught on. In 1957 Lazarus renamed his company Toys "R" Us. It grew steadily through the 1980s. In 1994 Lazarus retired and Michael Goldstein succeeded him as CEO of Toys "R" Us. Over the following few years, major retailers and online toy sellers like Target and Wal-Mart started to challenge the Toys "R" Us empire. Along with this new threat, the company weathered several years of down holiday sales, which contributed to a growing negative reputation for missing the boat on profit opportunities.

In 1998 Goldstein resigned after Wal-Mart surpassed Toys "R" Us as the largest toy retailer in the United States. The next CEO, Robert Nakasone, served only 18 months before being replaced by Eyler. The Toys "R" Us board was looking for a long-term solution and had talked with Eyler on and off for more than a decade. Nakasone had tried to recruit Eyler to be his No. 2 in 1998 and even negotiated to purchase Schwarz to get him. After Nakasone's departure, Eyler was still at the head of the candidate list because of his glowing reviews from key suppliers such as CEOs Alan G. Hassenfeld of Hasbro and Jill Barad of Mattel. Expectations were high, and Eyler didn't disappoint.

After a long string of earnings disappointments and management turmoil, Eyler came on board noting that customer service, store appearance, and merchandise appeal were the most critical points to address at Toys "R" Us. This was not surprising after coming from upscale toy vendor FAO Schwarz, where image was everything. His idea was to utilize some of the magic that was a mainstay at FAO Schwarz but at a price level that was appropriate for Toys "R" Us. Up to this point, shopping at these two stores was like night and day. Schwarz was like shopping in heaven with toy demonstrations for the parents, play areas for the kids, and specialty items unavailable anywhere else. Toys "R" Us, on the other hand, had a negative persona brought on by its warehouse style and poor treatment of customers, who often had to negotiate tall shelves and wrestle cumbersome boxes to get to the toy they sought.

Toys "R" Us opened its flagship store, in New York City's Times Square, in November 2001. The massive, dazzling new store was considered to be among Eyler's most notable accomplishments as CEO. It featured such attractions as an indoor Ferris wheel able to take 600 people a day for a spin, a life-size two-story Barbie townhouse with its own elevator, a 30-foot-tall animatronic dinosaur, and a version of the Candy Land board game big enough to double as a candy store. Although some insiders criticized the spectacle's $35 million cost, Eyler felt that the money was well spent, given that an average of 1.5 million people make their way through Times Square every day of the year. He also saw the flagship store as a key part of the critical task of changing the company's image. He had already initiated sweeping revisions in many existing Toys "R" Us stores. In addition to providing a better toy selection, he introduced many new toys that were available only from Toys "R" Us. He remodeled the stores' physical layout, adding toy-demonstration areas and placing toy displays in cul-de-sac sections instead of relying on the old warehouse-length aisles. The changes affected 167 stores in 2000 and 308 more in 2001.

Eyler was also credited with upgrading the Toys "R" Us employee areas, which reportedly improved morale. The happier employees got new bright-red uniforms and were much more willing to provide friendly service to their customers. With Eyler's presence and influence, the days of unhelpful sales clerks and Christmas-eve exasperation were over.

In the early 2000s Toys "R" Us continued to be a leading retailer of toys, children's apparel, and baby products in stores and through its Web sites. As of February 1, 2003, the company operated 1,595 retail stores worldwide. Its 1,051 U.S. locations included 681 toy stores under the name Toys "R" Us, 183 infant-toddler stores under the name Babies "R" Us, 146 children's clothing stores under the name Kids "R" Us, 37 educational specialty stores under the name Imaginarium, and four Geoffrey stores that offered products from Toys "R" Us, Babies "R" Us, and Kids "R" Us. The company also sold merchandise through its Web sites at www.toysrus.com, www.babiesrus.com, www.imaginarium.com, and www.giftsrus.com.

RETAILING STYLE

Coworkers and analysts described Eyler as an innovative and passionate marketer with entrepreneurial leadership and the energy needed for the toy market. The asset of having been a chief executive officer at several companies in various environments made him a leading candidate for Toys "R" Us. When he came to their table, he brought a reputation for commitment to customer focus, existing toy industry relationships, and experience heading up profitable electronic commerce and catalog businesses. Eyler's critics noted that during his career he had not led any major turnarounds and had never displayed great numbers. For example, while he was at FAO Schwarz, sales grew from $60 million in 1991 to $225 million in 1999, but profits were meager. Industry colleagues and press stories about Eyler seemed to agree, however, that if he had suffered some failures, they had only made him a better retailer.

See also entry on Toys 'R' Us, Inc. in *International Directory of Company Histories.*

SOURCES FOR FURTHER INFORMATION

Almanac of Famous People, 8th ed., Farmington Hills, Mich.: Gale Group, 2003.

Desjardins, Doug, "Back in the Center of the Toy Universe," *DSN Retailing Today*, October 2003, p. 6.

"Executive Business Briefing," United Press International, November 18, 2002, p1008322w2374.

Goldberg, Steven T., "Retailing's Comeback Kid," *Kiplinger's Personal Finance Magazine*, November 2001, p. 60.

Johnson, Jay L., "Eyler, the Fix-it Toy Man," in "The 10 New Leaders," *Retail Merchandiser*, May 2001, p. 16.

Newsmakers, Issue 3. Farmington Hills, Mich.: Gale Group, 2001.

Prior, Molly, "Eyler Arrival Boosts Morale," *DSN Retailing Today*, October 2003, p. 32.

———, "TRU's Eyler Touts Sound Growth Plan," *DSN Retailing Today*, June 18, 2001, p. 3.

"Toys 'R' Us: Beaten at Its Own Game: Under Heavy Pressure from Wal-Mart, the Chain May Sell Off Stores and Shift Focus," *BusinessWeek*, March 29, 2004, p. 89.

"Toys 'R' Us Braces for a Holiday Battle," *Fortune*, December 22, 2003, p. 60.

—Patricia McKenna